A Guide to the
Maximus Poems of
Charles Olson

A Guide to the
Maximus Poems of
Charles Olson

George F. Butterick

UNIVERSITY OF CALIFORNIA PRESS
Berkeley • *Los Angeles* • *London*

University of California Press
BERKELEY AND LOS ANGELES, CALIFORNIA

University of California Press, Ltd.
LONDON, ENGLAND

ISBN 0-520-03140-7
LIBRARY OF CONGRESS CATALOG CARD NUMBER: 75-27921
COPYRIGHT © 1978 BY
THE REGENTS OF THE UNIVERSITY OF CALIFORNIA

PRINTED IN THE UNITED STATES OF AMERICA

Acknowledgment

The Maximus Poems, published by Jargon/Corinth Books, is copyright
© 1960 by Charles Olson. Passages are quoted herein by the kind
permission of Theodore Wilentz and Jonathan Williams. *Maximus
Poems IV, V, VI*, originally published by Cape Goliard Press, is
copyright © 1968 by Charles Olson. *The Maximus Poems: Volume Three*,
originally published by Grossman Publishers, a division of the Viking
Press, is copyright © 1975 by the Estate of Charles Olson and the
University of Connecticut. Previously unpublished material by Charles
Olson among his papers at the University of Connecticut Library is
copyright © 1978 by the University of Connecticut. Other previously
unpublished material by Charles Olson quoted herein is copyright ©
1978 by the Estate of Charles Olson.

It's not a reference
it's an inner inherence

—Charles Olson, note among
his papers, October 1969

Contents

Introduction

I

Charles Olson writes at the close of his *Mayan Letters,* "The trouble is, it is very difficult, to be both a poet and, an historian."[1] The burden may be just as great upon the reader. The major difficulty, and it can be discouraging, is the large amount of reference needed to populate a poem that seeks to occupy and extend a world. The *Guide to the Maximus Poems* provides the scholarship useful for reading these poems which are as complex and allusive as Pound's *Cantos.* It consists of a series of annotations, moving through all three volumes of Olson's epic work, page by page, line by line, identifying names of persons and places, foreign words and phrases, and supplying the precise sources of the many literary and historical allusions and borrowings. It is an act of scholarship of the most fundamental and traditional sort, a handbook or companion to the poems, as well as, it is hoped, the basis for continuing work on them. It does not seek to analyze or interpret, but to allow the reader to participate actively in the poems, find his or her own meaning, exercise one's own judgment along the lines of Olson's own principle of *'istorin,* "to find out for oneself."

There are almost 4,000 annotations in all, identifying references ranging from local Massachusetts history to the poet's literal dreams, Algonquin legends to the cosmology of Whitehead, contemporary literary life to Arabic angelology. The notes draw from all conceivable sources, including the extensive body of papers left behind at the poet's death. Unpublished material from among those papers, as well as material in various libraries and in private hands, is called upon to throw new light on individual lines or entire poems. Letters written

1. *Selected Writings,* p. 130. The statement was written October 1953, in the midst of the poet's wrestlings with the direction the *Maximus Poems* might take.

by Olson are made use of; tape recordings of his readings and lectures; classroom notes; interviews with persons who actually appear in the poems; and, not least of all, conversations with the poet himself concerning the poems.

The *Guide* was begun as a doctoral dissertation at the State University of New York at Buffalo, at a time when Olson was habitually confused in academic circles with Elder Olson and when only one volume of the poems had been published. It owed its original inspiration to John Hamilton Edwards and William W. Vasse's invaluable *Annotated Index to the Cantos of Ezra Pound*, first published by the University of California Press in 1957. There are, however, important differences. A main and immediate departure from the form of Edwards and Vasse's *Index* is the adoption of a "chronological" structure. Whereas those scholars present their entries in alphabetical order, the annotations are arranged here not alphabetically, but in order of appearance, page by page, poem by poem. The *Guide* does include an index to all names and foreign words in the poems, but this is given apart from the annotations, as an appendix, where it may be used concomitantly with the annotations as the need arises. This is in part because certain items contain no single word or even words that could be suitably indexed for ready identification. An example would be, "Ships / have always represented . . ." (*Maximus* I, 79),[2] where in addition, as in many entries of this kind, the reader coming upon it in the poems alone would hardly feel it necessary to check in an index for an annotation, the item itself not being puzzling or conspicuous. However, following along in the order of the *Guide*, he sees that this, too, is a borrowing. The same is true for "the country not discovera" (I, 85), where one might have assumed a typographical slip, or "the history of weeds / is a history of man" (I, 94). Indeed, one of the results of this undertaking has been to reveal the surprisingly wide extent of such borrowing, thereby raising certain fundamental

2. *Maximus* I will be the abbreviation adopted throughout this *Guide* for the first collected volume of the poem, *The Maximus Poems*, published in 1960. *Maximus* II, then, will stand for *Maximus Poems IV, V, VI* (1968), and *Maximus* III for *The Maximus Poems: Volume Three* (1975). These designations are not to be confused with the sections of the early poems, those prior to *Maximus IV, V, VI*.

questions as to the nature of Olson's poetry and the limits of originality in art in general.

Regarding the scope or content of the annotations, degrees of both selectivity and elaboration have been necessary. Some entries will appear as bare dictionary or gazetteer entries; others more as footnotes, as might be found at the bottom of a page of a school anthology edition of Eliot's *Waste Land*. Thus, "Georgetown" (I, 45) is simply identified as "Town in Massachusetts about eighteen miles northwest of Gloucester"; but for "Nike" (I, 15), it is not enough to note she was the winged Greek goddess of victory. A reference to an epithet from Hesiod's *Theogony*, "fair-ankled Nike," will enlighten these lines:

> I know a dress just sewed
> > (saw the wind
>
> blow its cotton
> against her body
> from the ankle
> > so!
> it was Nike

Reference is made throughout to other of Olson's writings, and lines and passages from those quoted as part of the annotation, wherever such might further illuminate portions of *The Maximus Poems*. Consultation with the poet has enabled identification of the more highly personal references, including dreams. If the obvious appears to have been annotated, the author begs the reader's indulgence. What is commonplace for one time and place, like Necco wafers (III, 84) or an "Eskimo Pie" (III, 113), may not be so obvious to an Australian reader or in the next century. Consistency was thought to be a value.

Bibliographical documentation is given wherever necessary or useful. Occasionally a guide to pronunciation is offered. But in all cases, only sufficient information pertinent to the poems has been allowed. The author has not followed the lead of one of his favorite annotators, James Savage in his edition of Winthrop's *Journal*, but has kept his asides to a minimum. With material as unique and occasionally idiosyncratic as Olson's, it was thought necessary to be as formal as possible, lest the author's own eccentricities be misjudged for Olson's.

On the whole, annotations are fuller and more relaxed than those in the *Index to the Cantos of Ezra Pound*. This is possible, in part, because there are about half the 7,500 entries Edwards and Vasse had to concern themselves with. Still, it was decided that too economical an entry, while providing a ready identification, can strain the reader's attention and become as objectionable and defeating as the subjective irrelevance it seeks to avoid. For example, the length, age, and size of crew of the fishing schooner Olson sailed on in 1936 is given (note to *Maximus* I, 38) in order to make, in some small way, the experience more imaginable. Or it certainly makes imaginative difference to know that the fishing grounds where Carl Olsen (I, 19) set his dories down with such confidence and accuracy, Brown's Bank offshore Cape Ann, has an area of some 2,275 square miles.

Some of the annotations in the *Guide* can only be expected to be of interest to the local historian. Nevertheless, facts relating to the history of Gloucester or of early New England matters are treated with the same respect as much more intrinsically interesting references and allusions—such as the account of Jeremiah Dummer and his concubines (I, 128) or the Gloucester sea-serpent (III, 59)—not only for sake of consistency or thoroughness, but because the poet must be considered as he considered himself—a serious historian, as well as poet, of Gloucester, Massachusetts.

Another function of this handbook, a major one in addition to identifying references and illuminating certain lines, is to identify the sources used in the writing of the poems, and to suggest how and to what extent the poet has made use of these sources, thus providing some understanding of his method of creation. It has therefore been considered desirable to quote the appropriate section of a source in its entirety, wherever such has been discoverable, in order to exhibit the extent of the borrowing, or if the section is indeed long, at least to note the extent of the borrowing. This will enable the reader to examine for himself whatever changes from the original might have been made—very often misspellings and similar errors that suggest the heat and haste of the imagination. The *Guide*, in this aspect, is an outline for a *Road to Xanadu,* John Livingston Lowes's study of the influence of reading on the imagination in the composition of Coleridge's "Ancient Mariner" and "Kubla Khan." One of the conclusions made possible is that what Olson writes about Herman Melville in *Call Me Ishmael* is entirely true for himself: "Melville's reading is a gauge of him, at all points of his life. He was a skald, and knew how to appropriate the work of others. He read to write. Highborn stealth, Edward Dahlberg calls originality, the act of a cutpurse Autolycus who makes his thefts as invisible as possible."[3]

Wherever possible, the exact edition Olson used is cited, even though another may be more readily or commonly available. In some cases, where the material is less clearly from a single or determinable source, but can be found in a variety of locations, sources are often only suggested. The reader is asked to "compare" (cf.) or consider a work as a possible candidate for the exact source, or is referred simply to a dependable authority that will confirm Olson's statements or that may cast additional light.

Equally important, in quoting from the sources, is to provide the context of a reference in order that the reference, its place and function in the poem, might be better understood. For example, the annotation to the section beginning "Hyssop, for him, / was the odor of meat . . ." (I, 94), not only identifies the reference contained in those lines, but in locating the source, reveals it to be an example, in its original context, of a family tradition that can be established as firm historical fact. As a matter of inheritance, then, it can be related not only to the section following, of Elizabeth Tuttle and her descendants, but also to the symbolic inheritance of heraldry earlier in the poem, and even to the genetic concerns underlying the quotation from Anderson, that "the history of weeds / is a history of man," also on that page. Another example is the passage on *Maximus* III, 78, where an otherwise hidden etymological pun on "God's flesh" and the root of "raw" is revealed. However,

3. *Call Me Ishmael,* p. 36. For Dahlberg's statement referred to, see chapter VII of *Can These Bones Live,* dedicated to Olson.

any comment or judgment beyond the recognition of facts such
as these, would be an act of criticism beyond the limitations
proposed.

The desire has been to treat Olson on his own terms, not only
in accordance with the principle of *'istorin* which allows the
reader to discover the pleasure and ramifications of the poems
for himself, especially the great spiritual attainment that characterizes the final volume, but the terms by which Olson would
have treated Melville, to whom he had devoted so much of his
life: "some canon such as Greg & Pollard have brought to
Shakespeare emendation," as he writes to Merton Sealts, 7
March 1952, in the face of Luther Mansfield's and Howard
Vincent's massive annotated edition of *Moby-Dick*. "And this be
of some use to the community—perhaps get it so clear that
others would have a gauge to do their own work by, . . . work in
the larger & more difficult area of annotation to such a work as
M[oby] D[ick]." Objecting to Mansfield's and Vincent's "mud-
dying" of the facts "due to misleading inclusions & exclusions,
by patently false emphases," he proposes to do a series of
"PRINCIPLES of EDITING" (begun, as will be seen, in his
copy of the Mansfield-Vincent volume) in which he would
make clear "in what way the presentation of the sources has to
be *governed*." These principles are summarized in Olson's
praise of Sealts's own work, notably his checklist of Melville's
reading, as well as that of Jay Leyda, compiler of *The Melville
Log*, a chronological summary of all that was then known about
Melville and his career:

> yr CHECK-LIST is exactly an *act of mind* precisely because
> it (1) presents the known facts; (2) recognizes that these are
> only the known facts, that others obviously also existed which
> have disappeared or have not yet been recovered; and (3)
> leaves those facts as facts, and does not claim to analyze Mel-
> ville's use of them
>
> LEYDA, likewise . . . leaves the historial facts as they are now
> known, as he has been able to make them known
>
> (neither you nor Leyda have at any point, so far as I can
> see, allowed yr work to "spread," to make featherings of it-
> self, to swell at all: you have looked upon the issues of yr
> labors as the evidence of the labor. And thus *you have done no*

other man any slightest wrong, have—if you have found corrections of others necessary—let that correction sit inside
the facts as you have righted them:
                                    these are the silences which
breed honor and dignity between men[,] which breed alert-
ness—which *justify* scholarship—which make it *a thing of
life* . . .

He goes on in the letter to praise George Lyman Kittredge's
"superb book on Chaucer" as a measure "of how to do *sources*
at the same time that you do not *intrude* on the writer's own act
of passage *from* the sources to his own created thing."[4]

The author has also found helpful or at least reassuring
some additional remarks by Olson in his copy of Mansfield's
and Vincent's edition of *Moby-Dick* itself, at the end of their 260
pages of notes. The few "Principles of Annotations" he begins
to set down there are not unlike my own:

    (a) all uncommon or contemporary allusions identified, and
        where from, M[elville]'s source
    (b) on sources in general
        (1) if it is clear where his came from, any other sources
            are only encumbrances

The notes break off, but what is there is perfectly apparent as a
traditional approach to textual illumination: no doubts or dis-
sension as to the value of doing such, no surprisingly radical or
angular approach; just direct and clean dealing with the facts,
along with the suspension of the subjective judgments and
comparisons more properly called criticism than scholarship.

The series of poems which the present *Guide* serves is not
linear and causal but a series more in the sense of Pierre
Boulez's serial music, which Olson discovered in 1951 and
which underlies his early understanding of the poems. Each
composition, or poem, "will have its own structure and its own
mode of generation on all levels."[5] Its form, like that of the

4. Kittredge's best known book on Chaucer is *Chaucer and His Poetry*, first published
in 1915, but perhaps Olson means F. N. Robinson's edition of Chaucer with compre-
hensive annotations, confusing that with Kittredge's *Complete Works of Shakespeare*,
both of which he had used in school and kept in his working library.
5. Boulez in "4 musicians at work," *trans/formation* (New York), I, 3 (1952), 170—
another portion from which Olson quotes in his letters of 13–14 June 1952 to Cid
Corman (*Letters for Origin*, p. 103).

cosmos, is "through everything / —it is sewn / in all parts, under / and over" (II, 173). There is no step by step ascent, as up the concentric circles of Dante's *Paradiso*. Rather, it is a Whiteheadian universe in which "the process of creation is the form of unity."[6] Still, the research reveals a kind of systematic progression, if on the level of scholarship and reference alone. The earliest poems contain nothing of the history of Gloucester save that known from having lived there as Olson did, hearing stories from Alfred Mansfield Brooks, director of the local historical society, or from the fishermen like Lou Douglas he grew up among. So the poems begin with Maximus circling like a gull (himself "the bird overhead" as is written in a letter to Vincent Ferrini),[7] and it is not really until "Letter 7" (I, 30), with a reference to William Stevens, the ship's carpenter, that the wing dips and touches. "Letter 10" (I, 45) begins what increasingly becomes the narrowing investigation—though even then it is Samuel Eliot Morison's *Builders of the Bay Colony*, a well-known and general enough study, that provides the background. The next "letter" quotes directly from the writings of Captain John Smith, the first such use of the early historians. However, poems that follow concern themselves with material not limited to Gloucester but drawn from such works as Brebner's *Explorers of North America*, the *Dictionary of National Biography*, *American Neptune* magazine, and an *Annual Report of the American Historical Association*, setting down the conditions of the larger America and reflecting Olson's earlier ambitions to write a capacious poem called *West*. Significantly enough, these opening poems of the series were not written in Gloucester; it is not until back in Gloucester in 1957, with the land, sea, and sources around him, that Olson begins his direct, single-minded investigation and possession of the city. One sees, then, in the course of the annotations, the process or progress of the investigation, the act of history that will take the poet from Morison through John Babson and Frances Rose-Troup to the town records themselves (I, 147) and, in 1966, to

6. Alfred North Whitehead, *Adventures of Ideas* (New York: Macmillan, 1933), p. 231.
7. See note in the *Guide* to *Maximus* I, 1, "Antony of Padua."

England and the original records of the Dorchester Company and the Weymouth Port Books.[8]

None of the *Maximus* poems were actually written in a library (save perhaps II, 57 and III, 20); but parts are certainly *of* the library. Olson was, after all, trained as a scholar before he became seriously a poet (no matter how "creative" his earlier life had inclined—acting, the dance, associations with Dahlberg and Pound). The remarkable thing is how extensively, continuously, and indefatigably he researched his subject. An example from the making of *Call Me Ishmael* is pertinent. Call slips from the Library of Congress preserved among his papers indicate Olson read or at least glanced through all of their holdings on the American whaling industry at the time of *Moby-Dick,* before reducing what he needed to a few paragraphs (pp. 18 and following of *Call Me Ishmael*). In the same way, the poet's numerous notebooks, along with thousands of loose sheets of notes and maps from his walls, contain much more information on Gloucester than ever makes its way into the poems.

At Black Mountain, where many of the early poems were written, the library was decidedly small, but the poet was able to work on occasion at the Sondley Library, an excellent reference collection within the Pack Memorial Library in Asheville, North Carolina. A pocket notebook from the spring of 1953, which evidently accompanied Olson there, contains early versions of and materials used in no less than six of the early poems, from "The Song and Dance of" through "Maximus, at Tyre and at Boston." He may have missed his Washington days, with the Library of Congress a short streetcar ride away, but he was able to order books via interlibrary loan from Duke University (Rose-Troup's *John White* was one) or the University of North Carolina at Chapel Hill. Later, there would be the town records

8. Olson had originally intended to undertake this investigation among the English records in the summer of 1957, but was forestalled by legal matters relating to the closing and sale of Black Mountain College. Although he eventually got to see the Dorchester materials firsthand almost ten years later, no direct use of the materials is made, despite hundreds of pages of notes, and no poems came from his work among them.

in the vault of the Gloucester City Clerk's office, deeds and wills
among the county probate records at Salem, an account book at
the local historical society, documents on microfilm, borrowed
family papers. He used libraries up and down the Massachusetts coast between Gloucester and Boston—from the Sawyer
Free Library (a brief walk from his house on Fort Square), the
Sandy Bay Historical Society in Rockport (where he bestowed
in exchange for assistance rendered an inscribed copy of the
first volume of *Maximus Poems*) and the Essex Institute at Salem
(where he tried to date one of the librarians), to the Widener
Library at Harvard, which he had used years before as a graduate student. It might be said his father had started it all, his feel
for the documents of history, by taking him as a boy to
Plymouth for its tricentennial celebration and, most of all, by a
gift of reproductions of Matthew Brady photographs, which
the poet claimed "cured [him] that early of romantic history"
(*The Post Office,* pp. 26–27).

One final caution. One must be very clear about what Olson's
understanding of history is. He writes in "Letter 23" (I, 100–
101),

> I would be an historian as Herodotus was, looking
>
> for oneself for the evidence of
>
> what is said . . .

The poems, then, are an act of investigation:

> Best thing to do is *to dig one thing or place or man* until you
> yourself know more abt that than is possible to any other man.
> It doesn't matter whether it's Barbed Wire or Pemmican or
> Paterson or Iowa. But *exhaust* it. Saturate it. Beat it.
> And
> then U KNOW everything else very fast: one saturation job
> (it might take 14 years). And you're in, forever.[9]

Williams calls himself a dog among dogs, and *Paterson* is what is
thrown up by his digging. And what is often as interesting as the
results, the facts, is the act itself. There was always something

9. "A Bibliography on America," *Additional Prose,* p. 11.

at bottom unsatisfying and flat about Pound's definition of an epic as "a poem including history." The form of *The Maximus Poems* is the act of history.

II

The poems to which this *Guide* is addressed are generally regarded as Charles Olson's major work, despite the more immediate popularity and influence of his theoretical essay, "Projective Verse." They were written over a period of almost twenty years, nearly the entire length of time that Olson was active as a poet. There are more than 300 poems in the series, varying in length from a single line to ten pages. Some stand independently, others depend for their meaning on their context within the series. They were begun as a succession of "letters" (the designation is used throughout the first volume, but only occasionally thereafter) to the poet Vincent Ferrini in Gloucester, where Olson had grown up, and through Ferrini to the city itself. As such, they provide a vehicle, a "great White Cadillac" (II, 43), for the public voice known as Maximus of the private individual Charles Olson, although eventually the distinction between public and private, Olson and Maximus, becomes inconsequential as the integration of person and place, man and his earth, is achieved. It is a series in the tradition of the long poem encouraged by Olson's immediate pedecessors ("inferior predecessors," he once called them in an outburst),[10] Ezra Pound in his *Cantos* and William Carlos Williams in *Paterson*, although it has its roots deep in its own supportive soil.

The *Maximus* series is certainly ambitious in its own right, focusing as it does on a single locality that serves as a microcosm by which to measure the present and the nation and which grows to encompass earth, heaven, and hell. Yet it has its origins in a proposal that Olson had entertained for a number of years previous and which was, if anything, even more ambitious. As early as 1945, when he made his decision to withdraw from

10. In a letter to Cid Corman, 23 November 1953 (*Letters for Origin,* p. 132).

partisan politics and be primarily a "writer," Olson had proposed a long poem for himself to be titled, simply, *West*—meaning the entire Western World of which the American West was an imaginative and geographical culmination. At the earliest point, in a notebook kept while on a working vacation with the Democratic party's National Committee in Key West, Florida, he even wished to begin the book on America (it was alternatively to be a series of narratives), literalist that he always was, with the *tall* tale of Paul Bunyan—a Maximus figure if there ever was one![11] It was to be a tale "of space," by the author who opened his *Call Me Ishmael* later that spring with the statement, "I take SPACE to be the central fact to man born in America, from Folsom cave to now. I spell it large because it comes large here. Large, and without mercy." And it was to be linked somehow to the earliest culture-hero Olson was aware of, Gilgamesh of Ur (meaning also an *ur*-world), as well as to the figure he called Bigmans—an obvious prototype, by name alone, of Maximus. Most extraordinary of all in tracing the roots of the *Maximus Poems*, only a few days later in the same notebook the poet proposed a "book" on Gloucester that would include many of the same characters, local fishermen and residents, who later turn up throughout the poems, among them Carl Olsen, Newman Shea, Howard Blackburn, Homer and Viola Barrett. He presages the work to come even down to the proposition of "rewriting" stories from James B. Connolly, which does indeed occur as "*3rd letter on Georges, unwritten*" (II, 107), almost twenty years later. Thus, as early as January of 1945, shortly before he would abandon party politics and declare his independence in the poem "The K," itself a "telegram" announcing his decision (written in Key West in Feb-

11. This sense of Bunyan as the embodiment of "giantism" or requisite heroic size, goes back to notes on representative figures of the American West—what might be termed evidence of Olson's first thoughts toward a book on the subject—which were made upon reading James Daugherty's *Their Weight in Wildcats: Tales of the Frontier* in Gloucester in the spring of 1940 (in notebook "#5 / Gloucester, Spring / 1940"). They are possibly what he is referring to when he writes to himself in 1945 of "notes on the poem to be called 'West' you wrote 4 yrs ago" (*OLSON: The Journal of the Charles Olson Archives* 5, Spring 1976, p. 11), which otherwise do not appear to have survived. The subject of large men interested him too, of course, on account of his own conspicuous size. For instance, in the summer of 1935 he made a point of reading in *Scribner's Magazine* a story by Thomas Wolfe entitled "Gulliver: The Story of a Tall Man."

For the roots of *The Maximus Poems* in *West*, see the notes and essays in *OLSON* 5.

ruary 1945, it was originally titled "Telegram"), the groundwork for *Maximus* was laid.

Olson's notebooks are not the only place the roots of *Maximus* are to be found. Maximus is the "prospective" hero announced in the very last pages of *Call Me Ishmael*, the study of Melville, myth, and America which Olson wrote over the spring and summer of 1945 after he had returned to Washington from Key West. Maximus's principle of *'istorin* and the "central quality" Homer imparts to his hero Ulysses—"*search, the individual responsible to himself*"[12]—are the same. Maximus, by the sheer boldness and grandeur of his title, is Ahab come "full stop." He is Western man at the limit of himself, who no longer has a frontier other than himself and his extricable past, no farther west to go but to dig in deeper where he stands, with the result that Gloucester is taken back, "compelled" to its founding in 1623 by migrating European man, back to the old Norse and the Algonquins, even farther back to the ice and Pleistocene man. The scope of *The Maximus Poems* is all outlined in the last pages of *Call Me Ishmael*.

Olson actually sketched out a projected poem to be called *WEST* shortly after writing *Call Me Ishmael*. It proposed to cover the history of Western man for the past 2,500 years, beginning with Ulysses and including other such archetypal figures as Faust and Christopher Columbus before focusing on particular American heroes such as Montezuma, Washington, and Daniel Boone, while ending with a figure "yet unnamed," who "carries in him the seeds of the way of life which shall replace the West." In later notes Olson names this figure the "Quetzalcoatl figure," after the Mesoamerican culture-hero, adding the fanciful name "Orpheus West"—to which "Maximus" is at least an improvement. The proposal for the poem becomes modified in 1947–48 into a planned book of narratives which Olson tentatively titled *Red, White & Black*, described as a book "on the morphology of the American kultur [after Frobenius's "*Kulturmorphologie*"] . . . the differing ways the Indian, white and the Negro found out how to shape a human society in the West." It was to be a book based on rigorous scholarly

12. *Call Me Ishmael*, p. 118.

investigation, what he would call in "A Bibliography on America" a "saturation job": "The job is, by the techniques of total research, to crack down any events or person so completely that you can, in the minutiae of the facts, find the elements of which the event or person are made and which make them significant to other men."[13] He received a publisher's advance and a second Guggenheim fellowship for the project, but was only able to develop a chapter or two. Plans for the poetic *West* were still alive on 27 May 1948, however, as witnessed by a note on *"The Long Poem"* dated then, in which the same hopes and heroes occur as previously. Interestingly, in another note from that period he even identified his Quetzalcoatl figure with William Stevens, the Gloucester shipwright who is called "the first Maximus" in "Letter 7" (I, 31), because "he was the first to make things, / not just live off nature," and who remains a hero of individualism and resistance throughout the poems.

During this time, Olson's interest in the roots of the West, coinciding with the necessity of finding his own place as a poet, took a shift in emphasis—away from Cabeza de Vaca, the Donner Party, and the gold-bearing lands of the American West, to the psychological and intellectual basis of Western man. He continued to search for alternatives to the war-weary, Bomb-ridden world in which he found himself, and to the mind that produced and promulgated it. He acquired a number of unlikely books for a modernist (soon to be self-declared "post-modernist") poet—Aristophanes, Athenaeus, Ausonius, Diogenes Laertius, Euripides, Herodotus, Hesiod, Ovid, Pausanias, Plutarch, Theocritus (significantly, no Plato or Aristotle). This is more likely the reading of an Edward Dahlberg, to whom in fact Olson occasionally announced his acquisitions, all obtained in second-hand bookstores in Washington between 1947 and 1949. (One of the reasons he acquired works of the Greek dramatists, as well as of Elizabethan and Jacobean playwrights at this time, was to forward his own interest in the drama—namely, "The Fiery Hunt" and other plays, and his proposal with Frank Moore to reinstitute a "Greek" theater.)[14]

13. "Guggenheim Fellowship Proposal, 1948," *OLSON* 5, p. 34.
14. See *The Fiery Hunt & Other Plays* (and editor's introduction), and "Olson in Gloucester, 1966," *Muthologos*, I, 169 and editor's note.

And it will be his reading of Sappho, as will shortly be seen, that led him to the discovery of Maximus of Tyre, whose name he adopts as hero for the poems. It was characteristic of Olson to start with such primaries. "Beginner—and interested in beginnings": he could recognize the quality in Melville because it was so present in himself.[15]

During this time also, the few years before *The Maximus Poems* were begun, Olson intensively read Homer, especially the *Odyssey,* and along with that Victor Bérard's study of the sources of Homer's poem in the manuals and place names of Phoenician sailors. Bérard's book, *Did Homer Live?,* curiously influenced at least two comparative literary undertakings of the twentieth century: Joyce's *Ulysses* and Pound's *Cantos* (Pound derives his guiding principle of the "periplum" from it). Olson read Bérard in the spring of 1949, perhaps because of Pound's earlier recommendation, but definitely while pursuing his own interests in the *Odyssey*. It encouraged him (as did the writings of Carl Sauer) to attend to geography and honor the local, while Bérard's discussion of the role of the *periploi* or navigational charts drawn from first-hand experience from the decks of the ships fostered the development of Olson's sense later in the *Maximus Poems* of "eye-view," a direct complement to the notion of *'istorin*, the Herodotean historian's "finding out for oneself."

It was at this same time that Olson began a long poem on civilizations, not *West* but a poem on the West, encouraged by his reading of Pound and a reaction to Eliot. It was to be his first poem on the scale of *Maximus,* and foreshadows that both in substance, measuring present civilization and cultural values by the past, and form. It was richly associational, using techniques of collage and juxtaposition, what Pound called the "ideogrammatic" method. Olson had taken to heart remarks by Eliot in the preface to his translation of Perse's *Anabasis* concerning "the suppression of 'links in the chain,'" although he added an openness that allowed the diverse elements to assume their own shape. He also contributed an outlook that was more heroic than what Eliot offered.

15. *Call Me Ishmael,* p. 14.

"The Kingfishers" was Olson's apprentice-piece, without the focus of a Gloucester and without a Maximus. It is, nevertheless, a major achievement, and might profitably be read as an introduction to *The Maximus Poems.* It was originally part of an even longer poem, written in February and March of 1949, called "Proteus." A more ambitious title on the surviving manuscript, "The First Proteid," emphasizes further the "change" announced in the poem's opening line. Later, as "The Kingfishers I & II," it was sent for possible publication to *Poetry London,* whose editors had recently issued a symposium devoted to Eliot. Included as part of "Proteus" was another significant early poem subsequently revised and published separately, "The Praises," which was collected with "The Kingfishers" in *In Cold Hell, In Thicket* and which draws upon at least one of the same sources, Plutarch's essay "On the E at Delphi." Reading the two poems together will give the reader an idea of the scope Olson was after. "Proteus" was not quite the *West* proposed by the poet earlier, but it does include a section on Quetzalcoatl, and features as well another of the heroes from the unfulfilled *West,* Cabeza de Vaca. In one early version of "Proteus," Cabeza "lost Europe's clothes" when he was shipwrecked on the shores of America and was reborn. As in his briefer occurrence in "The Kingfishers," he appears in the role of "healer" as opposed to the ravaging conquistadors.

"The Kingfishers" was a response to the diffident negativism of Eliot's *Waste Land* and even more so to his *Four Quartets,* echoes of which are to be found throughout Olson's poem.[16] Notes on back of an early draft indicate that Olson considered it an "Anti-Wasteland" (which encourages a reading of the title as an inversion of Eliot's use of the Fisher-King from Grail legend in his poem). And unlike the kingfisher, which serves only as a symbol in "Burnt Norton," Olson's is first conditioned in hard, unromantic facts as supplied by the *Encyclopaedia*

16. Olson had heard Eliot read selections from both poems at the National Gallery in Washington in May 1947 (with Dorothy Pound and St.-John Perse, among many others, also in the audience), shortly before leaving for a visit to Gloucester at which time the *Maximus Poems* would be conceived. He read *Four Quartets* at least as early as November 1945, copying out portions of "East Coker" and "The Dry Salvages" on November 22 in his notebook "Washington Fall 1945 I."

Britannica, before it takes on any secondary characteristics or symbolic coloration. Whereas Eliot descries the dryness everywhere, the desert of modern life, when Olson concludes his poem, "I hunt among stones," it is with some hope. The stones are those of the past, like the one at Delphi with the archaic E on it, or, fulfilling his own terms, the ones the poet was to pick out of the Yucatan soil with glyphs incised. "Christamiexcited . . . hit a real spot, which had spotted fr bus . . . then, yesterday, alone, hit further south, and smash, dug out my 1st hieroglyphic stone! plus two possible stela (tho, no crowbar, so no proof) . . ."[17] Olson's conclusion in "The Kingfishers" need not be read as symptomatic of the existential despair prevalent in Eliot's poem and in the Kierkegaardian era following World War II, but as an opportunity to will change, to act "by seizure" to recover values of the past, "possible usages" of the present, which had been allowed to "dribble out" unused.[18]

During the time Olson was working on "The Kingfishers"— or more precisely, between "Proteus" and the revision and division of that into two separate poems ("The Kingfishers" by July, "The Praises" by December 1949)—Olson discovered Pythagoras in the writings of Diogenes Laertius, part of his reading among the ancient Greek sources of the West, and sought to include him in a poem along with other Ionian or pre-Socratic Greeks—Thales, Heraclitus, Anaximander, Anaxagoras—as well as Homer. He writes in notes dated 28 October 1949: ". . . do a poem (as they [the Greeks] did) turning over their knowledge, converting to our needs, strictly limited to these SOURCES of the West, but turning the attention *backward* from them instead of, as usual, only as predecessors of classic greece, in order that their vision shall come forward *clean*

17. Letter to Robert Creeley, 17 March 1951, in *Mayan Letters, Selected Writings,* p. 90.

18. "Human Universe," *Human Universe,* p. 12: "It is unbearable what knowledge of the past has been allowed to become, what function of human memory has dribbled out to in the hands of these learned monsters whom people are led to think 'know.' They know nothing in not knowing how to reify what they do know. What is worse, they do not know how to pass over to us the energy implicit in any high work of the past because they purposely destroy that energy as dangerous to the states for which they work . . ." To act "by seizure" is one of the possibilities offered by *'istorin* (see "A Later Note on Letter #15," *Maximus* II, 79).

to now." "The Kingfishers" is such a poem, though in its final form, it contrasts the West with the rising East, in what Olson wrote to critic M. L. Rosenthal, 5 March 1968, is "an examination-confrontation of *America* as such versus predictions of & from the *East Wind*." As a poem, it brings together the facts of such a confrontation on a scale equal to the movement of continents.

The most difficult consideration facing Olson was the form a poem of this magnitude should take. "Projective Verse," concluding as it does with a proposal for epic and dramatic scope, was written partly in response to precisely such a problem. It was begun in February 1950, shortly before the first *Maximus* poem, and revised in July of that year. Olson had looked around him and realized that Pound and Williams, and especially Eliot (except for those helpful observations in his preface to Perse), would not suffice; he had to draw up his own *ars poetica*. In his earlier notes and proposals, the complexity, scope, and all but the methodology for *Maximus* are evident. In a second notebook kept during his sojourn at Key West in 1945, he writes, with a degree of consciousness that makes his early dismissal as a mere imitator of Pound on the part of superficial critics most irrelevant:

> Maybe Pound discloses to you a method you spontaneously reached for in all this talking and writing.
>
> What about doing [on] a smaller scope—the West? But he has already taken the same frame, as you will note from your notes on the poem to be called "West" you wrote 4 yrs ago.
>
> But should you not best him? Is his form not inevitable enough to be used as your own? Let yourself be derivative for a bit. This is a good and natural act. Write as the father to be the father.

By that time, too, Williams, whom Olson admired almost as much as Pound, especially for his classic *In the American Grain*, and who would later wonder uncomprehendingly why Olson did not call his poem *Gloucester* as he had named his epic of place *Paterson*,[19] had begun to publish the first sections of his long poem. These were the available models, the possible directions, although Olson found failure in both their attempts. In his most direct statement on the subject, a letter to Robert Creeley from 8 March 1951 (*Selected Writings*, pp. 81–84), Olson writes of Pound and Williams as representing two extremes—Pound limited by the "irresponsibility" of his ego and Williams by a naively pastoral view of a city, without the depth of time or history (in which "all ages are contemporaneous")[20] that Pound had accomplished. Olson, on the other hand, sought to achieve a hero and a place together, simultaneously, Maximus *of* Gloucester as Apollonius is of Tyana in Olson's play of that name, where the two become one, inextricably. Only then could there be a hero of sufficiently "projective" size.

Olson's actual hero derives his name from a little-known philosopher of the second century A.D. He discovered the historical Maximus of Tyre quite by accident in March 1949, while reading about Sappho in a collection of Greek lyric fragments translated by J. M. Edmonds, where passages with reference to Maximus's *Dissertations* are marked in the poet's copy. He then apparently sought out an English translation of the complete *Dissertations* in the Library of Congress and found Thomas Taylor's nineteenth-century version. Apart from some opening promises of interest, the bulk of the lengthy text is rather dry neo-Platonic eclecticism, and it is unlikely that Olson found Maximus's own words or thoughts of equal inspiration to his name, save perhaps for the attractive reduction of his chief ideas in an *Encyclopaedia Britannica* article that the poet also consulted, later making direct use of it in the withheld *Maximus*

19. "Olson does identify himself with Gloucester and the sailors, and it might have been a better poem if it had been more so. Maybe not calling it Maximus, but calling it Gloucester. It would have been more understandable. But he wants to call it Maximus. And what is the definition of Maximus? Maximus means the furthest development of something."—in Walter Sutton, "A Visit with William Carlos Williams," *Interviews with William Carlos Williams: "Speaking Straight Ahead,"* ed. Linda Welshimer Wagner (New York: New Directions, 1976), p. 41.

20. Ezra Pound, in his preface to *The Spirit of Romance* (London: J. M. Dent, [1910]), p. vi.

poem, "*A Note* (#35)."[21] It is most likely that Olson chose Maximus before he had a fully developed sense of Tyre as being an Old World analogue for Gloucester—the chief port of the Phoenicians the same way Gloucester was a center of the American fishing industry, and the last holdout against Alexander the Great's "universalism," forcibly connected to the mainland by a causeway as Gloucester was to be by a modern highway and bridge.

He was perhaps encouraged by the freshness of the figure, who like Apollonius of Tyana was not pawed to death in schools or over coffee tables and little referred to by historians or literary persons. He must have been drawn even more by the name, the sheer boldness of "The Greatest." It was a proposal sufficiently large to satisfy any of his ambitions. There was the long preoccupation with a figure of great physical size, from Bunyan and Bigmans, to James Merry who wrestled a bull in a Dogtown meadow in "MAXIMUS, FROM DOGTOWN—I" (II, 2–6), each reflecting the poet's own inescapable bulk. He stood 6'7" and massive rather than spindly or lanky. In later years he had the appearance of a standing bear. So much of Olson's own personality is in the figure of Maximus that it seems pointless to minimize the identity, even though it disquieted him early on, especially in regard to "Maximus, to himself" (I, 52–53), where it is possible to confuse the poet with the hero, the man with Maximus. It is not until "*Maximus of Gloucester*" from 1965 (III, 101) that he is able to declare the difference clearly: "It is not I, / even if the life appeared / biographical. The only interesting thing / is if one can be / an image / of man . . ." The alternative is posed at the conclusion of "Against Wisdom As Such" (*Human Universe*, p. 71): "Otherwise, we are involved in / ourselves (which is demonstrably / not very interesting, no / matter / who." Maximus, then, rather than a simple persona behind which the poet is concealed, stands forth as such an "image" or model "of man." The choice of the name is preposterous, in one sense, but it is not mere vainglory. Maximus, like his avatar Enyalion, represents possibility. Maxi-

---

21. *OLSON* 6 (Fall 1976), pp. 59–60, and editor's note on p. 74 there.

mus is the "size man can be once more capable of, once the turn of the flow of his energies that I speak of as the WILL TO COHERE is admitted, and its energy taken up."[22] Olson was fond of John Keats's statement that "A man's life of any worth is a continuous allegory," quoting it often. If Maximus reflects the poet's life, it is as a personality seeking completeness; as an allegorical figure, it must be on the order of Man-becoming-all-that-he-might-become.

As the poem progressed in its absorbing complexity, Olson periodically paused to examine the nature of his hero and sort its components. In a note written 3 December 1959, shortly after the poem "MAXIMUS, FROM DOGTOWN—I" was composed, he enumerated the various archetypal figures of which James Merry, the poem's hero, was an example, relating them to Maximus. The list includes Orion (a vulgar brawling "Irish" version of whom Olson celebrates in his *O'Ryan* series) and Hercules, who appears in *Maximus* both as the Phoenician prototype of Odysseus and as the "Glory of Hera" (which the name signifies), an aspect of Enyalion. There are also Gilgamesh, Samson, Odysseus himself, and Theseus, who appears in the poems only once (III, 132). All are described as "Bigmans types" or "Sons," with their monstrous opponents (such as Merry's bull) "the libido hung up on MA"—specifically, the Terrible Mother of Jungian interpretation. Beyond these heroes and monsters, "outside such," Olson suggests, stands "Maximus Anthropos" as "the MODEL of man without this STRIFE." He has numerous other names and guises throughout the poems—shipwright William Stevens, the androgynous John Smith, Enyalion, the Perfect Child, Odysseus, Hercules Melkaart, James Merry, Manes/Minos, even a "whelping mother." But whatever his manifestations, Maximus is a "person," in the sense that certain theologies speak of the divinity as a person, rather than, or in addition to, being an abstraction or principle or force.

All the evidence is that Olson did not intend, consciously, to write *The Maximus Poems* as it stands, a long series of epic

22. "The Gate and the Center," *Human Universe*, p. 21. In his *Paris Review* interview Olson says, "Maximus is, of course, a verb" (*Muthologos*, II, 120).

dimension. The poems were begun spontaneously, as a letter from Washington to Vincent Ferrini in May 1950, stirred by the news that Ferrini was planning a little magazine in Gloucester to be called *Voyager*. The first poem, "I, Maximus of Gloucester, to You," is undoubtedly the one which Ferrini acknowledges in his letter of 20 May 1950 to Olson by saying, in characteristically laconic fashion, "Thanks for the poem which we like and are sure that the townspeople will scream [about]." The poem was quoted at length in a letter to Frances Boldereff on May 17, the same date as a manuscript among the poet's papers, in keeping with Olson's practice at the time of sending out what was under hand, testing for some response or recognition. On July 22, while mentioning he had retained a carbon copy of the poem, he asks (as a courtesy) for it "back" from Ferrini, seeking Ferrini's permission to publish it elsewhere, since *Voyager* had gotten delayed owing to lack of funds (it would appear as *Four Winds* in 1952) and Olson now had an opportunity to include the poem in a chapbook the Golden Goose Press was interested in publishing. It was the heavily revised carbon copy that was sent Cid Corman for the first issue of *Origin* magazine, featuring Olson.

So the first *Maximus* poem made its appearance rather abruptly, despite the clear buildup previously of intentions and materials for a poem of considerable proportions. There was no indication or even hope that this was finally to be the poem proposed earlier as *West*. The next poems in the series came only intermittently, spread over the next three years, haphazardly. It is not until September of 1950 at the earliest (the exact date is uncertain) that Olson is moved to write a second "letter" of Maximus; the third not until the summer of 1952; and the fourth, "The Songs of Maximus," in early 1953. And it is not until the spring of 1953, one of the busiest times of the poet's life—just after he had prepared and delivered a series of background lectures on the "New Sciences of Man" for an "Institute" he had organized at Black Mountain, as well as fulfilling other duties at the College, while maintaining a voluminous correspondence—that Olson rallied his energies and fully concentrated his attention to sustain the long undertaking.

Not only is there a wide gap between the first few poems, and the uncertain or less than certain beginning, but even before the writing of "I, Maximus," Olson was preoccupied with other archetypes. In late March, probably two months before "I, Maximus," he had written an excellent poem called "The She-Bear," never published during his lifetime, perhaps because he felt it to be unfinished (a revision was attempted ca. 1959). It is addressed to the empowering female principle, also called Lady Mimosa, who is, among others, Callisto, mother of Arcas, the eponymous hero of Arcadia and—as the poet knew from his reading of Pausanias and Rhys Carpenter the year before—ancestor of Odysseus (Callisto is the Great Bear in the sky who guides Odysseus on his voyage in *Maximus* I, 78). The She-Bear is invoked, as Our Lady of Good Voyage will be in *The Maximus Poems,* to guide the hero as he begins the business of making civilization: "o goddess excellently bright"—echoing Ben Jonson—"look kindly / on this effort."

Just as the She-Bear is the Great Mother, Bigmans is the "Son." Immediately upon writing "I, Maximus," indeed not more than a few days later, Olson began what promised to be yet another long poem. This time the hero was Bigmans, modeled explicitly (as notes from January 1945 had already hinted at) on the Babylonian Gilgamesh as a "civilizer" or culture-hero.[23] This new poem included an invocation to the figure as arouser of cities, much like the Maximus of "I, Maximus." The poet continued to think about the Bigmans series until August of 1950, and, significantly, in notes for its continuation, never mentions Maximus, never connects the two.

"Bigmans I" may have been written only a day or two after the first *Maximus* poem. It was sent to Frances Boldereff approximately May 19, two days after Olson had quoted "I,

---

23. Olson stated in conversation with the author, October 1967, that he had originally come upon the name "Bigmans" in a poem by Samuel B. Greenberg, the poet from whom Hart Crane borrowed much. See "The Flower Soul," in "The Greenberg Manuscripts," ed. James Laughlin in *New Directions* for 1939, p. 368: "She roameth at thy side / In Bloom of Lust and pride / I to adore her ream / That shiners the Bigmans ween." The name is also used by Olson in "La Préface" from ca. May 1946 (*Archaeologist of Morning,* p. [43]).

Maximus" to her in a letter. During this time there is no indication the *Maximus* poems would continue, or become *West*. Bigmans, who in earlier notes had been a prototype of Maximus, now existed side by side with him. It is clearly a prepatory poem for something larger, with an invocation beginning: "Arouse yourself, Bigmans, / arouse cities . . ." (the same verb will appear in "Letter 2" of *Maximus*). It is as much the poet, of course, who is the slumbering giant, the man who always felt he had a late start in life, which seeks arousal.[24] Olson sent the poem to Boldereff with the remark: "i am not thru with it, don't know where it goes from here . . ." Even in a second section of "Bigmans," shared with Boldereff on August 8 (still long before "Letter 2" is written), Olson felt there could be no completing such a poem, although he realized that a work of that order would necessarily include the stories of others, the inherited myths and tales, as well as a man's own narrative (the autobiography the *Maximus Poems*, like Pound's *Cantos*, stands in place of):

> that to tell is only to begin to unravel what no man can complete,
> that one tale no matter how severely it is told depends
> on tales once told and tales to be told when his is added
> to the changeful narrative . . .

This Bigmans, a giant marveled at by children, is the civilizer of a new world "where waters have thrown up new land." He is to build the walls of a shining city (like *Glow-ceastre*?): "he built a wall around what ground / was new enough to wipe out wrongs: behold / the brightness of his wall, which shines like flesh . . ." It is like Olson's original New England, a "newing land," a fresh start, where "people can, my people, clean / themselves of postulations gone awry, of runners crusted, shelled / with gurry . . ."

The Bigmans series, however, was insufficiently focused and the poet was unable to sustain it. It breaks off shortly thereafter into an outline for a proposal called "BIGMANS III," dated 24 August 1950, in which Olson merely discusses the

---

24. See, e.g., "Maximus, to himself" (*Maximus* I, 52–53) and "Reading at Berkeley," *Muthologos*, I, 97–156. Olson often felt himself to be psychologically "late"; in notes from 8 March 1948 examining his recent dream-life (in notebook "Faust Buch #1"), he sees himself as a "mere son."

Charles Olson as an infant in his father's mail sack. See *Maximus* III, 21.
Photo courtesy Mrs. Mary Sullivan of Worcester, Mass.

"Over the Cut": summer campers at Stage Fort Park, Gloucester, ca. 1920. Probably the photograph referred to by Olson in *The Post Office* (p. 18). Olson is the young boy on the roof, far left, legs dangling; his mother is in the third row, sixth from left; his father is the middle figure of the front row. Behind him is his sister Lil, or Lizzie, Corliss. "Dotty the Beauty" is there, too, second row, third from left, as is "Daddy Scolpins" (Matt Scullins), far right of third row, leaning against the porch post with folded arms (see *Maximus* I, 109–110).

The "striker" or swordfish harpooner (*Maximus* I, 3) aboard the *Doris M. Hawes*, July 1936. Photo taken by Charles Olson.

Olson with father and mother before Oceanwood Cottage, Stage Fort Park, ca. 1927.

Vandla Hedges. See *Maximus* II, 133. Photo in Literary Archives, University of Connecticut Library, courtesy Philip Hedges.

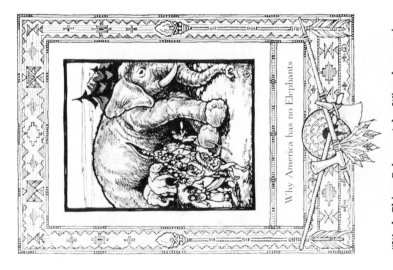

"Wash-Ching-Geka cut / the Winnebago nation out / of elephant . . ." (*Maximus* I, 135). From Olson's boyhood copy of *The Trot-Moc Book of Indian Fairy Tales.*

To my Grandmother
Christmas, 1939

Love,
Charles

From original in Literary Archives, University of Connecticut Library,
courtesy of Philip Hedges.

Olson outside his home in Washington, ca. 1946–47.

Olson reading *The Cantos of Ezra Pound* at Black Mountain, ca. 1949.

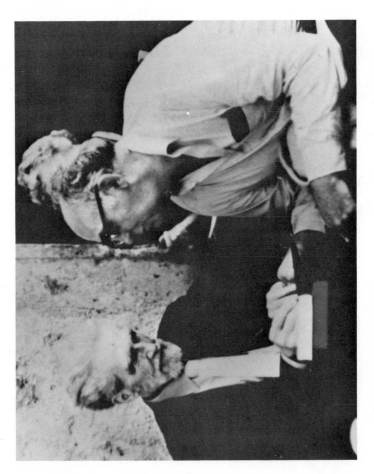

Ezra Pound and Olson at Spoleto, July 1965. Photo courtesy Joan Hart.

Olson at "Enniscorthy," Keene, Va., summer 1945.

Olson in San Francisco, 1957. Photo by Harry Redl.

Olson before his studio in Washington, ca. 1946–47.

"Helen Stein's eyes"—see *Maximus* I, 18. Photo in Literary Archives, University of Connecticut Library, courtesy Mary Shore.

Olson in Washington, ca. 1946–47.

Edward Dahlberg and Charles Olson in conversation, Washington, D.C., ca. 1946–47. Photo by Sam Rosenberg.

VINCENT FERRINI, East Gloucester author, and Mary Shore, secretary of the Cape Ann Society of Modern Art, founders of a new Cape Ann literary publication "4 Winds", are shown here arranging the display of Cape Ann literary works, past and present, in a Main Street window of the William G. Brown Co.　　(Photo by Wilhelm)

"In the plate glass of Brown's (that display) . . ." (*Maximus* I, 18). Clipping in Literary Archives, University of Connecticut Library, courtesy Mary Shore.

COMPLIMENTARY SCROLLS for retiring councillors Ben Smith (left) and Don Ross (right), both ex-mayors, are presented by Councillor Owen Steele.

Retiring Councillors Complimented

Eloquently describing their contributions to the city, Councillor Owen E. Steele last night presented a pair of framed scrolls to outgoing Councillors Donald J. Ross and Benjamin A. Smith II.

"Ex-Mayor Ross and I started out political life together here back in the early 1950's," Steele reminisced. "At 28 years of age he was elected a councillor, and at 31, mayor of Gloucester. He has always been a valuable contributor to political life. I know I speak for the whole council when I say I hope his retirement will be short."

Ross' speech of thanks was brief, but it contained what many thought ~~~ ~n indication that he would be back in political life before too many years had passed.

Smith, also an ex-mayor, was praised by Steele for his active political career. "As the first mayor under Plan E," Steele said, "Ben Smith did an outstanding job. His original administration did as much or more to further Plan E as any succeeding one."

"You make me feel like an old statesman, Owen," Smith replied. And he told how it had been his great pleasure to serve his city, first on the school committee, then as mayor and a councillor.

He expressed his gratitude to the city department heads and explained how they had helped him during his years in office. And he advised the two incoming councillors, Pierce N. Hodgkins and Elliott H.

Parsons, to use "these valuable men" for counsel.

Then glancing across the table at his long-time adversary, Councillor John J. Burke, Jr., Smith told the story of a man obsessed by fear, who "worried his life away" in apprehension that "something frightful was going to happen to him. "But," Smith said, "the object of his fear never came. The fear itself, like a beast in the jungle, devoured him, and he was unable to make any constructive move."

Steele then asked for a rising vote to pass the resolutions which had been inscribed upon the two councillor's scrolls. Every council member rose except Burke, who

remained solidly in his chair, staring at the table.

Burke's signature was also conspicuously absent from Smith's scroll, although both had been signed by every other councillor.

Before the council meeting began, Burke, with some pride, said that although he had signed Ross' scroll, he refused to sign Smith's. "I'm not a hypocrite," he said.

These brief ceremonies, scheduled for 5 p.m., were over by 5.30, and the council adjourned to the Tavern for a farewell dinner for Councilors Ross and Smith.

The scrolls were rendered by hand in script lettering by Franklin E. Hamilton, of the Department of Public Works.

The "complimentary scroll / handlettered / by Franklin E. Hamilton / of Public Works"—*Maximus* I, 142–144. Clipping from the *Gloucester Daily Times* among Olson's papers.

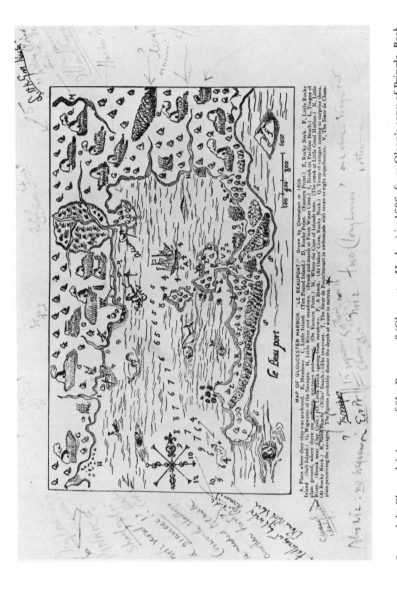

Samuel de Champlain's map of "Le Beauport" (Gloucester Harbor) in 1606, from Olson's copy of Pringle, *Book of the Three Hundredth Anniversary . . . of Gloucester*. See *Maximus* I, 151; also III, 85 and 100.

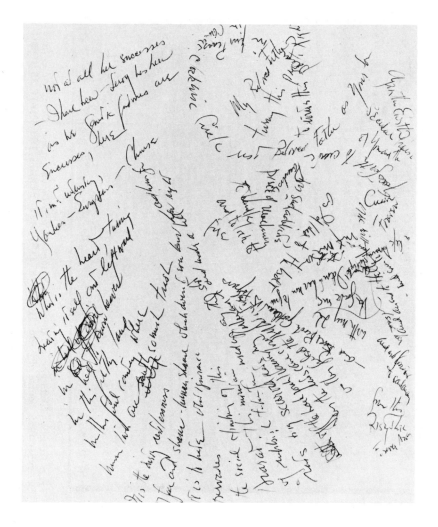

Original manuscript page of the poem beginning "I have been an ability . . ." (see *Maximus* III, 120–121).

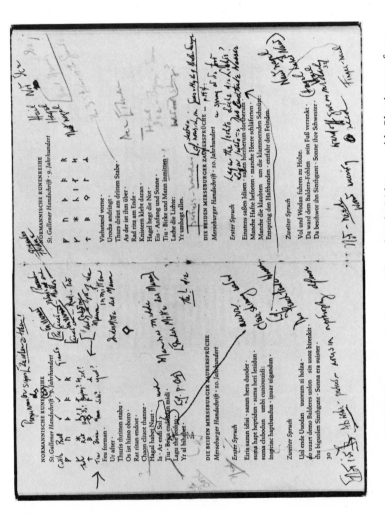

Pages from Wolfskehl and von der Leyen's *Älteste deutsche Dichtungen* with Olson's notes from December 1966. Source of poem "HOTEL STEINPLATZ, BERLIN, DECEMBER 25 (1966)," *Maximus* III, 179–180.

Original manuscript of "*Added to making a Republic in gloom on Watch-house Point" (*Maximus* III, 190), on the back of a letter from Joyce Benson.

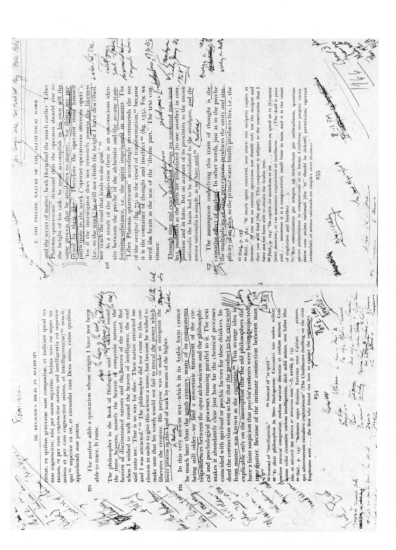

How Olson used his books: Jung's *Psychology and Alchemy* with notes in four colors of ink plus pencil, dated 1966, 1968, and 1969. Used for *Maximus* III, 116 and 228.

Olson in class at Buffalo, early 1964. Photo by Emilio Grossi in Literary Archives, University of Connecticut Library, courtesy Vincent Ferrini.

Olson on the porch of his home on Fort Square, Gloucester, 19 July 1969.

figure and sketches some goals: "What I must make Bigmans is, a discloser of, the root principle, that the PERSON accomplishes the SINGLE by way of the FACT that experience is always DOUBLE." Most important for the development of Maximus is a list of "Bigmans' figures" at the conclusion to this outline, which includes the Phoenician Herakles, Ulysses, Quetzalcoatl, and Cabeza de Vaca. The last two, as has been seen, are connected in earlier notes to the poet's *West* figure; the first two are direct forms of Maximus himself, who must wait until the poems acquire direction and momentum in the spring of 1953 to realize his identity and stand at full height.

III

The opening sections of *The Maximus Poems* were first published separately by Olson's former student at Black Mountain, Jonathan Williams, as part of his Jargon series. *The Maximus Poems / 1–10* appeared in October 1953, followed by *The Maximus Poems / 11–22* three years later, after money had been raised from patrons such as Caresse Crosby, Robert Duncan, Robert Motherwell, and M. C. Richards. The editions were handsomely printed in Stuttgart and limited to 350 and 375 copies apiece, respectively. Both volumes (with the exception of a revised version of the opening poem) were incorporated in the first major collection, titled simply *The Maximus Poems,* which was published in November 1960 by Jargon Books in association with Corinth Books operated by Eli and Ted Wilentz, proprietors of the Eighth Street Bookshop in Greenwich Village. To the two earlier volumes had been added another seventeen poems to make a third section, although there are no divisions in the text and no sections numbered I, II, III—a source of some confusion when *Maximus Poems IV, V, VI* appeared, and especially with *The Maximus Poems: Volume Three,* where the volume number was spelled out rather than designated by a Roman numeral in an effort to minimize confusion.

The poems in this first collected volume were written (with one exception to be cited later) between the spring of 1950 and July 1959, a period of more than nine years, the longest stretch in the series. They appear in the order in which they were written—that is, chronologically—in all but a few cases. Unlike many of the later poems, almost all of these were revised extensively from their original writing. As a series, they begin slowly, irregularly, the first poems, as has been noted, coming only intermittently. They pick up in April and May of 1953, when almost half of the volume was composed, until suspended and poems withheld or abandoned as the series threatened to become too diffuse and take on the entire area of the American West that the poet had proposed to himself in earlier projects like *West* and *Red, White & Black*—so that there were actually many more poems written than appear in the volume. At least fifteen additional poems (in various versions) were written at the time of Letters 5 through 22 but omitted from the series; more in October and November 1953, after Olson cut back, renumbered, and sought to begin again. There were still others occasionally thereafter (a "Letter #37" was reached in April 1957, a "Letter #43" that September).

Olson continued working on the series throughout the summer of 1953, pausing only to prepare a manuscript for Jonathan Williams (taking advantage of that opportunity to revise further), correct proofs of *Maximus Poems / 1–10* (from which he gave a reading at Black Mountain that August), and otherwise engage the steady demands of the college. His letters through June and July of 1953 to Cid Corman, Robert Creeley, and Jonathan Williams—his chief correspondents at the time—record the steady progress of the poems through Letter 33, which he reports to Corman on July 27 had been written—although it is not clear which of the surviving poems this actually is. (Because of revisions and repeated renumberings of the drafts, the same poem might have been numbered differently two or three times on the manuscript.)

He had no knowledge of where it would all lead. He writes to Creeley on May 3 after "The Song and Dance of" (I, 54–58) that he "can't figure how *long* the bloody bastard is going to occupy me." He lacked a clear conception of what he was seeking, playing it "by ear" day after day according to his own dictum (I, 2), and, as his letters reflect, constantly surprising himself with what came out under hand ("32 Maxes now alive!" he writes July 10 to Jonathan Williams). On June 24 he had written Williams—excited at having reached thirty poems and thanking him for having "pushed the button" by offering the opportunity to publish them—that it would take another year or more to "exhaust" the subject. Olson's letters to Creeley, especially, reflect the uncertainties as to the form and direction of the poem. He writes, for instance, on July 27: "I am even persuaded that I may abandon the Max thing where it is unless I can find out how to go by some such thing as I am attributing to you—a rhythm of meaning . . ." He reports he is both "badly stuck" and "terribly confused." Until finally, on September 24, he writes to Corman that the series "had got off its proper track (with #24, and through #33)," adding that "it has meant the hardest sort of both wandering away and cutting it." At this point he abandons the poems that sought to mislead him and which do not appear in the published volumes, so that on October 5 he writes to Jonathan Williams, "I finally broke, I believe, what was a stymie in the Maxes—& am off . . . on another run of 'em." On the same day he writes to Creeley: "am finally roving again, dropping 24–33 as they were—moving them ahead of me, perhaps . . ." Nothing more came of the poem at this time, however, mainly because of the distractions of running Black Mountain and upheavals in his personal life. It was during this time that he added a new wife and a son. He had also become interested in trying his hand at a book on Shakespeare, there were his reviews and essays for the *Black Mountain Review*, and other poems like the *O'Ryans*.

Many of the poems written but omitted from the first volume of *The Maximus Poems* have been published posthumously in the sixth issue of *OLSON: The Journal of The Charles Olson Archives* (1975). In those poems, figures out of the larger American history regularly appear, such as Aaron Burr, the murderous Harpe brothers, the robber-baron Daniel Drew, and Mary Ingles, survivor of Indian captivity on the Allegheny frontier.

There is a poem on the importation of slavery into the nation that adds dimension to the theme that had been introduced in "Letter 2" with the suggestion, "they hid, or tried to hide, the fact the cargo their ships brought back / was black" (I, 5), and continued more extensively in the John Hawkins passage of "Letter 14" (I, 62−63). Another goes as far afield as Cabeza de Vaca's wanderings through the Southwest. Certain of the poems are personal celebrations of love, such as Letter "25" or "The Fragment of a letter of Maximus to his wife." But all of them basically concern honor (as do Letters 19−22) and the conduct of human affairs—history in the sense of commentary and criticism, rather than actively "finding out for oneself." At the completion of this first long "run" of poems, Olson suggests the series's purpose in a letter to Frances Boldereff, 29 August 1953: "I guess these Maximus 'letters'—this poem—is the attempt to come to grips with this country which plagues us all, to try to run it down."

There was an attempt to force a conclusion to the series as early as February of 1954, in the form of three poems titled "Max X," "Max Y," and "Max Z" (of which only the manuscripts of "X" and "Z" appear to have survived among the poet's papers). Olson wrote to Corman on 24 September 1953 that "X" had been so designated, "simply, that when I did write it (two weeks ago) I hadn't, then, seen the path forward." And although he writes at that point that the path did show clear "last Saturday" (September 19, shortly after his reading of Rose-Troup's *John White* discussed below), little actual progress was made and other demands intervened. Frustrated with considerations as to proper subject matter and the inconclusive numbering and renumbering of the poems ever since the series had wandered "off its proper track," the poet declares the next poems, "Y" (written that October), and finally, in a hope to put an end to his difficulty once and for all, "Z." "Max Z," hurriedly written in pencil on 4 February 1954 and beginning "Honor is not now battle . . ." (continuing the theme begun in "Letter 20"), has as part of its title, "& end of the problem!" It was not, however, to be the case, or the solution.

"Letter 23" is the transitional poem of the early series, both chronologically and thematically. It was originally written in September 1953 (and is probably what gave Olson the confidence to write Corman and Creeley that September and October that the series was moving ahead again) and was possibly revised in 1958, thereby spanning both sides of the gap. It deals directly with the facts of Gloucester, introducing the notion of *'istorin,* the poet as Herodotean historian. The poem was made possible by Olson's realization following his discovery of Frances Rose-Troup's *John White,* that there was indeed—as he wrote Creeley on 13 September 1953—a "core" to the poems, and that it was precisely "that ground there, in front of my own damned porch" in Gloucester. In "Letter 23" itself, he locates his subject squarely and literally "in my own front yard" (I, 100).

The course of the poems up to this point is summarized in another letter to Frances Boldereff, 27 October 1953:

> . . . since June, the further "letters" of the Maximus Letters, have had me involved in one of the most difficult compositional times ever—done thru 23, solid, and mss ready since August, but, just at poem 23, even tho another fifteen at least done, I have stayed unsatisfied that the movement of the poem from that point is right
>
> And it is "history" (and of my own front yard, Gloucester) which has had me engaged blindly stupidly
>
> —yet know, have known, that, just here, 23, is the hump, of the book, however long, it may turn out to be . . .

It was something he had realized earlier in writing Corman on May 30 but had been uncertain how to effect it: "I figure, tho, all i have to do is to keep answering my own lead—to toe in. And that the bending back to G[loucester] ought always, actually, to give any reader a 'shape.' "[25] It was coming upon Rose-Troup, particularly her account of the site of the first permanent settlement of Dorchester Company fishermen on Cape Ann at Fisherman's Field in Stage Fort Park—redolent

---

25. *Origin,* 3d series, 20 (January 1971), p. 43.

with the memories of childhood for Olson—together with her evidence from the English port books of the early voyages, that leads Olson to rediscover the poem's original purpose in Gloucester and restore that as the focus of his attention. Thereafter, the poems fall upon the facts of Gloucester more relentlessly.

"Letter 23" is followed by a succession of poems written in Gloucester over the winter of 1957—58 which round out the volume, after Olson had closed Black Mountain and relocated permanently to Fort Square overlooking the harbor—although one of the poems (I, 138—141), interestingly, had first been written as notes made in June 1947 while the poet was in Gloucester and randomly gathering material toward a possible Gloucester book, once *Call Me Ishmael* had been published. This establishes the practice of withholding poems from the series and inserting them where appropriate (of which *"Letter 27,"* identified as "withheld," is the best example), allowing the chronology, like folders in a filing cabinet, to be held open at points while an appropriate piece written earlier is slipped into the new context. Similarly, there is the "Footnote" added to the poem "John Burke" written a full year earlier (I, 142—144), and the rearrangement for dramatic and transitional sake of the final poem in the volume, actually written before the two preceding it. But principally, overwhelmingly, the arrangement is chronological, and an important precedent in the preparation of the succeeding volumes.

IV

Maximus Poems IV, V, VI, the second volume of the series, was first published in London in November 1968 and was not available in the United States until the following April, when a photo-offset edition was released in conjunction with Grossman Publishers in New York.

The volume had originally been offered to Jonathan Williams and the Wilentz brothers of Corinth Books, publishers of the previous volume. Production of the new Jargon/Corinth book, however, progressed only as far as the typesetting, which was not done to Olson's satisfaction. He objected to the spacing of the poems, especially the spacing between lines, insisting there was too much "leading," whereas he demanded a page closer to the original handwritten or typewritten manuscript. Typical comments to the printer or to Eli Wilentz were: "Where in hell did anyone get the idea these *lines* are *not* as *written* . . . Oh Jesus! where *again* does such *ideas*—in the face of a *incredibly careful* mss—go fucking hay-wire?? . . . Here again *SHRINK LEADING!!!!* oh God it's too much! . . . *Note:* whoever directed the Printer to set this this way shld lose his fucking *head* . . . oh God whoever or however cld set such spaces? . . . Can't you see, Eli—or Mr Printer how stupid it wld be to *write* such lines *if* the spacing *were* so abominable?" As a result, production was abandoned, with hard feelings all around, since much time, money, and hope had been invested in the project.

The book was eventually given to Jonathan Cape in London for publication by its subsidiary, Goliard Press, originally founded by illustrator Barry Hall and poet Tom Raworth, both of whom Olson had met while visiting England in 1966. Cape was already planning to reprint *Call Me Ishmael* and *Mayan Letters* in their series of modern classics as well as to issue separate volumes of Olson's selected prose and poetry, and Olson was willing to consider the firm his major publisher. Moreover, Olson was content that the book was to be produced by Barry Hall, since Goliard Press had earlier published '*West*' (a later sequence than the proposed *West* from the 1940s) to his great pleasure.

Maximus IV, V, VI is divided into three sections, all but the first designated by Roman numerals, with the final "Fort Point section" distinct, as a kind of coda. This was the first indication, outside of letters to Jonathan Williams, that the poet had considered the previous volume as having a threefold division. The original proofs of this new volume had included the numeral IV before the text, but Olson immediately excised it. When asked why, he explained that he hoped the reader would feel invited to move more directly into the sequence. At the same time he also expressed hope that the absence of page numbers would permit the reader to more freely move about in the volume.

What the reader is struck with on seeing these middle poems for the first time after those of the previous volume is how the range opens up. There is an effort to drive back to roots, both of Gloucester as the end of migrating Western man,[26] and of man himself, back to the deglaciation and the sources of civilization. With that, the poems seek a consciousness prior to the rational mind the Greeks may have invented. (Seeds for this mythological and cosmological enlargement are buried in a single pivotal passage in the previous volume, in "Letter, May 2, 1959," *Maximus* I, 150: ". . . start all over step off the Orontes onto land no Typhon / no understanding of a cave / a mystery Cashes?") One finds material from old Norse, Vedic, Egyptian, Gnostic, Germanic, Ismaeli Muslim, and Greek sources, as well as local history. There are passages from Hesiod side by side with Algonquin tales, such as that of the enchantress who lusted after the serpent in a pond and is discovered by her husband (II, 21) or of the man who carried his house on his head and was the partridge who brings spring (II, 31). The scope is suggested by the map on the cover of the volume, which is not this time a U.S. Coast and Geodetic Survey of Gloucester but the whole earth when it was most nearly one, based on Alfred Wegener's theory of the origin of continents, although Gloucester continues to be the centripetal force whereby all is held in sway. One is also struck by the visual irregularity of the volume, the many short poems. Whereas in the first volume no poem is less than a page and a half, here one-third of the poems are ten lines or less, as Olson attempts by these "tesserae" (II, 99) to quickly and deftly fill out a poem that seeks to be as wide as a world.

As with the previous sections, this part of the sequence was not always as fixed as might be assumed nor as casual as it might appear to some readers. The underlying principle of a

26. See " 'I know men . . . ,' " *Muthologos*, II, 160–161: "I regard Gloucester as the final movement of the earth's people, the great migratory thing. . . . The migratory act of man ended in Gloucester. . . . Gloucester was the last shore in that sense."

predominantly chronological arrangement continues with a few exceptions, but there were changes and adjustments made all along the way. Enough evidence survives, notably tapes of readings and manuscripts and photocopies among the poet's papers, to trace—however quickly here—the development of *Maximus IV, V, VI*, thereby providing a further sense of Olson's method of composing his epic.

The earliest available evidence is a tape made of a reading at Harvard on 14 February 1962, during which the poet presented the opening sequence of Book IV through *"Cashes"* (II, 19), ten poems altogether. Most significant is the difference from the order of poems as they finally stand. In fact, in all of the early evidence there are minor variations in the series' order, until Olson makes a concentrated effort throughout the summer of 1966 to determine precise dates for all the poems and anchor them in place. On this occasion, upon reading *"Letter 27"* (II, 14–15), which was originally written much earlier at Black Mountain but withheld from the series until this point, he remarks: "Here's a kind of a game you get, playing with yourself. You start to put pieces, and cut . . . but this one was kind of fun to keep back." This casual attitude (for the benefit of the audience) is belied, however, by the pages of notes—reflecting many hours of effort—the poet would make in order to establish the original dates of composition for each of the poems, the original manuscripts of many of them having gotten misplaced in the general disorder of living and the constant production of new writing.

We are fortunate, also, to have a tape of a reading of the entire Book V at Goddard College on 12 April 1962, only a few weeks after the last poems in that section were written. At that point, the poet included in the series earlier versions of three poems later to be revised; omitted one poem included in the published volume; and only spoke of the *"3rd letter on Georges, unwritten"* (II, 107), as the "missing poem . . . I may not be competent to write."

Even more valuable evidence is provided by Olson's reading at the Vancouver Poetry Conference in August of 1963 of the entire volume of *Maximus Poems, IV, V, VI* as it then stood, a reading lasting more than three hours over two days, to a responsive audience. It went up through "*The River Map* and we're done" (II, 201–202), which he there calls "the last poem." From the tapes of the reading, it can be calculated that the manuscript at that stage of its development contained as many as twenty-four poems not present in the 1968 volume. These include a "Second Century Song," designated in some manuscripts as Maximus letter "#32." It was written at Black Mountain ca. 1954–1956 and is described at the reading as one of "two or three pieces that come in between" volumes IV and V, "a poem which has never yet found its place." Like "Letter #28: The Ridge" (published in 1969 in the magazine *Pacific Nation*), it was a stray that the poet never did find a place for.

Some of the poems omitted were indeed fragmentary or obscure ("The Rock / listens to itself / non-fallaciously" or "She vaulted onto his back"), but no more so, it might be argued, than some of the one-line poems that were allowed to stay ("Barbara Ellis, ramp"). And not all of the abandoned poems were weak or inferior to ones retained. One or two, such as "UPWARD CHOKING (on Dogtown)" or the one-liner "No matter how nicely you heist up your behind," drew delighted reactions from the audience at Vancouver; while another, "An Ode on Cape Anne," published in April 1963 in the *Yale Literary Magazine*, is also quite fine. There is no clearly discernible pattern to the omissions. It might be worth adding that while the present writer was visiting the poet for some weeks in June 1968 in Gloucester, Olson opened for the first time the proofs of *Maximus IV, V, VI* which had arrived weeks before from England, and while looking them over together, was asked why some of the specific poems known from the Vancouver tapes and the Prynne typescript (described below) had been left out. The poet suggested that there had been too great a proliferation of short or single-line poems as well as too high a concentration of Old Norse materials in the volume for his purpose. In other words, it was a thematic and formal decision, rather than any judgment on the quality of the individual poems.

In addition to those poems read at Vancouver as part of the series but later omitted, there are at least sixteen poems that

appear in *Maximus IV, V, VI* which were *not* read at Vancouver—
although most of them had been written by that time. These
include "*For 'Moira'* " (II, 12), "Bailyn shows sharp rise . . ." (II,
49), "*The View*—July 29, 1961" (II, 55), and others identified in
the notes to come. The most conspicuous and surprising absence is the final poem of the volume, "I set out now / in a box
upon the sea," a poem that could simultaneously end an epic or
provide a transition for whatever might be left to come.

The next important surviving evidence in considering the
development of *Maximus IV, V, VI* is the typescript of that
volume prepared for Olson through the resources of Jeremy
Prynne at Cambridge University in April and May of 1964.
Prynne, who had been in correspondence with Olson since
1961, providing him with information in various fields of
interest and supplying pamphlets such as the *Cambridge Ancient
History* fascicles along with neatly bound xeroxes of articles and
book chapters, offered to have a typed copy of the manuscript
made so that he might have an early opportunity to see the
poems. A comparison between the published poems and the
manuscript Olson sent Prynne via Jonathan Williams at the end
of March 1964 reveals more than thirty significant differences.
These include an occasionally different order for some of the
poems, early versions of six of them, the absence of others
(most noticeably, again, the final poem of the volume), and the
presence of thirteen poems later omitted (including one not
read at Vancouver). So it is clear that modifications continued
to take place in the volume at this stage as well. All of the changes
outlined here reveal the prolonged deliberation out of which the
poem was constructed, the artful putting together of things
"which had not previously / fit" (II, 157), until the desired sweep
of vision was achieved.

From the Prynne typescript we go to the Xeroxed page
proofs for the proposed Jargon/Corinth edition, typeset from a
new manuscript (including some of the Prynne typescript)
which Olson sent to Eli Wilentz in February 1965. The Xerox
copy was made by the poet before he returned the original
proofs with his corrections (and outbursts of dismay at what he
felt to be a ruinous typesetting job). Even at that late date there

are notable alterations in the sequence. For example, there is
the absence of two poems included in the final volume ("existed / 3000 / BC?" appearing on II, 111, and "Aristotle &
Augustine . . . ," II, 113). The poems "Bailyn shows sharp
rise . . ." (II, 49) and "τά περι του 'ηκεανου" (II, 92) occur in
still unrevised versions. There is also the presence of two
poems abandoned from the published volume—a poem with a
Norse theme beginning "Cunt the Underground passage . . . ,"
and yet another "Letter on Georges" (quite in addition to the
"3rd letter on Georges, unwritten," II, 107). This time it was an
article taken directly from the *Gloucester Daily Times*, written by
its waterfront reporter Jim Clark (the "Squibs" of I, 17) and
entitled "Young Fisherman Describes Rough Trip of Emily
Brown," for which the original newspaper clipping had been
sent to the printer as the manuscript. But most significantly, the
Jargon/Corinth volume, like the version read at Vancouver in
1963 and the Prynne typescript of 1964, also appears to end
with *"The River Map* and we're done"—so that the last poem of
the published volume is a late inspiration indeed, almost an
afterthought.

All the evidence indicates the volume was a developing
organism until its final publication. It was not to reach its
ultimate form until the summer of 1968, when Olson corrected
and returned the proofs to Barry Hall in London. Knowing
this, knowing there had been this path or process gave confidence to the editors asked to form the final volume out of the
materials left behind at the poet's death.

V

The third volume of the *Maximus Poems,* unlike its predecessors, was in fact not assembled into its final form by the poet
himself. It is a rare thing, certainly, in literary history that a significant part of the major work of a poet is put together by
hands and intelligences not the poet's own. It would be like
completing *The Faerie Queene* from stanzas (beyond the Muta-
bility Cantos) left behind at Spenser's death. Yet this is what

had been done with the final volume of the poems, following Olson's somewhat unexpected death in 1970, and some account might here be offered based on the present writer's involvement.

Shortly after he learned that he was dying of cancer, Olson appointed Charles Boer as his literary executor, and at the same time instructed Boer that there was to be a final volume in the *Maximus* series. My own involvement in the production of that volume began a few days later, when upon arriving at New York Hospital the evening of 19 December 1969, Olson telephoned me.[27] It was the first I knew of his hospitalization, and I realized that something was seriously wrong. He began speaking immediately about how it was not the "King," the pituitary gland governing growth and source of his giantism, that would get him in the end, after all, but "Lady Liver"—referring, I would learn a few days later, to the cancer centered in his liver.[28] He then turned to the matter of the *Maximus Poems*, as well as other of his writings which he wanted published. Instructions were minimal: he simply assured me that I would be able to identify the poems from among the papers. He also spoke, as on other occasions, of a separate volume of "alternate" *Maximus* poems, those withheld from the previous books. There was not time for many questions; I did not know exactly how sick he was or when death might occur. I realized later there was actually little more he could have said, even if we had several leisurely hours in which to discuss it. The fact was, he was faced with the same problem of the *massa confusa* which was his papers, the unordered accumulation of many years, as Boer and I later would be. It was one of the things bothering him over the last years, something he had tried to work out and alleviate, for example, during the few weeks I stayed with him in June 1968, when he had rented the apartment next door so the papers could be moved in and a sorting begun. Some years earlier he had even

27. See Boer's *Charles Olson in Connecticut* (Chicago: Swallow Press, 1975), an account of the poet's last days, esp. pp. 131 ff. It must have been the evening of the harrowing ambulance ride described therein that the telephone call was made (at 7:45, according to my note after receiving it).

28. See also Robert Duncan's letter to Jess Collins after his visit to Olson in the hospital, in *OLSON* 1 (Spring 1974), pp. 4–6. In a letter to Robert Creeley, 1 December 1951, Olson writes of "the pituitary . . . how we are kinged by this gland."

written Albert Glover to come with a station wagon and cart off the papers to set up an archive, but the plan did not work out. There were books to be made from among the piles in drawers, in cartons, on tables, all over floors (*A Special View of History* was only the first to emerge). At the same time he needed the decks cleared to get on with his daily work. He may have known he was dying that early, he certainly knew he was being gnawed from within by a physical discomfort or "toxicity" the local doctors were having no success in dealing with.

There were no further instructions, no detailed list of poems to be included; only the first poem—declared as such during the course of the poet's lectures at Beloit College in 1968 and confirmed by various notes among his papers[29]—and a last one, explicitly identified to Boer in person and in writing. Everything else was to fall into place between. The editors recognized this last volume was to be a continuation of the earlier two, picking up in the spring of 1963 where the "Fort Point section" of *Maximus Poems IV, V, VI* left off. The governing principle was to be that of chronology. Not only was this the arrangement of the previous volumes but there was ample evidence from the poet's papers of the extent to which this was so, the lengths to which he had gone to determine dates for the earlier poems. The editors in their efforts to date the poems would see, with a certain grim satisfaction at times, how the poet himself had labored for days in page after page of notes to regain a date for a manuscript long since parted from its original context. Often he was left with the same devices or evidence to achieve the date that we were—a postmark, a date to some note elsewhere on the sheet, the color of ink. Furthermore, a chronological arrangement was a sufficiently "neutral" one, in which the subjectivity of the editors would be least likely to play a part.

Olson told bedside visitors in the hospital that he had "finished" the *Maximus Poems,* though he also begged the doctors for ten more years to complete his work. One suspects the last poem, so much an escutcheon of losses, so concerned as it is with fatality and loss, was itself a compromise with fate. It was

---

29. See "Poetry and Truth," *Muthologos*, II, 8.

written six weeks before his death and was designated as the final poem in notes to Boer written in the margin of a copy of a book appropriately named *The Key,* which had been a gift to the poet in the hospital. There are wonderful grounds for a debate that might last as long as the poems themselves hold interest, in that the word "last," used in describing the poem in the written instructions, looks, some days or in certain slants of light, very much like "lost." However, it must be kept in mind that the poet himself told his literary executor directly from his death-bed, that it was indeed to be the *last* poem—no matter if one feels that the choice of it may have been a shrug in the face of fate.

There was no grand design, no "Canto C" planned years in advance, which would, when finished, "display a structure like that of a Bach Fugue."[30] Rather, notes throughout Olson's papers reveal, once the poem was launched, the repeated attempts to introspectively discern patterns (usually archetypal patterns, often related to aspects of the poet's psychic life)—supporting a reading of the poems that they are as much voyages of self-discovery as they are teachings or social commentary. There was also no evidence the poet had been thinking in terms of a division of the projected volume into sections, three or otherwise, as with the previous volumes. In the several instances he refers to the volume among his notes, it is always simply "Volume 3" or "Volume III." Only once, as the editors point out in their brief introductory note to the volume, does he speak of "Volume VII and thereafter"—a fact that reinforces the sense of the unplanned nature of the book.

The editors, however, were familiar with the poems that had been published by the poet himself to that date, including ones destined for the new volume which had appeared in magazines or as broadsides. Almost one-third of the final poems had been published by Olson before his death in scattered magazines, or read at readings or during interviews preserved on tape. None of these indicated a new or unexpected departure but served to support the continuation of the series in the direction indicated

30. William Butler Yeats reporting Pound's early plan for the *Cantos* in "A Packet for Ezra Pound" (1928), reprinted in *A Vision* (New York: Macmillan, 1938), p. 4.

by the second volume. In addition, Olson and I had talked at length those three weeks in 1968 I was with him, going through the first volume of poems page by page, as well as a chronology of his life, each day shortly after he awoke. He allowed it in all generosity and seriousness to be our "work" for the day, and tolerated my ceaseless questions as we discussed not only the texts at hand but plans for work to come. One of the things he hoped to do in the poems, for example, was pay greater attention to West Gloucester, which he had begun to do early in 1964 in poems in *Maximus* III, 24 and 26–27; Dogtown preoccupied him less, and he in fact puts it to rest in III, 195–196.

Boer and I also had the opportunity of surveying the entire extent of Olson's papers and examining his notes on the making of the first two volumes, before undertaking the task of going through the papers once again with the express purpose of singling out any poem that might conceivably have been a *Maximus* poem. Xeroxed copies were made of the typewritten ones and typescripts were made of the others in order to render them more accessible in the later stages of editing. Because of delays over a contract for the volume, there were many more opportunities to review the papers and the selections even after the final choice was made. Even so, some poems were missed— at least two, in this writer's opinion: one which had been thought too fragmentary (also surviving in several attempts, so that the poet himself appeared indecisive), but which I am now convinced should have been included. It emphasizes another dimension of the figure of Enyalion, who becomes a commanding presence in the later poems, and has an interesting tie as well to one of Olson's earliest poems.[31] It is hoped that it will be added to later editions. The other poem concerns the shipment of Gloucester goods to the colony of Virginia, indicating the extent of Cape Ann's commercial resourcefulness. However, none of these omitted poems alter in the slightest the scope, direction, and overall achievement of the volume as it stands.

---

31. A poem beginning "the salt, & minerals, of the Earth return . . . ," written in 1966 or 1967 in a notepad from the Mayflower Hotel in London, echoing the third from the last line of "The K" from 1945 (*Archaeologist of Morning,* p. [9]).

The poems were identified from the confused mass on the basis of subject matter. Confirmation was often supplied by a typed manuscript, but not every typed poem or fragment was included. One of the fundamental difficulties was to tell what was a poem and not prose or a note or a fragment. Olson's prose is itself often highly styled and poetic. For example, the poet's final piece of writing, the deathbed "Secret of the Black Chrysanthemum," so clearly a summation of dominant themes of the late *Maximus Poems* and of Olson's life over the final ten years, includes many specific references to matters already occurring in the *Maximus Poems*.[32] Yet he clearly identifies them as " 'Secret' notes" to Charles Boer rather than a poem. Further, it was written three weeks after the poem already identified to Boer as the final poem of the series. It might, of course, have been included as a kind of coda to the epic, but because there were no explicit instructions that this was to be the case, because there is no reference in it to Gloucester or to Maximus, and because of the intensely personal nature of the notes and their similarity to the many pages of notes so commonplace among the poet's papers, the decision was readily made not to include or append it to the volume.

More troublesome were some typed poems written in the period following his wife's death which do include the figure of Maximus but which seemed so private, the way many of the autobiographical poems or passages are not, that to include them would have in fact introduced a new theme, that of personal human love—not Maximus's love—into the poems. It was not ours to do. Nothing, save perhaps the last poem, indicates the poet would have done so. Indeed, every chance he had during his lifetime, whether in the published poems or those read at readings or during interviews—nothing indicates he thought to do so. In fact, in some of the poems it is not clear the subject is even the poet's wife, but rather an old friend, reflecting his acute loneliness and distress and further complicating the issue, leading the editors to realize how little likely it was that Olson himself would have included the poems or even

32. *OLSON* 3 (Spring 1975), pp. 64–92.

the theme, beyond the manner in which it appears, for example, in "Letter 72" (II, 53).

Identifying the poems to be included meant going methodically through the more than 250 document boxes which now house the assorted papers and records of Olson's life; the roughly 60 notebooks and notepads of the period from 1963 to his death (some 20 of the poems turned up there); the letters from over 500 correspondents, on the backs of envelopes of which poems were occasionally composed; and through the 1,500 books in Olson's library (a version of one poem, III, 192, was written on the back cover of a volume of verse by Barbara Guest; another poem, III, 72, appeared on the back page of Olson's working copy of *The Maximus Poems,* 1960). It took a year beyond the preliminary sorting done in the summer of 1970 on behalf of the Olson estate to prepare the materials for disposition according to Olson's last instructions, and it was clearly the only way to proceed. Olson's habits required it. He wrote on everything, whatever was at hand, including restaurant placemats, discount coupons from supermarkets, paper towels the nurse brought as he lay dying in the hospital, just as he wrote in his books, on his maps and Tarot cards, on the window frames and wainscotting of his apartment in Gloucester, on the walls beyond blackboards in the classrooms where he taught, and even inscribed money as souvenirs. He used the world around him as he found it with an extraordinary confidence. Some of the poems in the volume under consideration were written on check stubs and recopied, on blank checkbooks or envelopes torn open and spread flat, or on a card from a deaf mute portraying the hand alphabet of the deaf, undoubtedly handed to him in the street—the only things he might have had in his pocket at the time. In another case, a partially opened letter lay, presumably, at hand on the kitchen or bedside table. He began a poem (III, 190) on the back of the envelope and continued on to the back of the protruding letter, in which position it was found preserved among the papers, like a figure from Pompeii.

Even the poet himself lost the thread of the order of a manuscript written this way—of some consolation but little help to the editors. In one case, he copied the poem out longhand from its first hastily written appearance in a blank checkbook (the poet's scorn of money!), scribbled at night under street-lamps while out walking near the "Cut," his precinct. His attempt to copy the original begins neatly enough, but eventually the original sequence is lost, as if Theseus had dropped the thread on the floor of the labyrinth, and the poet makes in his small yellow notepad the best sense he could. He is imperfectly successful: his own question marks become part of the movement and meaning of the poem (III, 158). There is also an unfulfilled gap, a jump in sense between the lines "& tell you I have ____?" and "The river runs now . . ." which follows. It is not much noticeable and actually adds to the disjointed realism of the occasion, but it was hardly a calculated stroke. Such gaps in "sense" where chance is operative, or losses caused by the nature of the original manuscript, had not stopped Olson himself from incorporating the error into the poem on other occasions, at times capitalizing on it. There is, as an example, the unexpected pause occurring in the non-*Maximus* poem beginning "Snow White was always waiting . . . ," which resulted from the poet's typing of his own unclearly or incompletely revised holograph version.[33] Again, line lengths of certain poems were often determined by the size of a piece of paper or the room left to write on it. This indulgence of chance, which he elsewhere denounces as "I Ching-ness" (at least in its social implications),[34] is similar to his insistence, observed in the editor's notes to *Additional Prose*, of allowing the orthographic lapses to remain: "*no* damn it   the error is valuable."[35] There is also the instance observed by the editors in their introductory note to *Volume Three* of Olson's instructions to the printer of *Stony Brook*, the journal where the poem on III, 197–201 first appeared, *rejecting* the correction of a simple inconsistency in regard to the accenting of an Islamic name. Here the poet stubbornly defends the idiosyncratic and unique, the individualistic, as well as the truth-in-error Freud called "parapraxis."

33. *OLSON* 4 (Fall 1975), p. 18, and editor's note on p. 33 there.
34. "Theory of Society," *Additional Prose*, p. 22.
35. Note to "Mrak," on p. 95 of *Additional Prose*.

It might be quickly pointed out, however, that not all error regarding the poems need be tolerated. There are several minor typographical lapses in all three volumes (corrected in the poet's working copies of *Maximus* I and II, and in the corrigenda to *Maximus* III in *OLSON* 4, p. 113) that should stand corrected in future editions. Most important, the second "Letter on Georges" (I, 138–141)—which had been sent Jonathan Williams in 1960 lacking any clear statement of Olson's intentions—should be separately identified, according to the poet's instructions, and distinguished from the "1st Letter on Georges," within which it lies confused.

Olson occasionally expressed admiration for Li Po, the Chinese poet who wrote his verses on leaves plucked from a tree, which he afterward threw to the wind while moving ahead on horseback. Li Po's influence is perhaps seen in the case of another poem (III, 10), for which the original manuscript—typed on a short-lived leaf of inexpensive yellow paper the poet often used and apparently left out too long in the sun, near an unshaded window in the apartment—had disintegrated so badly (with chips and holes in it like a Dead Sea scroll) that the poet himself had to paste the brittle sheet on another of white typing bond and attempt to reconstruct it. He no longer had available the original handwritten manuscript written on pages torn from his copy of Lewis's *Latin Dictionary* and temporarily lost to the turmoil of living. Even following their discovery of the original, however, the editors decided to accept the poet's restored version as the more successful poem.

In the preparation of the volume, other difficulties abounded. In one case, a word near the end of a poem composed on a yellow legal-sized pad was written on the very bottom of the page, so that the word is lost to the pad's edge. There was no later typescript made for the poem, which is otherwise an excellent and interesting one (III, 211). It is unlikely the poet himself could have made the word out, unless to retrieve it from memory. In another instance (III, 95–96), three separate endings were attempted by the poet, none of them crossed out. Again, a handwritten manuscript that runs for eight pages in a fairly legible manner, a poem of obvious strength and significance (III, 117–121), suddenly enters a series of unreproducible and increasingly illegible spirals—like the "Rose of the World" poem (III, 104) only tighter, more involuted, more bewildering. The configuration printed on p. 121 of that third volume is only the first of those spirals, and is itself, owing to the strictures of print, only an approximation. After that point, the helixes become increasingly personal and confused—hopeless snarls on the page. It is inconceivable the poet would have himself published the sections, so the obvious compromise was made by the editors and the omission indicated by an ellipsis within brackets.

The most bewildering manuscript was of the long poem beginning on *Maximus* III, 145. An eight-page typescript was found among the papers together with a small group of other *Maximus* poems that had already been published in various magazines. Neatly typed, it was without title and the first line began somewhat abruptly (allusively, in medias res, without initial capital), though not unusually so. It was clearly a *Maximus* poem, datable by internal evidence to around 1966 or 1967, and the editors were prepared to include it as such. No holograph original was to be found. As the work of sorting and searching went on, however, a handwritten fragment surfaced, composed rapidly in red ink on the back and inside front cover of a small spiral-bound notebook which also contained the original handwritten version of "[to get the rituals straight . . ." (III, 173–174) dated 1966. The lines dealt with John White, Hugh Peter, and the settling of Gloucester, and some of them seemed to be a first draft of the opening lines of the typed poem, breaking off with the words, "Hugh Peter pastor North Church Salem before . . ." It was realized that this linked up with the opening lines of the typescript, which begins "going home to England . . ." Olson had apparently misplaced the original opening portion of the manuscript and had proceeded to type out what he had at hand (unless the remainder of the poem was originally composed on the typewriter—an unusual practice for the poet at this date, despite the proclamations of "Projective Verse"). Some weeks later, however, there came to light, folded in a notebook from another portion of the mass of

papers, what appeared to be still another, earlier portion of the
poem. It was written in the same rich red ballpoint ink as the
fragment in the notebook, on an invitation to the wedding of
poet Joel Oppenheimer, which bore the date 5 June 1966,
indicating the fragment was from the same time period as the
rest of the poem. This new portion seemed to serve as the true
opening section of the poem (its closing lines concerned the
place names of Cape Ann as reflections of its physical characteristics, the subject of the opening lines of the notebook
fragment) and was included as such by the editors. A similar
case of misplaced manuscripts occurred with the poem titled
"Stevens song" (see note to *Maximus* III, 30).

The editors were not always so successful. In one instance,
what appeared to be the sole surviving manuscript of a poem
(III, 35–36), a handwritten composition undated but from approximately 1963–64 (dealing with the figure of the Bulgar
who occurs in other poems as well as the poet's notes from that
time), had in fact also survived as a typescript (actually, two
typescripts and another holograph attempt). The typescript
revealed a slightly different line order and a decisively earlier
date, a date making its eligibility for inclusion in the present
volume doubtful. These had been attached to the back of a
group of original manuscripts from *Maximus* IV, V, VI and
overlooked. Another poem was not included because it was not
fully legible until a recording of Olson reading it became
available after the volume had gone into production. This was
the poem beginning "Her stern like a box . . . ," and is included
on the long-playing record not quite accurately titled *Charles
Olson Reads from Maximus Poems IV, V, VI*, which was not
released until 1975. It concerns the *Doris M. Hawes* caught in a
storm on her way back from Georges Bank, and as such is a
sequel to the story told in *Maximus* I, 38–39. The poem survives among Olson's papers in a single holograph version only,
written in pencil at the bottom of the typescript of the poem
that begins, "Between Cruiser & Plato . . ." (III, 205) from
1 January 1969. The editors sought to include it in the volume,
but it was not possible to make out every word (more conse-

quential in a poem this brief than in certain longer ones), as the writing had become smudged from careless handling of the manuscript and blotted by a grease stain. It is interesting to note that Olson himself had encountered the same difficulty and had to read "the 'something' of the full North Atlantic itself," when he attempted the poem for Gerard Malanga during his interview for the *Paris Review* in April 1969.[36] Fortunately, however, the poet had also read the poem only two weeks before—presumably from the same manuscript, but before it had been rendered illegible and the poem nearly lost—for the tape made by Barry Miles from which the record was produced, where the missing word, "*oasis* / of the full North Atlantic," can be clearly heard.

Precise dates for the poems, so necessary to maintain the chronological order, often had to be won from the chaos. This was possible for all but six or seven of them—and for some of those poems it was still possible to ascertain an approximate date by considering the pile of papers in which the originals had been found. But even here, with the chronological arrangement, there is some discrepancy and overlap, specifically in the case of four poems (III, 11−14) published by the poet as a group in 1964 but written in April of 1963, *before* the final poems of the "Fort Point section" as well as the very first poem of the volume under discussion. Still, because the poems are of value and were written and published by Olson so close in time to the others, it was felt best to include them, erring on the side of generosity rather than attempting to impose (as Olson did not) too restrictive a selection according to a principle that is finally mechanistic.

Despite these omissions, the edition makes available the poems that complete the series, those by which the reader needs to judge it, assembled according to the most commonplace and pragmatic principles while closely following the precedents established by the earlier volumes. If there are matters for future scholars to resolve or amend, it is hoped the present *Guide* will assist and encourage the effort.

36. See *Muthologos*, II, 150.

VI

Like most guides, this one will best reveal its structure in use. Still, a few preliminary directions are in order. The title for each poem is given first (or first line if there is no title), indicated by the symbol ▶ ; date and place of composition are supplied, and any other pertinent information. This is followed by the annotations in series, arranged page by page. A general form for entries can be established:

1. Page number from the appropriate volume of *The Maximus Poems* along the left margin (unless the item occurs as part of the title of a poem, such as "Maximus" or "Gloucester" in "I, Maximus of Gloucester, to You," when it will appear immediately following).

2. The item to be annotated, the name or phrase as it appears in the text, with enough of its content, a full line if necessary, so it can be readily located. If the annotation is to an entire passage, this is indicated by ellipses (e.g., *Maximus* I, 94, "Hyssop, for him, / was the odor of meat . . .").

3. The annotation itself, cross-indexed wherever necessary. Cross-referencing becomes more extensive as references accumulate throughout the poems, reflecting the complexity of the poems and the emerging patterns. References are annotated on their first appearance only. Not every subsequent occurrence of the name or phrase is noted but only those of immediate bearing on the reference at hand—in which case the reader is directed either to another appearance in the poems ("See *Maximus* I, 86") or to a note elsewhere in the *Guide* ("See note to *Maximus* I, 86 below"). Where the suggestion is to "See also *Maximus* I, 121 and note below," the reader is invited to look at both the page in *The Maximus Poems* as cited, and then the annotation to the item from that page, in the *Guide*. For possible additional appearances of a name or phrase, or in the case of the direction "q.v.," the reader is expected to consult the index for locations.

4. Shortened bibliographical references, if any, for which the full forms are to be found in the bibliography at the back. Olson's published writings are noted without the author's

name, sometimes in abbreviated form; otherwise both author and title are given.

It is hoped that all exceptions to the above are quickly self-evident. Running heads have been provided to assist the reader's eye in locating an annotation. Following the bibliography is the index to all three volumes of *The Maximus Poems,* an alphabetical list of all names of persons and places together with the volume and page numbers of each appearance. These are given in the fullest form to be found in the poems and spelled as they there appear.

Throughout the preparation of the *Guide to the Maximus Poems,* a number of people assisted in a great many ways. The author would now like to undertake the pleasantest task of all, and extend his thanks to all of them:

Most especially, Charles Olson, whose trust I hope I have fulfilled.

Also, the following friends for their repeated kindnesses, beginning with the members of my original dissertation committee—Robert Creeley, who served as chief adviser, allowing me the freedom to explore the poems for myself while lending encouragement whenever necessary, and who made available copies of his letters from Olson, now in the Washington University Library, St. Louis; John Clarke, who has my deep thanks, although he has since gained an acknowledgment greater than I could ever bestow, by having one of the final *Maximus* poems addressed to him; and Albert Cook, who brought Charles Olson to Buffalo and otherwise created a climate for the enthusiastic pursuit of poetry.

I am equally grateful to Donald M. Allen, to whom all readers of the New American Poetry are continuously indebted, and to Charles Boer, who faithfully served as executor of the Olson Estate and who kindly read a draft of this introduction, making numerous suggestions for improvement. Also, to Peter Anastas; Elizabeth Day, who helped on countless Gloucester matters; Vincent Ferrini; Albert Glover; Gerrit Lansing; Mary Shore; and Alexander Smith, whose patience and clarity helped prepare the index. John and Catherine Seelye also made some very valuable suggestions concerning the introduction; the shortcomings which remain there and throughout the volume are my own.

Without the advantage of Charles Olson's extensive papers, this *Guide* would be very much the poorer. They form the core of the Literary Manuscripts Collection at the University of Connecticut Library, which also includes the papers of Edward Dorn, Vincent Ferrini, and Michael Rumaker, all of which were of help on this project. Unless otherwise indicated, quotations from unpublished material by Olson in the course of the annotations are from this source and are published here with the library's permission. Other unpublished material appears with the permission of the Olson Estate.

The following other libraries kindly made available copies of letters, manuscripts, and tape recordings by Charles Olson: Goddard College Learning Aids Center; Harvard College Library's Poetry Room, Stratis Haviaris curator; Humanities Research Center, University of Texas at Austin; Lakehead University Library; Lilly Library, Indiana University; Lockwood Memorial Library's Poetry Collection, State University of New York at Buffalo, Karl Gay curator; The Poetry Center, San Francisco State University; Simon Fraser University Library; Spencer Research Library, University of Kansas; University of California at San Diego Library's Archive for New Poetry, Michael Davidson director; and University of Pennsylvania Library. Thanks also to the Beinecke Rare Book and Manuscript Library, Yale University, for a letter from Edward Dahlberg to Alfred Stieglitz.

And thanks to those individuals who generously and readily made available copies of their Olson materials: Joyce Benson, William Bronk, E. Hyde Cox, Robert Duncan, Monroe Engel, Brian Goodey, Brice Howard, Henry A. Murray, Robert Payne, M. L. Rosenthal, Anna Shaughnessy, Charles Tomlinson, Fred Wah, John Wieners, and Jonathan Williams.

The late Paul Blackburn, Edward T. Bloomberg, Frances M. Boldereff, the late Constance W. Bunker, John Cech, Cid Corman, Barbara Ellis, John Faulise, Joan Hart, Philip Hedges, Robert Hogg, John C. Larsen, Harry Martin, Ralph Maud,

Jean Radoslovich, Dan Rice, and Mildred S. Smith, all gave very specific assistance; and I am grateful to Jonathan Bayliss and the late Edward Dahlberg for permission to quote from their letters.

I am greatly obliged to the University of Connecticut Library and its staff for additional assistance, especially Richard H. Schimmelpfeng, director of Special Collections. The Sawyer Free Library of Gloucester and its staff also has my thanks, as do the Cape Ann Historical Society and the Buffalo and Erie County Public Library.

Sharp-eyed Clayton Eshleman copy edited the original manuscript for publication, raising pertinent questions and helping to improve it.

Very special acknowledgment is made to the University of Connecticut Research Foundation, Hugh Clark presiding, for providing funds for the typesetting of the manuscript.

And thanks above all to my sons and constant comfort, George Adam and Aaron, and my wife Colette, who actually solved one of the puzzles confronting the annotator by first discovering and then nimbly getting down on hands and knees to trace by finger tip the inscription identifying the "Aldermens polished granite statement" (III, 212) embedded in the side of the "Cut." In a somewhat obsessive project such as this, who could ask for more?

Chronology of the Life and Career of Charles Olson

1910   Born Charles John Olson, December 27, in Worcester, Mass., son of Charles (Karl) Joseph Olson, a letter-carrier, and Mary Theresa (Hines) Olson; raised in a tenement on Norman Avenue in Worcester.

ca. 1915 Begins summers at Gloucester with father and mother. By at least 1923 the family regularly occupied "Oceanwood" cottage on Stage Fort Avenue each summer, in what was known as Barrett's camp, above Stage Fort Park.

1917–24   Attends Abbott Street Grammar School, Worcester.

1924–28   Attends Classical High School, Worcester, where he is an honor student, captain of the debating team, and president of his class.

1928   Wins Northeast regional oratory championship that spring, and takes third place (despite bad cold) in National Oratorical Contest, Washington, D.C., May 26. Ten-week tour of Europe as a prize. Enters Wesleyan University, Middletown, Conn., upon return; while at Wesleyan he is an honor student (Phi Beta Kappa), editorial writer for the school newspaper, goalie on the soccer team, actor, orator, and candidate for a Rhodes scholarship.

1929   Attends the Gloucester School of the Little Theatre for the summer, performing in several productions.

1930   Works briefly for the C & R Construction Company on a reservoir project in Gloucester that July (see *Maximus* I, 21).

1931   Substitute carrier for the Post Office in Gloucester that summer and subsequent summers through 1934.

1932   Receives BA from Wesleyan in June. Performs with the Moorland Players in Gloucester that summer. Continues studies at Wesleyan in the fall, with a course (as an Olin Fellow in English) in American literature at Yale.

1933   Receives MA in English from Wesleyan in June, with thesis "The Growth of Herman Melville, Prose Writer and Poetic Thinker." Continues at Wesleyan that fall; begins search for Melville's library, going to Cambridge, Mass., for research among the Melville family papers, and by the beginning of 1934 has made enough progress for his teacher, Wilbert Snow, to arrange for an award of an Olin Fellowship in Economics to continue the work.

1934–36 Instructor of English at Clark University, Worcester. His father dies in August 1935 at 53 of a cerebral hemorrhage.

1936 Sails July 7 aboard the schooner *Doris M. Hawes* on a three-week voyage for swordfish on Brown's Bank. Meets Edward Dahlberg early August in Gloucester. Enters Harvard University in the fall as a graduate student and assistant in English and American literature. Courses taken at Harvard will include Frederick Merk's "The Western Movement."

1937 Returns to Harvard as an instructor and tutor (staff of John Winthrop House) there and at Radcliffe.

1938 July 1, first trip west, hitchhiking from Kansas City to San Francisco; returns leisurely by Greyhound (by August 14). Continues at Harvard in the fall as counselor in American Civilization (Winthrop House); course work for Ph.D. completed by the spring of 1939, first of three candidates in American Civilization program. "Lear and Moby-Dick" published with the help of Dahlberg, who selected it from a long paper written for F. O. Matthiessen's class. Living in Boston on Charles Street.

1939 Awarded first Guggenheim Fellowship in March for studies in Melville. Spends fall and winter with his mother in Gloucester; writes a first version of a book on Melville, which Dahlberg advises against publishing.

1940 Writes his first poems and an essay on myth in February while still at Gloucester; leaves for New York the next day. Meets the painter Corrado Cagli in May, and Constance Wilcock, who is to be his wife, the same month. Returns to Gloucester in June.

1941 October 1940 to April, living at 86 Christopher Street in Greenwich Village. May to July, publicity director for the American Civil Liberties Union. Beginning in November, serves as chief of the Foreign Language Information Service, Common Council for American Unity, New York (to September 1942).

1942–44 In September, begins work for the Office of War Information (OWI) in Washington; will serve as Associate Chief,

Foreign Language Division, until he resigns in protest, May 1944. Only publication for the government is a pamphlet in collaboration with Ben Shahn, *Spanish Speaking Americans in the War,* issued in 1943.

1944   Hired as director of the Foreign Nationalities Division, Democratic National Committee. Winter in Key West.

1945   In January, as a result of his service to the Democrats he is informally offered by party officials in Key West the posts of Assistant Secretary of the Treasury and the Post Office Generalship; disenchanted with politics, however, he turns down the offers. Writes the poem "The K." Starts *Call Me Ishmael* on April 13, finishes by August 6 (the bombing of Hiroshima) all but the introductory chapter on the whaleship *Essex,* which is written on a boat from Nantucket. Staying at "Enniscorthy," an estate owned by friend Adam Kulikowski near Charlottesville, Virginia, that summer. Returns to Washington (studio at 217 Randolph Place NE). Finishes "This is Yeats Speaking" that November.

1946   On January 4 begins visits to Ezra Pound in St. Elizabeths, which will last until the spring of 1948 (though with at least one visit beyond then). His first poems are published in *Harper's Bazaar, Atlantic Monthly,* and *Harper's.* In New York that spring to work as an agent for Polish interests at the early meetings of the United Nations Security Council. Lectures at the School of Political Action Techniques sponsored by the National Citizens Political Action Committee, Washington, June 26–29.

1947   Spring in Washington; March, *Call Me Ishmael* is published with the help of Ezra Pound and Caresse Crosby (Pound had sent the book to Eliot who found it "too American" and passed it on). Visit to Gloucester in June, lunch with Alfred Mansfield Brooks, director of the Cape Ann Historical Society: the *Maximus Poems* conceived. Leaves for West Coast on July 2, lecturing on poetry August 8 at the Pacific Northwest Writer's Conference at the University of Washington, Seattle. Goes from there to Sacramento and the Bancroft Library, Berkeley, for Sutter-Marshall and Donner Party material. Meets Robert Duncan and Carl Sauer.

1948   Returns from California to Washington, D.C. by early spring. Writes book on his father composed of three stories,

"Stocking Cap," "Mr. Meyer," and "The Post Office." Awarded second Guggenheim Fellowship for a book on the morphology of American culture to be called "Red, White & Black," a study of the differing ways the Indian, white settler, and Negro found to shape a human society in the American West. Writes "The Fiery Hunt," a dance-play based on *Moby-Dick*. Last political activity, supporting the nomination of Sen. Claude Pepper of Florida for President at the Democratic National Convention that July. Gives lecture on art at American University, Washington, July 29. Invited to Black Mountain College in September by Josef Albers; gives three lectures, asked to return one week out of every month to replace Edward Dahlberg (through the spring of 1949).

1949   His first collection of verse, *Y & X*, is published in February, through Cagli's suggestion, by Caresse Crosby's Black Sun Press. "The Kingfishers" written in Washington, February-March (final draft dated Black Mountain, 20 July). Reads at the Institute of Contemporary Art, Washington. Summer at Black Mountain; directs "Exercises in Theatre," August 28–29. Fall in Washington, writing. Seeks out Vincent Ferrini while on a visit to his mother in Gloucester, having read a poem by him in *Imagi*. Lectures at the Watkins Gallery, American University, December 15, to open an exhibit of "Drawings in the 4th Dimension" by Corrado Cagli.

1950   First *Maximus* poem "I, Maximus of Gloucester, to You," written that May in Washington as a letter to Vincent Ferrini. Ferrini sends some of Olson's poems to Robert Creeley, then planning a little magazine in New Hampshire, but Creeley turns the poems down, writing Ferrini that Olson is "looking around for a language, and the result is a loss of force." Olson responds to Creeley's rejection, and their correspondence, which will grow to an exchange of almost 1,000 letters all together, begins. April-May, takes the Cagli exhibit on the road (with a stop at Montevallo, Ala., enroute, to visit the author Robert Payne) to Black Mountain, where he repeats his Washington lecture and gives a reading. Returns to Washington. "Projective Verse" is published in *Poetry New York* in October. Mother dies in Worcester on Christmas Day.

1951   February to July in Lerma, Campeche, on the Yucatan peninsula; meanwhile *Origin* 1, featuring Olson, has appeared in April. Returns to Black Mountain at the invitation of the students, teaches through August (will remain as a faculty member, and later rector, until the closing of the school in 1956). Daughter Katherine Mary born October 23.

1952   Spring, receives grant for study of Mayan glyphs from the Wenner-Gren Foundation for Anthropological Research. Fall in Washington, on leave of absence from Black Mountain.

1953   *In Cold Hell, In Thicket* published by Creeley in Mallorca in March. Organizes an Institute of the New Sciences of Man, held at Black Mountain, March 7–28. First major run of *Maximus* poems, from Letters 5 on, also begun in March. Reads *Maximus* letters 1–10 and 11–22 for the first time, at Black Mountain in August. *The Maximus Poems / 1–10* published in Stuttgart by Jonathan Williams in October.

1954   *Mayan Letters* published in January. Meets Elizabeth Kaiser, a student at Black Mountain, who is to be his wife. Reads at the Charles Street Meeting House, Boston, September 11.

1955   Son Charles Peter born May 12.

1956   Writes "As the Dead Prey Upon Us," "The Lordly and and Isolate Satyrs," and "Variations Done for Gerald Van De Wiele." Closes Black Mountain in October; remains with wife and son, preparing the property for sale. Appointed by the court, assignee for benefit of the creditors of Black Mountain. *The Maximus Poems / 11–22* published that fall.

1957   Writes "The Librarian." That February gives readings at the San Francisco Museum of Art, the Poetry Center of San Francisco State College, and at Carmel Highlands; offers "A Special View of History" in five lectures for private subscribers. Returns to Black Mountain, and by June sells the property. In July moves with family to 28 Fort Square, Gloucester. Second run of *Maximus* poems begun late that fall with "a Plantation a beginning."

1958   Living in Gloucester, except for a period from June to November at Provincetown.

1959   "Maximus from Dogtown—I" written that fall.

1960   Reads at Wesleyan Spring Poetry Festival, April 19 (the first of his collegiate readings that will include Brandeis, Dartmouth, Goddard, Cornell, St. Lawrence, Brown, and later, Buffalo and Tufts). Reads April 30 in Toronto. *The New American Poetry* published in May, *The Maximus Poems* and *The Distances* in November. Reads at Hammond's Castle, Gloucester, September 3. Participates in Timothy Leary's research program on consciousness-altering drugs in Cambridge in late November, and again in January 1961.

1961   Receives Longview Foundation award for *The Maximus Poems*.

1962   February, reads at Magnolia, Mass.; gives Morris Gray reading at Harvard; reads again in Toronto. Summer in New York for six weeks, visiting with LeRoi Jones and Edward Dorn.

1963   Attends the Vancouver Poetry Conference, July 29–August 16, where he reads the whole of *Maximus IV, V, VI*. Assumes duties as Visiting Professor of English, State University of New York at Buffalo, that September, teaching courses in Modern Poetry and Myth and Literature, and living in Wyoming, N.Y., some 40 miles southeast of Buffalo.

1964   Wife killed in an automobile accident in Batavia, N.Y., March 28. Spends summer in Gloucester. Returns to Buffalo in September to teach until May 1965.

1965   Reads at the Festival of the Two Worlds, Spoleto, June 26 to July 2. Attends PEN conference in Bled, Yugoslavia. Reads and gives seminar at the Berkeley Poetry Conference, July 20–23. *Human Universe and Other Essays* published in a limited edition in August. Awarded *Poetry* magazine's Oscar Blumenthal-Charles Leviton Prize. Returns to teach at Buffalo in September, but after two weeks returns to Gloucester.

1966   Leaves Gloucester for London in October (will stay until February 1967). Reads for the Literarisches Colloquium at the Akademie der Kunstes, Berlin in December; suffers minor coronary attack some days later.

1967   *Selected Writings* published in March. Leaves London that month for Dorchester, England, to do research among the Weymouth Port Books on the early settlers of Gloucester.

Returns to London, reads at the International Poetry Festival, July 12. Flies back to Gloucester. Addresses the State University of New York Convocation in the Arts, Cortland, N.Y., October 20–22.

1968   Lectures and reads at Beloit College, March 25–29. Visits Donald Allen in San Francisco and Drummond Hadley in Tucson, returning to Gloucester in May. *The Maximus Poems IV, V, VI* published in London on November 28.

1969   In September visits Charles Boer in Connecticut and in October accepts the post of Visiting Professor at the University of Connecticut. *Letters for Origin* published in September. Shortly after Thanksgiving, admitted to Manchester (Conn.) Hospital; transferred to New York Hospital.

1970   Dies in New York, January 10, of cancer of the liver.

Notes to
The Maximus Poems, 1960
(*Maximus* I)

Notes on dedication and epigraph

Robert Creeley

(b. 1926), American poet and one of Olson's closest friends; described in the poems as the man who gave him "the world" (*Maximus* I, 52). Their relationship began in early April 1950, when some of Olson's poems were sent to Creeley, then planning a little magazine in New Hampshire, by their mutual acquaintance, Vincent Ferrini. Creeley, however, turned down the poems, writing Ferrini that Olson was "looking around for a language, and the result is a loss of force." Olson responded to the rejection, and their correspondence—which grew to an exchange of almost 1000 letters altogether, at times at a daily rate—began. The two men did not meet in person until Creeley arrived to teach at Black Mountain College in March 1954, four years after the initial letter. For some sense of the relationship, see, among published material, *Mayan Letters,* a selection of Olson's letters to Creeley from the Yucatan, and various interviews with Creeley collected in his *Contexts of Poetry.*

The epithet here offered Creeley occurred to Olson in a dream at Black Mountain. In a notepad among Olson's papers, appears the following from May 1969:

> the Figure of Outward means way out way out
> *there*: the
> 'World', I'm sure, otherwise
> why *was* the pt. then to like write to Creeley
> daily? to make that whole thing
> double, to
> objectify the existence of an
> 'Outward'? a[n] opposite to a
> personality which so completely does (did)
> stay at home? And so to *forward* a
> motion I
> make him—or in a dream 'heard' this
> 'name' of him (waking up & writing
> it on the white wall of South Lodge? in
> the night? And it is probably still there
> under
> new coats of paint like new coats. . . .

In a letter to Creeley, 14 December [1967], Olson also mentions how the epithet was written upon his awakening "on the wall of my bedroom at the end of South Lodge, black mt."

The phrase first was used by Olson in a poem entitled "For R.C." which he sent Creeley on 16 January 1953 and rewrote the next day: "the figure of outward . . . all things stand by him, and all the others / are the better known." In his letter to Creeley containing the poem, Olson reports how "the first senses of it got written in the dark on the white, and scratched-on, wall!"

All my life I've heard / one makes many

Actually exclaimed by a cook at Black Mountain, Cornelia Williams, while working in the kitchen of the college, and overheard by the poet. At the same time, a statement of one of the fundamental problems of thought and politics, the problem of "the One and the Many." Olson writes in a letter to Creeley, 1 June 1953:

> (this bright Cornelia, the cook,
> says today:
> all my life I've heard, "One
> makes many"
> and it sounded
> like the epigraph fit to go with the
> Figure
> Or to be
> IT! (christ, exactly, that's it . . .

In his copy of Whitehead's *Process and Reality,* p. 28, next to the statement, "the term 'many' presupposes the term 'one,' and the term 'one' presupposes the term 'many,' " Olson adds in the margin: "*exactly* Cornelia Wms, Black Mt kitchen, 1953." While in an autobiographical statement written in November 1952, Olson had stated: "that there is no such thing as duality either of the body and the soul or of the world and I, that the fact in the human universe is the discharge of the many (the multiple) by the one (yrself done right, whatever you are, in whatever job, is the thing . . ." (*Additional Prose,* p. 39). And in some early notes for the growth and shape of the poems, he calls the epigraph, "the dominating paradox on which *Max* complete ought to stand."

▶ I.1. I, Maximus of Gloucester, to You

Probably written in May 1950 in Washington, as a letter to Vincent Ferrini in Gloucester, after Ferrini announced on May 3rd that he was going to start a literary magazine to be called *Voyager.* It is undoubtedly the poem which Ferrini acknowledges in his letter of 20 May 1950 to Olson by simply saying: "Thanks for the poem which we like and are sure that the townspeople will scream [about]." An editor's note by publisher Jonathan Williams in the Jargon/Corinth edition indicates the present is a "revised" version of the poem. The original version, beginning "By ear, he sd," appeared in the first collection of the poems, *The Maximus Poems / 1–10,* published by Williams in October 1953. It was rewritten apparently before 22 March 1951 (Olson's letter to Cid Corman that date in Glover, "Letters for Origin," unpub. diss., p. 49), for its publication in *Origin* 1 that spring, but the evidence is that the rewriting began even earlier. A draft of the final version among the poet's papers is dated "may 17 L," the same day it is quoted at length in a letter to Frances Boldereff (a complete copy was sent her on 29 June 1950). The manuscript sent Corman for *Origin* was signed, significantly, "charles olson / stage fort avenue / gloucester" (i.e., the poet's boyhood home), although the poem was revised in Washington.

I.1. Maximus

In a biographical note for the anthology *New Writing in the U.S.A.,* written 12 August 1964, Olson has simply: "Maximus, Hero, a metal hot from boiling water, born in the winter, 1949–50, age 38–39." An archetypal figure, Jung's "homo maximus"; but also Maximus of Tyre, second century A.D. Greek eclectic philosopher, whom the poet had encountered by chance while reading about Sappho in J. M. Edmonds' translation in *Lyra Graeca* (letter to Monroe Engel,

ca. 15 April 1949; passages in the poet's copy marked).
Olson sent Frances Boldereff a quotation from Maximus'
Dissertations from Edmonds, in which Sappho's love of beautiful persons is compared to that of Socrates', ca. 29 March
1949. He then apparently sought out an English translation
of Maximus' writings.

The writings of Maximus of Tyre were translated by
Thomas Taylor, the first translator of Plato into English, as
The Dissertations of Maximus Tyrius (1804), which Olson said in
conversation he read in the Library of Congress a few
months before the writing of this poem. Evidence exists that
he sought his own copy in April 1949 through out-of-print
booksellers, but to no avail. Taylor writes in his Preface,
pp. iii–iv:

> Of Maximus, the author of the Following Dissertations,
> nothing more is known, than that he was by birth a Tyrian;
> that he lived under the Antonines and Commodus; that
> he for some time resided in Rome, but, probably, for the
> most part in Greece; that he cultivated philosophy, and
> principally that of Plato; and that he was one of those
> sophists who, like Dio Chrysostom, united philosophy with
> the study of rhetoric, and combined sublimity and depth
> of conception with magnificence and elegance of diction.
>
> I have said that he *principally* cultivated the Platonic
> philosophy, because from the twentieth dissertation it ap-
> pears that he preferred the cynic life to that of all others,
> thus placing the end of life in *practical* and not in *theoretic*
> virtue. . . .

See also the brief account of Maximus of Tyre in the *Encyclopaedia Britannica*, 11th ed., recommended to the author by
Olson in conversation, June 1968. There is no evidence that
Olson's knowledge or interest in the historical figure of Maximus extended much beyond these sources. Maximus is as
much a proposition, at the start of the poems, as anything
literal or referential.

During a reading of later *Maximus* poems at Goddard
College on 12 April 1962, the poet would remark:

> The general proposition is . . . this creature, Maximus, ad-
> dresses himself to a city, which in the instance is Glou-

cester, which then in turn happens to be in Massachusetts. I'm not at all impressed that there's necessarily any more Gloucester, Massachusetts in any meaningful sense than the creature is either me or whom he originally was intended as, which was Maximus of Tyre, a second-century dialectician. At least on the record what he wrote was *dialethi*, which we have I guess in the word 'dialectic,' meaning intellectual essays, or essays on intellectual subjects. And he mostly wandered around the Mediterranean world, from the center, the old capital of Tyre, talking about one thing—Homer's *Odyssey*. I don't have much more impression of him than that. I've tried to read his *Dialethi* and found them not as interesting as I expected. But he represents to me some sort of a figure that centers much more than the second century A.D.—in fact, as far as I feel it, like, he's the navel of the world. In saying that I'm not being poetic or loose. We come from a whole line of life that makes Delphi that center . . . and this I think is the kind of a thing that ought to be at least disturbed. . . . He is a transfer for me to that vision of a difference that Tyre is, or proposition that Tyre is, as against, say, Delphi.

Still later, Olson would tell Herbert Kenny ("I know men . . . ," *Muthologos*, II, 161–162): "why I chose to use Maximus of Tyre as the figure of speech, figure of the speech, is that I regard Gloucester as the final movement of the earth's people, the great migratory thing . . . migration ended in Gloucester. The migratory act of man ended in Gloucester . . . the motion of man upon the earth has a line, an oblique, northwest-tending line, and Gloucester was the last shore in that sense. The fact that the continent and the series of such developments as have followed, have occupied three hundred and some-odd years, doesn't take away that primacy or originatory nature that I'm speaking of. I think it's a very important fact. And I of course use it as a bridge to Venice and back from Venice to Tyre, because of the departure from the old static land mass of man which was the ice, cave, Pleistocene man and early agricultural man, until he got moving, until he got towns. So that the last *polis* or city *is* Gloucester."

In a notepad from 1961 among his papers, the poet provides this further understanding of the role of Maximus:

"the purpose of Maximus, the person who addresses himself to the City, is to measure: *the advantage of a single human figure*. I never thought of it before but the advantage of a single human figure is a practice I'd have said I might have acquired from Mayan stele, or that thigh bone of Quetzalcoatl, which I possess, on which a single warrior is carved."

I.1. Gloucester

City on Cape Ann, Massachusetts, on the Atlantic coast some thirty miles northeast of Boston; home of the poet, both where he grew up summers as a boy and where he would settle following the closing of Black Mountain College in 1957. It was settled in 1623 by emigrants from Dorchester, England, and in the late nineteenth century became, for a time, the principal fishing port in the United States. Useful recent introductions to Gloucester's history are Copeland and Rogers, *The Saga of Cape Ann* (1960), and Garland, *A Gloucester Guide* (1973), although the best work on early Gloucester is still John J. Babson's *History of the Town and City of Gloucester* (1860), reprinted in 1973. It should be noted that Gloucester can be considered—like its second century A.D. analogue in the poems, Tyre—to be an island, separated from the mainland by the Annisquam River, and only later connected to the continent and nation by a highway and bridge (see esp. *Maximus* I, 160 and II, 80).

Gloucester serves as a temenos or holy place in the poems, and contains hidden within itself a *polis* or ideal city—a "redeemable flower that will be a monstrance forever, of not a city but City"—which is to be struggled toward and attained, and which the poet will reveal by his act of imagination as well as personal investigation into the historical reality of the place or *topos*. In "MAXIMUS, Part II," written in 1957 shortly after Olson had returned to Gloucester after years of absence, he would identify the city as "a form of mind."

In a note from 10 February 1960 among his papers, Olson would write: "The interest is not in the local at all as such—any local; & the choice of Gloucester is particular—that is the point of the interest, particularism itself: to reveal it, in all possible ways and force, against the 'loss' of value of the universal . . . Tyre as (with Gaza) the only city which resisted Alexander's universalization." He also inquired of his audience at Goddard College, 12 April 1962: "Do you know, yourselves, enough of the history of Tyre to know that the only thing in the world that confronted the universalization that Alexander proposed—which I think is the great complement to the present—was Tyre? It so refused to be knocked down by this Macedonian athlete that it was the sole place in the world which bucked him, and it took Alexander . . . was it three or four years to reduce Tyre, and in order to get at her he built a mole from the mainland . . ." (Goddard tape).

Olson also wrote the following brief description of his intentions in *Maximus* in a draft of a letter to the Guggenheim Foundation in late January 1960, as the first volume was being printed: "Quickly, the poem is a man 'Maximus' addressing a city 'Gloucester' to induce its people, himself among them, to see and take life in and be a scale of which they, and their 'fishing,' say, the point is, are better examples than any outside or 'universal' reference; that the relevance lies in what is nearest, and most familiar, that the smallest or least can be lived in. . . ." And on a tape made for editor Donald Allen in August 1965, Olson offered this summary: "The whole intention of these poems in the earlier period was to address them as letters both to Mr. Ferrini (literally, I mean, in person) and by him to a whole social number of human beings which we really ultimately can call a city."

I.1. Off-shore, by islands hidden in the blood . . .

In remarks prefacing a reading of later *Maximus* poems in 1963 at the State University of New York at Buffalo, Olson described Maximus as "a person who speaks from further east than Gloucester to the city," i.e., from Tyre (recording at the Poetry Room, Lockwood Memorial Library). Maximus then is also a projection (more so because the poet is living in Washington while addressing Gloucester, the place of his youth). Later, Olson would realize, in an untitled essay written 14 March 1965 in a notebook among his papers, that "the 'hero' of my poem (Maximus of Gloucester) is in truth Maximus of Tyre. And thus, whether I liked it or not, at a very early point, in fact in the very first letter addressed to Gloucester, the position off-shore of Maximus is indeed an enormous expropriation of the other side of the Atlantic, the other side all the way back to man's first leaving the massive land continent of 'Asia' for Cyprus, the 1st 'island' in that aspect of Westward movement (Tyre of course is still more 'true' being that island only made into a peninsula when Alexander, to reduce her, for the first time in history—as late as 333 BC—built the mole. . . ."

Cf. the opening lines of "The Librarian" from 1957, a poem not considered properly a *Maximus* poem by the poet but certainly with similar materials:

> The landscape (the landscape!) again: Gloucester
> the shore one of me is (duplicates), and from which
> (from offshore, I, Maximus) am removed, observe. . . .

Consider also these lines on p. 4 of the poem at hand:

> I Maximus, say
> under the hand, as I see it, over the waters
> from this place where I am, where I hear,
> can still hear . . .

I.1. a metal hot from boiling water . . .

In his 17 May 1950 letter to Frances Boldereff quoting the poem, Olson speaks of himself as a "hard-boiled instrument, as metal hot from boiling water." And in his copy of *Origin* 1 marked "Working copy 1960," he adds at this point in the margin, "a scalpel"; while after "what is a lance" in the next line, is noted: "*the* instrument [make oneself a scalpel . . ."

I.1. the figures of / the present dance

Cf. "Projective Verse" (*Human Universe*, p. 54): ". . . from the root out, from all over the place, the syllable comes, the figures of, the dance." Also in his "working copy" of *Origin* 1 from 1960, Olson has: "the dancing 'floor' / the labyrinth the / churinga-act / the threshing- / floor, the / crawling / floor the . . . pathways of / the 'present dance.' "

I.1. Antony of Padua

(1195−1231), Franciscan friar and saint; patron of the Portuguese fishing community of Gloucester, and as such, annually celebrated each June. He was a noted preacher, famous for a "sermon to the fishes."

Cf. also the closing of Olson's letter to Vincent Ferrini, written 23 May 1950: "O my friend / in short, this is, the bird overhead is / Anthony of. . ." (*Origin* 1, p. 54).

I.1. 58 carats

No doubt an arbitrary figure—"50 carats" in the original version (changed here probably for sake of rhyme). Used in the sense in which the poet writes elsewhere, "the highest— 40 hours a day—price" ("Projective Verse," *Human Universe*, p. 54), or—although actually an allusion to a passage in W. C. Williams' *Paterson*—"WCW does lose his pearl, the 400 grams, the finest pearl of modern times" (" 'On Poets and Poetry,' " *Human Universe*, p. 64), lending specificity—in the present case to the suggestion that each one is, or has within, the necessary measure of his own condition.

I.2. my lady of good voyage

On top of the Church of Our Lady of Good Voyage on Prospect Street in the Portuguese community of Gloucester, overlooking the harbor, is an eighteen-foot statue of Our Lady holding a schooner as described. For an account of the statue and photographs, see e.g., Marden, "Gloucester Blesses Its Portuguese Fleet." She is the invoked muse of the poem, and, as Olson has said (conversation with the author, June 1968), "the poem is a voyage, and I want a good voyage."

I.2. said he, coldly, the / ear!

A statement of poetics, the ear of the poet: "the ear, the ear which has collected, which has listened, the ear, which is so close to the mind that it is the mind's, that it has the mind's speed . . ." ("Projective Verse," *Human Universe,* p. 54). In notes from the late 1940's on Ezra Pound's poetics, Olson writes: "The method of the verse, to register with such exactitude (by the ear) that what is made. . . ." Though equally and more simply, the phrase occurs in the sense of the common directive, to "play it by ear"—urging, that is, the spontaneous conduction of life: "MONEY, first—like SEX. They are the only things (things are so impossible) that any one has their eye on. And they both get to be nothing when they are no longer played by ear" (letter to Robert Creeley, ca. February 1951).

I.2. On the hill, over the water / where she who used to sing . . .

See the original version of "I, Maximus":

> Where, Portygee Hill, she sang
> and over the water, at Tarr's
> (the water glowed, the light west,
> black, gold, the tide
> outward at evening
>
> The fixed bells rang, their voices
> came like boats over the oil-slicks,
> like milkweed hulls . . .

There the "hill" of the present poem is specified as "Portygee Hill," the center of the Portuguese settlement of Gloucester, a high area around the church of Our Lady of Good Voyage. The bells are those of the carillon of that church, the first such in this country. They are further described in the original version as "fixed": though conceivably those of buoys, they are certainly the stationary bells of a carillon. In an early manuscript version, the line reads: "when the fixed bells rang by the Belgian came like boats"—the "Belgian" being a master carilloneur named Lefevre who made visits to Gloucester to play in the summer evenings. And "she who used to sing," while actually a woman named Mary Silveira, then a high school student, who did sing at carillon concerts (from, it is again specified, "Tarr's" Marine Railway on Rocky Neck, across the harbor from the church), it is equally Our Lady herself who sings, the muse of the poem.

The lines are filled out further by another letter to Ferrini, 2 July 1950, where Olson writes: ". . . the passage on how sounds USED to be, there, noticeably, from Tarr's Ralway, where I once worked, and used to go, of an evening; had my dory tied up there one night with too short a painter, and when I came out after a show (was also a player) there was the dory, oars gone, and itself standing straight up in the water! (Good painter!) I walked home the three miles or so that night!" (*Origin* 1, p. 61). As a young man, in the summer of 1929, Olson would row across the harbor from the beach near his house above Stage Fort Park, to work and study at the Gloucester School of the Little Theatre, which was located in a loft above Tarr's Railway (see also note to *Maximus* I, 60).

I.3. pejorocracy

Literally, 'worse-rule' (Latin *pejor,* and −ocracy, as in democracy, from the Greek *krateia*), a worsening form of government. Borrowed from Pound, Canto LXXIX of *The Pisan Cantos;* first used by Olson in "The Kingfishers."

I.3. street-cars, o Oregon, twitter / in the afternoon

See Olson's letter to Cid Corman, 28 May 1951, in Glover, "Letters for Origin," unpub. diss., p. 85: "Oregon, I *think,* if you know oregon like I know oregon, you'd, I think, think that it is still (the coast!) strangely frontier, where, a streetcar is as it was when it was NEW . . . instead of something . . . with a radio in every car. . . ." Streetcars in Washington, D.C., when Olson was living there in the late 1940's, and perhaps at

the time this poem was composed, had recorded music piped
in to "ease" the travellers.

In a letter to Bernard Kneiger, a friend of Corman's,
15 June 1953, Olson returned to the question of Oregon:

> . . . Of course! Yr original
> question was, why Oregon! wasn't it?
> And since it recurs again
> in letter 10 (abt James Conant asking Oregon to send its
> brightest!), I gather it is some fix in me of, how John Chap-
> man's apples do rot, despite, the beauty of, the land! (If
> you know that coast, fr, say, the Columbia south to Cres-
> cent City, Cal., you'll imagine why, to me, Oregon, is so
> beautiful . . .
>> May be Oregon has more import than I yet know. Writ-
>> ing to you like this, it occurs to me that I may have
>> thrown out some filament there in # 1 . . . that the in-
>> tent was more known to me than I yet know . . .

It may be simple enough: although localized in Gloucester,
this poem is to be a measure of the nation.

I.3. how shall you strike, / o swordsman

A "striker," to the Gloucester fishermen, is the swordfish
harpooner.

I.3. mu-sick

See also "ABCs (3—for Rimbaud)," written ca. June 1950:
"mu-sick, mu-sick—music / worse than war, worse / than
peace, & they both dead . . .," followed by "Who pleas for
the heart, for the return of, into the work of, / say, the running of / a street-car?"—where music or "mu-sick" and
streetcars are again closely related; passages on *Maximus* I,
13 likewise.

There is, in addition to the pun, an echo of a raspy popular song of the time entitled "Music, Music, Music."

I.4. faun and oral, / satyr lesbos vase

Suggestive of the classical Greek condition (an oral, i.e.
Homeric, pre-literate culture, and Lesbos, the island in the

Aegean, home of Sappho), though also classic psycho-sexual distortions. Cf. Olson's remarks in a letter to Creeley, 19 February 1952: ". . . it works out, doesn't it, that if you hide, or otherwise duck THE ORAL as profoundly phallic—if you try to ignore the piles of bones . . . you leave out the true animal bearing of the species and in the end—(to come back to my own beginning)—you pay for it by sex, and sex alone, becoming the only ORAL, and thus, the very inversion of the whole PHALLIC base—you get the present ultimate DE-LINQUENCE (example, Hitler, who, was a copralagnist [*sic*])."

I.4. o kill kill kill kill kill . . .

Conceivably an echo of *King Lear* IV.vi.191. Olson writes to Creeley, 29 November 1951: "Lear constantly repeats nouns and verbs, usually five or six times, the same word, as tho it was returning from the concave walls of a stiff, steel space: . . . Howl, howl, . . . is picked up by Kill, kill, . . . god, these words, RETURNING. . . ."

▶I.5. Maximus, to Gloucester: Letter 2

Written in the spring of 1951 and revised, with possibly an early version written in 1950. In a letter to Henry A. Murray from Lerma in the Yucatan, 4 June 1951, Olson writes: "a second letter from Maximus of Gloucester got written here, all about New England houses, & streets, for a new little gig out of Gloucester itself! (I am trying to get them to call it quite formally THE GLOUCESTER REVIEW, but I fear they'll go fancy, and call it FOUR WINDS, or something equally silly)."

In notes from ca. 1953 among the poet's papers, relating to the dating of the *Maximus* poems through "Letter #22," a date of March 1951 is assigned the present poem; at the same time, an early version entitled "I, Maximus (Letter #2)" is dated 2 June 1951, from Lerma. The poem is also dated from the spring of 1951 in a list prepared for editor Donald Allen, ca. 1958. A later note, however, made by the poet while preparing *Maximus IV, V, VI* for publication, reads: "Letter 2 written 1950? [after Labor Day at Cambridge—Oxford Md."; and in conversation with the author, June 1968, Olson stated the poem was written in 1950 while on vacation at the seashore at Cambridge, Maryland.

I.5. he was right: people / don't change . . .

In conversation, June 1968, Olson suggested this was the opinion of the writer Edward Dahlberg (see *Maximus* II, 36 and note), early friend and mentor of the poet, who was much given to aphorisms. Indeed, Olson wrote as early as 1939 or 1940 in his journals: "His [Dahlberg's] argument & justifications—we never change—same agonies, same urges, same aberrations, same pains at 40 as at 20. Only we acquire power to illuminate ourselves . . ."; while in a letter of 6 October 1949 to Dahlberg, Olson acknowledges that "one of the finest pieces of wisdom i acquired from you is, people do not change." The belief seems to have stayed with Dahlberg through most of his life, for he writes in a letter to Olson on 24 November 1954 (after this poem had been written): "You know how changeless man is. I am always the same, only more of it."

I.5. the house the street cuts off . . .

A house at 90 Middle Street, Gloucester, a handsome gambrel-roofed structure on the corner of Middle Street and Dale Avenue, facing the Library; known as the Hardy-Parsons House, it is owned by the Cape Ann Historical Association. In "A *Scream* to the Editor" in 1965, Olson would write that houses such as 90 Middle Street "live," calling attention to "the vigor of the narrow and fine clapboards on the back . . . that flatness right up against the street," and how such houses "have held and given light / a century, in some cases two centuries. . . ."

The story of the house was told Olson by Alfred Mansfield Brooks (1870−1963), director of the Cape Ann Scientific,

Literary and Historical Association, during their meeting in May or June of 1947 at which time Olson conceived of a long poem on Gloucester.

I.5. hid . . . the fact the cargo their ships brought back / was black

Black servants were quartered during the nineteenth century in the building at the rear of 90 Middle Street known as the Warren Apartments, since torn down to make way for a memorial garden in honor of Alfred Mansfield Brooks. E. Hyde Cox, Brooks' successor as director of the local historical society, reports to Olson in a letter of 5 November 1965: "So far as I can determine, no one is sure of the date of the apartments. 90 Middle dates from 1763 and is built around a still earlier house, but the apartment is thought to have been built at least 50 years later. . . ." In a return letter to Cox, 8 November 1965, protesting the destruction of that back building, Olson mentions that the matter of the servants had been part of his luncheon conversation with Brooks years previous.

Actual slave pens were reported by several local historians in a house owned by Gustavus Babson (see note to *Maximus* I, 145 below); e.g., David Babson, a descendant, writes in his "Maritime History of Gloucester," p. 61n.: "In the attic of this house, there are contrivances which were once used as slave pens so tradition states. Negro domestics were fairly numerous in Cape Ann in her commercial hey-day."

The theme of slavery is picked up again in "Letter 14."

I.5. the Library

The Sawyer Free Library, Gloucester's public library, at 88 Middle Street on the corner of Dale Avenue (across from 90 Middle). It was originally the Gloucester Lyceum, established in 1830, and received its present name in 1871 after a sizeable donation from Samuel E. Sawyer, a merchant of the town.

I.5. the light does go one way toward the post office . . .

The main branch of the U.S. Post Office in Gloucester, on Dale Avenue up from the Library.

I.5. the Unitarian church

86 Middle Street; formerly the First Church (Unitarian), built in 1828, now the Temple Ahavath Achim.

I.6. the lady

Our Lady of Good Voyage. The statue, standing between the twin cupolas of the church, faces seaward.

I.6. that false future she, / precisely she, / has her foot upon

Although most generally it is the church itself, orthodox religion, the statue rests upon, there is perhaps an allusion to the traditional pose of Mary in Christian iconography, in which it is Satan in the guise of a serpent that she has her foot upon, crushing its head in fulfilment of the prophecy— a reading encouraged by the mention of "sins" early in the section. Indeed, in a later long poem concerning Our Lady of Good Voyage entitled "The Horses of the Sea," from 12 March 1963, this is precisely the pose assigned her. Whether this is literally the case is uncertain, however, as it is not possible to see the base of the statue from below and no snake underfoot is evident in photographs of it; furthermore, in that later poem, Olson admits, "I'm not sure the Portuguese Virgin / of the church isn't standing then between the two blue towers / with feet as naked and as long as her hands / and no Enemy. . . ."

I.6. He / made the coast, and though he lost his feet for it . . .

Howard Blackburn (1859–1932), the most celebrated of the Goucester fishermen. For his story, as told by himself, see Connolly, *Book of the Gloucester Fishermen,* pp. 39ff.; also Garland, *Lone Voyager,* a full biography. Blackburn owned a bar at 289 Main Street (at present Blackburn Place) until the time of his death.

I.6. my other, the top of whose head a bollard clean took away . . .

Louis R. Douglas, Sr. (b. ca. 1855), a neighbor during Olson's early summers at Gloucester. Olson would later say that he considered Douglas "the man who made me a poet simply because of the nature of his language when I listened behind a stone wall to him and his brother from Newfoundland talk when I was four years old" ("I know men . . . ," *Muthologos,* II, 165). See also *Muthologos,* I, 196–197.

I.6. Chelsea Marine

The United States Naval Hospital at Chelsea, Mass., a community just north of Boston.

I.6. Santa Fe rose

A variety of hybrid rose is intended, named after the city in New Mexico.

I.6. the quiet one, who's died since . . .

Frank D. Miles, brother-in-law of Lou Douglas, Sr.

I.6. Eastern Point

The sheltering arm for Gloucester's harbor; its tip marks the entrance to the harbor from the east.

I.6. jacks

Red jacks (see *Maximus* I, 21), knee-high boots worn by the fishermen; originally made of heavy leather, watertight, and reddish brown in color.

I.6. Brace's Cove

On the east or Atlantic shore of Gloucester, below Eastern
Point; site of numerous shipwrecks in the days before vessels
were provided with electronic equipment (see esp. *Maximus* I,
21), as it was often mistaken in bad weather by mariners
for the entrance to Gloucester Harbor itself.

I.6. Lily Pond

Not the pond of that name today on the mainland west of
the Annisquam River, but what is now Niles Pond, formerly
Oceana Pond, on Eastern Point, separated from Brace's Cove
and the Atlantic by a narrow strip of land.

I.7. he with the muscle as big as his voice . . .

Carl Olsen (1886–1965). His story is told again by Olson
in a letter to the *Gloucester Times,* 28 December 1965, using
the nickname "Jim Chum" for the fisherman: ". . . which
Gloucesterman's dory-mate caught in the hooks of a trawl
and the man drew the trawl enough to loose his fellow but
he was gone for blood and the other had to heave him in a
fireman's lift over one shoulder and swim three miles in any
sea to their vessel."
See also *Maximus* I, 19 and 27, and notes.

I.7. Peak of Brown's

An area of Brown's Bank (see note to *Maximus* I, 19).

I.7. Bowditch

Nathaniel Bowditch (1773–1838), American mathematician and author of the *New American Practical Navigator,*
a guide for mariners first published in 1802 and still in use,
with revisions, today.

I.7. the Fort

Fort Point, a projection of land into Gloucester Harbor,
where in 1743 a breastwork and cannon had been set up to

protect vessels in the inner harbor; the poorer, predominantly Italian section of Gloucester, where the poet would settle upon his return to the city in 1957.

I.7. the small white house on Lower Middle

28 Middle Street, Gloucester (west of Washington Street). It would have been of special interest to the poet since it was a house he himself had stayed in briefly during the winter of 1940 (and "off the porch" of which . . .—see *Maximus* II, 1 and note).

I.7. the handsome brick with the Bullfinch doors

House at 21 Middle Street, home of Alfred Mansfield Brooks. Its main door has sidelights and a fanlight, here associated with the style of the architect Charles Bulfinch (1763–1844) of Boston. Garland tells us in his *Gloucester Guide*, pp. 105–106, that the house "was put here about 1850 by that inveterate mover and shaker, George Rogers, who bought the interiors of an 1820 house on Charles Street in Boston, and a 1790 house attributed to Charles Bulfinch on West Cedar Street, sailed them down to Gloucester, placed the Bulfinch atop the 1820, and built the brick shell around the two."

I.7. the Gas Company wharf

The former Gloucester Gas and Light Company wharf on the Inner Harbor, at the intersection of Duncan and Wharf streets.

▶I.9. Letter 3

The first version of this poem was written in the summer of 1952, in either Black Mountain or Washington, as a letter to Vincent Ferrini in response to a review of the first issue of Ferrini's magazine, *Four Winds*, in the *Cape Ann Summer Sun* for 18 July 1952 by the young editor of the newspaper, John T. Bethell. A copy of the review had been sent to Olson by Ferrini on 27 July and Ferrini received Olson's response before 11 August (date of his letter to Olson acknowledging the poem).

Olson wrote to Cid Corman on 24 September 1952, "I did not write a letter to the Gloucester Summer Sun, but I, MAX, 3 . . . was, in fact, started almost like a review" (*Letters for Origin,* p. 110). Earlier versions of the poem contain more explicit references to the review and the reviewer. Bethell had written, e.g., "*Four Winds* is, in the main, trivial and unpleasant. Some of its writing is poor, some inexcusable. There is a point in 'Sophie' when the young medical student comes face to face with a female, and is sick out the window into her garden. After reading *Four Winds,* you should see mine." Olson later observed, in "The Carpenter Poem I (Letter #33)," written 31 May 1955: "This is the letter to go with the other literary letters—#3, on the magazine the newspaper used that vulgarism about (than which there is no vulgarism which more betokens the mass-man). . . ."

An early version among his papers is inscribed by the poet, "for Dorie, who asked / Charles Aug 24 52"—i.e. Dori Billing, wife of Len Billing, a teacher at Black Mountain, who had asked Olson if he knew "how rare it was" growing up in Stage Fort Park (p. 10). The poem was rewritten by 29 April 1953, when the manuscript for *Maximus 1–10* was sent Jonathan Williams (Olson's letter "THURS–APRIL 29th?" to J. Williams).

I.9. tansy

Olson's description of the herb some years later in a note to editor Donald Allen, ca. 22 July 1963, is of some interest: "Tansy was brought on the bottom of bags in cargoes to Stage Head originally out of Dorchester's entry (at the mouth of the Wey) persons directly probably responsible William Derby and Thomas Purchase (though London ships also here at or at same time as transfer. It is strong (like goldenrod) and smells almost offensive with a pineapple odor. It doesn't grow anymore at the same place but that is due to more efficient mowers, and the desire (like blacktop) to have anything smooth and of one sort or character. We therefore celebrate TANSY MORE THAN BEFORE . . ."

I.9. Let them free the way for me, for the men of the Fort . . .

Cf. the earlier version, "Maximus, to Gloucester, Letter 3," published in *Four Winds* 2–3:

> Let them free the way for the men of the Fort
> to Middle Street, to buy the white houses . . .

The "white houses" here are those such as 90 Middle Street (see note to p. 5, "the house the street cuts off . . .") or, even more so, the one on Lower Middle mentioned on p. 7 above.

I.9. Cressy

Cressy's Beach on Freshwater Cove, near Stage Fort Park, Gloucester.

I.10. Did you know, she sd . . .

In conversation, June 1968, Olson said the question was asked him by the wife of one of his fellow teachers at Black Mountain College at the time (thus, Dori Billing—see note above).

I.10. Ravenswood

Ravenswood Park of more than three hundred acres, mostly forest, north of Western Avenue and Stage Fort Park, the area where Olson spent summers in his youth.

I.10. Fresh Water Cove

On the southwest side of Gloucester Harbor; named by Champlain when he landed there for water in 1606.

I.10. the Provinces

The Maritime Provinces of Canada—Nova Scotia, New Brunswick, and Prince Edward Island—which supplied Gloucester with many able fishermen.

I.10. three hundred sail could fill the harbor . . .

In the earlier published version, "376 sail."

I.10. the Races

The International Fishermen's Races held annually off Gloucester and Halifax, Nova Scotia, from 1920 to 1938. For a brief account, see e.g., Connolly, *Book of the Gloucester Fishermen,* pp. 254–273; his *Port of Gloucester,* pp. 275–291; and Copeland and Rogers, *Saga of Cape Ann,* pp. 196–198. See also *Maximus* I, 22.

I.10. San Pietro

The fiesta of Saint Peter, held by the Italian community of Gloucester each year (on the weekend closest to June 29, the saint's feast day), during which occurs the blessing of the fleet.

I.10. Town Landing

Area at the foot of Washington Street, off Rogers and near Commercial Street, on Harbor Cove.

I.10. Worcester

Birthplace of the poet (see also *Reading at Berkeley,* p. 4ff., and *The Post Office*); an industrial city in central Massachusetts, about eighty miles southwest of Gloucester.

1.10. Gloucester / is heterogeneous

"I am of the heterogeneous present and not of the old homogeneity of the Founders, and the West," Olson says, in writing about his mixed, immigrant parentage ("The Present is Prologue," *Additional Prose,* p. 39).

I.10. polis

The Greek city and concept of a city. In an unpublished essay entitled "The Methodology is the Form" written around the time of this poem, in 1952, Olson writes: "The question, now, is: what is our polis (even allowing that no such thing can be considered as possible to exist when such homogeneity as any Greek city was has been displaced by such heterogeneity as modern cities and nations are)?" His answer is, "the very whole world," not "a bit smaller than the whole damn thing"; it is "the State," "The System," the "totality," adding, that it is necessary "to invert totality—to oppose it—by discovering the totality of any—every—single one of us."

In a later essay, "Definitions by Undoings," written in the spring of 1956 at the same time as or part of the series of lectures given as "The Special View of History," Olson offered the word through its roots:

> . . . POLIS, then, is a filled up thing (in the passive as city, the community or body of citizens, not their dwellings, not their houses, not their being as material, but being as group with will, and that will is from the Sanskrit stem to fill or fulfill, and includes such words as plenus, plebes, po-pulus, publicus, thus our public etc., and manipulus, thus manipulate, ample, English full—and the Greek milk-pail *pella* or Latin pelvis which means a basin fr which our meaning of pelvis comes
>
> ((((maybe via plateia, and root PLA-T, place, flat plati-nos????? where can you find the meaning of Sanskrit *pur*
> ((Eng pure is fr purus
> Greek pur—to cleanse
> and fire Ger & Eng
> same!
> THE FIRE-CLEANSED FULL PLACE OF THE FIRE, THE PURE PLACE ist POLIS . . .

I.11. the Waiting Station

Wade's (formerly Francis' and Shurtleff's), a stationery store dealing also in newspapers, magazines, tobacco, etc., on Main Street in Gloucester. See also *Maximus* I, 18.

I.11. Magnolia

Community immediately southwest of Gloucester on route 1A heading towards Salem and Boston.

I.11. Al Levy

"Darb" Levy in earlier version. Gloucester policeman; probably Ralph A. Levie, or his brother Elliott, both on the local force in the late 1940's and early 1950's.

I.11. Annisquam-Lanesville

Bus serving the communities of Annisquam and Lanesville, respectively north and northeast of Gloucester, on Ipswich Bay.

I.11. the "Times"

The *Gloucester Daily Times,* the local newspaper.

I.11. the "Summer Sun"

A weekly supplement to the *Gloucester Times,* designed to accommodate Gloucester's tourist season. It carried the review of *Four Winds* which occasioned this poem.

I.11. my Tyrian

Maximus of Tyre (see note to *Maximus* I, 1).

I.12. the house . . . wearing its white face, its clapboard mask

The "house" is 90 Middle Street, with an echo perhaps of the "pasteboard masks" of *Moby-Dick,* Chapter XXXVI (Constable ed. I, 204).

I.12. Isolatos

Melville's term, describing the crew of the *Pequod*: "They were nearly all Islanders . . . 'Isolatoes' too, I call such, not acknowledging the common continent of men, but each Isolato living on a separate continent of his own" (*Moby-Dick,* I, 149).

I.12. I, Maximus, address you / you islands / of men and girls

In a late fragment, from ca. 19 October 1962, Olson would improvise (with an allusion to the oar of Odysseus):

> offshore by islands
> I, Maximus, an oar an oar
> stuck up into the sky
> and into the earth through to hell,
>   address you
> you islands, of men & plants

▶I.13. The Songs of Maximus

First version written at Black Mountain, 4 January 1953 (manuscript dated), and a copy sent to Cid Corman (letter that date in Glover, "Letters for Origin," unpub. diss., pp. 193−194) as well as to Vincent Ferrini for *Four Winds* (Olson letter, [4 January 1953]; Ferrini to Olson, 15 January 1953).

I.13. of all things to eat: dirty / postcards / and words . . .

Cf. "words even / are made to taste like paper . . ." ("In Cold Hell, In Thicket").

I.13. even the street-cars / song

See above, note to *Maximus* I, 3.

I.14. Seth Thomas

A clock of early American design, after the name of the original designer (1785−1859). Now a brand name.

I.14. Congoleum

A trade name for a floor covering, like linoleum. Cf. W. C. Williams, *The Great American Novel,* pp. 78−79: "You've seen this fake oilcloth they are advertising now. Congoleum. Nothing but building paper with a coating of enamel."

I.14. "In the midst of plenty, walk . . .

See the sixteenth-century English lyric which begins,

> Back and side go bare, go bare,
> Both foot and hand go cold . . .

from *Gammer Gurton's Needle* (which Olson played in during college). Used also by Ezra Pound in Canto LXXX.

I.14. the blessing / that difficulties are once more

Cf. the following from a letter by Olson to Robert Creeley, early 1951:

> Funny, the way, I like the odds against: even the plumbing. Don't fix. Figure, play it the way it comes out. Protest, I suppose. Work with how it comes, don't fix—or rather DON'T BUY. Even to beds, driving, Con crazy. make them. Take a spring, when one bed goes (I break em down, fast: 260 lbs, and the frame), make a wood base yrself, catch the spring with nails hooked over, and there it is. DON'T BUY—what they've got to offer. (Hell of a life for a woman, yes. And what I like is, the way she goes along. And not bomehian at all. Not at all. Fine. High. The wools, & shetland, cashmere, silver, smash. Keep dough for wine. Food. Movement. Beat em. Beat em by not needing them. The WAY.

Again in *Mayan Letters* (*Selected Writings*, p. 93), from a letter of 20 March 1951 referring to the earlier one: ". . . like I tried to say, about, *leaving* the difficulties, not removing them, by *buying* the improvements so readily available at the corner. You buy something all right, but what gets forgotten is, that you sell, in that moment of buying—you sell a whole disposition of self. . . ."

I.15. I know a house made of mud & wattles . . .

Cf. the opening lines of William Butler Yeats' "The Lake Isle of Innisfree":

> I will arise and go now, and go to Innisfree,
> And a small cabin there, of clay and wattles made . . .

In Olson's case the setting would be Lerma, on the Yucatan Peninsula, where he stayed for six months in 1951 engaged in archeological work among Mayan ruins, and from where he wrote Robert Creeley the letters quoted from above.

I.15. Nike

The winged Greek goddess of victory. But see esp. the epithet in Hesiod, *Theogony*, 1. 383: "fair-ankled Nike."

I.15. he looked, / the first human eyes to look again . . .

On 29 December 1952, a living specimen of the coelacanth, a primitive fish said to have existed 300 million years ago and considered an ancestor of the land vertebrates (including man), was reported discovered in the Mozambique Channel on the East African coast by James L.B. Smith, an ichthyologist. See "14-Year Hunt Yields 'Missing Link' Fish," *New York Times,* 30 December 1952, a clipping of which is among the poet's papers.

I.16. FAO

Food and Agricultural Organization, an agency of the United Nations.

I.16. Appleseed

Johnny Appleseed, born John Chapman (1774–1845) in Massachusetts, the American folk hero and agricultural missionary. In an essay from February 1952 entitled "History," Olson refers to "the 'Johnny Appleseed,' Johnny Lowdermilk foreign policy of the young Jackasses behind the 2nd Roosevelt" (alluding specifically to W. C. Lowdermilk, an American agronomist who helped to found the Soil Conservation Service of the U.S. Department of Agriculture and who was its assistant chief from 1939 to 1947, serving also as consultant to conservation projects abroad).

▶ I.17. Letter 5

Written April 1953 at Black Mountain. Olson wrote to
Vincent Ferrini on 9 April, a Thursday: "the enclosed, / is
what yr magazine (in last Saturday night) / provoked." However he did not include copies of the poem at this point—"I
had carbons, but, the damn carbons were sticking the rewrite,
so I finally wrote the whole thing straight on one bond"—
and did not send the letter until May 1st "—& 7 Maximus
letters later. . . . And in the meantime I have so rewritten
the 3 of them immediate to yrself (actually 6 & 7 only carry
on the argument breached at you fully in 5. . . ." He continues:

> It's all crazy. For—as from the start—you there are the
> nexus, Vince—from the beginning, 3 years ago.
> That this time I had to drub you—well, I hope you will
> find it in your heart to weigh it with the presiding fact
> to me, that I can't believe whatever the whole issue of
> these Maximus poems turns out to be, would have been
> at all, if you had not (if you did not now) be there
> I am immediately persuaded that it is one of those crazy
> doublets of experience—and please try to find your way
> to stay with me, in the endeavor.

Ferrini would have his first taste of the poems from Cid
Corman, who went to Gloucester at Olson's request to read
Maximus 1–10 to him (see note to *Maximus* I, 41).

A further sense of the writing and rewriting of this and the
poems immediately following can be had from notes found
among the poet's papers: "april 8 53 (wed—in midst of Maximus 5 6 7) . . . continued to stay on top of maxies—made the
long 8, and a sketched 9, thru Friday . . . a week ago Sunday,
when this run of Maxies started." Again: "april 23 53 (thurs
morn (in midst of rewriting MAX, after busting on letter 5) . . ."

I.17. as, in summer, a newspaper, now, in spring, a magazine

The *Cape Ann Summer Sun,* which occasioned "Letter 3";
and *Four Winds,* a literary magazine edited by Vincent Ferrini

and others in Gloucester from 1952 to 1953, the second issue of which appeared that spring. There were three issues of *Four Winds* in all, each with work by Olson, including early versions of the *Maximus* letters 2 and 3 and "The Songs of Maximus." This second issue was given the number 2–3, and dated Fall-Winter 1952–53.

I.17. Brown's

Department store on Main Street, Gloucester, where the magazine was sold and a window display set up. A photograph of Ferrini and Mary Shore, who was one of the editors of the first issue of the magazine—shown arranging the display of Cape Ann literary works in the store's window—appeared in the *Cape Ann Summer Sun* for 16–22 August 1951.

I.17. National Geographic

A heavily illustrated, popular magazine of natural science and tourism.

I.17. Gorin's

A "cut-rate" department store formerly on Main Street, Gloucester.

I.17. Rockport

Town northeast of Gloucester on Cape Ann noted for its art colony and shops for tourists.

I.17. Squibs

"Squibs from Waterfront," a regular column of interest to the fishing community, formerly in the *Gloucester Times*. Written by James P. Clark, waterfront reporter for the newspaper, it was signed simply "Squibs."

I.17. Antigonish

Antigonish County, Nova Scotia.

I.17. Chisholm's Wharf

Formerly on Wharf Street, between Pearce and Water Streets on Gloucester's inner harbor, owned by the Chisholm Fisheries Co.

I.18. what the people don't know . . . how infinite!

Woven in the attack is an allusion to an early book of poems by Ferrini entitled *The Infinite People* (1950), which takes as its theme the "common man."

I.18. if Lufkin has got over his scare, last summer, / when you were so sillily reviewed . . .

The first issue of *Four Winds* (Summer 1952) was sharply criticized in a review in the *Cape Ann Summer Sun,* 18 July 1952, by editor John T. Bethell (see note to "Letter 3," *Maximus* I, 4 above). Ferrini had written Olson on July 27: "This morning I went to Francis the magazine store & waiting station on Main St. & I noticed that all our drawings which he had displayed prominently in window were gone— he had sold the 15 copies we gave him & wont take any more! This the effect of the enclosed [a copy of the review]." In return, Olson sent an early draft of "Letter 3." Ferrini wrote again on August 11, acknowledging Olson's letter and adding: "FW is selling in rockport, brown pulled it out of his window where it was prominently displayed, and Francis, main bus terminal on main st wont touch it now."

Lufkin, a common Gloucester name, was apparently manager of a newsstand concession at the Waiting Station. In his "Reading at Berkeley," reading this poem, Olson interpolates: "Lufkin, behind whose diner . . ." (*Muthologos*, I, 121; for which, see "The Librarian" and letter of 22 April 1950 to Ferrini in *Origin* 1, p. 42).

I.18. the High School Flicker

The literary annual of Gloucester High School, containing essays and poems by the students. Olson himself wrote for his high school newspaper, the *Argus* of Worcester Classical High, and was editorial writer for the newspaper of Wesleyan University, also called the *Argus.*

I.18. Helen Stein

(1897–1964), a local painter, friend of Marsden Hartley and later of Vincent Ferrini and his co-editor Mary Shore.

I.18. Herman Melville

(1819–1891), the American author. Melville's first known literary composition appeared in a small local newspaper under the pseudonym "L.A.V."—which Olson as a Melville scholar was aware of. See his master's thesis, "The Growth of Herman Melville, Prose Writer and Poetic Thinker," pp. 8–9:

> With the crassness of Jerry Cruncher, the scholars have unearthed from a decent grave two "Fragments from a Writing Desk." These appeared in "The Democratic Press and Lansingburgh Advertiser" for May 4th and May 18th, 1839. . . . The first piece is written in a style that smothers one like a muff. It contains trash like "I see you reluctantly raise your optics from the huge-clasped quarto which encumbers your lap." He is quite correct in deciding to "terminate his tiresome lucubrations." The second fragment is a bit out of Tom Moore stuffed with a billet-doux, a mysterious fugitive, and a houri "reclining on an ottoman" and "lost in some melancholy revery."

I.19. Carl Olsen

A veteran fisherman, captain of the *Raymonde,* and successor to the most successful of Gloucester's fishing captains. See also the account of his heroism on p. 7 of *Maximus* I.

I.19. Brown's

Brown's Bank. Not the department store of the earlier line, but a fishing bank in the Atlantic directly east of Cape Ann and south of Cape Sable, Nova Scotia; about sixty miles long and forty miles wide, with an area of some 2,275 square miles.

I.19. Callaghan

Marty Callaghan, fishing captain. See also note to *Maximus* I, 22.

I.19. Bohlen

Captain Thomas Bohlin (1855–1910). For his accomplishments, see Connolly, *Book of the Gloucester Fishermen*, pp. 127–153, or Copeland and Rogers, *Saga of Cape Ann*, pp. 89–90; also *Maximus* II, 44 and 45.

I.19. Smith

Sylvanus Smith (b. 1829), successful fishing captain of the nineteenth century, author of *Fisheries of Cape Ann* (1915).

I.19. sight

A position in the crew of a fishing vessel.

I.19. the Raymonde

Eighty-four foot auxiliary schooner and dory trawler, built in Essex, Mass. in 1929.

I.19. highliners

The skipper (or his ship) who landed the most fish during a season. Olson writes in *Call Me Ishmael*, e.g., that Ahab "was an able skipper, what the fishing people I was raised with call a highliner. Big catches: he brought back holds barrel full of the oil of the sperm . . ." (p. 12).

I.20. Ferrini

Vincent Ferrini (b. 1913), Gloucester poet and editor of *Four Winds*. Originally from Lynn, Massachusetts, he settled in Gloucester in the late 1940's. A close friend of the poet, who "invoked" the first of the *Maximus* poems (see Olson's letter to Ferrini, July 1950, in *Origin* 1, p. 61, and note to "Letter 5" above).

See also Ferrini's *In the Arriving*, a long poem which he calls, in a letter of 1 February 1954 to Gene Magner (now in the Lockwood Library, Buffalo) and an undated letter to Larry Eigner from 1954, his "answer" to Olson.

In light of the fierceness of Olson's attack, the reader might consider his letters to Cid Corman for 21 October 1950 and 3 May 1951 on the function of an editor of a little magazine (*Letters for Origin*, pp. 2−11 and 48−52). Olson wrote concerning Ferrini in an early version of "Letter 5" among his papers:

> I charge you, friend but no co-worker, that, as worker,
>   you here show
> yourself not good enough to justify
> your entrance to the public domain . . .

Ferrini's account of their relationship was published as "A Frame" in *Maps* 4 (1971). See also note to *Maximus* I, 41 below.

I.20. hide in your cellar / (as a Portuguese skipper once had to . . .

"The Rat—a Portygee named Manuel Silva, skipper of the [blank], who received the name because he is said to have hid in his cellar on Portygee hill when the Portygees themselves were after him on his return from the voyage in which 14 of his crew were lost in the dories settin' their trawls." Olson heard the story while at sea from the crewmen of the *Doris M. Hawes* (q.v.) and recorded it in his "Journal of Swordfishing Cruise . . . July 1936."

I.20. Making frames over East Main St

Ferrini's picture-frame shop in East Gloucester.

I.21. highbush

A variety of blueberry.

I.21. Dogtown

An uncultivated section of Gloucester strewn with glacial deposits in the central part of Cape Ann; a deserted village, said to have its name from the dogs kept for protection by widows and elderly women who lived there during the latter part of the eighteenth century. It will become a focus of attention in the second volume of poems.

I.21. Old Salem Rd

In the western part of Gloucester, near where Olson spent summers as a youth; the first land route from Gloucester to Salem, running through the northern end of Ravenswood Park.

I.21. cut brush / at the new Alewife

As a young man of nineteen, Olson worked on the construction of the Babson Reservoir, which serves the city of Gloucester, at the site of what was known as the Alewife Brook (for a description of this brook and its various names, see Copeland and Rogers, *Saga of Cape Ann*, pp. 19–20). The reservoir was built by the C and R Construction Company of Boston, July through December, 1930 (see Myott, "Babson Reservoir—Built in Six Months"). According to Myott, who was consulting engineer for the project, before actual construction could begin, "the entire area occupied by the reservoir was cleared, grubbed and stripped of top soil and all organic matter" (p. 51). It would have been Olson's job to take part in this clearing.

See also, "Start Work On Alewife Brook Water Basin," *Gloucester Times*, 8 July 1930, p. 1:

> Work on the construction of the Alewife brook dam and reservoir for an additional water supply began yesterday with the arrival of a crew of about a dozen men with miscellaneous equipment, including bush scythes, bush hooks, pruning shears, axes, grub hoes, hatchets, etc., and material for portable buildings for tool sheds and tem-

> porary living quarters for some of the men. . . . Immediate work on this job will be the clearing of the reservoir site, an area of some 48 acres, of bushes and trees and the foreman states that from 150 to 200 men will be employed in order to get this done as quickly as possible.

There is no account in the newspaper, however, of the deception and sudden firing of the local men.

I.21. the grey-eyed one . . .

Epithet of the goddess Athena (*Athene Glaukopis*). The passage is an allusion to the *Odyssey* (VIII. 224−237), where Odysseus, after leaving Calypso's island by raft and after much difficulty, is cast ashore on the island of Scheria—as the Gloucestermen on the shores of Brace's Cove—covered with brine and mud. Athena appears to make him shine with handsomeness that he may be attractive to the princess Nausikaa who has come to the shore with her handmaidens to do laundry.

I.22. I was a letter carrier . . .

Olson served as a substitute carrier for the U.S. Post Office in Gloucester during summers from 1931 through 1935. See "Carrier Force Adds College 'Giant' to Fernwood Route," *Gloucester Times,* 11 June 1931, and *The Post Office.*

I.22. Anchor Inn

The Anchor Cafe on Rogers Street, corner of Pearce, Gloucester; since destroyed by an urban renewal project. Owned at the time by James H. Mason, former master mariner.

I.22. the Bluenose

Canadian racing schooner. It raced for the International Cup against the *Columbia,* captained by Ben Pine, in October 1923.

I.22. The Atlantic Supply wharf, "Piney's wharf", ...

The wharf of the Atlantic Supply Company, ship chandlers, was at Rogers Street on the east side of Harbor Cove and was managed by Ben Pine (1883–1953), captain of the schooner *Columbia* which raced the Canadian *Bluenose* off Halifax in 1923. Pine also won the final race for the International Fishermen's Cup held off Gloucester in 1938, accounts of which were publicized in *Collier's* magazine at the time (see, e.g., Connolly, "Pride of Vessel").

I.22. the first Race

The first International Fishermen's Race was held in the fall of 1920, off Halifax, as a result of a challenge sent Gloucester by a Halifax newspaper proposing to match a Candian vessel against the fastest Gloucester fishing schooner for a cash prize and trophy for the winner. See also note to *Maximus* I, 10.

I.22. the Puritan

A two-masted schooner built at Essex, Mass. in 1922 to race in the International Fishermen's Cup races, but wrecked before she had an opportunity to enter a race, on Sable Island.

I.22. the Elizabeth Howard

Schooner, 137 feet long, built in 1916.

I.22. the Henry Ford

Schooner, 138 feet long, beaten by the *Bluenose* in 1922. It was lost in 1928.

I.22. the Breakwater

The Dog Bar Breakwater at Eastern Point; constructed in 1904 of large granite blocks, it protects Gloucester's outer harbor.

I.22. Hugh Hill

Hugh Creighton Hill (b. 1906), English poet. He had three poems in *Four Winds* 2−3, the title of each beginning with "triangle": "Triangle in Comfort," "Triangle in Friendship," and "Triangle in Space-Time."

I.22. the Columbia

Schooner built in 1923. It participated in one International Fishermen's Race, under Captain Ben Pine against the *Bluenose* in October of 1923, before she was lost with her crew of twenty-two men in a gale off Sable Island four years later. On the hard luck encountered by the racing schooners, see, e.g., "The Hazards of the Fisheries," *37th Annual Report of the Fishermen's Institute*, pp. 9−11.

I.23. Sable

Sable Island, a narrow island in the Atlantic southeast of Halifax, N.S. See also *Maximus* I, 121 and note below.

I.23. a trawler, a few years back, / caught her nose . . .

Thomas, *Fast and Able*, reports the incident briefly, p. 9:

> At about 2 a.m. on New Year's day, 1928, the Canadian beam trawler Venosta, Capt. G. M. Myrhe, while dragging about 40 miles west southwest of Sable Island, got her gear entangled in wreckage. With powerful engines and winches of the trawler pulling the taut cables, there slowly emerged from the sea, like a phantom ship, two masts with no topmasts. Slowly the form of the vessel came into view, rolling and pitching but on an even keel. The crew of the trawler were in danger of having their sides battered in by the wreck, but suddenly the steel cables holding the wreck snapped and she slowly sank from sight. While the vessel was afloat, the powerful floodlights of the trawler were thrown on the derelict. An eerie sight greeted the watchers. No signs of humans could be seen. The vessel seemed in good condition, the major portion of her rigging was intact, but no sign of a name could be made out. The rough seas prevented any attempt in keeping the vessel afloat and to ascertain if any bodies were in the cabins. All aboard the

steamer seemed to think she was the Columbia, but this fact
will never be known.

See also, "Hull Afloat for Short Time Then Sank Again,"
37th Annual Report of the Fishermen's Institute, pp. 12–13,
photo on p. 14. Connolly, *Port of Gloucester*, pp. 300–302,
identifies the vessel raised as the *Columbia* in his account.
Olson preserved a clipping of the first magazine appearance
of the Connolly report, "Hail & Farewell, Columbia!," in a
scrapbook from his youth, as well as other clippings about
the fishermen's races.

I.23. Sterling's Drug

Drug store on the corner of Main and Pleasant streets
in Gloucester.

I.23. the school-boy Renaissance

A passage in Olson's review of Ernst Robert Curtius' *European Literature and the Latin Middle Ages* concerning "the
Nine boys (now shrunk to one little Peter) . . . that is to say . . .
their schoolboy Renaissance" (*Human Universe*, p. 156) suggests that when Olson speaks of "the school-boy Renaissance"
in this poem, he has in mind a particular kind of magazine,
represented by *Nine*, edited in London by Peter Russell from
1949 to 1956, which he characterizes in a letter to Corman
as "a deliberate (& most english, urbane decision, that, culture
(not art, notice) is taste, and that, by the king's grace, the way
to make a magazine is to be wholly professional abt, taste (and
that taste in precisely the inherited mold: why, for example,
there is so much of the Latin poets, in same, Rome being,
exactly the predecessor of, london as center of the new mercantilism (I am referring to Elizabethan London, which, was
the projector of, what we call British culture—of which same
culture NINE is as precise a new assertion of as is Winston
Churchill of feudal politics . . ." (*Letters for Origin*, pp. 48–49).
In his letters to Creeley during this period, Olson con-
tinually cites *Nine* as antipodal to his own concerns, referring
to "those roman idiots of london, nine, or whatever stupid

trojan aeneid nonsense . . . that cheap miltonic vulgarization of, the epos" (ca. 17 January 1953) and to its "cheap eclectic 'renaissance' " (23 March [1953]), while calling its sponsors "that Lavender Hill Mob" ([April 1953]). The Autumn 1951 issue of *Nine* was devoted to "Renaissance Poetry: Studies and Translations" and featured work by John Heath-Stubbs, Roy Campbell, and others (a prospectus for the magazine among Olson's papers includes the following remark, which alone would justify his hostility: "The 'rootless genres' of much contemporary writing hold little attraction for us. This seems to be an interval of minor poetry . . ."). Although in another letter to Creeley from April 1953, it is the literary or publishing and cultural scene in general that is criticized: "all this tidy little school-boy renaissance—Christ, I want to rear up and heave em all, London, and the Village, or the Universities. . . ."

I.23. "The Search"

A poem in *Four Winds* 2-3 by a Clem Graham. Its closing lines, especially, exhibit a vague "future" and sense of undefined progress or progress for its own sake:

> I listened to the people, all speaking
> Like rivers in their murmur, in their flow.
> I listened to America speaking.
> Go on, go on, it said. Our dead are dead.
> Forward, it said. Onward, onward, onward,
> And learn what to at the seige's end,
> For we are all there is, armed with ourselves,
> The fusion of our blood circulating
> In goals unending.

I.23. Steiner

Rudolf Steiner (1861–1925), Austrian theosophist. Ferrini published poems, and Mary Shore, his co-editor for the first issue of *Four Winds*, an essay, in *Proteus*, a magazine oriented toward the teachings of Steiner. It was edited by Frederick Heckel, who had a poem in the second issue of Ferrini's magazine.

I.23. to read sand in the butter on the end of a lead . . .

A substance such as tallow, inserted in a cleft in the bottom of the sounding lead, would bring up a sample of the sea-bottom—sand of various colors, shells, mud, impressions of rock, etc.—which revealed the nature of the coast.

I.23. that first day I sought you out . . .

Olson sought Ferrini out during a visit to Gloucester in 1949, having read in Washington "Two poems from *The House of Time*" by Ferrini, published that spring in the magazine *Imagi*. Ferrini remembers the meeting in "A Frame," *Maps* 4 (1971), p. 48: "We were living on Liberty Street near St Ann Church when coming home one night from the General Electric Company where I had been working for the last nine years, Peg told me about a Poet who had almost broken his head getting thru, and I could not fathom who it might have been and I was curious and sorry to have missed him. He came back the next night, a Giant! to pay a 'fan call' to another poet because he was smitten by a poem I had written and which had appeared in IMAGI. I was pleased by the size of the man and the compliment. I liked him right off, his manner of ease and his candid quality, he made himself immediately at home as though he had been a member of the family. I instinctively knew it was a turning point, then, and the next two times."

I.24. "The Three Turks Heads"

Three islands off the southeastern point of Cape Ann (now Thachers, Milk, and Straitsmouth Islands) were originally called "The Three Turks Heads" by Captain John Smith in his *Description of New England* (1616), commemorating an incident from his earlier adventures in which he claims to have beheaded three Turkish warriors in successive single combats. Smith (1580−1631), the English adventurer and early explorer of the New England coast, is a hero of these early poems. See also "Captain John Smith," *Human*

Universe, pp. 131–134, and "Five Foot Four, but Smith Was a Giant," *Additional Prose,* pp. 57–58.

I.24. what sticks out in this issue . . .

In this second issue of *Four Winds* appeared poems by Frederick Eckman, editor of *Golden Goose;* Frederick C. Heckel, *Proteus;* Leslie Woolf Hedley, *Inferno;* and Honoratio Ignacio Magaloni, *Poesia de America*—none of whom, save perhaps Eckman, have been heard from since.

I.25. life, / with a capital F

That is, *F*errini. Olson would later inscribe a copy of *Maximus Poems / 11–22* to Ferrini as follows: "like, the # 1 copy—'signed' [sign? (of it all? / for capital F."

Perhaps also an ironic allusion to Ferrini's practice at the time of spelling his name in print without capitals, in the manner of E. E. Cummings.

I.25. the shocking play you publish . . .

The play entitled "The Man Who Shot God" by Horace E. Thorner in that issue of *Four Winds,* pp. 28–54.

▶I.26. Letter 6

Written April 1953 at Black Mountain, by 13 April (Olson's letter that date to Robert Creeley).

I.26. Moulton cried up that day . . .

Cecil Moulton, captain of the schooner *Doris M. Hawes* on which Olson sailed in the summer of 1936. In his "Journal" kept during the cruise, entry for July 16th, Olson has recorded:

> . . . After dinner in the tide rips we struck the fish and I had my own little triumph. I went aloft on the port side for the first time. Hanging there vaguely considering the watery world there in the sun glare of the rips to port I saw fins. Surprisedly I looked again & excitedly sung out

"Port." We swung over on the helm and with nerves spiny and anxious I waited for Harry Fletcher to strike. He did, so hard & true, the pole followed the dart into the sword-fish's back. Away went the warp and buoy to starboard ready to be hauled when one of the two dories out had landed the fish he was playing. My first fish ironed and bleeding the blue depths red.

But that wasn't the end of my luck—beginner's, I suppose. By sighting one I had kept my promise to myself—thus to return the skipper his kindness & pay my to me precious passage. So I hung there my body quivering like the striker's pole when the dart goes home, quivering with the excitement of sighting a fish right out from under the gull-eyes of the whole masthead. I had somehow justified myself, even kept the faith with Melville. I know now the blood-beat there was in "Thar she blows." I was surprised afterward I hadn't called thus, instead of the correct cry, "Port." The feeling was so good I, with the human hunger for sensation and more of it whether it is success or passion or goods, wanted it again. I began to wonder if I could get three in succession or two in succession or two today. Of course I protected myself by assuring myself such a chance were impossible. Vaguely considering these wishes suddenly in the same direction, to port in the sun glare of the tide rips I thought I saw a purple shadow close to the surface. And then within a breath a fin broke water. I yelled again. We swung and missed and came about as I swore all the curses I knew and doubled them as we came up upon the fish until, quiet, bated, I waited the striker's thrust. It went in, half the strap, and buoy over two in succession were Mine! Could you blame me for gloating? It made my body run with joy to have the striker yell up to the mast head, "I guess we gotter git these college fellers for a crew." And Newman Shea crying down, "Good eye." And the skipper from the topmast, "Got any more of those glasses, Charlie?"

It was my day. To learn later that my pulling the fish out from under the long peaks over my head was due to the fact that fishermen on the mast head rarely try to pick one up in the sun's glare took me down not a jot. I got a shot of my two fish on deck and the swords now drag astern for the rest of the trip to be borne home like scalps or like the nuts of a bull, [quoting T. S. Eliot's "Gerontion"] to be eaten, to be drunk, to be divided.

See also *Maximus*, 38–39 and note.

I.26. that Englishman, / and mountain-climber

In conversation, July 1968, Olson only remembered him as one of two Englishmen met while travelling west in the summer of 1938: one, a man named Smith, a musician; and this one, an historian from Cambridge, whose name the poet had since forgotten.

I.26. Bright Angel Trail

In Grand Canyon National Park, Arizona.

I.26. the Colorado

The river flowing through the Grand Canyon.

I.26. Burke

Walter Burke (see *Maximus* II, 23), who lived at 19 Essex Avenue along the marsh lining the Annisquam River.

I.27. Hyperion / to the lump his men would have wheeled aboard . . .

See *Hamlet*, I.ii.139–140, where Hamlet compares his murdered father to his uncle Claudius:

> So excellent a King, that was, to this
> Hyperion to a satyr.

In an entry in his "Journal of Swordfishing Cruise on the *Doris M. Hawes*" for the 23rd of July, the young Olson saw a less grandly heroic figure than the portrait of Carl Olsen here and on p. 7 of the poems:

> . . . Olson [i.e. Olsen] is a brutish creature, of 6'3 and heavy in muscle and fat to 250, I suppose. He's hung heavily amidships with a belly as steadying as an anchor. His belly steadies his body as his nose does his face. It's one of those Scandinavian noses strangely like the Negro's—thick and squashed out at the mouth and small and close to the face at the eyes. His eyes, grayish, are animal and stupid. He has a voice like the grunt and bellow of a buffalo. There's

no lip movement—in this he is typical of all fisherman; but in his case the vocalization is in his chest and he speaks as you might imagine a cod would. If there were not such speed and beauty of movement to fish, you might think of Olson as like the fish he so craftily snares; the only one I think of like him is the monk fish. But he is in his hulk and ox-like stupidity a land beast. From the stories of him he is the primitive, too. His use of his strength is undirected and without meaning. When drunk—and he is that every hour ashore—he is uncontrollable; Cece Moulton tells the story of the night he tore his cell to pieces and bent bars and ripped away the ceiling because the jailers would not bring him a glass of water. As skipper he has the temperament of a child—*moody* & fitful.

I.27. Burke was raising his family . . .

In an unpublished earlier version of the poem: "Burke was raising his family in a shack over the marsh / back of Kent Circle. . . ."

I.27. Gorton-Pew

Gorton-Pew Fisheries Co., now the Gorton Corporation or Gorton's of Gloucester, Inc., Gloucester's largest employer; Olson worked for them as a boy in the summer of 1926.

I.27. young Douglas

Louis R. Douglas, Jr., foreman at Gorton-Pew Fisheries and son of the fisherman, "the top of whose head a bollard clean took away," of "Letter 2" (*Maximus* I, 6).

I.27. "pick-nicks", Pound roared . . .

Ezra Pound (1885–1972), who had also expressed his objection in a letter to Olson, 29 October [1946]: "Been fighting against pic-nic lunches for years."

Olson was one of the older poet's first visitors while Pound was being held at the District of Columbia jail to be tried for treason. These visits, beginning in early January 1946, continued after Pound was adjudged insane and unfit to stand trial, when he was transferred to St. Elizabeths Hospital; they lasted until the spring of 1948. In a letter to Peter Russell, 17 November 1949, now in the Poetry Room of the Lockwood Library at Buffalo, Olson wrote: "It is still a question swimming in my blood, but I found I had to cease seeing him in the spring of 1948 (I had been a sort of Achates from his arrival in the Federal Pen (has he not made it the 'Bughouse' to stand next to the 'Gorilla Cage' at Pisa?). Until that time, saw him once or twice a week, and kept sporadic notes on his conversation. What stopped me was a crux of things, of him and me." Pound himself wrote in a letter to his lawyer, Julien Cornell, in early 1946 that "Olson saved my life. Young doctors absolutely useless—must have 15 minutes sane conversation daily" (*Trial of Ezra Pound,* pp. 70–72). Cornell suggests that this "Olson" was one of the doctors at the hospital, but Albert Glover has correctly identified him as our poet ("Letters for Origin," unpub. diss., p. ix).

The notes Olson kept while visiting Pound are more extensive than the word "sporadic" in his letter to Russell might imply. Typed up after each visit and titled "Cantos," they begin 5 January 1946 ("I met Pound for the first time yesterday. I had seen him once before, on November 27, at his arraignment before [Judge] Bolitha Laws, when he stood mute. That day his eyes crossed mine once . . .") and continue until 9 February 1948. They are included with much else concerning Olson's relationship with Pound in *Charles Olson & Ezra Pound: An Encounter at St. Elizabeths,* edited by Catherine Seelye (1975).

Earlier, in the fall of 1945, about the time of Pound's return to the United States for trial, Olson had written a defense of him entitled "This Is Yeats Speaking," published in the *Partisan Review* early in 1946. But even before, he had felt the attractiveness of Pound the poet. While reading Pound's *Cantos XXXI-XLI* in Key West, February 1945, Olson wrote to himself in a notebook:

> Maybe Pound discloses to you a method you spontaneously reached for in all this talking and writing. What about doing [on] a smaller scope—the West? But

he has already taken the same frame, as you will note from
your notes on the poem to be called "West" you made
4 years ago.

But shud you not best him? Is his form not inevitable
enough to be used as your own? Let yourself be derivative
for a bit. This is a good and natural act. Write as the father
to be the father.

I.27. Con

Olson's first wife, Constance Wilcock (1919–1975).

I.27. S'Liz

St. Elizabeths Hospital, federal hospital-prison for the
criminally insane in Washington, D.C.; an abbreviation
frequently used by Ezra Pound.

I.27. the Anacostia

East branch of the Potomac river at Washington, D.C.
On the bank of the river in southeast Washington, adjacent
to St. Elizabeths, is a U.S. Naval Air Base.

I.29. the Laura Dysart

Possibly the *Laura Goulart,* a 107-foot long vessel built in
1921 at Essex, Mass., and owned by United Fisheries of
Gloucester.

I.29. the Magellan

An eighty-foot long trawler built in 1930 and owned by
Capt. Joseph D. Rose of Gloucester.

▶I.30. Letter 7

Written April 1953 at Black Mountain, after 3 April (an
early version of section 2 was written on an envelope bearing
the date 3 April 1953 and addressed to the poet at Washington, D.C.).

I.30. Marsden Hartley

(1877−1943), American painter. See also Olson's letter to the *Gloucester Times,* " 'A Beef' About Homer, Stamp": " . . . (if anyone [who] has the Feininger-Hartley catalogue of the Museum of Modern Art can see) that Hartley changed by going to places on Cape Ann alone and that his Maine thing, replacing the international style, dates at this time."

Hartley spent the summer and fall of 1931 in Gloucester, painting the landscape, especially the curious moraine of Dogtown, about which he wrote: "Dogtown (Gloucester) looks like a cross between Easter Island and Stonehenge— essentially druidic in its appearance. It gives the feeling that any ancient race might turn up at any moment and review an ageless rite there . . . sea gulls fly over it on their way from the marshes to the sea; otherwise the place is forsaken and majestically lovely as if nature had at last formed one spot where she can live for herself alone" (autobiographical note quoted in Museum of Modern Art catalogue of the Feininger-Hartley exhibit, p. 72). Olson did not know Hartley in Gloucester at this time, but did meet him about ten years later, probably through Edward Dahlberg. An interesting incident is related in a letter of 23 June 1950 to Robert Creeley (they had been discussing Hart Crane):

> Did do, come to think of it, a verse on hart: the 1st days i ever did same And it caused the most enigmatic business, between me and Marsden Hartley I was heart-broken, for Hartley had made it his business to find out my address on Christopher Street (god, what a darling of a room, with parquet floors, soap-stoned to their heart, And me alone, for the 1st time in my life, trying to go to mat with same) and, to my horror & surprise, come to see me in a new beautiful sea-green suit he'd bought where I used to buy mine, my Harrises, at Macy's Made-To-Measure, 35 bucks! There he was, at my door! It was his peak, the 1st or 2nd Walker Show, after his extraordinary 2nd birth (at 50, or so), the return to Maine. And I was his. I was so nervous, I made tea, but it was only orange slices in hot water, I had forgotten to add the tea, and didn't know it, the cups

were red Mexican clay, cheap, until he had gone! It went
all right, until I pulled out, in my green enthusiasm, the
Hart peom. He read it, slowly, sd no word, got up, took his
hat, and walked out!

It has bothered me, since that day. Damned if I know,
what went on. I still suffer over it.

For reproductions of Hartley's work, see McCausland,
Marsden Hartley, or, especially, the Museum of Modern Art
Catalogue of the Feininger-Hartley exhibit.

I.30. that carpenter

William Stevens, a shipwright who came to Gloucester in
1642 having been offered grants of choice land as an induce-
ment to settle, including eight acres at the Cut. A valuable
citizen and one of some prominence; he was, however, fined,
imprisoned, and deprived of his privileges as a freeman for
firmly speaking against royal interference in local government. See J. Babson, *History of Gloucester,* pp. 164–166, his
Notes and Additions, I, 75–77, and Copeland and Rogers, *Saga
of Cape Ann,* pp. 80–81.

Stevens' name appears to have been in Olson's consciousness as an exemplar of heroic virtue as early as 1948, when
it occurs among notes toward the proposed poem *West*
(which foreshadowed the *Maximus* poems), with this quotation (from Babson, *History of Gloucester,* p. 165) following:
"more regard to his substantial performance than the wages
he was to receive, and soe grew to poverty." This, then, is the
quality which makes Stevens eligible to be considered as the
"first Maximus" (see next page of poem).

I.30. Plymouth Plantation

The settlement at Plymouth, Mass., begun in 1620 by the
Pilgrims.

I.30. "the Cut"

The Blynman Canal, which provides an entrance to the
Annisquam River from Gloucester Harbor. For its history,

see Babson, *History*, pp. 7–9, or Copeland and Rogers, *Saga of Cape Ann*, pp. 177–180.

I.30. Morton

Thomas Morton (ca. 1590–1646), settled in New England in 1622; notorious for his maypole at Merrymount, he was banished by the Pilgrims in 1628 and later again by the authorities of the Massachusetts Bay Colony. See, e.g., Bradford, *History "Of Plymouth Plantation,"* pp. 284ff., or C. F. Adams, *Three Episodes in Massachusetts History*, I, 162ff.; Morton's own account is in his *New England Canaan* (1637).

I.30. Maverick

Samuel Maverick (ca. 1602–1670), settled in New England about 1624 and was dwelling at Winnisimmet, now Chelsea, when Winthrop and his fleet arrived in 1630. For his difficulties at the hands of the Puritans, see B. Adams, *Emancipation of Massachusetts*, pp. 256–265, and C. F. Adams, *Three Episodes*, I, 328–335.

I.30. Winthrop

John Winthrop (1588–1649), leader of the Puritan emigration of 1630 and governor of the Massachusetts Bay Colony.

I.30. Massachusetts Bay settlement

Founded by the Puritans in 1629.

I.30. Half Moon

Halfmoon Beach, a small well-protected, crescent-shaped beach on Gloucester Harbor below Stage Head and near the original settlement of Cape Ann at "Fisherman's Field" in Stage Fort Park.

I.30. Miles Standish

(ca. 1584-1656), military leader of the Plymouth Colony.

I.31. Verrocchio

Andrea del Verrocchio (1435–1488), Florentine sculptor and painter. His terracotta bust of Lorenzo de' Medici (1449–1492), prince of Florence and patron of the arts, is in the National Gallery in Washington, D.C., where Olson would have viewed it during his residence there.

Verrocchio means 'true-eye.'

I.31. Minnesota back

A football player.

I.31. "Why did you give him a black hat, / and a brim?" she queried . . .

The poet's wife, Constance, concerning the portrayal of Pound in the previous poem, p. 28.

I.31. Al Gorman

Alfred E. Gorman (1852–1931), a fish buyer. See also Olson's letter of 22 April 1950 to Vincent Ferrini, *Origin* 1, p. 42: ". . . the smell is of A. G. (he was known to all Gloucester as "the Wharf Rat" at the time I was a cartpusher on Gorton-Pew's Wharf)." Olson had recorded at length his impressions of Gorman in a composition written for an English course at Wesleyan. It was titled simply "Al Gorman," and included is the description of Gorman's rope for a belt and the other details in the poem:

> . . . He was shrunken and bent. A torn, grease-covered, tar splashed khaki shirt was partly covered by an old black vest, unbuttoned and hanging about his shoulders like a shroud. He had probably found the vest on a drowned body in the harbor or cast up upon one of the beaches. His dungarees were like the vest, but filled with holes and held up [with a] rope stolen from some tarred net out in the harbor, tied in a knot that had never been loosed, one could easily believe. . . .
>
> All the kids had been swarming about him like buzzards over a corpse. Some were brave enough to snatch at him

or make a pass to hit him but most of them kept their distance and kept yelling, "Hungry Al, the wharf rat, hungry Al, the wharf rat". The crews of the vessels, the mackeral splitters, and even the bosses were jeering and laughing at him. Yet the more they rode him the stronger he seemed. He straightened up a bit. There was something healthy about Al. His tanned and freckled face had the ruddiest glow, his eyes were as sharp as any miser's and the muscles in his arms were strong. He was sneering at them now. Like a cornered rat he was showing his teeth. I liked the fight in the old man and I wanted to cheer as he snapped out at them all, "You sons of bitches!"

Al died not so long ago. Even in death he remained the mystery he had always been. . . . it had been a story that he owned a mansion overlooking the harbor that no one but he and his sister had ever entered. The story circulated that the reason why the windows in this house were impenetrable with soot was that Al was too much of a miser to buy a chimney for the lamp. Other tales were current of his miserliness. It was claimed that he kept a lock on the sugar bowl and when he brought home the customary meal of a loaf of bread he wouldn't give his sister a slice until she paid for her share. The manner in which he made his reputed wealth was obvious. He sold fish. All the cod, mackeral, and haddock that he begged, found and stole about the harbor he would split, salt and pack in butts or barrels. These he sold to fish companies for clear profit—and the number of such butts through the years no one knows. And so the tales of Al Gorman, the wharf rat, circulated when his death was known. But Al had not finished. People gasped a few days later when they read his will—he had left $60,000 to the downtrodden sister! In death he had said, "Take your radios and your cars and your pleasures. You like to hoard those things. I want to get money. That's my hobby." Just as on that day I first saw him he fought back from the corner, so in death he hurled a challenge at those others. . . .

I.32. Mason Andrews

Charles Mason Andrews, Gloucester street peddler of the 1920's and 30's. For the account of his having lived in a hogshead, see the article, "Insists Upon Right to Live in

Hogshead," from the *Boston Post* for 18 January 1932, which Olson had clipped and preserved in a scrapbook:

> If a man chooses to live in a hogshead beneath the shelter of four towering pine trees, breathing in the pure fresh air he expects some day will give him back his health, should police, acting on complaint of citizens, drag him out at an early hour in the morning and threaten to send him to an insane asylum unless he goes to the city poor farm?
>
> Charles Mason Andrews, one of the best known characters of the city, who earns his daily bread by selling candy from a basket, wants to know why a man's home isn't his castle, be it a barrel or a mansion.
>
> "Mason," as everyone calls him, set up a pile of old debris by the side of the road in Concord street, opposite the old homestead where he was born. The old home was sold and he had no place to go, although he has many relatives locally and at Essex who are well fixed with worldly goods. Across the street Mason moved his few belongings.
>
> There he sought to reside in a hogshead, but police wouldn't let him stay there. Two cops hauled him out of his "home," locked him up in the station and then, next day, Andrews was told to "either go to the city home or be sent somewhere else."

This Gloucester character was also subject for another of Olson's college compositions, entitled "Mason," in which he writes:

> . . . I was sitting on one of the wharf-piles near the Rocky Neck shipyards. I had just finished a nerve-wracking rehearsal. I had stolen off to the pier head in the hope that the stillness of the evening on the harbor would creep into my being. It was so lonely and peaceful there. Suddenly an eye fastened itself upon me, a basket swung between my eyes and the water, and a voice boomed out, "Oranges, candy, nuts, shoe-strings, tonic, gum—." That basket was the only thing that kept me from tumbling into the harbor waters. . . .

I.32. Duncan St

Street in downtown Gloucester, extending from Main Street towards the waterfront. The Gloucester National Bank is on its east corner.

I.32. he used to wear a turquoise / in one ear, London . . .

Ezra Pound.

I.32. Whale's Jaw

A rock formation in Dogtown. In an early version of these lines, on an envelope bearing a post-office stamped date of 3 April 1953, Olson writes:

> I have no heat, it is spring, & I know little things
> this new Gloucester man has done which led me
> to his door one day I scratched a new car up
> trying to get it far enough in to Dogtown to see again
> the Whale's Jaw my father stood in (in a photograph)
> a smiling Jonah (or Jehovah himself,
> he looked . . . strong enuf[?], happy
> to have split it as it is split . . .

See also "Olson in Gloucester, 1966," *Muthologos*, I, 182–183.

I.32. Jonah

The Old Testament prophet swallowed by a whale.

I.32. Jehovah

The God of the Hebrews; Jahweh.

I.32. Marsden Hartley painted it / so it's a canvas glove

See "Whale's Jaw, Dogtown" (1931), oil on board, in the Museum of Modern Art catalogue of the Feininger-Hartley exhibit, p. 72.

I.33. Hartley . . . who used to stay too long at Dogtown . . .

Donald Allen, in a letter to the author, 4 June 1969, reports that Hartley's experiences painting the Whale's Jaw in Dogtown were described by him in a letter to Helen Stein, which Olson also had read.

I.33. my father . . . until all bosses struck him down . . .

See the poet's memoir of his father published as *The Post Office*, where the story of his father's "stubbornness" is fully told. In "Stocking Cap," e.g., Olson writes of "those queer obstacles he had a way of dealing with as a challenge and which made him such an attractive, tragic man. The stubborn side of it killed him in the end" (*Post Office*, p. 8). Also "The Grandfather-Father Poem" (*Archaeologist of Morning*, pp. 218–219):

> . . . on my father
> I'm afraid I am
> right, that he did fight
> rigidly the next generation of
> 'Irish' in the
> U S Post Office to
>
> 　mon grand
> 　Père: Paddy Hehir
> 　　"Blocky" Sheehan
> 　and the Postmaster,
> 　Healy, ran a travel agency
> 　　Pleasant Street
> 　　Worcester
>
> killed himself
> 'fighting'
> such men . . .

I.33. made palms of hands of gulls

See, e.g., "Gull" (1942–43), oil on board, in the Museum of Modern Art catalogue, p. 89.

I.33. a meal of fish a final supper

See probably "Fishermen's Last Supper" (1940–41), oil on board, in the Museum of Modern Art catalogue, p. 86 (also McCausland, *Marsden Hartley*, p. 51).

I.33. Crane

Hart Crane (1899–1932), the American poet. Among Hartley's paintings is a tribute to his friend entitled "Eight Bells' Folly: Memorial for Hart Crane."

I.33. Marseilles

The French port on the Mediterranean.

I.34. I only knew one such other pair of hands . . . aboard the Lafond's gill-netters.

On a plan of Gloucester Harbor and its wharves drawn by Olson among his papers, there is written:

> 'Long Wharf'—I first went 'fishing'
> from: Capt Bill Lafond, in
> the Eliza Riggs, son Randy
> [illegible] skipper, mate
> 'Jake'—& Dutchy
> Vegliano

This was when Olson was sixteen or seventeen years old (see *Maximus* III, 160).

I.34. Hartley's fingers gave this sense of soaking . . .

See the hands of figures in such paintings as "Fishermen's Last Supper" or "Adelard the Drowned, Master of the *Phantom*" and others in McCausland, *Marsden Hartley*, p. 51.

▶I.35. Tyrian Businesses

Written in the spring of 1953 at Black Mountain, probably by April 13th, judging from a letter to Robert Creeley, and definitely by 29 April, just before the manuscript of *Maximus 1–10* was sent to Jonathan Williams. The poem should be read in conjunction with Olson's essay, "A Syllabary for a Dancer" (*Maps* 4, 1971, pp. 9–15), written the previous August.

I.35. the one so far back she craves to be scalped . . .

The American dancer, Martha Graham (b. ca. 1894), whose
dances displayed such ritualistic violence. In an early version
of the poem there is added: ". . . and because nobody has
dragged her, / she has everybody do it, she does it, she makes
dance / a dragon"; while in "A Syllabary for a Dancer" is
written:

> We have a curious way, here in the States, of being furious
> about the doing of anything, if we do it at all. When we dance,
> for example. It is as though we thought to slay the Dragon
> we had to be as violent and thrashing as he is. . . . They don't
> even yet know how to sit down, how to dance sitting down!
> But don't be deceived by this ignorance, no matter how
> gross it appears in such monsters of the old will like a crea-
> ture such as Martha Graham (who is so far back she craves to
> be scalped and dragged over the ground and so, because
> nobody has dragged her, she has everybody do it, she does
> it, she makes dance an enemy!)

Olson first saw her perform in Washington in January 1949
(letter 2 February 1949 to Edward Dahlberg). He had sent the
Graham Company his dance-play based on *Moby-Dick* entitled
"The Fiery Hunt" for performance; on 24 February 1949 he
wrote author Robert Payne, "I saw the Co. here a month ago,
for the first time, and god help me, they are terrible, and will
murder the play."

I.35. that international doll . . .

According to conversation, October 1967, Madame Chiang
Kai-shek (b. 1892), known also as Mei-ling Soong. She
visited Washington as part of the war effort in 1943, when
she was the guest of President Roosevelt, and again in 1948,
though without official invitation or welcome, on behalf of
her husband's regime. Rumors of her imperious demands
and extravagance during her first visit were plentiful, including reports of her use of silk sheets.

I.35. that dead reason / of personality, the will of, like a seal . . .

Cf. "Syllabary for a Dancer": "Will was an assertion of personality, like the seal of the justice of the peace. The body was a shell. The mind was also an apparatus."

I.35. Tiamat

The primal mother of the Babylonian creation myth; the embodiment of "Chaos" in "Syllabary for a Dancer."

I.35. the land-spout's / put all the diapers / up in trees

An actual occurrence at Black Mountain; the diapers, newly washed, had been hung out to dry.

I.36. middle voice

See "Reading at Berkeley," *Muthologos*, I, 136: ". . . the 'middle voice,' which 'puts the diapers up in the trees,' which knocks your whole life out, even if you love and have babies who have diapers. And it was Wolpe who taught me that . . . I mean, I still don't know what it really means, but he says the thing that makes music work is 'the middle voice.' " Stefan Wolpe (1902–1972), pianist and composer, was an instructor at Black Mountain College from 1952 to 1956.

See also, "GRAMMAR—a 'book,' " *Additional Prose*, p. 29: "MIDDLE VOICE is old passive! (non-copulative!)"; also, in charting the ablative case with its function or condition, "removal or direction *away*," the connection is drawn, "ablative of means or instrument is *middle voice*."

I.36. There may be no more names than there are objects . . .

See "Syllabary for a Dancer": "It has become an important fact to a writer to recognize that language is simultaneously a sign and a sound. . . . One limit any of us writers are now re-imposing on our own medium (from this basic insistence on sign as factor as well as sound) is expressed in another quotation you have offered me from the Vedas, was it—that there may be no more names than there are objects. That will cover nouns adequately, and we can do the whole job by adding a like statement to cover verbs: there can be no more verbs than there are actions in the human universe."

I.36. a hollow muscular organ . . .

Definition of "heart" in *Webster's Collegiate Dictionary*, 5th ed., p. 459: "A hollow muscular organ, which, by contracting rhythmically, keeps up the circulation of the blood." Among the idiomatic phrases given under the main entry is "to have the heart," meaning, "To be sufficiently hard-hearted."

Among the poet's papers, in a group which included "Syllabary for a Dancer" and written at the same time as "Syllabary" and "Tyrian Businesses," are a series of "songs" entitled "Words, for Themselves," composed, like this section of "Tyrian Businesses," primarily of nouns and their dictionary definitions. One of these is as follows:

> between the coronal & sagittal sutures,
> the bregma)
> > And behind the oarlocks
> a man, rowing,
> standing up
> > Or,
> as it was for us, the
> simplest: a
> lugsail

Nouns, according to the poet in "Syllabary for a Dancer," are signs "of the objects which man has found important enough to give a name to."

I.36. a whorl of green bracts at the base / (ling

On the same page as the entry for "heart" in *Webster's Collegiate Dictionary*, p. 459, is the definition of "heather": "A species of heath . . . having a rose-colored calyx with a whorl of green bracts at the base; ling. . . ." At this point, the poet associates "ling" (which is also a fish of the cod family—see p. 45 of the poems) with Madame Chiang Kai-shek of the previous section, whose familiar name was Mei-ling (suggested in conversation, October 1967)—more clearly seen when the line that follows, "she is known as," is taken into consideration.

I.36. Weather / comes generally . . .

Cf. "The Dry Ode":

> The movement is, generally as, as weather
> comes from the west.

Also *Mayan Letters*, in *Selected Writings*, p. 86:

> is
> weather, here, as on the earth because
> the earth turns eastward, is
> all movements, as was the people's coming, is it from
> the west?

I.36. When M is above G . . .

See "metacenter" with accompanying illustration, a diagram of a ship's hull in water, in *Webster's Collegiate Dictionary*, 5th ed., p. 628: "The point of intersection (M in *Illust.*) of the vertical through the center of buoyancy (B) of a floating body with the vertical through the new center of buoyancy (B') when the body is displaced however little. When M is above the center of gravity (G) of the floating body the position of the body is stable; when below it, unstable; when coincident with it, neutral."

I.36. peltate / is my nose-twist . . .my / trophy . . .

From "nasturtium" in *Webster's Collegiate*, p. 662:

> [L., a cress, prop., nose-twist, in allusion to its pungency, fr. *nasus* nose + *torquere, tortum*, to twist.] *Hort.* Any of a genus (*Tropaeolum*, family Tropaeolaceae) of herbs bearing showy spurred red and yellow flowers and having pungent seeds and flower buds.

And "tropaeolum," p. 1072:

> [. . . fr. Gr. *tropaion* trophy. See TROPHY. So named because likened to ancient trophies.] *Bot.* Any of a genus (*Tropaeolum*) of tropical American diffuse or climbing pungent herbs with lobed or dissected peltate leaves and showy, variously colored flowers; esp., a garden species (*T. majus*), the nasturtium.

See also *Maximus* I, 93, "if the nasturtium / is my shield . . .," and *Maximus* III, 226 and 227.

I.37. totipalmate / is the toc . . .

On the same page as the definition of "tropaeolum" in *Webster's Collegiate*, p. 1072, is an entry for the "tropic bird," with an illustration: "Any of several totipalmate birds (genus *Phaëthon*) found chiefly in tropical seas, often far from land. The plumage is mostly white with a few black markings. The central pair of tail feathers is greatly elongated and the bill is bright-colored." Also "frigate bird," p. 401: "A long-winged totipalmate sea bird (genus *Fregata*), noted for its powers of flight and rapacious habits." Cf. the description of the frigate bird in *Mayan Letters, Selected Writings*, p. 69.

The original illustration and anecdote used in the poem appears in *Mayan Letters* (*Selected Writings*, p. 122):

> And that toc bird—the one I may have described to you, that picks its own tail away to beautify itself . . . leaving the end only, which is a peacock's eye—troubles this poor farmer, troubles him so, he stones them because, says he, can't look into the mirror of that tail, it frightens him, so he has to smash it!
>
> Which goes right to the heart of the matter. For that damned bird just does use its tail as though it were a mirror, switching it around like proud lady does her own—for admiration!

I.37. He had noticed, / the cotton picks easiest . . .

In conversation, October 1967, the poet suggested the reference was possibly to Eli Whitney (1765–1825), the inventor of the cotton gin.

I.37. He sd: Notice / the whiteness, not / the odor of / the dead night

Pages dated October 24th torn from a notebook from 1939 among the poet's papers, contain a list of agrapha, or sayings of Christ, among which occurs:

> A Moslem legend:
> "What a stench," said the disciples,
> when passing the carrion of a dog.
> "How white the teeth are!" said Jesus.

The legend may be found, e.g., in Ropes' article "Agrapha" in Hastings' *Dictionary of the Bible,* although the poet in conversation could not recall his exact source. It appears as well in Edward Dahlberg's *Flea of Sodom,* pp. 19–20, a manuscript copy of which had been sent Olson before publication: "passing crowds I exclaim, like the disciples, 'What a stench!', but let one oaf drop a smile on my vest, and I make Jesus' reply, 'How white the teeth are!' " Again, pp. 64–65 there: "It was a soul in its nauseous moan that chided the twelve disciples for exclaiming, 'What a stench!' when passing dog-carrion, by replying, 'How white the teeth are!' Had not Jesus, who doted on the white stole and the frankincense, been reared in Galilee whose twenty foul towns Solomon had guilefully presented to Hiram of Tyre?"

There is, then, an association to be made with lines from the later poem, "Maximus From Dogtown—II," written in 1959 (*Maximus* II, 9):

> . . . o Christ pick the seeds
> out of yr teeth—how handsome
> the dead dog lies!

—which, when related to the present lines, would place this story of Christ in further association with the previous references in this section to "seedling" and "teeth," as well as to cotton and the gin which separated seeds from the cotton tuft by means of iron "teeth."

I.38. the honey in the lion

Cf. Judges xiv.5–9, the account of Samson finding honey in the carcass of a lion he had slain.

I.38. "felicity . . .

From *Webster's Collegiate Dictionary*, p. 343, definition of "eudaemonia": "Well-being; happiness; esp., in Aristotle's use, felicity resulting from life of activity in accordance with reason." The definition occurs originally in Aristotle's *Ethics*, Book I.

I.38. "the vertical / through the center of buoyancy . . .

From the definition of "metacenter" in *Webster's Collegiate*, quoted above, note to *Maximus* I, 36.

I.38. the "Hawes"

The *Doris M. Hawes*, a 72-foot long auxiliary schooner on which Olson sailed in July 1936 on a three-week voyage for swordfish on Brown's Bank. It was built at Essex, Mass. in 1927 and carried a crew of twelve. For a sketch of the vessel, see Pierce, *Goin' Fishin'*, p. 213. See also note above to "Moulton," *Maximus* I, 26, as well as *Maximus* I, 91.

I.39. the striker out in the pulpit

For "striker" see note to *Maximus* I, 3. The "pulpit" is a "small platform with a waist-high rail around it on the end of the bowsprit" (Connolly, *Book of the Gloucester Fishermen*, p. 159).

I.39. Edgartown

Edgartown, Massachusetts, on Martha's Vineyard.

I.40. "The crooked timbers / scarfed together . . .

From the definition of "futtock" as found in *Webster's Collegiate*, p. 407. On the same page, below in the same

column, can be found the definition of "fylfot," or swastika.
For more on the swastika, its symbolism and relation to other
elements in this poem, see note to *Maximus* II, 11.

▶I. Letter 9

Written April 1953 at Black Mountain, by 9 April (see
below).

41. "I had to clobber him. . . ."

See Olson's letter to Cid Corman written 9 April 1953
from Black Mountain (*Letters for Origin*, p. 124):

> Been involved in a run of 4 new Max's (provoked by
> Ferrini's 4 whatever they ares)
> Done today. . . .
>   (These new Maxies rough up Vinc con-
> siderably—I was shocked by both the choice of things, &
> their putting together
>   (to put chowder before a Maximus—or at least
> such a one, as that one,
> #3!!
> But this is only a part of *the bigger wrong*. Hold his hand
> (tho I don't think he deserves forgiveness)
>
> I just hate
> that the necessities (at least as I take them
> are bigger
> than we are
>   only hate it, that he had to go & get
> caught in the wringer.

The "chowder" put before a *Maximus* was a poem by Curtis
Zahn, "Improvisation at a Seafood Grotto," which appeared
in *Four Winds* 2–3, pp. 19–20, immediately before Olson's
"Maximus, to Gloucester, Letter 3," and which in fact ended
with the word "chowder."

On 24 September, Olson wrote again to Corman (in
Glover, "Letters for Origin," unpub. diss., p. 221):

>   so then you
> must hie yrself to Gloucester & hold Vinc's hand! for i
> don't want him to suffer at being the target of #'s 5, 6, 7!
> Tell him, that, after all, to be a subject is better than not

to be! And that if he hadn't moved to Gloucester, he needn't have been! But that he did (even if now he has to suffer!) is why, in the 1st place, this poem got born! So the complex is larger than any hurt (I hope!!)

For it is a crazy thing abt life that those we strike (or sometimes overpraise) are most likely to be those who matter more to us than those we let off!

Certainly the assault stunned Ferrini—though he will immediately try to absolve and prove himself in his *In the Arriving* (1954), which he addressed directly to Olson, "whose drive, insight & perception are the mark of the / maker, the / Poet / with a voice most original, provocative & / contagious," and in which he declares, pp. 13–14, "love does not / judge / he / is / too   busy / making / anew"—and   certainly   Olson sensed the effect it would have. Cid Corman remembers the episode in his introduction to *The Gist of Origin*, pp. xxviii–xxix:

> The following day [after Olson's reading at the Charles Street Meeting House in Boston, 11 September 1954] Nick Dean, my photographer friend who had been a great help in setting up the reading, drove us out to Gloucester to the Ferrini place. It was destined to be a dramatic occasion, since it was the first meeting of Olson and Ferrini after appearance of the Jargon edition of Maximus 1–10. (I had already, reluctantly and regretfully, played assistant to Olson and gone, as he asked in the postcard sent me which is embedded in the poem, "to hold his hand," as it were, in delivering the volume. I had read the entire book to an audience that included Helen Stein, who also was fond of Vin. She had raged at Olson's attack and shredded him for humorlessness and callousness. But the dagger had fallen; Vin was profoundly hurt, of course. I despised myself, still do, for having been party to any of it.) I knew that a reconciliation was in the cards, but it was tense.
>
> We arrived just after noon and Vin came to the door.
>
> Charles crawled out, straightened up, strode to Vin, took him at once aside and in to a separate wing of the house, embracing him and asking for a drink. They joined us half an hour later in the extra-rented part of the soon-to-be-condemned house that was used as a sitting room. Larry Eigner had been alerted to Olson's coming and his father duly delivered him. Olson took a seat opposite Larry, in

his wheelchair by the fireplace. Vin was seated on the rug beside Charles. The big man read a little, upon request, from his poetry and asked if there were any questions. Larry, spasmodically trying to frame words (and C.O. frankly unnerved by the task of trying to cope with the garbled sounds), came out with, finally, as repeated by someone else in the audience, "Why did you attack Vinc in your poem?"

Olson flushed and the room was exceptionally quiet as he began to work out a reply, naturally in terms of the larger thesis involved and not as a personal attack. It wasn't quite coming off. At which point, unexpectedly, his wife, Con, who had been visiting in a nearby North Shore town, entered—to his transparent relief and joy. I never saw so large a man move so fast as he eagerly embraced her, and the scene ended there.

However, one must also take note of the continuing relationship of the two men: of the appearance of Ferrini restored, in *Maximus* III, 137–138; of Ferrini's persistent loyalty, as seen in a letter years later to the *Gloucester Times* which begins, "No city, none, has the kind of Chronicler as Gloucester has in Charles Olson . . ." (from 10 August 1967); or in his poems upon Olson's death. See esp. Ferrini's reminiscence entitled "A Frame," *Maps* 4, pp. 50–51:

When the first Maximus Poems came with Cid who had already warned me it had one poem that was severe with me, I was somewhat prepared, when I saw the copy he brought with him to a party at Helen Stein's studio on Marble Road . . . In the copy he gave us, he asked Peg "to forgive it." The news of it got around to my friends and they got on the warpath, they were ready to tear him apart. I remember that afternoon when about 15 friends assembled in my Liberty Street livingroom, and wait: listen to it, and I read the entire LETTER 5, and later pointing out where he was right and I had erred, wherein his philosophy differed from mine, but that what he had written was USABLE, in that he had said it so sharply, in extreme detail, and enlightening. I calmed them down when I read the first Maximus Poem in the book.

I was open to him and with him, but that line hurt deeply for its tart freshness and worse, alienation—"There is no place we can meet." It had the finality of the irreversible. I closed up a bit, I became cautious, afraid, my tongue

hesitated, the memory of rapids and the rough waters
were to be the way we worked together as friends, he had
one position, I another, he created a school, I none, his
verse became loose and open, mine tight, narrow, and as
sharp as the hook he used, none of us escape, when we go
fishing in the waters of living. . . .

Despite its unrelenting severity and somewhat overbearing
quality, it would be too easy to mistake the nature of the
attack. On a tape of a reading made for Donald Allen in
August 1965, Olson remarks that the opening of "Letter 9"
is "addressed to Cid Corman . . . asking him, because I was in
North Carolina and he was in Boston, to actually comfort
Ferrini that I meant no personal-ism at all in writing 'Letter
5' . . . which is solely devoted like a gadfly on the back of this
very beautiful friend and poet, who for years for me has
been both my friend and, for me, the poet or the seagull of
Gloucester in my own absence." While Ferrini himself has
observed, in remarks made at a Cape Ann arts festival in
1963 (quoted by Peter Anastas in his review, " 'The poem is
a record of a journey . . .' "): "With the 'Maximus Poems' . . .
Gloucester comes into its own. It's like it was, and it no longer
is. The stage has shifted a bit, but the ground is still the same
and always will be—love's—otherwise nothing can get
started. And history, a man's life, is the pivot. Error, personal and social, goes with it. Each sets up his own court of
Judgment. Maximus has his, you yours, I, mine."

See also note to *Maximus* I, 20 above.

I.41. Mallorca

Island in the Mediterranean off the coast of Spain, where
Robert Creeley lived in 1952–53 and operated the Divers
Press which first published Olson's *In Cold Hell, In Thicket*.

I.41. the news / that that book was in print . . .

In Cold Hell, In Thicket, published at this time by Robert
Creeley in Mallorca and issued as *Origin* 8. See "Reading at
Berkeley," *Muthologos*, I, 99: ". . . 'Letter 9' of the *Maximus*

Poems, which has to do with this same book [*In Cold Hell, In Thicket*], this beautiful book, which I love"; also p. 119 there: "The reference in it [in "Letter 9"] to a book which comes in, with its print, which is so brown, in this spring, which is so red and green, happens to be that book . . . it is the color of that print on that paper. . . ."

Creeley had written from Mallorca on 5 February 1953, enclosing a sample page from the book, which was in the process of being printed, and mentioning the almond trees were in blossom on the island. The book was not finished and shipped to Olson until 16 March, and the first copy arrived on 24 March, when Olson wrote to Creeley: "I cldn't even look at the poems, was all eyes for the THING, to hold it [in] my hand, to take in the incredible coincidence of the COVER, to look & look at what you had done with the pages (the delight of the type, the sitting of those pages . . . o, lad, this is THE HANDSOMEST. . . ."

Cf. also Olson's letter to Corman, 27 March 1953, upon receipt of *In Cold Hell* (*Letters for Origin*, p. 123): "the BOOK is beautiful—can't get over what a job the lad did the 1st time he took such a task in hand . . . and the type, and the page, reads like cream (i think Robt is rite, when he sez, it's human, that book, feels like humans made it. . . ."

Robert Duncan has written of that first edition of *In Cold Hell* (in catalogue 33 of The Tenth Muse bookshop, San Francisco, 1970, p. 18): "The physical volume was and is for me a numinous object."

I.42. in another spring, / I learned / the world does not stop / for flowers

The allusion is to Olson's first book *Call Me Ishmael*, a study of Melville and the writing of *Moby-Dick*, which was published in March, six years previous. At a reading at Goddard College on 14 April 1962 (preserved on tape), he would say: "My interest in actually doing that book on Melville was to arrest the West. In fact I was so disappointed when everything didn't stop, it knocked me out for five months. I couldn't imagine how the world could have this book and not

[laughs] catch up!" In a letter to Ann Charters, 14 February
1968, Olson also writes concerning the first appearance of
Ishmael (*Olson/Melville*, p. 11): "I had hoped of course that
the World would stand still!"

I.43. Bond's Hill

In the western part of Gloucester near Western Avenue
and the area where Olson spent summers as a boy, some 180
feet high overlooking the Annisquam River.

I.43. the Annisquam

Tidal river dividing Cape Ann, connecting Gloucester
Harbor on the south with Ipswich Bay on the north.
"Although several small brooks flow into it, the river essentially is a salt-water estuary, open to the sea at both ends. The
tide flows in and out at each end, with a rise and fall of eight
to twelve feet" (Copeland and Rogers, *Saga of Cape Ann*,
p. 177).

I.43. Alfred at Ashdown

Alfred the Great (849–901), king of the West Saxons who
defeated the Danish invaders at the battle of Ashdown, on
the Berkshire downs, in 871.

I.43. aprino more, Asser says

Latin, 'like a wild boar.' From *Annales rerum gestarum Alfredi
magni* (ca. 893), a life of Alfred the Great by Asser, bishop of
Sherborne, who died about 910. See e.g. Stevenson, *Asser's
Life of King Alfred*, p. 29: ". . . demum viriliter aprino more
Christianas copia contra hostiles exercitus . . ." ['at last, like a
wild boar he manfully led the Christian troops against the
hostile army'].

I.43. versus / my own wrists and all my joints, versus speech's connectives . . .

Cf. "Syllabary for a Dancer": ". . . the writer has been
forced, today, to re-awake his attention to the kinetics of

words, to the syllables as the eyes and fingers of his medium, to the nouns & verbs as the torso and limbs, to the connectives as the ankles and wrists of speech. . . ."

I.44. who threw Guthrum back . . .

An early version (unpublished) contains more of the historical details:

> . . . what threw back Guthrum
> when he even had Gloucester,
> and stole off to Chittenham
> at Twelfth Night (holed Alfred up in the swamps
> until spring

Guthrum (d. 890), Danish king of East Anglia, was defeated by Alfred in a battle at Edington in 878.

I.44. Glow-ceastre

Gloucester, England; in Old English, *Gleaw-ceaster*. See, e.g., Babson, *History of Gloucester*, p. 51: "Gloucester in England is situated in the Vale of Gloucester, on a gentle eminence rising on the east side from the river Severn, about thirty miles from the junction of that river with Bristol Channel. It was founded by the Britons, who named it Caer Gloew; which signifies the "Fortress of Gloew,' a prince of the county of which the city was the capital. Under the Saxons, the name became Gleaucestre,—the etymon of the present appelation. Some writers say that the name is derived from the British words *glaw*, 'handsome'; and *caer*, 'city.' "

I.44. Athelney swamp

In Somerset county, England, southwest of Gloucester; where Alfred withdrew after being beaten by the Danes in a sudden attack in January 878 at Chippenham. He remained at Athelney through the rest of the winter, to reemerge in the spring to decisively defeat the Danes at Ashdown.

▶ I.45. Letter 10

Written April 1953 at Black Mountain; a copy was sent to Robert Creeley on 13 April 1953. Any revisions would have been made by May 1st, when the manuscript of *Maximus 1-10* was sent off to Jonathan Williams (letter of that date to Vincent Ferrini).

I.45. John White

(1575–1648), organizer of the Dorchester Company, which established a settlement at Cape Ann in 1623, and author of *The Planters Plea* (1630). See, for this poem, chapter II of Morison's *Builders of the Bay Colony*, "Master John White, of Dorchester," pp. 21–56, in which the question of the motives for colonization is likewise raised and examined.

I.45. cod, ling, and poor-john

Morison, in his chapter on John White in *Builders of the Bay Colony*, p. 24, writes of "Dorchester as a clearing point for the dried fish (cod, ling, and poor-john) which the neighboring fishermen brought from Newfoundland every autumn . . ."

I.45. Naumkeag

Indian name for Salem. John White writes that Nahum Keike "proves to bee perfect Hebrew . . . by interpretation, *The bosome of consolation* . . ." (*Planters Plea*, p. 14). Salem, similarly, means 'peace.'

I.45. Conant

Roger Conant (ca. 1592–1679), governor of the Dorchester Company's settlement at Cape Ann from 1623 to 1626, when he and the body of the settlers abandoned the site and moved to Naumkeag, eventually settling what was to become Beverly.

I.45. Beverly

City next to Salem on the Massachusetts coast, some twelve miles southwest of Gloucester and eighteen miles northeast of Boston, settled by Conant about 1626.

I.45. Bass River

Early name for Roger Conant's settlement at Beverly, from the river separating Beverly from Salem, Mass. Conant removed there after difficulties with Endecott in Naumkeag.

I.45. a later Conant

James Bryant Conant (b. 1893), president of Harvard University from 1933 to 1953, who favored a broader social and geographical composition of the school's student body. He was appointed High Commissioner to West Germany from January 1953 to 1955. See also "Reading at Berkeley," *Muthologos*, I, 115: ". . . I think Conant was a stooge, of a creation of a false state, the West German state."

I.45. that first house . . .

Morison, *Builders*, p. 36: "Although Governor Endecott was instructed by the Company to be tender to the 'Old Planters' (Conant's company), and to accord them equal rights with the new, almost his first act of authority was to remove the frame of their 'great house' from Cape Ann to Naumkeag for his own use. . . ."

I.45. Stage Fort

On Stage Head (q.v.) on the western shore of Gloucester Harbor. It received its name from the fishing stage set up thereabouts by the Dorchester settlers and from fortifications built at the time of the Revolutionary War and rebuilt during the War of 1812.

I.45. Endecott

John Endecott (ca. 1589–1665), first governor of the Massachusetts Bay Colony.

I.45. Anne Bradstreet

(1612–1672), American poetess. For a photograph of her house, which was built in 1607 at North Andover, Mass., see Morison, *Builders*, opposite p. 334.

I.45. Georgetown

Town in Massachusetts about eighteen miles northwest of Gloucester.

I.45. Rowley

Massachusetts town about thirteen miles northwest of Gloucester.

I.45. Ipswich

Town in Massachusetts about ten miles northwest of Gloucester.

I.46. Tudor

Style of architecture characteristic in England during the reign of the Tudors (1485–1603), the royal family which included Elizabeth I.

I.46. Elizabeth

Elizabeth I (1533–1603), queen of England from 1558 until her death.

I.46. that Endecott, the "New", should have used it . . .

See Morison, *Builders*, p. 38: "In July and August [1629] there were three simple but important ceremonies that accomplished this practical break with the Church of England. We may imagine them as taking place in Endecott's 'great house' [the one removed from Cape Ann, belonging to Roger Conant] . . . About thirty heads of families, having formed a church covenant, spent the morning of July 20 in prayer and preaching, and in the afternoon elected Higginson and Skelton their teacher and pastor by ballot, the two ministers having admitted that they had no right to officiate as such without an 'outward calling' from the faithful."

I.46. Higginson

Francis Higginson (1586–1630), minister of Salem.

I.46. where my own house has been

Olson would write to Joyce Benson, 16 June 1966: "I was raised in a house which is the ear on the g of Stage (Fort) on the back cover of [*The Maximus Poems*, 1960]." This was "Oceanwood" Cottage on Stage Fort Avenue, behind Stage Fort Park, where Olson stayed summers as a boy with his parents. A two-story frame cottage with a screened-in porch, it was part of a small development known locally as summer "camps" (see *Maximus* II, 136 and note).

I.46. the Adventurers

Merchant "adventurers," as they were called; in this case, the Dorchester Adventurers, members of the joint-stock Dorchester Company which supported John White's plans for a settlement in New England.

I.46. 3000£

The figure is John White's, from his *Planters Plea*, quoted in Morison, *Builders*, p. 27: ". . . for the planting of a Colony in New England there was raised a Stocke of more than three thousand pounds . . ."

I.46. Clyde Beatty

(1904–1965), American circus performer and showman.

I.46. James

James I (1566–1625), king of England, successor to Elizabeth I.

I.47. State Street

Financial center in Boston.

I.47. Washington

The federal government, Washington, D.C.

I.47. "Beggarly"

Beverly, Mass. See Morison, *Builders*, p. 36: "Thither [to Bass River] removed the old planters, to establish a quiet village which in their lifetime grew into the township of Beverly—'Beggarly,' as the Salemites called it, to Roger Conant's great grief." See also note below to "Budleigh," *Maximus* I, 151.

I.47. 1A

State highway; an alternate route between Boston and Gloucester, passing through Beverly. Before the construction of route 128 (q.v.), the main highway into Gloucester from Boston.

▶I.48. Maximus, to Gloucester, Letter 11

Written April 1953 (begun ca. April 9 or 10, according to Olson's letter to Robert Creeley on the following day) and rewritten that June (letter to Creeley, June 19) as well as again on August 11 (note among poet's papers).

I.48. The rock reads ...

Tablet Rock, some thirty feet high in Stage Fort Park, with a bronze plaque, approximately ten feet from the base, inscribed:

On this site in
1623
A company of fishermen and farmers from Dorchester, Eng.
under the direction of Rev. John White founded
The Massachusetts Bay Colony

---

from that time the fisheries the oldest industry in the commonwealth
have been uninterruptedly pursued from this port

---

here in 1625 Gov. Roger Conant by wise diplomacy
averted bloodshed between contending factors
one led by Myles Standish of Plymouth
the other by Capt. Hewes
a notable exemplification of arbitration
in the beginnings of New England

---

placed by the citizens of Gloucester 1907

For a photograph of the plaque, see Pringle, *Book of the Three Hundredth Anniversary*, betw. pp. 144–145.

I.48. the Short Chimney

Miles Standish, a nickname derived from Hubbard's account of the confrontation at Stage Fort (see *Maximus* I, 112, and note below).

I.48. Capt Hewes

Leader of the settlers of the Dorchester Company in the dispute with the Plymouth settlers over the fishing stage at Cape Ann (*Maximus* I, 112 and note).

I.48. the cemetery where my father does, / at least where I say he does . . .

Washington Cemetery on Western Avenue, Gloucester, near Stage Fort Park (according to conversation, October 1967), whereas Olson's father is actually buried in the Swedish Cemetery, off Webster Avenue, Worcester, Mass.

I.48. the Breakwater

See note to *Maximus* I, 22.

I.49. "Tragabigzanda" / was what I heard . . .

The Turkish princess, Charatza Tragabigzanda, for whom John Smith named Cape Ann, in memory of the kindness shown him while held in captivity at Constantinople in 1603. See his *Description of New England* (1616) in *Travels and Works,* I, 204.

The background for the poem is set forth at greater length in a letter to Robert Creeley, ca. 10 April 1953:

> . . . yesterday, tried all day to see what i cld do with a crazy biz of Smith's (Capt John)
>
> he entered into my picture at 12, when three of us were crawling around Tablet Rock at our usual game, of stalking each other: bang-bang. When suddenly out from behind a bush, comes this voice crying, "Tragabigzanda! Tragabigzanda." And big—like I'd only heard some barker, or a traveling Jesuit come for hell-week to the church, use. Yes, and one other: an old ham had played "Lightning" for twenty years, and gave it the juice, whatever the line was. Well, here, in our own preserve, altogether private to ourselves (except for couples necking, or screwing, we'd stumble on, in same bushes—and be all put out) was something real crazy, real—new, this guy hollering this word
>
> We dropped to the ground like the trained Indians we were, eh? And came up to the bush on our bellies, real smooth. And parted same as deftly as Henry Ware or Paul Cotter had taught us to
>
> And by god if there wasn't John Smith all got up in ruff & armor, a bristling bastard (more Captain Shrimpe, that quondam drummer, as Morton had it Standish was, than the Admiral of New England, quite another man than that little Pricke from Plymouth), and Smith supporting some swooning Turkish Princess on his arm (she also dressed, a moth-eaten Elizabeth, from a bad movie)
>
> and the two of them taking instruction from a third bird in modern clothes, the director, we found out, of the Tercentenary Pageant (we later got jobs as part of the towns-people, with square shoes, and that damned collar, etc.)

but it was that noise, repeating itself—he didn't
have it right—"TRAG ...
                    a BIG
                    ZANDa,
                    all over the top of the rock,
and the echo (which we had good control of, and he
didn't) slopping out to the sea
         It was a bizness, to have "history" come bang into
the midst of our own game!

Years later, Olson would note with surprise in his copy of
the program of that 1923 tercentenary celebration, that the
role of Princess Tragabigzanda in the pageant had been
played by Natalie Hammond, mother of John Hays Hammond, Jr. Olson continues in his letter to Creeley:

> A very sad feller, this Smith. Was another of those lads
> I was getting at in that thing off to you a couple of days
> ago, got ground out of the N.E. deal because he was Old
> England, not the on-coming Commonwealth, even tho it
> was he named it Massachusetts, even, for that matter,
> named her New England first—and as well made (in his
> several books) the only solid sense about the difficulties,
> as well as the virtues of, that coast. His accuracies (this
> supposed liar, who told such tales of wars in Bohemia, and
> winning such a fair lady as Tragabigzanda he named Cape
> Ann as her cape, until Prince Charles reduced that, along
> with all the Algonquin names Smith had so scrupulously
> recorded (also for the first time, getting the orthography
> down in English)—he pegged the difference between the
> Maine coast and Mass Bay so rightly (1616) that you read
> it as you know that difference to this day.
>   Well, he got run over. The Pilgrams refused his prof-
> fered help (they took Standish, instead, that squirt). All
> Smith could get was fishing chances—which were not what
> he was after: he was after all the economies the situation
> offered, did want to "plant" a Plantation, found a country.
> His trouble was he was wholly secular. And for almost
> 25 years (the Virginia part of his story lasted 2!) he beat
> and beat against the Puritan tide, and lost.

Olson goes on to quote Smith's poem, "The Sea Marke" (see
Maximus I, 69−70), and says: "it is wild, that the prose of
this struggle, there, the founding (or such verse) is such a

sign of the battling went on: Morton & Smith writing so (right out of W. Shax, Gent., etc.). . . ."

I.49. Capt Shrimpe

Miles Standish, a nickname given by Thomas Morton in his *New English Canaan* (1637): " . . . the whole number [Morton's partisans at Merrymount], (had the rest not bin from home, being but seaven,) would have given Captaine Shrimpe (a quondam Drummer,) such a wellcome, as would have made him wish for a Drume as bigg as Diogenes tubb, that hee might have crept into it out of sight" (Force, *Tracts*, II, 95).

I.49. wrote down / Algonquin so scrupulously

In his *Description of New England*, Smith is careful to record the native names of locations along the New England coast (see, e.g., *Travels and Works*, I, 192).

I.49. before the small-pox took them all away

Morison, *Builders of the Bay Colony*, p. 13, writes: "It was fortunate for the Pilgrims that a pestilence among the Indians of Massachusetts Bay . . . had decimated the tribes along our coast in 1617–18. From Maine to Cape Cod, and westward to the country of the Narragansett and the Nipmuc, there was only a pitiful handful of natives to dispute the white man." John Smith notes, "it is most certaine there was an exceeding great plague amongst them; for where I have seene [in 1614] two or three hundred, within three yeares after [1617] remained scarce thirty. . . . But what disease it was the Salvages knew not till the *English* told them; never having seene, nor heard of the like before" (*Travels and Works*, II, 933). See also *Maximus* I, 103 and note, 151; II, 24, 178.

I.49. where I have learned another sort of / play

See *Maximus* I, 60 and note.

I.50. Smith was writing such things as: / "for all their discoveries I can yet heare of . . .

John Smith, *New England's Trials* (1622), in *Travels and Works*, I, 265:

> Thus you may see plainely the yearely successe from *New England* . . . which has bin so costly to this kingdome and so deare to me, which either to see perish or but bleed, pardon me though it passionate me beyond the bounds of modestie, to haue bin sufficiently able to foresee it, and had neither power nor meanes how to preuent it. By that acquaintance I haue with them, I may call them my children; for they haue bin my wife, my hawks, my hounds, my cards, my dice, and in totall my best content, as indifferent to my heart as my left hand to my right . . . Not for that I haue any secret encouragement from any I protest, more then lamentable experiences: for all their discoueries I can heare of, are but pigs of my owne sowe; nor more strange to me then to heare one tell me he hath gone from *Billings*gate and discouered *Greenwich, Grauesend, Tilbery, Quinborow, Lee*, and *Margit* . . .

I.50. from his Sea-Grammar, . . .

John Smith, *An Accidence; or, the Pathway to Experience for Young Seamen* (1626), in *Travels and Works*, II, 804:

> Some it may be will to say, I would haue men rather to feast then fight. But I say the want of those necessities, occasions the losse of more men, then in any English fleet hath bin slaine in any fight since [15]88: for when a man is ill sicke, or at the poynt of death, I would know whether a dish of buttered Rice, with a little Cinamon and Sugar, a little minced meate, or roast beefe, a few stewed Prunes, a race of greene-ginger, a flap Iacke, a can of fresh water brued with a little Cinamon, Ginger, and Sugar, be not better than a little poore *Iohn*, or salt fish, with oyle and mustard, or bisket, butter, cheese or oatemeale pottage on fish dayes, salt beefe, porke and pease, and sixe shillings beere. This is your ordinary ships allowance, and good for them are well, if well conditioned; which is not alwayes, as sea-men can too well witnesse . . .

In his *Advertisements for the Unexperienced Planters of New England* (1631), Smith calls the *Accidence for Young Seamen*, "my Sea-Grammar" (*Travels and Works*, II, 950). See also *Maximus* III, 171.

I.51. "The quarter Maisters", he declares, . . .

From Smith's *Accidence for Young Seamen*, in *Travels and Works*, II, 790: "The *quarter Maisters* hath the charge of the hold for stowage, rommageing, and trimming the shippe; and of their squadrons for their Watch. A Sayne, a Fisgigg, a Harping iron, Fish-hookes, for Porgos, Bonetos, or Dorados, &c. and rayling lines for Mackerell."

▶I.52. Maximus, to himself

Written April 1953 at Black Mountain (letter 1 May 1953 to Vincent Ferrini). An early version among the poet's papers is entitled "Tyre," with the body of the poem enclosed entirely within quotation marks.

I.52. I stood estranged / from that which was most familiar

Cf. Heraclitus' "Man is estranged from that with which he is most familiar," which Olson will choose as the epigraph for his *Special View of History*.

I.52. achiote

(Sp. from Nahuatl *achiotl*), the seed of the annatto tree which yields a reddish dye. Klaus Reichert, in his notes to the poem in his edition of Olson's *Gedichte*, p. 101, suggests the poet uses the word in the sense of sharp or "peppery."

I.52. doceat

Teaching, or 'to teach' (from L. *docere*); one of the three functions of literature according to Rudolf Agricola as quoted in Pound, *Make It New*, p. 8: "Ut doceat, ut moveat, ut delectet." Pound adds that the divisions "had, I suppose come down from antiquity." Also in Pound's *Jefferson and/or Mussolini*, p. 101, and his *ABC of Reading*, p. 66.

I.52. from one man / the world

Robert Creeley, according to the poet in conversation, October 1967. In a letter to Cid Corman, 24 November 1951, Olson writes concerning Creeley: "I have learned more from him than from any living man . . ." (*Letters for Origin*, p. 87). See also above, note to dedication.

I.53. arrogance

Cf. *Special View of History*, p. 30: ". . . the word [humilitas] is an old Indo-European root meaning arrogance, actually (from rogo, to ask a question to or of something, to make a demand which has to be answered. And because the demand is made of yourself (that with which you are most familiar) it turned over, and became that horror and practice of western man, humility."

▶ I.54. The Song and Dance of

Written April 1953 at Black Mountain (letter 1 May 1953 to Vincent Ferrini); sent as "#13" to Robert Creeley on 15 June of that year.

I.54. In the present go / nor right nor left . . .

There is a possible echo of Pound, Canto XXVIII, "go neither to the left nor the right," but variants of these lines in earlier versions among the poet's papers suggest more plainly the political connotations of "right" and "left": "In the present / be neither right nor left nor center / (Which is the victim / of either)," or "how are they choices / in our own hands, neither / to right nor to left, / nor at all in the middle . . ."; as does p. 73 of the present volume where the poet writes of the "left" and the "right" breeding "the worst." Olson wrote to Corman, 13–14 June 1952, of "the approximate identity of the Right and the Left, that—'Conspiracy' "

(*Letters for Origin*, p. 102). And much later, he would ask his audience at Berkeley, "is there or is there not a Great Business Conspiracy called America and Russia?" ("Reading at Berkeley," *Muthologos*, I, 112).

The poet in conversation, June 1968, suggested he had also faintly in mind the use of American Indians in battlefield communications during World War I, which proved confusing to the Germans—drawn apparently from his reading the previous September of Webb, *Great Plains*, on the sign language of the Plains Indian (pp. 68ff.)—with much gesturing to the "right" and "left"—which later served as the basis for the U.S. Signal Corps. As telephone operators, also, for the U.S. Army, the Indians simply spoke in their native languages, which puzzled German counterintelligence efforts. The relation of this to the poem seems faint indeed, but it does perhaps account for the association with Indians in the lines that follow.

I.54. the "Germans"

The rigid, systematizing mind; possibly Nazi Germany in its attempt to reclaim for its own purposes myth and cultural symbols from the past. In another context, Olson writes to Robert Creeley, 4 June 1952: "what I was getting at by 'German' is the severity of his mind. . . ."

I.54. the wild / clementine, the coarse hair in the middle . . .

An American Indian ceremonial bundle. "Clementine," intended as a plant (apparently the columbine), suggests also the heroine of a popular American western ballad. The following early version of the lines appears among the poet's papers on an envelope postmarked Stuttgart, 21 April 1953:

> seeds of the wild columbine,
> a coarse horsehair
> and half of a peyote bean
>
> And the Germans won't get you but the bundle will
> if you use it
> for social purposes

I.54. Altschuler / taught us how to fight Indians

Joseph A. Altsheler (1862–1919), American author of adventure novels for boys. There are several series, including the Great West and The French and Indian War. In the preface to '*West*', Olson writes: "Actually as in fact it was reading and playing it out as a child in redoubts we imagined trenches and trees at the foot of Fisher's Hill we were sure had been a part of earlier Indian wars the books of James Altschuler [*sic*]. . . ." See also the letter to Creeley quoted in note to *Maximus* I, 49: "We dropped to the ground like the trained Indians we were . . . And came up to the bush on our bellies, real smooth. And parted same as deftly as Henry Ware or Paul Cotter had taught us to." Henry Ware and Paul Cotter are characters from Altsheler's *Eyes of the Woods* and other novels (see *Maximus* II, 107 and note below).

I.54. Barbour, / Ralph Henry

(1870–1944), American author of books for boys; many, such as *The Half-Back* (1899), *For the Honor of the School* (1900), or *Behind the Line* (1902), with an emphasis on sports.

I.54. sports

A multiple pun. "Sports" in the colloquial sense of individuals of a gay or casual life-style; more evident in earlier versions, e.g. one sent Robert Creeley, 3 May 1953: "what sports are, how they breed only / blondes, / Muscle Beach, / and tin horns." Sports also in the sense of athletic events, spectator sports. Olson writes to Corman, 13–14 June 1952, of "the spectatorism which both capitalism and communism breed . . ." (*Letters for Origin*, p. 103). Also in the biological sense: "as though Rimbaud were a sport of nature and not a proof" ("Human Universe," *Human Universe*, p. 11). See, e.g., Boyd, *Genetics and the Races of Man*, p. 53: "The existence of dominant and recessive genes makes it possible for us to understand the phenomena referred to by breeders as sports, or throwbacks. In such cases an offspring displays a character found in ancestors more or less remote, but not exhibited by the immediate parents."

I.54. merchandise men, / who get to be President . . .

In conversation, October 1967, Olson stated he had in mind Harry S. Truman (1884−1972), president of the United States from 1945 to 1953, who was a haberdasher for a short time as a young man. Also helpful, perhaps, is that the following lines:

> He was a man made a bank
> of the present . . . He's got
> Confederate money
> on his hands—for cereal ad
> prizes!

appear in an unpublished poem originally titled "The Capitalist."

I.54. An-yan

An-shan, city in southern Manchuria, center of China's iron and steel industry in the 1950's; with possible pun (by which past and present are contrasted, in keeping with the rest of the poem) on Anyang, the capital of the Shang Dynasty of ancient China (suggested by poet in conversation, October 1967). Anyang was known to Olson from at least Childe, *What Happened in History*, p. 161, judging from notes among his papers from ca. 1953.

I.55. the race / does not advance . . .

Cf. Emerson's statement from "Self-Reliance": "Society never advances. . . . It undergoes continual changes . . . but this change is not amelioration."

I.55. Miss Harlow

Jean Harlow (1911−1937), American film star.

I.55. Jericho's / First Citizens

A U.S.-British archeological expedition uncovered at Jericho in Palestine north of the Dead Sea, seven Neolithic portrait heads made by covering skulls with plaster as described. Among his papers Olson has two clippings related to the discovery: "A Unique Discovery" from the *Illustrated London News* for 18 April 1953, and an article entitled "Ancient Skulls Found in Jericho" from an unidentified American newspaper, containing an Associated Press dispatch dated April 12.

I.55. "Always the land / was of the same beauty . . .

Description of the islands of the Caribbean by Columbus, as preserved by Andres Bernaldez in his *Historia de los Reyes Catolicos*; here quoted from Brebner, *Explorers of North America*, p. 5. In speaking of the geographic knowledge at the time of Columbus, Brebner writes: "The north, men understood, held volcanoes, Judas on his annual day's holiday near the mouths of Hell, icebergs, and implacably hostile natives called Skraellings. The soft islands of the Caribbean were a far cry from this, and their gentle inhabitants seemed appropriate dwellers for the Spice Islands of the East. 'Always the land was of the same beauty,' wrote Columbus, 'and the fields were very green and full of an infinity of fruits, as red as scarlet, and everywhere there was the perfume of flowers and the singing of birds, very sweet.' Even the pigeons 'had their crops full of flowers which smelt sweeter than orange blossom.'"

I.55. The Isles / of the Very Green

The islands of the Greek Archipelago, the Cyclades; so called, according to Bérard, in "the inscriptions of the Pharoahs" (*Did Homer Live?*, p. 36 et passim).

I.55. Meneptha

Menerptah, Egyptian pharoah of the XIXth Dynasty, who reigned from about 1225 until his death in 1215 B.C.; son and successor of Rameses II (q.v.). Spelled Mineptha by Bérard. See also *Maximus* I, 147, and note below.

I.55. Cyprus

Island in the eastern Mediterranean, birthplace of the goddess Venus (see note below to *Maximus* I, 57).

I.55. True Verte

Variation on the "Isles of the Very Green" (*verte* is French for 'green'). From the subtitle to Bérard's *The Phoenicians and the Odyssey*, as cited at the beginning of *Did Homer Live?*, p. 11: "Les Isles de la Très-Verte. – Mer Rouge et Méditerranée."

I.56. "Of an infinity of fruits...

Columbus' description continued from Brebner, *Explorers*, p. 5, quoted above.

I.56. the Lotus

Not the Buddha who is often depicted as seated in a lotus blossom, but Homer, who wrote of the *lotophagoi* (lotus-eaters) in Book IX of the *Odyssey* (in an earlier version of the poem sent Creeley on May 3rd, Olson has it more plainly: "the Lotus Eaters, it then was, Cyrenaica . . ."). See also the final chapter of *Call Me Ishmael* where Olson writes of Homer as a preparation for Columbus and the discovery of the New World: "Homer was an end of the myth world from which the Mediterranean began. But in Ulysses he projected the archetype of the West to follow. It was the creative act of anticipation. . . . Homer gave his hero the central quality of the men to come: *search, the individual responsible to himself*" (pp. 117–118).

I.56. Cyrenaica

Ancient coastal region of North Africa; approximately modern Libya. Bérard identifies the lotus-eaters as Berbers living around oases south of modern Tunis (*Did Homer Live?*, p. 132).

I.56. "And the singing of birds . . .

Columbus' description continued from Brebner, *Explorers*, p. 5, quoted above.

I.56. As another such had it, / a writer, love was . . .

Stendhal, in his *On Love*, p. 71: "I advise the majority of people born in the North to skip the present chapter. It is an obscure dissertation upon certain phenomena relative to the orange-tree, a plant which does not grow or reach its full height except in Italy and Spain." And again, p. 85: "Not to love, when given by Heaven a soul made for love, is to deprive yourself and others of a great blessing. It is like an orange-tree, which would not flower for fear of committing a sin. . . ."

I.57. it gave warmth, / he sd . . .

Columbus is intended, but actually spoken by Francis I of France in mocking Spanish ambassadors' fears that the French sought expansion into Spain's new world territories. Quoted as such in Brebner, *Explorers*, p. 131: "Francis I mocked the Emperor's ambassadors and held his ground. He planned no war, 'but the sun gave warmth to him as well as to others.' "

I.57. the nerve ends / stay open on this horst . . . an American sd they did . . .

Ezra Pound is the "American," speaking of the Tuscan aesthetic in his "Cavalcanti" essay (*Make It New*, pp. 348–349): "The senses at first seem to project for a few yards beyond the body. Effect of a decent climate where a man leaves his nerve-set open, or allows it to tune in to its ambience, rather than struggling, as a northern race has to, for self-preservation to guard the body from assaults of weather." Olson writes in a letter to Creeley, ca. February 1952: ". . . where the skin can stay, open, needs no encasement of, its nerve ends, the Master saideth." See also "In Cold Hell": "roots lie, on the surface, as nerves are laid open. . . ."

In the present poem, it is Mexico that is referred to; an early version reads: "The way, Yucatan, they still grow / in the ex-sea soil, in that pumice dust . . ." See also "To Gerhardt, There, Among Europe's Things," written 28 June 1951, while Olson was in the Yucatan: "on this horst / on the heat Equator, a mediterranean sea / to the east. . . ."

I.57. And ice, volcanoes, Judas / on his one day holiday . . .

From Brebner, *Explorers*, p. 5, quoted in note to p. 55 above. The account of Judas is originally from the relation of St. Brendan's voyage, the *Navigatio Brendani*, written around the tenth century (see e.g. Colum, *The Voyagers*, pp. 47–81). See also *Maximus* I, 78, and note.

I.57. Venus

Roman name for Aphrodite, Greek goddess of love, born in the waters off Cyprus. See *Call Me Ishmael*, p. 105: "THE EPILOGUE of the '56 Journal [Melville's *Journal Up the Straits*]. Off Cyprus, on his way from the Holyland to Greece, Melville can no more imagine a Venus to have risen from these waters than 'on Mt. Olivet that from there Christ rose.' "

I.58. the hat-makers of La Rochelle . . .

See Brebner, *Explorers*, p. 141: "Specifically, however, it was the hat-makers who became the stimulators in Europe of a demand for beaver-skins . . . The precise requirements of the hat manufacture were somewhat technical, but the basic consideration was that the downy hairs of beaver fur possessed in unrivalled fashion the gift of natural coherence into an extremely durable felt. So durable was it that in the late seventeenth century beaver hats made at La Rochelle were returned there after their French wearing to be remade for sale in Spain, whence they were again returned to be prepared for Brazil and for the last time to be used for trade purposes by the Portuguese in Africa."

La Rochelle is a seaport of France on the Atlantic coast. For the role fish and furs generally played in the early exploration and settling of North America, see Brebner's chapters VII and IX.

▶I.59. Maximus, to Gloucester: Letter 14

A first draft written at Black Mountain by 29 April 1953 (letter to Jonathan Williams, 'THURS—APRIL 29th?"); probably a final version by August 1953 (*Letters for Origin*, p. 128; letter to J. Williams, August 29th).

I.59. John Hawkins

(1532–1595), English naval commander and slave-trader.

I.59. "to unite in one lustre, / as stars" it says . . .

Webster's Collegiate Dictionary, 5th ed., p. 217, under "constellate": "To shine with united radiance; to unite in one luster, as stars."

I.59. the lard pail of ice cream . . .

A dream, one of a series of recent ones the poet had recorded on an envelope postmarked 2 March 1953 (this dream from a "Thursday," possibly March 5th).

I.59. that movie-house, / Boston . . .

The former RKO Keith Memorial on Tremont Street. Following a reading at the Poetry Center at San Francisco

State on 21 February 1957, at which this poem was read, Olson commented: "the old Keith . . . you came out on Washington Street and you went in on Tremont, or was it Boylston . . . I don't know whether it's still there . . . but it used to have . . . those phoney stars with lights. Lovely. You felt as though the whole thing was just pricked out like a colander."

I.60. "to tend to move / as though drawn" . . .

Possibly "-tropism" in *Webster's Collegiate*, 5th ed., p. 1072: ". . . denoting *tendency to turn, affinity for* . . . as in helio*tropism*"—which is characteristic of the sunflower (as is noted under the entry for "heliotropism" in *Webster's*).

I.60. The old charts . . .

Studies of the human figure such as those by Leonardo da Vinci based on the theory of proportion according to Vitruvius. "The classic proportional figure of man, bound by a circle, legs and arms spread to cut the circle into four arcs— a sudden geometric and annunciative man measurer and to be measured" ("Apollonius of Tyana," *Human Universe*, p. 26).

I.60. one taught us / how to stand in crowds . . .

In the summer of 1929, Olson studied at the Gloucester School of the Little Theatre and was taught, by a Mrs. Constance Taylor, posture exercises based on the system of body coordination and muscle control developed by Bess M. Mensendieck. For a description of the method, see her *It's Up to You*, or *Look Better, Feel Better*. See also note to *Maximus* I, 2.

I.60. Tarr's Railway

A marine railway (where vessels are hauled up a runway above high tide for repairs and painting) at the Tarr and Wonson paint factory; the Rocky Neck Marine Railway, Rocky Neck Avenue, tip of Rocky Neck, the loft of which served as the Gloucester School of the Little Theatre.

I.61. seeking, / like Euclid, / the ape's line . . .

A complex cluster. First, Euclid, the Greek geometrician who lived about 300 B.C. (in conversation, October 1967, Olson suggested he may have had somewhat in mind a line from a sonnet by Edna St. Vincent Millay, "Euclid alone has looked on Beauty bare"—in her *Collected Sonnets*, p. 45). While the "ape's line"—esp. in conjunction with "pithecanthropus" which closes this section of the poem—is suggestive of the "load line" or axis of weight distribution in regard to human posture, as in the following discussion of *Pithecanthropus erectus* from a text known to Olson: "The shape of the human femur has generally been regarded as a result or sign of the erect posture . . . As shown by Walmsley (1933), the lateral condyle (at the distal end of the femur) is the weight-bearing condyle in modern man, and in Pithecanthropus too the load line passes from the head of the femur through the lateral condyle. In Neanderthal man the load is distributed equally on both, whereas in the gorilla the medial condyle is larger than the lateral and the load line passes through it" (Gates, *Human Ancestry*, p. 79). This may be put in relation to the Mensendieck method described above, which offers "the stance fit for crowds" (indeed Mensendieck's *Look Better, Feel Better*, p. 71, discusses the advantages of her Balanced Standing Position: "You can use it when you stand waiting for a train, bus, elevator, or while talking with another person.").

I.61. a sash weight . . .

Note from 15 June 1953 among the poet's papers: ". . . this weight of the sexual (as exhausted) which is that sashweight I miss in myself—the weight of reality I take it I go more & more away from, in my self & work ('the primitive,' WCW called it)."

I.62. Because of the agora America is . . .

The phrase occurs, perhaps for the first time, in a letter written 25 April 1953, to an English writer, Ronald Mason, whose book on Melville Olson had warmly responded to in "Materials and Weights of Herman Melville" (a portion of another letter to Mason concerning the "marketing" of literature occurs in *Maximus* I, 72), where it appears amidst a discussion of the use made of Melville by critics and scholars: "The moral struggle, here, anyhow, is a crazy one, just because of the agora America is."

I.62. the Banks / which the Basques, maybe, / first found

The fishing shoals in the Atlantic, part of the continental shelf; specifically the Grand Banks southeast of Newfoundland and several smaller banks west of the Grand Banks. Andrews, e.g., *Colonial Period of American History*, I, 94n., reports: "The French Basques, with their seaport at St. Jean de Luz, and the Spanish Basques or Guipuzcoans, with their seaport at San Sebastian, were undoubtedly among the earliest to frequent these waters, and were records extant could probably be traced back for two or three centuries earlier. Brereton, *Briefe and True Relation*, mentions a 'Baske-shallop' in 1602; Champlain met Basques up the St. Lawrence as far as Tadoussar in 1610 . . . ; the Pilgrims saw 'Biskay shalops, fitted with both sails and ores,' in 1623. . . ."

I.62. Pytheas

Pytheas of Massalia (Marseilles), Greek explorer of the fourth century B.C., the first Greek to visit and describe the Atlantic coast of Europe, including England. He reported, according to Strabo, an island called Thule, which he described as northernmost of the British Isles, six days north of Britain, a region "in which there was no longer any distinction of land or sea or air, but a mixture of the three like sea lung, in which he says that land and sea and everything floats, and this [that is, the mixture] binds all together, and can be traversed neither on foot nor by boat" (Stefansson, *Great Adventures and Explorations*, p. 21).

Olson's knowledge of Pytheas comes first from Stefansson's book, "the one I call Pytheas' (!)" (letter to Brian

Goodey, a geographer, 25 September 1968), which he read
as early as 1947 or 1948. Notes made on the book, and on
Pytheas' sludge, are to be found in a notebook from that time
among the poet's papers.

In *Mayan Letters,* Olson writes: "*ultima Thule,* was the outer-
most reach of the world to the ancients, was, to the Greeks,
Thoule, or Thyle" (*Selected Writings,* p. 96).

See also *Maximus* I, 78, 84, 151, etc. and "A Maximus
Written to Throw Back a Hex," section quoted in note to
Maximus I, 78.

I.62. treasure: one fifth / to the crown, of all . . . jewels & pearls

From the commission granted Richard Hawkins in 1593,
as quoted in the *Dictionary of National Biography,* IX, 224:
" 'To attempt some enterprise against the king of Spain, his
subjects and adherents, upon the coast of the West Indies,
Brazil, Africa, America, or the South Seas, granting him and
his patrons whatever he should take, reserving to the crown
one-fifth part of all treasure, jewels, and pearls. . . .' "

I.62. Negroes, / it turned out, / were pearls . . .

John Hawkins, while a young man, "learned 'that negroes
were very good merchandise in Hispaniola, and that they
might easily be had upon the coast of Guinea' " (*Dictionary
of National Biography,* IX, 212).

I.62. His father / was old fashion . . .

William Hawkins (d. 1554?), father of John Hawkins. "In
or about 1528, in command of his own ship . . . he sailed for
the Guinea coast, where he traded with the negroes for ivory
and other commodities; and afterwards, 'arriving on the
coast of Brazil, used there such discretion and behaved himself so wisely with those savage people, that he grew into
great familiarity and friendship with them.' In a second
voyage (c. 1530) 'one of the savage kings of the country was

contented to take ship with him and to be transported into England,' Hawkyns leaving behind in the country, as a pledge of his safety, 'one Martin Cockeram of Plymouth.' This Brazilian king was brought up to London and presented to Henry VIII at Whitehall, and a year later sailed with Hawkyns on the homeward voyage. Unfortunately he died on the passage out, and it was feared that Cockeram's life might be in danger. The savages were, however, 'persuaded of the honest dealing of our men;' the hostage was safely restored, and Hawkyns returned to England with his 'ship freighted and furnished with the commodities of the country. . . .' " (*Dictionary of National Biography*, IX, 227–228).

I.62. Sierra Leone

Country on the west African coast, visited by John Hawkins for slaves (*Dictionary of National Biography*, IX, 213–214).

I.63. "for a crest: / "a demi-Moor . . .

The success of John Hawkins' slave-trading won him a grant of a coat of arms: "sable, on a point wavy a lion passant or; in chief three bezants: and for a crest, a demi-Moor, proper, in chains" (*Dictionary of National Biography*, IX, 214 and see the illustration in Markham, *The Hawkins' Voyages*, xi).

I.63. for some of those who built / white houses

See *Maximus* I, 9, and note to *Maximus* I, 5.

I.63. "On board, San Juan de Lua . . .

From the entry for John Hawkins in *Dictionary of National Biography*, IX, 215: ". . . they had on board at San Juan de Lua fifty-seven negroes 'optimi generis,' each valued at 160 *l.*, or a total of 9,120 *l.* (Schedule of property lost, *State Papers*, Dom. Elizabeth, liii.) . . ."

San Juan de Lua is a small island protecting the harbor of Vera Cruz, Mexico, where John Hawkins was attacked by a Spanish fleet in 1568. Hawkins presumably had intended to sell the slaves, the *"optimi generis"* (Latin 'finest products'), at Vera Cruz.

I.64. Dorchester Company

The joint-stock company organized in 1623 by John White and merchant adventurers of Dorchester, Eng., to establish a fishing plantation at Cape Ann.

I.64. Cape Ann

The northern promontory of Massachusetts Bay on which Gloucester is located. Originally named Cape Tragabigzanda by Captain John Smith on his voyage of 1614, but changed to Cape Ann by Prince Charles in honor of his mother, the wife of James I of England.

I.64. "the name of Hawkyns, / in its French form Haquin . . .

Quoted from the entry for William Hawkins, *Dictionary of National Biography*, IX, 228, without change.

I.64. Sir Richard

Sir Richard Hawkins (ca. 1562–1622), son of Sir John Hawkins, grandson of William Hawkins. He planned a voyage

> which, in his conception, was to surpass any yet made. This was not only a voyage round the world, arriving at 'the islands of Japan, of the Philippines, and Moluccas, the kingdoms of China and East Indies, by the way of the Straits of Magellan and the South Sea,' but he designed principally, he tells us, 'to make perfect discovery of all those parts where he should arrive, as well known as unknown, with their longitudes and latitudes, the lying of their coasts, their headlands, their ports and bays, their cities, towns, and peoplings, their manner of government, with the commodities which the countries yielded, and of which they have want and are in necessity . . .' This was a project quite beyond his predecessors, Drake or Cavendish, whose principal end was to prey on

the Spaniards, and who had been driven to sail round the world mainly by force of circumstances. There is nothing in Hawkyns's actions to show that his object was different from theirs; though when he wrote, thirty years afterwards, he may have persuaded himself that his voyage was primarily intended as one of scientific discovery. The ship in which he determined to go was built for his father in 1588, and named, in the first instance, the Repentance; afterwards the queen, admiring her graceful form, had ordered her to be renamed the Dainty, and as such she had sailed in the expedition to the coast of Portugal in 1590, and again in the voyage to the Azores in 1592.

I.65. the bay of San Mateo . . .

At the mouth of the Esmeraldas River, northwest of Quito, Ecuador; site of Richard Hawkins' naval engagement with a Spanish fleet in 1594. See *Dictionary of National Biography*, IX, 224: "The fight lasted through three days, till Hawkyns was carried below severely wounded. The ship was then almost knocked to pieces, with fourteen shot under water, seven or eight feet of water in the hold, and the pumps smashed; many of the men killed, many more wounded, and the rest mad drunk. . . ." Hawkins surrendered to the Spanish commander, who sent his glove as a pledge to guarantee life and safe return to England, but the Englishmen were detained and Hawkins himself was removed to Spain where he was, in violation of the agreement, thrown into prison.

I.65. wolf-tits . . . fit to raise / feral children

As Romulus and Remus in Roman legend.

▶I.67. Maximus, to Gloucester: Letter 15

First version written 8 May 1953. In a note from the "Night of Sun-Mon May 9–10 (?)," Olson asks himself, "why, now as I write is, my mind full of Blackburn? and some wish to remove any beating of him—to write him a letter taking back that poem, done yesterday, Max # 15?" For the role of Paul Blackburn in the poem see note to p. 68 below. Another note among the poet's papers indicates the poem was re-written June 17th that year.

I.67. It goes to show you. It was not the "Eppie Sawyer" . . .

See *Maximus* I, 7, where Olson had made the statement, "Bowditch brought the Eppie Sawyer / spot to her wharf a Christmas morning"—here corrected using H. Bowditch, "Nathaniel Bowditch," pp. 104–106:

> Bowditch's return from his fifth and last voyage, on Christmas Day 1803, has been considerably dramatized. Nathaniel I. Bowditch, in the *Memoir* of his father (1839) [Vol. IV of la Place's *Mécanique Céleste*], says:
>
> In his last voyage, Dr. Bowditch arrived off the coast in mid-winter, and in the height of a violent north-east snow-storm. He had been unable to get an observation for a day or two, and felt very anxious and uneasy at the dangerous situation of the vessel. At the close of the after-noon of December 25, he came on deck, and took the whole management of the ship into his own hands. Feeling very confident where the vessel was, he kept his eyes directed towards the light on Baker's Island, at the en-trance of Salem harbor. Fortunately, in the interval be-tween two gusts of wind, the fall of snow became less dense than before, and he thus obtained a glimpse of the light of which he was in search. It was seen by but one other person, and in the next instant all was again impenetrable darkness.   Confirmed, however, in his previous convic-tions, he now kept on the same course, entered the harbor, and finally anchored in safety. He immediately went on shore, and the owners were very much alarmed at his sudden appearance, on such a tempestuous night, and at first could hardly be persuaded that he had not been wrecked.

In a footnote he adds:

> Upon this occasion, he had given his orders with the same decision and preciseness as if he saw all the objects around, and thus inspired the sailors with the confidence which he felt himself. One of them, who was twenty years older than his captain, exclaimed, 'Our old man goes ahead as if it was noon-day.'

A good deal has been made of this dramatic episode by various writers . . . Let us examine Bowditch's own journal of this voyage, preserved at the Peabody Museum in Salem . . .

Dec.

20   Begin with brisk breeze; passing clouds. A 8 P.M. quite moderate. At midnight hard gale sprung up from W. . . .

24   Begins gentle breeze & pleas. Middle brisk breeze, thick rainy weather. Latter part moderate to foggy.

25   All this day very foggy, at 4 P.M. cleared up a little (running . . . in the Lat. of Baker's Island) Saw Eastern Point of Cape Ann: at 7 P.M. came to anchor in Salem. . . .

On the twenty-fifth the wind was northeast with continuing fog but no mention of snow, and Eastern Point was seen during the afternoon. Until 1831 there was no lighthouse on Eastern Point, but there was a beacon—a large ball erected on a mast—as was on Baker's Island from 1791 to 1798 when the light-house was built there. Having sighted Eastern Point he would know where to find Baker's Island and Salem harbor. To do this in a fog is no mean feat in itself, one may suppose; but how did it become so exaggerated in the account in the *Memoir*? The clue probably lies in the footnote; apparently Nathaniel I. Bowditch got the account from the sailor whose words are quoted; he remembered the snowstorm of the twentieth, and confused it, thirty-five years later at the age of eighty-five, with the foggy night of the twenty-fifth.

The ship "Putnam" was a three-masted vessel of 260 tons built in Danvers, Mass. in 1802; the "Bay" is Massachusetts Bay; and Baker's Island is about seven miles from Salem in Massachusetts Bay. For Eastern Point, see note to p. 6 above. An island in the Indian Ocean, Ile de France is since known as Mauritius; while Sumatra is the island, part of Indonesia, south of the Malay Peninsula. It might be noted, however, for sake of accuracy, that shoes, which Olson says was cargo for Sumatra and Ile de France, was a cargo on Bowditch's first voyage not the fifth voyage, the one here described (see H. Bowditch, p. 108, and chart on p. 102; also *Mécanique Céleste*, IV, 28). The voyage to Sumatra and Ile de France was indeed the fifth one, but the cargo was pepper and coffee, not shoes (Berry, *Yankee Stargazer*, pp. 136–137).

In reading "Letter 15" at the Poetry Center of San Francisco State College on 21 February 1957, Olson calls the earlier account of Bowditch and the *Eppie Sawyer* in "Letter 2," the "story I was raised with . . . information which I knew as a boy."

I.68. He sd, "You go all around the subject . . .

Paul Blackburn (1927–1971), American poet. "The conversation in Letter 15 occurred in several exchanges of letters Charles and I had in 1951. It was not Black Mountain, since I never went to BMC. He was in Gloucester and I was in E. 22nd St., NYC. I'd just come to Charles' work that year, via *Origin* and manuscript versions, since one of the major ways of getting the news about in those days was to send poems to one another. . . . On first coming to Charles' work, of course I found it difficult, and wanted to question the basis of his constructions, my own work being in a much more formative stage at that point, so that what comes out as crit/ in the conversational form, and a lovely redaction it is, was more a probe imbedded in whole paragraphs of talk about the texts themselves, or the ways to come at a poem. The following lines re: the poem as sleeping car which wraps you in cellophane and takes you there, i.e., you do not TRAVEL that way, came also out of that correspondence" (letter from Blackburn to the author, 12 February 1968). Olson wrote to Blackburn, 28 December 1958 (letter at University of California at San Diego Library): "Did you know, e.g., that one of the Maxies (the one abt Smith previously, & Pullman cars . . . turned all on *you*? Probably you do, for one section includes direct quotes from you?"

I.68. Pullman

Railroad car with accommodations for sleeping. Typical advertisements for such, as can be found in magazines of the day, made claims which stressed the comfort of the ride—

e.g., *Time*, 20 April 1953, p. 12: "Go Pullman: comfortable, convenient and safe"—which, even if true, would be offensive to a man who had written, *Maximus* I, 14, "the blessing / that difficulties are once more."

I.68. Rhapsodia

In the sense of the Greek *rhapsōidia*, 'songs stitched together,' i.e., the technique of epic poetry. Olson writes in a letter to Robert Creeley, 25 October 1950: "How to sew (rhapsode: was, how abt that: (the sound, I mean): meant, to sew together!)" See the following passage from the *Encyclopaedia Britannica* (11th ed.) article, "Homer," marked by Olson in his copy:

> The recitation of epic poetry was called in historical times "rhapsody" (ῥαψῳδία). The word ῥαψῳδός is post-Homeric, but was known to Pindar, who gives two different explanations of it—"singer of stitched verse" (ῥαπτῶν ἐπέων ἀοιδοί), and "singer with the wand" (ῥαβδός). Of these the first is etymologically correct (except that is should rather be "stitcher of verse"); the second was suggested by the fact, for which there is early evidence, that the reciter was accustomed to hold a wand in his hand—perhaps, like the sceptre in the Homeric assembly, as a symbol of the right to a hearing.

Also Carpenter, *Folk Tale, Fiction and Saga in the Homeric Epics,* which Olson had read in the late 1940's: "The Greek epithet *rhapsode,* or 'song-stitcher,' admirably conveys the patchwork technique of the oral compositor, working with metrical rags and ribbons which he can sew together to make hexameters" (p. 15).

I.69. John Smith's latest book . . .

"ADVERTISEMENTS / For the unexperienced Planters of / *New-England,* or any where . . ." was published at London in 1631 and is reprinted in *Travels and Works,* II, 917–966. Its "Epistle Dedicatorie," with its dedication to "*GEORGE Lord Arch-Bishop of CANTERBVRIE*" and "*SAMVEL Lord Arch-Bishop of YORKE,*" is dated 1630 by Arber (II, 920).

I.69. Smith (refused / as navigator by / the Pilgrims . . .

Smith had offered his services to the Pilgrims, but they declined, "to save charges," according to Smith, "saying my books and maps were much better cheape to teach them, than my selfe" (*Travels and Works,* II, 941 and 892).

I.69. THE SEA MARKE

As in *Travels and Works,* II, 922, with three minor differences in punctuation and spelling.

Olson has said that " 'Letter 15' is a use of a poem of John Smith which argues a condition of poetics at the date it was written . . ." (tape made at the Vancouver Poetry Conference, 14 August 1963), and has called Smith "that great successor to William Shakespeare" (*Muthologos,* I, 142), "the psyche that split off and went to America at exactly that moment of Shakespeare, Daniel, and Campion" (author's notes from class at Buffalo, 1 December 1964).

See also, especially for what follows in the poem, "Captain John Smith," *Human Universe,* pp. 132–133:

> Why I sing John Smith is this, that the *geographic,* the sudden *land* of the place, is in there, not described, not local, not represented—like all advertisements, all the shit now pours out, the American Road, the filthiness, of graphic words, Mo-dess . . .
> god, to get the distinction, across! so that even Ezra Pound stops praising ads, for some silk stocking, in the error of his anger, at the bland, not getting that the age of usury which followed from the time of cant is worse, worse than he knows, worse than even himself in jail (he is nowhere in such danger as us who aren't!), that even his own act is now ad-writing, that where he got it—say Elbert Hubbard—that his age of distraction is total, that energy, as a component, is not enough, not enough, Ezra, even though the syllables (nickel nickel) . . . .

For more on Smith see also note to "Tragabigzanda," *Maximus* I, 49, and *Maximus* I, 121–127.

I.70. And for the water-shed, the economics & poetics thereafter?

See "A Later Note on Letter XV" in *Maximus* II, 79.

I.70. Villon

Francois Villon (1431−ca. 1463), the French poet; subject of an opera entitled "The Testament of Villon," and much praise, by Ezra Pound. Pound has written in "How to Read," e.g.: "After Villon and for several centuries, poetry can be considered as *fioritura,* as an efflorescence, almost an effervescence, and without any new roots. . . . One must emphasize one's contrasts in the quattrocento. One can take Villon as pivot for understanding them. After Villon, and having begun before his time, we find this *fioritura,* and for centuries we find little else" (*Polite Essays,* p. 175). See also his *ABC of Reading,* pp. 104−105.

I.70. Fra Diavolo

Commonly, the popular name for an Italian brigand, Michele Pezza (1771−1806); though here an allusion to Elbert Hubbard, who termed himself "Fra Elbertus" and published a journal entitled *The Fra.* Olson has a page torn from an issue of *The Fra* among his papers, an article entitled "Hide-Bounders," addressed to "you Advertising Hustlers" and written in that gamey "American" style favored by Pound.

I.70. Elberthubbardsville, / N.Y.

I.e., East Aurora, New York, a community seventeen miles southeast of Buffalo, where Elbert Hubbard (1856−1915), popularizer, homilist, and moral imperialist, founded the Roycroft colony, modeled after that of William Morris in England. It included a press that reprinted classics (though not Villon). Hubbard himself was the author of innumerable essays and stories, the best known of which is "A Message to Garcia." One of his collections, *The Romance of Business* (1917), included an essay entitled "The Science of Advertising."

I.70. Raymond's

Department store on Washington Street, Boston. Its newspaper advertisements were loud and brash, featuring Uncle Remus characters proclaiming bargains in a simulated rural "Yankee" or backwoods dialect.

I.71. Brer Fox

Ezra Pound, a nickname given him by T. S. Eliot, after the character in the Uncle Remus stories of Joel Chandler Harris. Pound in turn called Eliot, "Old Possum."

I.71. Rapallo

Town in northwestern Italy; residence of Pound from 1924 to 1945, and to which he returned after his release from from St. Elizabeths Hospital.

I.71. Quattrocento-by-the-Beach

The fifteenth century, height of the Italian Renaissance so admired by Pound: "Quattrocento, 1450–1550, the vital part of the Renaissance" (*Make It New*, p. 282).

This section is "addressed" to Pound.

I.71. # / 429

1429, date for the arrival in Italy of Georgius Gemistus, Greek Platonist who encouraged Cosimo de' Medici to found an academy for classical learning at Florence; i.e., the start of the Italian Renaissance. See Olson's bibliography in *Mayan Letters* (*Selected Writings*, p. 129): "Ezra Pound, *Guide to Kulchur*, just because it razzledazzles History. And any Learning. But its loss is exactly that. Plus the poet's admitted insistence he will stay inside the Western Box, Gemisto, 1429 A.D.,

up"—although in *Guide to Kulchur*, p. 224, Pound simply
says Gemisto came to Italy in "the 1430's." See also *Maximus*
II, 23:

> The Renaissance a
> box
>
> the economics & poetics
> thereafter . . .

I.71. the American epos, 19- / 02

In a letter to the poet Philip Whalen, 13 December 1957,
Olson wrote: "At Homer's date *epos* (about equal to *logos*
and *muthos*, with what shadings now lost) was WORDS
THEMSELVES"; and in a notebook begun "Sunday Sept 15
1957" he wrote: "epos means words—without accompani-
ment of song or lyre & without being acted out (contrasted
to *ergon*)."

In conversation, October 1967, the poet suggested the
year 1902 could be a date for the start of national advertising. In his essay "History" from 1952, Olson speaks of the
appearance of "that special American phenomenon, PRO-
MOTION. . . . sometime, say, around the beginning of the
20th century, a principle of pumping up wants, of turning
them into cravings, of creating artificial or super-abundant
human wants." The specific year 1902 may also be intended
to mark America as "the New Empire," by using the date of
Brooks Adams' study of America's emergence as a world
power entitled *The New Empire*, which Olson would review
in the summer 1954 issue of the *Black Mountain Review* (see
also *Maximus* III, 66−67).

I.71. Barton

Bruce Barton (1886−1967), American advertising executive. He was a founding member of Batten, Barton, Durstine
and Osborn, one of the nation's largest advertising agencies.

I.71. your lost, you / found, your / sneakers

An early version has: ". . . your lost, your / found, you / seekers"—possibly, especially since followed in the poem by "o Statue," a faint echo or variation of "Give me your tired, your poor, your huddled masses yearning to breath free . . . ," the inscription at the base of the Statue of Liberty.

I.71. the best / is soap. The true troubadours / are CBS.

From an early manuscript of "Letter 15":

> .. . the best
> is soap
>> As the old dog sd, and meant it, the best writing is
> right there, the true troubadours
> are CBS

Pound is "the old dog." In a letter to Creeley, ca. February 1951, Olson wrote: "it should be no wonder that Ez, at the same time he carries on a conspiracy to reform finance . . . says radio commercials are the best verse being now writ— VILON [sic], or some soap . . ." Pound may have stated his views *viva voce*, possibly during one of Olson's visits to him in St. Elizabeths, when "we batted around the radio, the movies, the magazines, and national advertising, the 4 Plagues of our time" (*Charles Olson & Ezra Pound*, p. 89). Pound himself had written in "A Retrospect," however: "Consider the way of the scientists rather than the way of an advertising agent for a new soap" (*Literary Essays*, p. 6).

CBS is the Columbia Broadcasting System, the radio and television communications network.

I.71. Melopoeia

One of the three ways by which language is "charged or energized," according to Pound. See, e.g., "How to Read" (*Polite Essays*, p. 170): "MELOPOEIA, wherein the words are charged, over and above their plain meaning, with some musical property, which directs the bearing or trend of that meaning." In *ABC of Reading* he writes: "There are three kinds of melopoeia, that is, verse made to sing; to chant or intone; and to speak" (p. 61; also *Make It New*, p. 368).

I.71. Cokes

Coca Cola, the widely advertised soft drink. "Busy people pause for Coke" or "The Pause that Refreshes" were typical slogans (back covers of *Time*, 16 March and 13 April 1953, respectively).

▶ I.72. Letter 16

Written May 1953 at Black Mountain, between 10 May (see note below) and 23 May (a letter to Corman for that date in Glover, "Letters for Origin," unpub. diss., p. 212, reports: "Been on the Max kick still. Thru #22, now.").

I.72. "not to crowd you. But what do we have / but our wares?

"No artist is ever an aesthetician," writes Olson in his "History" essay, "he is—and this is where he is at one with everyone—a man offering his goods."

The passage in the poem itself was first written in a letter to Ronald Mason (see note to *Maximus* I, 62), 10 May 1953:

> Not to crowd you, but, what do we have but our wares? and our market, things being what they are, are our "friends," eh?
>
> (The literary mart is barter alone, it has got so primitive— like New England was, at its start
> > (and it amused me, last night, to learn that Malthus based his notions on the statistics of abundant births in the Mass Bay Colony!
> > > ((How abt that?!

Olson had begun his letter to Mason telling about the circulation of his manuscripts among friends and editors, enclosing a poem which had just been rejected for publication by Robert Payne.

I.72. Malthus

Thomas Robert Malthus (1776–1834), English economist, author of *An Essay on the Principle of Population* (1798), in which he writes—although without specific reference to the Massachusetts Bay Colony—that "In the northern states of America . . . the population has been found to double itself, for above a century and a half successively, in less than twenty-five years. Yet, even during these periods, in some of the towns, the deaths exceeded the births, a circumstance which clearly proves that, in those parts of the country which supplied this deficiency, the increase must have been much more rapid than the general average" (Everyman's ed., I, 7). From this, Malthus derives his famous proposition that population, if unchecked, increases in a geometric ratio, whereas food supply increases only in an arithmetic ratio.

I.72. Bowditch (later) ran Harvard . . .

While an insurance executive after retiring from active sea-trading, Nathaniel Bowditch was elected in 1826 to the Corporation of Harvard, a group of seven men who controlled the college. Under pressure and criticism from Bowditch, the president of the school, John Thornton Kirkland (1770–1840), resigned, and needed economic reforms were effected. See the account in H. Bowditch, "Nathaniel Bowditch," p. 109.

I.72. Agyasta

Agastya, Indian saint with superhuman powers. See Zimmer, *Myths and Symbols*, pp. 113–114:

> He is famous especially for the marvels accomplished by his digestive juices. . . . Now Agastya one day put the devouring tropical solar heat of his gastric energy to a major test: he swallowed the entire ocean. His intentions were good and the deed a brave one, but incidentally it had the effect of depriving the earth and all beings of the necessary life-maintaining water. That was what made

it necessary for the Ganga, the celestial river, a kind of Milky Way, to descend from the sky. The story goes, that there had been a group of demons annoying certain brahmin hermits by constantly disturbing their sacred ascetic routines. They would be chased into the ocean, but by night would emerge, as fresh as ever, and harass the holy men. The latter, in desperation, appealed to the celebrated saint. Agastya solved the problem at a stroke by simply swallowing the sea. But now the earth was left without its water, and all its creatures were brought to the point of perishing. When a person tries to be particularly helpful, he sometimes causes more trouble than he resolves. So it was, at any rate, in the case of Agastya with his boundless digestive fire.

See also *Maximus* III, 46: "the river / of Agyasta does not / fall it washes all / away."

I.72. about to start on his fourth voyage . . .

From H. Bowditch, "Nathaniel Bowditch," p. 107:

About to start on his fourth voyage he wrote to his future wife from Boston, 22 July 1799:
It was with the greatest difficulty we obtained our compliment of men, & a curious set of them we have, on the list are Tinkers, Tailors, Barbers, Country schoolmasters, one old Greenwich Pensioner, a few negroes, mullatoes, Spaniards &c &c &c but they will do well enough when properly disciplined.

I.73. who was the first "trustree" of others' monies . . .

See H. Bowditch, "Nathaniel Bowditch," p. 108:

In 1817 Mrs. Eliza Wetmore . . . and her brothers Samuel and Joseph Orne established the Orne Fund in memory of their deceased brother Charles Henry Orne, for the support of the ministers of the First Church in Salem, and the following trustees were appointed: Jonathan Hodges, Nathaniel Bowditch and George Cleveland. This is said to mark the beginning of professional trusteeship. Before that time men who had money in trust merely added it to what they had from other sources, and if financial disaster overtook them the money in trust shared the common fate of their funds. . . . Perhaps Bowditch's experience as supercargo gave rise to the idea that each trust should be kept rigidly independent of every other—a set of water-tight compartments as it were—so that a loss or a gain in one could not affect another. At all events, this must have been how supercargoes managed their finances, for on any voyage a considerable part of the cargo was made up of independent "adventures" entrusted to the supercargo to dispose of at the best advantage.

I.73. that most neglected of all / economic law . . . the good drives the goods / after the worst

A variation of Gresham's law that bad money drives out good, as well as of the common proverb, the good is the enemy of the best.

I.73. what he called it howling, / over another's pay- / cock . . .

Ezra Pound, Canto LXXXIII of *The Pisan Cantos,* speaking of William Butler Yeats:

> downstairs composing
> that had made a great Peeeeacock
>   in the proide ov his oiye
>   had made a great peeeeeeecock in the . . .
> made a great peacock
>   in the proide of his oyyee

While "pejorocracy" occurs in Canto LXXIX (see note to *Maximus* I, 3).

I.73. Cressy

Cressy's Beach (see note to *Maximus* I, 9).

I.74. Stephen Higginson (1743- / desc. of Francis Higginson . . .

From "Letters of Stephen Higginson," p. 704: "Stephen Higginson was born in Salem, Mass., in December, 1743. He was a descendant of Rev. Francis Higginson. . . . He had considerable acquaintance and standing in England. Happening to be in that country in 1774, he was examined by a committee of the House of Commons on the subject of American fisheries and some other colonial matter." In a footnote on the same page of the article: "The examination will be found in Force's American Archives, Fourth Series, I, 1645–1648."

All the information drawn from Higginson's letters had been copied by Olson into a pocket notebook, probably at the Sondley Library in Asheville, which the poet then worked from in making the poem. For Francis Higginson, see note to *Maximus* I, 46.

I.74. In Cong., was found frequently acting with / Hamilton . . .

"Letters of Stephen Higginson," p. 705: "He is found frequently acting with Hamilton, as he did in later years. On the other hand, he was strongly hostile to Robert Morris, and is found voting in favor of every suggested investigation of his department."

Alexander Hamilton (1757–1804) was a member of the Continental Congress at the time, and Robert Morris (1734–1806), the financier, was its superintendent of finance from 1781 to 1784.

I.74. Was chief instrument in suppressing Shay's / Rebellion

"Letters of Higginson," p. 705: ". . . he became one of his [James Bowdoin, the governor of Massachusetts] principal advisers in dealing with the Shays Rebellion, the successful suppression of which was largely due to his exertions."

Shays Rebellion was a popular insurrection in western Massachusetts in 1786–87, brought about by economic distress.

I.74. Enemy of Hancock

"Letters of Higginson," p. 706: ". . . he opposed the re-election of Governor John Hancock and endeavored to show that he had wavered discreditably in the crises of 1776 and 1788." John Hancock (1737–1793), the statesman and patriot, was governor of Massachusetts in 1780–85 and again 1787–93.

I.74. "the high Federalist of the 'Essex Junto' . . .

"Letters of Higginson," p. 707, where the editor of the letters points out that ones numbered 48 through 51 in the collection "show a curious transaction—the high Federalist of the 'Essex Junto' selling arms to the Virginia arsenal of 1799, built . . . for the protection of the State from those Federal encroachments against which the Virginia resolutions of 1798 were directed; or, if this is not effected, showing his correspondent how they can be sent to Toussaint L'Ouverture with great profit, and with the connivance of the Government, while the Secretary of State is assured that his Federalist friend has concluded not to send them thither."

The Federalist Party favored adoption of the Constitution and supported Hamilton's financial program; the Essex Junto, composed of representatives from Essex County, Mass., was the dominant group in that party, protecting the class interests of the New England merchants and shipowners. Timothy Pickering was its spokesman in Congress. See also *Maximus* II, 196–198.

I.74. in Letter 49, to Timothy Pickering . . .

"Letters of Higginson," p. 825: ". . . I think that, with the aid of the Herald, and the permission of the Secretary of the navy, I can arrange to furnish Touissaint with some arms, lead and flints.—I have a consignment of 4000 stands from Europe intended for the state of Virginia on Contract, according to a sample in the hands of the Executive. a part of them have been delivered at Richmond, 1320 Arms and 1536 Cartridge Boxes, which do not prove so well finished as the sample and are rejected, though confessedly very good and from one of the best factories in Prussia." While in a footnote at this point is added: "J.G. Jackson, in the debate of January 30, 1817, speaks of European arms which the state of Virginia obtained from *Swann* of Boston about 1798, as having proved worthless. . . ."

Timothy Pickering (1745–1829) was Secretary of War in John Adams' cabinet in 1795; Adams (1735–1826) was the second president of the United States, from 1797 to 1801.

Towards the end of that letter by Higginson is written, p. 826, "it will indeed pass off without notice" and so forth, as quoted in the poem. While the statement beginning, "Toussaint, at this time . . . ," is from a footnote to Higginson's Letter 50 on p. 827: "Toussaint l'Ouverture at this time was waging in Santo Domingo a fierce war against the French general André Rigaud."

Pierre Dominique Toussaint L'Ouverture (1743–1803) was the leader of the revolt in Santo Domingo, the island in the West Indies, which eventually established the republic of Haiti. He defeated André Rigaud (1761–1811), also born in Haiti, the leader of mullato forces, in a civil war in 1799.

I.75. same Higginson / to Adams

"Letters of Higginson," pp. 778–779, with slight changes:

> Those who built Vessels soon after the peace, whether for the fishery, or foreign Trade, have suffered more by the reduction in their value, than their earnings will pay; and in the old Towns, the unusual profits from the fishery, the first years after the Peace, were consumed in expences, which They were formerly strangers to. But those, who lived upon Cape Cod, and along the south Shore, who retained their old habits of industry and frugality, applied their gains to increase their Business. . . . even the last year, the cod fishery on the south Shore was a living business; but in the old Towns, They took less fish, expended much more, and had little or nothing left to support their families. There is a strong probability, that this business

will, from the causes mentioned, be in a good degree transferred from the north to the south Shore. This may be, in a national View of no great importance; but the Towns of M Head and Gloucester &c may be much distressed, before they recover those habits, which alone can make them to be flourishing and happy. . . .

"M Head" is Marblehead, Mass., a town some fifteen miles southwest of Gloucester on the coast.

I.76. Letter #27, to Pickering . . .

"Letters of Higginson," p. 790: "At Salem They are quiet and united, approve of the Treaty [John Jay's treaty with England, 1794] generally, but wish not to have any meeting. At Newburyport they are also united and may express their approbation. At M' Head and Cape Ann &c. they are all quiet and think very well of the Treaty. At portsmouth a protest is going on against their Town meeting which will be signed by all the best men and sent on to the President soon."

Newburyport, Mass., is northeast of Gloucester on the Merrimac River; Portsmouth is in southeastern New Hampshire.

▶I.77. On first Looking out through Juan de la Cosa's Eyes

A first version was written in early May 1953 at Black Mountain (letter to Jonathan Williams, "sat may 6? 7? 8?"), and rewritten shortly before 27 July 1953 (letter that date to Robert Creeley). The title echoes that of John Keats' sonnet, "On First Looking into Chapman's Homer." One early version was sent Creeley on 10 January 1954 for publication in the first issue of the *Black Mountain Review,* and another preserved among the poet's papers is entitled "On First Looking out of Balboa's Eyes," making the allusion to Keats' poem even closer.

Juan de la Cosa (ca. 1460–1510) was a cartographer and early explorer of the West Indies. He sailed with Columbus in 1493 as captain of the *Niña* and "Chief Chart Maker." A map of the world attributed to him—the "mappemunde" of the poem—bears the inscription, "Juan de la cosa la fizo en el puerto de S:mj^a en año de 1500," and, unlike Behaim's globe, includes the New World. For a reproduction, see Paullin, *Atlas of the Historical Geography of the United States,* plate 10.

I.77. Behaim

Martin Behaim (ca. 1436–1507), maker of the Nuremberg globe, 1492, the earliest terrestrial globe extant, which included several legendary islands such as St. Brendan's but portrayed nothing of the New World, depicting instead the eastern coast of Asia (including Cipangu and Candyn) as only about eighty degrees distant from the Azores. For a reproduction, see Paullin, *Atlas,* plate 8.

I.77. insula Azores

The islands in the North Atlantic west of Portugal. They appear on Behaim's globe as "insula dos Azores."

I.77. Cipangu

The name for Japan common in the fifteenth and sixteenth centuries, appearing as such on Behaim's globe.

I.77. Candyn

Island south of Cipangu on Behaim's globe, in the area of what were later to be known as the East Indies and Spice Islands.

I.77. de / Sant / brand / an

St. Brendan's, legendary island in the Atlantic southwest of Portugal; as it appears on Behaim's globe.

I.77. St. Malo

Seaport in northwestern France on the English Channel from which Breton fishermen sailed to the coast of North America in the fifteenth and sixteenth centuries.

I.77. Biscay

Maritime province in northern Spain, from which Basque fishermen sailed.

I.77. Bristol

Seaport in southwestern England; its merchants encouraged the extension of the English fisheries in the North Atlantic and the exploration of the New World.

I.77. Heavy sea, / snow, hail . . .

From Nathaniel Bowditch's journal of his fifth voyage (see *Maximus* I, 67 and note), as quoted in H. Bowditch, "Nathaniel Bowditch," p. 105:

> Dec.
> 20 . . . Heavy sea, snow, hail &c.
> 21 A[t] 8 A.M saw a tide rip, sounded, had 20 fath. decreased from that to 15 & 10, wore ship. Found we had been drifted near the shoal of George's.

I.77. Cap Raz

Cape Race, promontory of southeastern Newfoundland (as spelled on Hakluyt's map of 1587 in Paullin, *Atlas,* plate 14B).

I.77. Gades

Latin name for Cadiz, the city in southwestern Spain on the Atlantic, founded as a Phoenician (Tyrian) trading colony.

I.77. Cash's

Cashes Ledge, fishing shoal about eighty miles east of Cape Ann.

I.77. spelt

A kind of wheat; perhaps its grains or the beer made therefrom, or crumbs of bread from a meal, spilled upon the table.

I.77. portulans

Early coastal charts drawn from the actual experiences of pilots and mariners. See the chapter on *portulans* and *periploi,* "Sailors' Manuals," in Bérard, *Did Homer Live?,* pp. 139–167. Olson writes in "Captain John Smith": "it's a different thing, to feel a coast, an ancient thing . . . what men had to have before Pytheas, to move . . ." (*Human Universe,* p. 133).

I.78. What he drew who drew Hercules / going by the Bear . . .

See Bérard, *Did Homer Live?,* pp. 189–191. Hercules in this case is the Phoenician Herakles, or Hercules-Melkaart, whom Bérard identifies as a prototype of Odysseus. He is depicted on numerous intaglios found on the Italian and Sicilian shores of the Mediterranean as a sailor, "shown half-recumbent on a raft, from which pitchers are hanging," often with the design of a star overhead. Bérard then goes on to compare this picture with that of Odysseus in Book V of the *Odyssey* (11. 270–277), where Odysseus has been instructed by the sea-nymph Calypso to keep the "Bear," or the Big Dipper, on his left hand as he sails away from her island.

I.78. Sable

Sable Island. See notes to *Maximus* I, 23, and 121.

I.78. You could go any coast / in such a raft as she taught . . .

See Homer's *Odyssey,* Book V, where Calypso, after having received a message through Hermes that it is Zeus' will that Odysseus depart, assists Odysseus in building the raft which is to carry him away from her island, and supplies him with food and drink and "a store of dainties" for the voyage (11. 228–267). The section, "determined though he had been . . . to stick to what men eat / And wore," is derived from the same source. Calypso had hoped to make Odysseus immortal if he would remain with her, but his mind is set on returning to Ithaca; i.e., he remains a man, and is fed accordingly, not the nectar and ambrosia which both Calypso and Hermes eat, but food and drink "such as is meat for men" (1. 197). And later, as the raft is overturned by the storm, it is only after Odysseus abandons the clothes the goddess had given him but which weigh him down, that he can save himself; i.e., he is only able to survive when he "sticks to what men wear."

I.78. And Europe, / was being drained / of gold

From Brebner, *Explorers of North America,* p. 10, who is giving the background to Columbus' voyages: "there were too many middlemen on the route by the Levant, and Venice and Genoa, not Spain, controlled the Mediterranean and took the last profit. Besides, Europe was being drained of gold, and by all reports that coveted commodity was much more plentiful and much less valued in the East."

I.78. Bacalhaos

The Portuguese and Basque word for cod, the name given to the northeast coast of America because of the large number of the fish in that region. As such, it attests to the early presence of Portuguese and Basque fishermen on the coast. See "Reading at Berkeley," where, in response to the question, "But didn't Cabot find that the Indians used that word?," Olson replies, "Certainly, because the Portuguese were ahead of Cabot. That's one of my points in that . . ." (*Muthologos,* I, 148).

I.78. Norte

North (Spanish); also with the sense, as used in Mexico, of strong north wind.

I.78. Pytheus' sludge

See note to *Maximus* I, 62; also *Maximus* I, 84.

I.78. Judas-land

Where St. Brendan the Navigator saw an apparition of Judas (see note to *Maximus* I, 57); probably Iceland. A mermaid and various monsters were among other things reported sighted on the voyage. The linking of Pytheus and Brendan's "Judas-land" also occurs in "A Maximus Written to Throw Back a Hex":

> ... into the ice,
>
> into Judas-land, out of
> the sludge which the
> trinity of air, water
> and sky ...

I.79. Tierra, / de bacalaos

Land of cod-fish (Spanish), as it appears on early maps; e.g., the Gastaldi map of 1546, in Paullin, *Atlas,* plate 12B.

I.79. Verrazano

Hieronymus da Verrazano, brother of Giovanni (ca. 1485–ca. 1582), the Italian mariner who explored the Atlantic coast of North America from Florida to Nova Scotia for France between 1523 and 1524. Author of a map, based on his brother's explorations, on which the inscription occurs.

I.79. Mud Bank

A translation of "Limo Lue" (see below), derived from Latin *limus,* 'mud'; though "Limo Lue," in the orthography of the times, was actually "Le Molve," or French for cod-fish.

I.79. "sounding / on George's / 25 fath. sand. . . .

From Bowditch's journal quoted in H. Bowditch, "Nathaniel Bowditch," p. 105:

[Dec.] 23   Sounding on George's 25 fath. sand.
              At the same time spoke the Brig Albion
              Packet John Dogget who told us Cape
              Ann was 80 leag. dis.

George's is the fishing bank 190 miles east of Cape Cod; with an area of approximately 8,500 square miles, it is "the largest and most important fishing ground near the coast of the United States and is second to none in the western Atlantic except the Grand Bank of Newfoundland" (Rich, *Fishing Grounds of the Gulf of Maine,* p. 99).

I.79. Terra nova sive Limo Lue

Terra nova sive le molve, Newfoundland or the Land of Cod-Fish, as it appears on the 1529 map of Hieronymus Verrazano based on his brother's explorations. Reproduced in Paullin, *Atlas,* plate 13.

I.79. Corte Real

Either of the Cortereal brothers, Gaspar or Miguel, Portuguese mariners who discovered the coast of Labrador and Newfoundland in 1500–1502. Both were lost; Gaspar first, in the process of exploration, and Miguel after setting out to find his brother. "Corte Real . . . who is the Portygee who never came back, Corte Real, Number Two" ("Reading at Berkeley," *Muthologos,* I, 151), would seem to indicate Miguel is meant. See Brebner, *Explorers,* p. 112.

I.79. Bertomez

An entry in a notebook among the poet's papers indicates the name is to be found on the Maggiolo map, ca. 1519. The map, plate 11A in Paullin's *Atlas,* bears an inscription, near land identified as "bacalnaos," in orthography difficult to transcribe: "tepaqfoydes cubesiapor[?] bertōmez." Olson's notes indicate he would translate this as "discovered by Bertomez." However, in an article by Henry Harrisse on the Cabots, which, curiously, Olson is known to have read (see below, note to "On ne doit . . . ," *Maximus* I, 81), it is pointed out that old maps and mappemundes name that region "Terra que foy descubierta por bertomes" or, "Tierra de los Bretones," the Land of the Bretons. "Bertomez," then, in the orthography of the times, is the Bretons, not an individual Portuguese or Spanish explorer's name as Olson seems to suggest. Sailors from Brittany are known to have been early in the waters of the North Atlantic.

I.79. Cabot

John Cabot (1450–1498?), Venetian explorer in the service of English merchants of Bristol, who discovered Newfoundland in 1497 and may have been lost on his second voyage in 1498. His son, Sebastian, was also a mariner.

I.79. Respecting the earth, he sd, / it is a pear . . .

"By the way, this is Columbus . . . Not Van Allen . . . that Van Allen Belt . . ." (*Muthologos*, I, 152). From the letter by Christopher Columbus on this third voyage (1498), as quoted in Brebner, *Explorers,* p. 13: "His thoughts swiftly wove themselves into a mystical and novel cosmogony to account for his newly discovered hemisphere. 'I have come to another conclusion respecting the earth, namely, that it is not round as they describe, but of the form of a pear, which is very round except where the stalk grows, at which part it is most prominent; or like a round ball, upon one part of which is a prominence like a woman's nipple, the protrusion being the highest and nearest the sky. . . .' "

I.79. Ships / have always represented . . .

From Brebner, *Explorers,* p. 6: "Ships have always represented a large capital investment, and the manning and provisioning of them has always been costly."

I.80. It was the teredo-worm / was 1492 . . .

See Brebner, *Explorers,* pp. 7 and 15: "the ocean was stormy and forbidding enough, but the Caribbean with its tornadoes and its coral reefs was worse. Its waters swarmed with the teredo-worm, which could riddle a ship's hull in a single voyage . . . Columbus, however, risked everything in storm-racked ships, 'pierced with worm-holes, like a bee-hive', to follow the shores until they should open before him in the passage to India." The report is actually from Columbus' letter on his fourth voyage, of 1502, though this is not specified in Brebner. The teredo is a small mollusk that bores into the bottoms of wooden ships.

I.80. 1480 John Lloyd, the most expert shipmaster . . .

From Brebner, *Explorers*, p. 108: "The English effort began, so far as we know, on 15 July 1480, when John Lloyd, 'the most expert shipmaster of all England', on behalf of John Jay and other merchants, set out from Bristol 'to the island of Brasylle in the western part of Ireland, to traverse the seas'. He was out nine weeks before storms and shortage of supplies forced him back to an Irish port, but he found no 'Brasylle.' " The original account is given in the *Itinerarium* of William of Worcester, written about the time of Lloyd's voyage.

It should be explained that "Brasylle" is not the modern South American state, but a legendary island of the fifteenth and sixteenth centuries, said to lie off the southwestern coast of Ireland.

I.80. Ladies & / to the bottom of the, / husbands, & wives . . .

Cf. the once-popular American ballad, "The *Titanic*," with its improvised refrain,

> It was sad when that great ship went down,
> It was sad when that great ship went down,
> Husbands and wives and little children lost their lives,
> It was sad when that great ship went down.

(This version from Friedman, *Viking Book of Folk Ballads*, p. 323. See also, e.g., White, *American Negro Folk Songs*, pp. 346–347.)

I.80. 4,670 fishermen's lives are noticed.

The figure is approximate. One early version of the passage reads: "or the 3,570 each year / they throw flowers to . . ."; another: "five thousand seven hundred and twenty-nine lives / are noticed . . ."

Tibbets, *Story of Gloucester*, e.g., gives the figure 4,534 recorded lost by 1916, although the *Encyclopaedia Britannica*, 11th ed., under "Gloucester," says "From 1830 to 1907, 776 vessels and 5242 lives were lost in the fisheries . . ."—which probably should be 4242, for Atwood writing in 1945 says, "Since 1830 Gloucester has lost at sea, as I write, 4,836 men and 1,026 ships" (Northeast of Boston," p. 278).

I.80. each summer, at the August full / they throw flowers . . .

The ceremony described is central to "Maximus, to Gloucester, Sunday, July 19" (*Maximus* I, 152 and note).

I.81. On ne doit aux morts nothing / else than / la vérité

Voltaire writes in a letter to M. de Grenonville, 1719: ". . . on doit des égards aux vivants, on ne doit aux morts que la vérité" (*Oeuvres Completes*, I, 9n), which can be translated: 'One owes respect to the living; one owes the dead only the truth.' Olson's source, however, is Harrisse, "The Outcome of the Cabot Quater-Centenary," an essay correcting erroneous speculations about the Cabots, which ends with that portion of the quotation from Voltaire. References in a notebook from the time of this poem indicate that Olson had read the Harrisse article.

▶I.82. The Twist

Written at Black Mountain in May 1953, as will be seen from dream material cited in the notes; definitely by July 18th, when mentioned in a letter of that date to Robert Creeley.

The "twist" of the title refers also to the nasturtium or 'nose-twist' introduced on p. 36 of *Maximus* I.

I.82. Tatnuck Sq

In Worcester, Massachusetts.

I.82. Paxton, for May-flowers

Town about five miles northwest of Worcester. In "Stocking Cap," Olson describes going with his father on such trips, mentioning there, too, the pleasure of picking Mayflowers and walnuts (*Post Office*, p. 5).

I.82. Holden

Community northwest of Worcester.

I.82. And my wife has a new baby . . .

A dream—according to a note among the poet's papers—from early May 1953.

I.82. he and I distinguish / between chanting . . .

Likewise a dream, in which appeared one of those figures who, in "ABCs—2," "lie / coiled or unflown / in the marrow of the bone"—in this case, Ezra Pound in the guise of the "Master" (conversation, June 1968). The dream, from early May 1953, is recorded in notes the poet made at the time: "Pound's dist. between chant & letting the song lie in the thing itself—& I planting zenias etc. for him in the wet soil (indoors!) of his house." In "The Bezel" (1962), Olson has written: "the opposite of rational forms is not irrational but a difference of discourse. The play lies rather in the genetic and the morphological (as it was said to me in the dream [by the same master who instructed me throughout, & whom I celebrate—properly, I believe—as Grandfather] between chanting and letting the song lie in the thing itself and there canting off what the poem turns out to be."

I.82. As I had it in my first poem . . .

Not "I, Maximus," or Olson's first published poem, but probably one entitled "Marry the Marrow" from ca. 1945–

46, which is itself based on a poem written in Gloucester at the time of the "St. Valentine's Day Storm" (see below), i.e. February 1940. It includes the following lines:

> Structure! least steel, most liquid:
> The Annisquam and the Atlantic
> At high fulfilled the land,
> Brimmed and eased it.
> Stretched fabric across the hips of the earth,
> French cut,
> Discovering the global curve beneath.

The earlier poem, written in the poet's notebook "#4 Cambridge & N.Y. Winter–Spring 1940," has the same basic theme of the Annisquam tides and begins:

> Between the river and the sea I
>   sit writing,
> The Annisquam and the Atlantic
> My boundaries, and all between
> The moors of doubt and self-
>   mistrust maintaining
> A perilous structure of landness
>   against the flood
> of northern war and native
>   smug content. . . .

Two other attempts later in the 1940's to revise the early poem, "Purgatory Blind" and "New England March," survive. See also *Maximus* II, 129–"wrote my first poems . . . at Kent Circle"—and note.

However, it should be noted that the image of the tide does appear in "The K," which is Olson's first significant poem, written in the spring of 1945 and published in *Y & X* in 1948.

Olson had written in a letter to Robert Creeley, 28 November 1951:

> . . . [Con] reminding us of a thing (the very 1st po-em) done Gloucester, on Annisquam River, in which I had used as image which, as I tried to locate the thing (knew she did not mean 'tidal rivers rushing', that dream) it came out, this day, thus (Mr Fraud!):
>
>   French but chias
>   (the

original, and as of herself, Miss Wilcock, as, once, I saw her . . . in a French job, brown, cut on the bias . . .

I.83. Newton

Newton Square, Worcester. The trolley line went west, away from Norman Avenue where the Olsons lived, along Pleasant Street and through Newton Square.

I.83. the Severn

River in southeastern England which flows into the Bristol Channel. The "Worcester" and "Gloucester" of these lines are the English cities, the original namesakes for those in New England. Among notes amid the poet's papers is written: "the Severn (as binding Worcester to Gloucester as the Annisquam binds my own psyche."

I.83. Bristow

Bristol, England, at the mouth of the Severn River, as often spelled in the seventeenth century. However, in this instance, John Smith's name on his 1614 map of New England for what appears to be a settlement on the coast approximately where Salem and Beverly now are, as well as for "a great Bay by Cape *Anne*" in his *Description of New England (Travels and Works,* I, 232).

I.83. the landscape / I go up-dilly . . .

Cf. the dream recorded in a notebook from 1953 among the poet's papers:

> Sun. Aug 16 [1953] . . . The landscape of the dream was the same one—of Boston to Gloucester (this time G to B)— I have often had, which is not 1A or the B & M train, but a sort of fairy-tale landscape, up & down
>
> (English ballad abt up-down, down-town   town???)
>
> other experiences on this train (with a shift to elevated, at end) But had gone when I was awake. . . .

See, perhaps, the English nursery rhyme, "Daffy-down-dilly is new come to town . . ." ("down-dilly" occurs on *Maximus* I, 106)—although that "dilly" is the daffodil. In another sense, "dilly," according to the *Oxford English Dictionary*, is "A familiar term for the diligence or public stage-coach of former days"—which might be appropriate, too, for the trolley or the Boston & Maine Railroad train. Indeed, one of the examples given in the *OED* of its usage is curiously relevant to the poem: "Beginning gay, desperate, dashing down-hilly; / And ending as dull as a six-inside Dilly!" (from Thomas Moore's *Fudge Family in Paris*).

I.83. It rained, / the day we arrived. . . .

The first summer Olson came with his parents to stay at Gloucester, in 1915 or 1916. See also *Maximus* II, 136:

> . . . the first night we came to Gloucester
> . . . with the rain
> which I had seen
> out Johnny Morgan's Candy Kitchen window
> the afternoon previous . . .

Johnnie Morgan's confectionery at 80 Western Avenue was on the south side of what later was to be called Stacey Boulevard, along the harbor near the Cut. For a photograph of Morgan's shop around the time of the Olsons' arrival in Gloucester, see Garland, *Gloucester Guide*, p. 128.

I.83. She was staying, / after she left me . . .

Another dream. In a notebook from 1953, Olson records it:

> *Thurs May 15*
> Dreamt Con had left me, & was living in an apt house which was both Bohemia & a gingerbread house—the rooms on different levels, & the sense of the life lived in the house, like little people might in a cake
> I came with Kate to look her up, sort of the morning she moved in. And there was a heavy woman, a sort of nurse or companion to her . . . who tried to prevent me from seeing her. [With] Kate sort of hidden behind her,

I got sore, & was ready to sock this woman, when she told me what room Con was in—48-50, I think was the room (It was going around looking for it that I had this sense of the place as gay, & candy. At first I thot the typewriter I cld hear was Con. But it wasn't. The dream cut off when I got to the room.

Approaching the apt, I noticed a house next door which I quickly thought was a gangster's hideout. And just then the back of some gangster I did recognize (a tout or bookie) was seen going in the door.

I.84. Charles St

In Boston. Olson had rooms there in his final year at Harvard. The Macomber mentioned in the previous line was a cousin of Constance Wilcock, Olson's first wife (interview with her, April 1974).

I.84. next door / a man in a bowler hat ...

Dream material (conversation, October 1967); apparently a continuation of the dream recorded above.

I.84. Schwartz ...

Lester B. Schwartz, who lived on Essex Avenue at Kent Circle, Gloucester, where Olson was staying with his mother the winter of 1939–40. See also Olson's notes dated 3 May 1956 for a lecture at Black Mountain, quoted in Charters, *Olson / Melville*, pp. 86–87: "And I remember exactly the place and hour of my first attempt to write down how I understood myth to be—on the Annisquam River, winter, 1939, with Schwartz's mother-in-law, in whom I took great phantasy pleasure, in the same house!" What follows in those notes is of further relevance: Olson speaks of the power of dream as it appears in the poem "ABCs (2)," then continues "And the boat did swerve then [alluding to a line from that poem], just because Schwartz's mother-in-law and I and all my people were, even then, involved in avoiding the

yelping rocks
where the tidal river rushes"

(see "the dog-rocks" of *Maximus* I, 85 and note; also the original dream quoted in note to "the dog . . . tore the bloody cloak," *Maximus* III, 33).

I.84. dobostorte

A many-layered Hungarian pastry.

I.84. the St Valentine / storm

A snowstorm throughout the northeast on St. Valentine's Day, 14 February 1940, especially heavy on Cape Ann. Headlines in the *Gloucester Times* the next day read: "Worst Blizzard In Years Hits Bay State—Paralyzes Traffic: Northeast Gale Piles Up Huge Drifts in 17-Inch Snowfall." The film-maker Stan Brakhage, writing to his wife of his visit with Olson in a letter of 17 May 1963, says: "He showed me the house where he had left his mother that awful night written of as St. Valentine's Day Storm, wandered down to the bay to be bombarded by sheets of ice blown in from the sea" (*Metaphors on Vision*, p. [85]).

I.84. ice   wind   snow   (Pytheus) one

See *Maximus* I, 62 and note.

I.85. the whole Cut / was a paper village . . .

Apparently also dream material. In his notebook for 1953, Olson recorded for the "Night of Sun-Mon May 9–10 (?)": "Outside, in the street, it was early morning . . . (rest is gone) A damned unpleasant dream—myself, weak throughout—strong feeling of mother (something, in that village—house, Gloucester?—of my father? the houses of the village were strong (like that cardboard village I had as kid). . . ."

I.85. my Aunt Vandla

Vandla Hedges (1875–1948), of Wellesley, Mass., older sister of the poet's father.

I.85. the Third Ave El

Elevated railroad in lower Manhattan, torn down by the city of New York in 1954 (although plans for the razing had been discussed in the spring of the previous year, at the time this poem was written).

I.85. the Bridge

The Blynman Bridge over the Cut at Western Avenue; site of the annual memorial services for fishermen described in *Maximus* I, 152–154.

I.85. the country not discovera

The region John Smith was to name "Bristow" or Bristol (see p. 83 and earlier note), appearing as such on his chart in *Description of New England* (1616) which relates the old place names with his new ones (*Travels and Works,* I, 232).

I.85. Blynman

Rev. Richard Blynman, the first minister of Gloucester, who was authorized by a vote of the town in May 1643 to cut a canal through the beach and marsh which then obstructed access to the Annisquam River from Gloucester Harbor. See the history of the Cut, now officially known as Blynman's Canal, in Babson, *History of Gloucester,* pp. 7–10, or in Copeland and Rogers, *Saga of Cape Ann,* pp. 177–180.

I.85. the dog-rocks

See also "ABCs (2)": "the yelping rocks / where the tidal river rushes." These are rocks along the shore of Gloucester Harbor near the entrance to the Cut. They are named such in allusion to the Scylla of the *Odyssey,* Book XII, which is described as a barking dog (see also "Charybdeses" in *Maximus* I, 152).

▶**I.87. Maximus, to Gloucester, Letter 19 (A Pastoral Letter**

First written May 1953 at Black Mountain, apparently by May 18th (letter to Robert Creeley, May 19th).

I.87. relating / to the care of souls, / it says . . .

Webster's Collegiate Dictionary, 5th ed., p. 726, definition 2 under "pastoral": "Relating to the care of souls, or to the pastor of a church."

I.88. the clouds / of all confusion

Echo, perhaps, of the fourteenth-century English mystical work, *The Cloud of Unknowing.*

I.88. turned, / as He did, / his backside

Probably an allusion to Exodux xxiii. 23, where God says to Moses: "And I will take away mine hand, and thou shalt see my back parts; but my face shall not be seen." The passage would have been in Olson's mind from his reading of the Mansfield and Vincent annotated edition of *Moby-Dick* for review in the spring of 1952. In his copy of that edition, following the lines which end chapter LXXXVI, "The Tail," p. 377—" . . . how comprehend his face, when face he has none? Thou shalt see my back parts, my tail, he seems to say, but my face shall not be seen. But I cannot completely make out his back parts; and hint what he will about his face, I say again he has no face"—Olson has written: "cf. excellent note to." This note, on p. 786, which Olson has also marked, suggests the reader compare those lines from the novel with the passage from Exodus.

▶**I.89. Letter 20**

First written May 1953 at Black Mountain, apparently by May 18 (letter to Robert Creeley, May 19).

I.89. Newman Shea

A Gloucester fisherman, former president of the Gloucester Fisherman's Union and member of the crew of the *Doris M. Hawes* when Olson sailed on her in 1936 (see note to *Maximus* I, 38). See also "Projective Verse" (*Human Universe*, p. 57): "as Newman Shea used to ask, at the galley table, put a jib on the blood, will ya"; and especially, "Morning News":

> What I remember most
> is the smell of Shea's tobacco.
> And his talking, before breakfast,
> of "Kunrudd", as he pronounced it,
> of Kunrudd, and that book
> whose title he could never get straight.

Joseph Conrad (1857–1924), the English novelist, was himself a seaman and author of books with the sea as a setting.

I.89. until five years ago . . .

In an early version, Olson had written:

> . . . until five years ago, to make a guess
> at the date she lost
> her last stitch
> of clothes

Presumably, it is honor that is being spoken of.

I.89. the Tree / of Battles

Notes among his papers clearly related to this poem indicate the poet had looked up the suffix "-machy" in his copy of *Webster's Collegiate Dictionary*, 5th ed., for which is given: "[Gr. *machē* battle.] A combining form denoting *contest between* or *by means of*, as in logo*machy*" (p. 600). There is, however, no mention there of a "Tree" in connection with battle.

Possibly, in light of what follows in the poem, a genealogical or heraldic order is intended (a genealogical or family "tree"); perhaps even a reference to "The Battle of the Trees," a Welsh poem discussed in Graves, *White Goddess*, pp. 27ff., with its "tree alphabet," which—like heraldry— is a hierarchic order. Or "Tree of Battles" could be taken as an Old English or Old Norse kenning for 'warrior,' such as is suggested by Snorri Sturlusson in the Prose Edda, chapter 31 (see also Brodeur, *The Meaning of Snorri's Categories*, p. 146, who discusses the very phrase 'tree of battle' as "the image of a man standing straight and immovable in combat").

I.89. palette fess nombril / base

See the entry for "escutcheon" in *Webster's Collegiate*, 5th ed., p. 340:

> The surface, usually shield-shaped, on which armorial bearings are displayed. The ground of the escutcheon is called the *field* and its tincture is mentioned first in blazoning. The upper part is the *chief*, the lower part the *base*, and the sides *dexter* and *sinister*, respectively on the right and left of the wearer of the shield. Other points (see cut) are: A, B, C, *dexter, middle*, and *sinister, chief points*, respectively; D, *honor*, or *color, point; E, fess*, or *heart, point; F, nombril* or *navel*; G, H, I, *dexter, middle*, and *sinister, base points*, respectively.

For "palette"—often spelled pallette—see note to *Maximus* I, 94.

I.89. Red Rice

Jack Rice, brother of painter Dan Rice, both students at Black Mountain College at this time. The incident related occurred while Rice and his friend, Hanna, were undergoing training as U.S. Marine paratroopers during World War II (conversation with Dan Rice, January 1970). M-12's suggest American automatic rifles in use at the time (more precisely, M-14's).

See also the early version of the lines among the poet's papers:

> ... yet it was just those two,
> together, who had tried trust
> between them, even to knife wounds
> in Rice's calves, and a loss of a piece
>   of ankle bone
> of Hanna, from training each other
> to stand it,
> at twenty paces (with the knife)
> and a hundred yards (with the M-12 ...

Cf. the portrait of Jack Rice at that time in Dawson's *Black Mountain Book*, p. 128.

I.90. Stephen Papa

Landlord at 86 Christopher Street in Greenwich Village, where Olson lived in 1941.

I.90. Expresso

Espresso, the Italian coffee.

I.91. paul-post

Pawl-post (see also *Maximus* II, 101).

I.92. Earp

Wyatt Earp (1848−1929), gunfighter and lawman of the American West. See Lake, *Earp, Frontier Marshall,* mentioned by Olson in "Billy the Kid."

▶I.93. Maximus, at Tyre and at Boston

First written May 1953 at Black Mountain, apparently by May 22 (letter that date to Robert Creeley), though possibly by May 19 (letter to Creeley).

Tyre was a chief city of the Phoenicians and one of the leading ports of the eastern Mediterranean; home of the historical Maximus. See also notes to "Maximus" and "Gloucester," *Maximus* I, 1.

I.93. Honor, or color, point . . . middle chief . . . heart

Divisions of an escutcheon (see note to *Maximus* I, 89).

I.93. the nasturtium / is my shield

See *Maximus* I, 36 and note.

I.93. cantus firmus

(L.) 'fixed or firm song.'

I.94. the history of weeds / is a history of man

From Anderson, *Plants, Man and Life,* p. 15:

> Fennel, radish, wild oat, all of these plants are Mediter-
> raneans. In those countries they mostly grow pretty much
> as they do in California, at the edges of towns, on modern
> dumps and ancient ruins, around Greek temples and in
> the barbed-wire enclosures of concentration camps. Where
> did they come from? They have been with man too long
> for any quick answer. They were old when Troy was new.
> Some of them are certainly Asiatic, some African, many
> of them are mongrels in the strictest technical sense.
> Theirs is a long and complicated story, a story just now
> beginning to be unraveled but about which we already
> know enough to state, without fear of successful con-
> tradiction, that the history of weeds is the history of man.

Anderson's book calls attention to the necessity of dis-
tinguishing between cultivated plants and weeds in order to
determine the origin of cultivated plants, and with that,
the origin and organization of civilization, its dates and
migrations.

I.94. Helmet / palette breastplate tasses tuille

The illustration of "Plate Armor" in *Webster's Collegiate
Dictionary,* 5th ed., p. 59 under "armor," contains all the items
mentioned. The pieces of armor correspond to sections of
the escutcheon mentioned in *Maximus* I, 89 and 93.

I.94. Hyssop, for him, / was the odor of meat . . .

From Matthews, "Family Tradition and History," p. 193:

> Ten years ago the late Rev. Dr. James D. Butler, of Madison, Wisconsin, wrote to "The Nation": There is an old tradition in my family that J. B., an ancestor born at Boston in 1655, would never eat roast pork, and gave as the reason for his dislike that its odor brought back to him a sickening whiff of wind from a woman he had seen burned alive at the stake on the Common when he was a 'prentice boy. This story I heard in the twenties— perhaps as early as 1820—at the table of my father, who in 1770 was old enough to have heard and understood it, if told by his grandfather, whose birth was 1713, and who was himself the grandson of the J. B., the original eye- witness of the tragedy on the Common.
>
> For three quarters of a century Dr. Butler vainly sought for confirmation of this tradition, and not until 1899 did he succeed. On September 22, 1681, according to Increase Mather, a negress named Maria was burned to death. . . .

This account is presented in the source as an instance of how family traditions may turn out to be based on historical fact. The reference, then, when its original context is recalled, provides a link with the symbolic inheritance of heraldry in the earlier sections of the poem—as well as in the previous poem—and to the matter of Elizabeth Tuttle and her descendants.

Hyssop, the fragrant plant, is also sprinkled and burned as incense in ceremonies of the Catholic Church and was used in purification ceremonies by the Hebrews.

I.94. Elizabeth Tuttle

Elizabeth Tuttle married Richard Edwards in 1667; they were divorced in 1691. Her descendants—Jonathan Edwards and those that followed—were taken by eugenicists to be the bright contrary to the Jukes family, the Jukes having pro- duced criminals, drunkards, etc., while the Edwards family such men of genius and contribution as Jonathan Edwards

(1703−1759), philosopher, theologian, and preacher; Aaron Burr (1756−1836), the American statesman, whose mother was the daughter of Jonathan Edwards; Ulysses S. Grant (1822−1885), American general and president; and Grover Cleveland (1837−1908), president of the United States, descended from Edwards on his mother's side.

The theory was first presented by Winship in *Jukes-Edwards: A Study in Education and Heredity* (1900). Such a theory, however, can only be maintained, as Clarence Darrow pointed out in "The Edwardses and the Jukes," by ignoring the fact of Elizabeth Tuttle.

▶ I.96. Letter 22

First written May 1953 at Black Mountain, between May 19th (see below) and the 22nd (letter that date to Robert Creeley), and see also note to "Letter 16" above (*Maximus* I, 72).

Blocks of material indented in the poem and introduced by an open parenthesis—"Trouble with the car . . . ," "She lost her finger . . . ," and "I swung the car to the left . . ." —are from a series of dreams from the same night, as recorded in a notebook of Olson's from 1953:

> May 18−19 (Thrs morn):
>   a confusion of dreams, the marked one (it woke me) of Con allowing her little finger to be cut off—offering it for some sort of social end, not clear.
>   At first I had no knowledge of what it was she did give up, in this operation. When I saw her holding something (a wad of cotton or so) I thot it was her hand. But then it was clear it was her little finger. And she seemed almost proud of how little mutilated her hand looked.
>   My cry was, "O, why did you do it, you were so perfect?" And I was overwhelmed, that she should have, crying, "You were so perfect" . . .
>
> It was a big feeling, of loss, of sorrow, of sadness.

> ———————
>
> A later dream was some sort of celebration over her operation. . . .
>
> ———————

Without connection to either of above, I think, there was a business of me & the auto. 1st, going to the left to get up over a sort of loading platform (5 ft up) presented itself on the whole front of a hill in front of me
(Con was with me, & seemed surprised (?) I solved the problem by going to the left, on an end run.

I took the car to a garage, or something—it needed repairs—& they gave me (for $1) something for it. Which I started to eat. And it turned out to be a polishing cloth. And yet I keep eating it it was that good. And it was that heavy (material & color) cloth Karen Weinrib wears (as a sort of billowing cover
[housecoat? the mother-cover?]

At this point there is also a sort of party [maybe a twin to the other?]
         and some guy comes in & sits down (two?) who is not of it
         But Con, my memory is, seems to think it's all right (the hostess, anyway, has to call Doyle Jones, to figure where to seat this stranger) . . . A guy named Goomeranian (& Syrian or Armenian . . . appears (I think I woke up at that point)

There follows an analysis of these dreams and their confused images. At the end is written: "Omnivore—amor vore."

I.96. chaos / is not our condition

Cf. "Human Universe": "If unselectedness is man's original condition (such is more accurate a word than that lovely riding thing, chaos, which sounds like what it is, the most huge generalization of all, obviously making it necessary for man to invent a bearded giant to shape it for him) but if likewise, selectiveness is just as originally the impulse by which he proceeds to do something about the unselectedness, then one is forced, is one not, to look for some instrumentation in man's given which makes selection possible" (*Human Universe*, p. 9).

I.96. man is omnivore

"Man, as we know him, is omnivore!" wrote the geographer Carl Sauer to Olson in a letter prior to May 1952 (mentioned also in Olson's essay "Culture" from ca. August 1952). Kroeber, too, writes in his *Anthropology,* p. 77, in a passage marked by Olson in his copy: "He [man] is quite extraordinarily able to thrive on any one of a variety of different diets. In fact he may well be classed with the bears and the pigs as omnivorous." See also *Muthologos,* II, 101.

I.97. "Satie, enough"

Spoken in a dream; no reference to the composer Erik Satie (1866–1925) is intended (Olson in conversation, October 1967).

I.97. stopping the battle

In a letter to Robert Duncan, 31 May 1955, Olson would write of the " 'celtic' image of the poet's act: stopping the battle, to get it down. And I am only now again finding out what that means—christ, what a goddamn idea anyhow, holding up one's hand, and everybody suddenly ceasing what they are doing, and lending ear!" See also "Reading at Berkeley," *Muthologos,* p. 119: ". . . the old Irish doctrine: that the real boss of the kingdom is the poet . . . The only person that can stop Enyalion [q.v.]." The description is probably from Graves' discussion of the ancient Celtic concept of the poet (*White Goddess,* p. 22): "When two armies engaged in battle, the poets of both sides would withdraw together to a hill and there judiciously discuss the fighting. In a sixth-century Welsh poem, the *Gododin,* it is remarked that 'the poets of the world assess the men of valour'; and the combatants—whom they often parted by a sudden intervention—would afterwards accept their version of the fight, if worth commemorating in a poem, with reverence as well as pleasure."

Cf. Diodorus Siculus, V.31.5 (Oldfather trans., III, 179–181):

> Nor is it only in the exigencies of peace, but in their wars as well, that they obey, before all others, these men

[Druids] and their chanting poets, and such obedience is observed not only by their friends but also by their enemies; many times, for instance, when two armies approach each other in battle with swords drawn and spears thrust forward, these men step forth between them and cause them to cease, as though having cast a spell over certain kinds of wild beasts. In this way, even among the wildest barbarians, does passion give place before wisdom, and Ares stands in awe of the muses.

▶ I.99. Letter 23

Although not the "Max X" which Olson mentions in a letter to Robert Creeley on 13 September 1953 as having been written "two days ago," drawing from Rose-Troup's *John White*, at least a first version of the present poem was undoubtedly written around the same time—also the time of Olson's letter of September 10th to historian Frederick Merk (see note to Merk below). There was another poem designated "Max Y," which Olson announces to Creeley on 5 October 1953 as having been "added to the Max told you I had done. Thus am finally moving again, dropping 24–33 as they were . . . and turning more directly in at new 24 (X), and Y making 25 . . . ," and this may refer to the present poem, since an early version of "Letter 23" was called "Letter #25" in manuscript (although another manuscript has it designated as *"Letter 12"*—an indication of the extent of the reorganization underway—and it was read on a tape for Creeley as late as December 1958 as "Letter 24"!).

The poem was apparently rewritten at a later date. A note in the poet's copy of *The Maximus Poems* (1960) dates it at 1958.

An earlier "Letter 23" (on Aaron Burr) was written by 1 July 1953 (letter to Corman that date in Glover, "Letters for Origin," unpub. diss., p. 213), but was cut back because of Olson's feeling that the whole series had wandered "off its proper track" (to Corman, 24 September 1953, in Glover, p. 220).

I.99. The facts are: / 1st season   1623/4   one ship, the Fellowship . . .

From Rose-Troup, *John White,* p. 68: "the *Fellowship* of Weymouth, 35 tons, Edward Cribbe, master . . ." Rose-Troup's data on the *Fellowship* comes in a discussion of the Dorchester Company's third attempt or "season," therefore Olson's question mark after "Cribbe" and directive "cf. / below, 3rd season." Rose-Troup does not say that Cribbe was captain of the *Fellowship* for the first season, though this can be inferred from evidence presented (Rose-Troup's list on p. 69 and White's statement quoted on p. 66); for "below, 3rd season," see *Maximus* I, 116 and 117.

I.99. John Tilly to oversee the fishing, / Thomas Gardner the "planting"

Rose-Troup, *John White,* pp. 85–86: "They employed John Tilly to oversee the fishing and Thomas Gardner the planting on the mainland, for at least a year . . ." According to Babson, *History of Gloucester,* pp. 41–42, "A John Tylley was admitted a freeman in 1635: probably the same person who, in 1636, was taken by Indians on Connecticut River, and barbarously murdered. Thomas Gardner is said to have come from Scotland. He settled in Salem; became a freeman in 1637, and representative the same year."

I.99. all the evidence is, that the Plymouth / people, aboard the Charitie . . .

From Rose-Troup, *John White,* pp. 69–70:

> James Sherley, agent for the Plymouth Plantation, resident in London, wrote on 25th January, 1623/4, that the Plymouth Adventurers had raised a new stock "for the setting forth of the ship called the *Charitie* with men and necessaries for the plantation." This ship, after a voyage of *about* five weeks, reached Plymouth. She brought Winslow, the Sheffield Patent, Lyford and cattle. Altham says Winslow was at Cape Ann in April, 1624, so she would have sailed most probably from London, the nearest port

to the agent's residence, about the middle of February, 1623/4. . . .

I.99. Lyford

John Lyford was the first clergyman to arrive at Plymouth, but his stay there proved troublesome and he was expelled along with John Oldham (q.v.). He was invited in 1625 to be minister to the Dorchester Company settlement at Cape Ann.

I.99. Winslow

Edward Winslow (1595–1655), author of *Good News from New England* (1624), later became a governor of the Plymouth Colony. He came to Plymouth on the *Mayflower* in 1620, returning to England on business in the fall of 1623 and coming back the following March, bringing a patent for Cape Ann (which later proved worthless) and "3. heifers & a bull, the first begining of any catle of that kind in ye land" (Bradford, *History "Of Plymouth Plantation,"* p. 189—marked in Olson's copy).

I.99. Weymouth

Seaport in Dorset, England, seven miles south of Dorchester on the English Channel, from which the Dorchester Company vessels sailed.

I.99. Westcountry

The southwestern counties of England, especially Bristol and the seaport towns of Devonshire; the center of England's seafaring life.

I.99. It was this fishing stage which was fought over . . .

See *Maximus* I, 112 and note below.

I.100. literally in my own front yard, as I sd to Merk . . .

Frederick Merk (b. 1887), American historian and professor at Harvard, where Olson took his course entitled "The Western Movement." See Maud, "Merk and Olson," *Athanor* 2 (1971).

Olson had written him from Black Mountain, 10 September 1953:

> Again I have the distinct pleasure to write to you. This time, it is to ask you if you can advise me about the state of knowledge about what is, in fact, the very ground I was raised on: Fishermen's Field, Cape Ann.
>
> I am engaged in a work which pivots from that field, and wish to saturate myself on all the history of it which is now known. And I wonder if you will be good enough to spare me some of your time to say whether recent scholarship has attacked some of the questions I shall pose below. . . .

In his questions following Olson mentions, "the latest usable work I have found is that done, and published before 1930, by Mrs Frances Rose-Troup, on the 'Early Settlements', on 'Roger Conant', and on 'John White'," and asks if there might be "any further work beyond hers" on "the economic history of the planting of Massachusetts north of Plymouth 1622–1637." He closes the letter by saying:

> . . . As you well know, you are the pivot of my respect for history. And if I turn to you again, it is just because it is a joy to register, once more, my deepest respect.
>
> And anything you can give me back—or direct someone else, if there is someone who happens also to have come into this time with a distinct economic, rather than religious attention—shall be exceedingly helpful.
>
> As I say, I have put it thus specifically, not to point any of the pieces at you, but to suggest the sort of saturation that *my own front yard*—literally, that field was where I grew, our house being on "Stage Fort Avenue", Gloucester!—bred in me.

Merk's response of 27 September 1953, suggesting pertinent titles, is among the papers in the Olson Archives.

I.100. "fishermans ffield"

The location of the Dorchester Company settlement on Cape Ann in 1623, in what is now Stage Fort Park, Gloucester. See Rose-Troup, *John White,* p. 90: "Stage Head, the name of a promontory above Gloucester Harbor is supposed to have been the scene of this incident [the fight over the fishing stage], while 'ffisherman's field', mentioned in a grant of 1642, is thought to be the spot where the attempted land settlement was made." Babson writes, "That spot is plainly marked by tradition; and other evidence is not wanting to indicate the place. It is on the north-west side of the outer harbor. It was well chosen for planting, as the soil is good, and the tract is less rocky than any other of equal extent lying along the shore inside of the Cape. With reference to its early use, probably, it received the name of 'ffisherman's field,' by which it is designated in the early records of the town" (*History,* p. 40). See also *Maximus* I, 106 and note.

I.100. <u>muthologos</u> has lost such ground since Pindar . . .

From Thomson, *Art of the Logos,* pp. 18–19:

> So far as we know, the first to distinguish between Muthos and Logos, was Pindar. 'Surely marvels are many,' he says, 'and methinks in part *Muthoi* adorned with cunning fictions beyond the true Logos do deceive the minds of men.' Here Muthos, the false Story, is contrasted with Logos, the true. Again he says, 'I think that the Logos of Odysseus'—what people say about him, his fame—'is greater than his tribulation because of the sweet-versing Homer. For his fantasies and winged art carry a certain majesty upon them; Poesy steals away the judgments of mankind by her *Muthoi,* and a blind heart is most men's portion.' Here again Muthos is the false Story. It is from this usage that 'myth' has come to mean (in the words of the New English Dictionary) 'a fictitious narrative.' The reason for the choice of Muthos rather than Logos to designate the fictitious narrative is fairly clear. It is Homer's word, and it is of certain Stories in Homer that Pindar is thinking when he says that their charm blinds us to their falsity. Even Plato, one is rather surprised to learn, makes no distinction

between the words in his ordinary use of them. It is only when the need arises to discriminate between the false Story and the true, between imagination (as in what we call the Platonic myths) and demonstrable fact, that he follows Pindar and calls the false a Muthos. Yet the converse does not hold, and in normal usage Logos did not mean a true story. It means simply a Story.

See also Olson's use of *"muthologos"* in "Poetry and Truth," *Muthologos*, II, 37–38.

I.100. I would be an historian as Herodotus was . . .

Thomson points out that Herodotus was called "the *Muthologos*" by Aristotle, and that "What it all comes to is this, that for the audiences which harkened to the Stories a Muthos was a Logos, and a Logos a Muthos. They were two names for the same thing" (*Art of the Logos*, p. 19). Thomson had previously made the clarification on p. 17 that

> Logos did not originally mean 'word' or 'reason,' or anything but merely 'what is said.' This meaning it never lost, although in its long strange history it acquired many others, and it remained the usual designation for the kind of tale we are to consider. We shall therefore regularly use it in that sense. For some reason Homer avoids Logos, preferring Muthos; but Muthos with him means 'what is said' in speech or story exactly like Logos in its primary sense. . . . The question of truth or falsehood did not arise. This is worth remembering when we speak of Greek mythology. An early Greek, an average early Greek, would not have admitted that there was much in what we call his 'mythology' that was in the modern sense mythological at all.

He adds further, citing the difference between Herodotus and Thucydides, p. 23:

> Nothing matters to the Story Teller but the Story. If he lets his disbelief in that appear, he may be giving proof of superior intelligence, but it will in general be a bad thing for his art. It is assumed by the Story Teller and his audience that the story is true; destroy that assumption and you destroy his method. Herodotus is perfectly well aware of this. He is critical enough, and this often comes out in

his comments on a Logos. But in telling the Logos itself criticism is suspended, the atmosphere of belief is carefully and beautifully preserved. It is this which makes the real difference between him and Thucydides, who saw that his business was to destroy the *Muthodes,* the Mythic element in history, the Logoi, because they cared nothing for accuracy. It was the business of Herodotus to save them.

In a note, p. 237, Thomson also explains that ἱστορίη (which Olson transcribes elsewhere as *'istorin*), as it is used by Herodotus, "appears to mean 'finding out for oneself,' instead of depending on hearsay. The word had already been used by the philosophers. But while these are looking for the truth, Herodotus is looking for the evidence."

See *A Special View of History,* esp. p. 20; also *Maximus* III, 79; and "On History" from the Vancouver Conference, 29 July 1963, where Olson says (*Muthologos*, I, 3):

> Obviously the word "history" is a word—unless you take it to root—which doesn't have any use at all. And the root is the original first use of it, in the first chapter if not the first paragraph of Herodotus, in which he says "I'm using this as a verb *'istorin*, which means *to find out for yourself . . .*" After all, Herodotus goes around and finds out everything he can find out, and then he tells a story. It's one of the reasons why I trust him more than, say, Thucydides, who basically is reporting an event. . . . So, that idea of breaking that word so that we don't talk about a *concept* "history"— that's why I offered the damn thing . . .

Also, "Letter to Elaine Feinstein" (*Human Universe,* p. 97) and "A Bibliography on America" (*Additional Prose,* p. 13), for this use of the term *'istorin*. For the distinction between Herodotus and Thucydides developed further, see "It Was. But It Ain't."

I.101. Altham says / Winslow / was at Cape Ann . . .

From Rose-Troup, *John White,* p. 70, where the fact is used as evidence to establish the date of the sailing of the *Charitie* (see the passage from Rose-Troup quoted in note to *Maximus* I, 99 above).

Emmanuel (possibly Samuel) Altham was captain of the pinnace *Little James* which carried settlers to Plymouth. See also *Maximus* II, 108–110.

I.101. Sir Edward Coke

(1552–1634), lord chief justice of England. In debates in the House of Commons he argued against royal patents—such as the one granted in 1620 to Sir Ferdinando Gorges (ca. 1566–1647) for all territory in North America between the 40th and 48th parallels—which would allow monopolization of the New England fishing industry. See, e.g., C. F. Adams, *Three Episodes of Massachusetts History*, I, 123—129.

▶ I.102. a Plantation a beginning

Written winter 1957–58 at Gloucester; an early version was begun in September 1957, as there is a notebook among the poet's papers with "I (begins after 'a begin a Plant': Sunday Sept 15, 1957)" on the cover. The title is from the passage by John Smith quoted on p. 104 of the poem (see also note below).

I.102. "the Snow lyes indeed / about a foot thicke ...

From John White, *Planters Plea*, p. 29, in answering the objection, "But New-England hath divers discommodities, the Snow and coldnesse of the winter, which our English bodies can hardly brooke ...": "The cold of Winter is tolerable, as experience hath, and doth manifest, and is remedied by the abundance of fuell. The Snow lyes indeed about a foot thicke for ten weeks or there about; but where it lies thicker, and a month longer as in many parts of *Germany*, men finde a very comfortable dwelling."

I.102. Fourteen spare men ...

"Spare" in the sense of extra. The ship was double-manned, "that (by the helpe of many hands) they might dispatch their voyage, and lade their Ship with Fish while the fishing season lasted, which could not be done with a bare sayling company. Now it was conceived, that the fishing being ended, the spare men that were above their necessary saylers, might be left behind with provisions for a yeare; and when that Ship returned the next yeare, they might assist them in fishing, as they had done the former yeare; and, in the meane time, might employ themselves in building, and planting Corne . . ." (White, *Planters Plea*, p. 68; also quoted in Rose-Troup, *John White*, p. 64).

I.102. Stage Head

Rocky bluff projecting into Gloucester Harbor, behind which is Stage Fort Park.

I.102. Pat Foley

A letter carrier from Worcester, Mass., and friend of Olson's father (*Muthologos*, I, 145, and *The Post Office*, p. 41).

I.102. fishing worke

From John Smith's statement quoted in note to *Maximus* I, 104.

I.103. The ship which brought them / we don't even know / its name . . .

It is possible that Olson is using only White and Babson for this poem, for Rose-Troup states clearly on several occasions that it was the *Fellowship* which White describes as having brought over the fourteen "spare" Dorchester men— unless the poet has misread or misremembered her statement on p. 67 of *John White* that "The ship sent the previous year [1623/4] was, we know, the *Fellowship*, but the name of the converted Flemish Fly-boat [of the season 1624/5] cannot be supplied, as the entry in the Weymouth Port Book is illegible"; or has confused, at this point, the "voyage of discovery" (see note to *Maximus* I, 116) prior to 1623 with the "Fishing Voyage" of 1623/4, and her statement on p. 69, "that the 'voyage of discovery' was made by an unknown ship." This will appear corrected in the poems, *Maximus* I, 116, where Rose-Troup is definitely used, though there still seems to be a discrepancy among the dates, in part due to the difference between the Old and New Style calendars of the time.

I.103. Bilbao

Basque seaport in northern Spain. Babson suggests, *History of Gloucester*, p. 32n, this is where the Dorchester Company vessel returned to sell her cargo (White states only that the market was in Spain).

I.103. Champlain

Samuel de Champlain (1567–1635), French explorer. In 1606, on his second voyage to Cape Ann, he mapped Gloucester Harbor, naming it Le Beau Port, and found some two hundred Indians dwelling thereabouts. By the time the Dorchester settlers arrived in 1623, John White reports, *Planters Plea,* p. 25, there had occurred "a three yeeres Plague, about twelve or sixteene yeeres past, which swept away most of the Inhabitants all along the Seacoast, and in some places utterly consumed man, woman & childe, so that there is no person left to lay claime to the soyle which they possessed." See also *Maximus* I, 49 and note.

I.104. Her cargo brought / the Spanish market . . . 200 / pounds.

The figure is from White's *Planters Plea* (see note below).

I.104. "have set up", / said Smith . . .

From John Smith, *The Generall Historie of Virginia, New-England, and the Summer Isles* (*Travels and Works*, II, 783): "There hath beene a fishing this yeere [1624] vpon the Coast about 50. English ships: and by Cape *Anne*, there is a Plantation a beginning by the Dorchester men, which they hold of those of *New-Plymouth,* who also by them haue set vp a fishing worke. . . ."

I.104. the ship alone / small fiftie tunnes . . .

See White, *Planters Plea,* p. 39:

> The first imployment of this new raised Stocke [the 3000£ raised by the Dorchester Company; see *Maximus* I, 46 and note], was in buying a small Ship of fiftie tunnes, which was with as much speed as might be dispatched towards *New England* vpon a Fishing Voyage: the charge of which Ship with a vpon a new sute of sayles and other provisions to furnish her, amounted to more than three hundred pound. Now by reason the Voyage was vndertaken too late; shee came at least a moneth or six weekes later then the rest of the Fishing-Shippes, that went for that Coast; and by that meanes wanting Fish to make up her lading, the Master thought good to passe into *Mattachusetts* bay, to try whether that would yeeld him any, which he performed, and speeding there, better then he had reason to expect: having left his spare men behind him in the Country at *Cape Ann,* he returned to a late and consequently a bad market in *Spaine,* and so home. The charge of this Voyage, with provision for fourteene spare men left in the Countrey, amounted to above eight hundred pound, with the three hundred pound expended vpon the Shippe, mentioned before. And the whole provenue [profit, returns] (besides the Ship which remained to us still) amounted not to aboue two hundred pound . . .

Also quoted in Rose-Troup, *John White,* pp. 65—66.

▶ I.106. Maximus, to Gloucester

Written winter 1957—58 at Gloucester; an early version probably in 1953 (see final note to *Maximus* I, 107 below).

I.106. the widow Babson

Isabel Babson (ca. 1577—1661), an early settler on Cape Ann. For a notice of her and her descendants, see J. Babson, *History of Gloucester,* pp. 59—61, and his *Notes and Additions,* I, 5—8; also R. Babson, *Actions and Reactions,* pp. 3—5.

I.106. Middle Street

In downtown Gloucester. Roger W. Babson, e.g., the statistician, was born and raised at 58 Middle Street.

I.106. Joppa

Section of Gloucester towards the eastern shore of Cape Ann, between Eastern Avenue and Good Harbor Beach. James Babson had property at the corner of Joppa Road and Eastern Avenue, and John J. Babson wrote his *History of Gloucester* there in 1855–60.

I.106. Wellesley Hills

Community west of Boston near Wellesley, Mass.

I.106. Babson had his Institute there

The Babson Institute of Business Administration at Babson Park, Wellesley, Mass., founded in 1919 by Roger W. Babson (1875–1967), American business millionaire and statistician. His autobiography, *Actions and Reactions,* was first published in 1935 and revised in 1949.

I.106. Hupmobile

American automobile popular in the 1920's.

I.106. Jeffrey Parsons whom the historian Babson . . .

(1631–1689), an early settler. John J. Babson, in his *History of the Town of Gloucester* (1860), reports: "In April, 1655, he bought of Giles Barge an acre and a half of land in Fisherman's Field. He also bought, about the same time, a house and land at the same place, which had once belonged to George Ingersol, and still earlier to George Norton. There he fixed his residence; and descendants still live around the spot first occupied by their ancestor" (pp. 120–121). In *Notes and Additions,* I, 50, Babson quotes Parsons' will in which he leaves to his son, "the three acres whereupon his house stood, three acres of planting land at the south end of his field (formerly called by the name of fisherman's field) . . ."

I.106. what Babson called it, the only hundred acres . . .

See John J. Babson, *History of Gloucester*, p. 40: "It was well chosen for planting, as the soil is good, and the tract is less rocky than any other of equal extent lying along the shore inside of the Cape . . ."; but especially his letter in Thornton, *Landing at Cape Ann*, pp. 83–84: "On the north-west side of the outer harbor of Gloucester is a tract of land, containing about one hundred acres, more or less, which, in our early town-records, is called 'ffisherman's field. . . .' On the seaward side it has two coves, one of which is very small, formed by the projection of a rocky bluff into the harbor. This bluff is called Stage Head, and tradition affirms that this is the place where the operations of the first fishing company at Cape Ann were carried on. . . . One of the objects of the fishing company just mentioned, was to combine fishing and agricultural employments; and for the latter no spot more favorable than 'ffisherman's field' could be found on our shores, as it is less rocky than any other tract of equal extent on the borders of the harbor. It was also convenient for their fishery. . . ."

I.106. Somerset

Somersetshire, county of southwestern England on the Bristol Channel.

I.106. Dorset

Dorsetshire, county on the southern coast of England; Dorchester is its center.

I.106. the ridge which runs from my house straight to Tablet Rock

The house is the one on Stage Fort Avenue behind Fisherman's Field that Olson lived in while a boy (see also

Maximus I, 46 and note). This same ridge is subject of a poem, entitled simply "The Ridge," which was written at the same time as "Letter 27" but likewise withheld (see *OLSON* 6, pp. 47–51, and note on pp. 71–73 there).

For Tablet Rock, see note to "the rock I know by my belly and torn nails," *Maximus* I, 48.

I.106. the Company house which Endicott / thought grand enough . . .

See *Maximus* I, 45 and note.

I.107. an house built at Cape Ann . . .

See Richard Brackenbury's deposition in Thornton, *Landing at Cape Ann*, pp. 79–80:

> . . . at Salem we found liueing, old Goodman Norman, & his sonn: William Allen & Walter Knight, and others, those owned that they came ouer vpon the acco^t of a company in England, caled by vs by the name of Dorchester marchants, they had sundry houses built at Salem, as Alsoe John Woodberye, M^r· Conant, Peeter Palfrey, John Balch & others, & they declared that they had an house built at Cape Ann for the dorchester company, & haueing waited vpon M^r· Endecott, when he attended the company of the Massathusetts pattentees, when they kept theire court in Cornewell Street in London I vnderstood that this company of London haueing bought out the right of the Dorchester marchants in New England, and that M^r· Endecott hat power to take possession of theire right in New England, which M^r· Endecot did, & in perticuler of an house built at Cape Ann, which Walter Knight & the rest, said they built for Dorchester men: & soe I was sent with them to Cape Ann to pull downe the said house for M^r· Endecott's vse, the which wee did . . .

Quoted also in Rose-Troup, *John White*, pp. 118–119.

I.107. Beverly

See note to *Maximus* I, 45.

I.107. Conant Norman Allen Knight . . .

See, e.g., the list in Thornton, *Landing at Cape Ann*, p. 63. Also Rose-Troup, *John White*, pp. 103–104, although she lists thirteen original settlers (Olson says on *Maximus* I, 108 that only eleven are known): "Among these we can certainly place Roger Conant, John Woodbury, Peter Palfrey, John Balch, William Trask, John Norman and his son, John Tilly, Thomas Gardner, William Allen, Walter Knight, Thomas Gray, and, almost certainly, John Gray."

I.107. a rented house / on Fort Point

The poet's house at 28 Fort Square, to which he had moved from Black Mountain with his wife and son in the summer of 1957.

I.107. Cape Ann Fisheries

Dealers and processors of wholesale fresh and frozen fish, formerly in operation on Fort Square.

I.107. backwards / of a scene / I saw the other way . . .

I.e., from his earlier house at Stage Fort Avenue or from Stage Head itself, which overlooks Gloucester Harbor and Fort Point from the west.

I.107. He left him naked, / the man said . . .

In a notebook from 1953 among the poet's papers is written: "May 27–28 (over to Thurs, had dream of myself naked as reported in Max # 25. . . ." The dream appears as follows in the withheld "Maximus Letter #25" (*OLSON* 6, pp. 10–11):

I must make it known, now that I have had the great dream
have waked from the shock of myself confronted with
myself, I standing, before my own eyes, naked, and charging
myself with what? There I was, and I was he, and it was me,
just as I am, the exact body. And we stared at each other.

I do not know that we asked anything, I, of him,
or he, of me. Yet we did look at each other, we were
sibs. And the I who was naked had a single look.

The I who dreamt was as I have been, a host,
with people, things around me, was surprised,
looked out from the edge of a crowding of the real. And separate
only as a scratch is red, and conspicuous, on skin.
Was a looking figure, not liking to be looked at,
as, it was clear, this new one did not mind. This

was the charge he wore upon him like his nakedness,
it was this that made the other—me—awake.

▶ I.109. So Sassafras

Written winter 1957–58 at Gloucester.

I.109. Europe just then was being drained . . . ,

Cf. *Maximus* I, 78, "And Europe / was being drained / of
gold . . . ," and note above.

I.109. Ralegh

Sir Walter Ralegh or Raleigh (ca. 1552–1618), the English
adventurer. He supported the colonization of Virginia and
backed Pring's voyage after sassafras—which at the time was
considered an important remedy, esp. for syphilis or the "pox"
(see note to Pring below).

I.109. Gosnold

Bartholomew Gosnold (d. 1607), English navigator. He
made a voyage to the coast of North America in 1602 in com-
mand of the *Concord,* sailing from what is now Maine to
Martha's Vineyard (which he named) and returning to
England with a valuable cargo of furs and sassafras. See esp.
J. T. Adams, *Founding of New England,* pp. 36–37, and
Moloney, *Fur Trade in New England,* p. 17.

I.109. Pring

Martin Pring (1580—ca. 1626) made a voyage to the North American coast from Maine to Cape Cod, where he obtained sassafras, in 1603. See the account of his voyage in Levermore, *Forerunners of the Pilgrims*, I, 65: ". . . the Country yieldeth Sassafras a plant of sovereigne vertue for the French Poxe, and as some of late have learnedly written good against the Plague and many other Maladies."

I.109. mines John Smith called these are her silver / streames

Smith, *Description of New England,* in *Travels and Works,* I, 194: "But this is their Myne; and the Sea the source of those siluered streames of all their vertue. . . ." Quoted also in Innis, *Cod Fisheries,* p. 68n.

I.109. Sable

Sable Island (see note to *Maximus* I, 23)

I.109. Isle Shoals

Isles of Shoals, a cluster of small islands and rock ledges about sixteen miles north of Cape Ann, off Portsmouth, N.H. Originally called Smith's Isles by John Smith who visited them in 1614 (*Description of New England* in *Travels and Works,* I, 206).

I.109. make $1000 per / man per 7 months . . .

See Smith, *New Englands Trials* (1620) in *Travels and Works,* I, 242: "For to make triall this yeare, there is gone six or seuen sayle from the west Countrey, onely to fish, three of which are returned; and (as I am certainly informed) haue made so good a voyage, that euery Sayler for a single share had twenty pounds for his seuen moneths worke, which is more then in twenty moneths he should haue gotten had he gone for wages any where." Smith's figures are quoted also in Innis, *Cod Fisheries,* p. 72n.

I.109. Indians / occasionally bloody ... poor / john Tilly

See note above to *Maximus* I, 99, and Phippen, "The 'Old Planters,' " p. 189:

> In the year 1636 Tilley was on a trading voyage as master of a bark and while coming down the Connecticut River, ... very imprudently left his vessel, in a small canoe, with one assistant, on a fowling excursion along the banks of the river. He landed about three miles from the fort, and was stealthily watched by the Indians in ambush, until he had discharged his gun, when a large number of the savages arose from their covert and took him prisoner without chance of resistance, and at the same time killed the man left in charge of the boat. His inhuman captors tortured him by first cutting off his hands, and a while after, his feet also; notwithstanding which, it is said, he survived for three days, and won the admiration of the Indians by the manner in which he endured their cruel tortures.

The account is originally told in *Winthrop's Journal*, I, 194.

I.109. John Oldham

(ca. 1600–1636), a trader who came to Plymouth in 1623 on his "particular" as Bradford says, on his own account and not part of the general body of Plymouth associates. He became a center of discontent, along with Lyford (q.v.), and was banished. Later he was invited to be a trader with the Indians on behalf of the Dorchester Company settlers at Cape Ann.

I.109. 69 lusty men Bradford called Weston's

Thomas Weston (ca. 1575–1646), leader of a group of merchant adventurers in London which supported the voyage of the Pilgrims in 1620. In 1622 he launched a private venture to New England, probably without a patent. His company landed at Plymouth, where they were tolerated by the Pilgrims and their immediate needs cared for until they could find a suitable location of their own. Bradford writes, *History*, p. 149: "So as they had received his former company of 7. men, and vitailed them as their owne hitherto, so they also received *these* (being aboute 60. lusty men), and gave housing for them selves and their goods; and many being sicke, they had ye best means ye place could aford them." Weston's party eventually settled at Wessagusset, the present Weymouth, on Massachusetts Bay, but without success.

I.109. Bradford

William Bradford (1590–1657), Pilgrim Father and governor of the Plymouth Colony, author of the *History of Plymouth Plantation 1620–1647*. Olson had already used his *History* for the poem, "There Was a Youth Whose Name was Thomas Granger" (1947).

I.109. Medici

Powerful ruling family of Renaissance Florence. In *Maximus* III, 41 later, Olson will similarly speak of Winthrop as a prince, a "wanax" of ancient Mycenae.

I.109. Monhegan

Monhegan Island off Pemaquid Point, Maine, a few miles out to sea southwest from Penobscot Bay. A fishing station in the early 1600's; reached by John Smith in April, 1614.

I.109. Damariscove

Island off the coast of Maine, west of Monhegan. Bradford reports, "about y^e *later end of May* [1622], they spied *a boat* at sea . . . a shalop which came from a ship which M^r· Weston & an other had set out a fishing, at a place called Damarinscove, 40. leagues to ye eastward of them, wher were y^t year many more ships come a fishing" (*History*, p. 137).

I.109. Weston Thompson Pilgrimes grabbing . . .

For Bradford's sense of pressures upon him to secure territory on Cape Ann for fishing purposes, see his letter of 8 September 1623 from Plymouth:

We have write to the counsell [for New England] for an
other patente for cape Anne to weet for the westerside of it,
which we know to be as good a harbore as any in this land,
and is thought to be as good fishing place; and seeing fishing
must be the cheefe, if not the only means to doe us good;
and it is like to be so fite a place, and lyeth so neer us; we
thinke it verie necessarie to use all diligence to procure it;
and therefore we have now write unto you and the counsell
againe about it, least our former letters should not be come,
or not delivered, of which we have some suspition; M^r
Weston hath writen for it, and is desirous to get it before us;
and the like doth Mr Thomson; which is one spetiall motive
that hath moved us to send over this messenger fore named
[Winslow] . . .

(Marsden, "A Letter of William Bradford and Isaac Allerton," p. 296; quoted also in Rose-Troup, *John White*, p. 87).

David Thompson or Thomson (d. 1628?) received a grant
from the Council for New England in 1622 for land on the
coast of Maine, and settled near the mouth of the Piscataqua
in 1623. See C. F. Adams, *Three Episodes*, I, 191–193, also
Bradford, *History*, pp. 185 and 251.

I.109. Richard BUSHROD

(d. 1628), a mercer or haberdasher of Dorchester, Eng.
He obtained a license from the Council for New England on
behalf of himself and other merchants of Dorchester, which
would enable them to explore the possibilities for a settlement in New England. See Rose-Troup, *John White*, p. 59:

> Bushrod was to act as their representative in applying for
> the necessary authority. The result of this is enclosed in the
> Records of the Council for New England under the date
> of 18th February, 1622/3:—
>> Whereas Mr. William Darby of the Towne of Dor-
>> chester, Agent for Richard Bashrode of the same,
>> Merch^t., and his Associates, propounded unto the
>> Councell that the said Mr. Bashrode desired that either
>> himselfe or some one of his Associates might bee admit-
>> ted a patentee, and for that they purpose to Settle a plan-
>> tacion in New England, they now prayed to have a Ly-

cence granted unto them to send forth a Shippe for Discovery and other Imployments in New England for this yeare, which the Councell ordered accordingly. . . .

Bushrod and his associates, including John White, were to form the nucleus of the Dorchester Company which sponsored the settlement of Cape Ann.

I.109. George derby

William Darby or Derby (b. 1588?), member of the Dorchester Company (see Rose-Troup quoted above). Here confused with George Way (q.v.).

I.109. FISH pulling all of Spain's bullion out

See Innis, *Cod Fisheries,* on the relationship of fishing to the rise of mercantilism. On p. 52, e.g., he writes: "England was able, in part because of her relatively shorter distance from Newfoundland and in part because of the nature of fish as a foodstuff, to secure a strong and continuous hold on a product by which she obtained a share of Spanish specie and the products of the Mediterranean. Cod from Newfoundland was the lever by which she wrested her share of the riches of the New World from Spain." Elsewhere he quotes Sir Edwin Sandys arguing in Commons "in support of a bill for 'freer liberty of fishing,' partly on the ground that expansion and increased sales in Spain would increase imports of specie to England. It was an industry 'of 200 ships and 10,000 men, 8,000 marryners, and bringes in great store of bullion from Spaine' " (p. 74).

I.109. Our Lady / of bon viaje

Our Lady of Good Voyage ("viaje" is Spanish, though "bon viage" appears commonly enough in English writings in the sixteenth and seventeenth centuries). See *Maximus* I, 2 and note.

I.109. old man B

Charles Homer Barrett (1869–1959), mayor of Gloucester in 1915–16 when Olson first came as a boy to spend summers there. He built the summer "camps" where Olson and his parents lived, while he himself lived on Western Avenue, a neighbor and friend of the family. He served as Superintendent of Highways from 1918 to 1924. The poet wrote in a letter to the author, 6 March 1968: "They *all* got tarred including Homer in a real City Hall Scandal here back while I was out of Gloucester—all over the papers, names etc,—I suppose say in the late 40's early 50's???"

For a photograph of Barrett, see Pringle, *Book of the Three Hundredth Anniversary,* opposite p. 92.

I.110. Daddy Scolpins

A Matt Scullins or Scollin, from Boston; one of "the two brothers" described in *Maximus* II, 137, "who owned the American Oil Company courted / the two beauties of the camps / —& one walked away with the darker." He married Dorothy Purcell of Gloucester, dark-haired "Dotty the Beauty" of the poem (both identified in another letter to the author, 12 March 1968, and in conversation, June 1968).

A sculpin is a large-headed, broad-mouthed fish: "what Gordon Boone and I used to catch / was rockcod, when we didn't get nothing but daddysculpins, / those bloated, freckled bags / of wind" (fragment from 1952–53 among the poet's papers).

I.110. Big Train

After Walter "Big Train" Johnson (1887–1946), baseball player, pitcher for the Washington Senators from 1907 to 1927. See Olson's use of the nickname in his poem for Fielding Dawson, "pitcher, how . . ." (*Archaeologist of Morning,* p. 207):

    . . . as you pitch

    . . . how would you say
    how far back you are reaching from,
    say, big train, from; the dirt . . .

Used here with also a pun on train-oil.

I.110. the Cod Kings of Eng- / land

See Innis, *Cod Fisheries,* p. 103n: "The fishing ships became trading ships and West Country admirals were able to act as tyrants over the population and became known as 'kings.' "

I.110. tarvia

Trade name for road surfacing material.

I.110. our fireplace made / of pavingstone . . .

Cf. also "As the Dead Prey Upon Us" (1956), speaking of the poet's mother: "She sits by the fireplace made of paving stones."

I.110. Cally-o

Callao, seaport of Peru.

I.110. Bilbow

Occasional sixteenth- and seventeenth-century spelling for Bilbao (q.v.).

I.110. St Kitts

Island in the West Indies.

I.110. corfish

See note below to *Maximus* I, 117.

I.110. Spicks

The Spanish. See the account of this trading activity in Innis, *Cod Fisheries*, pp. 76ff.

I.110. & do and do and do

Echo of *Macbeth*, I.iii.4−10, which ends:

> Her husband's to Aleppo gone, master o' the *Tiger*.
> But in a sieve I'll thither sail
> And, like a rat without a tail,
> I'll do, I'll do, and I'll do.

I.110. Virgini-ay

Virginia, spelled as pronounced in sea-chanties or folk songs.

I.110. Fayal

One of the islands of the Azores.

I.110. Surinam

Dutch Guiana, colony in South America. J. Babson reports, *History*, p. 567: "Boston vessels traded to Surinam as early as 1713 . . . but it is not known that any Gloucester vessel engaged in the trade till about 1790, when, it is said, Col. Pearce sent a vessel there." R. Babson and Saville add, "Cape Ann practically controlled the Surinam trade of the young American continent. Col. Pearce who had a sheep farm in Dogtown sent the first vessel to Surinam in 1790. This trade reached its heights about 1858, preceding the Civil War. Gradually this romantic foreign trading gravitated to Salem and finally to Boston" (*Cape Ann Tourist's Guide*, pp. 113−114).

I.110. optimis generis

See *Maximus* I, 63 and note.

I.110. Osquanto

Also Squanto or Tisquantum (d. 1622), Indian inter-
preter for the settlers at Plymouth, "who there fell sick and
died. Not long before his death he desired the Governor
of Plymouth, who at that time was there present, to pray
for him, that he might go to the place where dwelt the
Englishmen's God . . ." (Hubbard, *History of New England*,
p. 76). Also Bradford, *History*, p. 155: "In this place Squanto
fell sick of an Indean feavor, bleeding much at ye nose (which
ye Indeans take for a simptome of death), and within a
few days dyed ther; desiring ye Govr to pray for him, that
he might goe to ye Englishmens God in heaven. . . ."

I.110. Rummage the ship

See the quotation from John Smith's *Accidence for Young
Seamen, Maximus* I, 51.

I.110. Boston / is where the best fish / go . . .

See, however, Innis, *Cod Fisheries*, p. 79: "Dry fish were
sent from fishing areas to Boston, and from thence the merchantable grades were dispatched to Lisbon, Bilbao, Marseilles, Bordeaux, Toulon, and other French ports, the
refuse grades going to the West Indies." Earlier he had
written, p. 75n: "Poorer grades of fish were sent to Boston"
(underlined by Olson in his copy).

I.111. O specie

See note to "FISH pulling all of Spain's bullion out,"
Maximus I, 109.

I.111. run bank clerks / for Council

Robert D. Tobey, bank teller who served on the Gloucester city council, 1953−56.

I.111. kench

James B. Connolly's text for illustration 210 in Church, *American Fishermen,* defines the term as follows: " 'Kenched' to press out the pickle. When thoroughly pickled, the cod are taken from the salt butts and put through a process called 'water hawsing,' to remove superfluous pickle. This consists of stacking them in heaps—or kenching, the fishermen call it—to press out the pickle not absorbed by the fish." Morison identifies a kench as a "salting box" (*Builders of the Bay Colony,* p. 26).

I.111. Clancy

Harold C. Clancy, a Gloucester junk dealer remembered for his appearances in local parades and celebrations and writings to the newspaper. He ran for the city council, without success, in 1957.

▶I.112. History is the Memory of Time

Written winter 1957–58 at Gloucester. The phrase is John Smith's, from his *Advertisements for the Unexperienced Planters* (*Travels and Works,* II, 948) "In all those plantations, yea, of those that we have done least, yet the most will say, we were the first; and so every next supply, still the next beginner: But seeing history is the memory of time, the life of the dead, and the happinesse of the living; because I have more plainly discovered, and described, and discoursed of those Countries than any as yet I know, I am the bolder to continue the story . . ."

I.112. Mormons

Members of the Church of the Latter Day Saints, founded in 1830. Persecuted like the Pilgrims for religious convictions, they sought a free homeland in the West in the days prior to and during the great Gold Rush of 1849–50.

I.112. 10 boats New England waters / the year before . . .

From Innis, *Cod Fisheries*, p. 72: "In 1621 the number of ships for New England increased to 10, in 1622 to 37, in 1623 to 40, and in 1624 to 50." Olson's figure for 1623, 45 vessels, can be accounted for by a note on that page in Innis, where he quotes John Smith: "In 1623 'went from England onely to fish, five and forty saile and have all made a better voyage than ever.' "

I.112. Damariscove

See note to *Maximus* I, 109.

I.112. Piscataqua

River in southern Maine, forming part of the boundary between Maine and New Hampshire. A settlement was established at its mouth by David Thomson (q.v.) in 1623.

I.112. That year the STAGE FIGHT . . .

See the account from Hubbard's *History of New England* quoted in Rose-Troup, *John White*, pp. 89–90:

> In one of the fishing voyages about the year 1625, under the charge and command of one Mr. Hewes, employed by some of the west country merchants, there arose a sharp contest between the said Hewes and the people of New Plymouth, about a fishing stage, built the year before about Cape Ann by Plymouth men, but was now in the absence of the builders, made use of by Mr. Hewes his company, which the other, under the conduct of Captain Standish, very eagerly and peremptorily demanded: for the company of New Plymouth, having themselves obtained an useless patent for Cape Ann, about the year 1623, sent some of the ships which the adventurers employed to transport passengers over to them, to make fish there, for which end they had built a stage there, in the year 1624. The dispute grew to be very hot, and high words passed between them, which might have ended in blows, if not in blood and slaughter, had not the prudence and consideration of Mr. Roger Conant, at that

time there present, and Mr. Peirce his interposition, that
lay just by with his ship, timely prevented. For Mr. Hewes
had barricadoed his company with hogsheads on the stage-
head, while the demandants stood upon the land, and
might easily have been cut off, but the ship's crew, by
advice, promising them to help them build another, the
difference was thereby ended. Capt. Standish had been
bred a soldier in the Low Countries, and never entered
the school of our Saviour Christ, or of John Baptist, his
harbinger; or if he was ever there, had forgot his first
lessons, to offer violence to no man, and to part with the
cloak rather than needlessly contend for the coat. A little
chimney is soon fired; so was the Plymouth captain, a man
of very little stature, yet of a very hot and angry temper.
The fire of his passion soon kindled, and blown up into
a flame by hot words, might easily have consumed all,
had it not been seasonably quenched.

Quoted also in Thornton, *Landing at Cape Ann,* pp. 45–46.
 Bradford also records the incident by saying, "some of
Lyfords & Oldoms freinds, and their adherents, set out a
shipe on fishing, on their owne accounte, and getting y^e
starte of ye ships that came to the plantation, they tooke
away their stage, & other necessary provisions that they had
made for fishing at Cap-Anne ye yeare before, at their great
charge, and would not restore ye same, excepte they would
fight for it" (*History,* I, 420; quoted also in Rose-Troup,
John White, p. 89). According to Bradford, the delay which
enabled the Dorchester men to seize the stage was caused by
a delay in Winslow obtaining and bringing the charter (see
Maximus I, 99 and note) and by being forced to employ
a drunken ship-master named Baker (*History,* p. 202).
 Rose-Troup, elsewhere commenting on the accounts of
Hubbard and Bradford, adds: "Bradford represents the
people who had seized the stage as belligerents to whom
the Plymouth men, so meek and mild, had, so to speak,
turned the other cheek, but Hubbard gives a different
and more racy story of the scene" (*Roger Conant,* p. 9).
See also *Maximus* I, 48.
 The Reverend William Hubbard (1621–1704) was minister of Ipswich, Mass. He settled in New England in 1635,

and was personally acquainted with Roger Conant and possibly heard the tale from him. His *General History of New England from the Discovery to MDCLXXX* was first published in 1815.

I.113. Capt Peirce

William Peirce (d. 1641), master of the *Charity*. That the ship was one hundred tons, see Bradford, *History*, p. 147.

I.113. the crook Allerton

Isaac Allerton (ca. 1586–1659), agent for the Plymouth Colony and an owner of the *White Angel*. He did not prove to be a satisfactory agent; Bradford says, for instance, that "though M$^{r.}$ Allerton might thinke not to wrong y^e plantation in y^e maine, yet his owne gaine and private ends led him a side in these things . . . ," and further claims the Plymouth settlers were "kept hoodwinckte" and "abused in their simplicitie, and no better than bought & sould, as it may seem" (*History*, pp. 340 and 347–348).

I.113. the Little James . . . the / White Angel . . .

The *Little James* was a pinnace of about forty-four tons, built for the Plymouth settlers and designed, according to Bradford, "to stay in the cuntrie" (*History*, p. 171). She had already been damaged in a storm off Damariscove Island (see *Maximus* II, 108–110), but salvaged and rebuilt. For the *White Angel*, see Bradford, *History*, p. 243: "The other was a great ship, who was well fitted with an experienced m[aste]r & company of fisher-men, to make a viage, & to goe to Bilbo or Sabastians with her fish. . . ."

For Bilbo or Bilboa, see *Maximus* I, 103 and note; San Sebastian is a port in Spain, on the Bay of Biscay.

The account of the towing of the *Little James* by the *White Angel* and her capture, occurs in Bradford, *History*, pp. 244–245:

> The lesser ship had as ill success, though she was as hopfull as ye other for ye marchants profite; for they

had fild her with goodly cor-fish taken upon yᵉ banke, as full as she could swime ... The m[aste]r was so carfull being both so well laden, as they went joyfully home togeather, for he towed yᵉ leser ship at his sterne all yᵉ way over bound, and they had such fayr weather as he never cast her of till they were shott deep in to yᵉ English Channell, almost within yᵉ sight of Plimoth; and yet ther she was unhaply taken by a Turks man of warr, and carried into Saly, wher yᵉ m[aste]r and men were made slaves, and many of yᵉ beaver skins were sould for 4ᵈ· a peece.

Bradford, however, mentions nothing about the *Little James* and the *White Angel* being present at the dispute between Standish and Hewes; while Hubbard mentions only Captain Peirce's interposition. However, Ford, in his edition of Bradford (I, 314n.), does point out that the *Little James* "may have been the first of the vessels ... designed to be built by the Council for New England, to lie upon the coast for the defense of merchants and fishermen employed there, and 'also to waft the fleets as they go to and from their market.'" As such, it would have been available to assist Peirce or Standish.

I.113. conantry

See reference to James B. Conant, *Maximus* I, 45–47 and note.

▶ I.115. The Picture

Written winter 1957–58 at Gloucester.

I.115. Ambrose Gibbons

(d. 1656), settled at Piscataqua and served as agent for Captain John Mason. In 1679, in a dispute over the territory granted Mason in March 1621/2—which included Cape Ann—Mason's heirs claimed that Gibbons took possession of the territory for Mason in 1622 or 1623, but that he was ousted by the Massachusetts Bay Company in 1630 (see Dean, *Capt. John Mason*). This Gibbons later served as assistant to Francis Williams, governor of Maine (Hutchinson, *History of Massachusets-Bay*, I, 93). Both Baxter and C. F. Adams suggest he is the brother of Edward Gibbons (d. 1654), who was with Morton at Merrymount (Baxter, *Trelawny Papers*, p. 349n; C. F. Adams, *Three Episodes*, I, 354). See also the sketch of him in Scales, *Piscataqua Pioneers*, pp. 84–86.

I.115. John Mason

Captain John Mason (1586–1635), the founder of New Hampshire, was governor of Newfoundland from 1615 to 1621 and member of the Council for New England. He received, with Sir Ferdinando Gorges (q.v.), several grants of land from the council, including a patent for "all the land from the river Naumkeag around Cape Ann to the river Merrimac" in March 1621/2, and in August of that year a grant for all land between the Merrimac and Kennebec rivers, under the title of the Province of Maine. Delayed from settling this territory by European wars, in 1629 he received a separate grant for the territory extending from the Merrimac to the Piscataqua, which he called New Hampshire.

I.115. John Watts took salt / he said Morton said / was his . . .

Watts, employed as factor for the Dorchester Company, was accused of taking salt—necessary for the preservation of fish caught—shallops, and other provisions stored by Plymouth fishermen on Ten Pound Island in Gloucester Harbor. See the account in Rose-Troup, *John White*, pp. 99–103, but especially the document of testimony in answer to the charges, published by Ford in the *Proceedings of the Massachusetts Historical Society*, LXIII (1910), pp. 493–496, reprinted in *John White's Planters Plea*: "For this defend.ᵗ [Watts] sayed that when the said salt was taken by this defend.ᵗ in New England aforesaid one Mʳ Morton then dwelling in New England aforesaid claymed the said salt as belonging unto him or as comitted to his charge."

The episode, here useful for dating the Dorchester Company presence at Cape Ann, will appear again in *Maximus* II, 74 and 106, and III, 45.

I.115. Hastings . . . misled the Donner Party

Lansford W. Hastings (1819–1870), author of *The Emigrants' Guide to Oregon and California* (1845). Olson calls him "that first of advertising men" in *A Bibliography on America* (*Additional Prose*, p. 8). He was the self-appointed guide who encouraged the party of American "emigrants" or pioneers, led by George Donner (ca. 1784–1847) and his brother Jacob, on its way to California from Illinois, to take a turn-off from the established trail, a detour around the Great Salt Lake, which led to their disaster. The account is vividly told in Stewart, *Ordeal by Hunger*; see also DeVoto, *Year of Decision*.

I.115. Ten Pound Island

At the entrance to Gloucester's Inner Harbor, in plain view of Fort Square; a low crest of rock some three and a half acres in all.

I.116. THE PICTURE . . .

The facts which follow have been gathered out of Rose-Troup's *John White*. Thus for "voyage of discovery, ship unknown," see her p. 69: "A clear exposition of the facts is therefore essential, but must be prefaced by a statement that the 'voyage of discovery' was made by an unknown ship." This was the voyage, made probably prior to 1623/4, for which a license was applied for by Richard Bushrod (see *Maximus* I, 109 and note), for the purpose of determining the possibility of a permanent fishing plantation at Cape Ann. That John Watts may have been factor or agent on this voyage is Olson's own suggestion.

For details of the 1624 season, see John White in Rose-Troup, pp. 65–66, although she gives the date of 1623—a discrepancy due to the different calendars in use. That the *Fellowship* was thirty-five tons, see p. 68 of Rose-Troup.

For the season of 1625, see Rose-Troup, p. 66, again quoting John White: "the next yeare was brought to the former Ship [the *Fellowship*] a Flemish Fly-Boat of about 140. tunnes," which "returned with little more than a third part of her lading: and came backe . . . directly for *England* . . ." Rose-Troup suggests on p. 68 that "It is possible that the Fly-boat was the *Pilgrime* . . ."

For season 1626, see Rose-Troup, pp. 67–68, though again there is a discrepancy in dating, due likewise to the transition from old to new-style calendar. That the *Amytie* was thirty tons and captained by Isaac Evans, see p. 68: "the *Amytie*, 30 tons, Isacke Even, master . . ." That she carried six cattle, see p. 70: "The *Amytie*, in 1625/6, carried six rother beasts . . ."

Cf. also Mrs. Rose-Troup's chart on p. 69 of *John White*: The ships sent out by the Dorchester Company were:—

> 1623/4   The *Fellowship*.
> 1624/5   The *Fellowship* and the *Pilgrime*.
> 1625/6   The *Fellowship*, the *Pilgrime*, and the *Amytie*, the latter laden with kine.

For the final voyage, of 1627, "backed by eleven enthusiasts," see Rose-Troup, p. 98, where she also quotes from a license authorized by the Privy Council to "transporte out of this kingdom, vnto the Plantation of New England, the nomber of twentie Rother Catell . . ." This is followed by her discussion of John Watts and the salt (pp. 95ff.), in which she says that one of the importances of that account is "It supplies the names of the Adventurers and the places at which they resided, and shows that after the greater part of them had relinquished their active participation in the adventure, it was carried on by eleven enthusiasts."

I.116. and there be / 11 years until fishing once more . . .

In 1638/9, when Maurice Thomson would apply to the General Court of the Colony of Massachusetts Bay for permission to establish a fishing plantation at Cape Ann. See *Maximus* I, 156 and note.

I.116. le Beau Port

Name for Gloucester Harbor given by Champlain, as it appears on his map of 1606 (see note to *Maximus* I, 151).

▶ I.117. The Record

Written winter 1957–58 at Gloucester.

I.117. Weymouth Port Book

Records of the seafaring activity at the port of Weymouth, England, preserved in the Public Record Office. They are referred to by Rose-Troup to provide additional information concerning the Dorchester Company's voyages to Cape Ann. See her *John White,* pp. 66–69.

I.117. Here we have it—the goods—from this Harbour . . .

From Rose-Troup, *John White,* p. 68:

> To the account of this venture [the third attempt of the Dorchester Company as described by White] we are able to add a little information from the Weymouth Port Books. Sir Walter Erle and Company intended to ship six rother cattle, under a special warrant from the Privy council, on the *Fellowship* of Weymouth, 35 tons, Edward Cribbe, master, sailing 23rd January, 1625/6. For some reason, probably because of the leak, they were taken out and shipped on the *Amytie*, 30 tons, Isacke Even, master, sailing on the 27th February following. The *Amytie* made her home port about 1st August, 1625, and the *Fellowship* followed about 11th September. The amount of dry fish, corfish, train oil, quarters of oak and skins of 'fox, racons, martyns, otter, muskuatche [muskrat] and beaver' unloaded by Richard Bushrod and Company and by William Derby and Company, were of considerable value, greater than White's account leads us to expect.

I.117. "so hote this time of yeare . . .

Anthony Parkhurst, report on the English fishing fleet in Newfoundland (1578), as quoted in Innis, *Cod Fisheries,* p. 35n: "In early August we learn the weather was 'so hote this time of yeare except the very fish which is laid out to be dryed by the sunne be every day turned it cannot possibly be preserved from burning.' " The shore fishery was that near the coast, where the catch could be put on shore to be cured.

I.117. Banks fishery, where fish are large and always wet . . .

From Innis, *Cod Fisheries,* p. 26: "At a later date the bank fishery was described as beginning in April and being over by July. The fish were large and 'always wet, having no land neere to drie,' and were called 'core fish.' "
See also "the Banks," note to *Maximus* I, 62.

I.117. the oil of seal, whale or cod . . .

Again Innis, p. 32n: " 'Traine' or 'trayne' was an abbreviation of 'traine oil'—the oil of seal, whale, or cod."

I.119. The above is calculated from Capt Richard / Whitbourne's list . . .

Whitbourne made several voyages to Newfoundland between 1579 and 1615; his "Observations as to the *Newfoundland* fisheries, 1622" were printed in Smith's *Generall Historie of Virginia, New England, and the Summer Isles, 1624* (*Travels and Works,* II, 776–781), and include "The charge of setting forth a ship of 100. tuns with 40. persons, both to make a fishing voyage, and increase the Plantation"—the list from which Olson makes his calculations. The list is also given in Innis, *Cod Fisheries,* p. 57n.

I.119. Rev John White's / statement of the cost . . . £225

White says only, "The charge of the Voyage, with provision for fourteene spare men left in the Countrey, amounted to above eight hundred pound, with the three hundred pound expended vpon the Shippe, mentioned before" (*Planters Plea*, p. 39; quoted in Rose-Troup, *John White*, p. 65). He does say, however, that wages and provisions for the thirty-two men left the following season cost 500£ (*Planters Plea*, p. 40; Rose-Troup, *John White*, p. 67). A notesheet among the poet's papers indicates that it was from these figures that Olson calculated the cost for fourteen men as being 225£.

▶**I.120. Some Good News**

Written winter 1957−58 at Gloucester. Its original title, "Good News! fr Canaan," makes the allusion to Edward Winslow's tract, *Good News from New England* (1624), more apparent.

I.120. the same side Bradford, / the fall before . . .

See Bradford's letter of September 1623, quoted in a note to *Maximus* I, 109.

I.120. Biskay

Biscay, the Basque province (see note to *Maximus* I, 77).

I.120. Breton

Of Brittany in northern France, home of fishermen.

I.120. Cabot

See *Maximus* I, 79 and note.

I.120. Georges / (as the bank was called as early / as 1530 . . .

Walter H. Rich in *Fishing Grounds of the Gulf of Maine* writes, p. 99n:

> The earliest record of this name (Saint Georges Shoal) that the writer has found appears upon a map discovered

in the library of Simancas, in Spain, where a chart said to have been made by a surveyor sent out to Virginia by James I of England, in 1610, was found in 1885 or 1888, after having long before disappeared from England. This chart is thought to embody, besides the work of Champlain and other foreigners, the information contained in the English charts of White, Gosnold, Pring, and probably of Waymouth's Perfect Geographical Map. It is thought to have been drawn by Robert Tyndall or Captain Powell.

(See Brown, *Genesis of the United States*, II, 460, and reproduction of the map between pp. 456−457 there.) Notes from ca. 5 February 1958 in a notebook among Olson's papers indicate he had made use of Rich for the information here on Georges.

I.120. Aragon

Region of northeastern Spain; formerly a separate kingdom until united with Castille under Ferdinand and Isabella in 1479. Like England and Portugal, its patron saint was Saint George.

I.120. Portyngales

Obsolete or archaic appearance of 'Portuguese,' common in the sixteenth century and before. Chaucer, e.g., uses "Portyngale" for Portugal in the epilogue to the *Nun's Priest's Tale*.

I.120. Old Man's Pasture

Fishing grounds about five miles southeast of Cape Ann.

I.120. Tillies / Bank

Fishing grounds about twenty miles east by south of Cape Ann.

I.120. Levett / says "too faire a gloss" . . .

Christopher Levett (see *Maximus* I, 133 and note), in his *Voyage into New England* (1628) in Levermore, *Forerunners,* pp. 630–631:

> Thus have I relaited unto you what I have seene, and doe know may be had in those parts of NEW-ENGLAND where I have beene, yet was I never at the Mesachu-sett, which is counted the Paradise of NEW-ENGLAND, nor at CAPE ANN. But I feare there hath been to faire a glosse set on CAPE Ann. I am told there is a good Harbour which makes a faire Invitation, but when they are in, their entertainment is not answerable, for there is little good ground, and the Shippes which fished there this yeare, their boats went twenty miles to take their Fish, and yet they were in great feare of making their Voyages, as one of the Masters confessed unto me who was at my house.

I.121. Quack

Indian name for what Levett was to call York, Maine; he describes it as "about two leagues to the east of Cape Elizabeth," on the coast.

I.121. Sable / Island

One hundred and eighty miles southeast of Halifax, Nova Scotia, on the northern sea route between Europe and America. It is estimated to have been at least one hundred miles long in the sixteenth century, but because of the steady encroachment of the sea, is now only about twenty miles long and barely a mile wide, with treacherous, shifting shoals. See Rich, *Fishing Grounds,* p. 104n:

> "Pedro Reinel, a Portuguese pilot of much fame" (Herrara), made a map in 1505 showing Sable Island, feared and dreaded by all fishermen even in those days, where he called it "Santa Cruz." Jacomo Gastaldi, an Italian cartographer, in 1548 shows it "Isolla de Arena." Sir Humphrey Gilbert, or his historian, says that the Portu-guese had made an interesting settlement here for ship-

wrecked mariners. This, "Upon intelligence we had of a Portugal who was himself present when the Portugals, above thirty years past [thus before 1553] did put upon the island neat and swine to breed, which were since exceedingly multiplied."

George T. Bates, on his map of "Ships Wrecked on Sable Island, The Graveyard of the Atlantic" among the poet's papers, notes that "Sable Island was so named by the French from its sands. It was called by the Portuguese and Spanish 'Isle Faguntes' and 'Santa Crus,' and by the Italians 'Isolla del Arena'. . . . The first voyage to North America for the purpose of colonization was made in the year 1518 by Baron de Lery et de Saint Just. No actual settlement was made at that time but it seems that the Baron left a number of live cattle on Sable Island. Other animals, including horses, sheep and swine survived early, unrecorded wrecks on the island of later, but ill-fated attempts at settlement by various European countries."

I.121. Smith, / at Monhegan, / 1614 . . .

See Smith's *Description of New England* (1616) in *Travels and Works*, I, 187: "In the moneth of Aprill, 1614. with two Ships from *London*, of a few Marchants, I chanced to arriue in *New-England*, a parte of *Ameryca*; at the Ile of *Monahigan*, in 43½ of Northerly latitude: our plot was there to take Whales and make tryalls of a Myne of Gold and Copper. If those failed, Fish and Furres was then our refuge. . . ."

I.122. Columbus

Christopher Columbus (1451—1506). See above, notes to *Maximus* I, 55—56 and 79—80.

I.122. Grant

Ulysses Simpson Grant (1822—1885)—nicknamed "Sam"— American general and president. He was appointed commander of the Union army by Lincoln in 1863. See also note to p. 125 below.

I.122. the Divine / Inert, the literary man . . . said / it has to be / if princes / of the husting . . .

See "Equal, That Is, to the Real Itself," *Human Universe,* p. 122:

> I pick up on calm, or passivity, Melville's words, and about which he knew something, having served as a boatsteerer himself, on at least his third voyage on a whaler in the Pacific. He says somewhere a harpoon can only be thrown accurately from such repose as he also likened the White Whale to, as it finally approached, a mighty mildness of repose in swiftness is his phrase. Likewise, in handling Ahab's monomania, he sets up a different sort of possible man, one of a company which he calls the hustings of the Divine Inert.

For Melville's statement on the "Divine Inert" and "princes of the hustings," see *Moby-Dick,* chapter XXXIII (Constable ed., I, 182):

> For be a man's intellectual superiority what it will, it can never assume the practical, available supremacy over other men, without the aid of some sort of external arts and entrenchments, always, in themselves, more or less paltry and base. This it is, that for ever keeps God's true princes of the Empire from the world's hustings; and leaves the highest honors that this air can give, to those men who become famous more through their infinite inferiority to the choice hidden handful of the Divine Inert, than through their undoubted superiority over the dead level of the mass.

For Melville's sense of "private passivity," see *Maximus* I, 126 and note.

I.123. the / Androgyne

See also "Five Foot Four, but Smith Was a Giant" (*Additional Prose,* p. 57): ". . . a 350 year inability of the American 'soul' obviously, to allow in still the difference John Smith was, from anyone else and from the great Shove America was, and has been, from the beginning. He is still some waif, presiding over Atlantic migration like a 5 foot 4 lead figure, Mercury or an Hermaphroditus of the whole matter."

Also in the sense defined in a letter to Cid Corman, 9 February 1951 (*Letters for Origin*, p. 28): the "combination" which is "that of documentarian & the selectivity of the creative taste & mind."

I.123. the simulacrum / Time Magazine / takes for male . . .

Time, a popular weekly magazine "of news and opinion," founded in 1923. Its self-excited manner and language was originally modeled on the assumed "Homeric" virility and grandeur of the Victorian Lang-Leaf-Myers translation of Homer. It can be further said to "play coy with identity" by the anonymity of its articles.

I.123. Caesar's / dream, / that he'd been intimate / with his mother . . .

Olson had written in a letter to Michael Rumaker, 23 December 1956: "Know thyself. Baloney. Know the world (Caesar fucked his mother, in a dream, and the soothsayer sayeth, Caesar, you shall rule the world!)" See also "Reading at Berkeley," *Muthologos*, I, 145: "The world is not differentiable. Caesar's dream is true. It's your mother, like, that's all. And you're the father if you are."

From Suetonius' life of Julius Caesar in his *Lives of the Twelve Caesars*, Gavorse trans., p. 6:

> While he was Quaestor it fell to him by lot to serve in Farther Spain. While there, . . . he came to Gades, where he noticed a statue of Alexander the Great in the temple of Hercules. At the sight of it he drew a deep sigh, as one displeased with his own shortcomings, in that he had as yet performed no memorable act, whereas at his age Alexander had already conquered the whole world.
>
> He soon after made earnest suit for his discharge, in order to seize the first opportunity to compass greater enterprises at home within the city. The following night he was much disquieted by a dream in which he imagined he had carnal company with his own mother. But hopes

of most glorious achievement were kindled in him by the soothsayers, who interpreted his dream to mean that he was destined to have sovereignty over all the world, his mother whom he saw under him signifying none other than the earth, which is counted the mother of all things.

I.123. Corinth / burning down / produces bronze

See *Call Me Ishmael,* p. 38, on the writing of *Moby-Dick*:

> Through May he continued to try to do a quick book for the market: "all my books are botches." Into June he fought his materials: "blubber is blubber." Then something happened. What, Melville tells:
>> I somehow cling to the strange fancy, that, in all men hiddenly reside certain wondrous occult properties—as in some plants and minerals—which by some happy but very rare accident (as bronze was discovered by the melting of the iron and brass at the burning of Corinth) may chance to be called forth here on earth.

Also quoted by Olson in "Lear and Moby-Dick," p. 165. On p. 40 of *Call Me Ishmael,* he explains, "Melville and Shakespeare had made a Corinth and out of the burning came *Moby-Dick,* bronze."

I.123. my Cabbage, we / baked potatoes / Fisher's Hill

See also the poem "ABCs": "my friend Cabbage, with whom to bake potatoes up / Fisher's Hill." In a notebook designated "Key West II: February-March 1945" among the poet's papers, is written: "When I was a boy I had a companion I had made up like all kids do. His name was Cabbage. We baked potatoes together. He got me over childhood. Melville got me over adolescence. . . ."

Fisher's Hill was in a field behind Olson's home on Norman Avenue in Worcester, Mass.

I.123. Smith, / who came to Monhegan / to catch whales. . .

See quotation from Smith's *Description of New England,* note to *Maximus* I, 121, and the passage following in *Travels and*

Works, I, 188: "And 40 leagues westwards were two French Ships, that had made there a great voyage by trade...."

I.124. Pemaquid

Peninsula on the coast of Maine between the Kennebec River (Boothbay Harbor) and Penobscot Bay, permanently settled by the English in 1625.

I.124. the Continental Shelf / was Europe's / first West...

The fishing banks of the north Atlantic are part of the submerged continuation of the continent itself which is known as the continental shelf.

I.125. "vainglorious", / they put Smith down / as...

Actually it was not the Pilgrims (who hired Standish instead—see *Maximus* I, 69 and note), but Smith's companions in the Virginia colony who felt him to be "vainglorious." George Percy, specifically, one of the councilors and early governors of Virginia, wrote in his "Trewe relacyon" that Smith was an "ambityous, unworthy and vayne glorious fellowe" (quoted in B. Smith, *Captain John Smith,* p. 158).

I.125. Mongols

The central Asiatic people; especially those of the thirteenth century under Genghis Khan, notorious for their fierceness.

I.125. Grant / still is a name / for butcher...

Grant was so called in Northern newspapers during the War between the States for the heavy losses he allowed his own troops to suffer in the battles of the Wilderness, Spotsylvania and Cold Harbor, at the beginning of his so-called "hammering campaign" to maintain relentless pressure on Lee's forces in May and June, 1864. See, e.g., Pratt, *Short History of the Civil War,* p. 305.

See also "abt the dead he sd . . ." (*Archaeologist of Morning,* p. [192]):

> . . . abt Grant

> I sd Butcher I read
> Kenneth Williams
> on Grant . . .

And then, Kenneth P. Williams, *Lincoln Finds a General.*

I.125. Clotho Lee

Robert E. Lee (1807−1870), general of the Confederate forces in the American Civil War, fated to defeat by the industrial superiority of the northern states. Clotho is one of the three Greek fates, the spinner of the web.

I.126. sd the / literary man, from hidden places / sprang / the killer's / instrument . . .

See *Moby-Dick,* chapter LX (Constable ed., I, 357), from the last paragraph:

> . . . as the profound calm which only apparently precedes and prophesies the storm, is perhaps more awful than the storm itself; for, indeed, the calm is but the wrapper and envelope of the storm; and contains it in itself, as the seemingly harmless rifle holds the fatal powder, and the ball, and the explosion; so the graceful repose of the line, as it silently serpentines about the oarsmen before being brought into actual play . . .

Also the description of the act of harpooning, chapter LXII (II, 7−8).

See also *Maximus* I, 122 and note, and cf. *Call Me Ishmael,* p. 15, on Melville: "He had a pull to the origin of things, the first day, the first man, the unknown sea, Betelgeuse, the buried continent. From passive places his imagination sprang a harpoon."

I.126. Browns

See note to *Maximus* I, 19.

I.127. a mark for all / who on this coast / do fall . . .

See Smith's poem, "The Sea Marke," quoted on *Maximus* I, 69—70.

I.127. the Channel

A gully in the Atlantic west of Georges Bank, separating that from the shoals of Nantucket.

I.127. Middle Ground

Fishing bank north of Sable Island and east of Halifax, Nova Scotia.

I.127. Pollock Rip

Fishing grounds southeast of Cape Cod.

I.127. the De-Hy

Fish processing (through dehydration) plant on the State Fish Pier, Gloucester.

▶**I.128. Stiffening, in the Master Founders' Wills**

Written in 1958 at Gloucester, by early March when the manuscript was sent to John Wieners for his magazine *Measure*. The following note appears on the inside front cover of Olson's copy of Whitehead's *Process and Reality*: "*Stiffening in the Master Founders' Will* [fr Brooks Adams' The Emancipation—of *Massachusetts*—ignorance, of *greed*."

I.128. Descartes

René Descartes (1596—1650), French philosopher and mathematician.

I.128. Boston's / settling

What was variously called Shawmut or Trimountaine, shortly to be named Boston, was settled by Puritan immigrants from England, led by John Winthrop, in 1630.

I.128. yellow sweetings

A variety of apple, first grown by William Blaxton or Blackstone (1595–1675), the earliest settler of what was to be Boston, on the western slope of Shawmut (Beacon Hill). See "Reading at Berkeley," *Muthologos*, I, 102: ". . . Richard [sic] Blackstone of the *Maximus Poems,* who grew the Blackston apple, in fact, on Beacon Hill, before Boston was." See also *Maximus* III, 153.

I.128. Quakers

The religious sect also known as the Society of Friends. They began settling in Massachusetts in the 1650's and came into immediate conflict with the Puritan establishment, both because of the aloofness of their social customs and the essential religious difference between their belief in direct private revelation and the Puritan hierarchy of ministers.

That Quakers were sold as slaves by the Puritans, see the account in B. Adams, *Emancipation of Massachusetts,* pp. 304–348, of two children who were sentenced to be sold to satisfy a debt imposed on their Quaker parents who had been persecuted to death. No Quakers are known to have been burned to death on Boston Common—now a park in downtown Boston—although Quakers are said to have been hanged and buried there (C. F. Adams, *Three Episodes,* I, 408; II, 550–51). Perhaps the reference here is confused with the burning of Maria (*Maximus* I, 94).

I.128. Mrs. Davis's cookbook

Adelle Davis, advocate of health foods, author of cookbooks such as *Let's Eat Right To Keep Fit* (1954). It would seem to be her enthusiasm for her cause (or that of her followers) that prompts Olson's analogy.

I.128. Cartesian monads

Monads are actually part of the system of the German philosopher Gottfried Wilhelm von Leibnitz (1646–1716), not that of Descartes.

I.128. Jeremiah Dummer

(1681−1739), agent for Massachusetts in England. The Massachusetts Historical Society has a copy of his sermon, *A Discourse on the Holiness of the Sabbath Day*, on which is a note in the hand of Jeremy Belknap: "In his latter days he grew a Libertine & kept a Seraglio of Misses round him to whom he was lavish of his favours. Col. S.—who was in England in 1738 went in to wait upon him at his Seat in Plastow on a Sunday after Church & found him with his Ladies sitting round a Table after dinner drinking Raspberry Punch. As he entered ye room he observed a confusion in Mr Dummer's countenance & ye Girls fled out of ye Door like Sheep—almost over one another's back. . . ." ("Letter—Book of Samuel Sewall," *Collections of the Massachusetts Historical Society*, p. 305n).

I.129. Anne Hutchinson

(1591−1643), center of a religious controversy in the Massachusetts Bay Colony. Called to appear before the General Court led by Governor Winthrop in November 1637, she was accused of holding gatherings for women at her home each Thursday, at which she "disparaged all our ministers in the land that they have preached a covenant of grace," or direct inspiration from God, enthusiasm in that sense. See the account of the trial, which resulted in her banishment, in B. Adams, *Emancipation of Massachusetts*, pp. 236−245.

I.129. God made right hands . . .

From a discussion of a statement from Kant's *Prolegomena to Any Future Metaphysics* in Weyl, *Philosophy of Mathematics and Natural Science*, p. 97n:

> Kant has been interpreted as follows: If the first creative act of God had been the forming of a left hand, then this hand, at the time even when it could be compared to nothing else, would already have possessed that definite character of the left one (in contrast to the right one)

which can only intuitively but never conceptually be apprehended. This is incorrect, as Leibniz points out, if we intend this to mean that something else would have happened had God created a 'right' hand first, rather than a 'left' hand. One must follow the process of the world's genesis further in order to uncover a difference: Had God, rather than making first a left hand then a right hand, begun by making a right one and proceeded to form another right one, then He would have changed the plan of the universe not in the first but in the second act, by bringing forth a hand which was equally rather than oppositely oriented to the first-created one.

I.129. M'Head

Marblehead, Mass.

I.129. East Anglia

Region of southeastern England composed of Norfolk and Suffolk. John Winthrop was from Groton in Suffolk.

I.129. another man, when young, / by fields from Shottery . . .

William Shakespeare, as he occurs in the thoughts of Stephen Dedalus in James Joyce's *Ulysses*, p. 207:

> He has hidden his own name, a fair name, William, in the plays, . . . A star, a daystar, a firedrake rose at his birth. It shone by day in the heavens alone, brighter than Venus in the night, and by night it shone over delta in Cassiopeia, the recumbent constellation which is the signature of his initial among the stars. His eyes watched it, lowlying on the horizon, eastward of the bear, as he walked by the slumberous summer fields at midnight, returning from Shottery and from her arms.

See also the association of elements in "Reading at Berkeley," *Muthologos*, I, 119: "The greatest poet of mars in the language . . . is William Shakespeare. I discovered that in wyoming, lower case *w*, last year. No Cassiopeia in the air overhead. No J O Joyce in—anywhere."

Shottery, the site of Anne Hathaway's cottage, is a village a mile west of Stratford-on-Avon. It might be worth noting that Olson himself visited the cottage while in England in 1928.

I.129. Mistress Hathaway

Anne Hathaway (1556–1623), wife of William Shakespeare.

I.129. Cassiopeia

A constellation of the northern hemisphere, shaped somewhat like the letter W.

I.130. "A family", he says, / "is a little / common wealth . . .

John Winthrop, "A Declaration in Defense of an Order of Court Made in May, 1637," in *Winthrop Papers*, III, 424.

I.130. Tenhill farm

Ten Hills, Governor John Winthrop's estate of some six hundred acres at Medford along the Mystic River. Near the site where William Blackstone planted his apple trees (see note to "yellow sweetings," *Maximus* I, 128 and note; also *Maximus* II, 57 and note, and III, 153).

I.130. "one-third, / my son, you will see come / annually . . .

See the deed of Gov. John Winthrop to John Winthrop, Jr., in *Winthrop Papers*, IV, 416:

> And allso all that parcell or necke of land now inclosed parte of my farme in Charlton called Tenhills lying ouer against the oyster banck, conteyning about thirty acres more or lesse. To have and to hould all the said lands and premises with their Appurtenances vnto the said Jo: Winthrop my sonne and Eliz: his wife during their liues . . . Provided allways and Reserved out of this present Grant vnto me the said Jo: Winthrop Marg[are]t my wife for the Terme of our liues and the longer liver of vs one third

parte of all such fruit as shalbe yearly growinge vpon the said necke of lande.

I.130. neat Rother / beasts

Rother, from the old English *hryðer* meaning 'ox' or 'cattle,' is common in the seventeenth century. It appears on several occasions in John White's *Planters Plea*. Rose-Troup notes that "Rother cattle are horned beasts." Also, probable pun on "neat," likewise meaning cattle.

I.130. Canaan

The promised land of milk and honey of the Israelites. The early settlers, with their conscious religious tradition, looked upon New England as their land of promise, a new Canaan. Cf. the title of Thomas Morton's *New English Canaan, or New Canaan.*

I.130. Cane

Cain, the first murderer; the eldest son of Adam and Eve who killed his brother Abel.

I.130. Moses

Leader of the Israelites into Canaan from their captivity in Egypt; founder of Hebraic monotheism, with its belief in a God who is transcendent yet who has made a covenant with his people. See, perhaps, Brooks Adams' preface to the 1919 edition of *Emancipation of Massachusetts,* in which he writes of the contrast "between Moses the law-giver, the idealist, the religious prophet, and the visionary; and Moses the political adventurer and the keen and unscrupulous man of the world. And yet it is here at the point at which mind and matter clashed, that Moses merits most attention. For Moses and the Mosaic civilization broke down at this point, which is, indeed, the chasm which has engulfed every progressive civilization since the dawn of time" (p. 8). See also part III of *Call Me Ishmael,* titled "Moses" and written principally from notes taken on Freud's *Moses and Monotheism.*

I.131. Corinth

See *Maximus* I, 123 and note.

I.131. skeigh

Defined in *Webster's Collegiate Dictionary*, 5th ed., p. 931, as "*Scot.* Shy; mettlesome; proud" (underlined in Olson's copy).

I.131. enthusiasm / is sedition . . . dishonours / parents

Winthrop's charge against Mrs. Hutchinson (see B. Adams, *Emancipation of Massachusetts*, p. 237).

I.131. the tailor's sewing

Epic song. See note to "Rhapsodia," *Maximus* I, 68.

I.132. cattle fattening / as they didn't / on the other shore

Rose-Troup, *John White*, p. 99n: "It is recorded that the kine grew into greater bulk in New England than in Old."

▶I.133. Capt Christopher Levett (of York)

Written winter 1957–58 at Gloucester, probably ca. February 1958 as an entry in a notebook containing an early version of the poem indicates the poet was reading Levett's *Voyage* on 12 February 1958. Christopher Levett (1586–ca. 1632) was an early settler on the coast of Maine. He received a grant for six thousand acres, on which he intended to build a city to be named York after his original home, the city in England. After exploration, he settled in 1623 at a place called Quack by the Indians—since identified as Portland harbor—naming it York, where he built a fortified house. He returned to England to get his family in 1624, and left behind some ten men, four of whom were of Thomas Weston's company of 1622 which settled at Wessagusset (Baxter, *Trelawny Papers*, p. 102n). See Levett's *Voyage into New England, 1623–24* (1628); also Baxter, *Christopher Levett, of York*. See also *Maximus* I, 120–121 and note.

I.133. Portland

City on the coast of Maine, about eighty miles north of Gloucester.

I.133. Levett says only, / 1624, I left / some men myself, and Plymouth / people fish . . .

See Levett, *A Voyage into New England,* in Levermore, *Forerunners and Competitors of the Pilgrims and Puritans,* p. 631: "But it seemes they have no Fish to make benifit of, for this yeare they had one Shippe Fisht at PEMAQUID, and an other at CAPE ANN, where they have begun a new Plantation, but how long it will continew I know not."

I.133. "House Island"

Site of fortified house built by Levett, 1623–24, in Portland harbor. See Levermore, *Forerunners,* p. 620n: "Dr. Baxter identifies the site of this building with an island, called House Island, near Cape Elizabeth, and gives good reasons for thinking that its name is derived from Levett's house." See Baxter, *Trelawny Papers,* p. 251n.

I.133. Conant's / house was timbers . . .

See *Maximus* I, 45. J. Babson writes, *History,* p. 44: "Some remains of the house are said to be contained in an old building, still standing, at the corner of Court and Church Streets" in Salem. R. Babson and Saville say the house is supposed to be standing now in the rear of the House of Seven Gables in Salem (*Cape Ann Tourist's Guide,* p. 117). This is the Hathaway House, built in 1682, located on Hardy Street (see esp. F. Conant, *Life of Roger Conant,* p. 7; also Emmerton, *Chronicles of Three Old Houses,* pp. 40–47).

See also *Maximus* II, 137:

> . . . the Dorchester Company house, which was probably
> up in the field over Settlement Cove like a fortress
> or Christopher Levett's at Portland on an island
> to have room around it and sight in an enemy
> country on shore

I.133. our / eyes which look / to strike

See also "Letter 6" above, and note to "how shall you strike, / o swordsman," *Maximus* I, 3.

I.134. "I have obtained a place / of habitation . . .

From Levett, *A Voyage into New England*, in Levermore, *Forerunners*, p. 620: "And thus after many dangers, much labour and great charge, I have obtained a place of habitation in NEW-ENGLAND, where I have built a house, and fortified it in a reasonable good fashion, strong enough against such enemies as are those Savage people."

I.135. About seven years / and you can carry cinders / in your hand . . .

That is, around 1630 or after the arrival of the second wave of colonists under Winthrop and the establishment of the Puritan commonwealth. In an early version in a notebook among the poet's papers, there appears:

. . . Levett dead, in 1630,
Smith in 1631: about seven years

and you can carry cinders
in your hand . . .

Cf. *Maximus* III, 41, which begins: "7 years & you could carry cinders in yr hand / for what the country was worth . . ."

I.135. Wash-Ching-Geka

The trickster-hero of the Winnebago Indians, a Siouan tribe originally centered in Wisconsin south of Green Bay; spelled Wakdjunkaga in Radin, *The Trickster*. The poet's source is a story, "How Wash-Ching-Geka Destroyed the Elephant and why Elephants are no longer Native American Animals," from a small booklet entitled *The Trot-Moc Book of Indian Fairy Tales* issued as a promotional device by a Massachusetts shoe manufacturer, which the poet had kept since a boy.

I.135. "the fish, / sd Levett, which we there saw . . .

From Levett's preface to his *Voyage into New England* (Levermore, *Forerunners,* pp. 609−610): "I have omitted many things in this my discourse, which I conceived to be Impertinent at this time for me to relate, as of the time of my being at Sea, of the strange Fish which wee there saw, some with wings flying above the water, others with manes, eares, and heads, and chasing one another with open mouths like stone Horses in a parke . . ." "Stone" is used in the sense of an animal not castrated.

I.135. Out, / is the cry of a coat of wonder

Cf. the early version of the poem in a notebook among the poet's papers, where there appears:

> . . . the most   as we now cry, out, way
>
> out, is the coat of wonder
> turned inside out . . .

Also, another early version (unpublished), entitled "How Small the News":

>   Out,
>
> is a cry, the coat of wonder
> turned inside. You've treated us
>
> so cheap . . .

▶I.136. 1st Letter on Georges

Written winter 1957−58 at Gloucester.

I.136. February night, or August / on Georges . . .

The account of a storm on George's Bank in February 1862 which makes up the body of this poem, is taken, with only minor changes throughout, from Proctor, *The Fishermen's Memorial and Record Book,* pp. 54−59, where it is titled "On Georges in the Terrible Gale of February 24th, 1862.

The experience of one who was there for the first and the last time." It begins:

> On the morning of February 14th, we started, and, in a glorious run of twenty-four hours, sighted the fleet on the Banks—nearly a hundred sail, riding at their anchors, half a mile, and in some instances, a mile apart. It was a pretty sight, and the fine, clear weather, rendered it highly enjoyable. We could distinctly see the men at the rail pulling in fish, rapidly as hands and arms could move. Soon our position was selected, anchor down, and the crew busy getting ready to try their luck.
>
> The cold, to one of my constitution, was intense, and pierced into the very marrow of my bones, although thickly clothed. But this deep sea fishing was so exciting that I stood at the rail sometime a full hour, without changing my position, pulling in the big codfish, and occasionally a halibut. . . .

Some pages later in this source is an account of another storm on George's—this time in August of another year—during which 128 men were lost: "The Terrible Gale of Sunday, August 24, 1873. Its Fearful Consequences!" Thus the two months, "February night, or August . . . ," in the introductory lines.

I.136. South Shoal

Fishing grounds in the Atlantic off the southwest edge of George's Bank near Nantucket.

▶ I.138. [Sch. Ella M. Goodwin . . .]

The poet pointed out in conversation, June 1968, that this section beginning with "Frost: 25 miles off the Highlands," is in fact a separate poem, a second "Letter on Georges," which through a printing error was not set apart from the preceding "1st Letter on Georges."

The main narrative—which begins, "Went out of Gloucester in the winter . . ." on p. 138, and ends, "He went down in the / Bay of Islands with all hands," p. 141—is by Lou

Douglas, whose own story is told on p. 6 of "Letter 2." Notes
to the left of that are the comments of Frank Miles, Douglas'
brother-in-law and the "quiet one" of "Letter 2," who also
made the voyage on the *Ella M. Goodwin*. Both men, living
near each other on Western Avenue above Stage Fort Park,
were neighbors of Olson's parents and occasional visitors at
the cottage on Stage Fort Avenue. It was sitting among them
one evening in Gloucester while visiting his mother before
leaving for the West Coast for a lecture and research, that
Olson heard the story and recorded it, adding statements
from another fisherman who was on the voyage, Ben Frost,
together with his own notes—probably, in fact, on 15 June
1947, the same time he wrote similar accounts of other fishing captains (William Greenleaf and Morton Selig) and their
voyages, also drawn from conversations with Douglas and
later preserved with *Maximus* materials from the late 1950's
among the poet's papers (one page of the original two-paged
manuscript of the present piece is typed on back of a draft
of a letter to Professor George Savage, Northwest Writers
Conference, 12 June 1947). So that, this is the first example
of a section of the poem written years earlier and incorporated into the chronological order of the series.

I.138. Frost

Ben Frost, fisherman who sailed aboard the *Ella M. Goodwin;* visited by the poet for his recollection of the episode
(see *Maximus* I, 141 and note below).

I.138. the Highlands

Fishing shoals near George's Bank.

I.138. Boston Post

Newspaper which carried a report of the incident. See
note below to p. 139.

I.138. South Shoals

See note above to "South Shoal," *Maximus* I, 136.

I.138. South Channel

Fishing grounds on the western edge of George's Bank.

I.138. Miles

Frank Miles. See also *Maximus I*, 6 and note.

I.138. the Chicago / theatre fire

A fire at the Iroquois Theater, Chicago, 30 December 1903, which cost 571 lives.

I.138. Lynn

City in Massachusetts about ten miles northeast of Boston.

I.139. the Cultivator

Cultivator Shoal on the northwestern part of George's.

I.139. Boston Post / Sat. Jan. 7, / 1905, / p. 2

See "Big Wave Swept Men Overboard" on p. 9 of that issue of the *Boston Post*:

> GLOUCESTER, Jan. 6.—John W. McKenzie, 20, was lost from the schooner Ella M. Goodwin, which arrived today, when he and three others were washed overboard Wednesday in South Channel, although another big wave washed back the others.
> The schooner was under a two-reefed foresail, riding sail and outer jib, heading northward. The gale, with falling snow, was then at its worst, and the seas were lashed to tremendous heights.
> Nine men were on deck at the time. Three, John W. McKenzie, Frank Miles and Robert W. Lee, were to the leeward, swaying up the forepeak. Suddenly the man at the wheel, Edward Rose, called out a note of warning. A tremendous sea, white capped and vicious, as high as the mastheads, arose from the depths and hurled itself against the craft, broadside on, with incredible swiftness. It struck the vessel a staggering blow, beneath which she reeled and quivered. Hundreds of tons of water flooded the deck.

The men at the peak halyards, McKenzie, Miles and Lee, taken in the act of overhanding on the peak halyards, were swept to the windward and over the vessel's sides by the irresistible onrush. Another, Leslie Sholds, standing to windward, suffered this same fate.

The chances for saving these four men in the teeth of hurricane and snowstorm seemed beyond human endeavor. But the back wash of the sea which carried them helplessly into its trough threw them violently back, excepting McKenzie. A swirl of snow curtained him from the gaze of his comrades.

McKenzie was born in Bear River, Digby county, N.S., but was brought up in Shelburne, where his relatives reside.

I.140. Bear River, Digby / County

Village in the southwestern county of Nova Scotia near the Bay of Fundy.

I.140. Shelburne

Town in southwestern Nova Scotia about sixty miles south of Bear River.

I.141. Bay of Islands

Inlet of the Gulf of St. Lawrence on the west coast of Newfoundland.

I.141. "to sway"—old English for / to hoist

See, e.g., the entry for "sway" in *Webster's Collegiate Dictionary*, 5th ed., p. 1006: "ME. *sweyen*, prob. fr. ON. *sveigja* to bend, swing, sway. . . . *Naut.* To hoist or set up;—often with *up.*" See Douglas' use of it in the narrative, bottom of *Maximus* I, 139, "swaying up the forepeak"; also in the *Boston Post* article quoted above.

I.141. Ben Frost at Institute

The Fishermen's Institute at 8 Duncan Street, Gloucester, was a social welfare organization for fishermen, and included living quarters. "16 Institute," which occurs below on the same page, would be Frost's room number there.

For a photograph of the building, see Charters, *Olson / Melville*, p. [46].

I.141. looard

Leeward.

▶ I.142. John Burke

Written January 1958 at Gloucester (date of newspaper article quoted below), with later revisions (early version read on birthday tape for Robert Creeley, December 1958).

I.142. John Burke did not rise / when Councilman Smith . . .

See "Retiring Councillors Complimented," *Gloucester Daily Times*, 3 January 1958, p. 1:

> Eloquently describing their contributions to the city, Councillor Owen E. Steele last night presented a pair of framed scrolls to outgoing Councillors Donald J. Ross and Benjamin A. Smith II.
>
> "Ex-Mayor Ross and I started out political life together here back in the early 1930's," Steele reminisced. "At 28 years of age he was elected a councillor, and at 31, mayor of Gloucester. He has always been a valuable contributor to political life. I know I speak for the whole council when I say I hope this retirement will be short."
>
> Ross' speech of thanks was brief, but it contained what many thought was an indication that he would be back in political life before too many years had passed.
>
> Smith, also an ex-mayor, was praised by Steele for his active political career. "As the first mayor under Plan E," Steele said, "Ben Smith did an outstanding job. His original administration did as much or more to further Plan E as any succeeding one."
>
> "You make me feel like an old statesman, Owen," Smith replied. And he told how it had been his great pleasure to serve his city, first on the school committee, then as mayor and a councillor.
>
> He expressed his gratitude to the city department heads and explained how they had helped him during his years

in office. And he advised the two incoming councillors, Pierce N. Hodgkins and Elliott H. Parsons, to use "these valuable men" for counsel.

Then glancing across the table at his long-time adversary, Councillor John J. Burke, Jr., Smith told the story of a man obsessed by fear, who "worried his life away" in apprehension that "something frightful was going to happen to him. "But," Smith said, "the object of his fear never came. The fear itself, like a beast in the jungle, devoured him, and he was unable to make any constructive move."

Steele then asked for a rising vote to pass the resolutions which had been inscribed upon the two councillor's scrolls. Every council member rose except Burke, who remained solidly in his chair, staring at the table.

Burke's signature was also conspicuously absent from Smith's scroll, although both had been signed by every other councillor.

Before the council meeting began, Burke, with some pride, said that although he had signed Ross' scroll, he refused to sign Smith's. "I'm not a hypocrite," he said.

These brief ceremonies, scheduled for 5 p.m., were over by 5:30, and the council adjourned to the Tavern for a farewell dinner for Councillors Ross and Smith.

The scrolls were rendered by hand in script lettering by Franklin E. Hamilton, of the Department of Public Works.

An accompanying photograph shows the scroll being presented. Olson saved the clipping among his papers.

I.142. inspectio / and judicium

Descartes' terms from his *Principles of Philosophy* as used in Whitehead, *Process and Reality*, esp. pp. 67 and 113n. "Inspectio" amounts to immediate intuition; "judicium," the faculty of judgment, logical analysis, or "inference."

I.142. the judge / or mischievous woman . . .

Also "the judge / or goddess of all mischief," *Maximus* I, 143. See Whitehead, *Process and Reality*, p. 497: "Throughout the perishing occasions in the life of each temporal Creature, the inward source of distaste or of refreshment, the judge arising out of the very nature of things, redeemer or goddess of mischief, is the transformation of Itself, everlasting in the Being of God."

I.143. Esop

Aesop (ca. 620–560 B.C.), the Greek fabulist.

I.143. the ponderous Harvard fullback

Ben Smith (b. 1916), Gloucester city councilman (later U.S. Senator, 1960–62), who graduated from Harvard in 1939.

I.143. she holds a city in her hair

Any of the goddesses or great mothers, such as Cybele, who are protectoresses of cities and are represented with a city, its walls and turrets, for a crown. Olson had been impressed by a description of such a figure in a letter from Robert Duncan, 14 August 1955, from Mallorca: "Ibizia was a Carthaginian colony and the ceramic figures from this period are magnificent. This goddess crownd with the walld imperishable city clutches in one hand to her breast a miniature lamb—in time we see her again holding the miniature child-lamb." In a poem called "The Horses of the Sea," dated 12 March 1963, in a notepad, Olson has the following: "Barcelona, is true, Duncan / told me, the Kathydrall / has a Virgin / with literally the walls / of a city forming the / crown which sits on / her head . . ."

I.144. A FOOTNOTE TO THE ABOVE

Originally a separate poem (it was not included when the earlier portion was first published in May 1959), entitled simply "A *Maximus* 'note' "; possibly written for Canadian poet Raymond Souster, who had published "John Burke" in *Combustion*. The manuscript sent Souster is inscribed "for Ray, January 1959–who wanted a 'note'!" and is described in an accompanying letter of 22 January 1959 as "a later 'Maximus' " which "explains" such things as Olson's use of proper nouns in the Burke poem (in Lakehead University Library).

I.144. Yana-Hopi

Distinct tongues. For Yana, spoken by a North California tribe of that name, see Sapir, *Language*, passim; for Hopi, language of those southwestern Indians, see Whorf, *Language, Thought, and Reality*.

I.144. in Maximus local / relations are nominalized

Also in "Postscript to Proprioception & Logography" (*Additional Prose*, p. 21):

> nominal-ize   all local relations are
> nominalized

See Sapir, *Language*, p. 118:

> . . . just as there are languages that make verbs of the great mass of adjectives, so there are others that make nouns of them. . . . But are there not certain ideas that it is impossible to render except by way of such parts of speech? What can be done with the "to" of "he came to the house"? Well, we can say "he reached the house" and dodge the preposition altogether, giving the verb a nuance that absorbs the idea of local relation carried by the "to." But let us insist on giving independence to this idea of local relation. Must we not then hold to the preposition? No, we can make a noun of it. We can say something like "he reached the proximity of the house" or "he reached the house-locality." Instead of saying "he looked into the glass" we may say "he scrutinized the glass-interior." Such expressions are stilted in English because they do not easily fit into our formal grooves, but in language after language we find that local relations are expressed in just this way. The local relation is nominalized.

I.144. the topological as a prime . . . metric then is mapping . . . congruent means of making a statement

This, like the poet's suggestion in Jonathan Williams' note at the end of the Jargon/Corinth edition that the "Figure of

Outward" strides "forth from the domain of the infinitely small," is derived from the language of contemporary mathematics. Cf. the following from "Equal, That Is, to the Real Itself," *Human Universe,* p. 120:

> ... it is my experience that only some such sense or form as the topological includes, able to discriminate and get in between the vague *types* of form morphology offers and the *ideal* structures of geometry proper, explains Melville's unique ability to reveal the very large (such a thing as his whale, or himself on whiteness, or Ahab's monomania) by the small.
>
> The new world of atomism offered a metrical means as well as a topos different from the discrete. Congruence was spatial intuition to Kant, and if I am right that Melville did possess its powers, he had them by his birth, from his time of the world, locally America. As it developed in his century, congruence, which had been the measure of the space a solid fills in two of its positions, became a point-by-point mapping power of such flexibility that anything which stays the same, no matter where it goes and into whatever varying conditions (it can suffer deformation), it can be followed, and, if it is art, led, including, what is so important to prose, such physical quantities as velocity, force and field strength.

See also the use and relation of "topological," "proximities," and "mapping" in the review of Havelock's *Preface to Plato*: "that we require *mapping*. By topological law that the *proximate*: a microcosm is literally as absolute as the other one. . . ." (*Additional Prose,* p. 53).

For these passages, see Weyl, *Philosophy of Mathematics and Natural Science,* esp. pp. 67–80, a discussion of non-Euclidean, projective geometry, as well as, on p. 86, the significant statement: "*Only in the infinitely small may we expect to encounter the elementary and uniform laws,* hence the world must be comprehended through its behavior in the infinitely small." Gloucester would then be "the infinitely small."

I.144. Mr. Foster

Or Doctor Foster. From the English nursery rhyme:

> Doctor Foster went to Gloucester
> In a shower of rain;

He stepped in a puddle
Right up to his middle,
And never went there again.

I.144. "And past-I-go / Gloucester-insides . . .

From Sapir, *Language,* p. 119n:

> In Yana the noun and verb are well distinct, though
> there are certain features that they hold in common which
> tend to draw them nearer to each other than we feel to be
> possible. But there are, strictly speaking, no other parts
> of speech. The adjective is a verb. So are the numeral,
> the interrogative pronoun . . . and certain "conjunctions"
> and adverbs (e.g., "to be and" and "to be not"; one says
> "and-past-I go," i.e., "and I went").

▶I.145. Letter, May 2, 1959

Written that date, in Gloucester.

I.145. 125 paces Grove Street . . .

This section, through "Kent's property / Pearce," is a
mapping of the area of Gloucester formerly called Meeting
House Plain, near the early settlers' first meetinghouse, just
east of the Annisquam River and about a mile north, via
Washington Street, of the harbor. See J. Babson, *History of
Gloucester,* pp. 191-192:

> There is nothing in the town-records about the erection
> of the first Meeting-house; but these records show that the
> first settlers had a place of public worship, and they cor-
> roborate the tradition which points out the spot on which it
> was located. An order passed for assigning a piece of land
> for a burial-ground, Feb. 8, 1644, says "that, at the end
> of these lots (viz., Mr. Blynman's, Thomas Jones's, Thomas
> Kent's, and Tho. Skillings's, betwixt and the old meeting-
> house place) shall be half an acre laid out for a common
> burial-place." This language will perhaps justify an infer-
> ence, that, even at this early period, the second Meeting-
> house had been built, and that the one mentioned in the
> order was erected by earlier inhabitants than Mr. Blynman
> and his company. In a grant of land to Sylvester Eveleth,

recorded next after a grant bearing date December, 1648, allusion is made to his house on Meeting-house Hill: and in April, 1653, it is recorded that Christopher Avery and John Collins measured the Meeting-house plain, and found it "39 rods from the creek and William Evans's fence; and from the north-west corner of Goodman Wakley's fence to Mr. Perkins's fence, 20 and a half rods; and from Mr. Perkins's garden fence over straight east to Goodman Wakley's fence, 17 1-2 rods." From these allusions, and other notices of the Meeting-house Plain of subsequent date, it appears probable that a house of worship was erected, soon after the incorporation of the town, on or near the spot occupied by three successive buildings for this purpose, about half a mile north of the place indicated as the site of the first one.

Also, T. Babson, "Evolution of Cape Ann Roads and Transportation," p. 305:

On February 8, 1644, the selectmen voted to set aside a half acre for a common burial place between lots owned by certain citizens and "the old meeting house place." This, and references in the records to "Meeting house hill" and later to "the meeting house plain" suggests that the first church building (about 1633) was near the old burying ground on Centennial Avenue (which was first called "Burying Ground Lane"),—some say it stood on what is now Curtis Square. . . .

Grove Street, above Oak Grove Cemetery, runs into Washington Street opposite Curtis Square and Centennial Avenue.

The section was originally written on back of an air letter from Scottish editor Alex Neish dated 9 April 1959, which Olson apparently had in his pocket at the time.

I.145. Oak Grove Cemetery

Cemetery off Washington Street near Grove Street.

I.145. Wallis property

John Wallis (d. 1690) and his sons. See notice of the family in J. Babson, *History of Gloucester,* pp. 175–176, 452.

I.145. White (as of 1707/8)

Reverend John White (1678–1760), minister of Gloucester (not to be confused with John White, the "Patriarch
of Dorchester"). He had a grant of land "just below the plain
on which his meeting-house stood," on which he built his
parsonage around 1704 (244 Washington Street near Centennial Avenue). "He removed from it, several years before
his death, into the house which he built and occupied during
the remainder of his life, on the lane leading to the old
burying-ground. His former dwelling was bought by James
Stevens, who kept a tavern there till 1740; when he sold
it to Capt. William Ellery, who continued it as a house
of entertainment several years" (Babson, *History*, pp. 230–
231). This house, now known as the White-Ellery House,
was moved in 1947 from its original location to the other
side of Washington Street, to make way for the construction
of Route 128.

Olson, by specifying "as of 1707/8," has in mind White's
first built house, the one sold to William Ellery, before it was
moved.

I.145. Centennial

Centennial Avenue extends from Washington Street at a
point opposite Grove Street south to Western Avenue near
the Cut.

I.145. Whittemore

Whittemore Street extends west from Washington Street
towards the marshes along the Annisquam River.

I.145. Kent's property

Thomas Kent (d. 1658), according to Babson, "had a house
and land near the burying-ground, recorded under the year
1649 . . ." (*History*, p. 110). This burying-ground was the one
located near what was Meeting House Hill.

I.145. Pearce

The early settler John Pearce (d. 1695), who "had land on the narrow projection, between Mill River and Annisquam River, which was formerly called 'Pearce's point' " (Babson, *History*, p. 125).

I.145. 70 / paces / hill falls . . .

This maps the area known formerly as Meeting House Hill, approximately where the Route 128 traffic circle now is, site of the early settlers' second and subsequent meeting-houses. The string of O's in this section is the printer's approximation of what in the original manuscript and first published version of the poem, was drawn more clearly to represent the "old stonewall."

I.145. Babson / house

Located at 245 Washington Street, southwest of the Route 128 traffic circle; it was built about 1740 by Joseph Allen and later acquired by Gustavus Babson. For a photograph, see R. Babson, *Actions and Reactions*, following p. 180.

I.145. Meeting House / Green

The common ground in the area of Meeting House Hill, site of Gloucester's early meeting-houses. Also called The Green. See, e.g., Copeland and Rogers, *Saga of Cape Ann*, pp. 19–20, 25–26.

I.145. Bruen

Obadiah Bruen. See the notice of him in J. Babson, *History*, pp. 65–66:

> He came to Plymouth with Rev. Richard Blynman . . . As nearly as can be ascertained, his residence in Gloucester was on the south-west side of the Meeting-house Green. . . . He sold all his possessions here in September, 1650, and went to New London, of which place he was

the recorder many years. . . . In company with about fifty families from Connecticut, he emigrated to Newark, N.J.; which place he bought of the Indians in 1667, and where it was the purpose of the settlers, as they declared, to establish a church and commonwealth . . .

There is a notice of him also in Caulkins, *History of New London*, pp. 155–156.

I.145. Eveleth

Sylvester Eveleth (d. 1689). See *Maximus* I, 147 and note.

I.145. Marsh St

North of what was Meeting House Hill, intersecting Washington Street.

I.145. Perkins

William Perkins (1607–1682), minister of Gloucester after Richard Blynman (q.v.). In his notice of Perkins, Babson writes: "He settled in Gloucester in 1650. In September of that year, ten acres of land at the head of Mr. Blynman's lot, called the Plains, were granted to him. . . . He also had the marsh reserved for teaching elders, and bought of Obadiah Bruen 'all that was his right in Gloucester. . . .' He remained in Gloucester till 1655; when he sold his houses and land here to Thomas Millett, sen., and removed to Topsfield, where he died May 21, 1682" (*History*, pp. 193–194).

See also mention of his property in note to Sylvester Eveleth, *Maximus* I, 147.

I.145. Millett

Thomas Millet or Millett (d. 1676) and his son Thomas (1633–1707). Babson reports, *History*, p. 116: "In 1655, Millet bought of William Perkins, who had been a teaching elder in the church here a few years, all the property the latter owned in the town. . . . His oldest son Thomas, born in 1633, had land of his father, lying near the old Meeting-house Plain in 1655."

I.145. Ellery

William Ellery (1694–1771) who bought the Rev. John White's house. See Copeland and Rogers, *Saga of Cape Ann*, p. 26: "The only landmark at The Green itself which still survives is the old Ellery House. It formerly was located on the south side of The Green, but when traffic Route 128 was constructed in 1953 the old house was moved to the other side of Washington Street, north of the traffic circle, where it still stands."

There is a notice of Ellery in Babson, *History*, p. 84.

I.145. Bruen . . . had already shifted from Piscataqua to Plymouth . . .

Not in Babson or any of the Gloucester historians. Entries in a notebook designated "I April, 1959" among Olson's papers, indicate his source is a document in the Massachusetts State Archives (Vol. 3, document 441a), concerning the sale of property at the Piscataqua settlement in Maine: "The Document of Thomas Larkham Pastor of the church of Northam on Piscataquack which he had of Obadiah Bruen 'of Cape Anne Alias Glocester' which had been granted sold assigned & sett over to the said Obadiah 'Bruen' by Richard Persivall 'now or heretofore of Shousbury(?) in old England' by a writing dated the 22nd of October 1635 . . . & Bruen had sold Larkham May 4th 1640. . . ." Olson adds: "*BRUEN*, then, was a previous plantation man at another fishing station, Quack, from *1635* to *1640!* And was of Cape Anne by or before date this document, September 13th, 1642. Thus Plymouth only after *May 4th, 1640*." That Bruen went to New London and then to Newark, however, is from Babson (see note on Bruen above).

I.146. hauling / marsh grass by gundalows possibly old Venetian

See T. Babson, "Evolution of Cape Ann Roads and Transportation," p. 314: "Flatboats called gundalows (a corruption of gondola) were used extensively in New England's tidal rivers for many years, especially for bringing salt hay from the marshes." See also Copeland and Rogers, *Saga of Cape Ann,* p. 233, and Taylor, "The Piscataqua River Gundalow."

I.146. Stefansson

Vilhjalmur Stefansson (1879–1962), arctic explorer. See his theory of the progressive northward movement of the centers of civilization as set forth in his *Northward Course of Empire*; also note to "novo / siberskie slovo," *Maximus* I, 151.

I.146. it isn't 67 years yet that the First Parish (Unitarian) preach- / er of the anniversary sermon . . .

See the sermon delivered by the Rev. Daniel M. Wilson on 21 August 1892 at ceremonies commemorating the 250th anniversary of the incorporation of Gloucester, in *Memorial of the Celebration of the Two Hundred and Fiftieth Anniversary.* The sermon begins, p. 38:

> In any account of the institutions of Gloucester we must reckon with the influences of the great sea. The salt breath of it, the mystery and power of it, and the sadness of it have interfused themselves with the life of the people and are potently with us in the celebrations of this day and week. We can no more exclude the sea from our thought than we can from our sight when we walk the ways of this town. . . . Then, also, with the wealth of the sea the prosperity of the town has ebbed and flowed. The Lord, in this matter, took a hand, as Minister Chandler firmly believed. "The scaly herds and finny tribes, moved by God's guidance," he wrote, "come voluntarily to the hooks and are drawn from their native element." This is a comforting assurance to the tender-hearted residents of this place who may be troubled at

the thought their support is at the expense of the suffering of the lower creatures. . . .

On p. 42 of the sermon, he speaks about Meeting House Hill,
Meeting House Green, and Meeting House Plain.

I.146. Zebulon

Rev. Wilson's anniversary sermon began with a quotation
from Genesis, XLIX. 13: "Zebulon shall dwell at the haven
of the sea; and he shall be for a haven of ships . . ."
(*Memorial of the 250th Anniversary*, p. 38).

I.146. John Trask Orator dedicated his address . . .

The Rev. John L. R. Trask of Springfield, Mass., gave an
address at the anniversary celebration, entitled "The Gloucester of Yesterday and the Gloucester of To-morrow." See
Memorial of the 250th Anniversary, p. 103:

> This Address Is Dedicated
> to the
> Memory of My Father and Mother
> who were born and married in Gloucester,
> and whose ashes rest in the sacred dust of the dear
> and venerable town.

I.146. his text Chapter XX the, Wonder-working Prov- / idence . . .

From Trask's address, as it appears in *Memorial of the 250th
Anniversary*, p. 113:

> In Chapter XX. of "Wonder-Working Providence,"
> Mr. Edward Johnson, the author, gives the following
> quaint and graphic account of the settlement whose years
> of eventful history we commemorate this day. The chapter
> is headed thus: "Of the planting of the one and twentieth
> church of Christ at a town called Glocester." "There was
> another town and church of Christ erected in the Massa-
> chusetts Government upon the Northern Cape of the Bay,
> called Cape Ann, a place of fishing, being peopled with

Fishermen till the reverend Mr. Richard Blindman came from a place in Plemouth Patten called Green Harbour with some few people of his acquaintance and settled down with them, named the town Glocester, and gathered into a Church, being but a small number, about fifty known. They called to office this godly reverend man whose gifts and abilities to handle the word is not inferior to many others, labouring much against the errors of the times, of a sweet humble heavenly carriage; this town lying out toward the point of the Cape, the access there unto by land becomes uneasy, which was the cause why it was no more populated; their fishing trade would be very beneficial had they men of Estates to manage it, yet are they not without other means of maintenance having good timber for shipping and a very sufficient builder, but that these times of combustion the seas throughout hath hindered much that work, yet there have been vessels built here at the town of late. . . ."

I.147. Stevens

William Stevens, the ship's carpenter mentioned on *Maximus* I, 31 as "the first Maximus." Babson, likewise, identifies Stevens as the "very sufficient builder" from Johnson's *Wonder-Working Providence* (*History*, pp. 165–166 and 188). See note to *Maximus* I, 30, and Stevens' frequent appearances later in the poems.

I.147. Peoples of the Sea

Name given invaders of Egypt during the latter half of the second millennium B.C., part of a great migration of peoples in the eastern Mediterranean at the time. They were defeated by Meneptha or Merneptah (see note to *Maximus* I, 55) around 1230 B.C. Bérard identifies them as including the Greeks: "The Achaeans are mentioned for the first time in the inscriptions which celebrate the victories of the Pharoah Minephta (1234–1224) over barbarians of the North, whom the Pharoahs styled the 'Peoples of the Sea' " (*Did Homer Live?*, p. 38).

I.147. Kadesh

Ancient city on the river Orontes in Lebanon. Egyptian forces under Ramses II fought the Hittites there in 1288 B.C.

I.147. Ramses II

(1304–1237 B.C.), Egyptian pharoah of the XIXth Dynasty.

I.147. these Englishmen . . . Bristol Z. Hill Wm Barnes Gloucester . . . Holgrave, Dorset.

List of names of early settlers of Gloucester with the places of their residence before emigrating to New England. The full names are: Zebulon Hill, William Barnes, William Addes, Christopher Avery, Jeffrey Parsons, William Southmead, Osman Dutch, William Stevens, Thomas Millet, and John Holgrave; while the locations given are almost all towns or counties in southwestern England, the West Country. Entries in a notebook identified by the poet as "III: real *goods*," make it possible to locate Olson's sources for this information. For all the names except John Holgrave, Banks' *Topographical Dictionary of 2885 English Emigrants* was used; that Holgrave was from Dorset is from Banks' *Planters of the Commonwealth*, appendix.

I.147. Sylvester / Eveleth Eveleigh Yeverleigh . . .

From Babson, *History*, p. 91:

> Sylvester Eveleth—or Everleigh, as he himself wrote it, and which agrees with the present English orthography—may have come from the county of Devonshire, England, where the name existed about the time of the settlement of New England. The name is said to have been anciently spelled Yeverleigh, and to have belonged to an estate, which, at an early period, was in the family of Clifford before it was adopted as a family cognomen. This settler had recorded to him in Gloucester, under date of December, 1648, "twelve acres of swamp and upland on the north side of the Millpond." Immediately following

this record, mention is made of "his house, on the Meeting-house Hill, having Capt. Perkins's lot on one side, and the highway on the other." He was a selectman in 1648, a freeman in 1652, and a representative in 1673. . . .

I.147. Millett sold to Allen

Joseph Allen (ca. 1653–1724). In a notebook, "I April, 1959," Olson discovers from the Gloucester town records: "1723, Thomas Millett sold to Joseph Allen for 481£, on the westerly side of the Meeting House Green." Babson only reports that "Joseph Allen came to Gloucester in 1674. He was a blacksmith, and was encouraged to settle here by an immediate grant of land and a common right. In 1675, he bought of James Davis, sen., a house and land near the Meeting-house" (*History*, p. 55).

I.147. Meeting House Hill

See notes to *Maximus* I, 145, "70 / paces . . ." and "Meeting House / Green." Although the extension of Route 128 from Boston had been formally opened the previous December, at the time of the writing of the poem construction and landscaping was continuing at the traffic circle which marks approximately the old Green today.

I.148. uroboros

Symbol of the perfect whole, "the circular snake, the primal dragon of the beginning that bites its own tail . . ." (Neumann, *Origins and History of Consciousness*, p. 10).

I.148. Zen arch- / er

See, e.g., the description in Herrigel, *Zen in the Art of Archery*, pp. 36–37:

> . . . the bow is held up with arms at nearly full stretch, so that the archer's hands are somewhere above his head.

> Consequently, the only thing he can do is to pull them evenly apart to left and right, and the further apart they get the more they curve downwards, until the left hand, which holds the bow, comes to rest at eye level with the arms outstretched, while the right hand, which draws the string, is held with the arm bent above the right shoulder, so that the tip of the three-foot arrow sticks out a little beyond the outer edge of the bow—so great is the span.

While on p. 35 of the book it is explained, "When drawn to its full extent, the bow encloses the 'All' in itself"—like the uroboros.

I.148. Frances / Rose-Troup

(b. 1859), English historian, author of several studies dealing with the early history of New England, especially *John White, the Patriarch of Dorchester and the Founder of Massachusetts* (1930), which offers fresh material on the Dorchester Company's efforts to settle at Cape Ann.

I.148. Weymouth Port Book/ No. 873

See note to *Maximus* I, 117.

I.148. 128

State highway Route 128.

I.148. Riverdale / Park

Between Washington Street and Mill River, immediately north of Route 128 and Meeting House Hill; site of a housing development.

I.149. the smell / as the minister said . . .

See the Rev. Wilson's sermon quoted in note to *Maximus* I, 146.

I.149. the rubbish / of creation

Cf. Herman Melville in *Journal Up the Straits,* quoted in *Call Me Ishmael,* p. 98:

Barrenness of Judea

Whitish mildew pervading whole tracts
of landscape . . . bones of rocks,—
crunched, knawed, & mumbled—mere refuse
& rubbish of creation . . .

I.150. the ludicrous reference to Wm Hubbard by the / tercentennary preacher . . .

The reference in the Rev. Wilson's sermon is actually to "Mister Chandler"—the Rev. Samuel Chandler, an early minister of Gloucester—not to the Rev. William Hubbard, the historian. Moreover, Wilson actually spoke at Gloucester's 250th anniversary ceremonies, and is not, therefore, a "tercentennary" preacher; his sermon was, however, also printed in Pringle, *Book of the Three Hundredth Anniversary,* giving rise to Olson's error.

I.150. Five Pound Island

Island in Gloucester's Inner Harbor near the head of the harbor, now covered by the State Fish Pier. Like Ten Pound Island, it is said to have gotten its name from the price paid by the early settlers to the Indians.

I.150. State Pier

The State Fish Pier, over one thousand feet long with a four-story cold storage building and processing plant. It extends from the mainland at the head of Gloucester's Inner Harbor into the harbor to and including what was formerly Five Pound Island.

I.150. A. Piatt Andrew

The A. Piatt Andrew Bridge carrying Route 128 over the Annisquam River; named for the congressman Abram Piatt Andrew, Jr. (1873–1936), representative from Massachusetts from 1921 to 1936. It was built in 1950.

I.150. Samuel Hodgkins

(b. 1658), an early settler. He was given authorization by the town in 1694 to conduct a ferry between the east bank of the Annisquam River to its west bank at what is now Rust Island. See T. Babson, "Evolution of Cape Ann Roads and Transportation," p. 308:

> Hodgkins was required to keep a good canoe to carry over single persons and a boat that would carry two horses at a time in bad weather and three in good; fare, one penny per person, two-pence for a horse. The town fathers considered a bridge over the river at this point in 1759, but decided it was not feasible. Meanwhile the Hodgkins family conducted the ferry for over a century. Now we have the bridge,—which ought to have been named for the Hodgkins ferry.

See also J. Babson, *History*, pp. 215–216, and Copeland and Rogers, *Saga of Cape Ann*, p. 183.

I.150. the fathometer / was invented here

Olson has among his papers a clipping from the *Gloucester Daily Times*, undated: "That the first fathometer was invented and patented by Herbert Grove Dorsey, a Gloucester man with the U.S. Coast and Geodetic Survey. He received the patent for his invention on April 24, 1928."
See also *Muthologos*, I, 190.

I.150. Orontes

River in western Syria, running into the Mediterranean north of Tyre. Kadesh was located nearby, as was Mount

Casius, site of Zeus' battle with Typhon (the river itself was also known as Typhon by the ancients).

I.150. Typhon

A monster of Greek mythology, child of Earth and Tartaros. He fought and disabled Zeus, imprisoning him in the Corycian Cave, but was defeated in turn after Zeus' rescue. The final battle took place on Mount Casius at the mouth of the river Orontes. See *Maximus* II, 94 and 95, and III, 49, and respectives notes.

I.150. Cashes

Cashes Ledge (see *Maximus* I, 77 and note), but see also notes to *Maximus* II, 7 and 94 for the pun with Mount Casius (more clearly seen if pronounced "Cashes").

I.150. "but that these times of combustion . . .

See Edward Johnson quoted above in Trask's sermon, note to *Maximus* I, 146.

I.151. Mr. Edward Johnson

(1598–1672), came to New England in 1630. He is the author of *The Wonder-Working Providence of Sion's Saviour in New England* (1653/4), quoted in Trask's sermon.

I.151. the Boulevard

Stacey Boulevard or Esplanade along Western Avenue east of the Cut, overlooking Pavilion Beach and Gloucester's Western Harbor.

I.151. R.O.T.C.

Reserve Officers' Training Corps, a military training program for college and high school students, in effect at Gloucester High School at the time.

I.151. Pytheas's sludge

See note to *Maximus* I, 62.

I.151. novo / siberskie slovo

Novo-Sibirskiye Ostrova, the New Siberian Islands, an archipelago in the Arctic Ocean, part of the Soviet Union. There is an early version of the poem among the poet's papers in which occurs:

> . . . as Steffansson couldn't
> stomach the dead end of his own prop-
> osition, in the ice
>
> of Barents or is it Chuckchee Sea   Novoy Sibirski Ostrov?

See also *Maximus* III, 37:

> the waters
> of the Atlantic
> lap the shore, the history
>
> of the nation rushing to melt
> in the Mongolian ice, to arrive
> at Frances Rose-Troup Land, novoye
>
> Sibersky
> slovo . . .

I.151. Canton

Port of southeastern China. For the importance of the Canton market in the late eighteenth and early nineteenth centuries, see Morison, *Maritime History of Massachusetts*, pp. 44ff., 64ff.

I.151. Surinam

See note to *Maximus* I, 110.

I.151. she said Richard / Bushrod George Way . . .

See Rose-Troup, *John White*, pp. 92–93: "It was to further this undertaking [a plan for a second attempt to found a settlement at Cape Ann] that, in 1627, White started a joint adventure with Richard Bushrod, Gilbert Loder, William Derby, Bernard Troup, George Way. . . ."

For Bushrod, see also note to *Maximus* I, 109; George Way (d. 1641?) was a glover from Dorchester, Eng.

I.151. Conant said Budleigh

See Roger Conant's petition to the General Court (1671) in Phippen, "The 'Old Planters' of Salem," p. 146:

> . . . Now my umble sute and request is vnto this honorabel Court onlie that the name of our towne or plantation may be altred or changed from Beuerly and be called Budleigh. I haue two reasons that haue moued me vnto this request. The first is the great dislike and discontent of many of our people for this name of Beuerly, because (wee being but a smale place) it hath caused on vs a constant nickname of beggarly, being in the mouths of many . . . Secondly, I being the first that had house in Salem (and neuer had any hand in naming either that or any other towne) and myself with those that were then with me, being all from the western part of England, desire this western name of Budleigh, a market towne in Deuonsheer and neere vnto the sea as we are heere in this place, and where myself was borne. . . .

I.151. she said so much train oil . . .

See also *Maximus* I, 117 and note.

I.151. some even entered as 'coats' . . .

See Rose-Troup, *John White*, p. 68n: "Some of the furs are entered [in the Weymouth Port Books] as skins, the others as 'coats', presumably the latter were bought from the Indians who had made them up for their own wear."

I.151. Freshwater Cove

See note to *Maximus* I, 10.

I.151. Tolmans field

Near Tolman Avenue, north of Cressy's Beach between Western and Hough Avenues, Gloucester.

I.151. the old Steep Bank where Kent Circle . . .

See T. Babson, "Evolution of Cape Ann Roads," p. 311: "There was formerly a small hill just west of the canal's exit about where Kent Circle now is, and the road going toward Salem passed in back of it. It was necessary to go a few hundred feet up Essex Avenue to make the circuit. I have the year 1868 as that in which this obstruction was levelled, although further improvements seem to have been made in this area around 1892. We can guess that it may have been composed in part of material excavated from the canal."

Kent Circle is located at the intersection of Essex Avenue with Western Avenue.

I.151. Apple Row

Old road along the orchards of the higher ground above Essex Avenue, beyond the marshes of the western side of the Annisquam; approximately present Bond Street.

I.151. Agamenticus Height

On the west side of the Annisquam, overlooking the marshes and mud flats of the river, and north of Bond Street or Apple Row, opposite what was Meeting House Hill.

I.151. the river and marshes show clearly . . .

On the map of Gloucester harbor, or *le Beau Port*, drawn by Samuel de Champlain in 1606. See the map in Pringle, *Book of the Three Hundredth Anniversary*, opposite p. 36, with the following explanation printed below it: "Place where our barque was . . . Troop of savages coming to surprise us . . . Sieur de Poutrincourt in ambuscade with some seven or eight arquebusiers . . . Sieur de Champlain discovering the savages . . ." Also in *Fishermen's Own Book,* pp. 8–9. Both are annotated in Olson's copies.

The pattern of figures with which the poem ends—denoting the depth of the harbor, probably in fathoms—is from this map.

I.151. the Beach

The beach along Gloucester's Western Harbor; specifically, Pavilion Beach, northwest of Fort Point.

I.151. Harbor Cove

On the western side of the Inner Harbor, next to Fort Point; at its head was the Town Landing.

I.151. "Washington" St

The early road, since named Washington Street, which linked what was in 1642 (see *Maximus* I, 156 and note) the center of town—the Green where the meetinghouse was built—and the harbor area. Washington Street today extends from the beginning of Main Street (near the Town Landing, head of Harbor Cove) to the Route 128 traffic circle (fomerly Meeting House Green), and beyond there, crossing Mill River, to communities on the other side of Cape Ann along Ipswich Bay.

I.151. Mill River

Tidal inlet of the Annisquam River reaching just north of Meeting House Hill and crossed by the present Washington Street.

I.151. Fore Street

Also Front, now Main Street.

I.151. Vinsons Cove

Also Vincent's Cove. On the west side of the inner harbor, near Vincent Street; named for William Vinson (ca. 1610–1690), who had property on that location.

I.151. East Gloucester Square

East Main Street and Highland Street, east of Rocky Neck.

I.151. Sieur de Poutrin- / court

Jean de Biencourt, Sieur de Poutrincourt (ca. 1557–1615), visited North America in 1604 and returned in 1606 to serve as lieutenant-governor of Port Royal, Acadia (now Annapolis Basin, Nova Scotia). He accompanied Champlain on a brief exploration of the coast south of Port Royal that last year.

I.151. Rocky Neck

Peninsula on the eastern shore of Gloucester Harbor opposite Fort Point and Harbor Cove.

▶ I.152. Maximus, to Gloucester, Sunday, July 19

Written 19 July 1959, at Gloucester. The poem concerns an annual memorial procession and ceremony for Gloucester fishermen lost at sea. See, e.g., the account in Copeland and Rogers, *Saga of Cape Ann*, p. 180: "While the Cut is primarily a travel convenience, it also has become the scene of a ceremony of simple beauty and great significance. Each year, on a Sunday afternoon in August, relatives and friends of the fishermen gather at the Cut to throw bouquets of flowers on the outgoing tide, in memory of those who have been lost in ocean tragedies. The flowers are carried out to sea by the tide and thus are spread over that one big grave." A service was held the day of the poem, which the poet apparently attended, for there is a program of the ceremony for that date preserved among his papers.

I.152. they stopped before that bad sculpture of a fisherman . . .

The Fishermen's Memorial, a statue in the heroic manner, of a fisherman crouched at the helm, on the Stacey Esplanade just east of the Cut, erected by the people of Gloucester in 1923; site of the annual ceremony.

I.152. "as if one were to talk to a man's house . . .

From Heraclitus, fragment 126, Burnet trans. (in Auden, *Portable Greek Reader*, p. 77): "And they pray to these images, as if one were to talk with a man's house, knowing not what gods or heroes are."

I.152. the Bridge

The Blynman Bridge over the Cut. See *Maximus* I, 85 and note.

I.152. Charybdises

Charybdis, a whirlpool off the Sicilian coast, described in the *Odyssey*, Book XII. It was opposite Scylla (see *Maximus* I, 85 and note).

I.153. the transformations of fire are, first of all, sea . . .

From Heraclitus, fragment 21, Burnet trans. (in Auden, *Portable Greek Reader*, p. 71): "The transformations of Fire are, first of all, sea . . ."

I.153. "as gold for wares wares for gold"

Heraclitus, fragment 22, Burnet trans. (in Auden, *Portable Greek Reader*, p. 71): "All things are an exchange for Fire, and Fire for all things, even as wares for gold and gold for wares."

I.153. a successful man . . . a famous man . . . a man of power, these are the damned by God

See *The Wisdom of Laotse*, p. 317: ". . . a successful man cannot give another person his salary, a famous man cannot donate his fame to others, and a man in a high position cannot give his power to another. Holding that power, a man is frightened when he has it and worried lest he should lose it. And these people go on forever without ever stopping to see what it is all about. These are the damned by God." Written on endpapers in Olson's copy of Laotse are two passages from the present poem, indicating the volume was on his table, in use, when the poem was being composed.

I.153. Yellowstone Park

Yellowstone National Park in northwestern Wyoming, Idaho and Montana; volcanic in origin, with geysers and boiling springs.

I.153. Jim Bridger

(1804–1881), fur trader, frontiersman, scout. He was the first white man, as far as is known, to visit the Great Salt Lake in Utah, in the fall of 1824.

I.154. Men are so sure they know very many things . . .

Heraclitus, fragment 35, Burnet trans. (in Auden, *Portable Greek Reader*, p. 72): "Hesiod is most men's teacher. Men think he knew very many things, a man who did not know day or night! They are one."

I.154. it is said, / 'You rectify what can be rectified,' . . .

The source is Chuangtse's "Imaginary Conversations Between Laotse and Confucius," in *The Wisdom of Laotse*, pp. 317–318, continuing from the section quoted above: "Resentment, favor, give, take, censure, advice, life and

death—these eight are means for correcting a man's character, but only one who comprehends the great process of this
fluid universe without being submerged in it knows how to
handle them. Therefore, it is said, 'You rectify what can be
rectified.' When a man's heart cannot see this, the door of his
divine intelligence is shut."

▶I.155. April Today Main Street

Written 27 April 1959 at Gloucester (dated in notebook
among the poet's papers).

I.155. Duncan

Duncan Street; runs southeast from Main Street towards
Duncan's Point and the harbor.

I.155. Joe, / the barber

Joseph S. Lacerda, owner of a barber shop formerly on
Duncan Street near Main, which earlier had belonged to the
Frederickson brothers.

I.155. the Fredericksons' / shop

The Frederickson Brothers barber shop formerly on Duncan Street, owned by Adolph and Harold Frederickson.

I.155. Mrs Galler

Mrs. Geller, owner of the Sterling Drug Store, Main
Street, corner of Pleasant.

I.155. Weiners

Gordon M. Weiner, proprietor of Sterling Drug Store
(listed as such on a sign above the door, which suggests how
the topic may have come up in the poet's conversation with
the "cigar woman" and "greeting card clerk").

I.155. Vinson's Cove

See note to *Maximus* I, 151.

I.156. Sao Paolo

Sao Paulo, city in southeastern Brazil near the coast.

I.156. the spring

Vinson's Spring, named, like Vinson's Cove, for the early settler. Babson reports (*History*, p. 174) that this Vinson or Vincent owned several lots of land, and "on one of which, probably, was the spring that perpetuates his name." The spring was near the harbor, for records reported elsewhere by Babson speak of "Spring Cove, alias Vinson's" (*Notes and Additions*, I, 18), while Dexter reports that an early map of Gloucester "uses the name Spring Cove for what is now called Vincent's Cove," and that on other maps, "the present Main Street is labelled Spring Street" ("Relationship of Natural Features to Place Names," pp. 146—147). An adtisement in the front of Pringle's 1892 *History of Gloucester* for the Vincent Spring Pharmacy at 266 Main Street places it "directly over the site of the original Vincent Spring."

I.156. Eveleth / was a baker in Boston . . .

Sylvester Eveleth (see note to *Maximus* I, 146). See Babson, *Notes and Additions*, I, 25: "He was the only emigrant to New England of this name, and appears first, according to Mr. Savage, as a baker at Boston in 1642." The information is also in Baxter, *Trelawny Papers*, p. 351n.

I.156. the General Court: / what Endecott / and Downing / divided, April that year . . .

See Babson, *History*, pp. 50—51: "At a General Court, October, 1641, commissioners were appointed to view and settle the bounds of Ipswich, Cape Ann, and Jeffries' Creek (now Manchester); and the Deputy-governor (Mr. Endicott), and Messrs. Downing and Hathorne, deputies from Salem, or any two of them, were appointed to dispose of all lands and other things at Cape Ann. Pursuant to this authority, as the town-records declare, 'the first ordering, settling, and disposing of lots, was made by Mr. Endicott and Mr. Downing, commissioners, 2d month, 1642.' "

The General Court, the legislative assembly of the Massachusetts Bay Colony, met at Salem; John Endecott was Deputy Governor at the time, and Emanuel Downing, brother-in-law of John Winthrop, was a deputy from Salem.

April was the second month according to the calendar in use at the time, thus "2 mo 42."

I.156. Duncan's Point

Projection on the western side of Gloucester's inner harbor, near Fort Point and Harbor Cove, and opposite Rocky Neck. Named for Peter Duncan (ca. 1630–1716) who bought land there in 1662. For the fishing stage on Duncan's Point, see Babson quoted in a note to *Maximus* I, 158.

I.156. stating / it was Mr Thomson's . . .

See the record of the General Court for 22 May 1639 in Shurtleff, *Records of the Governor and Company of the Massachusetts Bay*, I, 256: "For encouragement of Mr Morrice Tomson, marchant, & others, who intend to pmote the fishing trade . . ." Quoted also in Babson, *History*, p. 49.

I.157. the staple intended / said Smith

See his *Description of New England* in *Travels and Works*, I, 194: "The maine Staple, from hence to bee extracted for the present to produce the rest, is fish . . ."

I.157. the silver ore / codfish

See "mines John Smith called these are her silver / streames," *Maximus* I, 109 and note.

I.157. "It was ordered . . . that a fishing / be begun . . .

Continued from the entry for 22 May 1639 in Shurtleff, *Records of the Massachusetts Bay*, I, 256: "It is ordered, that a fishing plantation shalbee begun at Cape Anne, & that the said Mr Tompson shall have place assigned for building of houses, & stages, & other necessaries for that vse, & shall have sufficient land alowed for their occations, both for their fishing, & for keepeing of cattle, & for corne . . ." Also in Babson, *History*, p. 49.

I.157. that the Scotch border / had been crossed December / 1640 . . .

See entry for that date in *Winthrop's Journal*, II, 19: "About the end of this month, a fishing ship arrived at Isle of Shoals, and another soon after, and there came no more this season for fishing. They brought us news of the Scots entering into England, and the calling of a parliament, and the hope of a thorough reformation, etc., whereupon some among us began to think of returning back to England." Winthrop writes in June 1641 of the effect of the English Civil War on the settlement in New England (*Journal*, II, 31): how it "caused all men to stay in England in expectation of a new world, so as few are coming to us, all foreign commodities grow scarce, and our own of no price. . . . These straits set our people on work to provide fish, clapboards, plank, etc."

See also "Isle Shoals," note to *Maximus* I, 109.

I.158. Osmund Dutch

Or Osman Dutch (ca. 1603–1684), resided on the easterly part of Gloucester Harbor. See the notice of him in Babson, *History*, p. 83; also, *Maximus* II, 60–61, and III, 65.

I.158. William / Southmead

See the notice of him in Babson, *History*, pp. 162–163: "William Southmeade was one of the early settlers, and had a grant of the lot on which Mr. Thompson's frame stood. . . . The death of our settler is not recorded; but it occurred before 1649, when an inventory of his goods and chattels was made by Christopher Avery and William Addes. The augurs, tools, and other instruments, mentioned in the inventory, authorize the conjecture that he was a ship-carpenter. His widow married William Ash, and probably left town with him about 1651."

I.158. Thomas Millward

(ca. 1600−1653), an early settler. See the notice in Babson, *History*, p. 118: "Thomas Milward, a fisherman, was one of the selectmen in 1642. No grants of land are recorded to him; though he sold, as early as May, 1642, two acres in the Harbor to Robert Elwell. He removed to Newbury, where he resided in 1652, when he sold his farm at Fresh-water Cove to Samuel Dolliver of Marblehead. He died in Boston, Sept. 1, 1653."

I.158. Newbury

Massachusetts town some twenty miles northwest of Gloucester near the mouth of the Merrimack River.

I.158. There is evidence / a frame / of Mr Thomson's / did / exist . . .

See Babson, *History*, p. 50: "Our town-records, under date of 4th month, 1650, say, 'Will Southmead hath given him that psell of land in the harbour upon which Mr. Tomson's frame stood;' 'provided, yet if Mr. Tomson or his agent shall demand it, that then, upon compensation for the charges about it, this said grant is to be surrendered up.'" On p. 569, Babson writes, "Standing on the spot where Mr. Thomson set up the frame for his fishing, the beholder finds himself in the centre of a seat of the fishing business, which, for activity, enterprise, and extent, has no equal on this continent, and perhaps is not surpassed by any in the world." In a note he adds, "This spot, it seems, must have been

Duncan's Point. It was granted to William Southmeade; and went, with his widow, to William Ash, who sold it in 1651 to John Jackson; from whom it passed, in 1662, to Peter Duncan."

Evidence on pp. 27 and 39 of a notebook among the poet's papers, "II May, 1959 (2nd Such Book / Gloucester Sources, started: May 15, 1959," indicates Olson directly consulted the town records in addition to Babson, though this would have been after the present poem was composed. The legal language in the poem ("ux," Latin for 'wife,' and "alia," a spelling of *alias*, 'other' or 'also known as'—referring to the wife of William Southmeade who later married William Ash) is to be found in the original records of the town. Indeed, an earlier notebook, "I April, 1959," reveals Olson took notice, in time for this poem, of "goodwife Southmate alia Ash" (p. 1).

I.159. "Me Osmundū Douch . . .

Entry in *Note-Book Kept by Thomas Lechford, Lawyer*, p. 114: "Me Osmondū Douch De Capae Annae in nova Anglia, nautā tener' et firmit^r obligar' Will^o Hooke mercatori in 40^{ti}, Dat' 18.5.1639, coram Tho: Milward & meipo.

Condičoned for the payment of 20^{ti} to Mr Hooke at Mr Maverick's house in Nodill's Island 17 Julij.p^{r}x^o. [1s.6d.]"

I.159. Grace, / my love . . .

Letter of Osmund Dutch to his wife, as recorded in the *Note-Book Kept by Thomas Lechford*, pp. 112–113:

> Good wife, my love remembered to you in the Lord, These are to lett you understand that God be praysed I am well in health heere in this Country at the time of the writing this letter, and so I hope are you in health together with our Children. Seing it hath pleased God to blesse me heere in this land since I came last, I thanke God, I have cleared 40 £ and shall be able to make good provision for to intertaine you & my children, as I hope in the Lord. Therefore I desire you would by all meanes come over to me wth the children by the f[all] or as soone as you can the next spring . . . And if you want any thing more to come

forth, or to make yor better provision, then I shall take order wth my partner Mr Millard of Noddill's Island, who is my partner in the fishing trade wch we now are setting upon . . .

Noddle's Island is now East Boston.

I.160. 1641: Abraham Robinson / Thomas Ashley Willm / Browne . . .

From entry in Lechford's *Note-Book*, pp. 406–407: "Joseph Armitage of Lynne lets a shallop of 3 tunnes or thereabouts unto Abraham Robinson Thomas Ashley & Willm Browne of Cape Anne fishermen until 29.7.px with the tackling & appurtenences & they are to pay 3£ in money or good & merchantable dry fish to the said Joseph at the end of the said terme therefore & redeliver the said shallop wth the same appurtenences at Lynne."

I.160. a Biskie shallop

From Biscay; a Basque vessel or style of vessel, as it appears in accounts of the early explorers and settlers of the North Atlantic coast. See note to *Maximus* I, 62 on the Basques. Olson has underlined the phrase in Gabriel Archer's report of Gosnold's voyage in his copy of Lever-more, *Forerunners*, I, 44.

I.160. Biskie Island

Now known as Rust Island, on the west side of the Annisquam River. Tradition does not explain its earlier designation.

I.160. 128 bridge

Bridge on route 128 over the Annisquam River at Rust Island; officially, the A. Piatt Andrew Memorial Bridge (see *Maximus* I, 150 and note).

This poem would almost seem to have been written in reaction to the following remark by Thomas Babson which

concludes his "Evolution of Cape Ann Roads" (p. 328):
"But today's big story for the Cape is that it has at last been
joined to the continent by Route #128. The great hope is
that it will help to bring in new industry to supplement the
fisheries." (A note in Olson's copy, however, indicates that he
had been reading the essay on 2 June 1960, after the poem
was written.) The extent of Olson's distrust and bitter feelings at the time are evident in a fragment on the back of an
envelope postmarked 2 December 1959: "Agh Gloucester /
you are ugly / your streets are / your buildings / your
young / you have gone / out 128 / to the nation / & you
stink / as it does . . ." And he would write in 1960, in a note
among his papers, that "128 ends Gloucester as a sea city.
After this, what is she but another part of the nation?"

Notes to
The Maximus Poems IV, V, VI, 1968
(*Maximus* II)

▶ **II.I. Letter # 41 [broken off]**

Written in March 1959; a number of early versions are preserved among the poet's papers: a rough first draft in notebook dated 18 March 1959, another version in notebook written 21 March 1959 and entitled "An Arabesque," and a longer and much revised, typed early version.

II.1. she said it was an arabesque . . .

Mrs. Mildred (Shute) Smith, a librarian at the Sawyer Library in Gloucester, whose mother owned a guest house at 28 Middle Street where Olson arranged for his own mother to stay in the winter of 1940 when the summer cottage at Stage Fort Park grew too cold. According to Mrs. Smith in an interview, June 1971, it was Olson himself, with scarf wrapped around head and hat, who would cry out "Arabesque!" and leap over the porch railing of the house, long legs flying, into the snow.

II.1. St Valentine Day's storm

See *Maximus* I, 84 and note; also *Maximus* II, 129.

II.1. She hadn't seen me / in 19 years

That is, since February 1940, the time of the St. Valentine Day's storm. In the typed earlier version among the poet's papers, the passage appears: "that wld be 19 years ago last month" (further securing March 1959 as the date of the poem).

II.1. the Orontes

See *Maximus* I, 150 and note; also *Maximus* II, 81 and note.

II.1. the East African rift

A deep double fault in the earth's crust, extending from Syria in the north (the area of the river Orontes), through the Jordan Valley and the Red Sea, down into central Africa.

II.1. like he said the volcano anyone of us does / sit upon

In conversation, June 1968, the poet suggested "an early work by Jung" was being referred to. See then Jung's *Integration of the Personality*, p. 12:

> "Normal" man convinces me, even more than the lunatic, of the powerful autonomy of the unconscious. The psychological theory of the psychoses can take refuge behind real or imaginary organic distrubances of the brain and thus invalidate the importance of the unconscious. But such a device is not applicable to normal humanity. What is actually happening in the world is due not merely to "dim remnants of formerly conscious activities," but to volcanic outbursts from the very bottom of things.

II.1. Yellowstone

Yellowstone National Park (see note to *Maximus* I, 153), where the celebrated geyser known as "Old Faithful" is located.

II.1. Where it says excessively rough moraine

A map in Shaler, *Geology of Cape Ann*, opposite p. 608, showing "Bands of excessively rocky moraine" along Commons Road, Dogtown.

II.1. The war of Africa against Eurasia . . . Gondwana

The drifting of continents according to the theories developed by Eduard Suess (1831–1914) and Alfred Wegener (1880–1930). See the cover of *Maximus IV, V, VI* and Olson's note verso title page, written September 1968. See also Wegener, *Origin of Continents and Oceans*; Wilson, "Continental Drift"; and possibly Velikovsky, *Earth in Upheaval*, pp. 89–92, where in discussing the formation of the African Rift he mentions Suess' theories (p. 90): "Suess brought to geology the now generally accepted concept of Gondwana land, a continental mass that occupied the larger portion of the Indian Ocean, and that in relatively recent subsidence was torn apart and drowned. The subsidence of the Gondwana continent could have caused a strain on western Asia and Africa, and under this tension the land must have been rent and the Great Rift formed." Olson was aware of the theory to some extent as early as 1939, from his reading of Thomas Mann's *Joseph and his Brothers*, when he wrote in a notebook (designated "#3"): " . . . refer back to that incalculable point of time when 'Lemuria' in its turn only a remnant of the old *Gondwana* continent, sank beneath the waves of Indian O."

In the earlier version among the poet's papers, the lines read:

> The war of Eurasia
> against Africa has only
> just begun. Gondwana
> has bumped her until Alps
> and Anti Taurus stuck up . . .

▶II.2. MAXIMUS, FROM DOGTOWN—I

Written 20 November 1959 (manuscript dated) after a visit to Dogtown with Michael McClure, Donald Allen and LeRoi Jones earlier ("Olson in Gloucester," *Muthologos*, I, 194). In his foreword to the first publication of the poem (1961), Michael McClure writes:

> Late November 1959, standing in Dogtown Meadow, Massachusetts with Charles Olson, he told the story of Merry the handsome sailorman. Around us in the cold rocky fields where once farms & houses stood, women, far away, bent picking ground growing evergreens for Xmas florals. Charles told me the story of the handsome stocky man—pointing to a rock & patch of ground—"Here" he said "where the bull's enclosure was . . ."

> John, or was it Andrew, Merry had a bull calf. He wrestled him on Sunday afternoons for sport & entertainment. Merry was proud of his body strength. He had a sailor's wiry stocky strength. Sunday after Sunday, before the people, as the bull calf grew, Merry wrestled him. At last the bull became large and the sailor tapered off and quit the sport. Merry, by his own mind or perhaps by what he heard or saw on the faces or tongues of the Dogtowners became disturbed. Was he, the sailorman, afraid or too

weak to continue with the bull? He made a great announcement that Dogtown people should come out on Sunday
and see him fight again. Saturday night he drank—and
thought upon Sunday's battle and thought to practice with
the bull to try his strength and test his ingenuities and
learn what he might for the spectacle. There must have
been some fear . . .

II.2. The sea was born of the earth without sweet union of love . . .

See Hesiod, *Theogony*, 11. 131 – 133 (Evelyn-White trans.,
p. 89): "[Earth] bare also the fruitless deep with his raging
swell, Pontus, without sweet union of love. But afterwards
she lay with Heaven and bare deep-swirling Oceanus . . ."

II.2. Okeanos the one which all things are and by which nothing / is anything but itself, measured so

The phrase, "nothing is anything but itself measured so,"
first occurred in a dream the night of 17 June 1958, as
recorded in a notepad from that time:

> Everything $^{issues}_{comes}$ fr the
> Black Chrysanthemum
> & nothing is anything but itself
> measured so
>
> . . . Chrysanthemum
> chrysos = gold anthemum = flower
>
> the Black Gold / the Black Sun
>   the Golden Flower etc

See also "Experience and Measurement" from 1966 and the
deathbed "Secret of the Black Chrysanthemum" in *OLSON*
3, pp. 59 and 64-74, as well as "Poetry and Truth," where
Olson gives this account: "I have the superstition that human
beings have, that when they hear something that matters to
them, it's true. . . . I once was told this, by myself, to myself,
by no body or thing that I could identify. I think I was asleep,
and it was a dream. But what got said was, 'Everything issues

from . . . , and nothing is anything but itself, measured so' "
(*Muthologos*, II, 51).

See also Heraclitus' fragment 59, Burnet trans. (in Auden,
Portable Greek Reader, p. 73): "The one is made up of all
things, and all things issue from the one."

II.2. love . . . which unnerves the limbs and by its / heat floods the mind . . .

Hesiod, *Theogony*, 11. 120−122 (Evelyn-White trans., p.
87): "Eros (Love), fairest among the deathless gods, who unnerves the limbs and overcomes the mind and wise counsels
of all gods and all men within them." Later, Olson would be
struck by what he felt to be a better translation of *lusimeles*,
the word which Hesiod uses to describe Eros—that which
'loosens the limbs' (see, e.g., "Reading at Berkeley," *Muthologos*, I, 147).

II.2. Vast earth rejoices

Hesiod, *Theogony*, 1. 173 (p. 91).

II.2. Okeanos steers all things through all things

See Heraclitus, fragment 19, Burnet trans. (in Auden,
Portable Greek Reader, p. 71): "Wisdom is one thing. It is to
know the thought by which all things are steered through all
things."

II.2. everything issues from the one

See Heraclitus, fragment 59, quoted in note to "Okeanos
the one which all things are" above.

II.2. the soul is led from drunkenness / to dryness

See Heraclitus, fragments 73−76, Burnet trans. (in Auden,
Portable Greek Reader, p. 74): "A man, when he gets drunk,
is led by a beardless lad, tripping, knowing not where he
steps, having his soul moist. . . . The dry soul is the wisest
and best."

II.2. the sleeper lights up from the dead, / the man awake lights up from the sleeping

Cf. Heraclitus, fragments 64, 77 and 78, Burnet trans. (in Auden, *Portable Greek Reader*, pp. 73–74): "All the things we see when awake are death, even as all we see in slumber are sleep. . . . Man is kindled and put out like a light in the night-time. . . . And it is the same thing in us that is quick and dead, awake and asleep, young and old; the former are shifted and become the latter, and the latter in turn are shifted and become the former." Cf. also, Ephesians 5:14: "Awake thou that sleepest, and arise from the dead . . ."; also, Maximus of Tyre: "Life is the sleep of the soul, from which it awakes at death" (*Encyclopaedia Britannica*, 11th ed., XVII, 927).

II.2. WATERED ROCK

Note, perhaps, the geological condition of Dogtown as described by Shaler, *Geology of Cape Ann*, p. 611: "The unsettled region of the great moraines, the section commonly known as 'Dogtown Commons,' contains an area of several square miles of land which at present has very little value. A thousand acres of this land in the center of the island should be reserved for water supply. This morainal matter is so permeable to water that wells of no great depth placed in the center of such a reservation would afford a sufficiency to supply all the settlements along the coast line." Two reservoirs have since been constructed on Dogtown (see note to "the new Alewife," *Maximus* I, 21, and II, 152).

II.2. Merry

James Merry (d. 1892), former sailor who fought the bull on Dogtown. Olson's source for this story is Snow, "Bullfight on Cape Ann." The story is also quickly told in Copeland and Rogers, *Saga of Cape Ann*, pp. 36–37, and first mentioned in Mann, *Heart of Cape Ann*, pp. 47–48.

It is of interest that Merry was six foot seven, exactly the same height as Olson.

II.2. Handsome Sailor

See Melville's *Billy Budd*, chapter 1: "In the time before steamships, or then more frequently than now, a stroller along the docks of any considerable sea-port would occasionally have his attention arrested by a group of bronzed mariners, man-of-war's men or merchant-sailors in holiday attire ashore on liberty. In certain instances they would flank, or, like a bodyguard quite surround some superior figure of their own class, moving along with them like Aldebaran among the lesser lights of his constellation. That signal object was the 'Handsome Sailor' of the less prosaic time alike of the military and merchant navies." Aldebaran, to which the Handsome Sailor is compared, is (significantly in terms of the poem) the eye of the constellation Taurus, the Bull; while the designation of James Merry as a Handsome Sailor is doubly appropriate, for a little later on in *Billy Budd* the Handsome Sailor is described as: "A superb figure, tossed up as by the horns of Taurus aginst the thunderous sky . . ."

II.2. "under" the dish / of earth . . .

This and much of what follows is from Neumann, *Great Mother*, pp. 221–222:

> While . . . Nut rises as vault of heaven over the earth conceived as a flat disk, the male deity Geb, she is, in her character of celestial cow, the feminine principle, identical with the primeval water and genetrix of the sun, whose rays, in conjunction with the rain-milk flowing from her breast, nourish the earth.
>
> . . . .
> To Nut as the upper vault corresponds Naunet as the lower vault, the counterheaven lying "under" the disk of the earth, the two together forming the Great Round of the feminine vessel. But Naunet, the counterheaven, through which the sun passes at night, is identical with Nut; for Nut is not only the daytime sky but also the western devourer of the sun that passes back to the east through her body, which is the upper night sky.

Thus Nut is water above and below, vault above and below, life and death, east and west, generating and killing, in one. For she is not only the lady "with the thousand souls," who "causes the stars to manifest their souls," but also the sow, who devours her own children, sun, moon, and stars in the west.

The Great Goddess is the glowing unity of subterranean and celestial primordial water, the sea of heaven on which sail the barks of the gods of light, the circular life-generating ocean above and below the earth.

II.3. down / the ice holds / Dogtown

See "The Cow / of Dogtown," *Maximus* II, 148–150 and notes.

II.3. Gee Avenue

Street in Gloucester, east from Washington Street, which becomes Commons Road running through Dogtown. Pronounced with a hard 'g.'

II.3. to whore . . . at three girls' houses

See Babson and Saville, *Tourist's Guide*, p. 38n (marked in Olson's copy):

> Molly Jacobs was quite a character, altho she seemed to have lived in various houses. According to the records, Molly Jacobs was the daughter of Isaac and Molly, having been baptized Jan. 31, 1763. She was a friend of Judy Rhines and Liz Tucker. The trio were the leading characters of Dogtown, who used to vamp the young men from the conservative families of the Cape. The First Parish records spell her name 'Moley Jakups'—She was one of a few who were responsible for the bad reputation which Dogtown once had when—in its later days—it was the 'red light' district of Cape Ann.

II.3. Pisces

The constellation; twelfth sign of the zodiac.

II.3. their boots or the horse / clashing the sedimentary / rock tortoise shell / she sits on . . .

Neumann, *Great Mother*, p. 301n: "Because she is related to the moon, for the moon feeds on the wine of the maguey . . . Mayauel often sits on a tortoise, the maternal beast of the moon and the earth, which withdraws into the darkness like the moon . . ." On p. 302, Neumann writes, "We have several times referred to the war-like figures accompanying the Great Mother, the male followers representing her destructive aspect." Also on that page, it is interesting to note in terms of the present poem, Neumann says, "It is possible that the battles of Oriental heroes and kings with wild animals belong to the same psychological sphere [of battle frenzy and the ecstasy of war]. Mastery of the beast in single combat is among the heroic deeds that accredit the king as such. . . ."

II.3. Jeremiah Millett's house

In Dogtown, on the Dogtown Road near Cherry Street, at the top of Gravel Hill (see Mann's "Map of the Town Parish Showing Dogtown Village in 1742" in his *Beginnings of Dogtown*). It is cellar no. 8 on Babson's map (*Tourist's Guide*, pp. 36–37). See also *Maximus* II, 37. Jeremiah Millet (b. 1716) was the great–grandson of Thomas Millet, one of the first settlers.

An early manuscript of the poem has "Joseph Winslow's house," indicating Olson had just begun his Dogtown investigation. Winslow lived further down that same Dogtown Road.

II.4. she is the goddess / of the earth . . .

Mayauel, Mexican goddess of the intoxicant made from the maguey, about whom Neumann writes in *Great Mother*, p. 301:

> Here again the goddess of intoxicating liquor is the Great Goddess, the Mother, goddess of the earth and the

night. It is therefore no accident that Mayauel is the earth monster, the goddess of the earth and the corn, and the night sky. As the goddess with the 'four hundred'—i.e., innumerable—breasts, she is the heavenly mother nourishing the stars who are the fish swimming in the heavenly ocean, and with whom the four hundred gods of the octli or pulque, her sons, are identical.

Pulque was forbidden to the young, and a drunkard showing himself in public was punished by death. It was taken in moderation at many festivals, but its true importance was that warriors drank it before going into battle and prisoners before being sacrificed. The magical power of the pulque was a means employed by the war goddess to make the men braver in battle, but it was also the symbol of the deadly power of the Feminine itself, in which intoxication and death are mysteriously interwoven. The Mexicans also believed that a man born under the sign of the pulque-medicine plant would be a brave warrior. . . .

II.4. in Spain / where he saw the fight

See Snow, "Bullfight on Cape Ann," p. 152: "In the year 1887 James Merry, one of the tallest and huskiest men who ever shipped out of Gloucester, sailed on a long voyage which included the Mediterranean. He went to several important bullfights while in Spain, and, with his handsome figure and great height, he rivaled the toreadors and matadors at every bullfight he visited. He never forgot the gleams of admiration from fair young señoritas nor the envious stares of the men."

II.5. the bios / of nature

Bios appears in Heraclitus' fragment 66 in a double sense: "The bow ($\beta\iota\delta\varsigma$) is called life ($\beta\iota o\varsigma$), but its work is death" (Burnet trans., in Auden, *Portable Greek Reader*, p. 73).

II.5. eternal / events

A term Whiteheadian in spirit, though not actually to be found in Whitehead's writings. Apparently derived from "eternal objects" and "event" in *Process and Reality*. See *Maximus* II, 79 and note.

II.5. shrinking solid rock

If this is an allusion to a geological theory of the contraction of the earth, it differs fundamentally from Wegener's theory of continental drift. See Wegener, *Origin of Continents and Oceans*, pp. 8-9:

> The theory first appeared in Europe. It was initiated and developed by Dana, Albert Heim and Eduard Suess in particular, and even today dominates the fundamental ideas presented in European textbooks of geology. The essence of the theory was expressed most succinctly by Suess: "The collapse of the world is what we are witnessing" . . . Just as a drying apple acquires surface wrinkles by loss of internal water, the earth is supposed to form mountains by surface folding as it cools and therefore shrinks internally.

II.5. A drunkard / showing himself in public / is punished . . .

See Neumann, quoted in note to "she is the goddess / of the earth," p. 4 above.

II.6. Then only . . .did the earth / let her robe / uncover . . .

Cf. perhaps Neumann, p. 220: "She is the goddess of Saïs, of whom Plutarch wrote: 'I am all that has been, and is, and shall be, and my robe no mortal has yet uncovered.' "

▶ II.7. ALL MY LIFE I'VE HEARD ABOUT MANY

Written 28 November 1959 (original manuscript dated). An early version is entitled "OCEAN, or the *TRAVELS* of MAXIMUS." The title is a variation of the epigraph to *The Maximus Poems*, "All my life I've heard / one makes many." There is also a possible pun on the name of the legendary ruler Manes, given the allusion identified below.

II.7. He went to Spain, / the handsome sailor . . .

Not only James Merry, another "handsome sailor," who visited the bullfights in Spain (*Maximus* II, 2 and 4, and notes), but also several of the other sailor-heroes who serve as prototypes for Maximus, including Manes (note below), Pytheus (*Maximus* I, 62; II, 81 and 92), and Herakles-Melkaart, worshipped at the Phoenician colony of Cadiz, who is himself a model for Odysseus (notes to *Maximus* I, 78 and II, 68).

II.7. he went to Ireland / and died of a bee . . .

Manes or Menes, the traditional founder of the First Dynasty of Egypt. In his bibliography to *Mayan Letters*, Olson includes L.A. Waddell, "who was sure that the Sumerians or the Hittites or the Trojans founded the British Hempire, and that Menes the Egyptian was Minos the Cretan and ended up dead, from the bite of a wasp, in Ireland, at Knock-Many, the 'Hill of Many,' in County Tyrone" (*Selected Writings*, p. 130). See Waddell, *Egyptian Civilization*, chapter IV, or his *Makers of Civilization*, pp. 286–291. In his Canto 97, Pound too writes from the same source: "By Knoch Many now King Minos lies."

In a letter to his old high school teacher Anna Shaughnessy, 31 March 1969, the poet would mention having "originally" used Muirhead's "Blue Guide" to Ireland to identify "the hill of Many [Menes-Minos] in Tyrone (KNOCK-MANY), as the 'site' of the landing, & the death—from the bite of a bee—of one aspect of the 'hero' of that poem of mine . . ." (though this would have been after the poem, as only in the 1962 edition of Muirhead—which Olson had borrowed from the Sawyer Library in 1969—does Knockmany, as an early Bronze Age cairn, appear).

In notes from ca. January 1965 for a Guggenheim Fellowship application among the poet's papers, Olson has written, describing the second volume of the poem:

> . . . voyaging Hero is unt[h]roned or perhaps better (he was stung by a bee and 'died,' in Ireland, and was buried in in the Hill of Knockmany) 'relieved' by arriving at an environment—Gloucester
>
>   he
> travels actually with an unrelieved Monster (-Brother!) the

'blue' monster [who is in fact of course the ancient dragon, or Sea-Monster, in this case Typhon as of Mount Cassius, and, on this side—on the U.S. side of "Cashes" ledge—is literally the famed "Gloucester Sea-Serpent" . . .

The hero is to be seen as part or embodiment of the great "migratory act of man," of which Gloucester is the last "shore" (see note on the figure of Maximus, *Maximus* I, 1), and as such reflects the same tradition that Graves reports (actually the same tradition Waddell utilizes), by which "the Irish Milesians originated in Crete, fled to Syria by way of Asia Minor, and thence sailed west in the thirteenth century B.C. to Gaetulia in North Africa, and finally reached Ireland by way of Brigantium (Compostela, in North-western Spain)" (*Greek Myths*, I, 296).

II.7. He sailed to Cashes / and wrecked on that ledge . . .

See *Maximus* I, 77 and 150, and notes; also the poem entitled "Cashes," *Maximus* II, 19. A pun of Cashes with Mount Casius (*Maximus* II, 94 and note) is likely (and suggested by Olson's 1965 notes quoted above).

II.7. he built a castle / at Norman's Woe

John Hays Hammond, Jr. (1888–1965), Gloucester inventor (see *Maximus* II, 174), whose castle built of European remains on Hesperus Avenue on the heights above Norman's Woe is now a museum open to tourists. The Olsons were frequent guests at the Castle (as were other figures prominent in the arts), and Olson would give a reading of his poems there in September of 1960.

Norman's Woe is a reef on the Magnolia shore of Cape Ann, beyond Freshwater Cove. Babson writes in his *History*, p. 12:

> On the westerly side of the harbor is Norman's Oh, or Woe; a large rock, lying a few rods from the shore, and connected with it by a reef of rocks, which the sea leaves bare at low water. The tradition, that a man named Norman was shipwrecked and lost there, has no other confir-

mation than that derived from the name itself. A William Norman was an early settler of Manchester; and a Richard Norman is shown, by the probate records of Essex County, to have sailed on a voyage from which he never returned home, some time before 1682. The doleful name applied to this spot may commemorate a misfortune to one of those individuals. It will recall to the minds of the readers of American poetry, if it did not suggest to the author, a pathetic ballad of one of our most popular poets.

The reef is the setting of Longfellow's "Wreck of the Hesperus."

▶ **II.8. A NOTE ON THE ABOVE**

Written 29 November 1959 (dated in Olson's notes).

II.8. the sirens sang: / he stopped his / ears with caulking / compound

Odysseus, a prototype of Maximus, encounters the Sirens in Book XII of the *Odyssey*. Circe had warned him to stop the ears of his men with wax so they would not be deceived by the sweet lies of the Sirens, while he himself was tied to the mast.

▶ **II.9. MAXIMUS, FROM DOGTOWN—II**

Written 5 December 1959 (manuscript dated).

II.9. the Sea—turn yr Back on / the Sea

Echoes *Maximus* I, 149:

> The sea
> is east The choice Our backs
> turned from the sea but the smell
>
> as the minister said
> in our noses . . .

II.9. the Harbor / the shore the City / are now / shitty, as the Nation / is

Only seven years before, in "Letter 3," Olson had made the plea (*Maximus* I, 11):

o tansy city, root city
let them not make you
as the nation is

II.9. the Princes / of the Husting

See *Maximus* I, 122 and note.

II.9. Medea

The enchantress who falls in love with Jason and aids him in gaining the Golden Fleece. She was the daughter of Aeetes, king of Colchis on the Black Sea.

II.9. J-son

Also, Jason, leader of the Argonauts in the quest for the Golden Fleece.

II.9. Hines / son . . . John Hines

The poet's mother's maiden name was Hines; his grandfather, John Hines (1846–1918), came from Ireland to the United States some time before 1872. See "The Grandfather-Father Poem" in *Archaeologist of Morning*, p. 216, where "black jack / Hines" stokes the furnaces of the steel mill with "black / soft / coal."

II.9. Black Sea

North of Asia Minor and west of the Caucasus Mountains. Colchis, where the Argonauts found the Golden Fleece, was at its eastern edge.

II.9. Jack Hammond

John Hays Hammond, Jr., who built the castle referred to on *Maximus* II, 7. See also *Maximus* II, 174 and note.

II.9. Carboniferous / Pennsylvania / Age

The geological period, part of the Paleozoic Era, characterized in Europe and North America by the formation of coal. The Upper Carboniferous period in America is known as the Pennsylvanian Age.

II.9. the watered / rock

See *Maximus* II, 2 and note.

II.9. Aquarian Time

Relating to the age of Aquarius, the Water-carrier, which in astrological terms marks the end of the Christian aion or era. See "Across Space and Time" and the source from which its materials are drawn, Jung's *Aion*.

II.9. fish was / Christ

For the fish as symbol of Christ, see e.g. Jung, *Aion*, chapter VI, "The Sign of the Fishes." Olson refers to such symbolism in the early poems, "Siena" and "Adamo Me," but see, esp. for the astrological aspect, "Across Space and Time": "The Fish swam in on the back of Christ . . ."

II.9. Christ pick the seeds / out of yr teeth—how handsome / the dead dog lies

See note to *Maximus* I, 37.

II.9. Migma

Greek μιγμα, 'mixture, compound.' See the note to the word, translated as "medley," in Plutarch's essay, "On the E at Delphi," in *Plutarch's Morals: Theosophical Essays*, King trans., p. 194: "The origin of the Gnostic μιγμα, out of which it is Christ's business to extract the seeds of life." Olson has written in the margin of his copy: "O Christ / pick the seeds / out of the migma."

II.9. Wyngaershoek hoik Grape Vine HOYK the Dutch / & the Norse / and Algonquins

Wingaersheek Beach, between the mouth of the Annisquam and the entrance to the Essex River. Pringle, *History of Gloucester*, p. 17 (marked in Olson's copy), writes:

> Wingaersheek almost universally accepted as the Indian name of Cape Ann, is repudiated by Dr. Trumbull, who says that the word is not Indian, or, if so, is changed in the spelling to such a degree as to make it unrecognizable. Prof. E. N. Horsford, the learned Norse antiquarian, comes to the rescue and says that the word 'Wingaersheek' is an undoubted corruption of the German name, low Dutch, Wyngaerts Hoeck, which occurs on many maps of the period between 1630 and 1670, especially in Ogilby's 'America.' Wyngaerts Hoeck is from Wyngaerten, and is the equivalent of what the Northmen designated as Vineland, and as Champlain, in his account of his visit here in 1606, says that grapes were found quite plentiful, the application may not have come amiss.

Later, Wingaersheek became known as "Coffin's Beach," according to Copeland and Rogers, but "when the summer settlement began in 1882, it apparently was thought necessary by those developing the property to have a new name. Consequently Wyngaerts Hoeck was revived, with a new spelling 'Wingaersheek.' That name presently came to be applied only to the southern end of the beach, at the mouth of the Annisquam River . . ." (*Saga of Cape Ann*, p. 203).

See also *Maximus* III, 43: "GRAPE VINE / HOEK wyngaer's / HOEK Dutch"; also, " 'I know men . . . ,' " *Muthologos*, II, 162–163 and note there.

II.9. He-with-the-House-on-his-Head

See *Maximus* II, 31 and note; also II, 141. It should be noted, because of the Norse-Algonquin connection hinted at in this poem, that Leland, the source of this figure from Algonquin legends, draws parallels beween the Algonquin tales and Norse myths throughout.

II.9. she-who-Lusted-After-the / Snake-in-the-Pond

See *Maximus* II, 21 and note, and II, 142.

II.9. The-Grub-Eaten-Fish-Take-the-Smell-Out-of-The / Air

See *Maximus* II, 4:

> . . . smoked fish
> in the same field
> fly-blown and a colony
> of self-hugging grubs—handsome
> in the sun, the mass
> of the dead and the odor
> eaten out of the air
> by the grubs . . .

II.9. aer . . . Ta metarsia

See Harrison, *Themis*, pp. 391–392, on the distinction made by Stoic philosophers between τὰ μετάρσια, the 'weather,' and τὰ μετέωρα, the heavenly bodies:

> The Stoic writer Achilles, going back probably to Posei-donios, writes thus:
>> τὰ μετέωρα are distinguished from τὰ μετάρσια thus: τὰ μετέωρα are the things in heaven and the other, as e.g. the sun and the other heavenly bodies and ouranos and ether: τὰ μετάρσια are the things between the air and the earth, such as winds.
>
> The gist of the distinction lies in the difference between *aer* and *aither*; τὰ μετέωρα are the holy blaze of *aither* which is uppermost, τὰ μετάρσια, thunder, rain, clouds, wind, are of the damp cold *aer*, the lower region of earthy mist. Of all the heavenly bodies the moon with her dew and mists is most akin to τὰ μετάρσια.

II.9. Jack / & Jill

From the familiar English nursery rhyme:

> Jack and Jill went up the hill
>   To fetch a pail of water . . .

II.9. the Ladder / come down to the Earth

See perhaps Harrison, *Themis*, p. 391, at the beginning of her discussion of *ta metarsia*: ". . . one step on the ladder from earth to heaven is what may be called the 'weather.' " At the same time, cf. Jung, *Psychology and Alchemy*, pp. 54–56, concerning the ladder of ascent in rites of initiation: "The initiations of late classical syncretism, already saturated with alchemy . . . , were particularly concerned with the theme of ascent, i.e., sublimation. The ascent was often represented by a ladder . . . The idea of an ascent through the seven spheres of the planets symbolizes the return of the soul to the sun-god from whom it originated . . ." The passage is marked in Olson's copy, and an entry in a notebook from 1956-57 indicates his earlier interest in it. See also "the ladders" of "As the Dead Prey Upon Us" (1956), on which "the angels / and the demons / and men / go up and down."

II.9. the Many who / know / there is One!

Cf. the epigraph to *The Maximus Poems*, "All my life I've heard / one makes many," and the poem, "ALL MY LIFE I'VE HEARD ABOUT / MANY," *Maximus* II, 7.

II.9. the City is Mother— / Polis

See the quotation from Jung in note on "MONOGENE" below, and the poem on *Maximus* II, 18.

II.9. Mary

The poet's mother.

II.10. Elizabeth

His wife.

II.10. MONOGENE

Given the context and the proximity to "COLLAGEN": the singlecelled genetic material from which the human species has evolved, originally from the sea (see *Maximus* II, 72 and 147). Also, however, the "only-begotten" son of the Gnostic tradition. See the treatise quoted in Jung, *Psychology and Alchemy*, p. 104 (marked in Olson's copy with exclamation points): "This same is he [Monogenes] who dwelleth in the Monad . . . This same [the Monad] is the Mother-City [μητροπολις] of the Only-begotten [μονογενης]." Jung continues, "The Monogenes is the Son of God," the integrated self, and adds, p. 105, that "The Monogenes is also called the 'dark light.'"

II.10. COLLAGEN . . . KOLLAgen / TIME

In an unfinished piece from 1959 entitled "AQUARIAN TIME AND THE ANGEL MATTER—I," among the poet's papers, Olson writes that "Collagen Time" begins "1614 Smith Monhegan and circum Shakespeare's Two Noble Kinsmen: when the American thing became unstuck from the previous world soul." The Greek *kolla,* root of "collagen," means 'glue.'

II.10. LEAP onto / the LAND

Cf. *Maximus* I, 150:
>start all over step off the
>Orontes onto land . . .

II.10. the greater the water you add / the greater the decomposition / so long as the agent is protein

Cf.: "Civilization is the holes in all things which suddenly stick together [?illegible] a protein collagen. The greater the degradation of the substance by hydrolysis the stronger the sheer" (from "AQUARIAN TIME AND THE ANGEL MATTER—I").

II.10. the carbon of four is the corners

See Jung, *Psychology and Alchemy*, p. 209: "Now it is . . . a curious 'sport of nature' that the chief chemical constituent of organic bodies is carbon, which is characterized by four valences; also it is well known that the diamond is a carbon crystal. Carbon is black—coal, graphite—but the diamond is 'purest water!' " (also in *Integration of the Personality*, p. 198).

II.10. protogonic

Olson defined this in conversation, 13 June 1968, as the "earliest conceivable possibility of creation."

II.10. Dogtown the <u>under</u> / vault . . .

See ". . . *under* / Dogtown . . . ," *Maximus* II, 2.

II.10. Annisquam

The Annisquam River. See *Maximus* I, 43 and note.

II.10. the Black Chrysanthemum / Ocean . . . the Black Gold Flower

This is the "golden flower" of Chinese and medieval alchemy, which will figure increasingly through the poems. See esp. Jung, *Psychology and Alchemy*, pp. 74–75 and note: "The solar quality has survived in the symbol of the 'golden flower' of Chinese alchemy. . . . The golden flower comes from the Greek χρυσανθεμον . . . and χρυσανθιον = 'golden flower,' a magical plant like the Homeric μῶλυ, which is often mentioned by the Alchemists. The golden Flower is the noblest and purest essence of gold." See also the Chinese text itself, *The Secret of the Golden Flower*, Wilhelm trans., and Olson's "Secret of the Black Chrysanthemum," *OLSON* 3, pp. 64–74.

Jung also refers to "the seeding-place of the diamond body in the golden flower," p. 104n. (both "seeds" and "diamond" occur earlier in the poem)—which seems to have encouraged some of the verbal play and associations in the poem, such as diamond and coal, coal and Blackstone (black stone) River flowing "under" the city of Worcester (see "An Ode on Nativity"), where the poet's own roots (Jack Hines) were buried.

The identification of Ocean with the Black Chrysanthemum here has been prepared for in the line "Okeanos the one which all things are . . . ," *Maximus* II, 2. See note there, and cf. *Maximus* I, 2 for the simply visual or descriptive aspect of this passage: "the water glowed, / black, gold . . ." (where a pun on "black gold," the oil slick on the surface of the water, might be forced), and also p. 3 of that first volume where the water of the harbor is described as "a black-gold loin"—out of which spring the "seeds" which eventually "flower" etc. The combinations are endless.

▶ **II.11. Maximus, / to himself, / as of "Phoenicians"**

Dated 22 December 1959.

II.11. the fylfot / she look like / who called herself / luck

Cf. *Maximus* I, 40:

> But a fylfot,
> she look like,
> who calls herself
> (luck

A fylfot, it is to be remembered, is a swastika (see note to "the crooked timbers . . . ," *Maximus* I, 40).

II.11. svas- / tika

Sanskrit 'swastika,' from roots *su*, 'well,' and *asti*, 'it is'—a sign of good fortune or luck.

From his reading of Simpson, *The Buddhist Praying-Wheel*, some years earlier, Olson was aware of the swastika as a wheel—or a screw propeller—and as "symbol of the sun, or the solar motion," including "the whole celestial movement [this last phrase underlined in Olson's copy], which revolves over our heads with such unerring constancy. It is this motion which brings day and night; it also brings the seasons, and with the seasons come the fruits of the earth" (pp. 278–279). With the swastika, then, come the elements of morning, luck, and weather in the earlier poem, "Tyrian Businesses" (which the present poem is a successor to), and the fruitful spring of "Letter 9" following it—as well as the "sun" which is the Golden Flower.

See also the discussion of the swastika in Harrison, *Themis*, pp. 525–526.

II.11. as the lumber / was broken up in the screw The mess of it astern . . .

See *Maximus* I, 39:

> Then there was the noise—and the ship suddenly
> acting as no ship ever did, as the blades of the screw bit
> into that wood,
> and as that wood chewed them up!
> We watched the mess of it
> astern going
> off in the wake as the vessel fell off so she felt like dead
> in the water.

II.11. Ling, / OUT (why was she put up with, / so long?

See *Maximus* I, 36, "ling, / she is known as," and I, 35:

> that international doll,
> has to have silk, when she is put up
> (why is she put up with?)
> in the white house . . .

and respective notes.

II.11. the padma . . . Is what ALL / issues from

The lotus of India, seat and birthplace of the gods. It occurs in Jung's discussion of the Golden Flower in *Psychology and Alchemy*, p. 104, where he writes of the "metropolis" as being feminine like the *padma* or lotus as well as the Golden Flower. See also note to "Okeanos the one which all things are," *Maximus* II, 2.

II.11. The GOLD / flower . . . BLACK

See "the Black Gold Flower" in the preceding poem, and note.

▶ II.12. For "Moira"

Written 15 December 1959 (original manuscript dated), with minor revisions later.

II.12. TO HELL WITH . . .

The poem is derived from the following passage in Jung's *Symbols of Transformation*, p. 67n, a long note on *Heimarmene* or "bitter necessity" in which reference is made to Lucius Apuleius' *Golden Ass*:

> The young philosopher Lucius was changed into an ass, that ever-rutting animal hateful to Isis. . . . In his prayer to Isis, Queen of Heaven, Lucius says (XI, 25): ". . . thy saving hand, wherewith thou unweavest even the inextricably tangled web of fate, and assuagest the tempests of fortune, and restrainest the baleful orbits of the stars." Altogether, the purpose of the mysteries . . . was to break the "compulsion of the stars" by magic power.
>
> The power of fate makes itself felt unpleasantly only when everything goes against our will, that is to say, when we are no longer in harmony with ourselves. The ancients, accordingly, brought εἱμαρμένη into relation with the "primal light" or "primal fire," the Stoic conception of the ultimate cause, or all-pervading warmth which produced everything and is therefore fate. . . .

A look at the original manuscript, in which the poem occurs at the bottom of a page following copious notes on the meaning of the word *heimarmene*, reveals how the poet did not simply borrow or appropriate such passages for his own use, but labored to earn them. The poems are not actually "found," but are most often the culmination of a process; they sift through and clear by their own necessity.

Moira, too, is fate, a man's 'lot' or 'portion' in the original Greek. Isis was the great goddess of Egypt, whose brother

Osiris was killed by Typhon or Set, the ass-headed god of evil.

▶ II.13. Maximus further on (December 28th 1959)

II.13. ffisherman's FIELD'S rocks

Field Rocks in Gloucester Harbor, about two hundred yards off Cressy's Beach, just beyond Freshwater Cove; named, as Olson indicates, for their proximity to Fisherman's Field in Stage Fort Park.

II.13. Gen Douglas

Genevieve Douglas, a childhood friend; daughter of Lew Douglas, Sr. (see *Maximus* II, 23 and note).

II.13. Hammond's

Hammond's Castle near Norman's Woe (see *Maximus* II, 7 and note).

II.13. Lausel woman, holding out a ladle?

The Venus of Laussel, figure on a paleolithic (Aurignacian) limestone relief found in the Dordogne, France, with arm extended holding a curved, ladle-shaped object. See photograph in Neumann, *Great Mother*, plate 2.

II.13. sluggish treadle up which nature / climbed

Cf. *Maximus* I, 127:

> anything
> nature puts in the sea
> comes up,
>
> it is cornucopia
> to see it
> working up a sluggish
> treadle . . .

II.13. Andromeda

Chained to a rock or sea-cliff as a sacrifice to appease a monster sent by Poseidon, whose Nereids her mother had offended. She was rescued by Perseus, who fell in love with her at first sight and slew the monster.

II.13. Norn . . .

One of the Norse fates. Neumann observes on p. 250n of *The Great Mother*: "The Norns are midwives: 'Tell me then, Fafnir . . . Who are the Norns who are so helpful in need, and the babe from the mother bring?' "

It might be noted that both Gen Douglas and her sister Irene were nurses.

II.13. Perseus

Greek hero, slayer of Medusa; on his return home, he rescued Andromeda and married her.

▶ II.14. Maximus to Gloucester, Letter 27 [withheld]

First written at Black Mountain at the same time as "MAXIMUS TO GLOUCESTER, LETTER # 28" (*OLSON* 6, pp. 47−51), published as "The Ridge" in 1969 (*Pacific Nation* 2), which Olson described when reading it at Cortland, N.Y. in 1967 as a "companion" to "*Letter 27.*" Probably written in early December 1954, judging from Olson's letter to Robert Creeley from 8 December 1954, in which he writes: "last night, two—count em—2 Maximuses . . . [indicates first one was begun after thinking "well, why not start there, where the ridge . . ."] . . . I have just finished the rewrite of the 2nd (which didn't go as good as the first) and I see I stole a line from you, even though it was not intended, and what I was searching for was the simplest, to say how we do have this sense of unity with our body . . ." (The date of late 1954 tends to be supported by a remark Olson makes concerning Whitehead, whose *Adventures of Ideas* figures in the poem, in some notes identified by Charters as being from a 1956 lecture at Black Mountain [*Olson / Melville*, p. 84]: "I am the more persuaded of the importance and use of Whitehead's thought that I did not know his work . . . until last year.") Early versions of "*Letter 27*" among the poet's papers are designated "Letter 31" and "Letter 32" and even "Letter 12." An entry dated 13 November [1957] in a notebook from 1956–57 speaks of a "2 day struggle" with Letters 27 and 28, indicating further revisions were made at that time.

II.14.　Rexall

A drugstore chain.

II.14.　Hines

Olson's mother's family name (see *Maximus* I, 9 and note).

II.14.　no bare incoming / of novel, abstract form

For this and much of what follows in the poem, see Whitehead's *Adventures of Ideas*. Thus, p. 242 of that volume: "it was the defect of the Greek analysis of generation that it conceived it in terms of the bare incoming of novel abstract form."

II.14.　welter or the forms / of those events

Whitehead, *Adventures of Ideas,* p. 240, summarizing a passage from Plato's *Timaeus*: " 'In addition to the notions of the welter of events and of the forms which they illustrate, we require a third term, personal unity.' "

II.14.　the stopping of the battle

See *Maximus* I, 97 and note.

II.14.　the precessions . . . the slow westward motion

Olson apparently looked up the term "precession" in his dictionary upon meeting it in Whitehead. See *Webster's*

Collegiate Dictionary, 5th ed., p. 780, for not only "precession" as that which "goes before," but also, under "precession of the equinoxes" there: "*Astron.* A slow westward motion of the equinoctal points along the ecliptic . . ."

See also note to "Weather . . . ," *Maximus* I, 36; also *Maximus* I, 121: "the motion / (the Westward motion) / comes here . . ."

II.14. There is no strict personal order / for my inheritance.

Whitehead, *Adventures of Ideas*, p. 242: "Our perception of this geometrical order of the Universe brings with it the denial of the restriction of inheritance to mere personal order."

II.14–15. No Greek will be able / to discriminate my body.

See *Adventures of Ideas*, p. 242, "It was the defect of the Greek analysis . . ." quoted above, and pp. 243–244:

> So intimately obvious is this bodily inheritance that common speech does not discriminate the human body from the human person. Soul and body are fused together. . . . But the human body is indubitably a complex of occasions which are part of spatial nature. It is a set of occasions miraculously coördinated so as to pour its inheritance into various regions within the brain. There is thus every reason to believe that our sense of unity with the body has the same original as our sense of unity with our immediate past of personal experience. It is another case of non-sensuous perception, only now devoid of the strict personal order.

II.15. Polis

See esp. *Maximus* I, 10 and note.

▶ II.16. The River—I

Written ca. 21 October 1960 (manuscript dated).

II.16. the fiord

The Annisquam River and its basin, as described by Shaler, "Geology of Cape Ann," pp. 543, 581.

II.16. the diorite man

The stone monster from the Hittite "Song of Ullikummi," created to rival Teshub, the storm-god. See *Maximus* III, 37 and Olson's comments in "Causal Mythology," *Muthologos*, I, 72ff. His source is Güterbock, "Song of Ullikummi," and "Hittite Religion" in *Forgotten Religions* (ed. Ferm); see also Güterbock, "Hittite Version of Hurrian Kumarbi Myths."

See also "Diorite stone," *Maximus* II, 51.

II.16. Obadiah Bruen's / island

Island in the Annisquam River basin on the west side of the river, north of Rust's Island; identified as such in early town records. Now Pearce Island. For Bruen, see note to *Maximus* I, 145.

II.16. the Cut

See note to *Maximus* I, 30.

II.16. the yelping rocks

See *Maximus* I, 85, and note.

II.16. Merry

See *Maximus* II, 2 and note.

II.16. True inclusions / of other rocks are not commonly met with . . .

From Shaler, "Geology of Cape Ann," pp. 608 and 607, and see also Shaler's map showing the distribution of granite and diorite, opposite p. 610:

> True inclusions of other rocks are not commonly met with in the granitic material. . . . The mass of diorite is apparently of an irregularly circular form, having its center at about the middle of the Annisquam Reach on Rust's Island. On all sides where the rocks outcrop, it is surrounded

by granitite, the two entrances of the Reach being the only places where it could possibly have cut the granitite. These entrances are narrow and are bounded on either side by granitite which is not porphyritic, which facts almost exclude the hypothesis that the diorite has cut the granitite.

On p. 606, Shaler had written:

In the vicinity of Squam River an area of diorite has been found occupying the position indicated upon the map. The depression occupied by Squam River is one of the most marked features in the topography of the region. On either side are high hills, and the center of the Reach is considerably below sea level, although it is much encumbered by glacial drift. To explain this valley was for a long time a difficult problem.

▶ II.16. The River—2

Written 14 November 1960 (early manuscript dated).

II.16. the Poles

See Shaler, "Geology of Cape Ann," p. 606: "It is difficult to determine which of these two rocks is the older. The region is so drift-covered that the contact can not be seen; but wherever it is approached the granitite becomes markedly porphyritic; in some places, however, as for instance on the hill called 'The Poles,' in Gloucester, the diorite exhibits the same phenomenon." Copeland and Rogers write, "In the old days the ledge near Washington Street was known, for some unrecorded reason, as The Poles" (*Sage of Cape Ann*, p. 184). Pringle in his *History of Gloucester*, p. 288, describes the Poles in Riverdale as a "symmetrically dome-shaped mass of rock."

▶ II.17. The Poimanderes . . .

Notes among his papers indicate Olson was unsure of the exact date of composition; probably March (as mentioned in the poem) of 1960, the year after "Letter, May 2, 1959," where he had been "chomping around" the streets of Gloucester, pacing, "measuring off distances" around Meeting House Plain.

The *Poimandres* itself is the first treatise of the Hermetic corpus and concerns the "Shepherd" of men (Poimen = 'shepherd'). See especially Jonas, *Gnostic Religion*, chapter 7, "The *Poimandres* of Hermes Trismegistus," in which he writes, pp. 147—148:

> The system of the *Poimandres* is centered around the divine figure of Primal Man; his sinking into nature is the dramatic climax of the revelation and is matched by the ascent of the soul, the description of which concludes the revelation. The antithesis of the creator and the highest God is absent here: the demiurge has been commissioned by the Father, and his creation seems to be . . . the best way of coping with the existence of a chaotic darkness.

The treatise and the figure is referred to also in Jung's *Aion* and *Psychology and Alchemy*, passim.

▶ II.18. Dogtown   the dog   town . . .

Written 15 November 1960 (early manuscript dated).

II.18. the mother city . . . METRO- / POLIS

See quotation from Jung, *Psychology and Alchemy*, in note to "MONOGENE," *Maximus* II, 10.

▶ II.19. Cashes

"I did it originally on a tape that Duncan and I made for Creeley for his Christmas, two years ago, two or three years ago [December 1958]. . . . The thing was picked off the tape I made, for publication" (Olson, on tape made at reading at Goddard College, 12 April 1962). Printed here with minor revisions from that first publication, September 1960, in Gael Turnbull's *Migrant*.

II.19. I tell you it's cruel. There was the Rattler ...

The poem was found in Goode's *Fisheries and Fishery Industries of the United States*, IV, 66−67:

> The following sketch, quoted from a Boston newspaper, contains a fair example of the fisherman's dialect:
>
> ... 'It's curious. Sometimes a vessel 'll go down's easy's nothin', 'n' then agin she'll live whar you wouldn't say th' wus a ghost of a show. Now, thar was the Rattler, pitchpoled over the shoals off Cape Ann at midnight, some thirteen years ago, in a gale of wind, 'n' come right side up 'n' got into port safe with every man on board,' and the old man paused and patiently waited for the usual—
>
> 'How was that, cap'n?'
>
> With a prepatory 'wall,' while a satisfied look overspread his face, the captain continued:
>
> 'One of the wust shoals on the New Englun' coast is 'bout twenty-two league off Cape Ann, called Cashe's Shoals; yet fur all that th'r ain't much said 'bout 'em, which I never could explain, fur more vessels uv gone down thar than on any shoal of the same size along the coast.'
>
> 'How large are the shoals?'
>
> 'Wall, sailin' either side a quarter'v a mile an' you're in sixty or seventy fathom, but right on the shoals, which is only a few rod across, the water ain't much over twenty feet deep. Why, it's so shaller I've seen kelp growin' up on top o' the water, an' when thar's a blow an' the big seas come rollin' in thar's I've seen 'em—a hundred feet choppin' down on the bottom—I tell *you* it's cruel. No ship could live thar in a storm, an' only smaller vessels can go over in calm weather. Wall, the Rattler, as I was a speakin' of, wus comin' 'long down the coast from Newf'n'land loaded with frozen herrin'. The night wus a black one, 'n the cap'n was off his reck'nin'. Leastways, fust thing any one knowed, a big sea lifted the vessel an' pitched her forrad. She struck her nose on the bottom, an' just then another big one struck her fair in the stern, an' lifted it clean over the bow; her masts struck an' snapped off, an' she went over the shoals an' floated in deep water on the other side, fair an' square on her keel, with both masts broke off to 'ithin fifteen feet o' the deck.'
>
> 'Where were the crew?'
>
> 'Oh, they were down below. They said it was all over

afore they knew what was up; they didn't sense it all at first. They said, all it was they was settin' thar 'n' then,' illustrating by a motion of the hand toward the ceiling and back to the floor; 'they struck the deck 'n then came down agin all in a heap on the floor. They got up on the deck, kind o' dazed like, an' thar she wus, a complete wreck.'

'How about the man at the helm?'

'Oh, he was lashed. But he said arterwerds, when he felt the old craft spinnin' over, he thought it was all over with him. He held on ter the wheel fur dear life an' never lost his grip; but I tell you that's a tremendous strain on a man.' And the old captain clenched his large muscular hands as if he, too, for a time, was being subjected to the same strain. 'He wus pretty nigh gone; but they unlashed him, took him down below, and did for him all they could. Arter they got into port, he was laid up fur a long time, but finally come round all right.'

'How did they manage to get into port with their vessel a wreck?'

'They had a fair wind, the current was in their favor, an' they finally fell in with a vessel that towed 'em in all right. That was the nar'rest 'scape I ever heerd of fur a vessel.'

'Their good angels were watching over the crew that night, sure. If any one but you, captain, had told me that story I must say I should have doubted it.'

'Wall, you needn't doubt it, for it's gospel truth, an' the man who owned the vessel was Andrew Leighton, of Glo'ster, an' the cap'n who sailed her was named Bearse.' And the veteran fish-dealer brought down his clinched hand upon an ice-chest that stood within reach with an emphasis that settled all debate more effectually than the most successful gag-law ever put in practice by the most astute politician.

In a note on p. 66 of that volume is written:

> The facts in the case are truthfully described. The Rattler, while returning to Gloucester from a voyage to Newfoundland, in January, 1867, was overtaken by a furious gale in the vicinity of Cashe's Ledge. She was struck by a heavy sea, thrown on her beam ends or rolled over, and finally righted with the loss of both masts. She arrived in Gloucester a few days later.

▶**II.20. like**   **Mr. Pester acknowledges his sinfulness...**

Probably written sometime in 1960, although confirming evidence has not been found; manuscript typed at the same time as the poems immediately preceding and following. After the initial "like," the poem is taken verbatim from *Records and Files of Quarterly Courts of Essex County,* I, 35.

▶**II.21. Of old times, there was a very beautiful / woman...**

Exact date of writing unknown. Taken from Leland, *Algonquin Legends of New England,* pp. 273−274, with small changes:

> Of old times. There was a very beautiful woman. She turned the heads of all the men. She married, and her husband died very soon after, but she immediately took another. Within a single year she had five husbands, and these were the cleverest and handsomest and bravest in the tribe. And then she married again.
>
> This, the sixth, was such a silent man that he passed for a fool. But he was wiser than people thought. He came to believe, by thinking it over, that this woman had some strange secret. He resolved to find it out. So he watched her all the time. He kept his eye on her by night and by day.
>
> It was summer, and she proposed to go into the woods to pick berries, and to camp there. By and by, when they were in the forest, she suggested that he should go on to the spot where they intended to remain and build a wigwam. He said that he would do so. But he went a little ways into the woods and watched her.
>
> As soon as she believed that he was gone, she rose and walked rapidly onwards. He followed her, unseen. She went on, till, in a deep, wild place among the rocks, she came to a pond. She sat down and sang a song. A great foam, or froth, rose to the surface of the water. Then in the foam appeared the tail of a serpent. The creature was of immense size. The woman, who had laid aside all her garments, embraced the serpent, which twined around her, enveloping all her limbs and body in his folds. The husband watched it all. He now understood that, the venom of the serpent having entered the woman, she had saved her life by transferring it to others, who died.

He went on to the camping ground and built a wigwam. He made up two beds; he built a fire. His wife came. She was earnest that there should be only a single bed. He sternly bade her lie by herself. She was afraid of him. She laid down, and went to sleep. He arose three times during the night to replenish the fire. Every time he called her, and there was no answer. In the morning he shook her. She was dead. She had died by the poison of the serpent. They sunk her in the pond where the snake lived.

One or two other attempts, with slightly different line lengths, were made to adapt the story from Leland to the poet's satisfaction.

See also *Maximus* II, 142.

▶ **II.22. They said she went off fucking . . .**

Manuscript dated "*Mon March 6* (1960? or 1961?)" The main source of the poem is Eckstorm, *Old John Neptune*, p. 35:

It was of Mahli Sessil, however, that Clara Neptune told the story that lingers most in memory. I give it in her own words, as taken down in 1918. "One pond down dere somewheres, old time Injuns campin' dere. One day old lady say, 'We goin' visitin'.'—'who?'—'She Mahli Sessil, old Johnny Neptune her father; she *m'deolénno*, witch. Well, she get wash and comb hair and fix self all up and walk right into pond; 'We go visitin',' she say. Long 'bout night she come back, out of pond. She been cross pond and visit mountain. Ev'ry mountain she have Injun man in it. Every Sunday she do that." Here is Mahli Sessil, who lived on my own street and who married a white man, a respected woman, who is presented in this disreputable liaison with a mountain! The place, as I ascertained by close questioning, is Marsh Bay in Frankfort, on the west side of the Penobscot River on U.S. Highway, No. 1. The mountain is Mount Waldo, which there slopes steep to the water. One can imagine Mahli Sessil calmly walking into the placid, tidal stream and emerging within the mountain so close beside it. The tale clearly enough is very old, passed down from generation to generation until, after her death, it was fastened upon Mahli Sessil.

A story of the liaison of a woman with a mountain also appears in Leland, *Algonquin Legends of New England*, p. 255, and probably supplied Olson with the detail of "the spirit / of that mountain":

> Of the old time. There was once an Indian girl gathering blueberries on Mount Katahdin. And, being lonely, she said, "I would that I had a husband!" And seeing the great mountain in all its glory rising on high, with the red sunlight on the top, she added, "I wish Katahdin were a man, and would marry me!"
>
> All this she was heard to say ere she went onward and up the mountain, but for three years she was never seen again. Then she reappeared, bearing a babe, a beautiful child, but his little eyebrows were of stone. For the Spirit of the Mountain had taken her to himself; and when she greatly desired to return to her own people, he told her to go in peace, but forbade her to tell any man who had married her.

See also *Maximus* II, 143 and 188.

▶ **II.23 A <u>Maximus</u>**

Written fall, 1960 (dated by Olson in notes among his papers).

II.23. Bowditch the Practical / Navigator who did use Other People's Monies as different from his Own

Nathaniel Bowditch, "who was the first 'trustee' of others' monies / who treated them as separate from his own accounts" (*Maximus* I, 73, and see also note to I, 7).

Other People's Monies is the title of a book by Louis D. Brandeis, a copy of which the poet owned.

II.23. the Actuarial the ReaL Base of Life Since

Cf. "And that a p. poor crawling actuarial 'real'—good enough to keep banks and insurance companies, plus mediocre governments etc" ("Letter to Elaine Feinstein," in *Human Universe*, pp. 96–97).

II.23. jass is gysm

"Pun is rhyme," writes Olson in the Feinstein letter of 27 April 1959 (*Human Universe*, p. 97). The elemental rhythms and sexual connotations that jazz, both the music and the word, has had from its earliest roots is emphasized ("jass" being an early, occasional spelling). Mathews' *Dictionary of Americanisms*, under "jazz," suggests the reader see also "jasm," defined (I, 899) as 'energy, enthusiasm,' which in turn is suggested to be the same word as "gism," 'semen.'

II.23. Pound

Ezra Pound. See *Maximus* I, 27 and note.

II.23. Ferrini

Vincent Ferrini. See Letters 5−7 in *Maximus* I, and notes to pp. 20 and 41 of that volume.

II.23. Hammond

John Hays Hammond, Jr. See *Maximus* II, 7 and note, and II, 174.

II.23. Stevens

William Stevens. See *Maximus* I, 30 and note; also *Maximus* II, 48 etc.

II.23. Griffiths

John Willis Griffiths (1809−1882), American naval architect, author of *A Treatise on Marine and Naval Architecture or Theory and Practice Blended In Shipbuilding* (1849) and other volumes. He designed the first "extreme clipper ship," the *Rainbow*, for the China trade. "Through his writings Griffiths did more than any one else to put shipbuilding in America on a scientific basis, in place of the 'rule of thumb' methods then in vogue" (*D.A.B.*, VII, 626).

II.23. John Smith

See note to "Three Turks Heads," *Maximus* I, 24, and *Maximus* I, 49–51, 69–70, 104, etc.

II.23. Conants

Roger and James Bryant Conant. See "Letter 10," *Maximus* I, 45–47 and notes.

II.23. Higginsons

Francis and Stephen Higginson. See *Maximus* I, 46 and note, and I, 74 and notes.

II.23. Hawkinses

John, William, and Richard Hawkins. See "Maximus, to Gloucester: Letter 14," *Maximus* I, 59–66, and notes.

II.23. Lew Douglas

See note to "my other, the top of whose head . . . ," *Maximus* I, 6, and note to "*Sch. Ella M. Goodwin* . . . ," *Maximus* I, 138.

II.23. Carl Olsen

See note to "he with the muscle as big as his voice . . . ," *Maximus* I, 7; also *Maximus* I, 19 and note.

II.23. Walter Burke

See *Maximus* I, 26–28.

II.23. John Burke

See the poem entitled "John Burke," *Maximus* I, 142–144, and note; also *Maximus* II, 52.

II.23. John White

See esp. *Maximus* I, 45 and note, and *Maximus* II, 187.

II.23. John Winthrop

See *Maximus* I, 30 and note; also I, 129 etc.

II.23. ekonomikos

Greek ὀικονομικός, from *oikos* 'house' and *nemein* 'to manage.'

II.23. the plum / the flower

See "Letter 9," *Maximus* I, 41–44.

II.23. The Renaissance a / box / the economics & poetics / thereafter

See "And for the water-shed, the economics & poetics thereafter," *Maximus* I, 70, and note to "Quattrocento-by-the-Beach," *Maximus* I, 71. See also *Maximus* II, 79.

II.23. the / "Savage God"

Among the poet's papers is a request dated 7 July 1960 from Paul Carroll, editor of the magazine *Big Table*, inviting Olson to participate in a symposium on "Post-Christian Man." The invitation reads in part:

> Although your contribution may assume whatever literary form and length you wish, may I offer two phrases by William Butler Yeats as possible focuses of discussion. The first: "Why are these strange souls born everywhere today . . . ." The second: "After us the Savage God." I see the symposium, then, as the discussion of a vital question: Is it a fact of contemporary culture that, during our century and especially during the years following World War II, the Christian image of man has been replaced by another image or other images?

Notes indicate Olson attempted a response, but gave it up, with what appears in this poem remaining as a result. The phrase itself occurs in the concluding paragraph of Book IV, "The Tragic Generation," in "The Trembling of the Veil" section of Yeats' *Autobiographies* (p. 430): "After Stéphane

Mallarmé, after Paul Verlaine, after Gustave Moreau, after Puvis de Chavannes, after our own verse, after all our subtle colour and nervous rhythm, after the faint mixed tints of Conder, what more is possible? After us the Savage God."

II.23. Agyasta

See *Maximus* I, 72 and note.

II.23. primitive ("buttocks

See "Fat Lady / Spain," *Maximus* II, 93—the steatopygic condition of the paleolithic Venuses.

▶ II.24. December, 1960

Written that date, in Gloucester.

II.24. Saco

Settlement on the river of that name in southwestern Maine, below Portland.

II.24. Ipswich

Massachusetts town northwest of Gloucester.

II.24. Annisquam

The Annisquam River.

II.24. Ipswich Bay

Body of water north of Cape Ann.

II.24. the Thatchers

Anthony Thacher and his family, who in 1635 were sailing from Newbury with the Rev. John Avery along the coast to Marblehead, when they were caught in a sudden storm and shipwrecked off Cape Ann, near what is now known as Thacher's Island. Only Thacher and his wife were saved;

all the others, including Thacher's four children and Avery's six, perished. For an account of the misfortune, see Babson, *History of Gloucester*, pp. 47−49; also Copeland and Rogers, *Saga of Cape Ann*, pp. 128−129.

II.24. Pennacooks

A confederacy of Algonquin tribes that occupied the basin of the Merrimac River and the adjacent region in north-eastern Massachusetts and the southern part of Maine. They had an intermediate position between the southern New England tribes mostly loyal to the English, and the Abnaki and others farther north who were under French influence.

II.24. Abnaki

An Algonquin confederacy formerly centered in the present state of Maine.

II.24. Casco Bay

Inlet of the Atlantic Ocean on the coast of Maine just north of Portland.

II.24. Cape La Have

On the coast of Nova Scotia near Lunenburg, about fifty miles southwest of Halifax.

II.24. Cape Sable

The southernmost point of Nova Scotia. A petition of Captain Andrew Robinson (see below) complains of attacks by Indians while fishing there (Babson, *Notes and Additions*, II, 87−88).

II.24. Fox Island

In Penobscot Bay at Vinalhaven Island, off the coast of Maine.

II.24. Casco

Settlement just north of Casco River on Casco Bay in Maine, which became Fort Loyall, Falmouth, and finally Portland.

II.24. the Wakleys

Thomas Wakley, an early settler of Gloucester, and his sons. "He and his son John had houses and land on the south side of Goose Cove; which, in 1661, they sold to Thomas Riggs, and, with another son (Isaac) and a son-in-law (Matthew Coe), went to Falmouth, Me., where they purchased a large tract of land, on which they settled, and remained till the destruction of the place by the Indians in 1675, when Thomas Wakley and his wife Elizabeth, and John and his wife and two children, were barbarously slaughtered by the savages. Elizabeth, daughter of John, was carried off; but, after some months' captivity, was taken by Squando, the Saco sachem, to Major Waldron at Dover, where she subsequently married Richard Scamman, a Quaker. Isaac Wakley was killed by the Indians, at Falmouth, in 1676" (Babson, *History*, pp. 174–175).

According to Willis, *History of Portland*, pp. 71–72, Thomas Wakley, Matthew Coe, John Wakley, and Isaac Wakley, received a deed of land from Richard Tucker in May, 1661 for two hundred acres at Back Cove, Falmouth. "These persons constituted one family; John and Isaac Wakley, were the sons of Thomas, and Matthew Coe married his daughter . . ."—and, as such, were part of the "same weave / of interlocking / pieces . . . and cross / marriaging" that Olson will note further along in the poem.

II.24. Freeport

Town on Casco Bay, about fifteen miles northeast of Portland.

II.24. Arthur Mackworth

(d. 1657), early settler at the mouth of the Presumpscot River in Maine, near what was to become Portland. See the notice of him in Baxter, *Trelawny Papers*, p. 213n.

II.24. Portland

The city in Maine on Casco Bay (see also *Maximus* I, 133 and note), known earlier as Fort Loyall and Falmouth. For its early history, including an account of the settlers from Gloucester, see esp. Willis, *History of Portland*, also Hull, *Seige and Capture of Fort Loyall*.

II.24. wasn't / for Champlain, when 200 / here, 1606 . . .

Champlain reported from Cape Ann: "We saw two hundred Indians in this place, which is pleasant enough; and here are many nut-trees, cypresses, sassafras, oaks, ashes, and beeches, which are very fine. The chief of this place, who is called Quiouhamenec, came to see us with another chief, a neighbor of his called Cohouepech, whom we entertained. Onemechin, chief of Saco, also came to see us there, and we gave him a coat, which he did not keep long, but presented to another because being uncomfortable in it, he could not adapt himself to it. . . ." (as quoted in Saville, *Champlain and His Landings at Cape Ann*, pp. 19−20, marked in Olson's copy; also in Pringle, *History of Gloucester*, p. 15).

For Champlain, see also *Maximus* I, 103 and note; for his trouble with the Indians, p. 151 of that volume and note; and for smallpox and the Indians, p. 49 there and note.

II.25. Nathaniel Wharf / whose mother was / a Mackworth / bought of Josselyn / whose mother was a Cammock . . .

Nathaniel Wharf, an early Gloucester settler, was "son of Nathaniel Wharf of Falmouth, Me., by his wife Rebecca, daughter of Arthur Macworth. The father died in 1673;

leaving Nathaniel, then eleven years old, who came to Gloucester . . ." (Babson, *History*, p. 178). This information can
also be found in Willis, *History of Portland*, pp. 54n, 97–98,
and 135.

Babson states further in his *Notes and Additions*, I, 86, that
"This settler bought of Henry Joslyn, Nov. 1, 1693, a house
and land between land of Timothy Somes and land of
Thomas Riggs, sen. . . ."

Henry Josselyn or Joslyn, according to Babson, was driven
from Falmouth in 1675 by Indian attacks, and was part of
"the first reflux of the tide of emigration which, about twenty
years before, began to set towards Maine from our town. His
name first appears here on the occasion of his marriage,
June 4, 1678, to Bridget Day. The next year, he had a grant
of land between the lot of Timothy Somes and Thomas
Riggs's house. In 1693, he appears to have sold this land,
and a dwelling-house standing on it, to Nathaniel Wharf "
(*History of Gloucester*, p. 108)

Henry Josselyn's father (d. 1683), also named Henry, married Margaret Cammock in 1643 (Baxter, *Trelawny Papers*,
p. 2n). She later had a parcel of land at Dogtown (see
Maximus III, 91–93 and 195–196).

II.25. Washington

Washington Street, Gloucester.

II.25. Gee

Gee Avenue, leading to Dogtown (see note to *Maximus*
II, 3).

II.25. Stanwood was cut / through to make Back Road

At the point where Gee Avenue and Stanwood Street
merge and become Commons Road, there is a road leading
south to Dogtown Road (at the foot of Gravel Hill) formerly
called the "back road"—as Mann says, "paradoxically," since
"it is nearer to civilization than either of the others." See the
map in Mann, *In the Heart of Cape Ann*, and his explanation

on pp. 14—15. The "back road" is now simply an extension of Cherry Street.

II.25. William Tucker

Probably the son of John Tucker, early Gloucester settler, born in 1690 (Babson, *Notes and Additions*, I, 82). That he and Nathaniel Wharf were neighbors in Dogtown was gleaned by Olson from the town records. His grandfather, Richard Tucker, was an agent and partner of George Cleave at Machegonne, later Portland.

II.25. George Cleave

First permanent settler of what was later to become Portland, Maine. He received a grant in 1636 from Sir Ferdinando Gorges for land "beginning at the furthermost poynt of a necke of land called by the Indians Machegonne . . . (wch together wth the said necke of land that the said George Cleave and the said Richard Tucker have planted for Divers yeares already expired) is estimated in the whole to be about fifteen hundred acres or thereabout" (*York Deeds*, I, i). See also Baxter, *Trelawny Papers*, p. 32n et passim, and Willis, *History of Portland*, pp. 17 ff.

II.25. Gorges

Sir Ferdinando Gorges (ca. 1566—1647), the English colony-maker. A leading member of the Council for New England, he received a grant with Captain John Mason (q.v.) for territory in Maine, and in 1639 procured a royal charter for the Province of Maine.

II.25. Capt Andrew Robinson . . .

(1679—1742), said to have invented the schooner in Gloucester in 1713. For his activities against the Indians, see Babson, *History*, pp. 137—140; also *Notes and Additions*, II, 87—88.

His sister Ann (b. 1684) married Samuel Davis in 1704 (Babson, *History*, pp. 136 and 255). Babson writes, p. 255, that this Davis "is probably the person of the same name, son of Isaac Davis of Falmouth, Me., who, with his brother John, is mentioned as living here in 1733." The historian, however, says little about Isaac Davis and Dogtown; again, Olson has his information from the original records.

II.25. South Thomaston

Town in Maine on the neck of land southwest of Penobscot Bay. Babson reports in his *History*, p. 139, that Andrew Robinson, while erecting a fort for the colonial government in Maine, "was taken sick with a lung-fever, which, after a short illness, caused his death. He was attended in his last sickness by one of his daughters, who deposited his remains in one corner of the fort," the site of which he identifies in a footnote as being in Thomaston, Me.

II.25. Father Lauverjat

French Jesuit missionary to the Penobscot Indians. His role as instigator of Indian attacks upon English fishing vessels is mentioned in Eckstorm, *Old John Neptune*, p. 79.

II.25. Cardinal Richlieu

Richelieu (1585–1642), the French statesman, who controlled French policy from 1624 until his death.

II.25. Falmouth

The settlement earlier known as Casco. It became Portland in 1786.

II.25. Ingersolls

George Ingersol (b. 1618) and his family. "He had a house in the Harbor, and owned land in several places; which he sold, and afterwards removed to Falmouth, Me. He was lieutenant, at that place, of the military force for protection against the Indians; and, in the attack of the savages in 1675, had a son killed, and his house burned. His letter, describing other destruction of life and property (that of the Wakleys, probably, who had also emigrated from Gloucester), is in our State archives [and is quoted by Babson in his *Notes and Additions,* I, 106−107]. . . . Joseph, the only son of George Ingersol known to have been born in Gloucester, went to Falmouth with his father, and became a joiner. He married there Sarah, daughter of Matthew Coe. He probably returned to Gloucester soon after the second destruction of Falmouth by the Indians; as he had a daughter Hannah born here in 1693. He died in 1718, aged seventy-two . . ." (Babson, *History*, pp. 106−107).

The later Ingersolls made their homes in Dogtown, along Dogtown Road: "Apparently the house Molly Jacobs lived in in more recent years was in 1741 the home of Joseph Ingersoll. George Ingersoll, the first settler of the name, had a son Joseph and a grandson of the same name, who married Mary Brewer in 1707. Their son Joseph was living in the town parish in 1740, and with his father signed the petition. His brother John lived in another part of the parish" (Mann, *Beginnings of Dogtown*, p. 24).

See also the notice of the Ingersolls in Willis, *History of Portland*, pp. 210−211. See also *Maximus* II, 42.

II.25 Rider

"Phineas Rider was here as early as 1649, perhaps before; and had his residence in the Harbor, near Governor's Hill. He left Gloucester in 1658, and went to Falmouth, Me.; where he was town-commissioner in 1670 and 1671. He lived there in 1675, before the destruction of the town by the Indians; but his name is not afterwards met with" (Babson, *History*, p. 130). According to Willis, *History of Portland*, p. 71, Rider received a grant of fifty-five acres in 1658 from George Cleeves at Back Cove, Falmouth.

II.25. Wakleys

See note to this Gloucester family above.

II.25. Coes

Matthew Coe and his family. A fisherman, he "lived in Portsmouth in 1640, but came to Gloucester before 1647 . . . After having resided here for several years, he sold his house and land to Thomas Riggs, in 1661, for forty pounds, and bought, with others, of Richard Tucker of Falmouth, Me., two hundred and ten acres of land on the north margin of Back Cove, in that place; where he died before 1675. He married Elizabeth, daughter of Thomas Wakley, in 1647 . . ." His daughter Sarah "married Joseph Ingersol of Falmouth, and returned with her husband to Gloucester, the native place of both, about 1690; having left Falmouth probably on account of the continual anxiety and alarm to which they were exposed from the hostility of the Indians, and their repeated murderous attacks on that place" (Babson, *History*, p. 69).

II.25. Riverdale Dogtown / proprietors / of New Gloucester

The Wakleys, e.g., had property below Goose Cove in Riverdale, the section of Gloucester along the Mill River; while the Ingersolls were located in Dogtown nearby.

The town of New Gloucester is about twenty miles north of Portland, founded in the 1730's by families from Gloucester seeking new land for agriculture. See the account of the emigration to Falmouth and the settling of New Gloucester in Babson, *History*, pp. 296−298, 302−306.

II.26. 1699 / 40 fishermen says the Frenchman / traveller

See Innis, *Cod Fisheries*, p. 116: "In May, 1699, Villebon noted that the English had ketches of 40 tons, and that they had secured one load of fish and had returned for a second." Earlier on that page, Innis states that "in Ipswich bay there were about six hundred men, at Cape Anne some forty fishermen's houses, at Salem four hundred houses, the inhabitants all fishermen and sailors."

II.26. Norridgewock / 1724 wiped out

An Abnaki settlement in Maine on the Kennebec River, destroyed in August of 1724 by an English force. Its destruction is mentioned in Eckstorm, *Old John Neptune*, p. 79, but see the vivid and dramatic restoration of the final scene in the same author's article, "The Attack on Norridgewock." It was another incident in the succession of intercolonial wars between the French and their Indian allies such as the Abnakis, and the English and the tribes loyal to them. They were colonial extensions of the European struggle for power and were not thoroughly ended until the Treaty of Paris in 1763 by which France gave up her claims in North America.

II.26. Father Rasles / dead among his notes

(1652–1724), French Jesuit missionary to the Abnakis. He lived thirty-four years among the Indians and compiled a dictionary of their language. See, e.g., the chapter "Père Sebastian Rasles" in W. C. Williams' *In the American Grain*; also Eckstorm, *Old John Neptune*, p. 187n: "Father Rasles was warned, so runs the Indian tradition, of the coming of the English to destroy the town. The unfinished letter found upon his own table after his death, fully bears out the tradition that a shaman foretold the attack upon the town in ample time for all to escape; but the priest ridiculed the warning . . ."

II.26. sd schooner / invented

See note to Andrew Robinson, *Maximus* II,25, and Babson, *History*, pp. 251–255, where the following account by Cotton Tufts in the Massachusetts Historical Society *Collections* for 1804 is reprinted:

> I was informed (and committed the same to writing) that the kind of vessels called "schooners" derived their name from this circumstance; viz., Mr. Andrew Robinson of that place, having constructed a vessel which he masted and rigged in the same manner as schooners are at this day, on

her going off the stocks and passing into the water, a by-
stander cried out, "*Oh, how she scoons!*" Robinson instantly
replied, "*A scooner let her be!*" From which time, vessels thus
masted and rigged have gone by the name of "schooners;"
before which, vessels of this description were not known in
Europe nor America.

There is a brief account also in Copeland and Rogers, *Saga of
Cape Ann*, pp. 83–84.

II.26. what John Winter / had made so / at Richmond's / Island

Richmond's Island in Casco Bay just off Cape Elizabeth,
Maine, was the site of a plantation granted in December
1631 to Robert Trelawny and Moses Goodyear, merchants of
Plymouth, England. John Winter (d. 1645), agent for Trelawny, was employed to manage the fishing and fur business,
which he did quite successfully. See the note on him in
Baxter, *Trelawny Papers*, p. 16n.

II.26 William Pulsifer / of John Pulsifer

Babson reports, *History*, p. 130: "John Pulcifer, or Pul-
sever, settled about 1680, according to tradition, near a spot
still occupied by one of his descendants, on the old road [now
approximately Atlantic Street] leading to Coffin's Beach. In
1688, he had a piece of land 'given to the house where he
lived.'" A lot on the north side of Jones River (now Jones
Creek) was granted to him in 1717 ("Transcript of Book One
of the Commoners' Records," p. 747).

The story of a Pulcifer captured by Indians is given in
Babson, *Notes and Additions*, I, 59–60:

> A tradition was current some years ago, that a man of
> this family was one of a number of fishermen, who were
> taken from two schooners by Indians, at Sheepscot River,
> Me., in the early part of the last century. The Indians
> fastened the men to stakes and then barbarously toma-
> hawked them all except Pulcifer, who was suffered to live,
> and, after three months' confinement among the savages,
> made his escape and returned home to Gloucester. His

mind was so much affected by the awful sight of the murder of his companions, and his other sufferings, that the mention of the word Indian would throw him into a paroxysm of fright. It is said that in one of these paroxysms he wandered about in the woods a week, having fled thither upon being told that some savages were near in a boat.

No William Pulsifer appears in Babson. It is possible that "William Pulsifer / of John Pulsifer" should read "*or* John Pulsifer" (although it is "of" in Olson's original typescript), especially since the source does not state which Pulsifer underwent the ordeal. A William Pulsifer owned a home in Dogtown, but that was later (see *Maximus* II, 161). Both Mann, *In the Heart of Cape Ann*, p. 22, and R. Babson and Saville *Tourist's Guide*, p. 26, report that the house on Dogtown occupied by Jeremiah Millet in 1740–41 was owned *later* by William Pulsifer.

II.26. Jones Creek

An inlet of the Annisquam River flowing around the north and west sides of Pearce's Island.

II.26. diorite / edge of meeting / with granite

See *Maximus* II, 16 and note, and map in Shaler, opposite p. 610.

II.27. farm boys / going / fishing

Cf. Babson's account of the emigration from Gloucester, Mass., which founded New Gloucester in Maine, beginning: ". . . the youth who had been brought up to husbandry must turn to the sea for support . . ." (*History*, p. 302).

II.27–30. the information of Mr Richard Yorke . . .

In his *Notes and Additions*, II, 90–92, Babson adds:

> The following document contains a particular account of the capture by the Indians of three of our fishermen at Cape Sable, that year [1713], mentioned in the *History*, page *380*.

> June 22. The information of Mr. Richard Yorke, of Gloucester, taken June 22, 1713, saith that on Tuesday, being the 2d day of this instant June, being at Cape Sable in a sloop on a fishing voyage, and being in a harbour called the Owl's Head, with my sloop, and Mr. John Prince, of said Gloucester, lying by me with his sloop, there came down to the water side, about three of the clock in the afternoon, two Indian men dressed in French clothing, with a kind of a white flag on a stick . . .

The account continues as quoted in the poem, with only a few minor differences in transcription.

Richard Yorke, son of the early settler Samuel York, died in 1718 at the age of twenty-nine. Owl's Head is a point east of Rockland on the coast of Maine at the lower edge of Penobscot Bay. John Prince (ca. 1677–1767) was a Gloucester sea-captain. Colonel Samuel Vetch (1688–1732) led an English force in the capture of Port Royal, the former seat of French Acadia.

II.30. James Davis, captured . . .

The information that follows was first written as marginal notes in Olson's copy of Babson, *Notes and Additions*, II, 91. For Davis, see note below.

II.30. Josiah Ingersoll . . . who m. Mary Stevens

See Babson, *Notes and Additions*, I, 40, notice of the Ingersolls: "Josiah, the next son [of "Samuel, eldest son of Samuel"], married Mary Stevens, Dec. 30, 1712."

II.30. Paul Dolliver . . .

From Babson, *History*, p. 257: "Paul Dolliver settled at Freshwater Cove, near Richard [surname omitted]. He married Mary Wallis, Feb. 11, 1713; and died about 1749 . . ."

For "cf *page 87 before*," see Babson, *Notes and Additions*, II, 87: "Paul Dolliver (*Hist.* 257) appears a little later than Peter and might naturally be associated with him as a near relative, but I am informed by John S. Webber, Esq., one of his descendants, that Paul came from the county of Cornwall, England, about 1710."

II.30. John Sadler

Babson offers no information other than his marriage: "John Sadler and Sarah Scott, of Rowley, were intending marriage April 11, 1713, and had a daughter Sarah born Oct. 1714" (*Notes and Additions*, II, 92; also mentioned in his *History*, p. 146).

II.30. Josiah Lane . . . m. 1713

See Babson, *History*, p. 112: "Josiah married Rachel York in 1713; after which nothing is known of him"; though later Babson is able to add in *Notes and Additions*, I, 41: "Josiah, son of the first John, married Rachel, daughter of Samuel York, Jan. 15, 1713. He died Nov. 23, 1747, aged fifty-eight."

II.30. James Davis, is probably the James IV . . .

From Babson's notice of the Davis family in his *History*, p. 77: "His son James, born in 1690, was twice married: first, in 1719, to Mary Haraden, who died June 22, 1753; and next to Mrs. Hannah Saunders. He became one of the most useful and honored citizens of his time. He resided at Squam, and was one of the deacons of the church there nearly half a century. He also filled all the civil offices held by his father and grandfather; serving the town as one of its selectmen for a long course of years, and for seven years as its representative. His death took place, Aug. 15, 1776."

▶ II.31. Maximus Letter # whatever

Exact date of writing unknown (certainly by 1963 when it was read at Vancouver, but probably written as early as 1959 or 1960). Borrowed from Leland, *Algonquin Legends of New England*, pp. 290−293, though somewhat compressed, i.e., "chockablock." The tale, as found in Leland, begins:

> Once a man was traveling through the woods, and he heard afar off a sound as of footsteps beating the ground.

So he sought to find the people that made it, and went on for a full week ere he came to them. And it was a man and his wife dancing about a tree, in the top of which was a Raccoon. They had, by their constant treading, worn a trench in the ground; indeed, they were in it up to their waists. Then, being asked why they did this strange thing, they answered that, being hungry, they were trying to dance down the tree to catch the Raccoon.

Then the man who had come said, "truly there is a newer and better way of felling trees, which has lately come into the land." As they wished to know what this might be, he showed them how to cut it down, and did so; making it a condition that if they got the game they might have the meat and he should get the skin. So when the tree fell they caught the animal, and the woman, having tanned the skin, gave it to the man, and he went his way. . . .

See also *Maximus* II, 141.

▶ **II.32. I forced the calm grey waters . . .**

Written early March 1961 (probably before March 6th— see note to following poem). An earlier version among the poet's papers (also read at Vancouver in 1963) begins:

> I forced the calm grey waters — Backward I compel
>   Gloucester
> the Sea-Serpent   to yield
>
>   I wanted her
> to come to the surface   I had fought her, below
> long enough   I shaped her out of
> the watery mass with mushroom eyes . . .

The manuscript is reproduced in *OLSON* 3, p. 58, where the editor's note explains the significance of "mushroom eyes." "Backwards I compell / Gloucester / to yield" has already occurred on *Maximus* II, 15, and a celebrated Gloucester sea-serpent was reported sighted on several occasions during the early nineteenth century (see Babson, *History*, pp. 521–523). See also *Maximus* II, 121, and III, 59–61, and notes.

▶ **II.33. Maximus, March 1961—2**

An early manuscript is dated "before Mon March 6"; the original version appears on the same page as other matter dated 6 March 1961.

II.33. by the way into the woods

The setting is Dogtown, along the "upper road." See *Maximus* II, 46: "... what I call the upper road was the way / leading by Joshua Elwell's to the wood-lots ..."; also *Maximus* II, 38 and note.

II.33. otter / ponds

Also located in Dogtown; part of a grant of land off the "lower road" there to the early settler Benjamin Kinnicum in 1719, as noted in the "Commoners Book Vol. 2, 1713–1810," p. 147.

II.33. show me   (exhibit / myself)

In conversation, June 1968, Olson spoke of this poem as resulting from or having to do with a revelatory experience made possible, as in the previous poem, through the consciousness-expanding drug, psilocybin, a synthetic form of the Sacred Mushroom of the Mexican Indians—which he had experienced a few weeks earlier, in February 1961, in an experiment conducted by drug researcher Timothy Leary (see "Under the Mushroom," *Muthologos*, I, 20ff., and Leary, *High Priest*, pp. 143ff.).

Along these lines, in his edition of Whitman's *Leaves of Grass*—which, from evidence in his copy, the poet had been reading in early 1961 (also see "Bill Snow" written February 1961, references there to Whitman's "Trickle Drops" and to the mushroom)—there occurs a marking that may be pertinent. By the poem "In Paths Untrodden," Olson makes the marginal note, "pond-side," and underlines as follows:

> In paths untrodden,
> In the growth by margins of pond-waters,
> Escaped from *the life that exhibits itself* ...;

while in "Bill Snow" he writes: "Under the mushroom there isn't ever a thing which isn't solely more of itself" (*Additional Prose*, p. 42).

▶ II.34. The Account Book of B Ellery

In a note to himself on the order of the poems, Olson indicates this was written by 28–29 March 1961.

Benjamin Ellery (1744–1825), the son of William Ellery (1694–1771) and grandson of William Ellery (d. 1696), both of Gloucester, was a merchant who made his home in Dogtown in the late eighteenth century (see also *Maximus* II, 152 and 200, and *Maximus* III, 168). His account book, a vellum-bound volume, is preserved (though uncatalogued) in the Cape Ann Historical Society's museum on Pleasant Street in Gloucester. It contains birth records of the family inside its front and back covers (faintly in pencil on the last page can be made out the signature "B Ellery"), in addition to the record of transactions, a good many of which are of supplies sold to sea captains. Its earliest entry is for 3 August 1769. In conversation, June 1968, the poet explained that the poem is made up of the categories of entries in the account book.

▶ II.35. A Maximus Song

Dated 6 March 1961.

II.35. Phryne

A Greek courtesan who lived in the fourth century B.C. See the portrait of her in Athenaeus' *Banquet*, XIII. 59 (marked by Olson in his copy):

> But Phryne was a really beautiful woman, even in those parts of her person which were not generally seen: on which account it was not easy to see her naked; for she used to wear a tunic which covered her whole person, and she never used the public baths. But on the solemn assembly of the Eleusinian festival, and on the feast of the Posidonia, then she laid aside her garments in the sight of all the assembled Greeks, and having undone her hair, she went to

bathe in the sea; and it was from her that Apelles took his picture of the Venus Anadyomene; and Praxiteles the statuary, who was a lover of hers, modelled the Cnidian Venus from her body . . .

See also Jung and Kerenyi, *Essays on a Science of Mythology*, p. 151.

▶ II.36. LATER TYRIAN BUSINESS

Dated 12 March 1961. See the earlier "Tyrian Businesses" in *Maximus* I, 35–40.

II.36. the Diadem

Cf. "Tyrian Businesses," *Maximus* I, 37:

> As my flower,
> after rain, wears
> such diadem

See also "the diadem of the Dog / which is morning," *Maximus* II, 123.

II.36. "morning" / after

Cf. "Tyrian Businesses," *Maximus* I, 37:

> The seedling
> of morning: to move, the problems (after the night's
>   presences) . . .

II.36. the 7 Angels of the 3rd Angel's / Sleep—the 7 / Words

Corbin, in his account of the progress of the soul according to the vision of Nasir Tusi (q.v.) in "Cyclical Time in Mazdaism and Ismailism," p. 154, writes of the angel "fallen behind himself. From third he has become tenth. To the Time of his stupor that he must redeem corresponds the emanation of the seven other Intelligences which are called the seven Cherubim or the seven Divine Words." "The decade [of angels that the soul encounters] is completed by three superior esoteric ranks corresponding respectively to the third Angel, to the *Tali,* and to the *Sabiq* (*Nafs* and *'Aql,* second and first Angels), the primordial pair from which issued the third Angel . . . and the Seven Cherubim Angels, or Words . . ." (p. 169n).

II.36. Eternal Events

See *Maximus* II, 5 and 79, and notes.

II.36. the Salivarating / Dog

Fenris, with the arm of Tyr in his mouth (see *Maximus* III, 34 and 63) or after the sword was thrust in his jaws after he was bound (there was so much slaver it formed a river called Von or Expectation); or possibly Cerberus, guardian dog of the Greek underworld, offspring of Typhon (q.v.). Hercules carried him off as part of his labors and while doing so, Cerberus' saliva fell upon the ground and there sprang up the plant aconite. Graves calls him the Greek counterpart of Anubis, the dog-shaped Egyptian god of the dead (*Greek Myths,* I, 124). But see esp. *Maximus* III, 47, beginning "Space and Time the saliva / in the mouth . . . ," where the allusion to Fenris is stronger.

II.36. God the Dog

A not uncommon pun, but see esp. the earlier "Tyrian Businesses," *Maximus* I, 37, "He sd: Notice / the whiteness. . . ," and note; also *Maximus* II, 9, "Christ o Christ pick the seeds / out of yr teeth—how handsome / the dead dog lies," and note.

II.36. the 1st / Angel—who / Adores. Only after / was there a "soul" / of the World—nafs

From Corbin, "Cyclical Time in Mazdaism and Ismailism," p. 150:

> The first schema is drawn from Iranian sources, particularly Nasir-e Khosraw. He describes the procession of the

five primordial archangelical hypostases, the first two of which are the Intelligence ('*Aql*) and the Soul (*Nafs*). This eternal motion which moves the being of the first Intelligence or Archangel is an eternal movement of adoration of the Principle, which eternally actuates it toward being. From this eternal movement of adoration, from this cosmic liturgy, the Soul of the World eternally takes its birth.

II.36. the Anima / Mundi

'Soul of the World' (Latin). See also "Causal Mythology," *Muthologos*, I, 91 and 93: ". . . the spirit of the world, which I have never been able to see as other than the figure of woman as she is such in the very phrase *anima mundi*. . . . I just meant the rather classic figure, which I . . . well, for example in the Tarot deck it's the *El Mundo*, card XXI is *anima mundi*. She's the Virgin . . . she's the whole works. She's it." See also Jung, *Psychology and Alchemy*, figures 8 and 91.

▶ II.37. for Robt Duncan, / who understands . . . —written because of him / March 17, 1961

Robert Duncan (b. 1919), the American poet. Olson called him "the Wings of poetry." They met initially in 1947, while Olson was in Berkeley doing research at the Bancroft Library on the California Gold Rush. As he himself reports it, in a note for Duncan's *Years as Catches*, he had previously read a poem by Duncan in the magazine *Circle*, and, "I, arriving in San Francisco, / to Kenneth Rexroth who as always generously met me at the / station who's / Robert Duncan? And thereby / flew off / to meet him." They were drawn closer together as contributors to *Origin* in the early 1950's and the *Black Mountain Review*, and through their correspondence. Duncan was invited to take Robert Creeley's place at Black Mountain College in the spring and summer of 1956, shortly before the school closed; he in turn invited Olson to read at the Poetry Center at San Francisco State College in February 1957. For a deeper sense of their relationship, see e.g. "Against Wisdom As Such" (*Human*

Universe, pp. 67–71) and Duncan's "Notes on Poetics Regarding Olson's 'Maximus.'"

In a letter shortly after this poem was written, Olson wrote to Duncan, in response to a letter from him dated 15 March 1961:

> You will of course know what happiness your letter brought
> Also power. Or at least I wrote a Maximus that day which (if I can get it finished) . . . has for title for Robt Duncan etc (1st time, I do believe, the directly personal has fitted

In his letter, Duncan had written that he had been lecturing on Olson and the *Maximus* poems, "and I got, grabbed out of the air where it had been waiting, or grabbed out of my heart where it had been wanted: Maximus as a magic opus—not as magical or imagination [next to these last words Olson adds markings and an exclamation point in the margin] but as a recipe that had to be followed, paced out to a locus as in *Letter, May 2, 1959* . . ."

II.37. Gravel Hill

Small prominence in Dogtown at the entrance of Dogtown Road from Cherry Street. See also *Maximus* II, 160–162.

II.37. Jeremiah Millett's

See, e.g., Babson and Saville, *Tourist's Guide*, p. 26: "On the Dogtown Road (which is reached from Riverdale via Reynard Street) starting in at Gravel Hill on Cherry Street—we find that in 1741 Jeremiah Millet lived in the house later occupied by the Pulcifers." And again, from the same source, p. 32: ". . . going up Gravel Hill to the right, we come to the site of an old street car at the left just beyond which there is a large turn in the road. At this turn, on the right, is 'Split Rock' which makes a break in the stone wall bordering the road. Directly beyond Split Rock was the town pasture thru which a brook runs. On the Split Rock side was located the William Pulcifer or Jeremiah Millet place."

See note to Jeremiah Millet, *Maximus* II, 3.

II.37. my 'writing' stand- / stump

Michael McClure (see next note) wrote to Olson, ca. 4 December 1959, "How great it was to see you leaned over your table in your finca writing a great action poem with your branch-quill, in Dog Town." Donald Allen, in a conversation with the author, May 1975, described the "'writing' stand" to which the poet had led his visitors that afternoon a year and a half earlier, as a flat board or plank, almost chest-high on Olson, nailed to a tree trunk and supported by a post and cross-beam. Olson demonstrated to his guests how he might write at the stand if he wished, with a tree branch serving as a pen. See also *Maximus* III, 22.

II.37. Michael McClure

(b. 1932), American poet. He had visited Gloucester with Donald Allen in November 1959, when Olson took his guests to Dogtown for an afternoon (see McClure's foreword to the original publication of 'Maximus, from Dogtown—I," quoted in a note to *Maximus* II, 2 above).

II.37. Don Allen

Donald M. Allen (b. 1912), editor of the anthology *The New American Poetry* (1960), which featured Olson's work, as well as such important early collections of Olson's writings as *The Distances* (1960) and *Human Universe and Other Essays* (1965).

II.37. Charles Peter

The poet's son, then a boy of four and a half.

II.37. David Cummings

Olson mentions in a letter to Edward Dorn, 29 November 1959: "Don A[llen] LeRoi Jones and a very nice guy from Albert Einstein Hospital named David Cummings drove them up . . ." Donald Allen reports in a letter to the author, 27 July 1975: "David Cummings wandered into a poetry reading on, I think, 9th Avenue near 42nd Street. He was curious about the beat writing scene, and since he had a large secondhand car soon became known as the 'chauffeur of the Beat poets,' driving them to readings in New England and then south to points in NJ and to Washington, as I recall."

II.37. the pile of rotting fish . . .

See also *Maximus* II, 4:

> like smoked fish
> in the same field
> fly-blown and a colony
> of self-hugging grubs—handsome
> in the sun . . .

II.37. Edward Dahlberg

(1900–1977), American writer and important early friend of the poet. In his *Confessions*, Dahlberg speaks of meeting Olson "around 1938, when I was living in East Gloucester"— a rooming house at 44 Mount Pleasant Avenue—though surely the date is earlier, in August of 1936. A letter from Dahlberg to the photographer Alfred Stieglitz written 12 August 1936 (now in the Beinecke Library at Yale) mentions the meeting and describes Olson as "very sensitive, one of those porous personalities who, I believe, will do something in his life."

Although Olson was only twenty-five and about to be a graduate student at Harvard when he introduced himself, and Dahlberg was ten years older, with three novels published and experience of literary society, the two men became close friends. It was Dahlberg who arranged for the appearance of Olson's first important publication, while associate editor of the magazine *Twice A Year*, by urging Dorothy Norman to accept for publication "Lear and Moby Dick," which he selected from a long paper Olson had written for F.O. Matthiessen's class.

The incident related in the poem occurred during a stay with Olson and his mother at Oceanwood Cottage in Gloucester around 1940. Both men were intently at work, Olson on Melville and Dahlberg on what was to be published as *Do These Bones Live*. Olson completed chapters of a book on Melville, which Dahlberg advised against publishing on the grounds the style was too allusive, too "biblical" (see *Muthologos*, II, 103; also Charters, *Olson / Melville*, p. 9), and had a hand in the shaping of Dahlberg's book, especially the material there on Melville and Shakespeare (see the high compliments addressed to Olson in *Do These Bones Live* and later *The Flea of Sodom*).

While working, they shared meals together. According to Olson (in conversation, June 1968), who was apparently oblivious to the slight, his mother offended Dahlberg by serving him "left-over" meats while reserving the choicer meats, such as pork-chops, for her son, her "growing boy." (Dahlberg remembered it as a meal of chicken in a letter to John Cech, 27 January 1972, heaped with other bitter recollections of Olson: "the one time I was Charles' guest at East Gloucester I was seated at the table, and I noticed that his mother served him with fried chicken and I a thin plate of orts. I spoke to Charles about this, and when he was upset he ruffed his auburn silken hair.") The incident continued to prey and was brought up years later, when Olson reminded Dahlberg of it in a letter of 23 April 1947. Dahlberg wrote back, April 25th: "Now, for the matter of paying some irreverence to your mother. You are again unjust: the one time I was your guest, I got the water and you the wine out of the Cana Pots. I am not a gross feeder, and what food is put before me does not matter, provided my host has the same frugal fare. You happen to be a rank eater, and if Plato and Socrates and the fable of Euripides and the dogs could not teach you that it is base to give your guest dingy food while you sit opposite him and eat large chines of beef, then your belly and your unflagging appetite should have given you such breeding and wisdom." Olson apparently persisted, for Dahlberg responded, 2 May 1947: "Now to speak as simply as I can about the time when I was your guest; does one have to be clever to make you understand that it is base to sit at table and eat better food than you offer your guest. Aldington told me that Gerhardt Hauptman once invited him to dinner; he set a bottle of vin ordinaire before Aldington while he drank rich Sauterne. You will be lenient if I find a dismal cleavage between Hauptman's socialism and his hospitality."

Yet their relationship continued into the middle 1950's. In his *Confessions*, Dalberg denies there had been any "fevered or scurfed quarrel" between Olson and himself. "For seven years I had received two or three letters a week from him, with the salutation: 'Edward, my Edward.' Then one day he came to see me, his head pained, the broad surfaces of his face gnarled and warped, and disclosed that he feared my influence was impeding him" (p. 259). Dahlberg had introduced him to notable figures in the arts, such as William Carlos Williams, Alfred Stieglitz, Ford Madox Ford, Waldo Frank, Marsden Hartley, among others. When *Call Me Ishmael* was published, Dahlberg had been enthusiastic about it and later defended it in "Laurels for Borrowers" (1951). It was through Dahlberg that Olson first was offered a position at Black Mountain College (see Duberman, *Black Mountain*, p. 307), and in "Projective Verse" Olson acknowledges that it was Dahlberg who "first pounded into my head" the basic lesson, "ONE PERCEPTION MUST IMMEDIATELY AND DIRECTLY LEAD TO A FURTHER PERCEPTION." Still, Dahlberg had little sympathy for the poetry of Ezra Pound and the moderns to whom Olson had turned.

For a fuller account of this relationship—in some ways as vital to Olson as his relationship with Pound—see Cech, "Edward Dahlberg and Charles Olson: A Biography of a Friendship." See also, "he was right: people / don't change," *Maximus* I, 5 and note.

II.37. a mother is a hard thing to get away from . . .

See, e.g., Olson's poems "As the Dead Prey Upon Us" and "Moonset, Gloucester" (though also, to be fair, Dahlberg's autobiographical *Because I Was Flesh*, which contains a memorable portrait of his mother, Lizzie).

II.37. Wordsworth . . . whose Preface is a 'walker' for us all . . .

William Wordsworth (1770–1850), the English poet. His *"Preface"* is that to the second edition (1800) of *Lyrical Ballads*, a collection of poems by himself and Coleridge, in which he writes, e.g., "the principal object, then, proposed in these poems was to choose incidents and situations from common life, and to relate or describe them, throughout, as far as was possible, in a selection of language really used by men. . . ."

II.37. Benjamin / Kinnicum's . . . five / very rocky acres . . .

Benjamin Kinnicum appears in Babson's *History* only on the list of settlers from 1701 to 1750 (p. 260), although Babson in his later *Notes and Additions* reports that there appears in Thomas Bray's will, 1692, a bequest of six pounds to "Margaret Kinnicum, wife of Benj. Kinnicum" (I, 10), while the marriage of Benjamin Kinnicum and Margaret Josline or Josselyn is reported in an entry for 1711 (II, 89). Olson's information concerning Kinnicum's acreage is from the town records themselves ("Commoners Book Vol. 2," p. 141, entry for 14 March 1717): "Laid out and sold to Benjamin Kenikom about five acres of very rocky Land. . . ."

II.37. John / Josselyn

(fl. 1638–1675), brother of Henry Josselyn, who was the representative of Mason and Gorges in Maine and author of two volumes dealing with New England based on his observations during two visits to the area: *New-Englands Rarities Discovered* (1672), an account of the plants and animals of the region, and *An Account of Two Voyages to New-England* (1674), in which the section quoted later in the poem appears.

II.37. his brother's son's daughter

Margaret Josselyn (b. 1687), daughter of Henry Josselyn, whose father, also named Henry (see note to *Maximus* II, 25), was the brother of John Josselyn.

II.37. Higginson

The Rev. Francis Higginson, minister of Salem (see *Maximus* I, 46 and note). For his observation concerning strawberries, see e.g. Babson, *History*, p. 44: "On Saturday, June 27, 1629, the ship 'Talbot,' with Rev. Francis Higginson and other passengers, who were sent over by the Massachusetts Company to Salem, anchored in our harbor; 'where,' says Mr. Higginson in his journal, 'there was an island, whither four of our men with a boat went, and brought back again ripe strawberries and gooseberries and sweet single roses.'"

II.37. North- / road, the one went to the woodlots

Commons Road in Dogtown; also known as the "upper" road. For "the woodlots," see note to *Maximus* II, 38.

II.37. Ann Robinson and her husband Samuel / Davis

See *Maximus* II, 25 and note; also II, 53 and 152. Samuel Davis' grant of about six and a quarter acres on 27 October 1713 is recorded in the "Original Records: Commoners Book No. 1," p. 205, and is noted by Olson in his notebook "D'Town Dec 8 1960 . . . Sat. JAN 14th, 1961 [still at it, Friday Jan 20th!] *ENDED* abt Feb 21st? 1961," p. 32.

II.38. the Gulf of Maine

Section of the Atlantic Ocean along the northeast coast from Nova Scotia to Cape Cod, including the Bay of Fundy and Massachusetts Bay; the prime fishing area for the Gloucester fishermen.

II.38. La Have

See *Maximus* II, 24 and note.

II.38. Lunenburg, / Nova Scotia

Fishing town about forty miles southwest of Halifax.

II.38. meadows on which we saw fish / being cured 1960

See "the pile of rotting fish," *Maximus* II, 37 and note, and II, 4 and note.

II.38. Gloucester's Meeting House / Green

See *Maximus* I, 145 and note.

II.38. green fields / to dry the silver wealth . . .

See John Smith's description of the New England fisheries as silver mines, *Maximus* I, 109 and note.

II.38. Wm Smallmans

Dogtown settler; his name appears only in the town records (see *Maximus* II, 46 and note).

II.38. Widow / Davis's (1741)

According to the survey of Dogtown made by Joshua (Josiah) Batchelder in 1741, Widow Ann Davis (wife of Samuel Davis) lived on Commons Road at the rear of Widow Lydia Canaby's residence (R. Babson and Saville, *Cape Ann Tourist's Guide*, p. 42; cellar number 32.) It would have been the dogs kept for protection by old widows such as these that gave Dogtown its name.

See also note to "Capt Andrew Robinson," *Maximus* II, 25.

II.38. James Marsh

Little is known of this early settler, who seems to have married into Dogtown through the Riggs family, one of the oldest in the area. The only mention of him in Babson is a notice of his marriage to Sarah Riggs in 1728 and the subsequent birth of their children (*Notes and Additions*, II, 112); however, Mann is able to report him as dwelling on Commons Road at the time of the plan of Dogtown made by Josiah Batchelder in 1741 (*Beginnings of Dogtown*, p. 28), and

Roger Babson, in his and Saville's *Tourist's Guide*, p. 42, states that "On the left beyond the brook [off Commons Road] are two cellars (R) and (T) close together, one marking the house of James Marsh." Marsh's name is not apparent in the town records and Olson's notes from the time indicate he knew little more about him than what is available in the published sources cited.

II.38. what the record says—the way leading by / Joshua Elwell's to, the wood-lots, divided 1721.

The "record" is the "Original Records: Commoners Book No. 1, 1707–1820," on p. 205 of which is recorded a grant of some eleven acres "lying on the South-westerly side of the way leading by Joshua Elwell's to the wood-lots" to a number of Dogtown settlers, 4 December 1727 (noted by Olson in his notebook, "D'Town Dec 8 1960 . . . ," p. 34).

Joshua Elwell (b. 1687), according to Mann, "was the father of Isaac, married Susanna Stanwood (daughter, I judge, of Andrew), and became the father of Cap. Isaac Elwell, at one time postmaster of Gloucester" (*Beginnings of Dogtown*, p. 28 and map). His house was along the Commons Road (see map in Mann), cellar number 30 on Roger Babson's map of Dogtown.

The "division of the wood-lots," critical for Olson's establishing a date for the settlement of this part of Dogtown, is described in Babson and Saville, pp. 27–28 (marked in Olson's copy):

> In addition to these families holding a fee title to the small walled-in farms which they occupied, including more or less pasture land, they were later given certain "cow rights" or "wood lots" on a large tract of over 1,000 acres which is now known as the "Commons Pastures." Thus, altho each family had its own home and garden, they all had an interest in the "Commons" where they cut wood and did a certain amount of pasturing. These wood-lots were laid out in 1722 and numbered 136 in all. They were from 10 to 20 rods wide and from 160 to 320 rods

long according to the location. . . . All these lots are shown
on a plan made by Major Mason in 1835.

See also John Babson's *History*, pp. 233–238.

II.38. My problem is how to make you believe / these persons . . . went off to fish . . .

Cf. the following from *The Fishermen's Own Book*, p. 37:

> Why the early fishermen should have sought such out-
> of-the-way places—always far up some river or creek—in
> preference to Gloucester harbor, whose convenience of
> access and adaptability to the business has given birth to a
> thriving and growing city, is left to conjecture. It may be
> that in those troublous times they selected them as being
> more remote from the sea, and affording greater safety
> from the depredations of piratical craft, which were then
> quite numerous, and also from the cruisers of the govern-
> ments with which the mother country was then at war. The
> location of their dwelling houses—of which forty desolate
> cellars remain, whose story none can tell—far removed
> from the shore, and always in some secluded spot, corro-
> borates this view, as does the tradition that they hauled
> their fish up on Dogtown Common to cure.

II.38. George Dennison's store

Babson says in his *History*, p. 298: "George Dennison first
appears here on occasion of his marriage to Abigail Haraden, Ja. 14, 1725. He had several children; and died
March 14, 1748, aged forty-eight. His son Isaac died April 2,
1811, aged seventy-nine; leaving a son Isaac, who was a
soldier in the Revolutionary War, and died June 21, 1841,
aged eighty." In his *Notes and Additions*, II, 107, Babson is
able to add: "He carried on considerable maritime business
at Lobster Cove and had his home on a retired spot in the
adjoining woods where descendants have lived to the present
time."

Copeland and Rogers, however, write more fully (*Saga of
Cape Ann*, p. 172):

> George Dennison, who built a house on the old road
> through the woods to Sandy Bay, about a mile from the

head of Lobster Cove, also operated a store there. It was
opened in 1732 and Mr. Dennison sold groceries, woolen
cloth, boots, fishing gear, and four brands of rum. . . .

In the eighteenth century the spot where the Dennison
store was located was not so out of the way as it may seem
to be today. It was on a main thoroughfare between
Planters Neck and Sandy Bay. It also was only about a mile
from Dogtown, by way of the Whale's Jaw path, and many
men then living in Dogtown worked on the fishing vessels
or in the shipyards at Lobster Cove. A road from Goose
Cove (Dennison Street plus a section of road not now in
use) also led into the Sandy Bay road near the Dennison
store. Hence it was an eighteenth-century traffic center.
The George Dennison house is still standing, in excellent
repair.

See also *Maximus* III, 168–172.

II.38. John Adams . . . actually born Alexander Smith

(1764–1829), member of the mutinous crew of H.M.S.
Bounty. He survived and settled on Pitcairn Island in the
Pacific following the mutiny, where his descendants may be
found today. For the identification of Adams as Smith of
Dogtown, see Bolton, "John Adams of Pitcairn's Island," and
Sargent, *Life of Alexander Smith.*

Olson apparently came upon this curious fact while working at the Sandy Bay Historical Society and Museum in Rockport where there is a drawing of Alexander Smith on display, for a note written on a folder from that society, from
around 1960, mentions that this Smith was the son of
Alexander Smith and Rebecca Gardner who lived on Dogtown's Back Road (cellar no. 6 on R. Babson's map); while in
a notebook from 1960 ("started night of May 27th, 1960 . . ."),
he enters, p. 90: ". . . work done Monday July 18, fr SBHS
lead of Alexander Smith ('John Adams' of Bounty) . . ."

II.38. Christian mate when sd crew / busted Bligh

William Bligh (1754–1817) was in command of the *Bounty*
when the famous mutiny led by Fletcher Christian, the
master's mate, broke out in 1789. He and loyal members of

the crew were set adrift in an open boat, but reached the island of Timor, north of Australia, after a voyage of 4,000 miles.

II.38. New Hebrides

Island group in the southwest Pacific.

II.38. Pegasus

The winged horse of Greek mythology, which sprang from the body of Medusa upon her death. He came to be considered a symbol of poetic inspiration, since it was a stamp of his hoof that caused Hippocrene, the fountain of the muses, to issue forth on Mount Helicon.

II.38. Hector

Champion of the Trojans in the *Iliad* who was slain by Achilles.

II.38. muthos

See note to *muthologos*, *Maximus* I, 100. For the relation of mouth to *muthos*, see Harrison, *Themis*, p. 328 and note; also "Poetry and Truth," *Muthologos*, II, 37–38.

II.38. the world / is an eternal event

See *Maximus* II, 5 and note.

II.38. this epoch solely / the decline of fishes

See note to "Aquarian Time / after fish," *Maximus* II, 9, for light on the pun.

II.38. Bayliss

Doris Bayliss, wife at the time of Jonathan Bayliss, friend of the poet and then comptroller of Gorton's, Inc., the leading Gloucester fish processing firm. Mrs. Bayliss conducted a nursery school in her home on Washington Street.

II.39–41. "on the coast of Maine / shop-keepers there are none . . .

From Josselyn's "Two Voyages to New England," verbatim, as quoted in Innis, *Cod Fisheries*, p. 117–118n.

In remarks made while reading the poem at the Vancouver Conference, 14 August 1963 (preserved on tape), Olson reveals something of his purpose: ". . . that damn passage of Josselyn is all that marketing and fishing and 'Bostonism' of the coast halfway from Dogtown down to La Have, so that you've got a built-in coast there with all that activity and the moving of the marketing as well." The passage, he continues, "is a piggy-back poem on the Duncan, and is a part of it."

▶ **II.42. Further Completion of Plat**

Written by 28–29 March 1961 (note by Olson to himself on the order of the poems). The poem is written from information obtained from the town records and Babson's *History* and its supplements. For the poet's sense of the origins and significance of Dogtown, see also "Olson in Gloucester," *Muthologos*, I, 187–188, 191.

Mann, interestingly, uses the same word for the map or plan of Dogtown in his *Beginnings of Dogtown* (p. 18): "The 'platt' of the embryo Fourth Parish shows that in 1741–2 there were 25 houses standing within the limits of what we now call Dogtown."

II.42. Lt James Davis . . . to share 4 / more 1728/9 . . .

Davis (1663–1743) was one of the early settlers of Dogtown. See the notice of him in Babson's *History*, pp. 76–77, and in the *Notes and Additions*, I, 15. Here the poet has consulted the local records for his information. In a notebook, "D'Town Dec 8 1960 . . . Feb 21st? 1961," p. 40, Olson had copied from the "Commoners Book Vol. 2," p. 51: "1728/9 Wm Smallmans land [to Lieut James Davis & *James Stanwood* 3 or 4 acres *between their own land & Wm Smallmans*."

II.42. James / Stanwood

(b. 1690), another early resident of Dogtown. Mann, *Beginnings of Dogtown*, pp. 23–24, writes: "On the right of the village street stood in 1740 the house of James Stanwood. He appears to have been the son of John and the grandson of Philip, the founder of the family on Cape Ann and in America. James Stanwood married Mary, the daughter of Lieut. James Davis, in 1712, and had two sons, James and William. In 1728 James Stanwood was admitted a resident of Falmouth, now Portland, Maine, but evidently did not settle there, unless the James whose name is marked on the plan is the son." The same information is in Babson's *History*, pp. 167 and 297, and his *Notes and Additions*, I, 75.

II.42. the first / 10 acres, May 23, 1717, are "of land and Rocks . . .

From the "Original Records: Commoners Book No. 1," p. 112 (recorded by Olson in his notebook designated "D' Town Dec 8 1960 . . . ," p. 96):

> May 23, 1717. Laid out by the seven men comittie to Leit. James Davis about ten acres of land and rocks (between Joseph Ingersons and Bryants) . . .

Also on that page, for the next day:

> Then laid out and sold by the seven men comittie to Leit John Davis about four acres of land, adjoining to his former land, on the south, and on the east . . .

The two grants add up to the "14 acres" referred to in the opening line of the poem.

II.42. Ingarson Ingersoll

See *Maximus* II, 25 and note.

II.42. Smallman

See also *Maximus* II, 38, and II, 46 and note.

II.42. Falmouth (Portland's) rearising

See note to Portland, *Maximus* II, 24.

II.42. James Demerit . . . married Mary Briant

Olson records this in his notebook "D'Town Dec 8 1960 . . . ," p. 88, apparently from the Commoners Records. Recorded also in Babson, *Notes and Additions*, II, 109, and in Gloucester's *Vital Records*, II, 101.

II.42. Mill River

Inlet of the Annisquam, just west of Dogtown. See note to p. 151 of *Maximus* I.

II.42. acres, intermingled with John Day's / and Ezekiel Day's

John Day (b. 1657), according to Babson, "had a house near Poles [q.v.] . . . The date of his death is not ascertained. He may have lived nearly to 1742; when Joseph Winslow was administrator of the estate of a John Day, who appears to have been his father-in-law" (*History*, p. 79; also *Notes and Additions*, I, 17).

Ezekiel Day (b. 1662) "received a grant of land to set a house upon, between Lobster Cove and Hogskin Cove, in 1694; and was one of the first settlers in that section of the town. He married Mary Rowe, Jan. 27, 1690; and died Feb. 18, 1725, leaving several children" (Babson, *History*, pp. 79–80).

Evidence of the "intermingling" of acres belonging to the Davises with those of the Days can be found throughout the town records.

II.42. Captain Andrew Robinson

See *Maximus* II, 25 and note.

II.42. Ebenezer died in 1732 leaving £3047

In the *History*, p. 77, Babson notes that Ebenezer Davis (b. 1681) "was engaged in mercantile employments, and was one of the first in town who entered extensively into such pursuits. The inventory of his estate, amounting to three thousand pounds, shows that his labors were not unrewarded." In his *Notes and Additions*, I, 15, Babson is more exact: "Ebenezer Davis, youngest son of the first James, also resided in the Fourth Parish, and there carried on his maritime business. His will was proved Nov. 27, 1732. In the inventory of his estate, amounting to £3047.7.2, I find '3—4 sloop Good Intent, 3—4 sloop Elizabeth, 3—4 sloop Dolphin, 1—2 cargo gone to Virginia, 6 silver spoons, £6, negro man, £95, and Straitsmouth Island, £225.'"

II.42. Elias . . . died / at 40 and already at sd age was worth / £4500 . . .

Elias Davis (b. 1694) "was a merchant of extensive business, which he probably carried on at Squam Harbor. He died about 1734, leaving sons Job and Mark, and an estate, valued in the currency of the time, when corn was worth six shillings a bushel, at upwards of forty-five hundred pounds" (Babson, *History*, p. 77). In *Notes and Additions*, I, 15, Babson provides the inventory of the estate, referred to by Olson:

> Elias, next son of Lieut. James Davis, born Jan. 26, 1694, left at his decease the largest estate that had been acquired by any citizen of the town at that time:—upwards of £4500. I suppose that his home was somewhere on the east side of Mill River, and that he carried on his business in that section of the town. The inventory of his estate mentions dwelling house, warehouse and wharf, and fishing room at Canso, a large amount of merchandise, and the following vessels:—

	Schooner	John,	£460
	"	Mary,	330
	"	Molly,	170
	"	Flying Horse,	150
3—4	"	Greyhound,	131.5
3—4	"	Elizabeth,	205.5

Canso is a town in Nova Scotia north of Halifax.

II.42. More on Joseph Ingersoll / to follow

Nothing really comes of this in these published poems except a brief mention in *Maximus* II, 152. Ingersoll does, however, appear in occasional notes and poem fragments among Olson's papers.

II.42. Deacon Joseph Winslow, who bought from his father-in-law / Day, in 1724

See note to John Day above; also Mann, *Beginnings of Dogtown*, pp. 20–21, where it is reported that Abigail Day, widow of John, "had a daughter Sarah who married Deacon Joseph Winslow, mentioned in the Dogtown book, as the good deacon was in 1742 the administrator of John's estate. . . . There is no doubt in my mind that the name 'Joseph Whiston' on the original plan is an error. The house is that of Joseph Winslow, as is shown by consulting the list of distances, it being a rod from James Stanwood's, on the opposite side of the street, while no distance is given for the house of Joseph Whiston, named elsewhere in the list." In his *Notes and Additions*, II, 95, Babson records, "Joseph Winslow and Sarah Day were married Dec. 24 [1719] . . ." The purchase of 1724 referred to is probably the transfer of property recorded in the "Transcript of Book Two of the Commoners' Records," p. 85.

▶ II.43. A Prayer, to the Lord . . .

Dated 28 March 1961.

II.43. like a good old Catholic

The poet was raised as a Roman Catholic, after his mother's faith (see, e.g., "Reading at Berkeley," *Muthologos*, I, 149, and *The Post Office*, pp. 34–35).

II.43. San Vitale

Church in Ravenna, Italy, begun in the early sixth century. The tomb of Dante, who died in Ravenna in 1321, is just outside the church of San Francesco in that city.

II.43. my great White Cadillac

It might be reported that Mary Shore of Gloucester and her husband had such an automobile at the time, which she said Olson enjoyed because "he could stretch his legs out in it." She also told this writer, June 1972, that the poet once mentioned to her that this poem had been written with her car in mind.

▶ II.44. <u>Bohlin I</u>

Date of writing not known. This is the first of two poems dealing with the exploits of Captain Thomas Bohlin of Gloucester. All the information but for the date of "September 30, 1893" can be found in Connolly, *Book of the Gloucester Fishermen*, pp. 145–146. Some months after writing a story about Bohlin and his schooner, the *Nannie C. Bohlin* (see notes to following poem), Connolly is introduced to the skipper himself in a barber shop:

> Bohlin was about to button his collar around his seventeen-inch neck. He was a short, powerful man, five feet five in height, and weighing one hundred and eighty-five pounds. "So, you're the man who wrote that story about the *Nannie?*"
>
> "About you and the *Nannie*," I amended.
>
> "Never mind me. In that story you said the *Nannie* sailed from Cape Sable to Eastern Point in fourteen hours and a half. Where'd you get your time?"
>
> "From two of your crew."
>
> "They told you fourteen hours and a half?"
>
> "One told me fourteen hours and thirty-five minutes, and one told me fourteen hours and twenty-five minutes. I thought either time fast enough, but I split the difference and called it fourteen hours and a half."
>
> "You did? Well, the *Nannie* sailed from Cape Sable to Gloucester—not to any Eastern Point outside but to anchor in the stream inside the harbor—in fourteen hours and twenty-five minutes. You'd ought to give the *Nannie* what was comin' to her."
>
> "I'll see to that, Captain, when next I write about her. Fourteen hours and twenty-five minutes—that was great going, wasn't it?"

> "The fastest goin' any vessel of her tonnage ever showed anywheres—a strong fifteen and a half knots for that last two hundred and twenty-odd miles. We raised the Yarmouth steamer that has a thirteen-knot schedule at eight o'clock in the mornin' and at one in the afternoon we had her hull down. It was maybe a bit choppy for the steamer— I ain't sayin' she was makin' her full schedule—but that's what the *Nannie* did on that last leg home from Norway."

The information is also condensed in Connolly's *Port of Gloucester*, p. 253: "The record of the *Nannie Bohlin* (Captain Tommy Bohlin) sailing from Cape Sable to Gloucester, 225 miles (sea miles) in 14 hours, 25 minutes, an average speed of 15.6 knots, stands unequaled for a vessel of anywhere near her tonnage. She was 102 feet on the water line, 117 feet over all."

For a photograph of Bohlin and the *Nannie C. Bohlin*, see opposite p. 210 in the *Memorial of the 250th Anniversary of Gloucester* volume. See also *Maximus* I, 19 and note.

For "the stream" of Gloucester Harbor see *Maximus* II, 144 and note.

▶ II.45. <u>Bohlin 2</u>

Written March 1961 (early manuscript dated).

II.45. Bohlin / hove to, once / loaded down / with pickled herring . . .

From Connolly, *Book of the Gloucester Fishermen*, pp. 277–278:

> A correction: Bohlin did once heave a vessel to after he started for home. He once left Newfoundland in winter with a cargo of pickled herring. Load a vessel deep with herring in pickle and you might almost as well be on a half-tide rock for any lift you will feel of her deck under you. Besides having both holds full Bohlin was carrying two hundred and seventy-five barrels of herring on deck.
> Bohlin met with heavy weather. The vessel was trying to wallow through it. The deck load began to go adrift. While securing the deck load one man was washed overboard and lost. To prevent further loss of life, not to speak of the loss of cargo to the owners, Bohlin hove her to long

enough to put fresh lashings to the deck load. The vessel was not his own *Nannie*. If it had been the *Nannie* (according to Bohlin) nobody would have been washed overboard and lost. She might have allowed a little loose water to come aboard, but she never allowed it to stay there,—not the *Nannie*.

II.45. all having breakfast / with their boots on . .

Connolly, *Book of the Gloucester Fishermen*, pp. 144–145, tells of a fictionalized account he had published of a race between Bohlin's schooner and an English racing yacht (the material of the previous poem), which Bohlin himself had been given to read:

> That story came out in *Scribner's Magazine* on a late September day. A friend of mine, Maurice Foley, who was also a friend and neighbor of Bohlin's, bought a copy of the magazine and passed it over to him with the suggestion that he take it to sea with him and read it. Bohlin was sailing early next morning for a Grand Banks halibut trip.
>
> Bohlin was gone six weeks. Some of his crew were standing up on the corner after they came home. Soon they were telling of how the skipper, whenever it was too rough to fish, would be sitting in the cabin reading a magazine story somebody wrote about him and the *Nannie*.
>
> "Something in that story Tommie didn't like I guess," said one of the crew, "because one day he gets up saying: 'Gettin' old am I? I'd like to have some of 'em alongside me in a breeze o' wind and I'd show 'em how old I was gettin'.' And comin' home this time—man, man! Drove her? The planks were that loose in her for'ard that we all had to wear rubber boots sittin' down to our meals."

Connolly's story, "Home Bound, The Nannie O," in which the name Ohlsen is substituted for Bohlin, was reprinted in his collection, *Gloucestermen*. In that story, p. 191, the skipper refers to his ship as being made of three inches of oak.

II.45. if Bohlin had sailed / the Lady of Good Voyage / or his own Bohlin instead / of Dr. Stimson's in / the ocean race

Bohlin was hired to skipper the yacht owned by Dr. Lewis A. Stimson of New York in a race across the Atlantic for a cup offered by the Emperor of Germany, and made an excellent showing despite the fact he competed against the fastest ships of the time, much larger vessels. The account can be found in Connolly, *Book of the Gloucester Fishermen*, pp. 147–169. Given the nature of the competition, it probably would not have made much difference if he had sailed his own *Nannie C. Bohlin*, or any other standard two-masted Gloucester schooner.

II.45. he'd a rolled down a hill / in a snow storm . . .

A story told about Bohlin in Thomas, *Fast and Able*, p. 79:

> The wonderful endurance of this man was demonstrated about two years before his death, on a Christmas morning. Capt. Bohlin trudged seven miles in Newfoundland snow, waist deep, laden with $5,000 in gold, silver, and paper, wearing a pair of heavy rubber boots and carrying a precious accumulation of clean clothes. A young mail carrier who went along to guide him to the spot on the shore where the motorboat was to take him off to his schooner, had had to beg to be allowed to stop for a rest. At the end of the seven miles, not knowing how he was to get down a 12 foot embankment at the bottom of which the boat waited, he lay down and rolled. He landed against a fence with laundry, money and boots intact; rose and waded through yards of slush to climb into his boat.

▶ II.46. Gee, what I call the upper road . . .

Exact date of writing not known, though probably 1961. Gee Avenue (see *Maximus* II, 3 and note) and Cherry Street are the two roads into Dogtown from Washington Street, Gloucester. The settlement of what was to be Dogtown was begun along these two roads; the poem, then, fixes the establishment of that community.

II.46. the way / leading by Joshua Elwell's to the wood-lots

From the town records; see *Maximus* II, 38 and note.

II.46. Cherry or the lower road . . . the way that / leads from the town to Smallmans now Dwelling house . . .

Also from the town records, an entry for 16 December 1725 in the "Original Records: Commoners Book No. 1," p. 174, for a grant of eight and a half acres to the early settler Ezekial Days' heirs "adjoyning to their own land . . . hemlock tree markt standing by the way that leads from ye town to Smallmans now Dwelling house. . . ." Recorded by Olson in his notebook, "D'Town Dec 8 1960 . . . *ENDED* abt Feb 21st? 1961," p. 103. William Smallmans (see *Maximus* II, 38), whose house is mentioned in the record, does not appear in any of the published histories of Gloucester.

Cherry Street, accessible from either Reynard Street or Poplar Street, runs parallel with Washington Street northward to join Gee Avenue where that turns into Commons Road.

▶ II.47. B. Ellery . . .

Probably written in 1961, apparently before December that year but definitely before the spring of 1962. In a note to himself on a manuscript of the poem, Olson writes: "This was a mss sent to Joel Oppenheimer when editing the *Kulchur* in which instead you placed the *7 Hinges.*" The original manuscript of "the hinges of civilization . . ." (*Additional Prose*, pp. 25−26) is dated 7 December 1961, while the piece appeared in *Kulchur* 5 in the spring of 1962. This poem would have been written before then.

Benjamin Ellery was the Dogtown merchant whose account book is used earlier by the poet (see *Maximus* II, 34 and note).

II.47. Cinvat Bridge

In Zoroastrianism and Mazdaism, the bridge the soul must cross on the Day of Judgment, which will lead to either Paradise or Hell, according to the fate of the soul. See also note to the soul's Angel, *Maximus* II, 71.

II.47. aer

Greek 'air.' See *Maximus* II, 9 and note.

▶ II.48. the winning thing

Probably written in 1961. Dated "March 31st?" on one early manuscript.

II.48. Stevens

William Stevens, the ship carpenter who appears in *Maximus* I as "the first Maximus" (p. 30). See notes to that earlier volume, pp. 30 and 147.

II.48. as late / as 1667, when signing the oath . . . Stevens / is listed as ship carpenter

See *Records and Files of the Quarterly Courts*, III, 431. Babson, *History*, p. 166, reports the episode as follows:

> [Stevens] was a member of the General Court in 1665, when the Colonial Government made a noble resistance to the proceedings of the commissioners sent over by the king to interfere in the legislation of the Colony, in a manner which was justly esteemed to be an infringement of Colonial rights and privileges. It was a grave offense, in those days, to speak evil of rulers; and discretion would have counselled silence: but the honest indignation of our townsman, spurning all restraint, found utterance in no softened terms of dislike. Four of his neighbors testified at a Quarterly Court in Salem, in 1667, to his declaring "that he would bear no office within this jurisdiction, nor anywhere else, where Charles Stewart had any thing to do; and that he cared no more for Charles Stewart than any other man, as king; and that he abhorred the name of Charles Stewart as king." For this bold and rash expression of his hatred of the king, the offender was sentenced to a month's imprisonment; to pay a fine of £20 and costs; and to be deprived of his privileges as a freeman.

See also *Maximus* III, 30.

II.48. his great- / granddaughter Susanna who became the mother / of David and William Pearce

Susanna Stevens (b. 1717) "married David Pearce, Jan. 20, 1736, and became the mother of two distinguished merchants of the town,—David and William Pearce" (Babson, *Notes and Additions*, I, 78).

For the Pearce brothers, see the notice in Babson, *History*, pp. 267–271; also, for David Pearce, *Maximus* II, 196–197 and note.

II.48. Stevens . . . is all over the Cut

Babson writes in his *History*, p. 165, that Stevens "had a grant of six acres on the Meeting-house Neck; but his residence was at the Cut, near the Beach, where he had eight acres of land."

II.48. previously to coming / to Gloucester this man had built the largest / ship then known in England . . . Spain's spies had sought to / buy him . . .

Babson, *History*, p. 165, quotes an extract from a letter written in 1632 by Emmanuel Downing to Sir John Coke:

> "Being last night at the Exchandge, I enquired what ship-carpenters Mr. Winthrop, the Governor, had with him in New England: when I was informed by Mr. Aldersey, lord-keeper's brother-in-law, and Mr. Cradock, that the Governor hath with him one William Stephens, a shipwright; soe able a man, as they believe there is hardly such an other to be found in this kingdom. There be 2 or 3 others; but, for want of their names, I could not be satisfied of them. This Stephens hath built here many ships of great burthen: he made the 'Royal Merchant,' a ship of 600 tonns. This man, as they enformed me, had more reguard to his substantiall performance than the wages he was to receive, and soe grew to poverty: whereupon he was preparing to goe for Spayne, where he knew he should have wages answerable to his paynes, had not some friends perswaded him to N. England, where he now lives with

great content. Had the state of Spayne obteyned him, he should have be'n as a pretious Jewell to them."

There is no mention, however, that the "Royal Merchant" was the "largest / ship then known in England."

II.48. as they had earlier tried to John Hawkins

Sir John Hawkins, while negotiating to obtain release of his captured crewmen (see *Maximus* I, 59ff. and notes), was offered a bribe by the Spanish to forsake his queen's service. See *Dictionary of National Biography*, IX, 216.

II.48. a life as large as John Winthrop Jr also refused

John Winthrop (1605/6–1676), eldest son of John Winthrop, the governor of Massachusetts Bay. Olson writes in an unpublished essay, "To Make Cold Nymphs Chaste Crowns": ". . . it was pressed on him that he had a major career waiting for him, if he'd give up his iron works at Saugus, or his investigations into minerals in Connecticut hills, and go back to Mother England! He'd be a flare in Parliament, his friends insisted!"

The younger Winthrop came to New England in 1631, and helped found Ipswich, Massachusetts in 1633. He left Ipswich the following year to return to England despite a petition from his fellow settlers to remain, although he later returned to become governor of Connecticut. Of a scientific mind, his career was not marked by political ambition.

II.48. even colonially / Stevens dwindled

After his trial in 1667 for speaking inconsiderately against the king, Stevens descended into poverty, while his wife, in a petition to the General Court for relief, represented her husband to be deranged. See Babson, *History*, p. 166; *Notes and Additions*, I, 76–77.

II.48. He lived here on the front / of the city 40 years, until the day / he ran away, age 70 . . .

There is no report of this in the published histories; Babson only says that Stevens first appeared in Gloucester in 1642, having previously lived near Boston and in Salem (*History*, pp. 164–165), while 1667, the mortgaging of his property, is the last date there is for him on record. Nor is the date of 1693 for his death—which appears later in the poem—to be found in the Gloucester *Vital Records* or any other source.

II.48. Andrew Robinson

See *Maximus*, II, 25 and 42, and notes.

II.48. Ingersolls

In his notice of George Ingersol and his descendants (see also note to *Maximus* II, 25), Babson notes that of the children, "George was a shipwright. He resided in Falmouth and Boston, and died in the latter place before 1730. Samuel was also a shipwright. He came to Gloucester soon after 1700, and settled on Eastern Point, where he built several small vessels" (*History*, p. 106). Again, in *Notes and Additions*, I, 40: "Samuel Ingersol was an active shipwright, having his place of business at Eastern Point, near that where Capt. Robinson built the first schooner."

II.48. Sanders

Nathaniel and Thomas Sanders (see the poem following). In his notice of the family, Babson writes (*History*, p. 241):

> Thomas Sanders and Nathaniel Sanders made their appearance in town, simultaneously, in 1702. Joseph Sanders, shipwright, is mentioned in 1708. . . . In March, 1704, [Thomas Sanders] had of the commoners an acre of ground between the head of the Harbor and Cripple Cove; and, in 1706, a piece of flats below where he built

vessels. He was a shipwright himself, and carried on the business of ship-building extensively. From the frequent occurrence of his name in connection with grants of ship-timber, it is evident that he was a man of great enterprise.

In an entry for 1702 in his *Notes and Additions* (II, 74), Babson has: "The first persons bearing the name of Sanders appear in town this year.... They were shipwrights, and were attracted thither without doubt by the great activity with which the business of ship-building began to be carried on about this time. Tradition reports that the family came to Gloucester direct from England, under inducements held out by one of its members on his return from a voyage to this country."

II.48. 1713, a schooner

See *Maximus* II, 26 and note.

▶ II.49. Bailyn shows sharp rise ...

An early version, dated 4 January 1964 and sent Eli Wilentz for the proposed Jargon/Corinth edition of *Maximus Poems IV, V, VI*, has only the first nine lines. It was revised after the poet had acquired William Baker's *Colonial Vessels* (Olson's note on flyleaf of his copy: "Bot pharmacy Essex [for 5 dollars] Halloween night October 31st 1967—luckily"). One of the few poems placed out of chronological order by the poet.

Bernard Bailyn (b. 1922), Harvard historian, is the author with his wife Lotte of *Massachusetts Shipping 1697–1714*, in which is noted, p. 51: "Gloucester maintained a small but steady production through the middle years of the period; in 1706 its production amounted to 17.3 per cent of the registered vessels and 12.8 per cent of the tonnage produced in that year by towns in the Bay Colony whose names were specified."

II.49. average / tonnage is 46.4

Bailyn, *Massachusetts Shipping*, p. 50: "The average capacity of all registered Massachusetts-built vessels of known tonnage was 60.4 tons, but the average of those built in Charlestown was 96.8 tons; Boston's average was 69.3. Most other towns of high production obviously built smaller vessles. Salem's average tonnage was 52.0; Scituate's, 48.2; Newbury's, 47.1; Gloucester's, 46.4."

II.49. William Baker, / 1962, is of the opinion . . .

See William A. Baker, *Colonial Vessels*, pp. 147–148: "It is probable that the assumed invention of the schooner at Gloucester in 1713 consisted of fitting the long known two-masted fore-and-aft Dutch rig—the fore and main mast combination—to a typical ketch hull."

There is a description of a ketch also in Babson, *History*, p. 251.

II.49. Gloucester records / 1702 show Nathaniel Sanders buying twelve trees . . .

Quoted in Babson, *History*, p. 249n:

> "Jany. 23, 1702.—then sold to Nathanill Sanders tweallf tres for one pound ten shillings; to be oak trees for his youse about ye Sloop he is going to build" (Town-records)
>
> "December, the 28th day, 1702.—then receaved of James Parsons, Jephery Parsons, John Parsons, and Nathanaell Parsons, a bond for to pay to the towne the sume of three shillings pr. tunn, if they do sell or dispose of the Sloop out of the towne which Thomas Sanders is a building for the above said Parsonses; and the said Parsonses is to pay to the towne three shillings pr tunn in case the s^d Sloop be sold or disposed of out of town before six years be expired after the Launching of the said sloop"(*ib.*).

▶ II.50. 23 School and 16 Columbia . . .

Original written on a card from the Gloucester tax collector's office and dated "May 1st." Referred to are houses on those Gloucester streets. As viewed by the author in the summer of 1967, 23 School, an old brick with ivy, had a large yard with much foliage, violets, and some myrtle; an addition at the rear and a side porch were of wood, and a wooden fence surrounded the yard. The house at 16 Columbia was wholly of wood, with worn paint. Columbia Street itself, running parallel to Prospect Street above the center of town, joins School Street as it descends from Prospect toward the Harbor. The houses noted are a few hundred yards from each other. The whole area would have been an easy walk from the poet's house.

Before reading the poem at Vancouver, Olson remarked: "The last time I was to Canada, on radio, an excellent Englishman did the research and had a beautiful text, but the announcer was a Canadian and a Hollywood type, and the first question he asked me was, 'What do you think of Imagism, Mr. Olson?' This poem . . . I support it has to do with that . . ." (tape of reading, 14 August 1963).

In a poem called "Naming," also read at Vancouver in 1963 but never published, the poet speaks of "the flowers of the houses of 28 School, 16 Columbia, and 12 Columbia."

▶II.51. the bottom / backward . . .

A manuscript sent editor Donald Allen is dated by Olson, "May, 1961."

II.51. cod bred in winter . . .

See, e.g., Goode, *Fisheries and Fishery Industries of the United States*, III, 74: "During the months of February, March, and April large schools of cod make their appearance on the bank. They are generally found on the 'winter fishing-grounds,' a part of the bank lying to the eastward of the shoals . . . This is essentially a spawning-ground for the cod, which appear to come on the bank from the southeast, as they almost invariably, after reaching the ground, move slowly to the north and west as spring approaches."

II.51. ice had dropped / Banks in the water

See T. Babson, "Evolution of Cape Ann Roads," p. 303: "The surface of the Cape was reshaped in the great ice age. The ice caps wore away a strip of softer granite to form the bed of the Annisquam River; and it lined up the ridges and valleys, the harbor and the general trend of the cape itself in a north-south direction. The melting ice dropped sand and rocks in a chain of spots on the sea-bottom, reaching north-east to Labrador; these are of course the fishing banks." The passage was marked by Olson in his copy.

II.51. orchards and gardens, / tenements / messuages

Common legal language in deeds of the seventeenth and eighteenth centuries. Cf. the deed of John Winthrop and his sons from 1630 (*Winthrop Papers*, II, 186): "all houses edifices buildinges yardes Gardens and Orchardes to the said mes-uages or tenementes belonginge or apperteyning . . ."; or the sale of land by John Jackson to Peter Duncan in the Gloucester town records ("Original Records," I, 73): ". . . one Messuage House or Tenement, one orchyard and garden with all the out housing commonages and Appurtenances thereunto belonging . . ."

II.51. Danish cylinders now descend to measure / paleontological times

Danish oceanographic research vessels or vessels equipped with Danish underwater devices. At the time, oceanographers from the Woods Hole Oceanographic Institute on Cape Cod were active in the fishing areas off Cape Ann, including Georges Bank (see, e.g., Wigley, "Bottom Sediments of Georges Bank").

II.51. when figureheads from East India brigantines / sat in formal gardens so that old maids held their stomachers . . .

In conversation, June 1968, the poet mentioned that these lines reflect a story told him by Alfred Mansfield Brooks, director of the local historical society. In a note among his papers, "Conversation 3 hrs with AMB Sat Dec 21 [1957?]," he had written:

> Parrott garden had Pearce vessel figureheads
> (spooky, sd Guy Cunningham
> wooden statues, sd the Patillo sisters, 100 & 96!

Also among the poet's papers is a page from a letter written 8 November 1965 to E. Hyde Cox, Brooks' successor as president of the Cape Ann Historical Association, with a passage concerning "the Patillo girls I believe it was, two old maids, one of whom told him [Brooks] they, as girls, going by that garden . . . I *hope* you *know* what Wm or David Pierce *did* have in that garden for *sculpture*? I mean not one of us wld now or ever succeed in such a brilliance (so scared the Patillo girls they used to *run* by like I & others used to, when being raised by 'Washington Cemetery' over on Western Avenue (simply out of the most boring superstitions, nothing as real as studded *that* garden, on Water Street . . ."

See Brooks' article, "The Pearce-Parrot Garden," which describes the garden of William Pearce, prosperous merchant at the height of Gloucester's West Indies trade in the eighteenth century, whose house was on Pearce Street in Gloucester (since obliterated by urban renewal) near the Inner Harbor.

II.51. I stand on Main Street like the Diorite / stone

See "Causal Mythology," *Muthologos*, I, 72–73:

> I'm going to spend some time in this fourth thing on the poem from which I myself steal that, which is "The Song of Ullikummi." Actually it comes to us as a Hittite version of a Hurrian myth. It's called "The Song of Ullikummi." And it's the story of how this aborted creature, whom the poem calls the Diorite Stone, started growing from the bottom of the sea, and grew until he appeared above the surface of the water and then, of course, attention was called to him and he continued to grow and he became so offensive to the gods, and dangerous, that they had to, themselves, do battle with him. "The Song of Ullikummi" is actually the story of that battle and who could bring him down. Because he had a growth principle of his own, and it went against creation in the sense that nobody could stop him and nobody knew how far he might grow. It's a marvelous Hesiodic poem. In fact, I prefer it to those passages in Hesiod that include the battle of Zeus with the giants and eventually with Typhon, because this creature is nothing but a blue stone, and the *stone* grows. . . . And

the Diorite, for me, this Diorite figure is the vertical, the growth principle of the Earth. He's just an objectionable child of Earth who has got no condition except earth, no condition but stone. . . .

See also "from The Song of Ullikummi" in *Archaeologist of Morning*, pp. 236–237, and Güterbock, both "The Song of Ullikummi" and "The Hittite Version of the Hurrian Kumarbi Myths."

▶ **II.52. JI 17 1961**

Written that date in Gloucester.

II.52. as John Burke / read the comics . . .

John J. Burke, Jr. (1906–1970), a former mayor of Gloucester and city councilman from 1954 to November 1959, when he resigned. The incident reported in the poem is a true occurrence, according to the poet in conversation, June 1968.

For a summary of Burke's career and character, the reader may wish to see "The many sides of John J. Burke Jr.," an editorial in the *Gloucester Daily Times*, 7 January 1970, p. 8, but see esp. the poem "John Burke," *Maximus* I, 142–144 and note.

II.52. 'okloloidoros

Greek 'οχλολοιδορος, 'he who rails at the people,' a nickname of Heraclitus (*Encycopaedia Britannica*, 11th ed., XIII, 309). In the chapter devoted to Heraclitus in the poet's copy of Diogenes Laertius' *Lives*, p. 376—next to the point in the text where Heraclitus, playing dice in the temple of Diana, rails at the Ephesians who flocked to look, "You wretches, what are you wondering at? is it not better to do this, than to meddle with public affairs in your company?"—Olson has written in the margin: "John Burke, reading the comic strips at the City Council!"

▶ **II.53. Letter 72**

Written ca. July 1961 (an early manuscript dated).

II.53. Hilton's

William Hilton, early Dogtown settler, had a house (cellar no. 29) on Commons Road between the Bennetts' and Samuel Davis'. He married Mary Tucker in 1711.

II.53. Davis' . . . the / garden of Ann

Samuel Davis, who married Ann Robinson in 1704 (see *Maximus* II, 25 and note, also II, 37).

II.53. Elizabeth

Possibly the poet's own wife, rather than an Elizabeth Davis or Elizabeth Hilton.

II.53. Nasir Tusi

Thirteenth-century Iranian theologian. See Corbin, "Cyclical Time in Mazdaism and Ismailism," pp. 158ff.

II.53. man is the fallen angel

As a theological concept—although the phrase itself does not occur—see Corbin, "Cyclical Time," p. 136 et passim.

II.53. Joshua Elwell

See *Maximus* II, 38 and note.

II.53. Bennett placed himself / above 75'

Anthony Bennett (d. 1691) and his sons. Mann, *Beginnings of Dogtown*, p. 29, writes:

> Abagail Bennett, whose name appears [on Batchelder's plan of Dogtown], was the widow of the first settler of the name, Anthony, who was a carpenter, and built and operated the mill at the outlet of Cape Pond brook, near Fox Hill and the home of Tammy Younger. The name "An-

thony Bennett" which appears on the plan at this point was that of his oldest son, and Stephen and John Bennett, whose name appears near that of Abagail Bennett on the upper Dogtown road, were sons of the second Anthony. At the time of the preparation of the plan, 1741, he was non compos and under the guardianship of his son John, while his mother, Abagail, who seems to have been evicted from the home at Fox Hill to make room for the family of the son, had been dead seven or eight years.

The figure 75', like those following in the poem, are from topographic surveys of Gloucester (New England Survey Service, Drawing No. 40194 and others), available from the City Engineer's office, which Olson had acquired for his researches.

II.53. Commons Road

North or "upper" road through Dogtown, running roughly parallel to Dogtown Road in the southern portion.

II.53. "to the wood-lots" (1727)

See *Maximus* II, 38 and note.

II.54. the Commons

Dogtown was at first a heavily wooded area with some pasturage where the early settlers shared rights for cutting wood and pasturing cattle and sheep. As such, it was known simply as The Commons or the Commons Settlement, and later, Dogtown Commons.

▶ II.55. The View—July 29, 1961

For Half Moon Beach and the Cut, see notes to *Maximus* I, 30.

▶ II.56. Descartes soldier / in a time of religious / wars . . .

Dated 10 September 1961 A slightly different version beginning "magic opus / emanations . . ." among Olson's papers (a copy also sent to Donald Allen) bears the same date.

Descartes (see *Maximus* I, 128 and note; also II, 79) served with several armies between 1617 and 1628 in the Catholic-Protestant wars of the time.

II.56. St / Sophia

Sophia is the Gnostic "Mother" or figure of Wisdom. She became identified with the Spirit of God, and was canonized as Saint Sophia by the Greek Christians (with the famous church at Constantinople named in her honor).

II.56. Fishermans / Field

See *Maximus* I, 100 and 106, and notes.

II.56. Fishermans / 2 acres

Not the whole of Fisherman's Field—which was, according to Babson, "about one hundred acres, more or less" (see note to *Maximus* I, 106)—but individual allotments.

II.56. The Shoreman

See Josselyn, quoted earlier, *Maximus* II, 40: "a shore man" was the member of the crew of a fishing vessel who "washes [the fish] out of the salt / and dries it upon hurdles pitcht / upon stakes breast high and tends / their cookery . . ."

▶II.57. In the interleaved Almanacks for 1646 and 1647 of Danforth

Exact date of writing unknown. Read at Vancouver in August of 1963. The poem, as indicated in the note following it, is from a footnote in John Winthrop's *History of New England* and can be found in the second volume of the Savage edition, p. 332, where, in a note to a statement by Winthrop concerning a harvest, Savage adds:

> Our author's note of time is not very precise, inasmuch as the whole month of August is given. What harvest he intends is conjectural. I suppose English, not Indian, corn, as wheat, rye, barley, &c. is meant. My indefatigable cor-

respondent, John Farmer, Esquire, has furnished me with the following extracts from the notes in the interleaved Almanacks for 1646 and 1647 of Danforth, that may to some extent indicate the progress of vegetation. . . .

Olson has made an exact copy, with one minor difference: "Apricocs" has been spelled in the poem "Apricocks."

In an early manuscript of the poem, the note "as in footnote / in *Winthrop's Journal*" continues, "as read in Cape Ann Scientific Historical & Literary Society's Museum Pleasant Street."

"Blackston's apples," it might be noted, were named after the Reverend William Blackstone who came to New England in 1623 and built a house and planted an orchard on the slope of West Hill, southwest of Beacon Hill, Boston, where he lived from 1625 to 1635. See also note to "yellow sweetings," *Maximus* I, 128.

▶ II.58. ta meteura . . .

Date of writing unknown. Read at Vancouver in August of 1963. *Ta meteura* are the heavenly bodies, distinct from *ta metarsia* or the 'weather.' See Harrison quoted above in note to "Ta metarsia," *Maximus* II, 9.

II.58. parsonses / field

What was once Fisherman's Field (q.v.). See also *Maximus* II, 136: "fisherman's / field, and the Parsonses made it their / village or homestead from shortly thereafter / until my father's time. . . ." In notes among his papers, Olson writes that Josiah Batchelder's map from 30 May 1741 "SHOWS Stage Fort Park to Western Ave as 'parsonses field'. . . ."

See also "Of the Parsonses," *Maximus* II, 63−64, and "*As of Parsonses or Fishermans Field . . .*," *Maximus* III, 130−131.

▶ II.59. Thurs Sept 14th 1961

An early manuscript, which has an additional fifteen lines at the end omitted from this version as "too poetic"

(Vancouver tape), is signed: "Charles Olson / written Thurs Sept 14th, from / 12:30 to / 2:15 (inc. / typed copy."

II.59. Elicksander / Baker . . .

See the unpublished "Done Fudging Gulls," which begins:

> If Savage is right
> Alexander Baker can
> be taken as the earliest
> person to put himself
> here after Stage Fort:

> Savage says Baker had
> "sat down at Gloucester
> on first coming" date
> 1635 permission to mi-
> grate on *Elizabeth &
> Ann* Wm Cooper Master
> the following:

> Alexander 28
> uxor Elizabeth 23
> Elizabeth 3
> Christina 1

> Plus this, that, when
> both the husband and
> wife were admitted the
> Boston Church October
> 4, 1645 five new child-
> ren of theirs were
> baptized, all in a
> day, with their birth
> dates recorded:

> Alexander   1635
> Samuel   1637
> John   1640
> Joshua   1642
> Hannah   1644

> Of these the last three
> would appear to be Gloucester
> born for certain and so
> presumably the first two

See then Savage, *Genealogical Dictionary*, I, 95:

BAKER, ALEXANDER, Boston, ropemaker, came in the Elizabeth and Ann, 1635, aged 28, from London, with w. Eliz. 23; and ch. Eliz. 3; and Christian, 1; had Alexander, b. 15 Jan. 1636; Samuel, 16 Jan. 1638; John, 20 June 1640; Joshua, 30 Apr. 1642; Hannah, 29 Sept. 1644; all bapt. 5 Oct. 1645, as he and his w. were adm. of the ch. the preced. day, was freem. 1646 . . . At Gloucester he had sat down on first coming; and in the gr. to Rev. Richard Blinman, 1642, the same ld. is giv. that had bef. been offer. to Alexander B. . . .

The original records of the town have also been consulted, specifically the "Transcript of the First Volume of Gloucester Town Records Commencing 1642," where one finds, p. 36, the spelling "Elicksander" Baker. All Babson has for this settler is that he "was owner of a house and land early, and may have been for a short time a resident" (*History*, p. 61).

II.59. Done Fudging

"Just to the north of the inner end of the Cut, where a ledge rises quite abruptly on the bank of the river, lies 'Dunfudgin.' When a boat was brought through the Cut three hundred years ago, the crew had to fudge it along with poles. As soon as they reached deeper water, however, with broader steerageway, they could ship their poles and hoist their sail; they were done fudging. Hence that became the name of the spot, a name which readily suggests welcome relief from tiresome struggles against tide and wind" (Copeland and Rogers, *Saga of Cape Ann*, p. 180).

See also note to "where . . . do they actually . . . impede each other," *Maximus* III, 214.

II.59. Conant children

Lot Conant, son of Roger Conant (q.v.), was born about 1624, "either at Nantasket or in the 'great frame house' at Cape Ann . . ." (Lapham, *Old Planters*, p. 16). Savage, *Genealogical Dictionary*, I, 440–441, reports that "Young, Chron. 24, gives him [Roger C.] four s. I think he had five; but even the assiduous fondness of Felt, in a Mem. of gr. dilig. filling fourteen pages of Geneal. Reg. II has not furnish. complete fam. acco." Savage includes—in addition to Lot—among the children, "Exercise, perhaps the third s. b. at Cape Ann, a. 1636, bapt. 24 Dec. 1637."

II.59. Woodbury

"John Woodbury came from Somersetshire in England. After a residence of three years here and in Salem, he went back to England on business, and returned in 1628. He was made a freeman in 1631, and filled various offices of trust in Salem, besides representing it twice in the General Court. He died in 1641, leaving a son Humphrey; the father, without doubt, of Humphrey, who removed from Beverly to Gloucester about 1677" (Babson, *History*, p. 43). Lapham, *Old Planters*, p. 50, writes: "Besides his son Humphrey, born in England about 1609, the records mention three children of John Woodbery—Hannah, Abigail, and Peter. It seems certain that he also had a son John, born about 1630. No record appears of the younger John Woodbery's birth or baptism, but this is not strange, since the lists of baptism and membership in the Salem Church are available only as far back as 1635." Savage, *Genealogical Dictionary*, IV, 634, reports the daughter Hannah was baptized on 25 December 1636.

II.59. Balch

Babson writes that John Balch "came from Bridgewater, England. He was admitted a freeman in 1631; and was a useful citizen of Salem, where he died in 1648" (*History*, p. 43). He had a son, Benjamin, born before 1631, reports Lapham, *Old Planters*, p. 92 (although the same author, pp. 89−90, says Balch's "youngest son," Freeborn, was born in 1631). Savage, *Genealogical Dictionary*, I, 101, reports his son Benjamin was born around 1629.

II.59. Stage Fort 1623/4 to 1626/7

The earliest settlement on Cape Ann, abandoned in a move to Naumkeag (Salem). See *Maximus* I, 45 and 107, and notes.

II.59. Alexander, born Done Fudging Jan 15, 1635/6

See Savage's record of births in note to "Elicksander" Baker above; that this son was born at Done Fudging is Olson's addition.

II.59. the father and mother had arr. Boston / in mid-summer . . .

See Banks, *Planters of the Commonwealth*, pp. 154–155, who reports that the *Elizabeth and Ann*, with Roger Cooper as master, "sailed about the middle of May and arrived at Boston in Midsummer, with one hundred and two passengers." Banks includes Alexander Baker, his wife and two children (together with their ages), in the passenger list.

II.59. the incorporation / of the Town

The town of Gloucester was incorporated in April 1642 at a meeting of the General Court under John Endecott and Emmanuel Downing (see *Maximus* I, 156 and note).

II.59. Sam'l, / born January 16, 1637/8; / John . . . Joshua . . . Hannah . . .

See Savage, *Genealogical Dictionary*, p. 95, quoted in note to "Elicksander" Baker above.

II.59. Ethan / Allen

(1739–1789), American Revolutionary War hero, leader of the "Green Mountain Boys," a band of irregulars. That he was a descendant of Joshua Baker, see the notice of Mary

Baker, granddaughter of Joshua, in Mackenzie, *Colonial Families of the United States*, V, 29 – used by Olson, judging from a reference in a notebook from the spring of 1959. Mackenzie reports Mary Baker married Joseph Allen in 1736/7 and became the mother of Col. Ethan Allen.

II.59. just about / day Endecott & Downing divided / Gloucester up

See note to *"incorporation* / of the Town" above, and *Maximus* I, 156 and note.

II.59. the Bakers / sold out, at Done Fudging, to / George Ingersoll

For Ingersoll, see note to *Maximus* II, 25. His purchase of Baker's land along the Annisquam near the Harbor is entered in the town records.

II.59. Ingersoll was still in Salem date / his father's will, 1644

See "Will of Richard Ingersoll of Salem, dated July 21, 1644; proved Jan. 2, 1644–5," in *Records and Files of the Quarterly Courts*, I, 76 (marked in Olson's copy).

II.59. Stephen / Streeter

This early settler "may have preceded the settlers of 1642, as Mr. Blynman's grant includes a lot 'primarily given' to him. He had a house here, but did not remain in town long after its permanent settlement; for, in 1644, he was residing in Charlestown" (Babson, *History*, p. 169).

II.60. goodmen / Baker & Streeter / the two get referred / to in jointure the / moment the Town is / found

The town of Gloucester was "founded" in April 1642, or, according to the calendar then in use, "2 mo 42" (see *Maximus* I, 156 and note). A grant of land recorded for that date in the town records ("Transcript of First Volume,"

p. 12) refers to "2 Acres of marsh of Thomas Skellins which were primarely given to Steeven Streeter and Alexander Baker." Actually, it is in a later entry—for "5 mo 49"—that Baker and Streeter are referred to as "goodmen" ("Transcript of First Volume," p. 29).

II.60. another / pair equally / holding together . . . Ingersoll / and Kenie

For William Kenie, Babson only gives: ". . . he had a house and land, which he sold to Thomas Prince in 1652; having previously removed to New London" (*History*, p. 110). Caulkins, *History of New London*, p. 291, states his age was sixty-six in 1662 and that he died in 1675.

Sale of their land indicates Kenie and Ingersoll had left Done Fudging for the Harbor by "10 mo 48." See "Transcript of First Volume of Gloucester Town Records," p. 18: "Item given one Acre of marsh and some what more lyinge on the west side of Ainesquam River butting upon Smiths ffields with Two Acres of marsh lying to it that he bought of goodman Kenie and goodman Ingason. . . ."

II.60. each is possessed / of a front / on Fore / street, / & the water, by / 1647 (Dec.

George Ingersoll or Ingarson is recorded in the town records as having land at the Harbor in an entry dated "10 mo 47," i.e. December 1647 ("Transcript of First Volume," p. 25). For Kenie's presence at the Harbor at that time, see pp. 19, 23 and 30 of that volume of records. In a notebook "opened March 20, 1961" among his papers, Olson enters, p. 9: "Ingersoll & Kenie were on Main Street with Thomas Ashley's (then Widow Babsons) between them . . ." He then draws a line to Kenie's name, adding "5 mo 49 4 acres 'bet Ingerson & Walker.'"

For Fore Street, earlier name for Main Street (also Front Street), see *Maximus* I, 151.

II.60. Osmund Dutch . . . his letter to wife Grace . . . July 18th, 1639

See *Maximus* I, 158—160 and notes. It might be noted that Dutch's reference to himself as a *"nauta"* at Cape Ann, 18 July 1639, is not actually from his letter to his wife but from a record of a legal transaction kept by the lawyer Lechford in his notebook.

II.60. Abraham Robinson / Thomas Ashley . . . Willm / Browne . . .

See *Maximus* I, 160 and note. Babson writes of Ashley: "A lot in the harbor is mentioned, in 1650, as once belonging to him. Thomas Ashley and his goods were attached in July, 1642, for William Addes and others" (*History*, p. 58); also, p. 59, that the Widow Isabel Babson (q.v.) "bought of Mr. Milward two acres that was Ashley's lot; a portion of which, situated at what is now 75 and 77, Front Street, continued in the family about a century and a half."

II.61. Thomas Lechford, / Notebook, page / 406

See note to Abraham Robinson, Ashley, and Browne, *Maximus* I, 160.

II.61. Wm / Southmeade / or Southmate / as possessing / Thompson fishery / stage . . .

See *Maximus* I, 158 and note.

II.61. Thomas Millward

See *Maximus* I, 158 and note.

II.61. the ministerial student Thomas / Rashleigh

Babson writes, *History*, p. 50: "From one writer of that period (Thomas Lechford), we learn that our territory was occupied in 1639. He resided in Boston that year, but soon after returned to England, where he published a work, in which he says, 'At Cape Ann, where fishing is set forward, and some stages builded, there one master Rashley is chaplain.'" Later, p. 189, Babson adds: "By whose invitation he came, whether by that of Mr. Thomson (if he, indeed, established a company here) or by that of settlers on the spot, can never probably be known. He was some time member of the church in Boston; and, in 1652, was officiating as minister at Bishop-Stoke, England."

See Lechford, *Plain Dealing*, pp. 106–107: "And at *Cape Anne*, where fishing is set forward, and some stages builded, there one master *Rashley* is Chaplain: for it is farre off from any Church: *Rashley* is admitted of *Boston* Church, but the place lyeth next *Salem*, and not very far further from *Ipswich*." In a note, p. 107, is added: "Thomas Rashley was admitted to the Boston Church, March 8, 1640, then called a 'student.'" See also Savage, *Genealogical Dictionary*, III, 508 (which a notebook from August 1959 indicates Olson also used), under Rashley: "*Thomas*, Boston, adm. of the ch. 8 Mar. 1640, called 'a studyent,' meaning in theology, no doubt, and next yr. at Gloucester, as we learn from Lechford, he exercis. as they say, in a prophetical way, and there perhaps m. but his s. John 'being a. six wks. old,' was bapt. at B. 18 May 1645. . . ."

II.61. the Divinity School which / Harvard college was 1639

Harvard was established by the Massachusetts General Court in 1636 and named Harvard College in 1639 in honor of John Harvard (1607–1638), a Puritan minister who emigrated to New England and who left books and half his estate to the college upon his death.

II.61. Curtis Square / (where / R R / cuts between / Burial Ground and / hill

That is, roughly the site of the first meeting house in Gloucester. See, e.g., T. Babson, "Evolution of Cape Ann Roads," p. 305 (marked in the poet's copy): "On February 8, 1644, the selectmen voted to set aside a half acre for a common burial place between lots owned by certain citizens and 'the old meeting house place.' This, and references in the records to 'Meeting house hill' and later to 'the meetinghouse plain' suggests that the first church building (about 1633) was near the old burying ground on Centennial Avenue (which was first called 'Burying Ground Lane'),—some say it stood on what is now Curtis Square. . . ." Curtis Square, just north of the Boston and Maine Railroad tracks, is reached either by Whittemore Street or by Centennial Avenue from nearby Washington Street.

II.61. Harbor / Cove

See note to *Maximus* I, 151.

II.62. if he mocks 28 / different sorts of / song . . .

See Townsend, *Supplement to The Birds of Essex County*, p. 170: "Mr. S. Waldo Bailey reported a Mockingbird that remained for nearly a week in Newburyport and sang exceptionally well. He was able to recognize the songs or notes of twenty-nine species of birds in its imitations."

II.62. no mocking bird / was here / 1635 1639 1907 . . . Mimus polyglottos

Both 1635 and 1639 are dates given earlier in the poem. There is no record of the appearance of a mockingbird at all—which would thereby include those years cited—on Townsend's list of sightings on p. 170 of the *Supplement*. The report that the mockingbird, or *Mimus polyglottos*, was an "Accidental visitor from the south," appears in Townsend's original volume, *Birds of Essex County*, p. 303.

II.62. But by 1920 / had increased so / was becoming almost . . . a resident

In Townsend's *Supplement*, which includes a chart listing sightings through 1919, the increase is noted. Whereas he had written in the earlier entry for mockingbird, "Accidental visitor from the south," he writes in his 1920 volume, pp. 169–170:

> Not uncommon visitor from the South.
> In the original Memoir I collected seven records of this bird for the County. Four of these birds were shot. In the last fifteen years I have records of at least twenty-five birds seen in the County and only one shot. This would indicate that the bird is more common as a visitor and that, as it is received more kindly, it stays longer and comes again. It is also to be hoped that it is extending its range and is becoming a permanent resident. The bird has been recorded at all seasons of the year, and it has nested and raised young several times. Mr. F.B. Currier found them nesting at Newburyport, in 1914. Four young grew to full size. A second pair nested the same year. In 1915, two pairs also nested; one in 1916; and two in 1917.

▶ II.63. Of the Parsonses

Written 29 September 1961 (early manuscript dated). The Parsonses were a family of early Gloucester settlers, all descendants of Jeffrey Parsons (1631–1689) who owned land in the area then known as Fisherman's Field (later Stage Fort Park), including the site of the summer "camps" where Olson stayed as a boy. See the notice of the family in Babson, *History*, pp. 120–125, and *Notes and Additions*, I, 49–56.

The poem includes excerpts from various deeds preserved in the Essex County Registry of Deeds in Salem, material in the town records in the City Clerk's vault in Gloucester, the poet's firsthand experience of the location, as well as records from an inner landscape. It begins with reference to a living descendant of the Parsons family who still possessed some of the original land of his ancestors.

II.63. George Henry's division with / his brother

George Henry Morse, Jr. (1896–1964), owner of the Parsons-Morse house (see below) at the time of this poem. A note among the poet's papers indicates he had interviewed Major Morse, retired from the U.S. Marine Corps, a few weeks earlier on 9 September 1961.

II.63. the / flat stone by a cherry tree

See, e.g., the probate order transferring land and property from Nehemiah Parsons to Anthony Morse in 1842—
bringing for the first time the Parsons property into the
Morse family—in the Registry of Deeds, Salem. It includes:
" . . . parcels of land situated on the Salem road in Gloucester, aforesaid, Viz. a certain piece of land thus bounded,
beginning at a stake by the wall and running thence Southerly to a flat rock near a cherry tree. . . ."

II.63. the Garden Nathaniel's, deceased / when Samuel fisherman . . .

See the deed of Samuel Parsons to Ebenezer Parsons also
recorded in the registry at Salem, 10 July 1732 (although
it was written in 1722):

> KNOW all men by these present that I Samuel Parsons
> of Glocester in the County of Essex in his Majesties
> province of the Massachusetts bay in New England Fisher-
> man (alias Coaster) for and in consideration of a Deed
> of exchange of about One acre of wood land from Ebe-
> nezer Parsons of the Same Town and County Tanner . . .
> Give Grant Assign Set Over and Confirm unto him to
> Ebenezer Parsons and his Heirs and Assigns forever
> about thirteen Rods of Land Scituate Laying and being
> with in the Township of Glocester Called the Garden
> bounded as followeth (Viz) by a Rock in the fence by the
> road by a Gutter Thence to a Rock which was Nathaniel
> Parsons dec[d] his Corner bound Thence Southeasterly
> to a heep of Stones which was s[d] Nathaniels Bound also
> thence Southwesterly to a Plumb Tree with Stones about
> it . . .

Nathaniel Parsons (1675–1722), fifth son of Jeffrey Parsons, "is supposed to have had his house near that of his
father, at Fisherman's Field, and there to have carried on the
agricultural and maritime pursuits in which, from the inventory of his estate, it appears that he engaged" (Babson,
Notes and Additions, I, 53). Samuel Parsons (1690–1761),
grandson of Jeffrey Parsons, built the Parsons-Morse house.

And Ebenezer Parsons (1681–1763) was the youngest son of Jeffrey Parsons.

II.63. the Morse / house

The Parsons-Morse house, which until 1967 was situated at 106 Western Avenue, above Stage Fort Park. Pringle, *History of the Town and City of Gloucester,* p. 320, writes: "The Parsons house, more familiarly known as the Morse house, on Western Avenue near the foot of Parsons's Hill, was built about 1713 by Samuel Parsons, a grandson of Jeffrey, the early settler, the timbers being cut near by. It has always remained in possession of his descendants, the present occupant, Isaac Parsons Morse, being the great great grandson of the builder, his wife being a descendant of Samuel, on her mother's side. Their son, George H. Morse and grandson Charles Parsons Morse are the sixth and seventh generation that have lived in the house." George Henry Morse, Jr. (see above), was the brother of Charles Parsons Morse and also of that seventh generation.

Olson lived in the Morse house one summer with his parents as a boy (see *Maximus* II, 136), and fought in vain to save it, years later, from demolition (the course of events is summarized in the headings of articles in the *Gloucester Times* from June through August, 1967: "Poet vs. practicality—Poet Olson proposes his Western Ave. memorial," "Wrecker gets house—Poet loses bid for memorial," "Save Morse house—Poet asks public to call council," and finally "Poet's appeal fails—Historic house nears oblivion").

II.63. 1 acre of / rocky ground . . .

See the deed of Eliezer Parsons to Solomon Parsons, written with his wife Mary, 19 January 1736/7, and received at the registry in Salem on 7 August 1741, which includes: "One Certain Peice of Rocky land containing about one acre be it more or less lying in said Town of Glocester where said Solomon Parsons's house stands & bounded at the Easterly corner with a heap of stones on the Westerly side of the

Highway near M[r] John Parsons's Orchard . . . Excepting M[r] John Parsons's land where his Well is & there to bound by said land as it is and no way to Infrindge on said Well Priviledges. . . ."

Solomon Parsons (1706–1799) was the son of John Parsons, born in 1693 and still living in 1762, whose father also named John (1666–1714) was the third son of Jeffrey Parsons. Eliezer Parsons (b. 1694) was another grandson of Jeffrey Parsons.

II.63. Gravenstein / russets Greenings and Northern / spies

Varieties of apples.

II.63. the "Spring House" / the Leach's now winter home . . . Stewart / and Mrs Leach . . .

H. Stewart Leach and his wife Marjorie, living at 179 Western Avenue.

II.63. Walter Cressy

(1858–1916), a contractor who owned property along Western Avenue west of the Parsons-Morse house.

II.63. Cressy- / Strong strongway Walter and Neal, and Bertha . . .

Roland B. Strong owned a gas station at 165 Western Avenue at the time Olson was growing up at the summer "camps" across the street (see *Maximus* II, 137), while living at 88 Western Avenue with his wife Bertha—daughter of Walter Cressy—and sons Walter and Neil.

II.63. Frontenac

Louis de Buade, Comte de Frontenac (1620–1698), governor of New France from 1672 to 1682 and again in 1689 until his death. See esp. Parkman's *Count Frontenac and New France under Louis XIV*.

II.64. Josie Boone

Friend of the poet's mother. A resident of Roslindale, outside of Boston, she spent summers in Gloucester like the Olsons (her name appears written by Olson on the back of a group photograph of Gloucester summer campers ca. 1920).

II.64. the Chocolate Soldier

An operetta composed by Oskar Straus in 1908, based on the play "Arms and the Man" by George Bernard Shaw, and popular in America through the 1930's. It was made into a movie in 1941.

II.64. Spring land

"Spring Lane" in earlier manuscript. A quitclaim registered in Salem in 1843 by George Parsons and others regarding the division of the estate of Andrew and Nehemiah Parsons, speaks of "the northeast half of a piece of land on the Western side of the Salem road, called Spring lane."

II.64. 8 rods W'ly it says . . .

A grant to James and Eliezer Parsons, 19 February 1724/5, of rights to twenty-two acres of an "herbage lot," as recorded in the "Original Records: Commoners Book No. 1, 1707–1820," p. 180. The lot is described as beginning at a rock about eight poles westerly from Samuel Parson's house, and proceeding "from the Rock first mentioned westerly to a great Rock by the Spring which is about 10 poles leaving the Spring comon: thence N. westerly . . . ."

▶ II.65. THE BEGINNINGS (facts

Written 15 October 1961 (manuscript dated).

II.65. Dutche mariner New England coast ... along with John Gallop ...

See also *Maximus* III, 79:

> Osmund Dutch, and John Gallop, mariners, their wages
> asked that they be paid to the Dorchester
> Co., July, 1632. Thus Reverend John White writing
> to John Winthrop at Boston locates
> Dutch and Gallop as on this coast or ferrying
> others across the Atlantic at a probable date earlier
> than 1630. With Abraham Robinson the two
> then constitute the probable earliest
> new coast types to follow
> the original Stage Fort few ...

For Osmund Dutch, see *Maximus* I, 158 and note, and II, 60, etc.; while John Gallop (d. 1675) is mentioned as being active along the coast by several of the early historians, such as Bradford and Winthrop. He figures in Babson's *History*, pp. 94–95, "only as the seller of upland in the Harbor, and of marsh at Little Good Harbor, before 1650. A John Gallop was an early inhabitant of Boston. He was a fisherman and pilot; and was some time wind-bound in Cape-Ann Harbor, in 1632, in a voyage to Piscataqua for the Colony Government, to gain information of some Englishmen at the eastward who had turned pirates."

II.65. Babson guesses Robinson might have come across from / Plymouth 1631

See Babson's *History*, pp. 46–47:

> The settlement of a large Colony within convenient dis-
> tance, and the growing intercourse between Old England
> and New, afforded increased advantages, and a greater
> inducement than had yet existed, for pursuing that busi-
> ness [fishing]; and no improbability forbids credence to
> the statement that a company from Plymouth came across
> the bay in search of a suitable place for a fishing-station,
> and found it on the shores of Cape Ann.
>   It is said that these men, led by a son of Rev. John
> Robinson, landed at Agassquam, and were so well satis-

fied with its harbor, and other conveniences for the
fishing-business, that they concluded to set up a fishing-
stage, and to make preparations there for the accommoda-
tion of their families. No means exist for determining the
year in which this took place. We know that a remnant of
Mr. Robinson's Leyden congregation were passengers
in one of the ships that brought Winthrop's company in
1630; and a letter in print, written in March of that year,
alluding to Mrs. Robinson as intending to come over,
authorizes the inference that she, with one or more of her
children perhaps, was among the passengers. If, therefore, this traditionary account of the first settlement of
Cape Ann may be received as a fact in our history, the
date of that event may be fixed about 1631.

See also the notice of Abraham Robinson, son of John Robinson, in Babson, *History*, p. 134; also *Maximus* I, 160, etc.

II.65. 1633 anyway Rev Eli Forbes says (1792) on authority /
"Vide ancient Mss" . . .

Babson continues on p. 47 of his *History*, after the passage quoted in the note above:

> That there were settlers here as early as 1633, who "met,
> and carried on the worship of God among themselves,
> read the word of God, prayed to him, and sung psalms,"
> may be asserted upon authority of the highest respect-
> ability; for the statement is made in a printed sermon
> of one of the most esteemed ministers of the town in the
> last century, who gives, in the margin, reference to an
> "ancient manuscript" to warrant his assertion.

Babson adds in a footnote:

> The sermon here alluded to was preached by Rev. Eli
> Forbes, September, 1792, on the occasion of re-opening
> the meeting-house of the First Parish after it had been
> thoroughly repaired. The text was from Exod. XX. 24,
> last clause. "Ancient manuscript:" these are the only words
> of the marginal reference. There is too much reason to
> fear that this precious document is lost beyond the hope
> of recovery, and that we must ever experience the vain
> regret that it was not published instead of the sermon.

II.65. 1636 old John (White) to new John (Winthrop) urge[i]ng . . .

See the letter of John White to John Winthrop from 16 November 1636, in *Winthrop Papers,* III, 321–323, esp. p. 322:

> I should besides thincke it very convenient and almost necessary to sent on for fishing which is the first means that will bring any income into your lande. Two or three good masters that might bring with them each halfe a dosen good boates masters and three or foure good splitters in all would keepe you a good number of boats at sea, and time would soone bring in many of your owne men to be fitt for that employment.

John White, it will be remembered, was the leading organizer of the Dorchester Company which sought to found a fishing plantation at Cape Ann in 1623, thirteen years before.

II.65. 1637: the longer you defer fishing . . .

From the letter of John White to John Winthrop, ca. 1637, in *Winthrop Papers,* III, 335–337, esp. p. 336: "The longer you defer fishing and vse of other means that may bring you in some supplys the more you weaken your body and will ere longe make it wholy vnfitt for those remedys which may helpe it now but hereafter will come to late."

II.65. Hugh Peter pushing 1639 . . .

Peter (1598–1660) arrived at Boston in 1635 and was given charge of the church at Salem. See his letter of ca. 10 April 1639 to John Winthrop in *Winthrop Papers,* IV, 112–113, in which he expresses concern for the state of the colony in the hasty, scattered manner typical of him, and proposes to seek help from the Dutch:

> . . . once agayne I say wee must looke out, wee want necessary linnen cum multis alijis, and a voyage to the West Indyes would find vs wintere worke in Cottone etc. fishing will not yet or to purpose, manu-factures cannot sine

manibus: I am sick to heare the complaynts graunt ships doe come, eyther wee are too many to bee serued by so few ships; or theire supply will not bee quadrate, or we shall want mony to take them of: these things I say not out of want of faith for my selfe, but loue to the country.

See also *Maximus* III, 146ff.

II.65. stages builded nautas turning / fishermen (Dutch example) / Millward . . .

See *Maximus* I, 158–160 and notes; *Maximus* II, 60–61 and notes.

II.65. young Gallop

A son of John Gallop is mentioned in a letter from William Hooke to John Winthrop, 28 January 1639/40 (*Winthrop Papers*, IV, 184).

II.65. March 1640 Craddock / shoving at Winthrop

Matthew Cradock (d. ca. 1644), a London merchant and first governor of the Massachusetts Bay Company. He writes in a letter to John Winthrop (*Winthrop Papers*, IV, 207–208): "I shall not troble you further at present but wish some serious course might be thought of howe Returnes may bee prouided whereby trade may bee Incoraged I speake not for aney partyculer end of my owne but for the publique good and ame of opynion to cherish a Magazine for Fish to bee the oneley way by Gods assistance. . . ." However, the letter is dated 27 February 1639/40 (March 1640, the date of another letter on that page, appears as the heading at the top of the page).

II.65. come Gloucester / into / Being: April SIXTEEN / Forty-two

Date of the incorporation by the Massachusetts General Court of Gloucester as a township. See *Maximus* I, 156 and note.

▶**II.66. On Bemo Ledge he fell ...**

Manuscript dated "Oct 16th." Bemo Ledge is at the southern entrance to Brace's Cove on the Atlantic shore of Eastern Point. See also "the ones / had to crawl up out of Brace's Cove ...," p. 21 of *Maximus* I, and note to "red Jacks," p. 6 of that volume.

▶**II.67. THE CUT**

Written 18 October 1961 (manuscript dated). For the "Cut," see note to *Maximus* I, 30.

II.67. March 13, 1638/9 ...

From Shurtleff, *Records of the Massachusetts Bay,* I, 253: "Mr Endecott was willed to send 3 to veiwe Cape Ann, wheth^r it may not bee cut thorow, & to certify how they find it." Copied by Olson in his notebook, "Gloucester Feb/59 ...," p. 1, before he had acquired his own copy of Shurtleff (the passage was later marked in his copy).

II.67. December 10, 1641 ...

From Shurtleff, *Records,* I, 345: "It is ordered, that they that cut the beach betweene Cape Ann & Annisquam shall have liberty to take sufficient toale as the Court shall thinke meete for one & twentye years."

▶**II.68. Scheria—?**

Dated 18 October 1961. The poem derives essentially from two passages in Pausanias' *Description of Greece* as translated by Frazer. First, the island of Scheria itself, home of the Phaeacians who befriended Odysseus when he was washed up from the sea after his escape from Calypso's island (see *Maximus* I, 78 and notes), appears in Book II of Pausanias (Frazer, I, 77–78):

> The Asopus, which I have just mentioned, rises in Phliasia, and flowing through the land of Sicyon falls into

the sea there. The Phliasians say that Asopus had three daughters, Corcyra, Aegina, and Thebe, and that from Corcyra and Aegina the islands called Scheria and Oenone received their new names . . . Phliasians and Sicyonians affirm that the water of the river is not its own, but comes from abroad: they say that the Meander, descending from Celaenae through Phrygia and Caria, and falling into the sea near Miletus, comes to Peloponnese and forms the Asopus.

The Meander has been confused in the poem with the Scamander, a river about 175 miles further north, near the site of Troy.

The section of the poem remaining is from Pausanias, VII. 5. 3—4 (Frazer, I, 334):

You would be charmed, too, with the sanctuary of Hercules at Erythrae, and with the temple of Athena at Priene. The attraction of the latter is its image; the charm of the former is its antiquity. For the image of Hercules is like neither the so-called Aeginetan images, nor the most ancient Attic images: but if ever there was a purely Egyptian image, this is it. A wooden raft floated from Tyre in Phoenicia with the god upon it; but how this happened is more than even the Erythraeans can say. When the raft reached the Ionian sea, they say that it came to anchor at the cape called Mesate ('middle'), which is on the mainland exactly mid-way on the voyage from the harbour of Erythrae to the island of Chios. The raft having come to rest at this cape, the Erythraeans on the one side, and the Chians on the other, strained every nerve to tow the image to their own shore. At last a man of Erythrae, Phormio, by name, who got his livelihood by the sea and by catching fish, but had lost his eyesight by some disease, dreamed that the women of Erythrae must shear their hair, and that with a rope woven of the women's tresses the men would be able to tow the raft ashore. The ladies of the burgesses would have none of the dream; but the Thracian women, bond and free alike, who dwelt in Erythrae, suffered their hair to be shorn. And thus the Erythraeans towed the raft ashore. So Thracian women are the only women who are free to enter the sanctuary of Hercules; and the rope made of their tresses is preserved by the people of Erythrae to this day. And what is more, they say that the fisherman recovered his sight and kept it for the rest of his life.

The confusion in the poem between Hercules and Athena comes from the passage following in Pausanias which describes a statue of Athena Polias (suggesting the poem was probably written from memory): "There is also in Erythrae a temple of Athena Polias, and a colossal wooden image of the goddess seated on a throne, with a distaff in either hand and a firmament on her head." In his notes on this section, Frazer points out that "As the image was said to have come from Tyre, it may have represented the Tyrian Hercules or Melcart. . . . The legend that the image floated to Erythrae on a raft is remarkably illustrated by a series of scarabs, on which Hercules is represented on his raft" (IV, 127). He goes on to describe the scarab of Hercules-Melcaart, the same which is to be found in Bérard, *Did Homer Live?*, pp. 189–191 (see note to *Maximus* I, 78).

▶II.69. My Carpenter's Son's Son's Will . . .

Exact date of writing not known. Read at Vancouver in 1963. Lt. William Stevens, according to Babson, *History*, p. 167, "was lieutenant of the military company here, selectman two years, and representative in 1692. He died Sept. 24, 1701, aged forty-two; leaving an estate, which consisted, in part, of an interest in three sloops, a negro woman and a boy, and the privilege called the Cut, the latter valued at £30." His grandfather (q.v.), first appears in *Maximus* I, 31: "That carpenter is much on my mind: / I think he was the first Maximus. . . ."

II.69. a certain previledged place / call the Cutt . . .

According to Babson, Lt. William Stevens "came into possession of the land of his grandfather at the Cut, and there without doubt had his home. He died Sept. 24, 1701: and at the time of his decease was the leading merchant of the town in maritime business, small as his investments in it were. According to the inventory his estate consisted of 'one-half of a deck sloop, £26; one-third of an open sloop, £155; two-thirds of another open sloop, £16; a negro woman, £18;

mulatto boy, £10; one-third of a ware house, £5; house and homestead, £78; privilege called ye Cut, £30 . . ." (*Notes and Additions*, I, 77).

Olson, however, has consulted the original record of the inventory at the Probate Court in Salem, which includes: "a certain previledged place called yᵉ Cutt wher vessels pass through for money   34-10-00" (i.e., thirty-four pounds, ten shillings).

II.69. comparison (for value) / house sawmill barn / 74£

This is the value assigned the real estate of Lt. William Stevens when it was divided among his surviving children on March 6, 1713. It, too, is from the inventory of Stevens' estate in the probate records in Salem: "The Dwelling hous and home steed and a very sorry old saw-mill and orchard belonging to it with one comonage or comon right 74-00-00." Also recorded in Babson, *Notes and Additions*, I, 78.

▶II.70. Maximus, at the Harbor

The entire poem is dated 23–24 October 1961, although a note by the poet on a carbon of Jeremy Prynne's 1964 typescript indicates the third section was actually "added Mon, Nov 6 1961—2 weeks later."

II.70. Encircling Okeanos

Okeanos is regarded by Hesiod both as "a continuous stream enclosing the earth and the seas" and as having "nine streams which encircle the earth" (*Theogony*, Evelyn-White trans., notes on pp. 135 and 137).

II.70. the ring / of Okeanos

The phrase occurs much earlier as "the ring of the sea," which gives the poem "The Ring of" from 1952 its title; cf. also the "wobbling ring" of *Maximus* III, 19.

II.70. Paradise is a person. Come into this world.

From Corbin, "Cyclical Time in Mazdaism and Ismailism,"
p. 165:

> We gain this impression [that "every concept . . . in the
> world of the universal has its counterpart in the world of
> the individual: a concrete person . . . outside of which this
> ideal or mental reality remains virtuality and pure ab-
> straction"] by juxtaposing propositions such as these:
> "Paradise is a *person* (or a human being)" . . . Around these
> propositions Nasir Tusi [see note to *Maximus* II, 53] de-
> velops an analysis which may well be called phenom-
> enological. To be in Paradise, or to come into this world,
> designates above all different modes of being and under-
> standing. It means either to exist in true Reality . . . , or,
> on the contrary, to "come into this world. . . ."

II.70. The soul is a magnificent angel. / And the thought of its thought . . .

Corbin, "Cyclical Time," p. 166: "More active than the
person himself is the thought that is the thought through
him, the word that is spoken by him (and personified in
him). And this thought of his thought is precisely what
Nasir Tusi calls the Angel of this thought (or of this word of
action)." Nasir Tusi is quoted in a footnote at this point:
"Every true thought, every truthful word, every good action
has a spiritual . . . entity—that is to say, the Angel . . . who
endows the soul, in its progressive rise, with the ability to
pass easily through the successive degrees of perfection and
return to its original source. Then this soul becomes a
magnificent Angel (*fereshta-ye karim*), and the Angels of its
thought, speech, and action become integral parts of it, setting their imprint upon it."

II.70. apophainesthai

Greek, 'that which shows forth.' From Corbin, "Cyclical
Time," p. 166: "the ἀποφαινεισθαῖ of the phenomenology
which shows *itself* the *phainomen*."

II.70. Norman's / Woe

See *Maximus* II, 7 and note.

II.70. Round Rock shoal

At the entrance to Gloucester Harbor on a direct line from the Dog Bar Breakwater.

II.70. Pavilion Beach

Beach along Gloucester's Western Harbor, forming the western shore of Fort Point; about a hundred yards from the poet's house.

II.71. Watch House Point

Early name for Fort Point. According to Babson, *History,* pp. 307–308, "a small rock-bound hill, that seems to stand as a sentinel to overlook the waters by which it is almost surrounded, and watch every movement upon their surface. Upon the south side of this hill, about midway between its summit and the shore, was erected [in 1743] the battery, which, in case of attack, was to protect the shipping and homes of our ancestors. . . . The locality was then variously called 'Stage Neck,' 'Neck Beach,' and 'Watch-house Neck;' and the point where the battery was placed, 'Watch-house Point,' from the watch-house which was probably set up there thirty or forty years before."

II.71. the soul, / in its progressive rise

See quotation from Corbin, p. 166n, in note above to "The soul is a magnificent angel."

II.71. passes in & out / of more difficult things . . .

Cf. Corbin, "Cyclical Time," p. 166n, quoted above: ". . . the ability to pass easily through the successive degrees of perfection and return to its original source."

II.71. the act which actuates the soul itself

Corbin, "Cyclical Time," p. 167: "The soul performs its actions and understands it only beginning with the act which actuates the soul itself."

II.71. it sends out / on the path ahead the Angel / it will meet

See the Mazdean concept of the Fravarti, the celestial prototype and tutelary angel of man, as discussed by Corbin in "Cyclical Time," pp. 131ff. In Mazdaism, the earthly human soul has a celestial counterpart, a Soul of Light (or Angel), its Destiny, which it encounters after death on the road to the Cinvat Bridge (for which, see *Maximus* II, 47 and note). The human being "attains to his angel only to be drawn with him into a new height," for these Angels, "far from being 'fixed,' multiply beyond themselves, always sending out another Angel ahead of themselves" (Corbin, p. 133).

II.71. its accent is its own mirage

Should read "ascent" for "accent." From Corbin, "Cyclical Time," p. 167: "The burgeoning and growth in the soul of the angelical or demoniacal virtuality is the measure of its ascent (*mi'raj*). . . ."

II.71. the Perfect Child

Corbin, "Cyclical Time," pp. 161–162: ". . . the Gnostic idea of the Imam as Anthropos or as the Perfect Child (*al-walad al-tamm*) who engenders himself in the secret of the cycles of the aeon, and who, in his eschatological Epiphany, is expected to be the ultimate 'exegete' of mankind, a member of the true posterity of Adam which he will lead back (*ta'wil*) to the celestial archetype in which it originated." And in a note on p. 162, Corbin writes of "the Imam *Qa'im* (the 'Perfect Child,' herald, or 'Angel' of Resurrection)."

▶**II.72. brang that thing out . . .**

Manuscript dated 3 December 1961 (though the poem is also dated 24 October 1961 elsewhere in Olson's notes).

II.72. the Monogene

See *Maximus* II, 10 and note.

II.72. the original unit / survives in the salt

Very likely the salt of alchemy, as well as the elemental salt of the sea. See, e.g., Jung, *Psychology and Alchemy*, pp. 244–245:

> The *Rosarium philosophorum* says:
>
> Who therefore knows the salt and its solution knows the hidden secret of the wise men of old. Therefore turn your mind upon the salt, for in it alone [i.e., the mind] is the science concealed and the most excellent and most hidden secret of all the ancient philosophers.
>
> The Latin text has "in ips*a* sol*a*," referring therefore to "mens." One would have to assume a double misprint were the secret after all concealed in the *salt*. But as a matter of fact "mind" and "salt" are close cousins—*cum grano salis*! Hence, according to Khunrath, the salt is not only the physical centre of the earth but at the same time the *sal sapientiae,* of which he says: "Therefore direct your feelings, senses, reason and thoughts upon this salt alone." The anonymous author of the *Rosarium* says in another place that the work must be performed "with true and not with fantastic imagination," and again that the stone will be found "when the search lies heavy on the searcher." This remark can only be understood as meaning that a certain psychological condition is indispensable for the discovery of the miraculous stone.

Jung writes in *Aion*, p. 161, that "Whenever an alchemist speaks of 'salt,' he does not mean sodium chloride or any other salt, or only in a very limited sense. He could not get away from its symbolic significance, and therefore includes the *sal sapientiae* in the chemical substance."

As early as *Call Me Ishmael* (1947), Olson wrote (p. 13): ". . . the beginning of man was salt sea, and the perpetual reverberation of that great ancient fact [is] constantly renewed in the unfolding of life in every human individual."

▶ **II.74. Going Right out of the Century**

Dated 19 November 1961. This is another version of the episode first reported in *Maximus* I, 115; it will recur, as a kind of motif, in *Maximus* II, 106, and III, 45.

▶ **II.79. A Later Note on / Letter # 15**

Written, as noted, 15 January 1962. See "Maximus, to Gloucester: Letter 15," *Maximus* I, 67–71.

II.79. meubles

French, 'furniture.' It may be of some small relevance that Pound writes of "furniture poetry" in *Make It New,* pp. 186 and 200.

II.79. after 1630 / & Descartes was the value

See *Maximus* I, 128, "Descartes, age 34, date Boston's / settling," and note.

II.79. Whitehead

Alfred North Whitehead (1861–1947), whose philosophy of process underlies the *Maximus Poems.* On a film made in March 1966 for National Educational Television distribution, Olson speaks of Whitehead as "my great master and the companion of my poems" (*Mutbologos*, I, 186). See especially Whitehead's *Process and Reality* (1929), which Olson first read in the spring of 1955, and *Adventures of Ideas* (1933). See also Olson's lecture at Black Mountain in 1956, published in Charters, *Olson / Melville,* pp. 84–90. He had met the philosopher himself at a dinner in Cambridge in 1938, while a graduate student at Harvard. The copy of

Process and Reality he acquired in February 1957 is one of the most heavily marked and annotated volumes in his library.

II.79. Herodotus's, / which was a verb, to find out for yourself: / 'istorin

See *Maximus* I, 100 and note; also "Poetry and Truth," *Muthologos*, II, 37–38.

II.79. traum

German, 'dream.'

II.79. Whitehead's important corollary . . .

The statement is not present in Whitehead as such, nor—as pointed out in note to *Maximus* II, 5—is there precisely such a term as "eternal event" in his writings. There are, however, separately in *Process and Reality*, "eternal objects" and "events." An eternal object "can be described only in terms of its potentiality for 'ingression' into the becoming of actual entities; and that its analysis only discloses other eternal objects. It is pure potential. The term 'ingression' refers to the particular mode in which the potentiality of an eternal object is realized in a particular actual entity, contributing to the definiteness of that actual entity" (p. 31). In more familiar terminology, "eternal objects" and "actual entities" correspond roughly to "universals" and "particulars" (pp. 65–66). An "event," meanwhile, is used "in the more general sense of a nexus of actual occasions [or entities], inter-related in some determinate fashion in one extensive quantum" (p. 101). "The word 'event' is used sometimes in the sense of a nexus of actual entities, and sometimes in the sense of a nexus objectified by universals. In either sense, it is a definite fact with a date" (p. 326).

In a discussion held in November 1963, Olson would speak of "that beautiful concept of Whitehead's, the eternal event that strikes across all object and occasion" ("Under the Mushroom," *Muthologos*, I, 58). See also Olson's poem, "The

Lamp" (*Archaeologist of Morning*, p. 221), from 1964: "only if there is a coincidence of yourself / & the universe is there then in fact / an event."

▶II.80. 128 a mole . . .

The original was written on an envelope postmarked Gloucester, 28 November 1961 (definitely by 12 April 1962, when read at Goddard College).

Highway route 128 is carried over the Annisquam River into Gloucester by the A. Piatt Andrew Memorial Bridge, thus linking Gloucester with the mainland.

II.80. a mole / to get at Tyre

The Phoenician city of Tyre had been an island close to the shore until a mole or causeway linking it to the mainland was built by Alexander the Great during his siege of the city in 332 B.C. The causeway, which still exists, has since been widened by deposits of sand so that Tyre is no longer the island it once was. For Tyre's analogous relationship to Gloucester, see notes to "128 bridge," *Maximus* I, 160, and esp. to "Gloucester," *Maximus* I, 1.

▶II.81. "View": fr the Orontes

Dated 15 January 1962, same day as "*A Later Note on Letter # 15*" (*Maximus* II, 79). Reading the poem at Goddard College shortly after it was written, Olson remarked: ". . . there's an earlier *Maximus* way back sometime, on Columbus ["The Song and Dance of," *Maximus* I, 54–58] in which this whole business of the fact that Cyprus . . . you know, that island just off this point of land that I'm talking about, where the Orontes River comes in at the northern end of Syria . . . This is a picture—there's been several pieces of the picture put down before. One is that the island of Cyprus . . . is very close to this point which is the Orontes River, which was the main manageable traffic, trading outlet of the whole of the old Near East to Mediterranean and Atlantic. And the first step, the first stop and first step, both weather-wise and sailing-wise, was the island of Cyprus" (Goddard tape).

For the river Orontes, see also *Maximus* I, 150 and note.

II.81. Typhon

See *Maximus* I, 150 and note, and *Maximus* II, 95 and note.

II.81. Helen, / said Herodotus . . .

Helen of Troy. See Herodotus, *Histories*, I. i and ff. Olson had included Herodotus in his *Bibliography on America* (*Additional Prose*, p. 5): "At least first chapter of *Histories* on sailors & rapes of several women (Europa, Io, Helen, etc.)"

II.81. Manes

See note to "He went to Spain . . . ," *Maximus* II, 7.

II.81. Minos

King of Crete before the Trojan War, son of Zeus and Europa (see *Maximus* II, 102 and 111 and notes below). Identified by Waddell as Manes (see note to *Maximus* II, 7).

II.81. Gades

See note to *Maximus* I, 77.

II.81. Pytheas

See *Maximus* I, 62 and note, and *Maximus* II, 92 and note. He most likely embarked on his westward voyage from Gades.

II.81. Portuguese / are part Phoenician(?

Phoenician traders from Tyre were active on the Iberian peninsula as early as the eighth century B.C. and founded a number of settlements, most notably the emporium at Gades.

II.81. Canary Islanders / Cro-Magnon

The Canary Islands make up an archipelago in the Atlantic about sixty miles west of the North African coast. They were taken by Spain in the early fifteenth century. See Note V, "The Crô-Magnons of the Canary Islands," in Osborn's appendix to his *Men of the Old Stone Age*, p. 506, for evidence of Cro-Magnon stock among the inhabitants of the islands at the time of their conquest.

See also *Maximus* III, 163–165.

II.81. Stations / on shores / And Sable

See *Maximus* I, 121:

> the motion
> (the Westward motion)
> comes here,
> to land. Stations
> (going back to sheep,
> and goats on Sable
>
> Island . . .

and note above.

II.81. England / an Augustine / land

Saint Augustine (d. ca. 613), first archbishop of Canterbury, led a mission from Rome to christianize England in 597.

▶ II.82. The Young Ladies / Independent Society / of East Gloucester . . .

Written 2 October 1960 (manuscript dated). The society referred to actually flourished in East Gloucester in the late nineteenth century. It had come to the poet's attention through an account published in the local newspaper, August 1960 (preserved among his papers), following the destruction by fire of a hall which the organization had built. See Wonson, "History of a Hall" (part one):

In 1863, during the height of the Civil War, a number of young ladies connected with the East Gloucester Baptist Church, which had just been organized, formed a society and devoted their efforts towards the payment of the debt on the chapel which had been erected for the use of the church, and for five years they worked for this object. On the extinguishment of the debt on the chapel, they realized the need of a hall in the village for entertainments and similar gatherings, and enlisting many others in the enterprise, they resolved to work for the erection of a building for that purpose.

They organized as "The Young Ladies Independent Society of East Gloucester," and for the next few years they continued their efforts, until they secured sufficient funds to warrant the purchase of land and the erection of a hall, and as the members married, their husbands were admitted to membership, as well as others of both sexes who were interested in the object of the society, until at one time the membership reached nearly 200.

In the second part of his story, Wonson gives some of the ways by which the Society raised funds: "by dues, fairs, dances, strawberry festivals, valentine socials and other forms of entertainments for money raising and sociability . . ."

▶II.83. patriotism / is the preserved park . . .

In a note to himself attempting to date the poem, Olson wrote: "patriotism is on back of letter June 1960." An earlier version, entitled "THE BALLAD OF PRESENT-DAY GLOUCESTER—OR MAGNOLIA, or annisquam—WRITTEN TO CALL ATTENTION TO THE YEAR 1960 AS THE CENTENNARY OF JOHN BABSON's HIS STORY OF GLOUCESTER WHOSE FATHER AT LEAST WAS NOT A RICH MERCHANT of STAM BOULI" and dated 14 June 1960, was sent to Mary Shore of Gloucester.

Blocked out are names of Gloucester persons alive at the time of the writing, most of them frequent commentators on local and national affairs through letters to the editor of the newspaper. The names, however, are present in manuscript versions and were also read at Goddard and Vancouver; they appear in these notes within brackets.

II.83. [John Black] / Magnolia pirate

John W. Black, Jr. (1893–1964), a Gloucester lawyer.

II.83. Oliver Viera

Oliver F. Vieira (b. ca. 1899), pharmacist, resident of Magnolia, Mass.; commander of the local American Legion post at the time.

II.83. Ralph Harland Smith

(1897–1968), a retired Ensign of the U.S. Navy living in Gloucester. He wrote turgid patriotic letters to the newspaper at a time when the city was embroiled in a controversy over the role of the John Birch extremist group in local affairs. In a letter to the editor of the *Gloucester Times* dated 12 October 1965 among his papers, Olson later wrote a "defense" of Smith: "Smith at least is a kind of Gloucester *at least* as old in mindedness as Timothy Pickering's objection to Gloucester, and I shall miss the attack style and quantity of his mind" (for Pickering, see esp. *Maximus* II, 198).

II.83. [Peter Smith] / borrows it . . .

(b. 1897), publisher of out-of-print books and writer of letters of a liberal persuasion to the local newspaper.

II.83. [Nancy Larter]

Author of a column in the *Gloucester Times* at the time, entitled "Keeping an Eye on Nature."

II.83. the Nancy Gloucester

See "The Skippers of Nancy Gloucester," a poem by Percy MacKaye, in Pringle, *Book of the Three Hundredth Anniversary*, pp. 131–141. MacKaye writes in an introductory comment: "By the Nancy Gloucester I typify those 300 years of sea life

which Gloucester has experienced and her three skippers
are the three centuries and each one tells his yarn."

II.83. Elspeth [Rogers]

Elliot C. Rogers (1902–1970), an attorney who authored
with Melvin T. Copeland (next entry) *The Saga of Cape Ann*,
which had recently been published. He was also an amateur
naturalist.

II.83. the former head of the Harvard Business School

Melvin T. Copeland (1884–1975), professor of administration and director of research at the Harvard Business
School, from 1909—shortly after the school was founded—
until 1953. He wrote a history of the school, *And Mark an
Era: The Story of the Harvard Business School* (1958).

II.83. Brookline

Suburb south of Boston.

II.83. Mr Brown / of Old Magnolia / made a pass

Brown was manager of the Maison de Blanc, a gift shop on
Lexington Avenue, Magnolia. See Olson's letter of 2 July
1950 to Vincent Ferrini in *Origin* 1, p. 61, concerning "the
time that fancy dan fr magnolia, Brown, picked me up—and
wanted to take me for a ride in Ravenswood!) My m   y."

▶II.84. Bk ii chapter 37

An earlier version written by early 1962 (read at Goddard
College in April) was published in *Yugen* that spring. The
poem is based on a book and chapter of Pausanias' *Description of Greece*, with Gloucester references in place of the
original ones. Markings in one of his copies of Graves'
Greek Myths (I, 107), indicate Olson had been reading a section on the Lernaean Hydra adapted from Pausanias and
then apparently turned to Pausanias' text itself.

II.84. I. Beginning at the hill of Middle Street . . .

See Pausanias' *Description of Greece*, Frazer trans., I, 129:

> 1. Beginning at this mountain, the grove, which consists mostly of plane-trees, reaches down to the sea. It is bounded on the one side by the river Pontinus, and on the other side by another river, called Amymone, after the daughter of Danaus. 2. In the grove are images of Demeter, surnamed Prosymne, and of Dionysus: there is also a small seated image of Demeter. These images are made of stone. In another temple there is a seated wooden image of Saviour Dionysus. There is also a stone image of Aphrodite beside the sea. They say that it was dedicated by the daughters of Danaus, and that Danaus himself made the sanctuary of Athena on the banks of the Pontinus. 3. The Lernaean mysteries are said to have been instituted by Philammon. The stories told about the rites are clearly not ancient. Other stories, I am told, purporting to be by Philammon, have been found engraved on a piece of copper fashioned in the shape of a heart. But these stories also have been proved not to be by Philammon.

II.84. the stream or entrance / to the inner harbor

"Stream" is capitalized in the earlier version published in *Yugen*. See *Maximus* II, 144 and note.

II.84. In the Fort . . . are the images of stone

There are no public monuments or "images of stone" on Fort Point, other than a bronze commemorative plaque on Watchhouse Point. Perhaps the poet would include shrines in the back yards of some of the private homes on the Fort, including a plaster statue of the Virgin Mary in his own, set up by the owner of the house.

II.84. a seated / wooden image of Demeter

One of the Great Mothers; Greek goddess of fruitfulness and mother of Persephone.

II.84. a church called / the Lady of Good Voyage

See notes to "On the hill, over the water . . . ," *Maximus* I, 2, and to "the lady," I, 6.

II.84. a stone image of Aphrodite by the sea

Aphrodite was the Greek goddess of love and sexual beauty. It should be noted that in the earlier version, there follows: "It explains the annual ceremony of Phryne appearing before the people and going into the water in her full and original beauty." See above, *Maximus* II, 35 and note, for Phryne; the story about her walking naked into the sea does not occur in Pausanias.

II.84. the special / Hydra called the Lernean monster

The Hydra, or water-serpent, was the child of Typhon (q.v.) and Echidne, and lived in a swamp at Lerna. It was said to have many heads and a dog-like body, and was slain by Hercules as his second labor. Pausanias writes: "At the source of the Amymone grows a plane-tree: they say that under this plane-tree the hydra was bred. I believe that this beast was larger than other water-snakes, and that its venom was so deadly that Hercules poisoned the barbs of his arrows with its gall; but I do not think it had more than one head" (Frazer trans., I, 130). See also Graves, *Greek Myths*, I, 107–109.

Lerna, in Greece near Argos, is like Gloucester, on the seacoast. For Gloucester's own water-monster, see *Maximus* II, 32 and 121 and notes, also III, 59–60.

II.84. tablets of Poseidon / written on copper in the shape of a heart

There is a series of commemorative plaques set up at various historical spots throughout Gloucester (on the Fort, in Stage Fort Park, etc.), though these are bronze and rectangular, not "copper in the shape of a heart." It is such plaques which give rise to the poem on *Maximus* II, 174.

▶ **II.85. the rocks in Settlement Cove . . .**

Written by early 1962 (read at Goddard College in April). In conversation, June 1968, the poet explained that "Settlement Cove" was his own designation for the spot where he felt the original Dorchester Company settlers probably first landed on Cape Ann, on the far western curve of the Western Harbor, sheltered by the bluff of Stage Head, a spot earlier known as Steep Bank Cove.

II.85. dromlechs, menhirs

Megalithic stones; "dromlech" apparently a confusion or fusion of dolmen and cromlech, corrected in *Maximus* III, 97.

II.85. Stacy Boulevard

An esplanade, lined with streetlights, along the Western Harbor on either side of the Cut.

▶ **II.86. my memory is / the history of time**

Date of writing not known. A variation of John Smith's original statement, "history is the memory of time" (*Maximus* I, 112 and note).

In a draft of a letter concerned with the publishing of *Maximus IV, V, VI*, Olson describes such brief poems as these as not "snippets" but, "in fact, hooks & eyes."

▶ **II.87. Peloria   the dog's upper lip kept curling . . .**

Written, as noted, 12 November 1961. For "Peloria," see Harrison, *Themis*, pp. 458–459, following a discussion of *ta meteora* and *ta metarsia* (see *Maximus* II, 9, and 58 and notes):

> Thunder and lightning, wind and rain, storm and tempest might fitly be classed as *peloria*, portents. . . . The word *peloria* covers, I think, both Earth-powers and Sky-powers, both Giants and Titans; but it is not a little interesting

to find that quite early the word differentiated itself into two forms. Dr Osthoff has shown that πέλωρ and τέρας—monster and portent—are one and the same. An examination of the uses of the two words shows that they are practically identical, only that—and this is for us the important point—πέλωρ tends to specialize towards what is earth-born, and τέρας in the form τείρεα tends to be used of heavenly signs.

Thus πέλωρ is one regular term for an earth-born monster and specially for a snake. . . . Finally, what is very interesting for us, we know of an ancient festival celebrated in honour of these primitive earth-potencies and called by their name *Peloria*. . . .

See also, perhaps, the definition of "peloria" in *Webster's Collegiate Dictionary*, 5th ed., p. 732, from Greek *pelōros* 'monstrous': "An abnormal regularity of structure occurring in normally irregular flowers."

II.87. sent flowers on the waves . . . Flowers go out to sea.

See "Maximus, to Gloucester, Sunday, July 19," *Maximus* I, 152–154 and note.

II.87. the mole / of Tyre

See *Maximus* II, 80 and note.

II.87. Malta

The island in the Mediterranean south of Sicily. See also *Maximus* II, 93 and esp. 94.

II.87. Marseilles

Port on the French coast; home of Pytheas, who travelled to what possibly was Iceland (see *Maximus* I, 62 and note, also *Maximus* II, 92 and notes). This poem, like the ones on *Maximus* II, 7 or 94, presents the Maximus figure, the voyager, in his several guises (Pytheas, Odysseus, Hercules, Manes, etc.).

II.87. From Iceland to Promontorium Vinlandiae

Viking voyages to the New World. On Icelandic maps of Sigurdur Stefansson (Sigurd Stephanius), ca. 1590, and Hans Poulson Resen, 1605, appears a north-pointing cape (probably northern Newfoundland) designated *"Promontorium Vinlandiae."* See the detail of Stefansson's map in the section on "The Earliest Maps of Massachusetts Bay and Boston Harbor" in Winsor's *Memorial History of Boston*, I, 39. See also Merrill, "The Vinland Problem," pp. 25–26, and Skelton et al., *Vinland Map*, pp. 203–206, 217, 221–222.

In conversation, June 1968, the poet explained that he was here identifying "Promontorium Vinlandiae" with Cape Ann, specifically its Stage Head.

II.87. Settlement Cove

See *Maximus* II, 85 and note.

II.87. a mappemunde

Latin, 'map of the world.' See also "On first Looking out through Juan de la Cosa's Eyes," *Maximus* I, 77–81.

▶II.88. In the Face of a Chinese View of the City

Written, as noted, 5 January 1962. Minor revisions from first publication in *The Floating Bear*. Before reading this poem at Goddard College, Olson remarked: "I was talking to the very man that I wrote this about, the City Manager, the other day, and I said 'I just published a poem about you, in New York, called "In the Face of a Chinese View of the City." ' He said, 'I don't know anything about Chinese.' 'Don't worry,' I said; 'Do you remember Confucius?' 'Oh yeah,' he said [with evident confusion], 'uh yeah, uh hum' [laughter from audience]."

The poem reflects issues under dispute in the town at the time.

II.88. the D P W

The Department of Public Works, in charge of snow re-moval in Gloucester. A sixteen-inch snowstorm on Christmas Eve, 1961, had left a problem. A review of the local news-paper for the weeks immediately prior to the writing of the poem reveals complaints of snow-clogged streets (the edi-torial on the day of this poem was "Snow on the Sidewalks") and reports of several minor accidents due to automobiles skidding on slippery streets (though no report of a boy having, as a result, "a broken / pair of eyes"—or "broken / side," as it reads in the earlier published version).

II.88. criticize . . . the Superintendent of Schools for the texts / he buys

Prominent in the local news at the time was a hotly con-tested campaign for three vacancies on the city School Com-mittee in which candidates alleged to be members of the ultra-rightest John Birch Society levelled charges that text-books in use in Gloucester schools were lacking in sufficient patriotic quality.

II.88. $5,000,000 a year's receipts for ex- / penditures

This would seem to be an actual figure. An editorial in the *Gloucester Times* for 2 January 1962, "Our Annual Report," p. 4, says "Gloucester budget this year may top $5 million."

II.88. the color of the lights on the Main / Street turns the lips of women blue / and all days are cheery too . . .

Another editorial, "The Christmas Lights," 23 December 1961, p. 4, speaks of the "cheery lights" of downtown Glou-cester. In "A *Scream* to the Editor," Olson would again decry the mercury-vapor streetlights of Main Street which "destroy the color of color / in human faces."

▶**II.90. while on / Obadiah Bruen's Island . . .**

An early, if not original, manuscript of this poem is written on the back of a note to the poet and his wife from their Gloucester friend Harry Martin, apparently in February 1961. The poem was among those read at Goddard College in April 1962.

For Bruen's Island, see *Maximus* II, 16 and note.

II.90. the Algonquins / steeped fly agaric in whortleberry juice . . .

On the back of an envelope from drug researcher Timothy Leary postmarked 23 December 1960, Olson had written: "steep dried specimens of fly amanita in whortleberry juice / haschish & *majoon*"; while in an unfinished essay from ca. 1962 among the poet's papers, entitled "Under the Mushroom," there occurs: "amanita muscaria / fly agaric to Algonquin Indians who probably used same but without any such organization as the southern Indians who called one bite or enough mushrooms to get to the autonomic nervous system 'God's flesh' . . ."

Fly agaric or the mushroom *Amanita muscaria*, mixed with whortleberry juice, was sufficiently well known among primitive peoples for its hallucenogenic properties. It was used by the old Norse (from whence came the fury of the Berserks) and by the Siberians (first reported by Strahlenberg in 1730; English translation, *An histori-geographical description of the north and eastern part of Europe and Asia*, published in London in 1736). The Siberians, for example, according to Marshall, *The Mushroom Book*, p. 49—apparently the source of Olson's note from ca. 1960 quoted above—"steep dried specimens of the fly amanita in whortleberry juice, and thus make a drink which produces an intoxication similar to that produced by the 'haschisch' and 'majoon' of the East." See also Wasson and Wasson, *Mushrooms, Russia, and History*, I, 190–214.

There seems to be no distinct evidence, however, to suggest that the Algonquins shared this practice. In conversation, August 1969, the poet explained that he was led to write the poem by the association of the method of diluting the mushroom's potency with whortleberry juice with the name of Whortleberry Hill, a prominence on the east side of the Annisquam River a little below Pearce's Island (formerly Obadiah Bruen's Island) where shell heaps left by the Algonquins have been found.

Moreover, it does not seem that the poet knew from experience whether the whortleberry juice did make a proper mixture. He writes in a postcard to Albert Glover, 20 August 1969, who had sought his advice: "I can't, for the life of my self tell you if whortleberry juice does cut Amanita. [I was told in Maine . . . that all one has to do is 'skin' fly agaric to take off its poison. But *above all* see the Wassons *Russia, History & the Mushroom* (for recipes)."

▶ II.91. Shag Rock, / bull's eye . . .

Written by early 1962 (read at Goddard College in April). A "Plan of the Harbour of Gloucester . . . May 1813" (Massachusetts Archives #1756)—a photostat of which is among the poet's papers—shows "Shagrock" off the western edge of Ten Pound Island in Gloucester Harbor. It can on occasion be seen from Fort Point. See also one of the "New 'Songs of Maximus'" in *A New Folder*, 1959, p. 99: "On Shagrock, / January / ice is / the new / high water / mark. . . ."

II.91. Round Rock Shoal

See *Maximus* II, 70 and note.

▶ II.92. τὰ περι τοῦ ᾽ηκεανοῦ

An earlier version, dated 17 January 1962, was read at Goddard College and sent to Eli Wilentz in 1965 for the proposed Jargon/Corinth edition. It was probably revised in 1967 or in the summer of 1968. The title, which can be translated from the Greek as "Round About the Ocean," is that of a work by Pytheas (q.v.) and is mentioned in the article on him in the *Encyclopaedia Britannica*, 11th ed.: "His work is lost, and we are left almost wholly in the dark as to its form and character, but the various titles under which it is quoted (*e.g.* Γης περίοδος, or τα περὶ τοῦ 'Ωκεανοῦ) point to a geographical treatise, in which Pytheas had embodied the results of his observations, rather than to a continuous narrative of his voyage" (XXII, 703).

II.92. Strabo

(ca. 63 B.C.–ca. A.D. 24) the Greek geographer. At the Goddard reading, Olson made the following remarks about Strabo in relation to Pytheas:

> ... Again, I think, second century. The geographer who's responsible for our knowing about Pytheas at all (the man of the fourth century B.C. who actually sailed out of Marseilles, and by the very thing which makes Strabo suspicious that he was a liar, Stefansson, who really knows— the present Stefansson, Vilhjalmur, who knows, like, the Arctic—says it's the best evidence of the fact that Pytheas was really in a certain season off the coast of Iceland in the fourth century B.C. Like, that's really *talk*! Instead of crap of Irish and Vikings. Like, everything was really in existence, in powerful ways, back before Alexander. I think there again I'm pushing, but don't be fooled by the universalization of the present. The work, the real work of the future has already been done! And the future that is proposed is a lie.

The phrase "learned man" is not to be found in the *Encyclopaedia Britannica* article, nor is it in the *Geography* of Strabo itself, although mention is made there of Pytheas' "scientific knowledge of astronomy and mathematics" (Jones trans., III, 175).

II.92. the Greeks / were the 'English' / of the Mediterranean, / as the Germans / were the Romans

In the earlier version, the Greeks are compared to the "Germans," which Olson explained as follows: "The distinction being drawn is between the Phoenicians, who are the

'English' of the Mediterranean, as against the Greeks, who are the 'Germans' " (Goddard tape). Cf. then, Bérard, *Did Homer Live?*, p. 98: "The Phoenicians were the English of the waters of the Levant, and after them the Hellenes became the Germans. . . ."

II.92. the White / Sea

The arm of the Arctic Ocean extending into northern Russia, though possibly that area described by Pytheas as surrounding Thule (q.v.), which was neither earth nor air nor water, but a gelatinous "sludge."

II.92. "travelled all over by foot"

From the *Encyclopaedia Britannica* account of Pytheas: "All that we know concerning the voyage of Pytheas (apart from detached notices) is contained in a brief passage of Polybius, cited by Strabo, in which he tells us that Pytheas, according to his own statement, had not only visited Britain, but had personally explored a large part of it ('travelled all over it on foot,' according to one reading of the text in Strabo, bk. iv. ch. i.). . . ."

II.92. And did it all with limited means and in a private / capacity

From the same *Encyclopaedia Britannica* account: "Some modern writers have supposed Pytheas to have been sent out, at public expense, in command of an expedition organized by the republic of Massilia; but there is no ancient authority for this, and Polybius, who had unquestionably seen the original work, expressly states that he had undertaken the voyage in a private capacity and with limited means."

II.92. Tanaïs

After visiting Thule and the adjoining regions, the *Encyclopaedia Britannica* article continues, Pytheas "visited 'the whole of the coasts of Europe' (*i.e.* those bordering on the ocean) as far as the *Tanais* (Strabo, bk. ii, ch. iv. I)"—which river the authors of the article unaccountably identify as the Vistula, flowing north into the Baltic Sea, though most authorities hold that the Tanais is the Don of southern Russia, flowing into the Sea of Azov north of the Black Sea.

▶II.93. Cyprus / the strangled / Aphrodite . . .

Dated 17 January 1962. This is a poem—like those on *Maximus* II, 81 and 87—of migration. Cyprus, on the trade route to the west, was a principal stepping-stone in the desemination of culture and civilization from the ancient Near East throughout the Mediterranean. For its role as birthplace of Aphrodite, see *Maximus* I, 55 and note.

II.93. Rhodes

Island in the Aegean off the coast of Anatolia. Like Cyprus, it was both an important stopping place for traders and had an early association with a goddess—in its case, Rhode, the female eponym of the island, daughter of Poseidon and consort of Helios the Sun.

II.93. Crete

Island in the Mediterranean and a center of ancient civilization; home of the Minoans, whose chief object of worship was the Great Mother (see, e.g., Levy, *Gate of Horn*, pp. 213–225).

II.93. the Mother Goddess / fr Anatolia

The earth mother, mountain mother, goddess of vegetation and mistress of the animals, most commonly known as Cybele, indigenous to the Near East since neolithic times.

II.93. Phrygian Attis

A young god like Adonis and Osiris; the consort of the Great Mother, Cybele. His worship was centered in Phrygia, in western Anatolia.

II.93. Malta

See *Maximus* II, 87 and note. For its role as a sacred island in neolithic times and the specimens of figurines of the Great Mother found there, see esp. Levy. *Gate of Horn*, pp. 131−138 and plates 17−18, and Hawkes, *Prehistoric Foundations of Europe*, pp. 152−155.

II.93. Fat Lady

Any of the full-breasted, steatopygic figurines of the Great Mothers of Aurignacian time, such as the "Venus" of Willendorf. See Levy, *Gate of Horn*, pp. 56−63 and plates 6, 17−18; also Neumann, *Great Mother*, chapter 9 entitled "The Primordial Goddess," pp. 94−119, and plates 1, 3, and 8.

II.93. Spain

At the western end of the Mediterranean, the final stop (Gades) before the Atlantic and the New World.

▶II.94. after the storm was over . . .

Written, as noted, 17 January 1962.

II.94. cave at Mt Casius

Sacred mountain in northern Syria, on the Mediterranean coast near the mouth of the Orontes. Its Hurrian name was Hazzi. According to Guterbock, "Hittite Version of the Hurrian Kumarbi Myths," pp. 130−132, it was the site of the battle between the Hurrian weather-god Teshub and the diorite monster Ullikummi, as well as the fierce encounter between Zeus and the monster Typhon. See also Guterbock, "Hittite Religion," in *Ancient Religions*, p. 104, and Graves, *Greek Myths*, I, 136.

Casius is apparently intended to rhyme with Cashes, the fishing bank near Cape Ann (see the appearance of "a cave" and "Cashes" together in *Maximus* I, 150—as well as "Orontes" and "Typhon" there; also *Maximus* II, 7 and notes). It might be noted, however, that when the poem was read at

Vancouver in 1963, Olson did not stress the pun and pronounce "Casius" like "Cassius," but (as preserved on the
tape) seemed to say all three syllables.

II.94. the blue monster . . .

The snakelike Typhon, another form of the Hydra as well
as the Gloucester sea-serpent. See Olson's description from
ca. January 1965 quoted in note to *Maximus* II, 7, "he went
to Ireland." Also the description of Typhon in Hesiod,
Theogony (Evelyn-White trans., p. 139): "from under the
brows of his eyes in his marvellous heads flashed fire, and
fire burned from his heads as he glared."

II.94. to go / for Malta . . . to arrive at Ireland

The monster follows the course of the migrating hero. See
Maximus II, 7, 81, 87, and 93.

II.94. grapevine corner

Cape Ann as a whole; or specifically Wingaersheek Beach,
on the north side of Cape Ann, west of the Annisquam. In a
letter to the author, 18 April 1966, Olson wrote:

> I can put you on to *Dutch* source I'm pretty sure—of
> probably *all* primary matter then at least available; and
> you at least should go there. It is O'Callaghan, I believe,
> editing them, & published as Documents of the History of
> the State of New York.
> Any way, look it up—& if you *would* be so kind, & I am
> right, keep your eye open as well to Dutch exploration of
> what in fact is, in *one* of their earliest voyages on this
> coast, out of Nieuw Amsterdam,   [in Dutch nominative]
> *Grapevine Corner*

The "Dutch nominative," translated here as "Grapevine
Corner," would be "Wyngaershoek" or "Grape Vine HOYK"
(*Maximus* II, 9). In "'I know men . . . ,'" Olson says about
Wingaersheek Beach: "The Dutch called it Wyngaerds
hoeck . . . Grapevine Corner, Grapevine Harbor. That was
their name. There's a great map, in the *Documents of New*

York, showing the peninsula as Wyngaerds Hoeck..."
(*Muthologos*, II, 162).

For the Dutch origin of Wingaersheek, see Winsor, "The Earliest Maps," in *The Memorial History of Boston*, pp. 56–58, where a note refers to the reproduction of a 1621 Dutch map on which Cape Ann is designated as "Wyngaerds hoeck," in *Documents Relative to the Colonial History of the State of New York*, edited by E.B. O'Callaghan. Winsor mentions that an earlier map prepared in 1614 from information obtained from Adrian Block's voyage of discovery along the coast of Connecticut north to Nahant Bay, which was the basis for the Dutch claim by the New Netherland Company, also has "Wyngaerds hoeck." A letter to the *Gloucester Times* by Mrs. Edward Gardner in the late 1950's, preserved among the poet's papers, well summarizes the Dutch connections. It is she who originally translates "Wyngaerds hoeck" as "Grapevine Corner."

There is also a Grapevine Cove on the Atlantic shore of East Gloucester, with a Grapevine Road (see next poem) running from there to the Harbor side of the peninsula.

▶ **II.95. to travel Typhon . . .**

Written 19 January 1962 (manuscript dated). For Typhon, see *Maximus* I, 150 and note.

II.95. from taking the Old Man's / sinews out . . . from Sister / Delphyne

See the account of the battle between Zeus and Typhon in Graves, *Greek Myths*, I, 134:

> Wounded and shouting, Typhon fled to Mount Casius, which looms over Syria from the north, and there the two grappled. Typhon twined his myriad coils about Zeus, disarmed him of his sickle and, after severing the sinews of his hands and feet with it, dragged him into the Corycian Cave. Zeus is immortal, but now he could not move a finger, and Typhon had hidden the sinews in a bear-skin, over which Delphyne, a serpent-tailed sister-monster, stood guard.

A hotel in East Gloucester from the 1890's through the 1940's was named The Delphine (see note below). See also, possibly, note to the Parenti Sisters, *Maximus* II, 97, one of whom was named Delfina.

II.95. building . . . at the corner of Grapevine Road & Hawthorne Lane

The Delphine hotel, formerly at 51 Eastern Point Road in East Gloucester. It was on the corner of Hawthorne Lane, near Grapevine Road.

II.95. Simp Lyle

Simpson Lyle, manager of The Delphine.

▶II.96. up the steps, along the porch . . .

Dated by the poet 18 January 1962.

II.96. greet Simp / with the morning's mail

For Simp Lyle, see previous poem and note. For Olson's post office career, see *The Post Office*, but also the note to "I was a letter carrier . . . ," *Maximus* I, 22, and to the poem which follows this.

▶II.97. people want delivery . . .

Written 18 January 1962 (manuscript dated). A similar story to the one in this poem is told by Olson in a letter to Robert Creeley from Lerma, 9 March 1951:

> It is post office as I, ex-letter carrier, believe in playing it: much human businesses abt same, gab, etc: the maids on my route always found my mouth ready for their cake or, for talk. As well as anyone else. Result: one day I came out to my truck—after an hour of coffee & gab with a painter named Sacha Moldovan (never heard of since) and a Jap store keeper named Susumu Hirota (a much better painter than Moldovan, whom M had taught to paint)—and thar be John Drohan, Foreman of Carriers, standing, with his watch out, and never, for the rest of the morning's run—

he stayed with me that day—saying a word. (Those peculiar ways the "people" have of getting things over!)

II.97. the Parenti Sisters

Delfina and Zoe Parenti, who owned a gift shop at 3 Eastern Point Road in East Gloucester, near Rocky Neck.

II.97. Susumu Hirota

Storekeeper and painter, resident of Rockport, Mass. (see note above). He was a member of the Rockport Art Association.

II.97. the McLeod sisters / who ran the Harbor View

Mrs. Minerva McLeod (MacLoud in the *Gloucester Directory* for 1932–33), superintendent, and Lottie McLeod, manager, of the Harbor View hotel at 19 Eastern Point Road in East Gloucester. The hotel, torn down in the early 1960's after it was damaged by fire, overlooked Wonson's Cove just below Rock Neck.

II.97. the corner of Rocky Neck Avenue

The main road on Rocky Neck. The corner referred to would be that where Rocky Neck Avenue joins Eastern Point Road, near the Parenti Sisters' shop.

▶II.98. the coast goes from Hurrian Hazzi to Tyre . . .

Dated 19 January 1962. Another migration poem; see also *Maximus* II, 7, 81, 87, 93, and 94. Mount Casius (see *Maximus* II, 94) or in Hurrian, Mount Hazzi, is on the seacoast about two hundred miles to the north of Tyre.

II.98. Athirat of the Sea

Canaanite goddess, consort of the supreme god El, as she appears on the Ras Shamra tablets. See Driver, *Canaanite*

Myths and Legends, pp. 10ff. and 95, and Harris, "Ras Shamra," p. 487, where the name is underlined in Olson's copy.

II.98. Judas waters

Treacherous waters, perhaps, but also see *Maximus* I, 57 and 78, "Judas" and "Judas-land," and respective notes.

▶II.99. tesserae / commissure

Written, as noted, 19 January 1962. A version among the poet's papers is titled, "To Build the Seamless Tower."

In reading the poem at Goddard College that April, the poet in response to questions from the audience explained "*tesserae*" as "the little pieces that are used in making a mosaic . . . all those pieces of stone and glass and color," and "commissure" as meaning "bound together"—adding, "actually, they're both in the Webster's" (Goddard tape, 12 April 1962). However, see also Jung, *Aion*, p. 77, for "commissure" as an astrological term: "The conjunction of the two [the planets Saturn and Jupiter] therefore signifies the *union of extreme opposites* . . . The conjunction took place in the middle of the commissure . . ." On p. 93, Jung speaks of "The northerly, or easterly, fish, which the spring-point entered at about the beginning of our era, is joined to the southerly, or westerly, fish by the so-called commissure"; and on p. 148: "two fishes, joined by a commissure (= the yoke). . . ."

It might be noted that in reading the poem at Vancouver in August 1963, "commissure" was pronounced "come ashore," perhaps echoing the close of the previous poem (though this is not the case on *Charles Olson Reads from Maximus IV, V, VI*, Folkways LP, 1975).

▶II.100. Lane's eye-view of Gloucester / Phoenician eye-view . . .

Written by 12 April 1962, when read at Goddard College. The Gloucester artist Fitz Hugh Lane (1804–1865), known for his marine paintings and lithographic views of Cape

Ann, is celebrated by Olson in "Light sits under one's eye . . ."
and also "An 'enthusiasm'" (*Archaeologist of Morning*, pp.
226–228), where the poet's sense of Lane's "view" is
discussed:

> Lane painted true color, and drew
> true lines, and 'View' as a prin-
> ciple he has also made true as a-
> gainst too easy (Dutch) or even a
> more brilliant landscape Turner,
> Constable (Guardi Canaletto Tie-
> polo even behind theirs)
>
What kept him 'local' or at least provincial
(and patriotic, literally, especially in his
ship scenes, and in fact his introduction of
ships into his scenes, when they weren't there,
and he added them

> was rather a weakness of selection,
> some selecting necessity his principle
> of View called for if his lines and color
> were to be like it first principle
>
Or some proposal or Vision like in fact Parkman
by making France-American his subject grabbed off. . . .

For the additional sense of Lane's "View" as "Phoenician,"
see the beginning of a poem entitled "TO CELEBRATE
WHAT HE STANDS ON . . ." among the poet's papers,
written 14 June 1960:

> Lane, who ate
> at 18 months old
> the apple of Peru
> and carelessly handled
> by a physician of the town
> was crippled for life, 1804
> to 1865 was kept thereby to
>
> a Phoenician eye VIEW:
>
>   periegesis
> periodos
>   periplus
>
> of Gloucester . . .

Lane thereby joins the ranks of Odysseus, Pytheas, and
other heroes of these poems who record their eye-witness

experience of the local. His paintings are—like the *periodos* of Pytheas or the *periplus* of Odysseus—narratives where, according to von Humboldt (quoted in Sauer, "The Morphology of Landscape," *Land and Life*, p. 318n), "physical geography and history appear attractively intermingled."

For more on Lane, see Wilmerding, *Fitz Hugh Lane* (1971). See also *Maximus* III, 118, and the use of "eye-view" by Olson in "Postscript to Proprioception & Logography," *Additional Prose*, p. 21, and note on p. 86 there.

II.100. 1833 14 october 443 Vessels at anchor in the harbor ...

This line had been written by the poet on a faded photostat of a map of Gloucester Harbor by John Mason mounted on a wall of Olson's flat at Fort Square. It was originally a notation by Mason on his "Plan of Gloucester Harbour" from "1833, 4 & 5," preserved in the City Engineer's office in Gloucester City Hall, and appears on the map between Fort Point and Rocky Neck, the area Lane's seven-gabled house as well as Olson's own rooms looked out upon.

Next to a linocut on p. 112 of Smith's *Fisheries of Gloucester*, captioned "View of the Old Fort and Harbor in 1837, Showing Grand Banker and Pinky at Anchor" and based on a Lane painting, Olson would add in 1968 in his copy: "Lane's eye view." And on the back of a photograph of Lane's painting of The Fort and Ten Pound Island from 1842 among his papers, Olson had written: "1833 ... is pure date to date all paintings or views."

▶II.101. Older than Byblos ...

Written by at least 12 April 1962, when read at Goddard College. What appears to be a first version was written on p. 114 of Olson's copy of Connolly, *Book of the Gloucester Fishermen*, where also, on p. 128, the phrase "the pawl post" occurs and was underlined by the poet.

Byblos itself was one of the chief cities of the Phoenicians. It was "by its own tradition the oldest city in the world, built by the god El, and the French excavations have shown an unbroken series of levels down to the Chalcolithic, if not earlier" (Harden, *The Phoenicians*, p. 28). Inscriptions from around 1000 B.C., in the formalized alphabet later adopted by the Greeks, have been discovered there.

▶II.102. CHRONICLES

Written 23 January 1962 (manuscript dated). For source of the title, see note to "Taurus" below.

II.102.   As Zeus sent Hermes / to draw Agenor's cattle . . .

The source is Graves, *Greek Myths*, I, 194–195:

> Agenor, Libya's son by Poseidon and twin to Belus, left Egypt to settle in the land of Canaan, where he married Telephassa, otherwise called Argiope, who bore him Cadmus, Phoenix, Cilix, Thasus, Phineus, and one daughter, Europe.
>
> Zeus, falling in love with Europe, sent Hermes to drive Agenor's cattle down to the seashore at Tyre, where she and her companions used to walk. He himself joined the herd, disguised as a snow-white bull with great dewlaps and small, gem-like horns, between which ran a single black streak. Europe was struck by his beauty and, on finding him gentle as a lamb, mastered her fear and began to play with him, putting flowers in his mouth and hanging garlands on his horns; in the end, she climbed upon his shoulders, and let him amble down with her to the edge of the sea. Suddenly he swam away, while she looked back in terror at the receding shore; one of her hands clung to his right horn, the other still held a flower-basket.
>
> Wading ashore near Cretan Gortyna, Zeus became an eagle and ravished Europe in a willow-thicket beside a spring; or, some say, under an evergreen plane-tree. She bore him three sons: Minos, Rhadamanthys, and Sarpedon.
>
> Agenor sent his sons in search of their sister, forbidding them to return without her. They set sail at once but, having no notion where the bull had gone, each steered a different course. Phoenix travelled westward, beyond Libya, to what is now Carthage, and there gave his name to the Punics . . . Cilix went to the Land of the Hypachaeans, which took his name, Cilicia; and Phineus to Thynia, a

peninsula separating the Sea of Marmara from the Black Sea, where he was later much distressed by harpies. Thasus and his followers, first making for Olympia, dedicated a bronze statue there to Tyrian Heracles, ten ells high, holding a club and bow, but then set off to colonize the island of Thasos and work its rich gold mines. All this took place five generations before Heracles, son of Amphitryon, was born in Greece.

The date of 1540 B.C. in the poem, while not in Graves, is apparently calculated from Graves' statement (based on Pausanias and Herodotus) that the events related occurred "five generations before Heracles . . . was born in Greece," according to the Parian Chronicle's date for the birth of Heracles (see *Maximus* II, 104 and note). Taking a generation to be forty years, as suggested by Forsdyke, *Greece Before Homer*, p. 58, the date of 1540 B.C. is then five generations or some two hundred years before the birth of Heracles in 1340. Elsewhere Olson identifies it as the date "of the 'rape of Europe' by the bull Zeus," i.e. the date for the supposed Phoenician occupation of Crete and the beginning of the westward migration from Tyre (in his "1st 'Essay' on the Phoenician History," quoted in part in note to *Maximus* II, 104).

As for the places referred to in this poem, Carthage was the famous Phoenician colony on the North African coast near the present city of Tunis; the Black Sea, to the north of Asia Minor, is connected to the Mediterranean by the Sea of Marmara and the Dardenelles; and Thebes is the city on mainland Greece, in Boeotia. Thasos is an island in the northern Aegean, and Ida was the sacred mountain above Gortyna in central Crete, where Zeus was said to have been raised.

II.102. Taurus, / King of Crete, / caught Tyre . . .

In his notes to the narrative quoted in the previous note, Graves observes, p. 197: "It is possible that the story of Europe also commemorates a raid on Phoenicia by Hellenes from Crete. John Malalas will hardly have invented the 'Evil

Evening' at Tyre when he writes: 'Taurus ("bull"), King of
Crete, assaulted Tyre after a sea-battle during the absence of
Agenor and his sons. They took the city that same evening
and carried off many captives, Europe among them; this
event is still recalled in the annual "Evil Evening" observed at
Tyre' (*Chronicles* ii. p. 30, ed. Dindorff)." John Malalas (ca.
491–578) was a Byzantine chronicler, born at Antioch.

II.103. Ousoos the / hunter

Phoenician hero mentioned in Sanchuniathon's history
(see next poem) as preserved by Philo of Byblus. See esp.
Paton, "Phoenicians," p. 893: "He first invented a covering
for the body from skins of wild beasts which he was strong
enough to capture. And when furious rains and winds occurred, the trees of Tyre were rubbed against each other and
caught fire and burned down the wood that was there. And
Ousoos took a tree, and, having stripped off the branches,
was the first who ventured to embark on the sea; and he con-
secrated two pillars to fire and wind, and worshipped them
and poured libations of blood upon them from the wild
beasts which he took in hunting." Paton adds that Ousoos "is
evidently a patron-god of hunters," and points out that he is
equivalent to Esau of the Canaanites.

Notes among his papers indicate that Olson at some point
also consulted Weill, *Phoenicia and Western Asia*, pp. 30–31,
concerning Ousoos.

▶ II.104. Sanuncthion lived / before the Trojan War . . .

Written by at least April 1962, when read at Goddard
College, and possibly as early as January of that year (see
note to "Libyans" below).

Sanuncthion ("I think I even have it misspelled," Olson
recognized reading the poem at Vancouver)—or correctly,
Sanchuniathon—was a Phoenician historian said by Por-
phyry to have lived "before the Trojan War." He "wrote in
the Phoenician language a history of his people and of their
religion, based on the records of the cities and the registers

of the temple and on record received from a certain Hierombalos (= Jerub-ba'al) priest of the god Ieuo (= Jahweh)," according to Paton, "Sanchuniathon," p. 178. Excerpts of his cosmogony have been translated by Philo of Byblos and preserved in Eusebius, *Preparatio evangelica*, i. 9; a summary is included in Paton's article. See also, *Encyclopaedia Britannica*, 11th ed., XXIV, 128; Paton, "Phoenicians," in *Encyclopaedia of Religion and Ethics*, IX, 887–897; Obermann, *Ugaritic Mythology*, p. xviii; and Weill, *Phoenicia and Western Asia*, pp. 30–31—all of which were consulted by the poet. Sanchuniathon's history was later translated by Charles Doria at Olson's urging and published in the magazine *Io* in 1969.

Concerning his misspelling of the name, Olson would write in a letter to Charles Boer, 7 June 1969: "I had two reasons for leaving the ignorance of Sanuncthion—both that Sanchuniathon is 'foreign' in its form & punctuation—& equally [or using my own inability to remember that correct form easily, I kept my own illiteracy to, in fact, *support* any other like person's glomming—[there are some few other instances where I have let stand etc—& if you will notice, immediately thereafter—or *somewhere* else [in "A Work," *Additional Prose*, p. 33] I *have* used it correctly!" On the back of his envelope to Boer he adds: "letting the illiteracy stand   Or taking a *preferable* sonic condition!" Notes among his papers from some of the sources given above indicate Olson had researched the subject at least two years earlier, in January 1960, and appears to have simply misremembered the name at the time of the poem.

The poem itself is an extension of the previous one, an investigation into the mythological evidence for the historical migrations and settling of the eastern Mediterranean during the second millennium B.C., what Cyrus Gordon in *Before the Bible*, p. 17, calls "the heroic age." As Graves suggests, "The dispersal of Agenor's sons seems to record the westward flight of Canaanite tribes early in the second millennium B.C., under pressure from Aryan and Semitic invaders" (*Greek Myths*, I, 196), and Olson himself would propose in his essay "A Work" written just a few months after this poem, a "new picture" of the Second Millennium, which he says "is the millennium of the general overthrow of the ancient settled world, which was neither East nor West, and the bringing into existence of what, even if unclear, comes through to us . . ." (*Additional Prose*, p. 34).

The purpose of the poem is made even more clear in a later essay found among the poet's papers entitled "1st 'essay' on the Phoenician History / Wednesday February 5 1964 / called '1540, or, Santhunctionus" (the name still not correct!), in which he writes:

> Despite absence (at present?) of archeological evidences—and the literary evidence does not seem to be added to, except for Canaanite poems, & other material, since the Paros stone . . . a good case could now be made [chiefly due to Cyrus Gordon's work on loan-words between Greek, North & Hebrew Semitic, and Egyptian, and his proposed identification (*last year*) of Linear A as "Phoenician"] that there may not in fact have been *any* so-called Cretan people, or rule . . . One has a possible 'fixed date' [for "Phoenician occupation, or exploration" of Crete] by way of the Parian "Chronicle" (supposing that 'stone' will test-out, which I could suggest may soon make more sense, due to mythological evidences as well as Gordon's language and loan-word studies): that a king Agenor was in power at Tyre at 1540 BC, the date of the "rape of Europe" by the bull Zeus, who carried her off to *southern* Crete; and that this "Agenor" had come to Canaan from Libya [who was his "mother"—and his "father," the myth says, was "Poseidon," which also makes queer sense when one notices that Herodotus says the Greeks acquired "Poseidon" as a god from Libya. . . . In any case I wish only to awaken an attention to a complex of movement at, say, 1540 BC, throughout the Mediterranean, which suggests greater entrances & furtherance of Indo-European plus Phoenician movement in late Helladic, just prior to the consolidations which begin the now so-called Mycenaean Age. . . .

II.104. Phoenicia, / before 1220 BC

This date marks roughly the appearance of the "Peoples of the Sea" (see below) and the rise of Phoenician sea-power.

Olson has amidst notes on Sanchuniathon from Obermann's *Ugaritic Mythology* and Weill's *Phoenicia and Western Asia* among his papers: "Sanchuniathon *before 1220* BC—in other words approx. at 'rise' of Phoenicians." Up until this time Phoenicia had been under the rule of Egypt, until the invasion of Palestine by the so-called "Peoples of the Sea" established the Philistines on the coast and permitted the independent flourishing of the Phoenicians.

II.104. 1183

See Forsdyke, *Greece Before Homer*, p. 28: "The date that has been generally accepted for the Fall of Troy, 1183 B.C. in modern terms, was established by Eratosthenes of Cyrene, Principal Librarian in the Museum at Alexandria at the end of the third century. He was not a professional historian, but an encyclopaedic scholar who wrote on many subjects, grammar, literature, philosophy, geography, astronomy, mathematics; and he was also a poet. His colleagues called him *Pentathlos* for obvious reasons, and more maliciously, *Beta* [see Olson's possible use of this, *Maximus* II, 113], because the all-round athlete was not expected to be first in any single event." The date is underscored in Olson's copy.

II.104. the Parian Chronicle

A marble tablet found on the island of Paros in 1627, containing an outline of Greek history from the reign of Cecrops, legendary king of Athens, to the archonship of Diognetus in the year 264 B.C. See esp. Forsdyke, *Greece Before Homer*, pp. 50ff.

II.104. a / Phoenician Melkart- / Hercules more than / 5 generations previous . . .

See Graves, *Greek Myths*, quoted in note to "As Zeus sent Hermes . . . ," *Maximus* II, 102; also Bérard, *Did Homer Live?*, p. 189: "The legendary voyage of Herakles in the Western Sea is known to us from Hellenic legends and myths. But in ancient times it was known that Herakles the traveller, the explorer of coasts, the tamer of monsters in the Western Sea, was Herakles of Tyre. This Herakles-Melkaart had been an earlier visitor to the very waters visited by Odysseus and he had sometimes used the same kind of sea craft: tradition had it that, like Odysseus, he had made rafts."

II.104. the Greek Hercules / (born 1340 BC, / by the Parian Chronicle)

See Forsdyke, *Greece Before Homer*, p. 32: "Herodotus says elsewhere that he counts three generations to a century. That would place Heracles at 1180 B.C. But Herodotus also says that Heracles lived 900 years before his own time, and that the Trojan War was little more than 800 years ago. These dates would be about 1340 and 1250 B.C." Olson has a portion of this passage underlined in his copy, with a note at the top of the page:

$$
\begin{array}{r}
440 \\
\text{Heracles} \qquad 1340 \text{ BC} \qquad \underline{900} \\
1340
\end{array}
$$

On p. 59, Forsdyke writes: "The Parian chronicler supports his much earlier date (= 895 B.C.) by the statement that Pheidon was eleventh in descent from Heracles." The final five words are underlined by Olson and at the bottom of the page he makes these calculations:

$$3 \times 4 = 12 \text{ generations}$$

$$
\begin{array}{llll}
11 & 895 & & \\
\underline{40} & \underline{440} & 1335 & (\text{ yes Hercules} \\
440 & & & \\
& & & \underline{1340!}
\end{array}
$$

II.104. Agenor / was said to come from Egypt . . .

Graves, *Greek Myths*, I, 194: "Agenor, Libya's son by Poseidon and twin to Belus, left Egypt to settle in the Land of Canaan . . ." See also note to Uganda below.

II.104. Libya—who herself / was the daughter of / the king of Egypt

Graves, *Greek Myths*, I, 191: "Epaphus, who was rumoured to be the divine bull Apis, reigned over Egypt, and had a daughter, Libya, the mother by Poseidon of Agenor and Belus." Libya's name survives as that of the land to the west of Egypt along the North African coast.

II.104. Indo- / Europeans

See e.g. "GRAMMAR—a 'book,'" *Additional Prose*, p. 30:

> They appeared circum 1750 BC—or 1800—out of South Russia and east to the Caspian, and, as they dispersed, carried those languages we have know thus (west to east):
>
>
>
> Baltic Slavic   Tocharian(!)
> Celtic Germanic Latin Greek Hittite Armenian Iranian
> Sanskrit   (Fr. Sp. Ital.)
>
>

II.104. Libyans (the least known / of all sources of serious inroads on / Egypt

Olson apparently consulted Sanford, *The Mediterranean World in Ancient Times*, p. 84: "Until the end of the thirteenth century the Hittite power in Asia Minor, and the Hittite and Egyptian control of the eastern coasts of the Mediterranean, checked the movements of the Aegeans and others who had learned to covet the wealth of the great cities. But the Sea Raiders in alliance with the Libyans [the sentence is underlined up to this point in Olson's copy], attacked Egypt early in the reign of Ramses II . . . The next great raid came in 1223 B.C., in the reign of Merneptah." A note in the margin of p. 67 of the volume indicates the poet had been reading it on 21 January 1962; it is possible, then, that the poem may have been written at the time of that reading or shortly thereafter.

For these same "Raiders / of the sea," see "Peoples of the Sea," *Maximus* I, 147 and note.

II.104. Uganda

Land in east-central Africa. Graves writes, *Greek Myths*, I, 197: "Agenor is the Phoenician hero Chnas, who appears in *Genesis* as 'Canaan'; many Canaanite customs point to an East African provenience, and the Canaanites may have originally come to Lower Egypt from Uganda."

II.104. non-Euclidean

"Any of several modern geometries that are not based on the postulates of Euclid, used especially in mathematical physics to describe spaces different from that of common experience" (*American Heritage Dictionary*). Used in the sense of "Indo-European," or even "non-Indo-European" (Hurrian, at least, is a non-Indo-European language); certainly in the sense of pre-Greek, pre-Western.

II.104. Hittite

The ancient Hittites, with their capital at Hattusas (Boghazkoy) in north-central Anatolia, were a major power throughout the Near East until about 1220 B.C., when they yielded to the attacks by the "Peoples of the Sea."

II.104. Hurrian

The Hurrians appear in Anatolia early in the second millennium B.C. and move from modern Kurdistan, in the mountains around Lake Van (q.v.), westwards across northern Mesopotamia as far as the Euphrates. In "A Work" from 3 May 1962, Olson would write: "The facts of the 2nd Millennium are loosely known. Around about 1800 things shook up. The main drive down on the older Mesopotamian-Egyptian-Indus world seems to start with Hurrian and then Hittite people, the latter at least certainly Indo-European, in and before that date" (*Additional Prose*, p. 34). See also *Maximus* III, 170.

II.104. there may be East African . . .

See Graves, *Greek Myths*, I, 197, quoted in note to Uganda above.

II.104. Semite Sailors

Specifically, the Phoenicians (see also *Maximus* II, 81).

II.104. Gondwannan

See *Maximus* II, 1 and note; also *Maximus* III, 162.

II.104. the Sumerians

The ancient non-Semitic, non-Indo-European people who flourished in the Tigris-Euphrates valley from the beginning of the fourth millennium to the end of the third millennium B.C.

II.105. the Persian / Gulf

Inlet of the Arabian Sea, between the Arabian Peninsula and Iran or Persia; into its northern end flow the Tigris and Euphrates rivers.

II.105. a black-haired previous people / dwelling among reed-houses . . .

The Semitic peoples inhabiting Ubaid (see *Maximus* II, 116 and note) and other sites in the Tigris-Euphrates valley before the coming of the Sumerians, though the Sumerians, too, referred to themselves as a "black-headed people" throughout their literature (see e.g. Kramer, *Sumerian Mythology*, pp. 42, 52, and 61; also Frankfort, *Birth of Civilization in the Near East*, p. 88). In a letter to John Clarke from 1965, Olson writes of possibly these same "'Black-Haired' people or something whom Arthur Keith somewhere proposes— from the Northeast . . ." (*Pleistocene Man*, p. 4).

▶ **II.106. John Watts took / salt . . .**

Written by April 1962, when read at Goddard College. See the fuller report of the incident, *Maximus* II, 74, and its first appearance in the poems, I, 115 and note. It will occur again in *Maximus* III, 45.

▶ **II.107. 3rd letter on Georges, unwritten**

Exact date of writing not known; the original was written in pencil on a page of notes concerning the typing of *Maximus IV, V, VI,* ca. 1964. It was not read at Vancouver in August 1963 and not sent Jeremy Prynne as part of the final manuscript of that volume for typing in March 1964. Nor had it been read at Goddard College in April 1962, where Olson commented instead, at the place in Book V which he had reserved for the poem still to be written:

> That missing poem, by the way, is a story I may not be competent to write. But it should be a story which . . . I know a man who wrote [it]. I'm involved in that problem, so I crib him on the—a very great writer, who won the running broad jump at the first modern Olympics, in Athens— James Connolly. What I'd like to do is what he can do and has done, which is to take a vessel from the eastern end of Georges Shoal, the northeastern end, and run it, at night, in an easterly, through the maze of shoals of the north end of Georges, without wrecking, and getting into clear water on the other side, and making the market in Boston. And it really takes experience I don't have. So I'll have to wait or see what I do with that problem of stealing it from Connolly.

See the "1st Letter on Georges," *Maximus* I, 136–138, and the poem beginning "*Sch. Ella M. Goodwin . . .*" on pp. 138– 141 of that volume, which is actually the second Georges letter, as is explained in note to p. 138. For the location of Georges Bank itself, see note to *Maximus* I, 79.

II.107. Winter Cod / Grounds on the Eastern End

Rich writes in *Fishing Grounds of the Gulf of Maine*, p. 100:

> During February, March, and April large schools of cod make their appearance on the bank. At this season these are found most abundantly on the "Winter Fishing Ground," a part of Georges lying eastward and southeastward of the North Shoal between the parallels of 41 30' and 42 00' north latitude and 66 38' and 67 30' west longitude. The area of this Winter Fishing Ground is about 1,000 square miles. This part of the bank seems entirely given over to the codfish, since it is too broken, sharp, and rocky to please the haddock. Depths here are from 30 to 40 fathoms, deepening away from the North Shoal. This area is essentially a spawning ground for the cod, which appear to come on the bank from the SE., as they almost invariably, after reaching the ground, move slowly to the N. and W. as spring approaches. This is in the direction of the shoals. As soon as the spawning season is over the schools of cod break up, but more or less fish are caught on different parts of the ground at all times of the year, though . rarely are they found so plentiful as when the winter school is on the ground. . . .

II.107. Henry Ware & Paul Cot- / ter in the Eyes of the Woods

Characters in the novel of that title by Joseph Altsheler (see "Altschuler," *Maximus* I, 54 and note), an adventure story for boys set in the Kentucky wilderness, in which a band of scouts (including Cotter and led by Ware) is pursued by vengeful Indians. Their names occur as boyhood heroes in Olson's letter to Creeley ca. 10 April 1953 quoted in note to *Maximus* I, 49.

II.107. James Connolly

James B. Connolly (1868–1957), who has written more about the Gloucester fishermen than any other writer. See esp., for this poem, the chapter "Driving Home from Georges" in his *Book of the Gloucester Fishermen*, pp. 115–139, concerning Captain Maurice Whalen's driving of his loaded vessel from Georges back to the Boston market. See also *Maximus* III, 94, and " 'I know men . . . ,' " *Muthologos*, II, 166—168.

II.107. Bohlin

See *Maximus* I, 19 and note, and poems *"Bohlin I"* and *"Bohlin 2," Maximus* II, 44 and 45.

II.107. Syl- / vanus Smith

See *Maximus* I, 19 and note.

II.107. Marty Callaghan ˙

See *Maximus* I, 19 and 22.

▶II.108. THE GULF OF MAINE

Exact date of writing not known; read at Harvard on 14 February 1962, offered to Henry Rago for *Poetry* magazine in a letter March 8th. Titled "The Ballad of the Gulf of Maine" in an early manuscript.

The poem is based on an incident mentioned only briefly in Bradford's *History "Of Plimoth Plantation"* (pp. 187—188), but more fully reported in letters of John Bridge and Emmanuel Altham published by Jameson in the Massachusetts Historical Society *Proceedings* for 1910—11. There are, however, felicitous departures from the source.

II.108. Altham says / they were in a pinnace . . .

In his letter to James Shirley concerning the wreck of the *Little James* in which the master and two crewmen were lost, Altham writes (Jameson, pp. 183—184):

> But cominge home to our ship I there found this news true thus farr, that Mr. Bridge our master was drowned and the two men, and the ship in a very strange manner spoiled   for thus it fortuned that upon the 10th of Aprill 1624 hapned a great storme and some of our cables that

we were mored withall gave way and slip of on the place
they were made fast to ashore and soe the winde and sea
being very high drave our ship a shore upon rockes where
she beate [a note at this point locates the site as Damariscove Island, Me.]. In the mean time being the night the
master and Company arose and every man shifted for
them selves to save life, but the master going in to his cabin
to fetch his whisell could not get in to any boate aboute the
ship the sea brake soe over the ship and soe by that meanes
before a boat could come the ship overset and drowned
him and the other two and the rest that were got into our
shallops that hung about the ship had much a doe to
recover the shore . . . for the ship oversettinge pich her
maineyard in to one boate where were 6 or 7 of our men
and soe sunke her for thoes that could then swim got to
the shore with much hurt the rest that could not swim
were drowned, and soe before the next morninge our ship
was quite under water sunke and nothing to be sene save
only the tops of her masts some times for the sea did rake
her to and fro upon the rocks . . .

See also "Altham says / Winslow / was at Cape Ann in
April, 1642," *Maximus* I, 101, and note.

For both Monhegan and Damariscove Harbor, see *Maximus* I, 109 and notes.

II.108. his wife / and Captain Bridge's, in London / reached by mail . . .

This material is not present in the source. There is a suit
for wages mentioned in the letters, but this was actually
brought by two crewmen accused previously of mutiny, not
the wives of Altham and Captain John Bridges, master of
the *Little James*. Bridges, whose letter was written before
the disaster, was drowned in the shipwreck; Altham, however, was not even aboard the vessel at the time, as the poem
suggests. Nor is the address that follows in the poem to be
found in the letters. All that is mentioned of the men's wives
is the following request by Bridges, touching enough in its
own way and which may have inspired Olson to consider
further the plight of the lost sailors' wives: "Sir yf my wife
mak bowld for to trubell you be for I cum hom let me in-

treat you for to firnesh hir for a woman may have maney occasions in hir husbandes absentes and rather I am to want
my self then she . . ." (Jameson, p. 181).

II.108. High Court Row and St by Chancery Light

While the address certainly sounds authentic, it does not
appear in Olson's source (see note to James Shirley below).
And while there were no actual streets in London with those
designations at that time (none such are mentioned in Stow's
Survey of London, 1603) or even later, the choice of names
suggests the area around the Inns of Court and the quarter
chiefly occupied by barristers and solicitors. Lincoln's Inn,
e.g., is off Chancery Lane, itself off Fleet Street.

II.108. 4 men / alone . . . dragged themselves up . . .

There is no basis for this in the source.

II.108–109. King James said We do approve . . . fishing is / the holy calling

According to Winslow, *Hypocrisie Unmasked* (1646), when
James I was informed of the Pilgrims' proposed venture, the
following interview took place: "what profits might arise in
the part we intended, (for our eye was upon the most Northern parts of Virginia,) 'twas answered, Fishing. To which he
replied with his ordinary asseveration, 'So God have my soul,
'tis an honest trade; 'twas the Apostles' owne calling' " (in
Young, *Chronicles of the Pilgrim Fathers*, pp. 382–383).

II.109. corfish

See *Maximus* I, 117.

II.109. James Shirley

A London goldsmith, treasurer of the merchant adventurers who supported the Plymouth colony. Captain Bridge
addressed him, "at his house in Crooked Lane" in London;

Altham, as "dwellinge on London bridg (at the Gold hors-show [horseshoe])" (Jameson, pp. 182, 189).

▶**II.111. existed / 3000 / BC? . . .**

Apparently written early in 1962. The original is on a royalty statement from Grove Press for *The Distances* bearing the date 1962. On a similar statement from 31 December 1961 appears the following notes:

> Lebanon
> scant excavation
>   existed
>   as early as
> *via Bahrain?*   3000 at
> 2500
>   Byblos   (Gubla)
> by early 2nd Mill.
>   Joppa, Acre,
>   (Jaffa) Dor & Ugarit

The poem represents, for the most part, a further investigation into relationships between mythological names and the historical migration of the ancient Phoenicians, as in the earlier "Sanuncthion" poem, *Maximus* II, 104–105.

II.111. from / Red Sea

Herodotus in his *Histories* (I. 1) says that the Phoenicians came from the shores of the "red sea," probably meaning the Persian Gulf.

II.111. Bahrein

Island in the Persian Gulf just off the Arabian coast; site of an early settlement linking the civilizations of the Indus Valley and those of the Tigris and Euphrates. Olson had among his papers a clipping from the *New York Times* from 17 May 1959 entitled "Ruins of Old City Found in Bahrein: Danish Expedition Unearths Traces of a Persian Gulf Civilization of 3000 B.C."

II.111. Poseidon

See esp. the section of Olson's "1st 'essay' on the Phoenician History" quoted in introductory note to *Maximus* II, 104.

II.111. Samothrace

Island in the northeastern Aegean, center of the worship of the Cabiri (see below), i.e. the Samothracian mysteries instituted by Dardanus. Elsewhere in his "1st 'essay' on the Phoenician History," the poet suggests that Poseidon may have had some special relationship to Samothrace, since in Homer (*Iliad*, xiii. 12) it is from that island that the god first, says Olson, surveys the plains of Troy.

II.111. Taurus

Bull-king of Crete who attacked Tyre (*Maximus* II, 102 and note).

II.111. the beetle / stuck in his / leg

In a notebook from 1953−54 among the poet's papers, the following is recorded, p. [22]:

> *June '54* Mon June 28th was awakened around midnight ... by dream of crabs or beetles on my leg—I a Negro—& Herman Melville telling a story of his adventures as sure as life!
>> It was my left leg & these beetles were between the surface of the leg in its situation & the actual skin of it—which I was interested to notice (when all the beetles had been finally shown up & crushed) was unflawed. . . .

Also among the poet's papers is a letter, probably to his wife Constance, dated 5 July [1954], in which he writes: "The dream a week ago was a double one, of tearing a beetle off my leg. But the thing which wowed me was the other part of this dream, in which, by god, Melville was more real than he ever was, and was telling me a like incident of his own adventures (I believe it was his own sick leg at Typee!" In further fragments among his papers, Olson has: "the beetle on my leg / was the father / stuck in me," and "the beetle of the hero / stuck on my leg." Charters reports the same dream in *Olson / Melville,* p. 59n: "Olson has said that once he 'dreamed of Melville with a scarab stuck in his leg, like a bloodsucker. The bite of Isis.' "

II.111. Minos

King of Crete, son of Zeus and Europa, brother of Sarpedon and Rhadamanthys (see also *Maximus* II, 102 and note). Also identical with Menes or Manes (*Maximus* II, 81).

II.111. Megiddo

Canaanite city of northwestern Palestine. In a summary of an essay by W. F. Albright for the *American Journal of Archaeology,* which Olson had been reading around this time (see "A Work," dated 3 May 1962, in *Additional Prose,* p. 34, and editor's note there, p. 89), Luce writes, p. 106, that a section "discusses the Canaanites before the seventeenth century B.C. The writer does not deal with the origin of the Phoenicians but shows that the Canaanites may well have been settled in Palestine and Southern Syria as early as the fourth millennium—towns which can clearly be dated before 3000 B.C. have Canaanite names (*e.g.* Jericho, Megiddo, etc.)."

II.111. Jericho

Canaanite city north of the Dead Sea. See also *Maximus* I, 55 and note.

II.111. Sarpedon

Brother of Minos and Rhadamanthys (see *Maximus* II, 102 and note).

II.111. Rhadamanthys

Son of Zeus and Europa, brother of Sarpedon and Minos (*Maximus* II, 102 and note).

II.111. Europa

Phoenician princess abducted to Crete by Zeus in the guise of a white bull. See "Europe," *Maximus* II, 102 and note.

II.111. Dardanus

Son of Zeus and Electra, founder of Troy. He introduced the cult of the Cabiri to Samothrace (Graves, *Greek Myths*, II, 260).

II.111. Electra

Daughter of Atlas; one of the Pleiades. She was the mother of Dardanus.

II.111. Atlas

One of the Titans, condemned by Zeus to support the heavens upon his shoulders.

II.111. Zeus

Sky-god of the Greeks.

II.111. Cabiri . . . the / 'great gods'

See Kerenyi, "The Mysteries of the Kabeiroi," who gives their characteristics as follows, p. 48, in a passage marked in Olson's copy:

> The first of these is that they are deities who are secret and must be kept secret. The fact that mariners in danger at sea invoked their help doubtless gives some indication of their nature. But we are not justified in regarding them as helper deities pure and simple, because they were called upon for help. They are precisely—and this is the only

characterization that the tradition permits—mystery deities "pure and simple." Their name in Greek is a foreign word. It was formerly held to be a Hellenized form of the Semitic "*kabirim*," "the Great," since the Greeks also called the Kabeiroi "the great gods". . . .

The *Encyclopaedia Britannica,* 11th ed., IV, 916, says "the name appears to be of Phoenician origin."

II.111. the 7 / great planets

For the ancients, there were only seven planets—the sun, the moon, Mercury, Venus, Mars, Jupiter, and Saturn—characterized by being in motion relative to the "fixed" stars. The Samothracian Cabiri were four in number, although according to Goethe, *Faust* part II, "there should really be seven of them" (quoted in Jung, *Psychology and Alchemy,* p. 148).

▶II.112. phalaropes / piled up on Thatchers . . .

Olson's source is an entry for *Phalaropus lobatus,* the northern phalarope or sea goose, in Townsend, *Birds of Essex County,* p. 164:

> This is the least rare of the Phalaropes, and it is a common bird along the northern coast of Maine. Mr. W. A. Jeffries reports an unusual flight of them in 1890, after a strong but short northeast wind. A flock of 300 was found about a mile off the shore at Swampscott, from the 12th of August to the 26th of September. With them Mr. Jeffries found a single Red Phalarope. On September 2d, 1899, there occurred a remarkable night flight of Phalaropes probably of this species, previously referred to in the lighthouse records . . . in which from 800 to 1000 killed themselves against Thatcher's Island Lights. On September 9th, 1904, between 12.30 and 4 A.M., a large flock was seen hovering about Thatcher's Island Lights and eight were killed. I had the opportunity of identifying one of these birds.

In his *Supplement,* pp. 9–10, Townsend adds the following interesting details:

A change has been made in the character of some of the lamps in the lighthouses during the last five years, which has apparently rendered them less destructive to birds. This is the case at Thatcher's Island where formerly, as shown in the original Memoir, a large, although decreasing number of birds was killed. Instead of ordinary kerosene lamps with their yellow lights there is now used a spray of kerosene oil and air, which brings a Wellsbach mantle to a white heat and produces a diffuse white light more like daylight. The keepers believe that the birds are able to see around them more easily and are not so dazzled as by the old lamps, and therefore none are killed.

Thatcher's Island, with twin lighthouses, was originally one of John Smith's "Three Turks' Heads" (*Maximus* I, 24 and note). It was named afterwards for a shipwrecked family (see *Maximus* II, 24 and note) and is just off the eastern shore of Cape Ann toward Rockport.

▶**II.113. Aristotle & Augustine / clearly misunderstood Anaximander . . .**

The original is written on an envelope with the date 13 April 1962 stamped on it by the local post office; thus a later manuscript bears Olson's note: "written *after* April 13/ 1962."

Anaximander (ca. 611–547 B.C.) was one of the Ionian philosophers. According to the *Encyclopaedia Britannica*, 11th ed., I, 944, which would seem to have influenced Olson, "his reputation is due mainly to his work on nature, few words of which remain. From these fragments we learn that the beginning or first principle (ἀρχή, a word which, it is said, he was the first to use) was an endless, unlimited mass (ἄπειρον), subject to neither old age nor decay, and perpetually yielding fresh materials for the series of beings which issued from it. He never defined this principle precisely, and it has generally (*e.g.* by Aristotle and Augustine) been understood as a sort of primal chaos." Olson refers to his map of the earth, in which the world is "locked tight in River Ocean which circled it . . . like a serpent with tail in mouth," in *Call Me Ishmael*, p. 118.

Aristotle (384–322 B.C.), the Greek philosopher, writes about Anaximander in his *Metaphysics* (XII, ii) and *Physics* (I, iv; III, iv); Augustine (A.D. 354–430), bishop of Hippo and a Father of the Church, writes about him in his *City of God* (VIII, ii).

For a similar use of *beta,* the Greek letter, and which may have encouraged the word play here, see Forsdyke quoted in note to "1183," *Maximus* II, 104.

▶II.116. off-upland . . .

Dated 17 June 1962. The poem resulted from a reading of Braidwood, *The Near East and the Foundations for Civilization,* and an original version actually occurs as a note on p. 30 of Olson's copy, where it is also clear that the locale of the poem is Dogtown, this time as a parallel to ancient Ubaid, a settlement four miles north of Ur on the Euphrates. The Annisquam River is, like the Tigris and Euphrates delta, lined by salt marshes, with the earliest settlements on the uplands nearby.

In speaking of man's earliest village settlements, Braidwood points out, p. 11, that these occurred on the hilly flanks above the Fertile Crescent of Mesopotamia, not in the Crescent itself. He continues, "These hilly flanks are grassy uplands . . . ;" Olson underscores the last two words, adding in the margin, "Dogtown?" On p. 36, Braidwood speaks of the expansion of Ubaid culture into "the riverine alluvium area of southern Mesopotamia," and mentions a "generalization Ubaidian culture pattern characteristic of the northwestern, northern, and eastern hilly flanks zone"—which the poet has marked, adding in the margin:

> off-upland,
>   4100
> [Dogtown]
> riverine
>   ('Squam /
> Orontes)

And on p. 37, in the margin next to a discussion of early settlements—which begins, "We have said that we suspect the geography of southern Iraq in early post-Pleistocene times was little different from its present state—that it was not the freshly drained Persian Gulf bottom of salty mud flats which some archeologists have claimed. The general culture and technological level we suggest for the Ubaid phase would have been *the earliest in which men could have managed life in the flat alluvial plain of the south, save on the very river banks alone"* (underlining is Olson's)—the poet adds the Gloucester examples of Planters Neck, Stage Fort, the Farms and the Mills of Riverdale, and Little Good Harbor. Gloucester, then, is seen as having its own "riverine" period along the mud flats of the Annisquam, equivalent to the Ubaid period of around 3900 B.C.

II.116. Squam

Common nickname for the Annisquam River; an abbreviated form of the Algonquin *Annisquam* or *Wannasquam*, which itself is said to be "descriptive of the harbor inside the mouth of the river," according to Copeland and Rogers, *Saga of Cape Ann*, p. 153. According to Sherwin, *The Viking and the Red Man*, I, 304, the designation means "beautiful water." Also serves as a shortened name for the village of Annisquam, on the banks of the river north of Riverdale (see also *Maximus* III, 134).

II.116. Old Norse / Algonquin

Appears in a marginal note on p. 37 of Olson's copy of Braidwood as corresponding to that earlier phase of Mesopotamian settlement described above. For Norse survivals in the language and mythology of the Algonquins, see Sherwin, *Viking and the Red Man*, and Leland, *Algonquin Legends of New England*; also *Maximus* II, 9.

▶ II.119. The earth with a city in her hair . . .

Dated "circum Sept 29th, 1962" in the poet's notes, though possibly written somewhat later since the original appears on an envelope with a note dated 29 October.

Cf. *Maximus* I, 143, "she holds a city in her hair," and note.

▶ **II.120. And now let all the ships come in . . .**

Written October 1962. An early manuscript is dated "Oct
10th or 12th," while a note by the poet elsewhere reads:
"after to let them all come in / Oct 2 weeks ago / (Oct 29th,
1962."

In a conversation with Ed Dorn in July 1965 (*Muthologos*,
I, 158–159), Olson states that the poem was "caused" by
Jeremy Prynne's having done Olson's research among the
Weymouth Port Books (q.v.) for him, and explains:

> . . . a Prynne man went and found all the goddamned
> records of all the boats that crossed the Atlantic Ocean
> after Columbus that might have bearing on entering Glou-
> cester Harbor. So that I wrote "And now let all . . ." just to
> get out of the trap that [his] having done that put me into.
> I still carry the stuff around in my bag, I didn't open it.
> 'Cause, I mean, I got to do that research now on the other
> end, the natural end of the stuff that you use for your own
> purpose. So I just sort of . . . : "Now let all the ships come
> in, let the fucking harbor be flooded with *all* the ships!"
> [Laughs.] And by the way, those aren't . . . and then
> there's "pity" and "love," and that's just pity and love.
> But then the others, "The Return," "The Flower," "The
> Gift," and "The Alligator," are ketches owned by a Glouc-
> esterman who built them. . . . And these are the four
> ketches he owned. Ketch is an old name for sloop, a
> fishing sloop—but they spell it in the record "catches,"
> and you know catches is song."

In the will of John Hardy of Salem, 1652, as recorded in the
Probate Records of Essex County, I, 147, occurs the following:
" . . . I giue vnto my son Joseph Hardy one quarter pt of the
old catch caled the returne: and one quarter pt of the new
Catch caled the gift: and one eight pt of the Catch caled the
flower. . . ." Also on that page is an inventory of Hardy's
estate (marked in Olson's copy): "one fourth part of the
Alegatter Catch, 30 li.; three fourths of the Catch called
Guift, 60 li; one halfe of the Catch called the Returne, 30
li. . . ."

▶II.121. HEPIT•NAGA•ATOSIS

Dated in manuscript, "c. Oct 11th or 13th." The title is taken directly from a plate in Leland, *Algonquin Legends of New England*, between pp. 274—275, showing the serpent of the pond visited by the adulteress (see *Maximus* II, 21). "At-o-sis" in Algonquin means "the Serpent," according to Leland.

II.121. they saw a Serpent that lay quoiled . . .

This is the Gloucester sea-serpent (who first appears in *Maximus* II, 32), which Babson reports "had been seen in our own waters even as early as 1639; when a visitor to New England was told 'of a sea-serpent, or snake, that lay quoiled up like a cable upon a rock at Cape Ann. A boat passing by with English aboard, and two Indians, they would have shot the serpent; but the Indian dissuaded them, saying, that, if he were not killed outright, they would be all in danger of their lives' " (*History*, p. 523).

The visitor referred to by Babson was John Josselyn (q.v.), and the story actually appears in his *Account of Two Voyages to New-England* (Mass. Hist. Soc. *Collections*, 3d ser., III, 228), not his *New-Englands Rarities Discovered*, which is the first systematic account of the botanical species of that portion of North America—although that is a more appropriate title for this poem. The error is in Olson's source—Kierman, *The Sea Serpent of Cape Ann*. See also *Maximus* III, 59–60, and note.

▶II.122. Barbara Ellis, ramp

Manuscript dated 12 October 1962. Barbara Ellis (b. 1923) of Gloucester was an acquaintance of Olson's through the Ferrinis. A robust, talkative woman, she described herself in an interview with the author, June 1971, as "outspoken" and "controversial."

Vincent Ferrini relates that he pointed out to Olson that there are several definitions of "ramp" in the dictionary, asking which one he intended in the poem; Olson replied, laughingly, "all of them!"

For one definition of "ramp," see *Maximus* III, 78, and for another appearance, see the poem *"position fr which to see"* from November 1962 in *OLSON* 4, p. 11.

▶II.123. the diadem of the Dog . . .

Written on an envelope postmarked 12 October 1962 and dated October 19th by the poet.

The "Dog / which is morning" would seem to be Sirius, the Dogstar. In notes from 24 March 1961, Olson has written:

> the *Diadem*
>   the Dog's Dripping
>   Saliva
>   *Sirius* . . .

(See also "the Salivarating / Dog" of *Maximus* II, 36, and *Maximus* III, 47, beginning "Space and Time the saliva . . .")

In another note, this from early 1964, the poet has written:

> the Diadem
> of the Dog   not how he smells, but
> is his   how handsome his teeth
>   *teeth*   are

—indicating "the Dog" here is also the one of "Tyrian Businesses" (see *Maximus* I, 37 and note, for the elements "diadem," "teeth," and "morning," as well as "dog"; also *Maximus* II, 9).

▶II.124. They brawled in the streets, trapped the night watchman . . .

Dated in manuscript "Nov (5th?)" Should read "tripped" the night watchman. The letter beginning "DEEREST SIR . . ." contained in the poem is, with a few omissions, from John Endecott, then deputy-governor of the Massachusetts Bay Colony, to Governor John Winthrop. It deals with a

series of misdemeanors by a number of Gloucester work-
men building a ship at the town under William Stevens (q.v.)
for a Mr. Griffin in 1643.

The letter is preserved in *Winthrop Papers*, IV, 417—418
(also in Babson, *Notes and Additions*, II, 64—65, but with
changes in spelling), where a footnote observes that Griffin
and Thorne, his mate, were shortly thereafter presented to
the General Court, and refers the reader to the Essex
County court records. Olson then turned to the *Records and
Files of the Quarterly Courts of Essex County*, I, 58—59, to complete the picture.

▶II.126. out over the land skope view . . .

Dated only "November" in manuscript, but probably written in 1962 since the poem was read at Vancouver the
following August. In that reading the poet pronounced
"skope" as "skopé," with the comment that the Greek word
was intended. In an undated note to himself, the poet has
written:

> our *scope* fr skopein
>   fr Skopos . . .
>   to look out, from a high place,
>   on
>   in my view / D't [i.e. Dogtown] . . .

See also *Maximus* III, 84 and note.

"Land scope" is of course a variation on "landscape," the
definition of which, as "a portion of land which the eye can
comprehend in a single view," Olson had adopted in "Postscript to Proprioception & Logography" (*Additional Prose*,
p. 21), adding under it, "to bring the land into the eye's
view"—which is one of the tasks in these poems. "View,"
then, becomes a specialized term for Olson (see e.g. "'View':
fr the Orontes," *Maximus* II, 81; *Maximus* II, 100 and note; and
Maximus III—in addition to p. 84—pp. 184, 192, and 193).

II.126. Alexander Baker's . . . land-bench

Along the east bank of the Annisquam River above Done
Fudging. See *Maximus* II, 59—60 and notes.

II.126. Apple Row

See note to *Maximus* I, 151.

II.126. The Sargents

William Sargent, early settler, and his sons, who had grants of land near Done Fudging on the western side of the Annisquam River. For a notice of the family, see Babson, *History*, pp. 148–150.

II.126. Hesoid said the outer man was the bond with which Zeus bound Prometheus

From an account by Zosimos of Panopolis, alchemist of the third century A.D., portraying the salvation of man by the Son of God who unites with man to lead him to the Father and the Abode of Light, as quoted in Jung, *Psychology and Alchemy*, p. 350. The "outer man" is the physical Adam, whose name symbolically reflects the four elements, while Prometheus is the spiritual or "inner" man or "Man of Light":

> Now when the Man of Light abode in Paradise, where blew the breath of Heimarmene, they [the elements] persuaded him, who was without evil and free from their activity, to put on the accompanying Adam wrought of the four elements of Heimarmene ... And he in his innocence did not turn aside; but they boasted that he was their slave. [Wherefore] Hesiod called the outer man the bond with which Zeus bound Prometheus. ...

The statement by Hesiod referred to occurs in the *Theogony*, ll. 613–616.

II.126. the suffering / is not suffered

In Zosimos' account, the Son of God "appeared even to the very feeble as a man capable of suffering and like one scourged. And after he had privily stolen away the Men of Light that were his own, he made known that in truth he did not really suffer ..." (*Psychology and Alchemy*, p. 352).

II.126. the foreknowledge / is absolute

The phrase is originally Milton's (*Paradise Lost*, ii, 557):

> Others apart sat on a hill retir'd,
> In thoughts more elevate, and reason'd high
> Of providence, foreknowledge, will and fate,
> Fix'd fate, free will, foreknowledge absolute;
> And found no end, in wand'ring mazes lost.

II.126. the father / is before the beginning of bodily things

Zosimos' treatise, as quoted in Jung, begins: "If you have meditated and lived in human community, you will see that the Son of God has become all things for the sake of devout souls: in order to draw the soul forth from the dominion of Heimarmene into the [realm of the] incorporeal, behold how he has become all—God, angel, and man capable of suffering. For having power in all, he can become all as he wills; and he obeys the Father inasmuch as he penetrates all bodies and illuminates the mind of each soul, spurring it on to follow him up to the blessed region where he was before the beginning of bodily things . . ." (*Psychology and Alchemy*, p. 347).

▶II.127. Part of the Flower of Gloucester

Written by at least 14 November 1962, when sent to Ed Sanders for publication in *Fuck You / A Magazine of the Arts* (Olson's letter of that date accompanying the poem, at Simon Fraser University Library; acknowledged in Sanders' November 29th letter to Olson).

The "Flower" is, of course, the "Black Gold Flower" (*Maximus* II, 10) which will grow "down / the air / of heaven" (III, 18), but also perhaps the ship, the ketch, called the "Flower" which is listed along with "The Return," "The Gift" and "The Alligator" (II, 120). It seems a remote possibility, but Olson tells Ed Dorn in 1965, "I'm going to write the rest of the Maximus . . . to include the last—well, I guess it's two; I've done two of those ships, and now I've got to do two . . ."

(*Muthologos*, I, 158). See also then, in these terms, "The Alligator" of *Maximus* III, 48.

II.127. Harbor Cove

Immediately east of Fort Point; see note to *Maximus* I, 151.

II.127. Inner / Harbor

Gloucester Harbor east of Fort Point, where it has narrowed to pass between Fort Point on the one side and Rocky Neck on the opposite shore; the center of Gloucester's waterfront activity, where the State Fish Pier and the dehydrating plant is located.

▶II.128. Veda upanishad edda than

Dated "after Oct 19th" in the poet's notes. The first three words are the names of three bodies of sacred learning: the Vedas, from the Sanskrit for 'knowledge' and secondarily the 'words' in which that knowledge is embodied, are the oldest texts of Hinduism; the Upanishads, said to mean 'secret wisdom' or that which is gained at the feet of a master, are later Vedic elaborations; and the Eddas, one in prose and another in poetry, are the primary sources for our knowledge of Old Norse mythology.

Otherwise, it can be said that the three titles appear in chronological order, and that all four words repeat a similar vowel sound. Also, as Olson would have known at least from his reading of Fowler's "Old Norse Religion," there are certain striking parallels between the Norse Eddas and the Sanskrit Vedas, which—despite a great difference in age—reflect a common Indo-European background.

It would seem, too, from a note made ca. 24 December 1963 among his papers, that the poet was aware that the word *Edda* may be related to *oðr* or *odhr*, Norse for 'poetry'; but it is not very likely that he was attempting an echo or pun of "other than" in the poem. Rather, the word "than" serves as a more interesting grammatical device, causing the reader to observe the commonality of the three hitherto discrete proper nouns. It triggers an anticipation of comparison, for which there is no comparison; the reader ordinarily expects with the appearance of "than," a comparison to some inequality, as in "more than" or "less than," though here the anticipation is not fulfilled. Instead, it is the essential equality of value of the three preceeding words, the unique but related bodies of lore, which is expressed—and at the same time their incomparable superiority to all or whatever else.

▶ **II.129. Wrote my first poems / and an essay on myth . . .**

The original poem is in a notepad with another dated 19 November 1962, so it was definitely written in late 1962.

For that which the poet considered to be his "first poem," see *Maximus* I, 82 and note. The essay on myth, likewise never published, was part of the uncompleted study of Melville undertaken with the help of a Guggenheim Fellowship in 1939. In a letter to Waldo Frank, 12 January [1940], Olson speaks of spending many weeks "reading and writing notes and passages towards what I think may be the most fruitful passage in the book, a long section on Melville and myth-making." (Notes on Melville and myth are to be found in his notebook "#5 Gloucester, Spring 1940.") In his letter of March 25th to Frank, he writes of having completed the "section on myth." At the same time, he reports he is "living in a house [on Kent Circle] which sets on a jut of land between the river which ebbs and floods under my eye out the east window and the sea which moves and rushes and breaks against the window to the south."

In notes for a lecture that was given at Black Mountain in 1953 as part of his preparation for the Institute in the New Sciences of Man, Olson speaks of that essay as his "second piece of prose" (the first probably being "Lear and Moby-Dick"), which he says was "written in a boarding house on the banks of a river which I have only recently discovered is a prime image of all my experience, of woman of birth of my own town of me—of who I am, the subject of my work has been what I there tackled the morning after a St Valentine's day blizzard of 26 inches of snow: the nature of myth." See also Olson's notes from May 1956, quoted in note to "Schwartz," *Maximus* I, 84, in which he says, "I remember exactly the place and hour of my first attempt to write down how I understood myth to be—on the Annisquam River, winter, 1939, with Schwartz's mother-in-law, in whom I took great phantasy pleasure, in the same house!"

II.129. Kent Circle . . . Kunt Circle

Just "over the Cut" at Western Avenue; formed by the bifurcation of Essex Avenue before it reaches Western Avenue along the Harbor, to allow westbound traffic easier access. The westbound lane curves around what was once Steep Bank Hill (see below), now a row of houses, to join Western Avenue, and an "inverted triangle"—the feminine symbol—results.

The pun had an even further although decidedly private significance for Olson, since one of the boarding houses in the row along Kent Circle—in fact mentioned in *Maximus* III, 213 as one of the " 'homes' of my 1st / poems—the Frazier Federal"—was where "Schwartz's mother-in-law" lived, and which was also, the poet revealed in conversation, June 1968, the site of a romance he had enjoyed during that winter of 1939–40.

II.129. there was a Dance Hall there / like literally ye Olde / West . . .

On the wall of the City Engineer's office in the Gloucester City Hall, which Olson had visited at least for copies of topographic surveys and to view the original of John Mason's map of Gloucester Harbor (see *Maximus* II, 100), is a framed photograph of a single-story wooden building with a sign identifying it as the "Alhambra." This is the dance hall mentioned in the poem, and on its weather-worn front was pasted a poster promoting a travelling show called "Pawnee Bill's Historical Wild West," with the location "Kent Circle" pencilled on the bottom of the photograph (it is mentioned in none of the published sources for Gloucester history known to Olson). The building housed a popular skating rink in the 1880's and was still standing in 1891, when a slight fire is reported (*The Gloucester Fire Department*, p. 240).

II.129. the St Valentine Day's / Storm

See *Maximus* I, 84 and note; also II, 1 and note.

II.129. writing / at the stile . . . age / 29

For "the stile," see poem following and note. Twenty-nine was Olson's age in the winter of 1939–40.

II.129. Steep Bank Hill

See *Maximus* I, 151 and note, for its location and a description.

II.129. Peter Anastas's Boulevard Sweet Shop

Peter Anastas, Jr. writes (postcard to the author, 9 December 1971): "My father bought The Boulevard Sweet Shop from Nick Cocotas (who then moved up Western Ave. to open the Boulevard Grocery—ah, those Greeks!) in 1931 and had it until 1949. 99 Western Ave. was the address. Apparently Charles made all his telephone calls there literally for years, and the other day my father said 'when I first knew Charles he used to come in with a raccoon coat.' "

II.129. as soon as the work / was over

Probably the beginning of the study of Melville that Olson had undertaken in the freedom afforded him by the Guggenheim Fellowship he had been awarded the previous March (see *In Adullam's Lair*).

II.129. the Canal

The Cape Cod Canal, joining Cape Cod Bay with the waters of Buzzards Bay, an inlet of Long Island Sound.

▶**II.130. the 1st lot from the Cutt**

Written ca. November 1962 (the original in the same note-pad as the previous poem). The poem deals with the early occupation of the area of Fisherman's Field near Kent Circle, using information derived from the town records.

In a notebook designated "II May, 1959 . . . Gloucester Sources, started: May 15, 1959," Olson records on p. 124, from the town records: "P Rider 2 A up ff lying next to the stile (bot of T Prince) & next to Collins on the other side" (the entry in the "Transcript of First Volume Commencing 1642," p. 27, reads: "2 Ackers of upland in the Ffishermans field lyinge next to the Stile . . ."). On p. 125 in the same notebook, Olson has: "the said Prince sold to P[hineas] R[ider] 2A in ff the 1st Lott from the Cutt bounded with John Collins his land on the further side & the highway on the N" (entry for 25 April 1655 in the town records).

Elsewhere among his papers, on a hand-drawn plan of property along Gloucester Harbor, the poet has written:

> "the 1st Lott from the Cutt . . ."—Th. Prince
> Ph. Rider, 1655—"lying next to the stile"
> p's'l [i.e. parcel] to sea added 3/12/1652

From his sketch it is apparent that "the sea added" in the poem refers to a triangular parcel of land which had been added to Thomas Prince's property in 1652, giving him access to the sea.

In another note, from ca. 1961, the poet mentions the "stile," which, he adds, "would have been about where the tennis court now is." The same area will be occupied in a different way in the next poem.

▶**II.131. I am the Gold Machine . . .**

Original manuscript dated "Nov 19th / or 20th." The poem was dated 19 November 1962 by the poet when published in the *Journal of Creative Behavior* in 1967, where there is also the note that it "can also be called the *Almadine*" (i.e. almandine), probably a reference to the "long red drop" of a jewel on line 15 of the poem.

The "Gold Machine" itself exists in both the alchemical sense—just as the poet later refers to "Al' chimiya the / Gold-making machine" (*Maximus* III, 200)—but also literally as a machine, a hydraulic dredge witnessed by the poet on a visit to the gold-mining areas of California in 1947 or 1948. In reading the poem at an International Poetry Festival in London, 12 July 1967, Olson remarked: "I should say that in California, the Canadians, when I was last there, were taking a million dollars, still, out of the land of the Gold Rush by using a machine—which is what I am proposing as image here" (tape of reading). He describes the machine in a letter to Robert Creeley, 18 February [1950]: "the deserts we found in and around Sacramento, where the gold Com-panies have, with their huge water shitting machines, spoiled the earth . . . they turn the top soil down under and pile on top of it, as their crawling machine goes along, all the crunched gravel and stone their water-test has proven not to contain gold, or the dust, of gold" (*Mayan Letters*, in *Selected Writings*, p. 72). In a later letter to Creeley, 3 September [1951], Olson would again write of "those fucking hoses they go over old gold fields with, to suck off, what's left (a million . . ." He describes the dredge further in "Letter #72" dated 6 October 1962, a few weeks earlier than the present poem (*OLSON* 4, p. 8):

> The gold machine
> which clanks all over Sacramento's
> fields, toward the north fork
> of the American River, a bug
> wilder than movies, or parts
> (shitting pissing eating parts)
> imagined by Rube Goldberg
> of Mars, taking $1,000,000
> each year now for the
> Canadian syndicate which
> —cleaning up after the
> Demolition. . . .

II.131. the V / running from the Rest House down the hill to the / Tennis Court

In Stage Fort Park, Gloucester, is a sizeable building containing a refreshment stand, rest rooms, and a patio with benches; while at the northern end of the park, near Western Avenue and towards Kent Circle, are public tennis courts. No distinct "V" as such connects the two, though the land does generally slope in the direction of the tennis courts.

II.131. as De Sitter imagined the Universe a / rubber face or elastic bands . . .

Willem de Sitter (1872–1934), Dutch astronomer. See his *Kosmos*, pp. 114–115, which entries in a notebook from November 1946 indicate Olson had read at that time:

> It is perhaps somewhat difficult to imagine the expansion of three-dimensional space. A two-dimensional analogy may help to make it clear. Let the universe have only two dimensions, and let it be the surface of an indiarubber ball. It is only the *surface* that is the universe, not the ball itself. Observations can only be made, distances can only be measured, along the surface, and evidently no point of the surface is different from any other point. Let there be specks of dust fixed to the surface to represent the different galactic systems. If the ball is inflated, the universe expands, and these specks of dust will recede from each other, their mutual distances, measured along the surface, will increase in the same rate as the radius of the ball. An observer in any one of the specks will see all the others receding from himself, but it does not follow that he is the centre of the universe. The universe (which is the surface of the ball, not the ball itself) has no centre.
>
> It is, of course, not essential that we have chosen for our illustration a rubber *ball*. We might just as well have taken any other surface, it is not even necessary that it should be a closed surface. Even a plane sheet of rubber might do just as well, if only the stretching to which it must be subjected to illustrate the expanding universe is the same in all directions.

In a letter to Robert Creeley, 7 April 1951, Olson wrote: "it broke, once, right in front of my own eyes, when I heard de Sitter lecture on the expanding universe (by the way, take a gander at his book KOSMOS, some day when you get a chance: a wonderful high-faced, spade-bearded, nervous dutchman, an active descendant of Riemann, Bolyai & Lubache[v]sky. . . ." In October 1931, while an undergraduate at Wesleyan University, Olson had attended a lecture by de Sitter entitled "The Size of the Universe," given as part of the college's centennial celebration. The poet told the story one class at Buffalo in the fall of 1964 of walking late into the lecture from debating practice and comprehending immediately, to his own amazement, all that de Sitter had to say. Indeed, notes taken by Olson during the lecture survive inside the front cover and on the flyleaf of his copy of Foster's *Argumentation and Debating*, which he apparently had with him that evening!

II.131. the Morse house over / Western Avenue

See *Maximus* II, 63 and note. Western Avenue marks the north and west boundary of the Stage Fort Park area.

II.131. Robert Duncan

See *Maximus* II, 38 and note. An appropriate choice, to be sure, since Duncan's life was devoted to the occult traditions, of which the precious stone or *lapis* is part.

▶II.132. In the harbor . . .

Dated 23 November [1962].

II.132. Can 9 Nun 8 . . .

Buoys of different shapes: a "can" buoy shows a flat top above water, a "nun" has a conical top, like a nun's habit. Numbers and locations can be had from the U.S. Coast and Geodetic Survey map no. 243, "Ipswich Bay to Gloucester Harbor." Can 9 is near Prairie Ledge off Freshwater Cove;

nun 8, at the center of Gloucester Harbor, north of Ten
Pound Island; nun 10 marks Mayflower Ledge west of Ten
Pound Island; and can 11 marks Babson Ledge off Fort
Point. They are all visible from the poet's house on Fort
Point.

▶II.133. Kent Circle Song

Dated "November 23rd" in the poet's notes. For Kent
Circle, see esp. *Maximus* II, 129 and notes.

II.133. My aunt Vandla's / village a carbuncular / (goiter) gambrel / Federal . . . a gold brooch / at their throat

See *Maximus* I, 85 and note, for mention of the toy
cardboard village the poet had been given by his aunt as a
boy; also *Maximus* III, 213, where the poet speaks of the
"Frazier Federal" and "the proud Monster Federal" along
Kent Circle (the Federal style in American architecture
appeared in the United States during 1783 to 1815, the
Federalist period), and "the Aunt Vandla gambrel" also
there, "that doll of the gambrel roof / of my Aunt Vandla's
toy village."

Aunt Vandla had goiter (in *Mayan Letters* Olson describes a
bird "with its gular pouch swollen like my Aunt Vandla's
goiter"), and the poet mentioned in conversation that she
customarily wore high-necked, frilled dresses with a brooch
at the throat to conceal the swelling (confirmed in conversation with her son, Olson's cousin Philip Hedges, May 1975).
Indeed, a photograph now in the Olson Archives through
the kindness of her son shows her, quite attractive, in just
such a dress.

II.133. the walls / all made of cake . . . into the oven with her

Reminiscent of the gingerbread house and old witch of the
Grimm's folk tale, "Hansel and Gretel." It might be noted
that Olson had at one time other feelings toward his aunt
than memories of the toy village she had given him. In a
letter to Waldo Frank, 12 January [1940], written while

staying at Kent Circle, Olson speaks of her as "a most hypocritical aunt[,] goiterous and sly, a most tristful quack, with eyes red-lidded like a hen's."

▶II.134. I swung out, at 8 or 10 . . .

Dated in notes, "Nov 23rd." The final lines were read at Vancouver, "in the 3rd bedroom / of the same."

II.134. Wellesley Hills

Home of Aunt Vandla (see *Maximus* I, 106 and note). The spacious house of Federal design at 48 Laurel Avenue in Wellesley Hills, similar to houses at Kent Circle in Gloucester (specifically, no. 6 Essex Avenue), with dormers on the third floor, still stands.

▶II.135. JW (from the Danelaw) . . .

Dated 23 November [1962]. The initials, "JW," are those of John Winthrop. The "Danelaw" is the name given to those districts in the north and northeast of England occupied by the Danish invaders during the ninth and tenth centuries, in other words the districts in which the Danes' law prevailed.

II.135. and as those words go down . . .

There apparently has been a passage left out of the original. In a note or draft of a letter from ca. 1964 among his papers, written verso a letter from Jeremy Prynne, Olson writes: "There is a passage missing in the John Winthrop poem on page—I didn't have it to hand when I was setting the poem finally. The poem in fact seemed just as well without it. It still does. But simply so that anyone might know what I did find so important which Winthrop said, here it is [crossed out] page of his Description of New England, volume 2 . . ." In another note from ca. 1964, on the same sheet as the original of "*3rd letter on Georges*" (*Maximus* II, 107), the poet writes: "I didn't purposely leave out the passage from Winthrop . . . I simply thought the poem didn't need it. But for anyone who wld like to know where it is (from the History of New England, Volume 2, p —" Unfortunately, both notes break off without identifying the passage.

II.135. Vedic

See *Maximus* II, 128 and note. Childe's remark in *What Happened in History* on Vedic India, p. 168, may be helpful (the passage is marked in Olson's copy): "The priests who sang [the hymns of the Rig-Veda] and performed the rites enjoyed essentially the status of any highly-skilled craftsman under Bronze Age barbarism; they were, that is to say, entirely dependent on the generosity of royal patrons, but not permanently attached to royal households, since rajas competed for their services. Yet they are the ancestors of the Brahmans who built up such a reputation as monopolists of magic and sole intermediaries between gods and men that they could at length claim to form the highest caste, superior even to kings." Also, Piggott, *Prehistoric India*, pp. 259–260, likewise marked in the poet's copy: "The *Rigveda* hymns reflect the aspirations and life of members of the upper classes of a society which, in common with other Indo-European communities, was formally divided into a three-fold grading of warriors, priests, and artisans—*Ksatriyas, Brahmans*, and *Vaisys*, comparable with the *milites, flamines*, and *quirites* of Roman society or the *equites, druides*, and *plebes* of the Celts of Gaul as recorded by Caesar in the first century B.C. But it is important to realize that the concept of *caste*, as known in later literature, is quite unknown in the *Rigveda*. The tripartite arrangement is perhaps an obvious enough division of responsibilities within a community, but its formal recognition is characteristically Indo-European."

II.135. a magistrate / in the mixed rule . . .

During a dispute between magistrates and deputies in the General Court of the Massachusetts Bay Colony over voting powers in September 1634, John Cotton preached a sermon

describing what he felt to be the nature of the commonwealth. The sermon is reported in Winthrop's *Journal*, ed.
Savage, I, 141; however, see the account in Miller, *Orthodoxy
in Massachusetts*, pp. 247−248 (marked in Olson's copy),
where the term "mixed government" is also used. Miller
reports that Cotton "preached at the opening session [of the
General Court], explaining the divine philosophy of Congregational rule, the Calvinistic theory of 'mixed government,'
and applying it conclusively to the case in hand: 'He laid
down the nature or strength . . . of the magistracy, ministry,
and people; viz—the strength of the magistracy to be their
authority; of the people, their liberty; and of the ministry
their purity; and showed how all of these had a negative
voice, etc., and that yet the ultimate resolution, etc., ought to
be in the whole body of the people. . . .' "

II.135. 1593 Arisleus' / Vision was published Basel

The "Aenigmata ex Visione Arislei et allegoriis sapien-
tum," collected in *Artis Auriferae quam chemiam vocant . . .* ,
which, according to Jung's bibliography of ancient volumes
containing collections of alchemical works by various authors
(*Psychology and Alchemy*, p. 467), was published in Basileae
(Basil) in 1593. Jung explains in a footnote on p. 315 that
"Arisleus is a corruption of Archelaos, owing to Arabic
transcription. This Archelaos may be a Byzantine alchemist
of the 8th or 9th century." Also on that page, Jung informs
us that in the "Visio Arislei," Arisleus "tells of his adventures
with the *rex marinus*, in whose kingdom nothing prospers and
nothing is begotten, for there are no philosophers there.
Only like is mixed with like, consequently there is no procreation." Winthrop, on the other hand, through Cotton,
proposes a thriving land through a truer mixture of
opposites.

▶II.136. proem

Dated 21 November 1962 when published in the *Journal
of Creative Behavior* and "November 21st (?)" in an early

typescript. However, the original was written on sheets now loose from a notepad immediately before "not the intaglio method . . ." (next poem), dated in another manuscript, "Friday / November 23rd / #6). The date of November 23rd for the present poem also appears among the poet's notes, so it is actually not out of chronological sequence here.

For its printing in the *Journal of Creative Behavior*, Olson had included the following "comment": "Proem is written as though it was just before or after the waters had receded—as though it were in fact Ukhnukl [i.e. Ukhnukh—see note to "holy Idris," *Maximus* III, 199] himself speaking: who the Ismaelites believe was the last one to contemplate directly the intelligible realities." The poet also added an "intervening comment": "The psychological is the real, of which the personal is the constant, and current expression. Into the water wade—and get your feet wet. Or plunge, straight across, into the island, on the outer shore. Or start, with the Castle, Perilous."

The focus of the poem is the area of Stage Fort Park, and recapitulates much earlier material in the series.

II.136. the first place the English as fishermen / Westcountry men used to settle on . . .

See *Maximus* I, 106 and notes.

II.136. importing / the large company house

This is "the Company house which Endicott / thought grand enough to pull it down and haul it all the way / to Salem for his Governor's abode" (*Maximus* I, 106). See also later in the poem, "the Dorchester Company house, which was probably / up in the field over Settlement Cove like a fortress . . ."; also, *Maximus* I, 45 and note. There is a tradition that materials for this house had been brought from England by the Dorchester Company settlers.

II.136. the original / 14 men

These are the Dorchester Company's "fourteen spare men the first / year who huddled / above Half Moon beach" (*Maximus* I, 102).

II.136. fisherman's / field

See *Maximus* I, 100 and 106 notes. That the land there was "divided among 17 men / in 1642" would have been calculated by the poet from the town records.

II.136. the Parsonses

See "Of the Parsonses," *Maximus* II, 63–64 and notes; also III, 185.

II.136. Barrett's

C. Homer Barrett. See "old man B," *Maximus* I, 109 and note, and III, 66–67.

II.136. his sister Lizzie Corliss's / henhouse

Lillian A. Corliss (b. ca.1862), sister of Homer Barrett.

II.136. Johnny Morgan's Candy Kitchen

See *Maximus* I, 83 and note.

II.136. up on Bond Street / with Bill Collins

William W. Collins, a letter carrier for the Gloucester post office and friend of Olson's father; he lived at 6 Bond Street northwest of Stage Fort Park, on the other side of Western Avenue.

II.136. the Morse's

The Parsons-Morse house. See *Maximus* II, 63–64 and notes.

II.136. the gambrel / the old schoolhouse of the Cut / which Ed Millett has had now for years

Edward G. Millet (1916–1965), at 94 Western Avenue.

II.136. the Park

Stage Fort Park.

II.136. the Cupboard

Refreshment stand in Stage Fort Park.

II.137. the Strongs

See note to "Cressy-Strong," *Maximus* II, 63.

II.137. Homer

Homer Barrett.

II.137. Roland has the oil & hop-top contract

Roland Strong (see note to "Cressy-Strong," *Maximus* II, 63). "Hop-top" is actually "hot-top," a road-surfacing material; like tarvia (*Maximus* I, 110), a tar mixture.

II.137. the two brothers / who owned the American Oil Company

See note to "Daddy Scolpins," *Maximus* I, 110; also III, 66.

II.137. John Parsons / orchard, and well

See "Of the Parsonses," *Maximus* II, 63–64; esp., for John Parsons' property, note to "1 acre of / rocky ground" there.

II.137. James Parsons house

James Parsons (1658–1733) was the eldest son of Jeffrey Parsons. Babson reports (*History*, p. 121) that "his residence was at the corner of the old road leading from the Manchester Road to Ipswich [approximately Kent Circle]; and the old house still standing there bore till recently indubitable marks of age, which render it probable that he was the builder."

II.137. Jeffrey, the original wampum / of the tribe . . .

Jeffrey Parsons (see *Maximus* I, 106 and note, as well as II, 63 and note).

II.137. his house which George Ingersoll / had owned and before him George Norton . . .

Babson reports that Jeffrey Parsons bought land in Fisherman's Field around April 1655, and also, "about the same time, a house and land at the same place, which had once belonged to George Ingersol, and still earlier to George Norton. There he fixed his residence; and descendants still live around the spot first occupied by their ancestor" (*History*, pp. 120–121).

For George Ingersoll, see note to the family, *Maximus* II, 25; for a brief notice of George Norton, who died ca. 1659, see Babson, *History*, p. 118.

II.137. Settlement Cove

See *Maximus* II, 85 and note.

II.137. Christopher Leavitt's at Portland

See "Capt Christopher Levett (of York)," *Maximus* I, 133–135 and notes.

▶II.138. not the intaglio method . . .

Dated, like the previous five poems, 23 November [1962]. In Canto 79 of his *Pisan Cantos*, Ezra Pound had written (itself based on Dante, *Paradisio*, XIII, 67–69):

> the imprint of the intaglio depends
> in part on what is pressed under it

the mould must hold what is poured into it
in
discourse
what matters is
to get it across e poi basta . . .

II.138. the luxurious indoor rink

The safe and enclosed; but consider Pound's remark in Canto 93 from the *Rock-Drill* section (p. 90): "Tho' the skater move fast or slow / the ice must be solid."

II.138. Saint Sophia

Holy Wisdom (see *Maximus* II, 56 and note).

II.138. our / lady of bon voyage

Our Lady of Good Voyage, the muse of these poems (see *Maximus* I, 2 and note).

▶II.139. mother-spirit to fuck at noumenon . . .

Dated by the poet, 25 November 1962.

II.139. Vierge / ouvrante

The "opening Virgin" (Fr.); specifically, a statue of the Virgin and Child whose front may be opened to reveal the additional figures of the Father and crucified Son carved within. The figure is taken by Neumann to be an example of the sheltering and positive Great Mother: "Seen from outside, the 'Vierge Ouvrante' is the familiar and unassuming mother with child. But when opened she reveals the heretical secret within her. God the Father and God the Son, usually represented as heavenly lords who in an act of pure grace raise up the humble, earth-bound mother to abide with them, prove to be contained in her; prove to be 'contents' of her all-sheltering body" (*The Great Mother*, p. 331). See plates 176—177 in that volume for a painted wood example from the fifteenth century.

▶**II.140. <u>Monday, November 26th, 1962</u>**

Written that date in Gloucester.

II.140. his nibs

In notes from ca. 1962 or 1963 among Olson's papers appears the following:

> . . . at the
> "Bridge" (Canal
> on Pipers
> Rocks
> there sat his
> Nibs: *Nibs*
> the espiritu
> santo the
> Nixie (*Nixus*
> the melosin-
> a (song-
> ster, the
>   Pipe-
>   er . . .

A playfully complex figure, as it takes shape through the poet's notes. In another fragment from 1962 or early 1963 occurs this portrait of the "pixie": "My father was a king, / with a mermaid's tail. And he sat now the other day / with a grin on his face contemplating me / finding out any of this . . . as though the whole time his only / purpose in being was to end up in the humorous / observation of me, that he never was my father at all / but this queer article of sub-being retaining a crown / on his head." In another fragment from the same time entitled "The Canal," Olson speaks of

> winter
> 1962−3 starting with that pip-squeak
> tucking his KeKrops' tail up under him
> and sitting so smugly . .
> on the 'dog-rocks' . . .

(Cecrops, the legendary first king of Athens, was traditionally pictured with a serpent's tail—see esp. Harrison, *Themis*, pp. 202−203.)

Later, on the back of a Cape Ann Bank check re-order form (the form itself dated "7−67") is written the following:

> NEB—he was who came to me out of the
> water And rose on his rock, gigg-
> ling (at me. ["Nebel" crossed out] Niflis-
> heim. Heaven him (its-
> self.

Again, in another note in a xeroxed copy of Heraclitus' *Cosmic Fragments* there occurs:

> limit—or psychopomp: my
>   Giggling ["Devil" or
>   King of the
>   sea
>   His
>   "Nibs"

NEB− is also the root of Neptune, king of the sea. In one of the poet's principal word-running "machines," the table of roots in Lewis, *Elementary Latin Dictionary*, p. 945 under NEB−, NVB−, there occurs: "*cloud, veil* . . . Lat. nebula, Neptunus, nimbus, nubes . . . Cf. Germ. Nebel." For *nebel* as the root of Niflheim, see note to "the statistical Nebel," *Maximus* II, 167.

And in fragments from an early version of "Golden Venetian Light" (*Maximus* III, 212−216), written at the Cut near Piper's Rocks, Olson would speak of having "previously dreamt" and "fantasied" the "Vainglorious Fisherman . . . Luck again, / with his boots on."

See perhaps also, "the pet child / of the lucky sea," *Maximus* II, 66, and definitely III, 62.

II.140. Piper's Rocks

In Gloucester Harbor, just west of the Cut. In a note from ca. 1959−60 among his papers, concerning "A map back room 2nd fl CAHist Mus / City Engineers office copy July 1, 1916 John H Griffen Engineer 1833 4 & 5 by John Mason," Olson writes: "my Dog rocks [see *Maximus* I, 85 and note] Mason calls 'Pipers Rocks.' " The name "pipers Rocks" is also evident on a photograph of a map of the Gloucester water-front in 1845, "Coppyed from J Masons Survey Scale One hundred feet to an Inch," likewise among Olson's papers.

▶**II.141. I   he who walks with his house on / his head . . .**

Written 27 November 1962 (early manuscript dated). A retelling of the Algonquin myth that first appears on *Maximus* II, 31.

▶**II.142. II   she who met the serpent in the pond . . .**

Written 27 November 1962 (early manuscript dated). A retelling of the Algonquin myth on *Maximus* II, 21.

▶**II.143. III   the woman who said she went out
every Sunday . . .**

An early manuscript dated "November 27th 1962." A retelling of the Algonquin legend on *Maximus* II, 22.

▶**II.144. into the Stream or Entrance to the Inner Harbor . . .**

In pencil (erased) on an early manuscript: "written Dec 6 . . . written Dec 9." Original on a Western Union telegraph envelope.

For the "Stream" of Gloucester Harbor, see Brooks, "A Picture of Gloucester About 1800," p. 335:

> Behind Ten Pound Island more than three quarters of the way into the harbor the eastern and western margins suddenly draw together leaving a narrow strait, the "Stream," between two rocky headlands. This is the entry to the safe, landlocked "Inner Harbor" where, since 1750 or before, practically the entire maritime business of the town, fisheries and foreign commerce, has been centered. On the port side of a vessel coming through the "Stream" rose the steep promontory where, 1743, "the town naked to the enemy," a breast work was thrown up and eight twelve-pounders set. Hence the name Watch-house Neck. Here in 1794, covering both Outer and Inner Harbors

and the "Stream" the United States Government built a real fort which now long gone, survives in the name of this part of Gloucester.

II.144. Head of the Harbor

The innermost reach of the Inner Harbor, past what was once Five Pound Island, now the Fish Pier, and near the point Main Street turns to become East Main Street.

II.144. Dutches Sloo

Named for Osmund Dutch, the early settler, whose residence Babson reports "was in the easterly part of the harbor; near the head of which, a miry place was long called 'Dutch's Slough' " (*History*, p. 83). Olson writes in a note from ca. 1959 among his papers: "Dutch's slough (sloo) wld be the salt creek which fills the marsh which runs from the head of the Harbor [between Water and Pearce streets] to the Little Good Harbor over which now the Stop & Shop squats." It appears as "Dutches slow" in the town records ("Transcript of Book Two . . . 1694 to 1752," pp. 117 and 218).

▶II.145. THE FRONTLET

Dated 9 December 1962.

II.145. Portuguese / hill

See note to "the hill, over the water . . . ," *Maximus* I, 2.

II.145. Our Lady of Good Voyage

See *Maximus* I, 2 and note, and note to "the lady," p. 6 of that volume.

▶II.146. Homo Anthropos . . .

Dated 10 January 1963. "Anthropos" (Greek 'man') is an archetypal figure, like the "Monogene" elsewhere in the poems, which occurs throughout Jung's writings—as does "homo maximus," the "Son of Man," Original Man, the whole man.

II.146. Potnia

The Greek ποτνια, which Liddell and Scott define in their *Greek-English Lexicon*, p. 1260, as 'mistress' or 'queen,' adding that it is "a poet. title of honour, used chiefly in addressing females, whether goddesses or women," as in ποτνια θηρῶν, 'queen of wild beasts.'

See, e.g., Harrison, *Prolegomena to the Study of Greek Religion*, p. 264: "The Earth-Mother and each and every local nymph was mother not only of man but of all creatures that live; she is the 'Lady of the Wild Things' (ποτνια θηρῶν)," which Olson has transliterated as "potnia theroun" in the margin of his copy. See also Rose, *Handbook of Greek Mythology*, speaking of the non-Hellenic character of the goddess Artemis, p. 113: "her association with wild animals connects her, not with any Greek deity, but with the Minoan goddess whom we commonly call the ποτνια θηρῶν or Lady of Wild Things, her Cretan name being unknown to us."

II.146. Potidan

See Graves, *Greek Myths*, I, 43: "Poseidon's name, which was sometimes spelt *Potidan*, may have been borrowed from that of his goddess-mother, after whom the city Potidaea was called: 'the water-goddess of Ida'—Ida meaning any wooded mountain.

Poseidon was god not only of the sea, but of springs and other inland waterways.

II.146. Theroun

From Greek θηρ or *ther*, 'wild beast.' See also note to "Potnia" above for the title *Potnia theroun*.

▶ II.147. to enter into their bodies . . .

Written 26 January 1963, judging from notes of that date in Olson's copy of Frankfort, *Kingship and the Gods* (the same source used by the poet in his own calculations elsewhere among his papers). The poem derives from the poet's reading in Frankfort, esp. pp. 24–32 of that volume which deal with the ancient Egyptian narrative of creation known as the "Memphite Theology," in which Ptah, god of the city of Memphis, is proclaimed creator of all.

On p. 28 of Frankfort's study, occurs the following section (much of it underlined in the poet's copy) dealing with the origins of the major gods in Ptah: "And the final phrase of the section closes the circle: while it has started by stating that the gods came forth from Ptah, objectified conceptions of his mind, it ends by making those gods 'enter into their bodies' (statues) of all kinds of material—stone, metal, or wood—which had grown out of the earth, that is, out of Ptah." In the margin above the passage, Olson has written:

> to cause them
> "to enter into their bodies"
> which also
> had grown out of
> Earth

—which becomes the start of the present poem.

The "father" in the final portions of the poem is Osiris; the speaker Horus, his son. The goddess Isis is the mother of Horus. Frankfort quotes a passage from the "Memphite Theology," in which the body of Osiris who has "drowned" in the Nile is drawn ashore and interred at Memphis (pp. 31–32): " . . . Osiris floated in his water. Isis and Nephthys perceived it. They saw him and were aghast. But Horus ordered Isis and Nephthys to grasp Osiris without delay and to prevent him from floating away. They turned their heads in time, and thus they let him reach land." Frankfort had clarified earlier this "drowning" of Osiris (p. 30): "But the word 'drowning' has connotations in connection with this god to which the straightforward translation cannot do justice. The paradox of Osiris . . . consists precisely in this—that in death the god becomes a center of vitalizing force. Hence the Nile, and especially the Nile in flood, count as a manifestation of him. Osiris' connection with the river is not, therefore, rendered adequately by the statement that he was destroyed by the water—that he was drowned. The god was in the waters, and we have translated the verb here 'to float.' "

Olson has underlined "to float" in this last passage, as well as sections from the Egyptian text given earlier, where an exclamation point is added in the margin.

II.147. of whom the Goddess / was the front

See "THE FRONTLET," *Maximus* II, 144.

II.147. the polyphony

The word occurs in Frankfort, *Kingship and the Gods*, p. 25, in the following context: "The various references to 'the land' [in the "Memphite Theology"] have to be understood with some appreciation of that polyphony of meaning which the Egyptians loved." Olson has underlined the last eight words, adding in the margin of his copy: "the polyphony of meaning which I loved."

II.147. the Monogene

See *Maximus* II, 10 and note; also II, 72.

▶II.148. The Cow / of Dogtown

Dated 11 February 1963. Frankfort points out in *Kingship and the Gods*, p. 162: "Egyptian texts of the most varied nature abound in metaphors, appraisals, and other expressions which relate to cattle. The king is 'a strong bull'; a queen-mother is called 'the cow that hath borne a bull'; the sun is 'the bull of heaven'; the sky is a huge cow."

II.148. Shaler says . . .

Nathaniel Southgate Shaler (1841–1906), prominent American geologist, in his report for the United States Geological Survey, "The Geology of Cape Ann," p. 549.

For Dogtown Commons, see note to "the Commons," *Maximus* II, 54.

II.148. he has already of course / made it clear . . .

Shaler's "Geology of Cape Ann," p. 548:

> From beneath the ice mass there came forth many streams
> of flowing water, bearing with them great quantities of
> detrital matter. At the time when these streams flowed
> the base of the ice was considerably beneath the present
> level of the sea. On the floor of that sea, immediately in
> front of the glacier, the whirling currents, originated in
> the ocean by the swift-flowing glacial streams, formed the
> peculiarly distributed mounds and valleys of stratified
> debris which we note as kames. These subglacial streams
> were rare on the part of Cape Ann which is now above the
> ocean level, for the reason that they were drawn away
> into the deep valleys which lie east and west of its elevated
> mass. We know by the facts exhibited elsewhere that sub-
> glacial streams, though occasionally appearing along all
> parts of the ice front, are most likely to find their channels
> in the depressions of the surface which lie beneath that
> front. Thus the kame deposits were probably accumulated
> on territory which now lies beneath the surface of the sea.

II.148. the Banks

See *Maximus* II, 51 and note.

II.148. the Upper Road

See "Gee, what I call the upper road," *Maximus* II, 46 and note.

II.148. the Whale-Jaw

See *Maximus* I, 32 and note.

II.148. Bob Lowrie

Robert E. Lowrie, a former resident of Gloucester and sociologist teaching at American International College, Springfield, Mass.

II.149. Shaler says: "On Dogtown Commons . . .

In his "Geology of Cape Ann," p. 549, picking up where the passage left off on the previous page of the poem (verbatim, except for the spelling of "bowlders" in the original).

II.149. Hough avenue

Road through Stage Fort Park.

II.149. the Barrett's

Home of Homer and Viola Barrett (q.v.) at 96 Western Avenue, above Stage Fort Park.

II.149. Ray Morrison

Raymond L. Morrison (1912–1969), whose house at 92 Western Avenue was next to the Barretts'.

II.149. Lizzie Corliss' hen house

See *Maximus* II, 136 and note.

II.150. Viola's true rubbish heap flower garden

Viola Barrett, wife of Homer Barrett. Of American Indian extraction, she is the "Indian woman" of "As the Dead Prey Upon Us." See also *Maximus* III, 67: "When I was a Blue Deer Viola Barrett was my mother. . . ."

It should be understood that Olson speaks approvingly of the garden, that such a garden is not careless or ill-kept. See Anderson, *Plants, Man and Life*, pp. 136–141, for a discussion of the dump heap garden.

II.150. Nut is over you

One of the Pyramid texts of ancient Egypt contains the following address to Osiris (quoted in Frankfort, *Kingship and the Gods*, p. 183n): "Thy mother Nut is spread over thee . . . She causes thee to be a god . . ." Nut is the sky, personified as a goddess; she is, then the "Cow of Dogtown." See also note to " 'under' the dish / of earth," *Maximus* II, 2.

II.150. Ptah

Chief god of ancient Memphis, creator of all (see notes to *Maximus* II, 147). He is identified with the Primeval Hill.

II.150. the Primeval Hill

In the "Memphite Theology" as summarized by Frankfort in *Kingship and the Gods*, p. 25, "the land of Egypt is proclaimed to have its being in the creator-god Ptah-Ta-Tjenen, Ptah 'the Risen Land.' . . . The 'Risen Land' possesses, again, a multiple significance. It alludes to the universal Egyptian belief that creation started with the emergence of a mound, the Primeval Hill, above the waters of chaos. Ptah, the fruitful earth, is one with this hill—the starting-point of all that is, even of life itself" (marked in the poet's copy).

II.150. the Cow of Heaven

Nut, the sky. See figure 34 in Frankfort, identified as "The Heavenly Cow and the Sun in Its Boat."

II.150. She leans / from toe to tip of hands . . .

Again Nut, the personified sky. See figure 35 in Frankfort, where the goddess is arched over the world, supported by her brother Shu, the god of air. The "Cow-sign" she makes with the earth must be her arched shape, like that of inverted horns.

▶II.151. <u>Stage Fort Park</u>

Probably written in late 1963, as drafts of the poem were found in a manuscript pile from that time among the poet's papers. It was definitely written by 4 January 1964, since Olson had written in a note elsewhere to himself: "or else see orig. mss. found / in mss pile (? on floor? Note Jan 4 1964 [Note to self—anyway to *determine date?*"

Stage Fort Park, west of the Cut and overlooking Gloucester Harbor, is the area where Olson spent summers when young.

II.151. when the land was then depressed below the level / of where the sea now is . . .

See Shaler, "Geology of Cape Ann," quoted in note to "he has already . . . made it clear," *Maximus* II, 148.

II.151. Merry mac

Pun on the Merrimac River (formation probably based on "Mighty Mac"—see *Maximus* II, 174 and note), which flows from New Hampshire across northeastern Massachusetts and into the Atlantic, about twenty miles northwest of Cape Ann.

II.151. choke-cherry trees

See also the lower half of *Maximus* II, 199.

▶II.152. Further Completion of Plat (before they drown / Dogtown with a reservoir, and beautify it)

Dated 16 February 1963. See the earlier *"Further Completion of Plat," Maximus* II, 42, from 1961. The Goose Cove Reservoir, which now occupies territory once part of Dogtown, was completed later in 1963. The poem summarizes much Dogtown material which has been presented earlier, most of which was originally copied by the poet from the town records into his notebook designated "D'Town Dec 8 1960 . . . ENDED abt Feb 21st? 1961." See also "Olson in Gloucester, 1966," *Muthologos*, I, 187–188.

II.152. Lower Road

See *Maximus* II, 46 and note.

II.152. Kinnicum, before 1717

See *Maximus* II, 37 and note to "Benjamin / Kinnicum's . . . five / very rocky acres."

II.152. Joseph Ingersoll

See *Maximus* II, 42 and note to the Ingersoll family p. 25 earlier.

II.152. Bryant . . . by 1717

See the grant of land recorded in the town records, *Maximus* II, 42 above and note.

II.152. Smallmans up at the end before 1725

See *Maximus* II, 46 and note; also II, 38.

II.152. Upper Road

See *Maximus* II, 46 and note.

II.152. Samuel Davis . . . 1713

See *Maximus* II, 37 and note; also II, 53.

II.152. William Hilton . . . before 1719

A grant of two and a half acres to Hilton is recorded by the poet in notebook "D'Town Dec 6 1960," p. 31, as listed in the "Commoners Book Vol. 2 1713–1810," p. 348, and dated either 31 March 1719 or 13 October 1719.

II.152. Elwell next above . . . 1719

See note to "the way leading by / Joshua Elwell's," *Maximus* II, 38; also II, 46.

II.152. Jabez Hunter, 1725

His marriage to Abigail Tucker in 1718 and their subsequent children is all that is recorded for this early Dogtown settler in Babson (*Notes and Additions*, II, 97); however, a grant of land to Samuel Davis in 1725, listed in the "Commoners Records," mentions Hunter (recorded by Olson in notebook "D'Town Dec 6 1960," p. 33).

II.152. The division of wood-lots . . .

See note to "by the way leading by / Joshua Elwell's . . . ," *Maximus* II, 38.

II.152. 1725 (Lower Road) "by the way that leads from the town to / Smallmans now Dwelling house"

See *Maximus* II, 46 and note.

II.152. 1727 (Upper) "the way leading by Joshua / Elwell's to the wood-lots"

See *Maximus* II, 38 and note.

II.152. the expanding period of Gloucester . . . directly after 1703

In a notebook "started night of May 27th, 1960," the poet has entered on p. 6: "Notes June 2 / 1960 . . . use Babson's (236) 1704 as control DATE." Some pages later in the same notebook, calculations indicate that—working from figures available in Babson's *History*, p. 542—the population of Gloucester twice doubled between 1704 and 1755, from 700 to 2,745 persons. Babson's 1704 figure is from the record of division of common land at that date (*History*, p. 236). Dogtown, then, comes into existence shortly thereafter, when the common land on that part of Cape Ann was divided, reflecting the growth in population.

II.152. Malthus' evidence on population

See *Maximus* I, 72 and note; also III, 64. In "Poetry and Truth," *Muthologos*, II, 10, Olson speaks of Gloucester having "spilled over" into Dogtown in its first leap of population—which he terms "Malthusian"—at the beginning of the eighteenth century. Since Malthus reported from his survey that "the population has been found to double itself, for above a century and a half successively [before 1798], in less than twenty-five years," Cape Ann, having quadrupled in the fifty years from 1704 to 1755 (as mentioned in preceding note), was indeed perfectly "Malthusian."

II.152. up through 1775 / (when B. Ellery

See *Maximus* II, 34 and note, and II, 200 and note. The period when Dogtown was still a home for fishermen and merchants like Ellery who sold them supplies. On the importance of Ellery in this respect, Olson has written in notes among his papers: "At least the *Gee Avenue* men were fishermen—& note how this is the period (*1726* anyway when the Davises—Ebenezer etc—are making money out of Mill River: and if B Ellery owns *2* schooners 1774—the Dolphin and the Britannia—& 'lives on D'town' (& the capt of his Dolphin is Andrew Millet!) why an evidence yet, of any change, 1726–1775."

▶II.153. Sequentior

Dated 22 February 1963. The title is derived from the Latin *sequor* 'to follow,' of which the closest form is actually *sequentur*. Used in the sense of 'that which follows' (although *-ior* is a comparative ending).

II.153. Smallmans definitely there 1721 [action of committee / on wood-lots . . .

This information is from the town records ("Transcript of Book 2, 1713–1810," p. 58): "Gloucester   December 19. 1721. The return of ye seven men comittie that were chosen Febry 24, 1720/21 to lay out the wood land in this town; and the account of the lots as they were laid out, is, viz . . . 20 lots laid out between Smallman's house and Sandy Bay and butting southerly on the path that leads from town to Sandy Bay." This represents an advance from the preceding poem,

where William Smallmans is known to have been on Dogtown only "before 1725." See also *Maximus* II, 46 and note.

II.153. spread, of time, on Lower Road / probably 4 years all told

That is, from the action of the committee in 1721 until the
grant of land to William Smallmans in 1725 (see previous
poem).

II.153. the Reverend John White . . . letter to the General Court . . .

When a new meeting-house was built on Middle Street in
Gloucester near the harbor, members residing in the northerly portions of the parish (which included Dogtown) peti-
tioned the General Court in 1738 for permission to be set
off as a separate parish. They pleaded, according to Babson,
History, p. 310, the inconvenience of travelling two or three
miles to the new meeting house, arguing "many of them are
seafaring men, and have no conveniences for going to meeting but on foot; which is very uncomfortable for elderly
people, women, and children."

The passage quoted in the poem is actually not by the
Reverend John White (see *Maximus* I, 145 and note)—not to
be confused with the earlier "Patriarch" of the Dorchester
Company—but is from "The Answer of the Subscribers in
behalf of the first Parish in Glocester to the Petition of Capt
Nathaniel Coit & others . . . ," signed by Epes Sargent and
Daniel Witham of Gloucester, and preserved in the Massachusetts Archives in Boston ("Ancient Plans, Grants, &c,"
III, 131). The relevant passage was copied by Olson in a
notepad in 1963 as follows: "That the Petitioners are most
of them Seafaring Men is allowed and many of them to the
number of about fourty are not rated more than fourteen
Pence apiece to the Parish Rate & several of them not rated
at all . . . and the rest of Parish not Petitioners are in Proportion to their number poorer than they, And if they have no
Conveniences to Carry their families to meeting, they have as

little to detain them in that Part of the Parish, and must remove to some other place where they may get their Bread on Shore since Trading & fishing fail with us by Reason of the Wars."

The passage is presented in the poem as an argument for the presence of fishermen on Dogtown, so far from the Harbor or the Annisquam (as Olson writes on *Maximus* II, 38, "My problem is how to make you believe / these persons, who lived here then, and from these roads / went off to fish . . . or were / mariners—sailors—and a few farmers"). It is made clearer by the following excerpt from a poem on the subject, written 3 February 1960, among the poet's papers:

> . . . To straighten things out,
> it was fishermen
> who lived on
> Dogtown, not old ladies
> or farmers. Or wood cutters . . .
> and if you examine
> the records of the squabble
> among the church people
> during 1741 to 1743
> you'll find Rev John White
> (who was caught in the middle
> in the fight over whether the First Church
> shld be at its first place,
> up there at this jointure
> of the two river-ways
> to go to sea,
> or down at the harbor
> where the bigger fishing
> was beginning to go)
> White in so many words
> pleads with the General Court
> of the hardships for the
> "fishermen" who as such
> lack the transportation
> to go the long distance
> to the new church . . .

See also "Olson in Gloucester, 1966," *Muthologos*, I, 187–188.

▶ **II.154. Licked man (as such) out of the ice . . .**

Probably written in 1963, when other Norse material is used, but the exact date of writing is not known; not read at Vancouver in August 1963.

II.154. the cow——

Audumla is the omitted name (see following poem and note).

II.154. Ymir

The primeval giant of Norse myth, from whose body the world was made.

II.154. Odin

The chief god of the Norse Eddas, the All-Father, ruler of heaven and earth.

II.154. Odin's mother / was the giant——.

Bestla is the name omitted (see note to "Audumla" in the next poem).

▶ **II.155. Gylfaginning VI**

Exact date of writing not known; not read at Vancouver in August 1963. *Gylfaginning* or 'The Beguiling of Gylfi' is the first part of Snorri Sturluson's Prose Edda and is a survey of Norse myth in the form of questions and answers. The sixth chapter of it—as Olson would have known from footnotes in Fowler, "Old Norse Religion," his source—contains the story which constitutes this poem.

II.155. a cow Audumla . . .

From Fowler, "Old Norse Religion," pp. 239–240: "The genealogy of Odin tells a great deal. Although he is the protean thread upon which everything is supported, the All-

Father, the God of Gods, the Many-Shaped, the Lord of Hosts—these and fifty other names are used of him—yet his mother is Bestla, the daughter of Bolthorr, a giant, and his father is Borr, or Burr, the son of Buri (or perhaps Burr himself), a *man* licked out of ice by the cow Audumla which had come into being to provide food for Ymir."

"Burr" is read as "Brrrr" on tape of Olson's interview with Inga Loven in Gloucester in August 1968 (*Muthologos*, II, 89), as if to emphasize the chilliness of "ice" in the preceding line.

II.155. iotunn

Norse for 'giant.' See also *Maximus* II, 165.

▶II.156. Heaven as sky is made of stone . . .

Probably written in early 1963 since apparently the same sources as used in the poems shortly following were consulted, but the exact date is not known; not read at Vancouver in August.

For heaven as made of stone, see perhaps Rose, *Handbook of Greek Mythology*, p. 26, who writes that Heaven (Uranos) "is not infrequently called Akmonides, *i.e.*, son of Akmon, the latter name being of somewhat uncertain meaning. It seems possible to take it as signifying 'unwearied,' but it has been ingeniously suggested that it is connected with Old Persian and Sanskrit *açman*, in which case it would mean 'stone'. . . ."

II.156. Diorite—ex- / granitite

See *Maximus* II, 16 and note.

II.156. Tartaros's threshold . . . is made of a metal native to itself

See Hesiod, *Theogony*, Evelyn-White trans., 11. 808−810 (p. 137): "And there are shining gates and an immovable threshold of bronze having unending roots and it is grown of itself." In a footnote, the translator adds, "*i.e.* the threshold is of 'native' metal, and not artificial."

It will occur again in "The Secret of the Black Chrysanthemum" (*OLSON* 3, p. 72).

▶II.157. All night long . . .

Written in early March 1963. The original is in pencil on the back of an envelope sent by the poet Ronald Johnson from London, postmarked 27 February 1963. In discussing the poem in class at Buffalo in November 1964, Olson remarked that it was literally based on a dream.

II.157. Eumolpidae

The descendants of Eumolpus, priest and poet who founded the Eleusinian mysteries in honor of Demeter; the hereditary guardians of the mysteries. See, e.g., "Eumolpus," *Encyclopaedia Britannica*, 11th ed., IX, 890, marked in the poet's copy.

▶II.158. the Vault / of Heaven . . .

Written in early March 1963, verso letter of 23 February from poet Ronald Johnson (in envelope postmarked London, 27 February 1963—see note to preceding poem).

The sky as "Vault of Heaven" is a concept held by many early peoples, including the Greeks, Norse, Egyptians and Sumerians.

II.158. the deformed horns

See chapter 14 entitled "The Power in Cattle: Procreation," and plate 38, of Frankfort's *Kingship and the Gods*, esp. p. 165 there, where he describes how the horns of the cattle of certain modern African tribes have been artificially deformed for ritualistic purposes, a living remnant of an ancient Egyptian practice.

II.158. to carry the impression to / Ptah

For the bull as messenger in ancient Egypt, see Frankfort, *Kingship and the Gods*, p. 167, where it is reported that the full title of the sacred bull of Memphis was "the living Apis, the Herald of Ptah, who carries the truth upward to Him-with-the-lovely-face (Ptah)." See also note to Ptah, *Maximus* II, 150.

II.158. Over the earth / is the Dome / of the sky

See, e.g., Rose, *Handbook of Greek Mythology*, p. 17:

> In order to understand the cosmological myths of the Greeks, it is necessary to realize what they, in early times, supposed the shape of the world to be. They began with much the same notion as all early peoples appear to possess, namely, that its real shape is that which as much of it as can be seen at once appears to have. Now this, unless the observer be shut in between long lines of hills, like an Egyptian, or confined to an island, or a group of islands, like the peoples of the southern Pacific, is a circle, more or less flat except where mountains or hills rise from it, and capped by the immense dome of the sky, which touches it at the horizon. . . .

▶II.159. turn out your / ever-loving arms . . .

Exact date of writing is not known; read at Vancouver in August of 1963. On a typed manuscript of the poem among the poet's papers is written: "date? (after early spring 1963?"

II.159. the triple-force

See perhaps Jung and Kerenyi, *Essays on a Science of Mythology*, p. 156, for the "triple form" characteristic of the goddess of the Eleusinian mysteries—Kore (virgin), Demeter (mother), and Hecate (moon)—indirectly "confirmed" by Hesiod: "The poet of the *Theogony* acclaims her as the mighty Mistress of the *three* realms—earth, heaven, and sea" (marked in Olson's copy).

II.159. Orge

In conversation, June 1968, Olson suggested that the author see the root *verg-* in Lewis' *Elementary Latin Dictionary*, where can be found the following, p. 952: "VERG-, VRG-, VALG-, *slope, press.* Gr. οργή . . . Lat. vergō, urgueō, virga, virgō; volgus, volgāris. . . ."—which includes, then, the Latin for "Vir- / gin" and "Vulgar," as well as the Greek "*Orge.*" Olson then apparently turned to his Liddell and Scott, *Greek-English Lexicon*, p. 1069, under ὄργια (which is marked in the margin of his copy): ". . . *orgies, i.e. secret rites, secret worship,* practised by the initiated alone, just like μυστήρια, a post-Hom. word; used of the secret worship of Demeter at Eleusis. . . ." Notes among his papers indicate Olson also looked up οργή ("natural impulse, one's temper, temperament"), as well as οργας, ὀργάω, γῆ, γαια, and αια (see their use in the next poem).

On an envelope from the poet Philip Whalen postmarked 26 January 1959, found in the poet's copy of Lewis' *Latin Dictionary*, is written:

> ὄργια
> *orgies* are *secret rites*
> practiced by the *initiates*
> *alone*, just like
> *mysteries* (μυϛτήρια
>   a post-Homeric word)
>   fr ϵργω (? *work?*)

> root of vulgar is VERG-which
> in Greek is ὀργη 'orge =s
> same as Homer's *thumos* (cf.
> Dodds) —— natural impulse

>   one's temper (temperament)
> [libido, no??]   nature
>   heart of men: lust, or
>   *to be rampant*
> —properly to *swell* & teem, *with*
>   *moisture*
> *Skt*: ÛRG̓ (ûrgâ
>   sucus vigor
> "ready to bear a crop"

In another note loose among his papers, the poet has written the following, likewise drawn from his Liddell and Scott, which further connects the elements of the poem:

Skt gaûs (terra)
>Germ. gau
>ὀργας
>on land by land opp. to *nausi* γε
>*the Orgas*
>>where on earth
>>ubi terrarum
>the earth or ground as tilled, a hump
>of earth

gaia
>a land, country
>thrown up to form a *cairn*
>aia
>>(A- original name of Colchis
>with or without cultivated
>fields [thus possibly wild
>well-watered, fertile *spot* of land, meadow-land,
>partially wooded. Such a tract
>between Athens,
>and Megara, reserved to
>Demeter, and Persephone, was called
>ἡ ὀργάς or, ιερα ὀργάς
>: 'marriageable'

In his copy of Pausanias' *Description of Greece*, Frazer trans., I, 137, a passage on "the Orgas, or sacred land of the Eleusinian goddesses," is also marked by the poet (as well as a note on the passage, III, 314).

▶II.160. "at the boundary of the mighty world" H. (T) 620 foll. . . .

Written March 1963 (dated "March, the holy month . . . LXIII" on p. 162). The quotation is from Hesiod's *Theogony*, quoted originally in Rose, *Handbook of Greek Mythology* (see note below to "*katavothra*," p. 162).

II.160. Gravel Hill

See *Maximus* II, 37 and note.

II.160. 'the source and end (or boundary'

Hesiod, *Theogony*, Evelyn-White trans., lines 736–737 (p. 133), "the sources and ends of gloomy earth," or 807–808 (p. 137), "the sources and ends of the dark earth."

II.160. the way that leads ... to Smallmans / now Dwelling house

See *Maximus* II, 46 and note; also *Maximus* II, 152.

II.160. the Lower / Road

See *Maximus* II, 46 and note.

II.160. she could / stick her head up out of the earth ...

Gaia at the birth of Erichthonios. See Harrison, *Themis*, p. 264: "It is at the birth of Erichthonios, the second great Athenian hero, that Cecrops is mostly represented in art, as on the terracotta in Fig. 63. Gaia herself rises in human shape from the earth; she is a massive figure with long heavy hair. She holds the child in her arms, handing him to Athena his foster-mother, to whom he stretches out his eager hands." See also, then, figure 63 in *Themis* (p. 263) showing Gaia, Athena, Erichthonios, and Cecrops.

II.160. 'father' Pelops otherwise known as Mud Face

Graves says Pelops' name means "muddy face" (*Greek Myths*, II, 404). He was killed by his father Tantalos and served up as food to the gods at a banquet, but was eventually restored to life by Zeus. His own children include Atreus and Thyestes. The Peloponnesus is named for him.

II.160. 'garden / tenement messuage orchard

See *Maximus* II, 51 and note.

II.160. this 'pasture' (B. Ellery to / George Girdler Smith . . .

From a deed preserved at the registry in Salem, Mass., which Olson had recorded in a notepad:

> Know all Men by these present, that I Benjamin Ellery of Gloucester in the county of Essex and commonwealth of Massachusetts yeoman—in consideration of one hundred and fifteen dollars paid by George Girdler Smith of the same Gloucester gentleman . . . do hereby grant sell and convey unto the said George Girdler Smith—a certain piece of land, situate and lying in the 4th parish of Glocester aforesd—beginning at the corner of Wm. Centers land near the house that formerly belonged to John Brewer, then running eastward as the brook runs to a corner wall joining to a pasture formerly Mr Pulsifers, now the property of the town of Gloucester aforesaid, thence northerly as the wall runs 'till it comes to the corner joining Millets pasture, thence westerly and southerly as the highway runs, thence southerly until it comes to the first mentioned bounds containing twenty acres be it more or less . . .

The original was signed 11 April 1799 and recorded at the Essex County registry on August 31st of that year.

For Benjamin Ellery, see *Maximus* II, 34 and note; George Girdler Smith was born around 1757 and died in 1810.

II.160. the Memphite lord of / all Creation

Ptah himself. See note to "to enter into their bodies," *Maximus* II, 147; *Maximus* II, 150 and note to "Primeval Hill"; and *Maximus* II, 158.

II.161. quid pro quo

Latin, 'something for something,' i.e., a substitute.

II.161. the end of the world

See possibly also *Maximus* II, 167 and note, for an additional sense.

II.161. the Otter ponds

See *Maximus* II, 33 and note.

II.161. There is a bridge / of old heavy slab stones . . .

The bridge is no longer in existence, the slabs not evident, following the extension and paving of Cherry Street around 1967.

II.161. the 'Back Road'

See *Maximus* II, 25 and note.

II.161. Jeremiah Millett's / generous pasture

See *Maximus* II, 3 and 37, and respective notes; also note to "this 'pasture' " above.

II.161. they called it / Bull Field, in the newspaper

Among Olson's papers is a clipping entitled "Flames Scorch Field: 3 Acres Are Burned Here," from the *Gloucester Daily Times*, 24 February 1960, p. 1, which begins:

> Gloucester firefighters battled three bush fires in five hours Tuesday afternoon.
> The biggest broke out at 2:35 off Cherry Street at the southern end of the "Bull Field" in Dogtown Common.
> Flames seared through briers, brush and brambles over a three-acre plot before being checked on the eastern bank of the Sportsmen's Club Pond.
> The fire started on a ridge off Cherry Street. Fanned by brisk northwest winds, it crept down the hill and across rough, rocky terrain to the side of the pond. . . .

The name "Bull Field" would have been of special interest to the poet because of the story of James Merry who wrestled the bull on Dogtown (see *Maximus* II, 2–6), though at a spot about a mile away from this "Bull Field."

II.161. it became Mr Pulsifer's and then, / 1799, the property of the town / of Gloucester

From Benjamin Ellery's deed of sale; see note to "this 'pasture,' " above. Both Mann, *In the Heart of Cape Ann*, p. 22, and R. Babson, *Tourist's Guide*, p. 32, report that the house occupied by Jeremiah Millett (*Maximus* II, 3 and 37) on Dogtown Road in 1740–41, was later owned by William Pulsifer. Nothing more, however, is said about this Pulsifer in the published histories.

II.161. Erechthonios

Erichthonios, son of Hephaestus, whose seed had accidentally fertilized Gaia whole he was attempting to rape Athena. When the child was born, Earth handed him up to Athena to be cared for (see "she could / stick her head up" above and note).

II.161. Dogtown Square

At the easternmost end of Dogtown Road, where it meets with Wharf Road. The location is marked by the initials "D.T.SQ." carved on a boulder.

II.162. Hellmouth

In discussing the location of the kingdom of Hades, Rose in his *Handbook of Greek Mythology*, p. 79, points out there was a tendency among early peoples to place the abode of the dead in the West, although, he adds, "this naturally did not drive out the local traditions of places which claimed to possess a Hellmouth of their own. . . ."

II.162. Gaia

Mother Earth, to the Greeks.

II.162. katavóthra

From Rose, *Handbook of Greek Mythology*, p. 18:

> . . . Hades is often conceived as being underground, to be reached through one of the many deep rifts in the strata of the Greek rocks, *katavóthra* as they are called in the modern tongue, such as the famous one at Tainaron near Sparta. Of this idea we have abundant evidence in the tales of Amphiaros, Orpheus, and especially of Herakles. Such double beliefs [hell as farthest west and also underground] are common enough; it is noteworthy that we find them blended together in at least one passage of Hesiod, where certain monsters are for a while confined by Zeus 'under the earth' but at the same time 'on the farthest verge, at the boundary of the mighty world.'

This last, of course, provides the opening for the present poem, and in his footnote to the passage Rose, p. 37, identifies the lines as from "*Theog.*, 620 foll."

II.162. the Mount, / which looks merry

This would have to be a local prominence only and not Thomas Morton's Merrymount, or Mt. Wollaston, many miles to the southwest of Dogtown, near present Quincy, Mass. and below Boston.

▶ II.163. [MAXIMUS, FROM DOGTOWN—IV]

Written in March 1963, the "same day or so" as the preceding poem, according to Olson in class at Buffalo (author's notes, 17 November 1964). The poem is based for the most part on the translation of Hesiod's *Theogony* by Hugh G. Evelyn-White, with checking by the poet in his Liddell and Scott *Greek-English Lexicon*, some injection of modern cosmological thought through Weyl and Whitehead, and with additional Norse and Vedic elements.

The original is written in a notepad containing two earlier attempts to explore the meaning of Hesiod's cosmology, including a poem called "The Birth of Beauty" from March 13. At Berkeley the poet would describe the present poem as "absolutely a reduction of Hesiod" (*Muthologos*, I, 115). See also "Poetry and Truth," *Muthologos*, II, 27, where after reading the poem, Olson says it contains "straight stealing from Hesiod's cosmology" with "Norse additions, or retentions from . . . what we call Indo-European myth and I'm trying to call cosmology."

II.163. a century of so before 2000 / BC

I.e., around the second millennium B.C. In "A Work" from the previous May, Olson wrote: "I stress the 2nd Millennium because it is clear that the series [of generations of gods] set themselves then, and though there are the wars of the Zeus and his brothers with the Titans, or Giants, who didn't rebel with the brothers, and therefore insert a curious mixed evil set who trouble thereafter all the established edicts of heaven and confuse the general cosmology, the fathers run out in the sons decisively in the 2nd" (*Additional Prose*, p. 34).

II.163. the year rebegan in / March

March, during which occurs the vernal equinox marking the beginning of spring, was the first month of the old Roman year until the adoption of the Julian calendar in 46 B.C. Here perhaps also with some relation to the change from the Old Style calendar to Gregorian or New Style. In his interview with Inga Loven, August 1968, Olson speaks of the "calendar in which the year began—the new year was on March 28th, if I'm not mistaken—so that the first month of the year was March" (*Muthologos*, II, 85).

See also the preceding poem, p. 162, for mention of "March, the holy month."

II.163. festival days . . . feral (Father's / Days

Possible pun on the *dies ferales* or Feralia, the Roman "festival of All Souls, kept from the 13th to the 31st of the month of Fe(b)ruary" (Harrison, *Prolegomena*, p. 49). It was "devoted to ceremonies of the worship of ancestors" (Harrison, p. 51).

II.163. wild untamed undomesticated hence wild

From the definition of "feral" in *Webster's Collegiate Dictionary*, 5th ed., p. 369: "Untamed; undomesticated; hence, wild; savage."

II.163. our father who is also in / Tartaros

Parallels the opening of the Lord's Prayer. Tartaros is the lower reaches of the underworld in Hesiod, "as far beneath the earth as heaven is above the earth," where the Titans get imprisoned for their revolt. Tartaros is also the father by Gaia or Earth of Typhon (see below).

II.163. Aegean- / O'Briareos whose exceeding / manhood . . . comeliness / and power

Briareos, or Obriareos, was one of the hundred-armed giants who fought with the Olympians against the Titans; he is brother of Cottus and Gyges. Rose points out in his *Handbook of Greek Mythology*, p. 22, that "according to Homer, men called him Aigaion," and that "Aigaion-Briareos seems to be connected somehow with the Aegean Sea; a possible suggestion as to his origin is that the octopus, a favorite subject of Cretan art, has contributed to his monstrous shape." Graves, too, notes in his *Greek Myths*, I, 32, that "Briareus ('strong') was called also Aegeon (*Iliad* i.403)," though he believes that "his people may therefore be the Libyo-Thracians, whose Goat-goddess Aegis . . . gave her name to the Aegean Sea."

Hesiod writes, in Evelyn-White's translation (*Theogony*, p. 125): "But when first their father was vexed in his heart with Obriareus and Cottus and Gyes, he bound them in cruel bonds, because he was jealous of their exceeding manhood and comeliness and great size . . ."

II.163. the reciprocal 1/137 one of the two / pure numbers out of which the world / is constructed

From Weyl's discussion of "absolute constants in nature" in his *Philosophy of Mathematics and Natural Science,* in which he writes (p. 287) of the "pure dimensionless number equalling approximately 1/137," and concludes: "For the moment we can say no more than that the construction of the world seems to be based on two pure numbers, α and ϵ, whose mystery we have not yet penetrated" (p. 289).

II.163. Earth 'came into being' / extraordinarily early, #2 . . .

See Hesiod, *Theogony,* 11. 116–117 (Evelyn-White, p. 87): "Verily at the first Chaos came to be, but next wide-bosomed Earth. . . ." But for "came into being," see esp. Rose, *Handbook of Greek Mythology,* p. 19: "Nor does Hesiod say that even Chaos had existed from all eternity, for he uses the word γενετο, 'come into being,' rather than 'was,' a term with which philosophers in later ages made great play."

II.164. appetite. Or / as it reads in Norse / hunger, as though in the mouth

Fowler, "Old Norse Religion," p. 247, writes that the Norse *Ginnunga Gap*—which he had identified with χαος on p. 239—"has been variously interpreted. It may mean 'yawning gap'; or, if *ginnunga* be the genitive singular of a proper noun, then it is the gap, or gaping void, or yawning open mouth, or gullet, of the being prior even to chaos. There are Vedic parallels, such as the source of all life in hunger."

II.164. stlocus

See the table of roots in Lewis, *Elementary Latin Dictionary,* p. 950, under STER-, STRA-, STLA-: "locus (old, stlocus; cf. Germ. Strecke)." On the blackboard of the classroom at Buffalo, Olson wrote:

sta- I.E. root of local

'*st*'locus (locative—demonstrative—where,
   ↗   not *what* Gloucester

fell out of use

(author's notes, 24 November 1964)—adding on another occasion that "stlocus" was the "lost Latin of 'local' " and that "*stl-* in 'locus' is *sta-*" (author's notes for 14 April 1965).

II.164. the land, country / our dear fatherland the Earth, / thrown up to form a cairn

See Liddell and Scott, *Greek-English Lexicon*, pp. 297–298, under γαῖα: "Poet. for γῆ. *a land, country*, in Hom., often, φίλην ἐς πατρίδα γαῖαν to one's dear father*land* . . . 2. earth, χυτὴ γαῖα *earth* thrown up to form a cairn . . ." And at the end of the entry: "Cf. αἶα."

See also note to "*Orge*," *Maximus* II, 159.

II.164. Uranos

The Greek 'Heaven.'

II.164. a i a / the original name / of Colchis

See αἶα in Liddell and Scott, p. 32: "Ep. form used for γαῖα . . . II Αἶα, ἡ, orig. name of Colchis, Soph. Fr. 774 . . ." Rose in his *Handbook*, p. 197, notes that "The original goal of the Argo [i.e. Colchis] is called Aia in Homer and many other other authors, *i.e.*, simply 'the Land' . . ."

Colchis, where the Golden Fleece was to be had, was on the eastern shore of the Black Sea below the Caucasus.

II.164. Kuban where those / inventors of the Vision— the / Civilizers . . .

A river and valley on the verges of the Caucasian Mountains (the area also of Colchis). According to Hawkes, *Prehistoric Foundations of Europe*, pp. 220 ff., what is called the Kuban Copper Age flourished there shortly after 2500 B.C.

In his copy of Whitehead, *Process and Reality*, pp. 292–293, after a section dealing with the theory of cosmic epochs which "provides the basis for a statistical explanation of probability" (Whitehead says, "In any one epoch there are a definite set of dominant societies in certain ordered interconnections"), the poet has written in the margin above the sentence, "The environment can be limited to the relevant portion of the cosmic epoch," which he has also underlined: "exactemente: pre-2300 BC—& possibly even pre-3250 Kuban-Terek) . . ."

Kuban also occurs in an unpublished essay from 11 October 1965 among the poet's papers as "the Founding City of civilized man," while in another essay, from ca. 1963, Olson writes of "incredible Kuban-Terh^{er}(nan source of the 'Warriors.' " Kuban, then, is to be taken as the home of Indo-European man.

II.164. the statistical

The term occurs throughout Whitehead's *Process and Reality*, esp. on p. 285, where in Olson's copy there is added an exclamation point and this marginal note: "March Monday one week after old Inaugural Day." (Other marginal notes on p. 291 include "source & end ('boundaries' " and "iotunns," confirming that Olson was reading these pages at the time the poem was written.) On p. 292, Whitehead writes of "that numerical character which a statistical theory of probability requires," which is underlined by the poet, with the comment in the margin: "*whiz.*"

Again, on p. 293, Whitehead writes: "The argument, as to the statistical basis of probability, then recurred to the doctrine of social order. According to this doctrine, all social order depends on the statistical dominance in the environment of occasions belonging to the requisite societies. The laws of nature are statistical laws derived from this fact." Olson has this last sentence underlined. Cf. also the later occurrence of "statistical" along with "End of the World" on p. 167 of this poem.

II.164–165. Tartarós / is beyond / the gods beyond hunger outside / the ends and source of Earth / Heaven Ocean's / Stream

See *Theogony*, ll. 736–737 (Evelyn-White, p. 133), and esp. ll. 807ff. (pp. 137–139): "And there, all in their order, are the sources and ends of the dark earth and misty Tartarus and the unfruitful sea and starry heaven, loathsome and dank, which even the gods abhor. . . . And beyond, away from all the gods, live the Titans, beyond gloomy Chaos."

II.165. O'Briareos / helped out by Poseidon . . .

Theogony, ll. 817–819 (p. 139): ". . . Briareos, being goodly, the deep-roaring Earth-Shaker made his son-in-law, giving him Cymopolea his daughter to wed."

II.165. those roots of Earth . . . the foundations of Ocean

Theogony, l. 728 (p. 133): ". . . above [the bronze fence around Tartarus and night spread 'in triple line all about it'] grow the roots of earth," while the phrase "Ocean's foundations" occurs in l. 816 on p. 139. See also the note below to "ep' 'Okeanoio '*Themethlois*," *Maximus* II, 168.

II.165. iotunns those who / strain / reach out are / hunger

Iotunns are the Norse giants or titans. Hesiod writes in his *Theogony*, ll. 207–210 (p. 95): "But these sons whom he begot himself great Heaven used to call Titans (Strainers) in reproach, for he said that they strained and did presumptuously a fearful deed." The word "Titan" comes from the Greek τιταίνω, 'to stretch, strain,' and is cognate with the Norse *iotunn*. Fowler, "Old Norse Religion," p. 239, writes: "The word *iotunn*, however, usually translated 'giant' . . . seems actually to mean 'devourer' or simply 'eater.' " See also *Maximus* III, 164, "Hunger Himself or Mouth-Without-The-World-To-Eat."

II.165. the last, the youngest child of Earth . . .

Theogony, 11. 820ff. (p. 139):

> But when Zeus had driven the Titans from heaven, huge Earth bare her youngest child Typhoeus of the love of Tartarus, by the aid of golden Aphrodite. Strength was with his hands in all that he did and the feet of the strong god were untiring. From his shoulders grew an hundred heads of a snake, a fearful dragon, with dark, flickering tongues, and from under the brows of his eyes in his marvellous heads flashed fire, and fire burned from his heads as he glared. And there were voices in all his dreadful heads which uttered every kind of sound unspeakable; for at one time they made sounds such that the gods understood, but at another, the noise of a bull bellowing aloud in proud ungovernable fury; and at another, the sound of a lion, relentless of heart; and at another, sounds like whelps, wonderful to hear; and again, at another, he would hiss, so that the high mountains re-echoed.

II.166. Shakti was shooting / beams of love directly / into the woman he wanted to be / full of love

It was the god Shiva, actually, who did the shooting, not Shakti, the active and creative power of the universe, which is feminine when personified. The source is Zimmer, *Myths and Symbols in Indian Art and Civilization,* p. 180:

> The moment Rāhu tendered Jalandhara's demand that the Goddess should be delivered to him—the Shakti of the universe to become the tyrant's principal queen—Shiva countered the colossal challenge. From the spot between his two eyebrows—the spot called "The Lotus of Command" (*ajna-cakra*), where the center of enlightenment is located and the spiritual eye of the advanced seer is opened—the god let fly a terrific burst of power, which explosion immediately took the physical shape of a horrendous, lion-headed demon. The alarming body of the monster was lean and emaciated, giving notice of insatiable hunger, yet its strength was resilient and obviously irresistible. The apparition's throat roared like thunder; the eyes burnt like fire; the mane, disheveled, spread far and wide into space. Rāhu was aghast.

II.167. it would take you one year / from the tossing . . .

Theogony, 11. 783ff. (p. 133): "It is a great gulf, and if once a man were within the gates, he would not reach the floor until a whole year had reached its end, but cruel blast upon blast would carry him this way and that. And this marvel is awful even to the deathless gods."

II.167. Tartaros / was next after Earth

Theogony, 11. 116–119 (p. 87): "Verily at the first Chaos came to be, but next wide-bosomed Earth . . . and dim Tartarus in the depth of wide-pathed Earth. . . ."

II.167. Earth / was next after hunger / itself

I.e., after Chaos (see note above, but esp. note to "appetite," p. 164).

II.167. the statistical Nebel / and "End of the World"

See Fowler, "Old Norse Religion," p. 239: "According to Snorri Sturluson's version of the primal act, the cosmic giant Ymir was generated in Ginnungagap by the mutual attraction and opposition of cold from Niflheim and heat from Muspellsheim"; while in a note on p. 247, Fowler says: "Niflheim (ON *nifl*; German *Nebel*, 'cloud') is known later as the home of the dead; and Muspellsheim is later the home of Sutr, who, in the end, destroys the ordered cosmos. *Muspell-* (the word occurs in ON, OS, OE, and OHG) may mean 'fire'; but it may also mean something like 'the end of the world.' "
For "the statistical," see note to p. 164 earlier.

II.168. Ocean / which is 9 times around / earth and sea

Theogony, 11. 787–791 (p. 137): "Far under the wide-pathed earth a branch of Oceanus flows through the dark night out of the holy stream, and a tenth part of his water is allotted to her. With nine silver-swirling streams he winds

about the earth and the sea's wide back, and then falls into
the main. . . ."

II.168. out of Ocean was born / 3000 / (when his wife was Tethys) / daughters

Theogony, ll. 363–366 (pp. 105–107): "For there are
three thousand neat-ankled daughters of Ocean who are dis-
persed far and wide, and in every place alike serve the earth
and the deep waters, children who are glorious among
goddesses."

II.168. Cottus and Gyes

Sons of Earth and Heaven, brothers of Briareos (*Maximus*
II, 163 and note).

II.168. ep' 'Okeanoio 'Themethlois / the lowest part the bottom tithemi

Theogony, 1. 816, where Evelyn-White, p. 139, translates
the phrase as "upon Ocean's foundations." According to
Liddell and Scott, *Greek-English Lexicon*, p. 665, Θέμεθλα
means 'the foundations, the lowest part, the botton.' τίθημι
also appears in the entry there, as a cognate, and means 'to
set, put, place.'

II.168. Θε

Θε in the version published in *Psychedelic Review*. See Rose,
Handbook of Greek Mythology, p. 21: "Themis is a word of
doubtful origin, but probably from a Greek root"; while in a
footnote on p. 38, Rose adds: "The root Θε, *put, make fast*;
but the exact meaning is very uncertain." See also Liddell
and Scott, p. 666, under Θέμις.

II.168. Ocean deems / himself

In class at Buffalo, Olson suggested a pun of "deems" with
Themis 'Order,' daughter of Uranos and Gaia (author's

notes, 21 October 1964), the root of which is Θε and which is cognate with " *'Themethlois*."

II.169. Night's house is right over / their heads . . .

Theogony, 11. 748–754 (p. 133): "Night and Day draw near and greet one another as they pass the great threshold of bronze: and while the one is about to go down into the house, the other comes out at the door. And the house never holds them both within; but always one is without the house passing over the earth, while the other stays at home and waits until the time for her journeying come. . . ."

II.169. Bifrost

The Norse "rainbow bridge" which joins heaven and earth (see Fowler, "Old Norse Religion," p. 241).

II.169. Styx's house and Iris the messenger are / bungled prettinesses . . .

Theogony, 11. 775–781 (p. 135): "And there dwells the goddess loathed by the deathless gods, terrible Styx, eldest daughter of back-flowing Ocean. She lives apart from the gods in her glorious house vaulted over with great rocks and propped up to heaven all round with silver pillars. Rarely does the daughter of Thaumas, swift-footed Iris, come to her with a message over the sea's wide back."

II.170. Kronos

Son of Heaven and Earth, father of Zeus.

II.170. in Tartarós / away from all the gods . . .

Theogony, 11. 813–817 (p. 139): "away from all the gods, live the Titans, beyond gloomy Chaos. But the glorious allies of loud-crashing Zeus have their dwelling upon Ocean's foundations. . . ."

II.170. Typhon . . . who would have come to reign over mortals / and immortals

Theogony, 11. 836–837 (p. 139): ". . . he would have come to reign over mortals and immortals, had not the father of men and gods been quick to perceive it."

II.170. the heat took hold on the dark-blue sea / when Typhon and Zeus engaged . . .

Theogony, 11. 844ff. (pp. 141–143):

> And through the two of them heat took hold on the dark-blue sea, through the thunder and lightning, and through the fire from the monster, and the scorching winds and blazing thunderbolt. . . . Hades trembled where he rules over the dead below, and the Titans under Tartarus who live with Cronos, because of the unending clamour [earlier, 1. 710, Hesiod uses, as Olson here does, "clangour"] and the fearful strife. So when Zeus had raised up his might and seized his arms, thunder and lightning and lurid thunderbolt, he leaped from Olympus and struck him, and burned all the marvellous heads of the monster about him. But when Zeus had conquered him and lashed him with strokes, Typhoeus was hurled down, a maimed wreck, so that the huge earth groaned. And flame shot forth from the thunder-stricken lord in the dim rugged glens of the mount, when he was smitten. A great part of huge earth was scorched by the terrible vapour and melted as tin melts when heated by men's art in channelled crucibles; or as iron, which is hardest of all things, is softened by glowing fire in mountain glens and melts in the divine earth through the strength of Hephaestus. Even so, then, the earth melted in the glow of the blazing fire. And in the bitterness of his anger Zeus cast him into wide Tartarus.

II.171. The life-giving earth / had crashed around in burning . . .

Theogony, 11. 693–697 (p. 129): "The life-giving earth crashed around in burning, and the vast wood crackled loud with fire all about. All the land seethed, and Ocean's streams and the unfruitful sea. The hot vapour lapped round the earthborn Titans. . . .”

II.171. it was this 'lava' . . .

The volcanic nature of the occurrence is suggested in Evelyn-White's footnote on p. 141, in which it is pointed out, "Pindar represents him [Typhoeus] as buried under Aetna, and Tzetzes read Aetna in this passage."

II.171. for all their great spirit, their / metathumos

Olson has either misread or substituted "*metathumos*" for Hesiod's ὑπερθύμους (*hyperthumos*) in line 719 of the *Theogony*, which Evelyn-White translates as "for all their great spirit" (p. 130).

II.172. Tartaros / which had been there as early as hunger . . .

Theogony, ll. 116ff. (p. 87): "Verily at the first Chaos ["hunger"] came to be, but next wide-bosomed Earth . . . and dim Tartaros . . . and Eros (Love) . . ."

II.172. Love . . . accompanied Tartarós / —as Night had Heaven the night / his son had hurled off his parts

The birth of Aphrodite is described in *Theogony*, ll. 176ff. (pp. 91–93):

> And Heaven came, bringing on night and longing for love, and he lay about Earth spreading himself full upon her. Then the son from his ambush stretched forth his left hand and in his right took the great long sickle with jagged teeth, and swiftly lopped off his own father's members and cast them away to fall behind him. . . . And so soon as he had cut off the members with flint and cast them from the land into the surging sea, they were swept away over the main a long time: and a white foam spread around them from the immortal flesh, and in it there grew a maiden. First she drew near holy Cythera, and from there, afterwards, she came to sea-girt Cyprus, and came

forth an awful and lovely goddess, and grass grew up about her beneath her shapely feet. Her gods and men call Aphrodite . . .

II.172. Love accompanied Tartarós / when with Earth . . . he made / Typhon

Theogony, 11. 821–822 (p. 139): "huge Earth bare her youngest child Typhoeus of the love of Tartarus, by the aid of golden Aphrodite."

▶II.173. I looked up and saw / its form / through everything . . .

Exact date of writing unknown. The original manuscript is undated but on a page from the same type of notepad and in the same color ballpoint ink as poems from the fall of 1962. The poem was definitely written by March 1964, when sent to Jeremy Prynne at Cambridge as part of the complete manuscript for typing. It was apparently not read at Vancouver in August 1963, though the tape of that reading may have been stopped short for a suggested intermission at that point.

▶II.174. One of the Bronze Plaques Which Decorate These / Shores

Exact date of writing is not known; the poem is not on the tape of the Vancouver reading in August 1963. For actual commemorative plaques set up in various locations about Cape Ann, see note to "tablets of Poseidon," *Maximus* II, 84 and note, although no such plaque or other public monument (except his own Castle, now a museum) dedicated to John Hays Hammond, Jr. does exist.

II.174. John Hays Hammond Jr . . .

The Gloucester inventor who "built a castle / at Norman's Woe" (see *Maximus* II, 7 and note). Day books kept by the butler at the Castle indicate Olson and his wife were regular guests there from the fall of 1959 through early 1962 (letter from Harry Martin to the author, 31 August 1971).

In the poet's library was a copy of a report on the works of Hammond issued by the Franklin Institute of Pennsylvania, a gift from Hammond to Olson, which contains all the information cited in the poem. Sheffield Scientific, which is mentioned, is part of Yale University.

II.174. Russia Cement

Russia Cement Company (later reorganized as Le Page's, Inc.), a glue manufacturing firm begun in Gloucester using fish skins and other waste from the local fish-processing plants.

II.174. Gorton Pew

Another of the principal Gloucester manufacturers; see *Maximus* I, 27 and note.

II.174. Mighty Mac Hammond

"Mighty-Mac" is the brand name used by the Cape Ann Manufacturing Company located in Gloucester, makers of boys' and men's outerwear.

▶II.175. A Letter, on FISHING GROUNDS . . .

Exact date of writing not known; not on tape of Vancouver reading in August 1963, but probably written in the spring of 1963.

The poem is based on an appendix to the report of the U.S. Commissioner of Fisheries for 1929, *Fishing Grounds of the Gulf of Maine,* by Walter H. Rich, agent of the Bureau of Fisheries. Olson had borrowed a copy from Rutherford H. Marchant of West Gloucester (acknowledged in the final lines of the poem), who was a marketing agent for the Bureau of Fisheries. The copy, kept by Olson, has the following note on its cover beneath Marchant's signature: "by usurpation from R.H. Marchant so long ago (note acknowledging my arrogation Sunday Sept 22nd 'LX VII."

The greater portion of the poem is taken verbatim from pp. 54–55 of Rich's document, except for a section on the Indian presence in the area of the Gulf of Maine woven in towards the end, and occasional minor changes such as "ragged" at the end of line 7 of p. 175 instead of Rich's "rugged" (possibly even a typographical error), or the addition of "glorious" (line 18 of p. 176) to Rich's simple "these waters."

Some of these changes on p. 176 serve to revise Rich's 1929 report, especially the addition (lines 8–9) of "but not now any / longer since the Horse Latitudes have shifted north." (The Horse Latitudes are belts of high atmospheric pressure, calms, and light variable winds, 30°–35° both north and south from the equator.) Other changes make possible the introduction of the Indians on lines 27–36 of p. 176. On p. 175, e.g., whereas Rich has "the neighborhood of Passamaquoddy Bay," Olson makes the change to "the neighbourhood of the original / Micmacs" (Rich having discussed in a note on his p. 61 the Micmac origin of the name Passamaquoddy). The Micmacs were the Algonquin tribe centered in Nova Scotia and New Brunswick around the Bay of Fundy, at the northern end of the Gulf of Maine; they extended westward into Quebec and south into Maine below Passamaquoddy Bay. Again on p. 175, lines, 29–30, whereas Rich has "These Fundy tides probably are the greatest in the world," Olson has "These Indian tides"— which will prepare the way for the Indian presence later on, where Olson breaks off from his source, in the section beginning "the mists of the Indians" on p. 176 to "the tales to tell in the continuous speech" (although the phrase "the fogs are especially noted" occurs in Rich). The poem then concludes with Rich once more.

II.176. Brown's Bank

Olson's addition to Rich's report. See *Maximus* I, 19 and note.

II.176. m'teoulin

Eckstorm, *Old John Neptune*, writes in a note on p. 5:
"*M'té-oul-ino*, or *Medé-oulino*, is the Penobscot word for a
shaman, or wizard. *M'te-*, *mede-*, means 'noise,' 'sound of
anything'; the root *-ol-*, says Dr. Speck, 'denotes something
hollow'; *-ino*, or *-winno*, is a 'person.' The m'téoulino is 'one
who makes a noise upon something hollow,' specifically, a
drum, which is the adjunct of the exorcist." She continues,
"*M'te-oulin*, a shortened form, stands in common use for
either the shaman or his magic, cause or effect." The word
is spelled *m'teoulin*, as in the poem, throughout her study.

II.176. the masques performed / in the waves

See Eckstorm, *Old John Neptune*, pp. 88–89, following a
discussion of the origin of the common Maine Indian name,
Neptune, and the Indian belief in mermen:

> In 1606, when De Poutrincourt came back to Port Royal
> after a cruise to the westward, he found that Lescarbot,
> who had remained there, had prepared a rousing welcome
> for him. Lescarbot, who was something of a versifier, had
> written a pageant called "Neptune's Theatre" and had ar-
> ranged a performance in which Neptune, six Tritons and
> four Savages had speaking parts and made joyous revelry,
> while the others gaped in admiration. It was, as Lescarbot
> says, "a ceremony absolutely new on that side of the
> ocean." But to the Indians it was much more than a
> masquerade. To see Neptune, with his crown and trident
> and fish's tail and all his attendant half-men, blowing
> horns, coming out of the water, would confirm their old
> beliefs and in a form more magnificent than they had
> imagined. They would hardly have been Indians, with
> their habit of bestowing new names upon important oc-
> casions, if they had not forthwith taken the name of Nep-
> tune, easy to speak, having an apparent meaning in their
> own tongue and applicable to their leading family of chief-
> tains, and adopted it as they did so many other foreign
> words. We have no direct proof that they did this at this
> time, but when we discover that only a century later the
> name was that of their head chief, sprung traditionally
> from the water half-men, we could hardly ask a better

way of accounting for it than by this pageant of Marc
Lescarbot, given in 1606, with its chief actor Neptune,
the God of the Sea.

II.176. 'Bahia fonda'

The Bay of Fundy (Sp.). See footnote in Rich, *Fishing
Grounds*, p. 56:

> "It [Fundy] was not clearly indicated by Verrazano (1524)
> nor in the report of Gomez (1525), who probably saw
> something of its entrance; but fog or other unfavorable
> circumstances may have prevented him from observing
> it more accurately; but we find in the first old Spanish
> maps, in the latitude where it ought to be, names like these:
> 'Rio hondo,' or 'fondo' (a deep river); or 'Bahia hondo'
> (a deep bay). . . ."
>
> Doctor Kohl, here quoted, further says: "On the maps
> of the seventeenth and early part of the eighteenth century,
> especially, it is written Bay of Funda. I believe that this
> name grew out from, and is a revival of, the old Spanish
> name 'Bahia fonda.' "

▶II.177. Maximus, to Gloucester, Letter 157

Exact date of writing is not known, but probably late
spring of 1963 after reading in Eckstorm, *Old John Neptune,*
as with previous poem. Not on tape of Vancouver reading
that August. A first version was written on endpapers torn
from the poet's copy of Lewis, *Elementary Latin Dictionary*—
like *Maximus* III, 9, from June 1963.

II.177. an old Indian chief as hant . . .

An earlier version of this opening section was also found
among the poet's papers:

                a haunt sitting
        Mr. Randazza
                paled
        and went into his house

                on the stone
        Mr Randazza's side
        of Fort Hill

an Indian chief
is buried there & there
the Indian chief
was sitting, 1959, on
the stone

Mr Randazza
went white & went into
his house

Both Thomas and Antonio Randazza, fishermen, were neighbors to the west of Olson at 29 Fort Square, on the Harbor side of the road, while closer to Olson's house, at 16½ Fort Square, lived Salvatore and Pauline Tarrantino and their family, in "the yellow house / on fort constructed like a blockhouse house" (*Maximus* III, 10).

Olson used "hant," a dialectal version of "haunt," previously in his poem "Move Over" from 1947.

II.177. Mr Misuraca

Probably Gaetano Misuraca, a neighbor from 19 Commercial Street, at the beginning of Fort Point.

II.177. Tarentines

Also spelled Tarratines. Micmac Indians from Nova Scotia who invaded the region of Penobscot Bay and held the territory for a few years in the early 1600's. See the account in Eckstorm, *Old John Neptune*, p. 75, where a communication from William F. Ganong is reported:

> The earliest known use of the name appears to be that in the account of the Sagadahoc Colony, 1607, where they are called TARENTYNS and identified with the Micmacs, for while the expedition was off Cape La Have, Nova Scotia, they saw the Indians, and the narrative reads, "we take these people to be the tarentyns" . . .
> As to the *origin* of Tarratines I am at a loss. The probability is very strong that it was a nickname given them by the New England Indians and adopted by the English of New England. The name Tarantyn bears a considerable resemblance to Abnaki roots for *trade* and as the Micmacs very early traded with the European fishermen on one

side and with the New England Indians on the other, it is possible they were called "the traders."

Eckstorm herself continues, p. 76:

> No nickname could have fitted the Micmacs better than that of the "Traders," Tarentyns; for the early accounts tell of the extensive commerce they had with the Indians of the western Maine coast in knives, kettles, coats and articles obtained from the French of Nova Scotia. They traversed the whole coast region exchanging these articles for corn, which they did not grow themselves; but they were never residents of Maine except for a brief interval, when they came in for a few years after the great pestilence of 1618–1619.

On p. 77 she speaks of

> the devastating plague which swept away more than three-fourths of the inhabitants of the coast. And then followed the invasion of the Micmacs, or Tarentyns, who for several years held the country east of the Penobscot. They were in possession when the English began to arrive in numbers, and they remained about ten years, during which time the Pilgrims and others correctly enough called the Indians of Penobscot Bay the Tarratines. About 1630 they withdrew and the old Etchemin population flowed back again into its accustomed haunts; but the name of Tarratines clung to the region and has been transferred to the more recent Penobscots, who are not of the same stock as the old inhabitants and who speak a different language.

These sections are marked in Olson's copy.

II.177. Wikings

The Vikings; spelled to reflect *wīcing*, an early appearance of the name possibly derived from O.E. *wīgend*, 'a warrior' (Collingwood and Powell, *Scandinavian Britain*, pp. 60–61, where it is spelled "wicking"). 1000 A.D. is the common round date for the earliest Norse voyages to North America.

II.177. these Sicilians / talk an Italian / which is Punic.

Punic is the language of ancient Carthage, closely related to Phoenician, while Sicily, only some 140 miles from Carthage on the North African coast, was the site of a number of Phoenician settlements and Carthaginian invasions, most notably by Hannibal in 409 B.C.

II.177. For the Tarantinos / where Micmacs . . .

"Were" in the original version written on the endpapers torn from Lewis' dictionary: "For they [the Tarantines] were / Micmacs spotted / first off Cape La Have. . . ."

II.178. the yellowing disease . . .

See C. F. Adams, *Three Episodes of Massachusetts History*, I, 1–4, esp. p. 2 on the suggestion that the epidemic of 1616–17 was a visitation of yellow fever: "This conjecture is based chiefly on the description of one of its symptoms, given long afterwards by Indians, then old, but, at the time of the sickness, young, who, speaking from distant recollection, said that 'the bodies all over were exceeding yellow, both before they died and afterwards.'" Adams goes on to show, however, that it was not actually yellow fever.

See also *Maximus* I, 49, 103, 151; II, 24; and " 'I know men . . . ,' " *Muthologos*, II, 163.

II.178. Penobscot Bay

Inlet of the Atlantic halfway up the Maine coast.

▶II.181. why light, and flowers? . . .

Written 23 May 1963 (manuscript dated "May 23rd").

II.181. Paul Oakley

(b. 1912), acquaintance of the poet living in East Gloucester at 115 Mount Pleasant Avenue, a large house high above the Inner Harbor; here viewed directly from Main Street at the top of Water Street across the harbor.

II.181. gardens ran / to the water's / edge . . .

Gardens such as the one alongside the Pearce-Parrot house on Water Street (see note to "when figureheads . . . ," *Maximus* II, 51).

II.181. the Virgin

Our Lady of Good Voyage, on top of Portuguese Hill (see e.g. *Maximus* I, 2 and note). The statue of the Virgin atop the the church is also plainly visible, like Paul Oakley's house on the other side of the harbor, from Main Street at the head of Water Street in Gloucester's business section. The lines of vision northward from that point to the statue and eastward to Oakley's house, form roughly, as the poem indicates, a right angle.

II.181. 90 Middle, the gambrel / which is sliced off . . .

See "the house the street cuts off . . . ," *Maximus* I, 5 and note.

▶II.183. Fort Point section

A note on a manuscript of this section title among the poet's papers indicates all the poems within were written in the spring of 1963. One small exception, however, will be the lower half of the poem on p. 199.

For the location of Fort Point itself, where the poet lived, see note to "The Fort," *Maximus* I, 7.

▶II.184. you drew the space in / reticule . . .

Exact date of writing unknown; the original (or at least an early copy) appears in a notepad among the poet's papers from 1963. Definitely written by August 1963 when read at Vancouver as "epigraph" to this Fort Point section.

II.184. Enyalion

Enyalios, the Cretan war god, whose name appears on the Linear B tablets found at Knossos (see Webster, *From Mycenae to Homer*, p. 105). In Homer, a name or epithet of Ares (*Iliad*, XX.69). He will become a strong presence in the later poems; see esp. the poem beginning "rages / strain / Dogs of Tartarus . . . ," *Maximus* III, 38−40.

Here, Enyalion already contains some of the complexity he later displays more fully: on the one hand he is Mars, on the other Vulcan or Hephaestus. In a note written ca. February 1964 among his papers, Olson has:

> Now spread the iron net
> Enyalion   *Monster of*
>   [actually *Vulcan*,
>
>   to catch Mars (ares
>   and Venus (Aphrodite)
>   at it . . .

while in conversation, June 1968, the poet spoke of the net in this poem as being that by which Hephaestus captured Mars and Venus *in flagrante delicto* (see *Odyysey*, VIII.266−367), although he did not explain how in the poem it is Mars (Enyalion) rather than Hephaestus who is to cast the net. In an early version of *Maximus* III, 38−40, also, Enyalion appears as a hobbled figure like Vulcan, so it is no mere lapse or confusion.

▶II.185. Civic Disaster

Written spring 1963, as mentioned in the poem.

II.185. Ed Bloomberg

Edward T. Bloomberg (b. 1903), manager of the local movie theater and an old acquaintance of the poet's. He had met Olson on Main Street a few weeks earlier, when they had discussed the state of local politics (interview, August 1967).

II.185. Dutchie

"Dutchie" Vegliano, neighbor of Olson's at 16 Fort Square, a house overlooking Watchhouse Point and Gloucester Harbor (see the photograph of him on his porch taken in June 1968 in Charters, *Olson / Melville*, p. [71]—the peach tree is there too, on p. [69], in a back yard at the beginning of the Fort near Commercial Street).

II.185. Sam Novello

Owner of the Ollevon (Novello spelled backwards) Net and Marine Supply Company on the hill (site of the fort described in the next poem) across Olson's backyard. The company's sign and nets, spread out along a fence, were plainly visible from the poet's porch.

II.185. Levasseur's / nursery

Paul A. Levasseur, a neighbor at 53 Fort Square and a tree-climber for Bartlett Tree Experts, a chain of nurseries with a branch on Route 127 in nearby Beverly.

II.185. Nelson's / pharmacy

Formerly at 276 Main Street (since changed owners), across from Ed Bloomberg's North Shore Theatre.

II.185. Nebuchad- / nezzar's tile of the lion / and the bull . . .

The "tile" referred to is possibly the glazed bricks on the pylons of the "Ishtar Gate" built by Nebuchadnezzar (605–562 B.C.), king of Babylon, presenting a pattern of bulls alternating with long-necked "lions" or, more appropriately, dragons, on an aquamarine background.

▶II.186. June 6th, 1963

Written that date in Gloucester.

II.186. the Head and Chariot / of the Maiden ...

See the photograph of the prehistoric bronze ritual vehicle, plate 28 in Piggott, *Dawn of Civilization*, a volume loaned to Olson by poet Gerrit Lansing, then living in Gloucester (conversation with Lansing, August 1967). Also, remarks there by T. G. E. Powell, in his chapter entitled "Barbarian Europe" (p. 339): "Further evidence of wheeled vehicles comes to light in Late Bronze Age graves of the Urnfield culture, so called from the spread of the rites of cremation and urn burial. The cult car above [in the photograph] (8th–7th century BC) was found in a cremation grave at Strettweg, Austria. The dominating female figure and some of her attendants may be forerunners of personalities in later Celtic and Teutonic myths."

II.186. Among the 8 / 24 pounders ...

The battery on Watchhouse Point (later known as Fort Point), installed in 1743 following an appropriation of money by the General Court "for the erection of a suitable breastwork and platform, and for eight mounted twelve-pounders. . . ." (Babson, *History*, p. 307). There would seem to be a discrepancy here between the poem and Babson over the size of the cannons, although it must be that the twelve-pounders of the original fortification had been replaced by larger guns, perhaps when taken over by the federal government (*Maximus* II, 198 and note), since Col. Totten's report (see *Maximus* II, 189 and note) mentions twenty-four pounders.

II.186. the Neck

Watchhouse or Stage Neck. See note to Watchhouse Point, *Maximus* II, 71.

II.186. the Orlandos

Either the house at 67 Commercial Street, where Fort Square begins, home of fishermen named Orlando in 1963 (according to Gloucester city directory), or most likely the Orlando Brothers Fish Company at 42 Commercial Street on the east side of the "neck" leading to the Fort (in either case, Commercial Street is "the road or entrance—*gorge*— / to the Fort").

II.186. the Exterior Slope

See Col. Totten's report, quoted in note to *Maximus* II, 189.

II.187. JOHN WHITE, / of Dorchester . . .

See note to *Maximus* I, 45.

II.187. Hanseatic League

A commercial federation of North German towns from the fourteenth to seventeenth centuries, including such other important trading centers as Bruges, in the heart of "Belgae" territory.

II.187. Bel- / gae

A Celtic people of northern Europe which have given their name to present Belgium; first mentioned by Caesar as forming the third part of Gaul, a territory bordering the Hanse towns.

II.187. "receptacle / for those of religious / purpose . . .

Paraphrase of a description of Roger Conant's purpose in settling Naumkeag, as given in Hubbard's *History of New England*: ". . . secretly conceiving in his mind, that in following times (as since fallen out) it might prove a receptacle for such as, upon the account of religion, would be willing to begin a foreign plantation in this part of the world" (quoted in Babson, *History*, p. 41; also in Rose-Troup, *John White*, p. 53).

II.187. 6 of the / 90 / of the Dorchester Co. / survived into / the New England Company . . .

From Rose-Troup, *John White*, pp. 114−115: "Six members of the old Dorchester Company appear among the subscribers to the new venture . . . ;" while on p. 447 she reports that there are two lists of the members of the Dorchester Company to be found in the Public Records Office, one of ninety names and a list by John White of one hundred and twenty-one (with two repeated). The New England Company (shortened from "the New England Company for a Plantation in Mattachusetts Bay") was formed in 1628 after the failure of the Dorchester Company on Cape Ann following Roger Conant's removal to Naumkeag.

▶II.188. into the hill went into / the hill every Sunday . . .

Exact date of writing not known, but what appears to be the original was written in a notepad from 1963 which contains another poem or fragment based on the bronze figure of the previous poem. It was definitely written by 16 August 1963, when read at Vancouver.

This is a third telling (see also the version on p. 143) of the Algonquin legend originally recounted on *Maximus* II, 22.

▶II.189. the distances / up and down . . .

Written early June 1963. An earlier version entitled "1st Fort poem, Col J G Totten's report," among the poet's papers, was written 4 June 1963, and the manuscript of the present poem is clearly from the same time.

In response to an inquiry concerning Fort Defiance in Gloucester (see *Maximus* II, 192 and note), Olson received a letter from the National Archives and Records Service, Washington, ca. 1959—preserved among his papers— informing him that "There is also a report of the condition of coast defenses made by Col. J. G. Totten on February 25, 1835. A negative photostatic reproduction of the portion of this report dealing with Gloucester can be furnished at a cost of $0.80." Olson promptly sent for the photostat, which is also among his papers. The relevant section of Totten's report is as follows:

> *Fort in Gloucester Harbor.*
>
> This is also a very small work, and is, also, in a very ruinous state. There is room for 10 guns. The wall is quite low, and the exterior slope of the parapet, which had been made nearly vertical, has fallen, in some places, & will require to be reformed throughout. Traverse circles of wood should be placed for the guns;—a new furnace built;—new gates. The two magazines, under the brick quarters, must be thoroughly repaired. A palisading must be carried acro[s]s the gorge;—
>
> The brick quarters require extensive repairs, both within & without: being repaired & barricaded; this building will afford a place of last resort to the garrison. An abatis should enclose the works. 7. 24 p^n guns lie on the terre-pleine. There are 2 rotten Burbuk carriages.

It is odd that Olson should have mis-rendered the date of the report of the poem, since at the top of his photostat he has plainly written, "*1835* [instead of the erroneous 1833] report on coast defenses, by Col J. G. Totten." In any case, the document is another evidence of the extent of Olson's researches into Gloucester history outside of published material.

▶ **II.190. Tantrist / sat saw**

Written June 1963, apparently outside the Sawyer Library in Gloucester (see "in front of the same Library . . . ," *Maximus* II, 196 and note). One early appearance of the poem is on a piece of paper along with notes on the palisading of the Fort (see previous poem); another, inside the back cover of the poet's copy of Jung's *Aion*.

On the Gratwick tape from November of that year, Olson would again speak of himself as a "tantrist," in the sense of being devoted to books, adding: "I mean I wouldn't touch the drugs [he had previously explained that after two successful experiences with psilocybin, he felt no need to continue exploration with drugs] because I'm a Tantrist. I know how books put you on. Like, literally, the book puts you on. The poem puts you on" (*Muthologos*, I, 46). It is a sense he probably derived from Jung's definition of Tantrist as "scholastic" and of *tantra* as a 'book' in *Aion* (the same volume, one might bear in mind, in which Olson wrote one of the original versions of the poem), p. 217n.

In "Poetry and Truth," too, Olson says (*Muthologos*, II, 44): "I suppose in the flux of the present I'm a Tantrist, and care for that order of showing, which as I understand it is text." And John Cech et al. quote him as late as 1969 saying, "I am a Tantrist—that The Word is a book / that life is a book" (*Charles Olson in Connecticut*, p. 13).

II.190. Lingam / of the City / Hall

The Gloucester City Hall on Dale Avenue, just a half block up from the Library, has a square though plainly phallic tower with cupola.

▶ II.191. I stand up on you, Fort Place

Most likely written in June of 1963. The poem appears both on the same manuscript as the one on *Maximus* II, 196–198, which is dated June 1963, as well as in a notebook from the same period including the poems "Why light, and flowers?" (*Maximus* II, 181) and "*The River Map*" (II, 201–202), the former dated May 23rd, the latter June 15th.

▶ II.192. rotundum . . .

Date of writing not known; read at Vancouver on 16 August 1963. The initial word is from Latin *rotunda*, 'round, circular'; commonly, a round building with dome. For those looking at the poems from a Jungian perspective, Jung points out that the *rotundum* is "the round, original form of the Anthropos" (*Archetypes and the Collective Unconscious*, p. 294; near a passage marked by Olson in his copy).

II.192. Fort / defiance / Hill

A map of Gloucester Harbor by John Mason in the Cape Ann Historical Society, which Olson dates on a photograph of it among his papers as having been drawn between 1832 and 1835, shows a fort and its blockhouse on Fort Point bearing the designation "Fort defiance Hill." It is the hill in back of the poet's house.

Also among Olson's papers is a photostat of a letter from a Major C. E. Blunt to General R. Delafield, Chief Engineer in Washington, dated 15 January 1866, which speak of a "Fort Defiance" overlooking Gloucester Harbor. The photostat was made available through the National Archives and Records Service and was sent along with another map of Gloucester Harbor drawn for the Chief of Engineers, 17 January 1866 (both sent to Olson in 1959). On this map, too, is shown a "Fort Defiance" on Fort Point.

▶II.193. Or Lindsay / roared upon the town . . .

Exact date of writing not known, but probably June 1963 (it was read at Vancouver that August).

The story concerns a British attack on Gloucester in 1775 under a Captain Lindsay in his sloop-of-war, *Falcon*. Although the story appears in a number of places, Olson's source is the fullest account, that of Babson in his *History*, pp. 393–396, too lengthy to reproduce here. It should be pointed out, however, that one of the more interesting words in the poem, the ship being "warped" away (p. 195)—which means to move a vessel by hauling on a line, or warp, attached to some fixed object as a buoy—appears exclusively in Babson, p. 396: ". . . the next day, to the great joy of the inhabitants, the ship was warped out of the harbor, and steered out to sea." Only Olson's figure of twenty-eight captured British marines is not in Babson (or any other account). The historian says thirty-five men were captured, several of which were wounded, one so severely that he died soon after. Twenty-four of these prisoners were sent to Cambridge to be interred, the rest had been impressed American seamen and were released to their various homes.

II.193. Pavilion Beach

On Fort Point (see *Maximus* II, 70 and note).

II.193. Pearce's Wharf

Later known as Central Wharf, "located roughly halfway between the foot of what is now Hancock Street and Duncan Street" (Copeland and Rogers, *Saga of Cape Ann*, p. 58). There, according to Babson, *History*, p. 268, David Pearce (see poem following) "had a distillery, oil-works, and stores for merchandise. At the head of the wharf, on Front Street, he built a large house, in which he resided till his failure. . . ."

II.193. 5 Lb Island

See *Maximus* I, 150 and note.

II.193. the Unitarian / Church

On Middle Street, Gloucester; built in 1738, occupying the site of the later one mentioned on *Maximus* I, 5.

II.194. Vincent's Cove

See *Maximus* I, 151 and note.

II.194. one of them / had such a short horn . . .

Babson's report is more direct (*History*, p. 395): "The attempt to set the town on fire was a very unfortunate exploit for the enemy: for, in addition to the capture of those who were engaged in it, the boatswain of the ship, in applying fire to the combustible matter prepared, carelessly allowed it to reach the powder-horn he was holding; which caused it to explode, and occasioned the loss of his hand."

▶**II.196.   13 vessels, and David Pearce's / Corporal Trim . . .**

Written June 1963, as mentioned late in the poem. Something of the historical background on which the poem is based is supplied by Pringle, *History of Gloucester*, pp. 84–85, the poet's apparent source:

> France and the United States, at the close of the Revolution, made a treaty of alliance, whereby the latter was to assist the former in defending her West Indian possessions. Between 1790 and 1800, France and England were at war, and England captured those islands. Instead of assisting France, our government, in 1794, entered into a commercial treaty with Great Britain [Jay's Treaty]. This greatly incensed the French. . . . Accordingly she entered upon a course of reprisals, and French privateers began to prey upon American shipping. Gloucester suffered from this to quite an extent, seventeen ships [not "13 vessels" as Olson says], valued with cargoes at $175,000, being taken. In 1798, the relations between the American and French governments became strained in consequence, and when hostilities seemed imminent, fifty-two men of Cape Ann shipped on board the sloop of war "Herald," to participate in what they thought to be certain war. Happily, another conflict was averted. The French spoilation claims arose from these depredations, inflicted prior to September 30, 1800. Demand was made by the United States on France for indemnification, but the latter government urged as a set off, broken faith in violating the treaty of alliance. This was acknowledged by the United States, and it was agreed on our part, to assume the payment of all claims arising from French depredations, and the matter was thus settled. Claimants have frequently petitioned Congress for reimbursement. Bills to this effect passed during the administrations of Polk and Pierce, but were vetoed. Efforts are being made at the present time by the heirs of original claimants, for the allowance of these sums so long unpaid which have been acknowledged as valid, settlement having been made in a few cases, and it is probable that in the course of time, the government will discharge all its obligations in this respect. During the warfare the French cruisers destroyed over 1500 American merchantmen with cargoes. [Gloucester, then, was hardly "possibly the sole place / which did suffer damages / from the French . . ."]

> Among the ships taken was one owned by David Pearce, the cargo of which, as entered at the Gloucester custom house, was valued at $19,000. He, at this time, was considered worth nearly $300,000, an enormous fortune for the times. This proved to be the beginning of a series of reverses. Shortly after, one of his ships, valued at $10,000, was lost in the Indian Ocean. Misfortunes came thick and fast, reducing him from affluence to poverty, in which condition his last days were passed.

The section is repeatedly marked in Olson's copy, and in the margin on top of p. 85 he has written: "17 ships lossed [sic], Gl., to French—in Jefferson's War—value 175,000$—though it is actually unfair and inaccurate to describe the war as "Jefferson's," since Jefferson was not to become President of the United States until 1801. He was only vice-president under Adams from 1797 to 1801, and before that, at the time of Jay's Treaty, had been in retirement at his Monticello estate. Moreover, as a republican Jefferson in fact had favored good relations with republican France; it was his Federalist opponents, friendly to England, and the persistence of both France and England in denying America's neutrality that led almost to outright hostilities. If it was anybody's "private war," it would have to be Hamilton's. It would be best to read that passage in the poem as simply an "undeclared war," which is more accurate.

David Pearce (ca. 1736–1818), whose vessel was among those lost, was one of the most prosperous merchants of Gloucester at the time. Babson in his *History*, p. 267n., says that "The amount of Mr. Pearce's property was once estimated by himself at three hundred thousand dollars; but his brother, the late Col. William Pearce, never considered him worth more than two hundred thousand. If that was its value, it must have been the largest estate ever accumulated in Gloucester." At his wharf (see preceding poem), according to Copeland and Rogers, *Saga of Cape Ann*, p. 58, David Pearce "had a distillery where cargoes of Surinam molasses were landed and converted into rum. He also had an oil works, for refining whale and fish oil, and warehouses for storing hogsheads of sugar, molasses, cocoa, coffee, and

other merchandise, large quantities of which were trans-
shipped from Gloucester by freighter to Boston."

There is a rather full notice of Pearce in Babson's *History*,
pp. 267–268, although it does not report that he "went
broke" four times, as Olson says further on in the poem. And
neither Babson nor Pringle provide the identity of the ship
lost by Pearce to the French as the "Corporal Trim" (Pringle
mentions the brig "Corporal Trim" as being owned by Fitz
Sargent, p. 93), so that Olson's source for this information is
not known.

II.196. Federalism

Morison's summarization in a chapter titled "Federalism
and Neutral Trade" in his *Maritime History of Massachusetts*,
p. 160, is appropriate: "New England Federalism believed
that the main object of government was to protect property,
especially commercial and shipping property; and it supported nationalism or states' rights according as the federal
government protected or neglected these interests of maritime New England."

II.196. Stars / and Bars

The flag of the Southern states during the American Civil
War.

II.196. Thomas Pinckney

(1750–1828), statesman and diplomat from South Carolina. He was minister to Great Britain at the time of Jay's
Treaty, in 1796 the Federalist candidate for vice-president,
and in 1797–1801 a Federalist representative in Congress.

II.196. Pickering of Salem

Thomas Pickering, prominent member of the Essex Junto
(see *Maximus* I, 74 and notes) and the "kept politician of New
England Federalism," its "mouthpiece" in Congress (in the
words of Morison, *Maritime History*, pp. 160, 167).

II.196. in front of the same Library / out of which I regarded City Hall / three days ago

See the previous poem beginning "Tantrist / sat saw . . ." (*Maximus* II, 190). The Sawyer Library is on the corner of Middle Street and Dale Avenue, just down the street from the Gloucester City Hall.

II.196. the Society of Mercy

A charitable organization like the English Legion of Mercy, founded in London in the 1890's, is intended, or more likely a religious order devoted to charity like the Roman Catholic Sisters of Mercy founded in 1827.

II.196. the maritime law of / port of proposed sale . . .

Olson had made the following notation at the top of p. 97 in his copy of Capt. Sylvanus Smith's *Fisheries of Cape Ann*: "who lost by the law of deviation (ins[urance] not cover them if supercargo changed port of sale fr port of destination / cf A M Brooks conversation Dec/57."

II.197. Madagascar

Large island off the southeastern coast of Africa in the Indian Ocean; formerly a French colony, now the independent republic of Malagasy.

II.197. until Universalism occurred / in Gloucester

The first Universalist church in America was founded at Gloucester in 1779 by John Murray as the Independent Christian Society, which rejected the standard Calvinistic doctrine that sin can only be expiated by eternal punishment, offering instead a belief in a final, universal salvation. For a full account see Eddy, *Universalism in Gloucester*; also, Babson, *History*, pp. 428—439, and Copeland and Rogers, *Saga of Cape Ann*, pp. 48—52.

II.197. the / Tyrian Lodge

A Masonic lodge established in Gloucester in 1770. For details of its formation, see Pringle, *History of Gloucester*, pp. 328–329. Among the signers of its charter were Joseph Warren and Paul Revere, both prominent in the early stages of the American Revolution. See Tibbetts, *Story of Gloucester*, pp. 15–16:

> Nor must I forget to tell you at this time of the institution in March, 1770, of Tyrian Lodge of Masons, one of the oldest Masonic lodges in the State, whose charter, precious document that it is, bears the signatures of General Joseph Warren, who fell five years later at Bunker Hill and of Paul Revere, whose early morning ride on the nineteenth of April, 1775, will go ringing down the ages as long as pluck and daring make the heart beat quicker at the recital of their deeds. . . . The history of this Lodge of Masons for now a century and a half is singularly interwoven with the best in the life of this town. Strange indeed that in 1770 this Lodge was instituted mostly by the men who the year before had learned of the faith of Universalism, whose corner stone rests upon the Fatherhood of God and the Brotherhood of Man, and who four years later were to become the first Universalist Society in the world. Strange, did I say?

II.197. the Sons of Liberty

Revolutionary groups that arose in 1765 to oppose the Stamp Tax; they led to the formation of the more coordinated Committees of Correspondence a few years later (see next note). Although neither Paul Revere nor Joseph Warren, who belonged to the Tyrian Lodge, seem to actually have been members of the Sons of Liberty, both were active among other pre-revolutionary groups closely related to the Sons of Liberty (Warren, e.g., helped organize with Samuel Adams resistance to the Stamp Tax, and Revere, who participated in the Boston Tea Party, rode by horseback to New York in the middle of winter in 1773 to report to the Sons of Liberty on the event.)

II.197. The Committee of Correspondence . . . was on board Mr. Lindsay's ship . . .

Babson has the Committee of Safety, which was an extension of the slightly earlier Committees of Correspondence: "On the 8th of August, [Lindsay] fell in with two schooners from the West Indies, bound to Salem; and, having made a prize of one, chased the other into this harbor. She was run ashore on the flats between Pearce's Wharf and Five-pound Island; and Lindsay, who had followed her as far as he safely could, came to anchor, and prepared to take possession of her where she lay. Before attempting this, however, he sent in a boat, with a flag; and the Committee of Safety went on board of his ship, where they were detained till they promised to release the schooner" (*History*, pp. 393–394). Earlier, p. 388, Babson reports that a Committee of Safety had been formed in Gloucester at the outbreak of the Revolution in April of 1775, consisting of "thirty-one of the most prominent and respectable citizens."

The Committee of Correspondence was a pre-revolutionary organization created in 1772 at a Boston town meeting to maintain communications with other towns and colonies. According to Morgan, *Birth of the Republic*, p. 57, in a passage marked by Olson, "the business of the committee was to prepare a statement of colonial rights, list violations (past, present, and future), communicate these to other towns, and invite similar statements from similar committees in return. Boston was proposing, in effect, a revival of the local Sons of Liberty who had organized in 1765 to proclaim their rights and to nullify the Stamp Act. But where the Sons of Liberty had been extralegal, the committees of correspondence would have the official blessing of the town meetings."

For Lindsay, see the previous poem and notes.

II.197. Fort Beach

See Pavilion Beach in previous poem, and note.

II.197. Al'Arabi's / circumvallum

Ibn al'Arabi (1165–1240), Arabic mystic and author of *Meccan Revelations*, a general text of Sufic beliefs and doctrines. See the report of his *circumambulatio* of the Ka'ba at Mecca in Meier, "The Mystery of the Ka'ba," esp. pp. 155–156, where it is told how he "journeyed in the year 1201/2 from his native Spain to Mecca and there, while walking around the Ka'ba, the famous cubical temple, had the crucial experience of his life." This was a mystical experience in which he meets "none other than himself . . . his alter ego, his transcendent self, the 'true I,' as a fourteenth-century mystic puts it. . . ."

Husaini, *Ibn al 'Arabi*, is somewhat more explicit (pp. 20–21):

> Once, while circumambulating the Ka'ba, he met a celestial spirit in the form of a youth engaged in the same holy rite, who showed him the living esoteric temple which is concealed under the lifeless exterior, just as the eternal substance of Divine ideas is hidden by the veils of popular religion. These veils the lofty mind must penetrate to reach the splendour within and partake of the Divine character and behold what no mortal eye can endure to look upon.
>
> Ibn al 'Arabi swooned at once. When he recovered, he was directed to contemplate the visionary form and to write down the mysteries that it might unveil to his gaze. Then the youth entered the Ka'ba with Ibn al 'Arabi and resuming his spiritual aspect appeared to him on a three-legged steed. The youth then breathed into the breast of Ibn al 'Arabi the knowledge of all things and once more bade him describe the heavenly form in which all mysteries are enshrined.
>
> Such is the reputed origin of the "Meccan Revelations" of which the greater portion was written in that town itself. . . .

II.197. Mr Oppen

George Oppen (b. 1908), American poet. Olson had just read an essay by him in the summer 1963 issue of *Kulchur* entitled "The Mind's Own Place," dealing with the responsibility of a poet to the political issues of his time, and had written a response in the form of a letter to the editor of the magazine (of which Olson was himself a contributing editor), though it was never sent. In it, he criticizes Oppen for assuming a position which, he says, is "Jeffersonian," a "closed system . . . in which patriotism—or the political—stays a fixed term, as the history does." Olson, on the other hand, insists "that you may have a politics when you also have epistemology and theology in the curriculum," and, consequently, that "history must go, and all analogy as well as itself as a special analogy, with it."

Oppen had written, "It is possible to find a metaphor for anything, an analogue . . ." (p. 3), and, "Alice wandered from her governess; Dorothy of Oz ran too late for the storm cellar and was caught in a Kansas cyclone. Together and contrastingly they dawned on our infant minds, and may have contributed to the aesthetic, if not social sentiment which went in search of the common, the common experience, the life of the common man. Or it may be, more simply, that a more open society made possible the literary career of the obviously non-aristocratic spokesman who, once he tired of Invocation to Someone Else's Muse, *had* to make his own poetry" (p. 6).

Both points of view are far too complex to adequately summarize here, and Olson's letter is especially aswirl.

Oppen had written a review of *The Distances* and *Maximus From Dogtown—I* for *Poetry* magazine in August 1962—generally favorable but with a few distinct reservations, most notably what he found to be an overriding presence of Pound in the poems—which would have given Olson further reason to take an interest in Oppen's essay. Oppen said in his review, "to encounter Olson's work, in spite of the currency of the phrase, is simply not an encounter with a new poetry." Olson had written to William Bronk six months before the present poem, 21 December 1962, in response to a query from him: "I do know Oppen, and though some of my friends thought his review of *The Distances* and *Maximus from Dogtown* . . . was the old business of measuring me by

Pound, and I thought myself he raced his motor on *Maximus from Dogtown*, I thought his picking "The Satyrs" for a voice which was peculiarly my own, true enough. (I haven't yet seen his poems at all . . ."

II.197. the heavens above / do declare / the handiwork / of the orbits

From Psalm 19.

II.198. the War of the World

Judging from repeated references in notes among the poet's papers, as well as from "The Secret of the Black Chrysanthemum" (*OLSON* 3, p. 66), this is Ragnarok, the war at the end of the world, in which Enyalion loses his hand to Fenris the wolf (see *Maximus* III, 33–34 and notes); also, perhaps, "the Civilized War" between Zeus and the Titans at the beginnings of creation (*Maximus* II, 171). It is, in other words, the war within creation itself. See also *Maximus* III, 99.

II.198. Fort Point / 1st Federally / and effectively fortified / 1794–1798

The fort which gave Fort Point its name (see esp. *Maximus* II, 186 and note) had been ceded to the Federal Government in 1794 (Garland, *Gloucester Guide*, p. 126).

II.198. The total price / lost by the city . . . $200,000

Pringle says the loss was only $175,000 (see initial note). Olson may have sought out the original documents of the case.

▶II.199. The lap / of the one of the two women . . .

The original version of the first section of the poem was written on the back of an envelope from the poet LeRoi Jones, postmarked 12 June 1963, and was read by itself at

Vancouver on 16 August 1963 and again at Buffalo on 4 October 1963 (recording at Lockwood Library). The second section was added later, written directly on a typescript of the first half possibly by late 1964, the date mentioned in that part of the poem (Olson's daughter visited him in Gloucester that Thanksgiving), although among notes to himself concerning the poem the poet has "1965?" In that case, it would have to have been by February 1965, when a manuscript was sent to Eli Wilentz for the proposed Jargon/ Corinth edition.

In the original manuscript of the first section there is an earlier opening, which makes clear that the two women referred to are the goddess Isis and her sister Nepthys: "The lap / of Isis, / and Nepthys the queen / of the underground / house." See the previous poem, *Maximus* II, 147, in which the two were called upon "to turn around, and be of some help." The poet's source here again is Frankfort, *Kingship and the Gods*, pp. 182–183: "The sister and wife of Osiris was Isis, the deified thrown [directly below this, Olson adds in the margin of his copy: "her 'lap' "] . . . She was the loving mother of Horus and the faithful companion and supporter of Osiris. Nephthys' name means 'Lady of the House,' and she was conceived as the spouse of Seth. But in mythology she appears almost exclusively in connection with Osiris, whom she and Isis succor and bewail."

II.199. underground house / wealth (money) . . .

Attributes of Pluto, Greek god of the underworld, whose name means 'wealth.'

II.199. my own house . . . at / Stage Fort Avenue

The cottage at 2 Stage Fort Avenue above Stage Fort Park, rented by the poet's parents for summers during his youth.

▶II.200. a Contract Entered Into . . .

Exact date of writing not known; definitely by 16 August 1963, when read at Vancouver.

The contract for mutual insurance, signed in 1774 by fifteen Gloucester shipowners including Benjamin Ellery (see *Maximus* II, 34 and note), is printed in Babson, *Notes and Additions*, II, 141–143:

> Whereas, for the better carrying on our fishing voyages and sustaining the losses that may happen therein. We whose names are hereunto subscribed, have agreed to make a common stock of our vessels, so that those persons that shall happen to lose any vessel during the term hereafter agreed on, shall be reimbursed, and by the owners of those vessels that shall not be lost, the whole of what such vessel shall be estimated at when put into the stock, except such a proportion as said vessel shall bear towards the whole of said stock . . . In witness of all which, each of the parties aforesaid have here to set down each of the vessels that he hath put in stock as aforesaid, and the real and estimated value thereof; and hereunto set his hand and seal this Sixth day of April, Anno Domini One Thousand Seven Hundred & Seventy-Four. . . .

In the list of vessels' names that follows, Benjamin Ellery is given as owner of the schooners *Dolphin* and *Britain* (elsewhere *Britannia*).

▶ **II.201. The River Map and we're done**

Manuscript dated "June 15th [1963—from fall 1959." "The 'River Map' is one of the legendary foundations of the *I Ching*, which in its present form derives partly from the twelfth century B.C. According to legend, a dragon dredged the magical signs of the 'River Map' from a river. On it the sages discovered the drawing, and in the drawing the laws of the world-order" (Jung, *Archetypes and the Collective Unconscious*, p. 359, marked in the poet's copy).

Olson's own "River Map," in which to find "the laws of world-order" and on which the poem is more literally based, is a "Plan of Squam River from the Cut to the Light House," prepared in August of 1822 by William Saville for the Canal Corporation mentioned later in the poem (Massachusetts Archives Maps and Plans No. 1797), a photostat of which is among the poet's papers.

Saville (1770–1853), who Babson describes as a "well-known citizen" of Gloucester, "was a schoolmaster in early life; next, a trader; and finally, for about twenty years, town clerk" (*History*, pp. 284–285).

II.201. the accuracy of his drawing of the Fort

Not on the same "River Map" or plan of Squam River from 1822, but Saville's "Plan of the Harbour of Gloucester from a Scale of 50 Rods to an inch May 1813" (Massachusetts Archives Maps and Plans No. 1756), a photostat of which is also among the poet's papers.

The map is unsigned but has been identified as that of William Saville's through a comparison of the handwriting with that of the signed map of 1822 (see *Maximus* III, 100; also III, 85).

II.201. wreck here flats Old Bass Rock channel . . .

On Saville's "Plan of Squam River." "Bass Rock," for instance, appears on the map approximately midway up the Annisquam, near what is now Thurston Point.

II.201. Annisquam / Harbor

At the mouth of the Annisquam just inside Ipswich Bay, at the community of Annisquam.

II.201. Obadiah Bruen's / Island

See *Maximus* II, 16 and note.

II.201. granitite / base

See "The River—I," *Maximus* II, 16 and notes.

II.201. Rocky Hill

On Saville's map. It appears on the east side of the Annisquam towards the Cut, where the Boston and Maine railroad bridge now is.

II.201. Castle Rock

The designation is not to be found on Saville's map or any other the author has consulted. There is only a cluster of three small rocks on the "Plan of Squam River," in the salt marsh west of the river and near a plank bridge over the Cut.

II.201. a Table / Rock / like Tablet

See note to Tablet Rock, "the rock I know by my belly and torn nails," *Maximus* I, 48.

II.201. a Canal Corporation

The Gloucester Canal Corporation was formed in February 1882 to finance the reconstruction of the Cut after storms and tides had filled it with sand over the years, in order that it might be reopened to navigation. See Babson, *History*, pp. 9—10; also, Copeland and Rogers, *Saga of Cape Ann*, p. 178. It was for this project that Saville drew his "Plan of Squam River" in August of that year.

II.201. kun

Trigram from the *I Ching*, or Chinese "Book of Changes," meaning 'earth,' the receptive, the feminine which receives "into itself the creative power of heaven" (Jung, *Archetypes and the Collective Unconscious*, p. 359).

II.201. Mill / Stream

Mill River, an inlet of the Annisquam (see *Maximus* I, 151 and note).

II.202. Alexander Baker's / goldenrod / field

See *Maximus* II, 59ff. and note to Baker there. Also *Maximus* II, 126.

II.202. specularia

The wild flower *Speculiaria speculum,* known as Venus's Looking Glass.

II.202. Sargents houses

See *Maximus* II, 126 and note.

II.202. Apple Row

See *Maximus* I, 151 and note.

II.202. a salt Oceana

Olson's designation for the tide-filled river and flooded marshes near Done Fudging (q.v.), after Oceana Pond, an early name for the fresh-water Niles Pond on Eastern Point. See also the later poem, "OCEANIA . . . ," *Maximus* III, 155–161.

II.202. Bonds Hill

See *Maximus* I, 43 and note.

II.202. the Diorite

See *Maximus* II, 16 and notes.

II.202. old hulk   Rocky Marsh

These appear on Saville's map. The "old hulk" is in the river off Wheeler's Point, the "Rocky Marsh" is near Goose Cove.

▶II.203. I set out now / in a box upon the sea

Exact date of writing not known; not read as part of the manuscript of *Maximus IV, V, VI* at Vancouver in August 1963. The lines appear to have been originally the final ones

of a longer holograph poem from ca. 1962 or 1963 among
the poet's papers, which begins:

> I navigate now without authority. Turn, great sun,
>   your disc upon me
> I must cut myself adrift, cut off
> my bull's horns, go where I have refund
> be not the special son of my mother,
> the evidence of my father, the pleasure
> that he had a son, go out into the abandonment
> I have so carefully neglected . . .

The opening and closing lines of this longer poem were
copied out again by the poet, at or around the same time
the poem was composed. They are written in the same red
ochre pencil as the longer poem in the flyleaf of Olson's copy
of Pritchard, *Ancient Near Eastern Texts:*

> I navigate now without authority. Turn, great sun,
>   your disc upon me
> I set out now
> in a box upon the sea

There are many mythological parallels to the hero's "box"
or ark, among them Odysseus' and Herakles-Melkaart's raft
and Osiris' and Perseus' own boxes in which they were cast
adrift—all of which figures appear at one time or another
throughout the poems. Even the coffin on which Melville's
Ishmael floats to salvation is a relation. See esp. Rank's list
in his *Birth and Death of the Hero*, p. 73 and n. Indeed,
markings in the same distinctive red pencil used for the
original longer poem as well as in Pritchard, occur in Olson's
copy of Rank, indicating he was using that text at the time
the poem was written.

Notes to
The Maximus Poems:
Volume Three, 1975
(*Maximus* III)

▶ **III.9. having descried the nation . . .**

Written in June 1963, and mentioned at the Beloit lectures in 1968 as the intended first poem of the third volume ("Poetry and Truth," *Muthologos*, II, 8). What is probably the original version occurs on a portion of endpapers torn from the poet's copy of Lewis, *Elementary Latin Dictionary* (1915 ed.), where it was apparently written by Olson (as notes on the same page indicate) while looking up *castrum*, which is part of the root of Gloucester (Caer Glow, Gleawe-castre, Gleucestre). Further, in his copy of the dictionary, Olson has at *specula*, meaning 'a look-out, watch-tower' (which he has underlined), the words "watch house point" added in the margin (p. 799). Also, under *speculor*, one of its meanings—'having descried'—is similarly underlined (p. 780).

These three lines were typed out as the opening section of a four-part poem from early 1963, the other sections of which were also originally on endpapers from Lewis' *Latin Dictionary* (a version of the next poem in the present volume was the closing portion). They were copied out again, separately, on other occasions—for example, at the end of the following note written in 1964 after the death of the poet's wife, which provides a definite date for the poem: "in *gloom* on Watchhouse Point / (cf June 1963 for Bet!)" They were again dated "June (Gloucester) 1963" when copied out amid notes from 26 November 1969 on p. 51 of the poet's copy of Piggott, *The Druids*.

For a hint of what it might mean to "write a Republic," see the following passage from a letter Olson wrote to Ralph Maud, ca. August 1966: ". . . that a poet, or a man who wld in fact write a republic [still so far as I can 'hear,' the real word for politics—res politius populus puberte public [the contrast *is* Aristotle, isn't it—his 'Politics'?!]"

For Watchhouse Point itself, see note to *Maximus* II, 71. See also the poems later in this volume, "Watchhouse / Point: to descry / anew" (III, 25), "*Added to / making a Republic / in gloom" (III, 190), and the closing lines of the next to last poem: "the inititation / of another kind of nation" (III, 228).

▶ **III.10. Said Mrs Tarantino, . . .**

A reconstruction of a poem originally written ca. June 1963; the final section of a four-part poem of which the preceding "having descried the nation . . ." was the opening portion. The typed manuscript, on cheap yellow paper, had deteriorated by the time the poet was ready to make use of it, and was pasted by Olson on another sheet while a reconstruction was attempted, apparently in February 1964 (judging from a note on the cover of his notebook "Started Sunday June 22nd [1969]"; another attempt at restoring the poem appears verso *Niagara Frontier Review* stationery), yielding this somewhat different version. The original manuscript, written like the preceding poem on the endpapers of the poet's copy of Lewis' *Elementary Latin Dictionary*, apparently had been misplaced by the poet (thus not available for his reconstruction attempt), as a note added to it reads: "found Tues. Sept. 10 1964."

For the Tarantinos of Fort Square, see *Maximus* II, 177 (written on the same endpapers from Lewis) and note.

▶ **III.11. Bona Dea (Athena / Polais) . . .**

This and the next three poems were written together on an envelope postmarked Boston, 23 March 1963, and mailed to Olson at Gloucester. On a xerox of the published poems, Olson has: "1963   written spring—April (?)."

Bona Dea, "the good goddess," was a Roman deity of fruitfulness, both of the earth and of women. Athena Polais (i.e. Polias, the error is corrected in the original manuscript), was the Greek goddess in her role as protectress of the city (the *polis*, same root as "polity"), most notably of Athens, and as such had a shrine in the Erechtheum (Pausanias I.26.6−I.27.1). There is no traditional connection between her and the Bona Dea.

III.11. The Big False Humanism . . .

See also Olson's attacks on humanism in "Human Universe" and, especially appropriate for this poem, *Letters for*

Origin, p. 127, where he writes Corman that "certain New Englanders have exposed the local . . . by demonstrating that the particular is a syntax which is universal, and that it can not be discovered except locally, in the sense that any humanism *is* as well place as it is the person, that another of Socrates' crimes (who was improperly punished) was, that he did give polis its death blow when he cried, Be, a Citoyen, du Monde, that just this again is one of the Greek things which we late citizens of Boston & environs . . . have shattered. . . ."

III.11. O'Connell's

O'Connell's Variety Store, proprietor John B. O'Connell, at 89 Washington Street (corner of Prospect Street), Gloucester.

▶III.12. The last man except conceivably / the Soviets . . .

Written late March or April 1963 (see note to previous poem).

III.12. Mao when he was / living in the Yenan cave community

Mao Tse-tung (1893−1976), leader of the People's Republic of China, directed the struggle against the forces of Chiang Kai-shek from the village of Yenang in the mountainous region of northern Shensi province from the end of the Long March in 1936 until his triumphant entrance into Peking in 1947. The caves in which Mao and his supporters lived are preserved as a national monument.

III.12. Richlieu

As the poet himself writes in a note on a xerox of the poem as published in *Trobar*: "In *fact* its Louis the 14th & Count Frontenac—& 1689 . . . Richelieu *was dead, 1642.*" For Cardinal Richelieu, see also *Maximus* II, 25 and note; for Frontenac, who actually masterminded the attacks on the English settlements, see *Maximus* II, 63 and note.

III.12. three attack-lines / of French and Indians . . .

For the attacks on Salmon Falls and Fort Loyall (Portland), see especially Parkman, *Count Frontenac and New France Under Louis XIV*, chapter XI, entitled "The Three War-Parties" (marked in Olson's copy). Also Hull, *Seige and Capture of Fort Loyall*, pp. 50ff.

Parkman writes that Frontenac "formed three war-parties of picked men, one at Montreal, one at Three Rivers, and one at Quebec; the first to strike at Albany, the second at the border settlements of New Hampshire, and the third at those of Maine" (pp. 208–209). He describes the bitterness of the winter, mentioning the frozen St. Lawrence River and the frozen Lake Champlain, encountered by Frontenac's first band as it advanced to massacre Schenectady, N.Y. There is no mention at all of White River, which is southeast of Lake Champlain in Vermont, in either Parkman or Hull. (Olson's original manuscript has "East Fork" of White River rather than "West Branch.") Frontenac's next attack was against the English settlement at Salmon Falls on the river of that name which forms the lower boundary between Maine and New Hampshire before flowing into the Atlantic at Portsmouth Harbor. The final attack was against Fort Loyall, where George Ingersoll, formerly of Gloucester, was the "chief military officer."

III.12. the Main St Gloucestermen . . .

For Gloucester settlers at Portland (known earlier as Casco and Falmouth), Maine, including George Ingersoll, see *Maximus* II, 24–25 and notes.

▶III.13. I believe in God / as fully physical . . .

Written late March or April 1963 (see note to *Maximus* III, 11).

III.13. Prêdmost

A village in central Moravia in Czechoslovakia, site of paleolithic remains such as the drawing of a woman scratched on ivory, reproduced as figure 4 in Neumann, *Great Mother*. Neumann's observations on p. 105 concerning this drawing may have a bearing on the poem. He has been discussing the more "sensuous" figures of mother goddesses and continues:

> With these figures contrast the "abstract" representation in which we discern an emphasis on the transformative character. The earliest example of this type is probably the Předmost scratched drawing of a female figure. While the elementary character makes for sculpture, the abstracting expression of the transformative character tends toward an ornamental design closely related to the tattooing and body painting whose purpose it is to transform and spiritualize the body.

A note by Olson on his xerox of the poem as published in *Trobar* corrects the erroneous accent: "actually Předmost."

▶ **III.14. I told the woman / about the spring . . .**

Written at the same time and on the same envelope as the previous three poems. An identification of the woman is possible, surprisingly, from remarks made by Olson on the Gratwick tape (along with still another poem written on that envelope), as Ilse or Elsa von Eckartsberg, who had been visiting Gloucester along with Timothy Leary and other members of the International Federation for Internal Freedom to consider a site for their research center (see "Under the Mushroom," *Muthologos*, I, 27 and note to "the House of the Rite" later in that discussion.) The spring referred to is evident, e.g., on U.S. Coast and Geodetic Survey map 233, "Gloucester Harbor and Annisquam River."

III.14. Freshwater / Cove

Between Stage Head and Dolliver Neck (see *Maximus* I, 10 and note).

III.14. Dolliver Neck

On the west side of Gloucester Harbor, just south of Freshwater Cove; site of a U.S. Coast Guard Station.

▶ **III.15. Main Street / is deserted . . .**

Written in the spring of 1963 (the original was found in an envelope among the poet's papers dated as such). Holograph manuscript only, beginning with a page 3, so that two earlier pages were apparently lost.

III.15. Stage Fort Park / where the Merrimac / once emptied . . .

See also *Maximus* II, 151 and note.

III.15. the Polls

See "the Poles," *Maximus* II, 16 and note.

III.15. more versant / on the western side . . .

From Shaler, "Geology of Cape Ann," pp. 548–549: "As a whole the kame deposits of Cape Ann form an imperfect fringe, extending from Andrews Point westward as far as Annisquam up to the part of the island which lies next to that inlet and thence to Eastern Point. . . . Deposits of this nature are, however, distinctly more abundant on the western versant of the island than on the eastern."

III.15. several of these areas / on Dogtown Commons . . . during the period / in which this district / was inhabited . . .

From Shaler, p. 549 (previously quoted in *Maximus* II, 149).

III.16. Great Hill

Elizabeth Day of Gloucester writes in a letter to the author, 29 September 1972: "Great Hill is the rise one climbs on the way to Rockport center, just beyond the Babson cooper shop museum. The rise is long and gentle but was considered too severe for the first road which wound around the hill, and when the railroad was built the company bought the road and built the wagon and foot road over the hill."

The designation appears as early as John Mason's "Map of Gloucester, Cape Ann," drawn in 1831.

III.16. the cellar / of Widow Day's / kame

The widow Jane Day, known also as "Granny" Day, lived on the northeast end of Dogtown Road. Her cellar hole is identified by the number 20 carved in a boulder at the site (correspondingly charted on Roger Babson's map of Dogtown in Babson and Saville, *Cape Ann Tourist's Guide*, pp. 36–37).

III.16. These high-lying / benches of drift material / where subglacial streams emerged . . .

From Shaler, p. 549 (quoted earlier in *Maximus* II, 149).

III.16. the paths of water green and rich / under the ice . . .

See Shaler, p. 548, quoted in note to *Maximus* II, 148; also *Maximus* II, 149 and 151.

III.17. the diorite / is included in the granitite . . .

Shaler, p. 607: "In several places, notably on the road to Coffin's Beach, and in the vicinity of Bond's Hill, on the west side of Squam River opposite the city of Gloucester, the diorite is in such a position as to indicate that it is included in the granitite. Owing to the abundance of drift, this point in any of these localities can not be definitely settled. The first impression was that we had here a great dike of diorite cutting the granitite; but every indication in the field points to the opposite conclusion, namely, that the granitite has burst up around this diorite, leaving it as an included mass."

III.17. the power in the air / is prana

Prana in Sanskrit is the life-giving 'breath,' the 'vital air.' Wilhelm and Jung, specifically, speak of "the power (air, *prana*)" in *The Secret of the Golden Flower*, p. 23.

III.17. the ice, / on top of the Poles, / on the throne ...

The Poles here are not only the Poles, or Polls, of Dogtown (*Maximus* II, 16 and note), but the North Pole, where the Bulgar is (see *Maximus* III, 35 and 44 and notes).

III.17. the plagioclase

Mentioned by Shaler (p. 606) as being part of the composition of the diorite in the area of the Annisquam River.

▶**III.18. Imbued / with the light ...**

Probably written originally in late December 1962, as different versions were found in a notepad from that time among the poet's papers. Other versions, including the present one—which thus represents a typical or compromise version—were found in another notepad, this time from late January 1963, where it appears on the same page as the poem following (the date 26 January appears elsewhere in the pad, while the page immediately following has the opening lines of the poem on *Maximus* II, 147, which can be dated 26 January 1963). The same poem was copied out on later occasions in slightly different arrangements, such as the one from 1966 on *Maximus* III, 178, and thus was a dominant image for the poet throughout these last years. See also the deathbed "Secret of the Black Chrysanthemum, *OLSON* 3, p. 64.

For the image itself, see *The Secret of the Golden Flower*, Wilhelm trans., p. 23 (marked in Olson's copy), though rather than the source, the text is probably the confirmation of an experience:

> Master Lu Tzu said: That which exists through itself is called Meaning (*Tao*). Meaning has neither name nor force. It is the one essence, the primordial spirit. Essence and life cannot be seen. It is contained in the Light of Heaven. The Light of Heaven cannot be seen ...
> The Golden Flower is the Light. What colour has the Light? One uses the Golden Flower as an image. It is the true power of the transcendent Great *One*. ...

▶**III.19. I looked up / and saw . . .**

Written early 1963 (see note to previous poem). Another version was read at Vancouver as the final section of the poem on *Maximus* II, 147, from January 1963.

III.19. Okeanos, / the wobbling / ring

The phrase is used previously in "Maximus at the Harbor" (*Maximus* II, 70) and much earlier in the non-*Maximus* poem, "The ring of."

▶**III.20. The shape of Weymouth . . .**

Typed manuscript dated "June (29th ?) 1963," with a holograph original written on back of an envelope postmarked 28 June 1963.

III.20. Alfred

See *Maximus* I, 43 and note.

III.20. The Grace / of Waymouth The Diligence . . .

Names of ships, their masters, cargoes and destinations, from the Weymouth Port Books (q.v.) for the year 1621, on microfilm sent the poet by Jeremy Prynne (ordered from the Public Record Office in London and received by Olson in early May—Prynne to Olson, 9 May 1963).

The "Mary gould" may either be the ship "Mary gold," i.e. "Marigold," or "gould" may have been her cargo. Rose-Troup reads John rather than William Blachford, a woollen merchant and stockholder in the Dorchester Company (*John White*, p. 450).

III.20. John Larsen . . .

No such name appears among those in the port books. This is John C. Larsen of Gloucester, now an attorney, then a highschool student who seems to have been present when the poet was laboring with the microfilm of the port records. He writes, 25 October 1973, in response to an inquiry from the author:

> In 1963 I was in my second year of high school in Gloucester. While I did visit Gloucester's Sawyer Free Library time and again, and I recall seeing Mr. Olson peering at some sort of microfilm through a viewer there, I do not think that the library was the place where he might have encountered me. At that time I was employed at Connors Pharmacy in Gloucester after school, evenings and weekends, and come to think of it I do remember Mr. Olson coming into the drug store on occasion. I am uncertain whether I ever told him my name, but the poem is evidence that I must have at some time or other. He was always thought of by most of us as a rather offbeat individual, with rather unusual tastes and interests. I recall, for example, selling him some rather obscure brands of cigarettes that he seemed to enjoy, such as Picayunes and Gauloises. The drug store had a soda fountain, and I do recall him sitting at it now and again. I do not recall ever getting into any extended conversation with him beyond my usual habit of being courteous and friendly with anyone coming into the store.

Considering the poem, however, the following reconstruction is possible. Having no such equipment of his own to read the microfilm that Prynne had ordered for him, Olson had gone to the Sawyer Library to make use of the microfilm viewer available there. It was while he was scanning the entries, seeking to identify the vessel used by the Dorchester Company for its preliminary voyage, the "voyage of discovery" (*Maximus* I, 116 and note), that he was encountered by young Larsen, known to him from behind the drugstore counter.

The microfilm has survived among the poet's papers. Seventeenth-century handwriting is highly cursive and difficult (esp. this with its Latin phrases and irregular spellings) and does indeed look to the modern eye like Arabic—what any bright young schoolboy might have said, if called over for a look.

The "unk   unk" that follows represents a difficult portion of the script or the poet's efforts at transcribing it (probably an abbreviation for "unknown"), while "nescio," which is Latin for 'I don't know,' is the poet giving up.

▶III.21. The Return to the Mail-Bag . . .

The original manuscript, of which only a typed copy has been found, is without a date or clear clue to a date. Judging from the "Age 52" of the postscript, which would seem to refer to the poet himself (it is also the same age as the poet's father at the time of his death), the poem may have been written sometime between 27 December 1962 and 26 December 1963, the period during which Olson was fifty-two years old.

The poem is based in part on a photograph of the poet's father dressed in his letter carrier's uniform and standing with his infant son in a mail sack hung from his shoulder (reproduced on the cover of *The Post Office*).

▶III.22. followed his sow to apples . . .

Probably written in late December 1963 at Wyoming, N.Y. (another version appears verso a poem entitled "Aprino More," dated 24 December 1963 and dedicated in memoriam to Alfred Mansfield Brooks).

The poem begins with an allusion to the founding of Glastonbury, England, by Glasteing, who discovered a sow he had been pursuing under an apple tree and settled with his family on the site. The story is originally found as a 12th-13th century interpolation in William of Malmesbury's *De Antiquitatae Glastoniensis Ecclesiae* (ca. 1130), although Olson's exact source is uncertain (see, e.g., Chambers, *Arthur of Britain*, pp. 122 and 265–266). Graves, in his *White Goddess*—which is a probable source for other matter in the poem, as will be seen—mentions only the white Sow-goddess of the ancient Celts who ruled mid-winter (Vintage ed., pp.58 and 195).

III.22. at the writing table . . . the three century gap

See, "on the north side" of Dogtown's Lower Road, "my personal 'orchard' / where I wrote with a crab-apple branch / at my 'writing' stand- / stump for Michael McClure" (*Maximus* II, 37); also, "exactly / 300 / years / writing / at the stile," in the Kent Circle poem, *Maximus* II, 129.

III.22. Glastonbury / thorn of Joseph from his staff . . .

Town in Somerset, England (in the Westcountry), said to be the burial place of Arthur, the legendary king of England; indentified with Avalon, which means 'appletree' and which is, like the Biblical "Paradise," an orchard. According to legend, the first Christian church in England was built there by Joseph of Arimathea, the rich Jew who buried Christ in the tomb and whose staff, when planted in the ground at Glastonbury, became a flowering thorn. This story, too, is found in William of Malmesbury and is mentioned in Graves, *White Goddess*, p. 181, as follows: ". . . the Glastonbury Thorn which flowered on Old Christmas Day (January 5th, New Style) and was cut down by the Puritans at the Revolution was a sport of the common hawthorn. The monks of Glastonbury perpetuated it and sanctified it with an improving tale about Joseph of Arimathea's staff and the Crown of Thorns as a means of discouraging the orgiastic use of hawthorn blossom, which normally did not appear until May Day (Old Style)."

III.22. his sister

Morgan le Fay, the fairy sister of Arthur, who carried his body to rest at Glastonbury.

III.22. Osier the Dane

The romance of Ogier the Dane and Morgan le Fay is mentioned in Graves, *White Goddess*, p. 483—and especially the note on that page:

The late mediaeval legend of Ogier the Dane proves that Avalon was understood as an island of the dead by the Arthurian romance-writers. For Ogier is there said to have spent two hundred years in the 'Castle of Avalon', . . It was nothing new for Ogier le Danois to live in Avalon. The name is merely a debased form of 'Ogyr Vran' which . . . means 'Bran the Malign' or 'Bran, God of the Dead'. . . .

III.22. Oberon

King of the fairies in Shakespeare's *Midsummer Night's Dream*. There is no traditional connection between this Oberon and the Arthurian legend, however (according to Stokes, *Dictionary of the Characters & Proper Names*, p. 234, the name "is doubtless taken from *Huon of Bordeaux*, a transln. by Ld. Berners of an old French romance"). Shakespeare's Oberon has "come from the farthest steppe of India" (II.1.69), while the Oberon of *Huon*, according to Stokes, "is a misshapen dwarf, of angelic visage, the son of Julius Caesar by the grandmother of Alexander the Great"!

III.22. Mallabron

Original manuscript not entirely clear: could be Mallabran, even Malla bran. Perhaps then related to "Bran the Malign" ('Ogyr Vran') whose name in turn is related to Ogier the Dane, according to Graves, *White Goddess*, p. 483n. In another version or fragment, Olson has after what is probably "Mallabran," "A spirit of the sea." The Celtic hero Bran was the son of the sea-god, Llyr or Ler.

▶ III.23. the authority of Cape Ann . . .

The original is written on a page torn from a copy of the magazine *Sum* from December 1963, edited in Albuquerque by Fred Wah, and has a later note added by Olson: "[was by bed side? and dates Jan (?) 1964? / or fall '63 . . ." The date would have to have been January 1964, or at least late the preceding December, since the magazine had been mailed from Albuquerque shortly before Christmas (conversation with Fred and Pauline Wah, June 1972).

III.23. the children buried the lovekin

See "The Librarian":

> (What's buried
> behind Lufkin's
> Diner?

Then, Olson's letter to Vincent Ferrini (*Origin* 1, p. 42), in which this dream is recounted:

> . . . two kids die, on my hands,
> down back of Lufkin's diner, between it (which was a Chinese Rest.) &
> Roger's St!

According to an article from early 1970 in the *Gloucester Daily Times* entitled "James and Virginia Kandres buy diner immortalized by poet Olson" (clipping in Olson file at Sawyer Library), Lufkin's Diner "originally opened on the west end of Main Street, but moved to its present location at the east end about 40 years ago. Andrew Lufkin, his wife, Mary, and Andrew Jr. ran the diner until a fire closed it."

III.23. the Abnaki

Indian tribe (see *Maximus* II, 24 and note).

III.23. the Micmacs

Like the Abnaki, a tribe found in Maine. See note to *Maximus* II, 175.

III.23. John Neptune / and other Indian shamans

See Eckstorm's *Old John Neptune and Other Maine Indian Shamans*, an account of the *m'teoulin* of the Maine Indians.

III.23. Bristowe

See note to *Maximus* I, 83. It also occurs in "The Librarian."

III.23. Bridge Street

A main street in Manchester, Mass.

▶III.24. Ships for the West Indies . . .

Written ca. January 1964 ("Saturday January . . . 64" crossed out verso last page of original holograph manuscript). See Babson, *History*, p. 384 (marked in Olson's copy):

> As early as 1732, a trade had begun with the Southern Colonies, and was continued to about the beginning of the present century. The voyages were made in the winter season, when there was no employment for vessels or men in fishing; and the business was conducted in a manner now little practised in any part of the world. In most cases, perhaps in all, no wages were paid to master or crew; but, in lieu thereof, the privilege of bringing home a certain quantity of Southern produce was granted to each one; who was also allowed, probably, to take out fish on private adventure; as, in the few invoices preserved, this article does not appear among the shipments by the owners. In these invoices, the principal articles are salt, rum, sugar, and molasses. . . . On these voyages, the rivers, creeks, and inlets of Virginia, Maryland, and North Carolina, were visited; and there the cargo was bartered in small quantities for corn, beans, bacon, live hogs, and other products of the country. . . .

Also Babson, p. 385: "The foreign commerce of Gloucester was also, for many years after its origin, carried on with the fishing vessels. . . . Of this commerce, we only know that it was of inconsiderable extent till about 1750; when we find notice of voyages to the West Indies, to Bilbao, and Lisbon. The West-India cargoes consisted of fish and other provisions, for which, sugar, molasses, rum, and coffee were returned. . . ."

III.24. Charleston

Chief port of South Carolina.

III.24. Walker's Creek

Inlet of the Essex River in the northern part of West Gloucester; named for Henry Walker (see notes below).

III.24. the West Gloucester / farmers by and about 1690 . . .

Babson quotes the town records where it is said that in 1690 "William Haskell, Jr., & Mark Haskell, made request to have liberty to set down a corn-mill upon a creek called Walker's Creek" (*History*, p. 202 and n.), which is indicative of the extent of farming activity. As to the prosperity of the farmers, in Babson's *Notes and Additions*, I, 35, it is mentioned of one, William Haskell, that "no person in town had left so large an estate as he had accumulated; though his neighbor, Henry Walker, who followed him to the grave in nine days, left a larger one." See also the notice of Henry Walker below, where it is mentioned by Babson that his estate was "the largest that had then been accumulated in town."

III.24. Cape Sable

See *Maximus* II, 24 and note.

III.24. Haskell Street

Possibly where William Haskell and his descendants lived in West Gloucester (see note below), because present-day Haskell Street is in East Gloucester, off East Main Street.

III.24. Richard Window's kitchen

See Babson, *History*, p. 179 (marked in Olson's copy): "Richard Window, a carpenter, had, as early as 1651, a house and ten acres of land near Walker's Creek; which, at a date not known, he sold to William Haskell. He was a selectman in 1654. In 1655, he bought of John Coit a house and land on the east side of the river, where he probably lived during the remainder of his life. . . ."

III.24. Haskells

See Babson, *History*, p. 99:

> William Haskell was born about 1620, and was connected with the family of Roger Haskell of Salem. He first appears in Gloucester in 1643; and, in 1645, mention is made of his land at Planter's Neck. He probably resided here for a few years following the last date; but the hiatus in the recorded births of his children affords ground for conjecture that he was not a permanent resident from that time. If he left town for a season, he had returned in 1656, and settled on the westerly side of Annisquam river, where he had several pieces of land; among which was a lot of ten acres, with a house and barn, bought of Richard Window, situated on the west side of Walker's Creek. His sons took up land on each side of this creek, which is still occupied by descendants.

Also Copeland and Rogers, *Sage of Cape Ann*, p. 205.

III.24. Henry Walker who married Abraham Robinson's / widow . . .

See Babson, *History*, p. 175 (marked in Olson's copy):

> Henry Walker is mentioned as an owner of land before 1650. He married, Sept. 26, 1662, Widow Mary Brown, who first appeared here as the wife of Abraham Robinson. He had his residence on the west side of Annisquam River, where a creek still perpetuates the name. He was selectman in 1667 and several subsequent years. He died Aug. 29, 1693: his wife died April 17, 1690. His estate, the largest that had then been accumulated in town, was appraised £922.10s., consisting chiefly of land. Having no children, he left legacies to the descendants of his wife by her two previous husbands . . .

Also Babson, p. 135: Abraham Robinson "left a widow Mary, who married William Brown, July 15, 1646; and, again becoming a widow in 1662, married Henry Walker in the same year, and died April 17, 1690." Again Babson, p. 65 (also marked): "William Brown was among the earliest settlers . . . He married Mary, widow of Abraham Robinson, in 1646; and died May 3, 1662, leaving a daughter Mary, born in 1649, who married William Haskell. His widow married, for her third husband, Henry Walker. His estate, which was considerable for the time and place (£223.7s.) was mostly left to his son-in-law, Abraham Robinson."

It would seem that it was his grandson, Andrew Robinson, that Henry Walker raised, and that Abraham Robinson II was raised by his stepfather William Brown, for Babson writes on p. 135 (in addition to just quoted passage from p. 65) that Abraham, son of Abraham Robinson, "on coming to maturity, received several lots of land bequeathed him by his step-father Brown. . ." Abraham's son Andrew, Babson reports, at the age of eleven years, "was living with his paternal grandmother, and her husband, Henry Walker, who left him, by will, a legacy of twenty pounds. In the vicinity of this early home, which was surrounded for many miles by a dense forest, he probably acquired the passion for hunting; which in manhood often led him several days at a time upon distant excursions, from which he always returned with abundant proof of his courage and skill" (*History*, p. 136). Moreover, Abraham Robinson II was born before 1646, his father's death; his mother married William Brown that year and upon his death, married, for the third time, Henry Walker, in 1662, when Abraham Robinson was at least sixteen—so Walker can hardly be said to have raised him.

The marriage of Henry Walker's step-daughter to William Haskell, son of William Haskell, is also reported by Babson in the *History* on p. 100 (marked by Olson): "William married Mary Walker, July 3, 1667; who died Nov. 12, 1715, aged sixty-six. She was the daughter of William Brown; but she took the name of her step-father, Henry Walker."

III.24. 40 fisherman houses / Cape Ann—1690

On p. 209 of his *History*, Babson reports thirty-one lots laid out on the west side of the Cut in 1688 to settlers, including five Haskells and Henry Walker.

▶ **III.25. Watch-house / Point: to descry / anew . . .**

Written ca. January 1964 ("Saturday January . . . 64" crossed out on original manuscript), on final page of original holograph manuscript of preceding poem.

See "having descried the nation . . . ," *Maximus* III, 1 and note.

III.25. *attendeo*

From Latin *attendo* (when used with *animum*), 'give attention, attend to.'

III.25. minutiae / hold & swim

See appearance of "minutiae" towards end of previous poem.

III.25. the electro-magnetic / strain

Terms from Whitehead, *Process and Reality*. See, e.g., p. 136 of that volume: "Our present cosmic epoch is formed by an 'electromagnetic' society . . ." (also Olson's use of the term in *Muthologos*, I, 60 and II, 52). And, "strain-feelings," about which Whitehead writes, p. 177: "A certain state of geometrical strain in the body, and a certain qualitative physiological excitement in the cells of the body, govern the whole process of presentational immediacy" (marked in Olson's copy), and especially, Part IV, Chapter IV, entitled "Strains."

III.25. Ut gard   Out-yard

Utgard (literally 'out yard') was the realm outside the home of the gods in the Norse cosmological view.

III.25. one house— / one father one mother one city

Consider perhaps Snell, *Discovery of the Mind*, p. 230 (marked in Olson's copy):

> There are, of course, even in the earliest layers of speech some seeds of abstractions, nouns which differ somewhat

from concrete nouns or names. Many words which were later regarded as abstracts began their career as mythical names. In Homer, e.g., fear appears as a demon, as the Frightener, the *Phobos*. The extent to which these words were understood as names, even after their mythic connotation had long worn off, is evident from the use of the article. Aeschylus, for one, does not use the article in combination with substantives of the type which Ammann calls *mono-semantica*, i.e. those nouns which, like proper nouns, describe something existing only once, as . . . earth, sun, heaven, and moon; or which refer to objects of which the speaker knows only one example: . . . house, city, father, mother.

▶III.26. <u>West Gloucester</u>

Written ca. January 1964 and sent to Ed Sanders for publication in his *Fuck You / A Magazine of the Arts* (letter from Sanders to Olson, 24 January 1964, acknowledging receipt), although this copy was subsequently lost and Olson had to reconstitute another from the original holograph manuscript.

West Gloucester is that area west of the Annisquam River and north towards Essex, Massachusetts.

III.26. Atlantic / Street

Off Concord Street in West Gloucester, towards Wingaersheek Beach, skirting the marshes along Jones Creek not those of Walker's Creek, which are considerably further west and north. The poet may have intended Concord Street itself, which does cross Walker's Creek.

▶III.28. William Stevens, / first to venture / on to the sea . . .

Written early 1964 (same red ink and paper as other material from January-February of that year); mentioned in a note among the poet's papers as having been written before the Enyalion poem (III, 38–40).

For Stevens, see *Maximus* I, 30, 147, and II, 48, and notes above. "First to venture / on to the sea" is an echo of the lines

concerning Ousoos the hunter, *Maximus* II, 103—which is
then completed by the last lines of this poem.

III.28. Salem Neck

The early settlement at Salem, Massachusetts. See, e.g.,
William Wood's description as quoted in Herbert Adams,
"Salem Commons and Commoners," p. 25: "Four miles
north-east from Saugus . . . lieth Salem, which stands on the
middle of a neck of land very pleasantly, having a South
river on the one side, and a North river on the other side.
Upon this neck, where the most of the houses stand, is very
bad and sandy ground. Yet, for seven years together, it hath
brought forth exceeding good corn, by being *fished* but every
third year."

III.28. the Sea / Fort, Massachusetts Colony
Records, 1633 . . .

See Shurtleff, *Records of the Governor and Company of the
Massachusetts Bay*, I, 113, entry for 4 March 1633−4:

> Vpon consideracõn of the vsefullness of a moveing ffort
> to be builte, 40 ffoote longe & 21 ffoote wide, for defence
> of this colony, & vpon the ffree offer of some gentlem̃
> lately come ouer to vs of some large som̃es of money, to be
> imployed that way, it is thought fitt that this matter shalbe
> moued to such men of of ability as haue not borne their
> p̄te in the greate charges of the ffoundacon of this
> colony . . .
>   There is x^t pmised Mr Steuens, for his care & expedicõn
> in this worke, to be pd when the worke is finished.
>   *Gyven & pmised towards the Sea Fort: . . .

(there follows a list of twenty-two men and their contributions).
   Olson is perhaps bluffing with the figures, probably not
having the text with him in Buffalo at the time of writing,
since the passage is marked in his copy.

III.28. sd Stevens / Sat down / on the Harbor front . . .

See especially Babson, *History*, p. 165:

> He was admitted a freeman in 1640; and, in 1642, appears in Gloucester as one of the commissioners appointed by the General Court for ordering town-affairs. His standing among the early settlers, and the importance of his aid in promoting the prosperity of the town, are sufficiently indicated by the extraordinary grant he received of five hundred acres of land lying between Chebacco and Annisquam Rivers. He also had a grant of six acres on the Meeting-house Neck; but his residence was at the Cut, near the Beach, where he had eight acres of land. He was a selectman several years . . .

III.28. old A & P

Probably the branch of the Atlantic and Pacific Tea Company, then a series of small neighborhood groceries, at 49 Washington Street (listed in 1928 Gloucester city directory); as distinguished from the large supermarket presently off Main Street.

III.28. the Stage Fort Apartments / built by a blind man . . .

On Western Avenue near Middle Street, built by Daniel Corveth, who lost his sight during the Second World War.

III.28. the Boulevard

Stacey Boulevard (see *Maximus* I, 151 and note).

III.28. about where Billie Wynn's / been working . . .

The Boulevard Grocery at 49 Western Avenue, owned by Nicholas S. Cocotas. Cocotas had previously owned the Boulevard Sweet Shop further down on Western Avenue, which he sold to Peter Anastas, Sr. (*Maximus* II, 129 and note). Benjamin F. Winn lived at 191 Western Avenue, Gloucester.

III.29. holding / the rights of the River's / passage

She also *Maximus* II, 69 and note. It would have been this Stevens' great-grandson Samuel, known as "Cut" Stevens, who owned the rights during "the River trade / of 1713" (see Babson, *History*, p. 167).

III.29. timber cut / for the apartments / of Boston (the River trade / of 1713)

See Babson, *History*, p. 6:

> The rocky surface of the town, which now presents many large tracts, offering scarcely a tree or bush to relieve the eye, was once covered with a fine growth of various kinds of wood: but the work of levelling it began when the town was first settled, and has been continued with unfaltering perseverance; till, at length, only in a few places are there any trees to be found. In addition to the wood cut for fuel for domestic consumption, and the timber felled for ship-building and for the construction of tenements in town, quite a brisk business was early carried on in the exportation of the article to Boston. A stray leaf of an old account-book reveals the fact, that in about three weeks, in 1711, over five hundred cords of wharf-wood were shipped to one firm in that place.

Again, on p. 380: "The division of the woodland, at that time [the beginning of the eighteenth century], enabled the people to cut large quantities of wood for sale; and the transportation of this article to market created a need for many vessels. This business increased so rapidly, that, in 1706, no less than thirty sloops were employed in carrying wood from one section of the town alone . . ." (identified in a note as Squam River, "as appears from the fact that that number of town-vessels paid, in that year, the annual toll for passing through the Cut").

Discussed also in Copeland and Rogers, *Saga of Cape Ann*, p. 14.

III.29. Deptford

Southeastern borough of London on the Thames; site of the royal dockyard in Pepys' time.

III.29. Hawkins

John Hawkins (see *Maximus* I, 59 and note).

III.29. Pepys commanded . . .

See the following entries from the *Diary* of Samuel Pepys (1633–1703), at the time Clerk of the Acts in the Navy office. First, 9 July 1663: "Sir W. Batten and I sat a little this afternoon at the office, and thence I by water to Deptford, and there mustered the Yard, purposely, God forgive me, to find out Bagwell, a carpenter, whose wife is a pretty woman, that I might have some occasion of knowing him and forcing her to come to the office again . . ." (III, 202). Almost a month later, 7 August 1663, in Deptford: " . . . I staid walking up and down, discoursing with the officers of the yard of several things, and so walked back again, and on my way young Bagwell and his wife waylayd me to desire my favour about getting him a better ship, which I shall pretend to be willing to do for them, but my mind is to know his wife a little better" (III, 241). Again, on 19 October 1664, Pepys writes: "Then I to my office, where I took in with me Bagwell's wife, and there I caressed her, and find her every day more and more coming with good words and promises of getting her husband a place, which I will do" (IV, 271). Then, 20 December 1664: "Up and walked to Deptford, where after doing something at the yard I walked, without being observed, with Bagwell home to his house, and there was very kindly used, and the poor people did get a dinner for me in their fashion, of which I also eat very well. After dinner I found occasion of sending him abroad, and then alone *avec elle je tentais a faire ce que voudrais et contre sa force je le fraisais bien que passe a mon contentment*" (IV, 311).

Next, 5 October 1665: ". . . down by water to Deptford and there to my Valentine [Mrs. Bagwell]. Round about and next door on every side is the plague, but I did not value it, but there did what I would *con elle* . . ." (V, 104). Also, 8 November 1665, Pepys reports: ". . . by water to Deptford, and there did order my matters so, walking up and down the fields till it was dark night, that je allais a la maison of my valentine, and there je faisais whatever je voudrais avec her, and, about eight at night, did take water, being glad I was out of the towne; for the plague, it seems rages there more than ever . . ." (V, 141). A similar episode occurs on 13 June 1666 (V, 328). Presumably it was all worth it for the Bagwells, for on 4 March 1666/7, Pepys writes: ". . . away to Deptford, and there I a little in the yard, and then to Bagwell's, where I find his wife washing, and also I did hazer tout que je voudrais con her, and then sent for her husband, and discoursed of his going to Harwich this week to his charge of the new ship building there, which I have got him . . ." (VI, 207).

Whether Olson read the episode in the diary itself or has it from some other source is not known.

III.29. as David had Uriah

See 2 Samuel XI. David had Uriah assigned to the most vulnerable spot in battle to be killed so that he could possess his wife, Bathsheba.

III.29. came to the Bay / fr St Swithins . . .

Presumably Stevens is intended, although—as Olson had already noted in *Maximus* I, 147—William Stevens came to New England from Stepney, another borough of London. In Bank's *Topographical Dictionary*—Olson's source for information on birthplaces of settlers in the earlier poem— only a Ralph Worley, a settler at Charlestown (in the Massachusetts Bay Colony) is listed (p. 103) as coming from the parish in London named St. Swithins.

III.29. he ventured / on to the sea in the trunk of a tree

Cf. Ousoos the hunter of Phoenician legend, also the first shipbuilder (*Maximus* II, 103 and note).

III.29. the Bark Royal was the ship he built . . .

Actually the *Royal Merchant* (perhaps another evidence Olson is writing from memory or in haste). See note to *Maximus* II, 48.

▶**III.30. Stevens song**

The original was begun on the torn front of an envelope bearing the postmark, Cambridge, Eng., 22 January 1964, which had apparently become separated from the body of the poem (it was found among the poet's papers separately), and was continued in the same spiral-bound notepad from February 1964 that contains "Statement for the CAMBRIDGE magazine" (*Additional Prose*, p. 56) dated February 1964, as well as both "wonis kvam" (*Maximus* III, 43) and a portion of an early version of the Enyalion poem (III, 38–40). A typescript of the opening portion (from "out of the fire . . ." to "shipbuilder / of England and") was later made by the poet. That only this opening portion was typed, suggests Olson may have been unable to locate the rest of the poem in the notepad at the time he was typing up his manuscript.

The Stevens of the title is the William Stevens of the previous poem and one of the chief heroes of the epic. See esp. "my carpenter," *Maximus* I, 30 and note; also *Maximus* II, 48 and note, where Babson's account of Stevens' stubborn resistance to the King is quoted.

The poem could possibly be also titled "The Quest of the New King of the Sea," as that appears on the original manuscript above "Stevens song" (no title is given on the typescript of this portion). The original begins, "out of the fire / the Phoenix . . . ," with that last crossed out.

III.30. 1683?

Date for William Stevens' death or disappearance (see *Maximus* II, 48—where Olson has "1693 Stevens dies"—and note).

III.30. his wife had to petition / the General Court for relief . . .

See *Maximus* II, 48 and note. The petition of Phillipa Stevens—in which she mentions "my husband having been absent about three weeks, in which time they came for the fine, and not as yet is he returned"—is printed in full in Babson, *Notes and Additions*, I, 76.

III.30. my own Father's / remarks to Paddy Hehir / and to Blocky Sheehan . . .

See "my father . . . until all bosses struck him down," *Maximus* I, 33 and note, and esp. *The Post Office*, p. 52: "I'm not sure they didn't inspect the life out of him first, having docked his pay, and that it wasn't on one of these inspections that he called Paddy Hehir or maybe it was Blocky Sheehan a son of a bitch." Paddy Hehir ("hair, the Irish pronounce it") was foreman of letter carriers at the postal station in Worcester where Olson's father worked; "Blocky" Sheehan was the Superintendent of Mails at the time.

III.30. that hemp you promised / for caulking the pinnace

These lines, which seem out of place in the poem, also occur as a single line ("that hemp you spoke of for caulking the pinnace") on a loose sheet from a different notepad, probably from a slightly earlier period (winter of 1962−63).

III.31. taking night collections / joining Swedish fraternal / organizations . . .

Olson writes in *The Post Office*, p. 52: "It took fourteen years. The demerits came first. Then the removal from the route. At that point they pulled another military move. They required him to tear off the three red stars from his sleeve, for the fifteen years he had served. For they had a final ignominy. I suppose it is possible they thought they could drive him out of the service altogether. Anyhow they assigned him to the lowest job there is, the job the greenest sub carrier gets, the night collection."

Again, *The Post Office*, p. 28:

> ... when the government of these States so failed him he was thrown back on that other rock of the immigrant, his foreign nationality organizations.... [Olson later tells us, pp. 53–54: "He joined the Carl the 15th Lodge, the Swedish American Federation. The paper "Svea" had helped in the struggle. He became a friend of Karl Fredin the editor. His Swedish began to come back. He began to get me to speak to their festivals. He became more and more involved."] To some degree he substituted Sweden for America as a focus for his curiosity, after the "Americans" failed him in his fight and he had to turn to the Swedish-American societies for aid. They are like mothers anyway, these societies, keeping their children back from the brunt of this country. They aid them but they also fondle them when they are hurt or cut to pieces as they so often are on the steel points of the society.

III.31. Senator David I Walsh

See also *The Post Office*, p. 53: "he fought back from the start. The senator was David I. Walsh. He tried to reach him. The congressman was Pehr Holmes, a Swede. He saw him. Promises, letters, meetings, articles...." Walsh (1872–1947) served us U.S. Senator almost continuously from 1919 to 1939.

III.31. Congressman / Hobbs

George R. Stobbs (1877–1951), representative in the U.S. Congress from Worcester from 1925 until 1931, when Pehr Holmes took over the job.

III.31. Pehr Holmes Mayor

Pehr Gustav Holmes (1881–1952), mayor of Worcester, 1917–1919; representative in Congress, 1931–1947.

III.31. there sits a wolf

Fenris, the wolf from Norse mythology (see further below in the poem and note to "your own living hand amputated," *Maximus* III, 47; also other references to dogs throughout the poems, such as on II, 36).

III.31. light or color, or fruits . . . ever a garden ever a walled place / not anything resembling Paradise

The word "paradise" is said to be etymologically derived from the Avestan *pairidaêza,* 'an enclosure, a place walled in,' as well as the Hebrew word for 'garden' or 'orchard' (see also *Maximus* III, 22). See e.g., "Paradise" in Cheyne and Black's *Encyclopaedia Biblica*, pp. 3569–70. Cf. also "Light is not color . . . Color is the Fruits / or the Four Rivers of Paradise" (*Archaeologist of Morning*, p. [223]), a poem written in January or February 1964.

III.31–32. Sneferu's / intended ship / imported forty shiploads of cedar logs

See, e.g., Pritchard, *Ancient Near Eastern Texts*, p. 227, from the Palermo Stone (marked in Olson's copy):

> Bringing forty ships filled (with) cedar logs.
> Shipbuilding (of) cedarwood, one "Praise-of-the-Two-Lands" ship, 100 cubits (long), and (of) *meru*-wood, two ships, 100 cubits (long).
> Making the doors of the royal palace (of) cedarwood.

Also discussed in Smith, *The Old Kingdom in Egypt*, p. 25, which Olson may have owned at the time of the poem's writing.

Among Olson's papers is the following note on a *Niagara Frontier Review* envelope, which could have been drawn from either Pritchard or Smith: "ships, shore-hugging still 1540 [record of shipping *from* Tyre dates 2750 when Sneferu, 4th dynasty pharoah, had 40 shiploads of cedar logs transported from Tyre to his ship-building works Cenoptic mouth of the Nile] . . ."

III.32. in 1954 AD, / when the funerary boat / of Kheops . . .

Kheops or Cheops was second king of the Fourth Dynasty of Egypt, which lasted from 2900 to 2750 B.C. See the report of the discovery of his solar barge by Kamal el-Malakh at the Great Pyramid of Giza in May 1954 (Love, "Cheops Treasure, Ship of the Dead, Found at Pyramid," p.4):

> Describing the first sight of the ship, Mr. el-Malakh said: "I saw what appeared to be a wooden floor below me. I closed my eyes to make them accustomed to the darkness. A second impression struck me. It was vapors, perfumes of the wood, sacred wood of the ancient religion.
> "A smell of incense mingled with the scent of wood. It was faint and mystic, like the odor of a cathedral. . . .

III.32. three kinds of way / by which the prince / is instructed . . .

See Havelock, *Preface to Plato*, pp. 108 ff. and esp. pp. 120–121 where he writes:

> . . . orally preserved communication was operating at three levels or in three different areas. There would be the area of current legal and political transactions; the issuance of directives which would accumulate as precedents. Here the governing class bore the main responsibility for oral formulation of what was necessary. Then there would be the continual retelling of the tribal history, the tale of the ancestors and how they behaved as models for the present. This historical task would be the special province of the minstrels. And finally there would be the continual indoctrination of the young in both tale and precedent through recital. They would be required to listen and to repeat and their memories would be trained to do this. These three areas overlapped and interpenetrated each other. Thus the prince or judge as he issued

rescripts and made decisions cast his performative utterance into the idiom of epic recital in which he had been trained from youth. . . . The picture drawn in Homer and Hesiod of the arbitrators holding the staff of office and giving judgment in the speaking place, of the prince who commands the speech which will resolve a quarrel and control a throng, is not Mycenaean but contemporary.

III.33. the dog . . . tore the bloody cloak . . .

See the following dream-notes from 1950 among the poet's papers:

> francoise [Boldereff ?], & boat which we were in which swerved to avoid rocks at entrance of Annisquam (a lot of goings on previously, now lost)
> c[onnie] & i watching something—but I sd, you must, you must watch it: it is very beautiful; a policeman trying to manacle a woman under her cloak; then she ran, he shot her, & she lay bleeding, while 3 or 4 dogs pawed & tossed her cloak, blood stained, while she lay in the green grass

Again, in a note in the margin of his copy of Jung and Kerenyi's *Essays on a Science of Mythology*, p. 131 (opposite passage on Hecate as a dog), the poet writes: "cf my dream of the golden cloak *torn* by dogs." See also the later *Maximus* III, 53.

First used in the poem "ABCs (2)" from June 1950 (and see also *Maximus* I, 85, and note to "Schwartz" on previous page there):

> . . . what bloody stumps
> these dogs have, how they tear the golden cloak
> And the boat,
> how he swerves it to avoid the yelping rocks
> where the tidal river rushes

III.34. when Tyr / put his hand / in Fenris / mouth

Again, see note to "your own living hand amputated," *Maximus* III, 47.

► **III.35. the / Bulgar—& / the 4 sons hidden / in the thigh . . .**

Actually written somewhat earlier than realized at the time of the editing of *The Maximus Poems: Volume Three*. Other versions of the poem, including copies dated 4 February 1963, were found after the book had gone to press clipped to the back of manuscripts from *Maximus IV, V, VI*. So that, in addition to the handwritten manuscript first found by the editors and transcribed for inclusion in their edition (on the back of which is a prose piece containing a reference to a project to be called *Kingfisher's Bird-Nest Poems*, which is also mentioned in a draft of a letter to Donald Allen in a notebook from ca. February 1964, thus suggesting that date for the poem), there is what is probably the original holograph version, written in pencil on two pages removed from a notepad. This was later copied out in red ink by the poet; and, finally, two typescripts—one ending "the Bulgar emerges / to take anything / up in his arms," the other "and hides in his father's brother's thigh" (with no room left on the page for "his own four sons")—were prepared. A note on one of the typescripts indicates Olson had in fact discarded the poem from *Maximus IV, V, VI*.

When asked by the author in 1968, regarding its appearance in the Enyalion poem (*Maximus* III, 38–40), who this difficult figure of the Bulgar might be, the poet replied that it was a figure of the rainbow of Egyptian origin, and that his source was "a late Jung." See then Jung's *Aion*, p. 123, where the quaternity of the four sons of Horus is discussed: "Mestha, Hapi, Tuamutef, and Qebhsennuf, who are said to dwell 'behind the thigh of the northern heaven,' that is, behind the thigh of Set, whose seat is in the constellation of the Great Bear. The four sons of Horus are Set's enemies, but on the other hand they are closely connected with him" (marked in Olson's copy). This region of Set or the "northern heaven," Jung identifies on the next page as the North Pole. On p. 132 Jung states that this quaternity "the ancients associated with fire," while on p. 135 he says that "the infernal fire is nothing other than the *Deus absconditus* (hidden God) who dwells at the North Pole and reveals himself through magnetism." There is no mention in *Aion*, however, of a Bulgar or the Bulgars, only a legend a few pages later in which the Old Bulgarian word *Osob*, 'individual, personality,' figures (pp. 146–147).

The Bulgars were a race of horsemen, akin to the Tatars and Huns, who made their appearance east of the Black Sea and below the Danube in the latter part of the seventh century A.D. The "Bulgar" might thus represent a migration from the outskirts of civilization or, as bearer of a new civilization, one of the New Civilizers (or new barbarians, "Unholy Barbarians" as Olson says at his Berkeley reading) to follow the earlier "Civilizers," the original Indo-European "inventors of the Vision" (*Maximus* II, 164), i.e. a continuation westward from Kuban of the primary Indo-European migration, an early stage of the second, or Northern, migration which Olson writes about in the final part of his "Vinland Map Review" (*Additional Prose*, pp. 66–68). In an essay fragment from ca. 1967 among his papers, Olson writes of the Bulgars as "Dorians" or invaders from the north: "Indo-European peoples on the move—at or before or soon after that date [1750–1700 B.C.]—& definitely *not* that 'last one' practically, say, of the Dorians—Bulgars—of *late* date, 1220 1st & then smashing Mycenae itself harsh & to the ground 1125. . . ."

There is additional, scattered evidence that the "Bulgar" is a figure out of the prismatic northern ice, rather than, e.g., in any way related to Bulga or Bolg, one of the many names of the Celtic sun and lightning god, even though the Celtic hero Cuchulain enters into the Enyalion poem along with the Bulgar (who may even be carrying Celtic "colors"—see notes to *Maximus* III, 38 and 40). In a poem written immediately before "[MAXIMUS, FROM DOGTOWN—IV]" (*Maximus* II, 163–172) in a notepad from mid-March 1963, Tartarus, the "place of monsters," is called "Bulgar land" and located "north north west"—in other words at the North Pole, where Hell was for the early peoples. In his copy of *The Secret of the Golden Flower*, at the sentence "The abysmal is in the north" on p. 72, Olson notes in the margin: "! wow as of the *Bulgar* / And the sons of *color* . . . ," while in a copy of Graves' *White Goddess* bought in December 1966, Olson adds in the margin of p. 185, "Bulgar," with a line drawn to "Corona Borealis" in the text. Another note, this time on the inside back cover of the poet's copy of Nasr, *Science and Civilization in Islam,* and dated 31 July 1968 after reading a section on the alchemical tradition (pp. 246ff.), is relevant: "So vertically is *not* a discussible thing: if it is happening that is all which can happen, that more strength shall exist in its '*polar*' / in its Bulgarian condition / the *Aurora Boreal Vision* . . . color(s . . ."

Further light may be provided by the following note written on the verso of an envelope air-mailed from Oakland, 10 May 1964, to Olson at Wyoming, N.Y.:

> to the t[op] of the w[orld] (wholly opposite to
>   e[nd] of the w[orld]—actually *outside*)
> & t[op] is the same as Bulgar's—or colorful sides of,
>   ? Set's [?] in Aion on
>   jewel [?] or
>   Almadine(?
>   —where ice, & COLOR
>   —sons—meet RED
>   spectrum?
>   light of the
>   *stars*

(The "Almadine" is the alchemical stone in *Maximus* II, 131, which the poet "wished / so strongly to show right away to Robert Duncan . . ."; it figures also in the earliest version of the Enyalion poem shortly following.) Finally, there is the following fragment found among the poet's papers: "the Bulgarian bridge where the king went down in his golden chariot"—presumably a solar myth, with the "Bulgarian bridge" being the rainbow.

III.35. Mill Pond

Section of Mill River in Gloucester, below the former site of the Riverdale Mills, where Washington Street crosses Mill River.

III.35. Riverview

Overlooking the Annisquam River from its east bank; off Wheeler Street, north of the Route 128 traffic circle at Washington Street.

III.35. Primitive Hill

Perhaps the "Primeval Hill" of Dogtown (*Maximus* II, 150), though possibly even specifically what is called Great Hill (*Maximus* III, 16) in Dogtown, which is the highest rise from there to the Atlantic.

III.35. Miss Barrett

Viola Barrett, wife of Homer Barrett (see note to *Maximus* II, 150). "Mrs Barrett" in the typed versions of the poem.

III.35. Bond's Hill

See *Maximus* I, 43 and note.

III.35. the Poles

Probably at one time "the Pool's," as the Pool family had a house near the top of Bond's Hill on Essex Avenue beyond Bond Street at the turn of the century. In any case, different from what is more commonly known as "the Poles" of Gloucester (*Maximus* II, 16 and note). Undoubtedly with a play here on North Pole (as in *Maximus* III, 17).

III.35. dropped land / into the bottom / as it left . . .

See also *Maximus* II, 51 and note.

III.36. the road to Balzarinis / pig farm

The Old Rockport Road off Eastern Avenue, south of Dogtown near the Gloucester-Rockport boundary. The pig farm, according to Esther Johnson, former town clerk of Rockport, was in back of Nugent Stretch at the base of Great

Hill in Dogtown, in the vicinity of the Babson cooperage (now a museum).

III.36. Demeter's pigs

Pigs were ritually sacrificed to Demeter, the Greek corn goddess and earth mother, in the Eleusinian mysteries. See, e.g., Jung and Kerenyi, *Essays on a Science of Mythology,* p. 165: "The pig is Demeter's sacrificial animal. In one connexion, where it is dedicated to the Eleusinian mysteries, it is called δελφαξ, the 'uterine animal' of the earth, just as the dolphin was the 'uterine animal' of the sea. It was customary for Demeter to receive a gravid sow as a sacrificial offering. The mother animal is a fit offering to the Mother Goddess, the pig in the pit a fit offering to her vanished daughter. As symbols of the goddesses, *pig* and *corn* are perfect parallels."

III.36. his father's brother's thighs

Horus' father was Osiris and Osiris' brother was Set, in whose thigh the sons were hidden (see opening note).

▶III.37. Astride / the Cabot / fault

Written February 1964, the day before "Enyalion" (see note to poem following) and definitely by March 2nd when sent, along with "7 years & you cld carry cinders in yr hand . . ." and the Enyalion poem which follow, to Tom Clark, then poetry editor of the *Paris Review* (Olson's letter to Clark that date, Spencer Library, University of Kansas).

For the Cabot Fault, a rift in the earth's crust from northern Newfoundland down to the Boston area and including Cape Ann, see Wilson, "Cabot Fault: An Appalachian Equivalent" (a xeroxed copy of which is among Olson's papers); also Wilson's "Continental Drift," p. 90. After reading the poem during his "Causal Mythology" lecture, Olson remarks: "I learned that, by the way, luckily in Vancouver, from one of the Vancouver people that I think isn't here today, Dan McLeod. He showed me in Vancouver a thing which I had never realized, that there's a split in the Atlantic Ocean, a fault which runs just where all my own attention has been—northeast—and that she runs right straight through Gloucester" (*Muthologos*, I, 72).

Two earlier holograph versions as well as a typescript of the poem (typed at an angle or "drift," as published here) survive.

III.37. one leg upon the Ocean one leg / upon the Westward drifting continent

The image is comparable to that of Antony as described by Cleopatra, which Olson, like Melville, was fond of (*Call Me Ishmael*, p. 71): "His legs bestrid the ocean" (*Antony and Cleopatra*, V.ii.82). The direct reference, however, concerns the theory of continental drift.

III.37. to build out of sound the wall / of a city

As the walls of Thebes were built by Amphion. See e.g. Pausanias, IX.5.4 (Frazer trans., I, 451): "Amphion sang and built the wall to the music of his lyre"—which Olson also refers to in an essay written at the time of the New Sciences of Man program at Black Mountain in 1953. In notes among his papers from ca. 1965 he would write: "the City's walls shall not stay up if the words, and the music, are not said right." See also *Maximus* III, 194.

III.37. the earth / rushing westward 2' / each 100 / years . . .

Should be two *centimeters* per *year* (or roughly six and a half feet per hundred years), if the figures are intended to be accurate. See the chart in Wilson, "Continental Drift," p. 94: "Distance from Mid-Ocean Ridge of some islands in Atlantic and Indian oceans is plotted against age. If all originated over the ridge, their average rate of motion has been two centimeters a year. . . ." Olson's source, however, may be a letter from Dan McLeod (who had first told him about the

Cabot Fault), undated but from this time, in which occurs:
"the depths of the channel in *Letter, May 2, 1959,* seem un-
believably shallow, tho the New Eng. coast has fallen 9 in.
and sea level risen 3 in., so it appears the Cabot Fault is
taking its turn in Gloucester. And wow!—since 1930, that
coast is drowning at 2 ft. per century." On the other hand,
Pauline Wah's notes from Olson's class at Vancouver,
8 August 1963, record the poet as speaking of the land mass
of North America moving northwestward at ¾ inch per
century (*OLSON* 4, p. 67), so Wilson may still be the source.

III.37. 500 years / since Cabot

John Cabot, for whom the Cabot Fault is named, sailed
in 1497 to Newfoundland (see *Maximus* I, 79 and note).

III.37. the / Azores

See also *Maximus* I, 77 and note. The islands are just east
of the Mid-Atlantic Ridge.

III.37. St Martin's / Land

Because divided like his cloak by the drifting of the
continents. St. Martin of Tours, while in the Roman army,
divided his cloak with a beggar to share its warmth and on
the following night had a vision of Christ. The patron saint
of France, he has no particular connection with the Azores.

III.37. the Mongolian ice

In the sense of a distant source, perhaps, or the ice itself
as a barbarian horde ("One cries Mongols"—*Maximus* I, 125),
although "Siberian" ice might be more appropriate in the
light of what follows.

III.37. Frances Rose-Troup Land

See *Maximus* I, 148 and note.

III.37. novoye / Sibersky / slovo

"Novosibressky / Slovo" in earlier holograph version. See *Maximus* I, 151 and note; also Wilson, "Continental Drift," caption to map on p. 100: "Rifting of supercontinent to form the Atlantic Ocean could have produced the Verkhoyansk Mountains in eastern Siberia. As shown on this map of the Arctic, the rift spread more widely to the south. The opening of the Atlantic Ocean and Baffin Bay separated Greenland from both North America and Europe. The continents were rotated slightly about a fulcrum near the New Siberian Islands."

III.37. to arise from the River

Presumably the Annisquam.

III.37. the Diorite Stone / to be lopped off the Left Shoulder

See *Maximus* II, 16 and 51 and notes. In the Hittite myth, it is actually on the right shoulder of the giant Ubelluri that the diorite man Ullikummi grows (Guterbock, "The Song of Ullikummi").

▶III.38. rages / strain / Dog of Tartarus . . .

Written February 1964 in at least three attempts, directly following "Astride / the Cabot / fault . . ." See Olson's remarks in "Causal Mythology," *Muthologos,* I, 76:

> . . . the day after I wrote this poem I read you first ["Astride / the Cabot / fault . . ."], I wrote this other poem. . . . It also is a footnote, like it's an example of another side of the literal study of mythology, which I spend a lot of time on, which is really archaeology on one side, or etymology on another. I found that in Crete, or in Greece at the time of Mycenae and Pylos and Tiryns, that the god who we know of as Ares or Mars was apparently called Enyalios. In this poem I abuse his name by using Enyalion. But the poem is based on the word Enyalion. And it's directly connected now to the struggle of the *imago mundi,* as a child of earth, with the bosses.

According to Liddell and Scott, *Greek-English Lexicon,* p. 489, the name Enyalios is used for 'battle' or 'the battle-cry' or 'warlike.'

A final version of the poem is dated 12 February 1964. A note on the last page of that manuscript reads: *"revised Feb 12th* / [prior to / *JW as King* poem / then (after JW) / Wonis kvam."

III.38. Guards of Tartarus / Finks of the Bosses . . .

Specifically, "the glorious allies of loud-crashing Zeus," Cottus, Gyes, and Briareus, who "had done that day, of the Civilized War, / their turn—for the Boss." They were the wardens of the Titans held prisoners in Tartarus for their revolt against Zeus. See *Maximus* II, 163ff., esp. 170, 171.

III.38. Enyalion

See *Maximus* II, 184 and note. In this poem, however, a composite in which several mythological figures are incorporated and transformed—even more so when earlier versions are considered. The next phrase, "he has lost his hand," reveals Enyalion also to be Tyr (see III, 34 and 47 and note), which is made more clear in another poem, beginning "belief—'War' . . ." and written 8 June 1964, where Olson has: "Enyalion . . . has already lost his right hand, / placed in the mouth of the Wolf . . ." While what appears to be the first version of the present poem also describes Enyalion as follows:

> Enyalion is the god of war   Enyalion
> is the son of Odin   Enyalion is the one caught in the trap
> in bed with Beauty. Beauty is the wife of Tartaros . . .

Referred to is the story of Ares caught in bed with Aphrodite by her husband, Hephaestus, who created a special net for the purpose—quite the reverse of that earlier *Maximus* poem in which it is Enyalion who is urged to "spread the iron net." However, in another version of the present poem, Enyalion, or Ares, is also spoken of in terms of Hephaestus: "hobbled," with a "dragged foot," who killed "the partridge" (for these allusions see III, 49 and note)—yet who also killed "the smith" (Hephaestus) himself. Further, Tyr is not "the son of Odin," as mentioned in the earliest version, Vidar is. So the images are continuously confused, reversed, or interwoven, until the new figure—who is also a *Wanax* and at times, as will be seen, has the traits of an ancient Irish hero—is created, an archetypal composite but also a unique and novel hero.

III.38. the High King

I.e., the Mycenaean *Wanax* (see previous poem and note there); also, to a lesser extent, the Irish *Ari-Ri* (note below). An earlier version reads: "the High King / is not a War Chief, he has Equites / to do that."

III.38. Equites

Latin 'horseman,' 'cavalryman,' or 'knight,' but see Webster, *From Mycenae to Homer*, pp. 11–12 and 98–99, for the Mycenaean *Eqeta*, the 'Counts' or companions of the *Wanax*, "who appear in Pylos and Knossos as grandees of noble family, and as military commanders with chariots, uniforms, and male and female slaves."

III.38. the glories of Hera

Literally, Heracles, whose name means 'the glory of Hera.' Hera was the wife of Zeus.

III.38. who takes off his clothes / wherever he is found . . .

According to Cross, "Celtic Elements," pp. 55–56:

> the unabashed exhibition of the human figure with the avowed purpose of eliciting admiration appears to have been a common practice among the early Celts . . . An early example is found in the *Táin Bó Cúalnge*, where it is said that Cuchulainn went forth "to show his beautiful, pleasing figure" . . . to the women and maidens attached to the army of Connacht. For this purpose he decorates his person with the most bizarre and barbaric magnifi-

cence. "Then the maidens begged the men of Ireland to
raise them upon the surfaces of shields above the shoulders of the men, to view Cuchulainn's figure" . . . Another
case, found in the Rennes manuscript of the prose
Dindshenchas, is connected with the death of the famous
King Niall of the Nine Hostages. While the king was on
an expedition in France, one Eochaid "advised the women
[of France] to ask that [Niall's] form might be shown to
them. Wherefore, after undressing, Niall displayed
himself to them" . . .

It might be pointed out that in a note from ca. 1966 among
the poet's papers Enyalion is once mentioned along with
Cuchulain: "Life is so fantastic You cldn't even come near it
in beauty You cld be beautiful. Enyalion was—Cuchulain
was say. . . ." And in his "Reading at Berkeley" Olson states
that the poem concerns the fact "some woman wanted to
have a look at whether Cuchulain looked as good as they
said he did . . ." (*Muthologos*, I, 111).

Also, in an early version of the poem written verso a first
version of "7 years & you cld carry cinders in yr hand . . ."
(III, 41), Olson has: "the High King / can strip in the middle
of Battle / and the war stop while Queen Cuntsiga / takes a
look at him . . ." In another version, the queen—this time
nameless—is mentioned as "passing by, in her retinue /
going counter-clockwise around the nation, stopping at the
hours / of the nation's organized parts . . ." The reference
here, in part, is to an ancient Irish custom concerning the
governing of the land by the *Ari-Ri*, or high king, whose seat
was at Tara, as described in Coon, *Story of Man*, p. 295:
"After his inauguration, the high king toured his land,
traveling clockwise around the island, with the sea on his
left hand, visiting all the sub-kings of different ranks, who
entertained him with great ceremony."

III.39. the earth / is the mundus

Mundus is Latin for 'the universe,' 'world,' 'earth.'

III.39. the color / of the god of war   is beauty

See "Reading at Berkeley" (*Muthologos,* I, 132): "If we don't know that War is Beauty, in the same sense that Venus took him to bed . . ."—referring to the story of Aphrodite's entanglement with Ares.

III.40. beyond the earth . . . far away from the rules of sea-faring

See Havelock, *Preface to Plato,* who writes that Hesiod "claims his function is to declare the *noos* of Zeus in minstrelsy 'taught' . . . by the Muses, this *noos* being in the present instance the rules of seafaring . . . , and that minstrels and harpists are of Muses and Apollo 'over the earth' . . ." (p. 112).

III.40. Ousoos

See *Maximus* II, 103 and note; also, III, 29.

III.40. where you carry / the color, Bulgar

See the earlier poem beginning, "the / Bulgar—& / the 4 sons . . ." (*Maximus* III, 35–36), and note to that. The "color" carried by the Bulgar, then, would seem to be that of the rainbow, but also note the discussion of "colors" in Coon, loc. cit. (marked with an exclamation point in Olson's copy): "It was easy to tell a man's rank because each was entitled to wear a different number of colors in his clothing. Slaves could wear but one, the fourth class two, and so on up to the king and queen, who wore six."

III.40. the law of the proportion / of its parts

The classic Greek concept of beauty. See e.g. Else, "Aristotle on the Beauty of Tragedy," pp. 184–185: ". . . in a beautiful and perfect whole the parts stand in due proportion to each other ($\sigma\upsilon\mu\mu\epsilon\tau\rho\iota\alpha$). And 'due proportion' means in the last analysis arithmetical or geometrical *ratio*; that is, συμμετρία = commensurability" (this last marked in Olson's copy).

▶ **III.41. 7 years & you cld carry cinders in yr hand . . .**

Written at the same time as the previous two poems (same typing, mentioned together in notes among the poet's papers, the three sent together to the *Paris Review*). For the opening lines, cf. p. 135 of *The Maximus Poems*—"About seven years / and you can carry cinders / in your hands for what / America was worth"—and note above.

III.41. wanax

The high king of the Mycenaeans. The word is found on the Linear B tablets; see esp. Webster, *From Mycenae to Homer*, p. 11. "Agamemnon was wanax of the forces at Troy" ("Causal Mythology," *Muthologos*, I, 96).

III.42. Good News / can come / from Canaan

See note to "Some Good News," *Maximus* I, 120.

▶ **III.43. vonis kvam . . .**

Written in Buffalo ca. February 1964. Original in notebook following *Maximus* III, 30–34, an early fragment of the Enyalion poem (III, 38–40), and the "Statement for the CAMBRIDGE magazine," which was dated when published February 1964; and before fragments of *Maximus* III, 51 from March. Typed around the same time as the previous two poems. See also Olson's note on his final manuscript of the Enyalion poem, quoted above in note to III, 38.

"Vonis kvam" would be "Old Norse-Algonquin" for the river Annisquam. See Sherwin, *Viking and the Red Man*, I, 304–305, where it is said that Wannasquam, spelled also Wonnesquam, is derived from Old Norse *vanns-kvam*, 'river cove or inlet.' Mentioned in conversation by Olson, June

1968, as his source. Although he apparently did not own this volume (only Sherwin's vol. 2), notes by the poet on an announcement for the first issue of the magazine *Set*, published 1961 in Gloucester, confirm his awareness of the etymology in Sherwin.

Annisquam Harbor, at the north end of the Squam River where it opens out into Ipswich Bay, is at the "back / of the Cape" from Gloucester.

III.43. Lobster Cove

First major indentation along the east bank of the Annisquam south from Annisquam Harbor.

III.43. Goose Cove

Below Lobster Cove, continuing south along the Annisquam to Gloucester.

III.43. Mill River

See *Maximus* I, 151 and note. The third major indentation, or "bump," of the Annisquam River from Annisquam Harbor to Gloucester Harbor.

III.43. Alewife / or Wine / Brook

See *Maximus* I, 21 and note. It flows into Mill Pond, the lower part of Mill River, and so might be considered a fourth "bump" for Annisquam waters.

III.43. GRAPE VINE / HOEK wyngaer's / HOEK . . .

See *Maximus* II, 9 and note.

III.43. Svenska

(Swedish) 'Swedish' or 'Swedes.'

III.43. ladder / of the Cut water / ran up hill

Cf. perhaps the following from "Maximus, from Dog-town—II" (II, 9):

> we will carry water
>
> up the hill the Water the Water to
> make the Flower hot—Jack
> & Jill will
>
> up Dogtown hill on top one day the
> Vertical American thing will
> show from heaven the Ladder . . .

III.43. bump / on earth's / tit

See Columbus' description in *Maximus* I, 79:

> Respecting the earth, he sd,
> it is a pear, or,
> like a round ball upon a part of which there is a prominence
> like a woman's nipple, this protrusion
> is the highest & nearest to
> the sky

▶III.44. The Condition of the Light from the Sun

Dated 14 February 1964 in a typescript sent to poet Charles Tomlinson. The original was written verso a State of New York paycheck stub dated 11 December 1963; it was copied out and sent Andrew Crozier in February 1964 for publication in *Granta*.

John A. Wells (b. 1908), to whom the poem is dedicated along with Alan Cranston, was a classmate of Olson's at Wesleyan University, where he was Phi Beta Kappa, captain of the basketball team, senior class president, and winner of a Rhodes Scholarship to Oxford (for which Olson was runner-up). He later became a lawyer and manager of political campaigns in the United States for the Republican Party. Cranston (b. 1914), on the other hand, was a liberal Democrat and eventually U.S. Senator from California. Olson first knew him in 1941, when both worked for the

Common Council for American Unity in New York. When Cranston was appointed chief of the Foreign Language Division of the Office of War Information following the outbreak of the Second World War, he hired Olson as his associate chief. He was controller of the State of California at the time of this poem.

Both men become figures of "Men of Power" (see *Maximus* III, 150 and note) for Olson. See the following recorded among the poet's papers: "Dreamt of Cranston night Thurs to Fri June 11th to 12th [1964] . . . If Cranston & John Wells are my own power drives, then this is who [what?] feels *old* in me now—& the I who dreams does not?"

III.44. the Bulgar and his sons . . .

See the earlier poem beginning "the / Bulgar—& / the 4 sons hidden / in the thigh . . .," *Maximus* III, 35–36 and note. Also, the Bulgar who carries "the colors," *Maximus* III, 40.

III.44. the Throne the Kingdom the Power

Echoes the close of the Lord's Prayer, "for thine is the kingdom, and the power, and the glory, for ever" (7 Matthew 13).

▶III.45. Signature to Petition . . .

Written in Buffalo or Wyoming, N.Y., ca. 10 February 1964 (one page of the original is verso a note from the English Department of the State University of New York at Buffalo from that date), in response to a request by Vincent Ferrini for the poet to add his name to a petition protesting an attempt by the Gloucester City Council to rezone Ten Pound Island for business purposes (see stories in the *Gloucester Daily Times* for 15 January 1964, 18 February, and esp. 21 February reporting the defeat of the proposal). Ferrini writes in his reminiscence "A Frame," *Maps* 4, p. 52, that when Olson "struck back at me for my

Utopia with that TEN POUND ISLAND poem and I asked him why," Olson responded with, "I don't sign petitions, I make them!"

III.45. John Watts took salt . . .

See *Maximus* I, 115 and note; also II, 74 and 106.

III.45. Admiralty Bundle, / of Court Papers 78639 . . .

Rose-Troup in *John White*, p. 99n., cites the following sources for her account of the salt controversy: "*Court of Requests* (Uncalendared) Bundle XVI. part ii. ditto Bundle 676, *Court of Request Decrees*, Book 35, fol. 314v, *Chancery Bills and Answers*, Charles I, 1636, Beale *v.* Dashwood." She does not mention any Admiralty Court papers. Olson would seem then to have invented this source, just as he approximates the number of shallops and tons of salt involved shortly below. (In a note made during his researches in England concerning the Dorchester Company, dated 16 April 1967, he writes: "It has taken a month more now, to reach this point. And that, curiously, involved a turn from port books to the Court of Requests. Which I, mistakenly, thought was Admiralty.") There were, according to Rose-Troup, eleven fishing boats and shallops and one hundred and seventy-one hogsheads of salt that Watts and White and the others were ordered to pay for.

III.45. Quahamenec

Also Quihamenec. See *Maximus* II, 24 and note.

III.45. John Smith's / earlier prognostication that / these silver waters . . .

See *Maximus* I, 109 and note.

III.45. Cicely

I.e., Sicily. The original manuscript has "Sicil . . ." begun but crossed out. Probably a fifteenth-century or "antique" spelling rather than any sense of the herb cicely is intended.

III.45. Pan Cake / Ground

See *United States Coast Pilot: Atlantic Coast, Section A*, 1950 ed., p. 321: "The best anchorage in the outer harbor for vessels coming in for shelter or bound to Gloucester is in Southeast Harbor, known locally as Pancake Ground." At another sentence on that page, "Southeast Harbor is the cove in the eastern part of Gloucester Harbor, northward of Black Bess Point and southward of Tenpound Island," Olson has added in the margin of his copy, "*Pancake Ground.*"

III.45. Armored Cruiser / Boston

Supplied by a letter of 31 November [1963] from Jonathan Bayliss, a Gloucester friend, to Olson at Wyoming:

> Two things have happened in Gloucester at once: Kennedy's death and the arrival of a missile cruiser that is a lot like JFK and beautiful to my eyes. It's anchored inside the breakwater, between Garland's house and Weld's. It has good old boyhood 8″ guns forward—2 turrets of 3 each—and guided missiles aft. Also a number of 5″ AA batteries. It is almost twice as heavy in displacement (17,000 tons) as the cruiser I used to desire.
>
> At the same time came a great blow that put a hole in the breakwater, flooded the Cut, and stranded the sailors who'd already come ashore. . . .
>
> It was a South-easter, and the *U.S.S. Boston* looked right into it. (I could have picked it up in my hand, dense as brick, and moved it like a locomotive in the bathtub.) . . .
>
> This is one of the biggest ships that's ever come inside the breakwater, as good as a frigate in the old days. . . .

III.46. the top of all tit

See Columbus' description of the earth "as a prominence / like a woman's nipple" (*Maximus* I, 79 and note). Also "earth's / tit" in *Maximus* III, 43.

III.46. the waters / do run down in bumped / courses

See the "bumps" in the earlier poem on p. 43 of this volume. Also, the account of Columbus and the Orinoco

River in Brebner, *Explorers of North America*, p. 13, Olson's original source for Columbus' description of the earth: "This time his landfall was the island of Trinidad, and here, at the mouth of the Orinoco, he thought he had found what God sent him out to see. The mighty outpourings of fresh water for miles into the sea convinced him that such a river could only flow from a continent, and presumably from the one withdrawn from the ken of man since Adam's sin and expulsion from the Garden of Eden, for there legend and theology agreed was the great terrestrial river-fountain." In a fragment in the same blue ballpoint ink as the original of this poem, on an envelope postmarked 17 January 1964, Olson writes of "The River Columbus thought / by the fact its current flowed / downhill (or was it uphill) / did prove he had struck the shores / of Paradise . . . turns out rather to be a / straight flow / down / of Agyasta. . . ."

III.46. the tiny Columbia ship

I.e., related to Christopher Columbus.

III.46. the sign of his name / as Christ-bearer

Christopher means 'Christ-bearer' (Late Greek, from a legend that St. Christopher carried Christ across a swollen river). Mentioned, too, in Brebner, *Explorers*, p. 10.

III.46. the Dove

Traditional symbol for the Holy Ghost. Appropriately, Columbus' name in Latin means 'a male dove.'

III.46. the river / of Agyasta

See *Maximus* I, 72 and note.

▶III.47. Space and Time the saliva / in the mouth . . .

Written in early March 1964. The original is verso the original holograph manuscript of the poem "West 4 and 5," which in typescript is dated 2 March 1964.

III.47. your own living hand amputated . . .

A fragment on the original manuscript more clearly identifies the hand as that of Tyr, the Norse god of battle who
places his hand in the mouth of the wolf Fenris as a pledge,
which then enables the fettering of the wolf although Tyr
loses his hand in the bargain. See, e.g., Fowler, "Old Norse
Religion," p. 248, and Davidson, *Gods and Myths of Northern
Europe,* p. 31; also *Maximus* III, 34, 38, 63, and 177. See, too,
the Salivarating Dog in *Maximus* II, 36.

▶III.48. the Alligator . . .

Written on the same sheet and at the same time as the preceding poem, with a later typescript. In that original version,
"heels" is crossed out and "balls" substituted.

In interpreting the figure of the alligator, it might be
noted that Chaos as "*the gaping jaws* of the crocodile" is
marked in Olson's copy of Liddell and Scott's *Greek-English
Lexicon,* p. 1713. Also, as the poet recognized in a commentary on a dream of his own from May 1958 concerning a
crocodile (in a notepad of such dreams and commentaries),
the beast is a type of chthonic animal. And it is into the waiting jaws of a crocodile that the fool from the Tarot pack is
about to step, in "A Foot Is to Kick With" (*Human Universe,*
p. 79).

▶III.49. Sun / upside down . . .

Holograph original in notepad written in Wyoming, N.Y.
and dated 9 March 1964.

The source for the poem is Graves' *Greek Myths,* I, 86–88,
a chapter entitled "Hephaestus's Nature and Deeds." As
Graves tells the story, the Smith-god "was so weakly at birth
that his disgusted mother, Hera, dropped him from the
height of Olympus, to rid herself of the embarrassment
that his pitiful appearance caused her. He survived this mis-
adventure, however, without bodily damage, because he fell
into the sea, where Thetis and Eurynome were at hand to

rescue him. These gentle goddesses kept him with them in an underwater grotto, where he set up his first smithy and rewarded their kindness by making them all sorts of ornamental and useful objects." In his notes, Graves adds:

> Hephaestus and Athene shared temples at Athens, and his name, if it does not stand for *hemero-phaistos*, 'he who shines by day' (i.e. the sun), is perhaps a masculine form of *he apaista* . . . , 'the goddess who removes from sight', namely Athene, the original inventor of all mechanical arts. It is not generally recognized that every Bronze Age tool, weapon, or utensil had magical properties, and that the smith was something of a sorcerer. . . . That the Smith-god hobbles is a tradition found in regions as far apart as West Africa and Scandinavia; in primitive times smiths may have been purposely lamed to prevent them from running off and joining enemy tribes. But a hobbling partridge-dance was also performed in erotic orgies connected with the mysteries of smithcraft . . . and, since Hephaestus had married Aphrodite, he may have been hobbled only once a year: at the Spring Festival.
>
> Metallurgy first reached Greece from the Aegean Islands. The importation of finely worked Helladic bronze and gold perhaps accounts for the myth that Hephaestus was guarded in a Lemnian grotto by Thetis and Eurynome, titles of the Sea-goddess who created the universe. . . .

The Corycian cave seems to be Olson's addition or perhaps confusion of the Lemnian grotto mentioned by Graves with that Lernean cave where the Hydra, offspring of Typhon, lived (see *Maximus* II, 84, 94, and notes).

III.49. connection to / the Dogs

See perhaps *Maximus* II, 123 and note, as well as the "dogs" in *Maximus* III, 53, and "the Dog" in the poem beginning "Space and Time . . ." (III, 47).

▶III.50. "home", to the shore . . .

The poet's typescript of his holograph original is dated 14 March 1964. The poem is based on a decipherment of the pictographs on the Phaistos Disk as reported in an abstract prepared by Cyrus Gordon for a colloquium held at Brandeis University on 5 March 1964 and sent to Olson shortly afterwards. See the following from that abstract:

> The two commonest words on the Disc, occurring five times each, are written HORN + BIRD ([pictographs reproduced]) and MAN + *te* ([pictographs]). The flying BIRD has been correctly identified with Linear A *ku* by B. Schwartz and S. Davis. But now we can explain the phonetic values of the Cretan signs acrophonically from the Northwest Semitic words depicted by the signs. Thus *ku* is derived from *kudr*, the Ugaritic and Syriac word for a bird of prey. Moreover, we know from Eteocretan that *r, l, m, n* and *s* were used vocalically. The archaic Praisos text has *krk* (pronounced *kṛk*) for the more familiar *kark* "town." Analagously, the Minoan word for "horn" would be *kṛn* instead of the usual Semitic for *ḳarn*. We therefore read HORN + BIRD *kṛ-ku* "town": a probable word appearing repeatedly in Eteocretan.
>
> The MAN sign, related in form to Linear A *pu/bu* ([pictographs]), can now be explained acrophonically from Ugaritic *bu-nu-šu* "man." The *te* ([pictograph]) is so read because of its resemblance to Linear A *te* ([pictographs]). The word MAN + *te* is thus to be read *bu-te* ... , the plural construct "houses" which can have the logically singular meaning "house, temple." The grammatically singular form is *bayt* "house" to judge from the HOUSE plan which seems to have the value *pa/ba,* in the repeated combination *pa-'i-to* ([pictographs/ Linear A script]) "Phaistos." Indeed Linear A *pa* ([script]) appears to be a simplification of HOUSE on the Disc.

Gordon concludes his paper by saying:

> ... The signs on the Apodulu libation bowl ... are relatively pictographic. Thus *ku* is [pictograph], clearly representing the flying BIRD. Now the *tu* sign on the bowl is [pictograph], obviously portraying an APPLE, which in Ugaritic is *tuppûh* ...
>
> In learning English, the pupil says "*a* is for *apple*"; in learning Minoan he should say "*tu* is for *tuppûh.*"

The ancient Minoan city of Phaistos, where the clay disk was discovered, was on the south shore of central Crete; the disk itself dates from around 1700 B.C. and, as Gordon points out, appears to be a ritual text associated with a shrine of Baal in the palace of that city.

▶III.51. Her Headland / over / the sea-shore . . .

Written ca. 20 March 1964, judging from notes on the same sheet as the start of a letter to the author, the final version of which was sent, dated March 20th.

See note to the previous poem.

▶III.52. To have the bright body of sex and love . . .

Holograph original written in blue ink on page torn from notepad, with the following note added in pencil: "oh yes see next sheet—& both were on top of the same folder in which notes on Blegen(?) were—on black table by fireplace." The poem was thus probably written in Wyoming, N.Y.— the Hooker house where the Olsons lived had a fireplace— and the note was apparently made by the poet when packing in order to leave, following the death of his wife in March 1964. A typescript later made by the poet has the following note at the bottom: "date? (In blue ink—abt period of Enya-lion—or *after* March 28th [i.e., the death of his wife] /////?????"

▶III.53. Maximus to himself June / 1964

The original manuscript has title "Maximus At Cut Bridge" crossed out. A note on that manuscript dates the poem more precisely: "written Thurs. June 4th—day we went to Grat-wicks."

III.53. where the tidal river rushes

The Annisquam River in Gloucester. Cf. *Maximus* I, 85:

> . . . the sight of the river
> exactly there at the Bridge
>
> where it goes out & in

III.53. the golden cloak

See *Maximus* III, 33 and note above.

III.53. no more dogs...

See *Maximus* III, 33, 49; also "the Dog" in *Maximus* III, 47 and note above; as well as *Maximus* II, 123 and note.

III.53. the fabric

Possibly with an echo of John Smith's use of the word (see *Maximus* III, 171 and note below; also III, 109).

III.53. Vessel / in the Virgin's / arms

See "my lady of good voyage / in whose arm, whose left arm rests / no boy but a carefully carved wood, a painted face, a schooner!" (*Maximus* I, 2)

III.53. no more dog-rocks / for the tide / to rush over...

See *Maximus* I, 85, "the dog-rocks / the tide roars over," and note.

III.53. not any time again / for wonder / the ownership...

Echoes "the wondership stolen by, / ownership" (*Maximus* I, 9).

▶III.54. Publish my own soul...

Dated 1 August 1964.

III.54. August my father's month

The poet's father died in August of 1935. In a note among his papers from ca. 1966, Olson has written: "My father born April 17th 1882... married January 23rd 1908 / 1st child—? December? 1908 / —& myself conceived March 27th 1910...."

III.54. the ions of March

Echo of the Ides of March, with probable, if oblique, reference to Jung's theory of synchronicity (see note to "solar piston ion force," *Maximus* III, 137).

III.54. my Mother and Father / were married in winter used an umbrella in the snow

In conversation, June 1968, Olson related an anecdote apropos these lines, concerning his parents' wedding trip to New York City, which he had included in his narrative *The Post Office*: "They arrived in a blizzard and stayed at the old Grand Central Hotel. One thing stood out that could be talked about and that my mother dwelt on with a blush. She had packed no button hook for her high shoes. My father had to go out in the storm and find some store open at that hour. He picked up their umbrella, one of the wedding presents, and when he stepped out into the snow he stepped, she delighted to put it, into a rice storm as well!" (p. 25).

▶III.55. I believe in religion not magic or science . . .

Written ca. August 1964 (original manuscript typed at the same time as the previous poem); mentioned in a letter from Robert Kelly to Olson, 7 August 1964.

See Olson's remarks on the Gratwick tape from November 1963: "You could correct Frazer's great founding statement of the nineteenth century on this [the role of religion], when he says that man goes through three stages—magic, religion, science. If you remember, that's Frazer's absolute fixed statement of why he's writing *The Golden Bough*—is to show how man was once in a magic stage, then was caught in religion, and now is in the stage of science. Well, that's only one term wrong—the stage [of] magic, so-called magic. That's inaccurate. There was no such stage as magic" (*Muthologos*, I, 40). Frazer writes in his final chapter of *The Golden Bough*, p. 711: "If then we consider, on the one hand, the essential similarity of man's chief wants everywhere and at all times, and on the other hand, the wide difference between the means he has adopted to satisfy them in different ages, we shall perhaps be disposed to conclude that the movement of the higher thought, so far as we can trace it, has on the whole been from magic through religion to science"; but see esp. the discussion of the terms in Malinowski, *Magic, Science and*

Religion, pp. 18–19, which Olson had been reading around this time.

▶III.56. fire it back into the continent . . .

Written ca. August 1964. Original manuscript typed at same time as previous poems; all three first published together in *Fubbalo* in September 1964.

▶III.57. the sky, / of Gloucester . . .

Original on a page torn from *Matter* 2, published July 1964; typed version dated "August 6th."

Cf. lines from "The Cow of Dogtown" (*Maximus* II, 148):

> The top of Dogtown
> puts one up into the sky as free-
> ly as it is possible, the extent of
> clear space and air, and the bowl
> of the light equalling, without at all
> that other, false experience of mountain
> climbed, heaven. . . .

▶III.58. The-Man-With-The-House-On-His-Head . . .

Written in Gloucester and dated 7 August 1964.

See the Algonquin legend retold as "Maximus Letter # whatever" (II, 31), and the mention, *Maximus* II, 9 of "He-with-the-House-on-his-Head."

III.58. the Otter Pond the / grant to Benjamin Kinnicum . . .

See *Maximus* II, 33 and 37, and notes above.

III.58. the road to / William Smallmans / now dwelling house

See *Maximus* II, 46 and note; also II, 152 and 160.

III.58. Dogtown <u>under</u> / City . . .

Echo of previous emphasis in "Okeanos *under* / Dogtown," *Maximus* II, 2.

III.58. Dogtown granite / -tite

See especially *Maximus* II, 16 and note.

III.58. the city to the shore

Cf. *Maximus* II, 147.

III.58. the banks

See *Maximus* II, 51.

III.58. Oceanographers Canyon

An actual designation: canyon of the ocean floor on the southern side of Georges Bank.

III.58. the / Child . . . Ocean's / Child

See *Maximus* II, 71: "The great Ocean is angry. It wants the Perfect Child." Also, "the pet child / of the lucky sea," *Maximus* II, 66.

III.58. Jupiter / furens

Latin 'raging, wild, furious,' an epithet not traditionally applied to Jupiter, the Roman Zeus, in the same way it is to Hercules (as in Euripides' *Hercules Furens*). More appropriate to Chronos (see note below).

III.58. Round Rock Shoal

See especially *Maximus* II, 70 and note, and II, 91.

III.58. the one from whom the Kouretes / bang their platters

I.e., Chronos. In the original, "for whom" is crossed out and "from" substituted. See, e.g., Harrison, *Themis*, chapter 1 entitled "The Hymn of the Kouretes," especially figure 3 on p. 23 there. The Kouretes were guardians of Zeus at his birth on Mount Ida who saved the infant from the wrath of his father, Chronos, by surrounding the cradle and with clashing of sword and shield preventing his cries from being heard. Harrison points out, "The Kouretes are *armed and orgiastic dancers* . . . Strabo says they are certain youths who execute movements in armour; it is especially as inspired dancers that they fulfil their function as ministers in sacred rites. 'They inspire terror by armed dances accompanied by noise and hubbub of timbrels and clashing arms and also by the sound of the flute and shouting.' "

▶III.59. The Feathered Bird of the Harbor of Gloucester

Written in Gloucester and dated 8 August 1964. Part of the original appears on a page of a letter from Jeremy Prynne, and the whole was later typed. The poem concerns the Gloucester sea serpent (see *Maximus* II, 32, 121, and notes above).

III.59. He was here, 1817 August 23rd . . .

This and all the details that follow—except for mention of Captain John Beach's drawing—have been selected from a small folder by Irma Kierman entitled *An Exciting and Authentic Narrative of the Visits of the Sea Serpent to Cape Ann . . .*, which had been sent to Olson's son by Mary Shore (acknowledged by Olson in a letter to her of 3 August 1960, in which he makes excerpts very much as in this poem) and used already for "HEPIT·NAGA·ATOSIS" (*Maximus* II, 121).

Kierman reports the visit by the Linnean Society to investigate sightings of the sea serpent by Gloucester citizens, who willingly testified before the committee of scientists. Kierman writes, "The concensus [*sic*] shows they saw something like a huge brown snake swimming around Ten Pound Island, as much at home as if it were plying the artificial castles of a goldfish bowl." Col. Thomas H. Perkins is reported as testifying, "As he came along, it was easy to see its motion was not like a common snake, but a caterpillar" And in other testimony by Matthew Gaffney, a ship's carpenter and local

sportsman who had a reputation as a sharpshooter, it is reported: "I had a good gun and I took good aim and I think I
must have hit him. He turned toward us immediately after
I had fired, and I thought he was coming at us, but he sunk
down and went directly under our boat and made his appearance at about one hundred yards from where he sunk.
He did not turn like a fish, but appeared to settle directly
down like a rock."

Kierman next presents a summary of the witnesses' accounts in the Linnean Society's report:

> The Society's finding was based on the concensus of
> answers made to its carefully worded questions put to a
> number of reliable eye-witnesses. A careful summary of
> the questions and the findings has been prepared by the
> Sandy Bay Historical Society of Rockport. It contains
> these colorful conclusions:
>
> Q. When seen? At what distance from the spectator?
> A. From two car lengths to 250 yards.
> Q. Was it in motion or at rest?
> A. Both; moving slowly, and sinking to the bottom like
> a rock, and turning swiftly doubling up in a U shape.
> Q. How fast did it move?
> A. Faster than any whale; a mile or more in three
> minutes.
> Q. What parts of the body were above water, and how
> high?
> A. The head and neck, many big bunches, and some-
> times many feet of smooth back.
> Q. If serpentine, were its sinuosities vertical or hori-
> zontal? That is, did it move sidewise like a land snake, or
> up and down like a caterpillar?
> A. All but one witness said "vertical."
> Q. What were its color, length and thickness?
> A. Dark colored; most say brown. Forty to 100 feet
> long; thickness of the body about half a barrel in circum-
> ference; two and one-half feet thick; size of a man's body.
> Q. Did it utter any sound?
> A. No.
> Q. Did it appear to pursue or to avoid anything?
> A. Not especially. It noticed boats when it was shot at
> and dove under them.
> Q. How many persons saw it?

A. Various numbers; once 200 were watching it at one time.

The author of the folder then reports a sighting of 28 August 1817 from the ship *Laura,* one of whose crewmen testified that the creature, which was headed northeast, " 'was much swifter than a whale; his motion was very steady and a little up and down. It had a head like a serpent and when it passed astern of the vessel it threw out several feet of tongue, resembling a fisherman's harpoon, several times, perpendicularly, and let it fall again.' "

Kierman concludes her *Exciting and Authentic Narrative* by reprinting a news item from the Salem *Register* for 23 August 1817, in which a seventeen year-old named John Johnston is quoted as saying, "The serpent's head did not look flat like a snake's, but rounded like a dog's." She then prints an interview of her own from 1947 with Judge Sumner D. York, who had been an eye-witness to the serpent over sixty years earlier, in which she asks him, "How did it really look? . . . No flames belching from its dripping jaws? . . . No forked tongue darting in and out? No fangs? No glittering eyes?"

> Judge York laughed gently and pushed the illustrator's dream of the sea serpent aside.
> "No. It was a creature like a snake at least 80 feet long with a rounded head like a dog's. You know, I've always had the idea in the back of my mind that there was some sort of food along these shores the serpent especially liked. Perhaps it was ripening seaweed . . . or some sort of small fish, like herring."

III.59. drawings exist / of his appearance . . .

The etching, "A correct View of the Town and outer Harbour of Gloucester, and the appearance of the Sea Serpent, as was Seen on the 14th August 1817—from the Original sketch of Capt John Beach Jr," hangs on a wall of the Cape Ann Historical Society. Olson owned a reproduction of the original.

▶**III.61. Coiled, / throughout the system . . .**

Written in Gloucester and dated 8 August 1964.

Again, the Gloucester sea-serpent is invoked; also Ty-phon, whose eyes showed "some glare" (*Maximus* II, 94), the serpent of the Algonquin legend (*Maximus* II, 21), and even the Midgard serpent of Norse mythology, who appears in poems omitted from the published series. On the original manuscript of the previous poem appears: "The jewel, in the dragon's / eye, the sea serpent's / gleam . . ." See, too, "HEPIT·NAGA·ATOSIS" (*Maximus* II, 121), which begins:

> entwined
> throughout
> the system . . .

▶**III.62. Right at the Cut . . .**

Written in Gloucester, early August 1964 (original seems to have been typed at the same time as poems dated 6−8 August that year).

The figure referred to is "his nibs" from the poem "*Monday, November 26th, 1962*" (*Maximus* II, 140), who had "crawled up" out of the Harbor and was "sitting on Piper's Rocks / with a crown on his head. . . ."

▶**III.63. The Wolf / slinks off . . .**

Written ca. 11 August 1964 (the date of a note verso original manuscript).

See esp. *Maximus* III, 31 and 47 and notes; also II, 36 and note.

▶**III.64. There was a salt-works at Stage Fort**

Written in Gloucester and dated 19 August 1964. Typed original only.

III.64. Elias Parkman / was the name of the salt-maker ...

See Babson, *History of Gloucester,* p. 120 (marked in Olson's copy): "Elias Parkman was of Boston in 1651. He is mentioned in our records without date, as purchaser of a house and land, in Fisherman's field, of Christopher Avery. In 1655, he had a grant of 'wood and timber from the run of water as runneth out at the beach by the salt-work; in consideration of which he is to let the town have salt, for their own proper use, 6d. per bushel cheaper than he sell out of town, for such pay as the town can pay him at pris currant.' If he resided in town at all, it was probably only for a brief period."

The information in the poem concerning this 1655 grant to Parkman is to be found originally in the Gloucester town records (see "Transcript of the First Volume ... Commencing 1642," p. 48). Olson has worked backwards from that point, tracing through the records the owners of the land in Fisherman's Field previous to Parkman, from Edmund Brodway to Giles Barge and Christopher Avery. So that, on p. 52 of that same volume of records, the land is recorded sold first by Brodway to Barge in December 1653: "Geils Burge Bought of Edmund Brodway 2 acres of upland in fishermans field William Colmans Land Liing on the west side and James Babsons Land on the east side and Buts upon the sea sothherly. . . ." Then on p. 43 earlier, the sale from Barge to Avery on 16 April 1655 is recorded: "Geils Berg sould to Christo— Avery 2 acers of Land Liing in fishermans feeld Lying Betwixt James Babsons Land and Samuel Dolevers Land and Buts to the sea side and Reacheth home to Thomas Verys Land and do Record it to him and his assigns for ever." Finally, on p. 57, the land is sold by Avery to Parkman, 22 March 1657: "Christopher Avery sold to Elias Parkman that house abovesaid with 2 akers of land in ffishermans ffield and 2 acers of land liinge at the head of the house lots in the head of the harbour at the ende of Thomas Princes lote northwest. . . ."

III.64. the land appears / initially to have been Thomas Millward's . . . the Thompson fish- / ery of 1638/9 . . . Dutch's letter to his wife . . .

See *Maximus* I, 156−160 and notes; also II, 60−61.

III.64. Trapiano / barks

Trapani, a salt-shipping port in western Sicily. "Nearly all the salt used for codfish comes from Trapani, in the Island of Sicily, while the mackeral salt is imported from the vicinity of Liverpool" (advertisement for Gloucester fish merchants John Pew & Son in *New England Magazine,* XII, 1892, p. 25).

III.64. The Bay

The Massachusetts Bay Colony.

III.64. cod . . . its silvermine

See John Smith's description, *Maximus* I, 109 and note; also *Maximus* I, 157 and III, 45.

III.64. vessels too were built (at Salem Neck)

See, e.g., *Maximus* III, 28 earlier, and III, 145.

III.64. Bay / had pine-tree monies of its own

Massachusetts established a mint in 1652 and issued silver coins with pine and other trees stamped on the obverse, which came to be known as pine-tree shillings (see e.g. Morison, *Builders of the Bay Colony,* pp. 150−153, with illustration).

III.64. as Malthus found

See *Maximus* I, 72 and note; also II, 152.

III.65. Castine

Maine town on the east side of Penobscot Bay, named for Baron de St. Castin or Castine (see *Maximus* III, 91).

III.65. the Bay's alertness, 1642

When Endicott and Downing, commissioners of the General Court of the Massachusetts Bay Colony, authorized "the first ordering, settling, and disposing of lots" which in effect created the town of Gloucester (*Maximus* I, 156 and note).

III.65. get Cape Sable . . . from / Indians and from French

The southernmost point of Nova Scotia. The entire province, save for Cape Breton, was ceded to England after years of fighting against the French and Indians by the Treaty of Utrecht in 1713.

III.65. halibut, in 1936, when the waters of the Atlantic had / still not warmed up swordfish too . . .

Olson would be reporting this from his own firsthand experiences on Georges Bank (see *Maximus* I, 26–27 and notes). For the Peak of Browns, see *Maximus* I, 7 and note.

III.65. Novy

Local slang for Nova Scotia or Nova Scotian.

III.65. Biscay

See *Maximus* I, 77 and note; also I, 120.

III.65. an island floating in the Western Sea

Cf. *Maximus* I, 77: "in the Atlantic, / one floating island . . ."

▶III.66. The NEW Empire

Typewritten manuscript only, written in Gloucester and dated "Thurs Aug 20th [1964]"; typed at same time as previous poem. The title (and the phrase recurring in final lines) is an allusion to Brooks Adams' *The New Empire*, which deals with the emergence of the United States as a world power at the close of the nineteenth century (see, e.g., Olson's introductory note to the Frontier Press reprint of the book and his review, "Brooks Adams' 'The New Empire,'" *Human Universe,* pp. 135–136).

III.66. Homey, over the Cut, Homer Barrett . . .

See *Maximus* I, 109 and note. "Over the Cut" was a familiar Gloucester expression for persons who lived in Gloucester west of the Annisquam River (see also below, "Charley Olson from over the like / Cut," III, 224).

III.66. Poliziano

Angelo Poliziano (also Politian, as spelled again later in the poem)—1454–1494—Italian humanist and friend of Lorenzo de Medici.

III.66. on the Fort, Neolithic family life

See below, *Maximus* III, 166.

III.66. Rank sayeth . . .

Otto Rank (1884–1939), psychoanalyst and author of *Art and Artist,* which Olson first read in the 1940's. See specifically Rank's selected writings issued under the title, *Myth of the Birth of the Hero,* pp. 300–301, in the chapter "Forms of Kinship and the Individual's Role in the Family":

> The transition from a primitive group-family (kinsfolk) to our present-day small family is characterized by the acceptance of the father's individual role of begetter of his children; this role was formerly denied him for religious reasons, the group's desire for immortality. This development changed the child from a collective being into a personal representative of a patriarchal-individual ideology. The transition phase was the matriarchy . . . Today with the enfeeblement of the *patrias potestas* and the strengthening of an individualistic tendency, the child is an individual for himself, although he is lawfully the father's successor and is claimed as a collective being by the State. Thus the three chief stages in the ideological

development of the child are: a collective being (mother), heir (of the father), private being (self).

III.66. Self, he says (hero, poet, psychoanalyst, in that / order . . .

Rank, *Myth of the Birth of the Hero,* p. 312:

> . . . a collective ideology has already given place to a family organization that finds immortality in children, and the individual ego can no longer free itself from this racial fetter. Finally, in a present-day man whose victorious individualism has precipitated the downfall of the father's rule and of the family organization, we find the same motive interpreted as a wish for the father's role, a motive that originally gave expression to the horror of it. . . . The poet-dramatist is the successor of the hero, in that he narrates the heroic deed as a recollection of the "good old times"; and the psychologist proves to be the poet's successor in that he interprets it anew for us today.

III.66. the Park

Stage Fort Park.

III.66. the Two Brothers of the American Oil / Co.

See *Maximus* I, 110 and note, and II, 137.

III.66. before Arizona came

Arizona was admitted to the Union in 1912.

III.66. power as child (collective guilt as collective soul)

See chapter XI of Rank's *Myth of the Birth of the Hero,* "Forms of Kinship and the Individual's Role in the Family." For example, on p. 299 Rank speaks of "the child's role as a collective soul-bearer," while on p. 300 he writes that among primitives the child "has not only more collective significance but also more religious significance, that is, the child guarantees the continuation of existence to the community, not only in the social sense but also in the meaning of the original belief in immortality." Also note following.

III.66. Responsible / (said Rank) for being fathers . . .

See e.g. *Myth of the Birth of the Hero,* p. 304: "we have briefly described the different stages of this parental attitude and have designated the employment of the child as 'heir' as the decisive turning point from the original concept of the child as a collective being to his present position as a free individual. At this stage of patriarchal culture, the child is no longer important as the bearer of the collective soul of the race, but as the individual successor of the personal immortality of the father."

III.67. When I was a Blue Deer Viola Barrett was my mother

See the dream-poem, "As the Dead Prey Upon Us":

> and the Indian woman and I
> enabled the blue deer
> to walk

> and the blue deer talked,
> in the next room,
> a Negro talk

> it was like walking a jackass,
> and its talk
> was the pressing gabber of gammers
> of old women

> and we helped walk it around the room
> because it was seeking socks
> or shoes for its hooves
> now that it was acquiring

> human possibilities

For Viola Barrett, the "Indian woman" of the dream (identified by the poet in conversation, June 1968), see *Maximus* II, 150 and note.

III.67. 1923, 300 years after

After the coming of the Dorchester Company settlers in 1623 and the founding of Gloucester.

III.67. Florence

Seat of the Medici, center of the Italian Renaissance.

▶III.68. The Cormorant / and the Spindle . . .

A typed manuscript—the basis for this published version—appears to have been made in August 1964, at the same time that other poems from that date (such as the two preceding ones) were typed. However, an earlier version may have been written as early as 1963, judging from an entry in a notebook from ca. 1966: " 'Republic' starting 1963: exact date of Crocodile & Spindle?" One holograph manuscript also among the papers bears no date but seems to be early (on notepad sheet from early 1960's), while still another is written on a book mailing envelope from the Gloucester publisher Peter Smith, but that unfortunately is also undated. In that version, which differs only in line arrangement, the poet has crossed out: "The Spindle / on which I once / and only once saw / a cormorant."

Both cormorants and the "Spindle" appear together as early as a poem from 13 August 1960. See also the appearance of a cormorant on Black Rock's "spindle" on *Maximus* III, 115.

The Spindle becomes "the fixed pole in the whirl of phenomena" in the poet's copy of *The Secret of the Golden Flower*, p. 7, where the phrase is underlined, with the following note dated 26 April 1969 in the margin, worded cautiously, even secretly, to preserve its special meaning for the poet: "my sp' _____ / & the (Bird) on it." For more on the Cormorant, see perhaps *Maximus* III, 184.

III.68. Black Rock

The *United States Coast Pilot,* 1950 ed., p. 321, identifies Black Rock as lying "100 yards off the western end of Rocky Neck." It is "bare at half tide, and is marked by a daybeacon, red oblong cage on iron spindle." The poet has underlined the last three words in his copy, with the note, "the *Spindle*," drawn to it in the margin.

▶III.69. COLE'S ISLAND

Written in Gloucester and dated 9 September 1964, almost six months after the sudden death of the poet's wife. There is, however, an earlier version, apparently based in part on a dream, written in a notepad between February 26th and March 6th, 1963. It begins:

> Death, I am paying my respects.
> You come out suddenly on the path
> as though I am a trespasser on your land.
> With your gaiters. Etc. The last time,
> just about here, when I drove in,
> in my car, with son, we scared
> two handsome pheasant . . .

Cole's Island is located in West Gloucester on the Essex River west of Wingaersheek and Coffin beaches, and is reached via Concord Street. It is not a true island, but attached to the mainland by marshes and a road. The area is secluded and thick with growth, though clearly identified by a sign, which also declares that it is private property and warns against trespassing.

III.69. Essex River

Western boundary of Cole's Island, originating at Essex, Mass., and flowing into Essex Bay and the much larger Ipswich Bay.

▶III.71. Hector-body . . .

Originally written in a notebook some time after 14 March 1964 (date on earlier page) but by 28 March 1964 when it was typed, in Buffalo or Wyoming, N. Y., with lines "got home again, / Wednesday / January 20th / 1965" added in blue ink in Gloucester to the typed manuscript. The original typescript has noted in red ink at the bottom: "follows Phaistos Disc poem [*Maximus* III, 50 or 51] . . . must date abt Week of March 28th"; mentioned as written 28 March 1964 in class the following year (author's notes, 9 March 1965). A copy, with the later lines added and a similar note on bottom, was sent Edward Dorn, 22 January 1965.

See Webster, *From Mycenae to Homer*, p. 94: "Two phrases can be dated by military practice. In strangely archaic lines Hektor says: 'I can wield to the right, I can wield to the left my dry cow. That for me is shield warfare.' Leumann rightly says that Hektor emphasizes his technique of mobile defence against Ajax' more static method with his body-shield, and regards this as the original use of the formula 'shield warfare', from which he traces several later passages. Hektor is here giving the new tactics of the hand-grip shield, which had been introduced at least by the time of the Warrior vase." By "Goddess-shield" following, then, Olson means the figure-eight shaped (goddess-shaped) body-shield of the Mycenaeans, made of cow-hide, which gave way to the round hand-grip shield of bronze. (See also the similar phrase in his 1962 poem beginning "As the shield goddess, Mycenae . . . ," *Maps* 4.)

III.71. the Knossian / who is compared to Enyalios

See Webster, *From Mycenae to Homer*, p. 105: "The Cretan Meriones, the owner of the boar's tusk helmet and regularly described as 'the equal of the murderous Enyalios' (the Cretan war god attested on the tablets) . . ." On p. 117, Webster also mentions that Meriones had a body-shield in addition to his boar's tusk helmet.

III.71. Helladic

Pertaining to Bronze Age Greek culture.

III.71. now moves on east from / west of Albany

I.e. towards Gloucester from Buffalo, where the poet had been teaching since September 1963. "Troy" in the earlier line thus is possibly a pun on Troy, New York, just north of Albany.

▶**III.72. Sweet Salmon . . .**

Written in pencil on the last page of the poet's copy of *The Maximus Poems* (1960) and dated 20 March 1965. This is the Celtic Salmon of Wisdom, "the tasting of whose flesh," Jessie Weston writes, "confers all knowledge" (*From Ritual to Romance,* p. 124). The passage is underlined in pencil in Olson's copy and a few pages later the corner of p. 130 has been folded down as a place-mark, where the following re-telling of the story of Finn occurs:

> Finn Mac Cumhail enters the service of his namesake, Finn Eger, who for seven years had remained by the Boyne watching the Salmon of Lynn Feic, which it had been foretold Finn should catch. The younger lad, who conceals his name, catches the fish. He is set to watch it while it roasts but is warned not to eat it. Touching it with his thumb he is burned, and puts his thumb in his mouth to cool it. Immediately he becomes possessed of all knowl-edge, and thereafter has only to chew his thumb to obtain wisdom.

The story is also told in Graves, *White Goddess,* p. 68.

The figure of the salmon will occur again in *Maximus* III, 187.

III.72. Cut the finest / on the bone.

Apparently a reference to a Paleolithic bone-carving. See the following note dated 1 December 1959 among the poet's papers:

> the genetic is
> "soft"—hard soft [salmon] is END, the END (was used to be
>   but not first, wisdom: First,
>   was *salmon*: cf such & such
>   bone carving   art mobilier
>   Frawnce, Perigordian
>   perhaps
>   Aurignacian
>   anyway

Again, in a poem from the same period among the poet's papers, beginning "OCEAN, and we shall fall . . . ," there occurs: "OCEAN is stags cut on a reindeer horn, with salmon entangled under their feet the female / SIGN OF LIFE carved in their sides, salmon is the softness of the wise . . ." (for which, see e.g., fig. 208 in Osborne, *Men of the Old Stone Age*). Also, in a poem for Fitz Hugh Lane entitled "TO CELE-BRATE WHAT HE STANDS ON / THE CITIZEN IDIOT OR THE IDIOGRAPHY / OF HIS BEING" from 14 June 1960:

> . . . the salmon
> of the first
>   reindeer
>   bone
>   carved
> to show wisdom

In a letter to Robert Creeley, 12 November [1967], Olson would write: "the Salmon my Paleolithic . . . ancestors . . . taught me *is* the performance—or was it my Irish love-potion? Yes, that, that was it: that activity, of the Salmon—& they certainly didn't, those Pleistocene Celts mean just fish . . . When love makes the sun inside us instead of   or in addition to, of course, the one out there all these essential two or three fish & animals [if that many] and that One Flower one flower which takes over suddenly & expose both the inorganic & the organic as organism, and autonomy then is what it is all about—is the possible Salmon."

▶III.73. Poem 143. The Festival Aspect

Both the original holograph manuscript, written in Buf-falo, and the published version are dated 29 March 1965.

Why "Poem 143"? There were thirty-six separate poems in the first volume (thirty-seven including the "Second Letter on Georges") and at least one hundred and forty in the second volume, including a "Letter 157" (*Maximus* II, 177), although Olson had not yet determined the final order or even complete contents of *Maximus IV, V, VI* by this time. Un-doubtedly a number arbitrarily assigned the poem, as a way of reminding the poet himself or the reader of the continuity of the series. In a note in his copy of Zimmer, *Myths and Sym-*

bols in Indian Art and Civilization, p. 69, Olson has: "Monday April 12th ['144' was Sunday]."

For "The Festival Aspect," see Zimmer, p. 185: ". . . let us consider one more of the 'Festival Aspects' of the great divinity [Shiva] whose 'Fixed or Fundamental Figure' is the lingam."

III.73. the three Towns

See Zimmer, *Myths and Symbols,* pp. 185–187:

> According to an ancient Vedic conception, the universe comprises three worlds (*triloka*), (1) the earth, (2) the middle space or atmosphere, and (3) the firmament or sky. These are called "The Three Towns" (*tripura*). Shiva as Tripurantaka puts an end . . . to the Three Towns. The story goes, that, once again in the course of history, the demons, titans, or anti-gods (*asura*), half-brothers and eternal rivals of the proper rulers of the world, had snatched to themselves the reins of government. As usual, they were led by an austere and crafty tyrant, who . . . had acquired special power by dint of years of fierce self-discipline. Maya was this tyrant's name. And when he had taken to himself the entirety of the created cosmos, he constructed three mighty strongholds, one in the firmament, one on earth, and one in the atmosphere between. By a feat of magic he then amalgamated his three fortresses into one—a single, prodigious center of demon-chaos and world-tyranny, practically unas- sailable. And through the power of his yoga he brought it about that this mighty keep should never be conquered unless pierced by a single arrow. . . .
>
> The bow of Shiva had, in the past, accomplished cele- brated deeds. . . . And so now again it is he who is peti- tioned to intervene to re-establish the divine order of the universe. His work, this time, is to be the annihilation, with a single shaft, of the universal stronghold of the demons, Tripura.

III.73. the Absolute

Zimmer, *Myths and Symbols,* p. 123: "The Absolute is beyond the differentiating qualifications of sex, beyond all limiting, individualizing characteristics whatsoever. It is the all-containing transcendent source of every possible virtue and form. Out of Brahman, the Absolute, proceed the energies of Nature, to produce our world of individuated forms, the swarming world of our empirical experience, which is characterized by limitations, polarities, antagonisms and co-operation."

III.73. delta / and lingam

See Zimmer, *Myths and Symbols*, p. 147: "The downward-pointing triangle is a female symbol corresponding to the yoni; it is called 'shakti' "; and also this note there: "Likewise, according to Greek lexicographers, the Greek letter Δ, delta, denotes (though upward-pointing) the female . . ." Zimmer's main text continues: "The upward-pointing triangle is the male, the lingam, and is called 'the fire' (*vahni*)."

III.73. the Lotus

See Zimmer, *Myths and Symbols*, p. 90 (marked in Olson's copy):

> When the divine life substance is about to put forth the universe, the cosmic waters grow a thousand-petaled lotus of pure gold, radiant as the sun. This is the door or gate, the opening or mouth, of the womb of the universe. It is the first product of the creative principle, gold in token of its incorruptible nature. It opens to give birth first to the demiurge-creator, Brahma. From its pericarp then issues the hosts of the created world. According to the Hindu conception, the waters are female; they are the maternal, procreative aspect of the Absolute, and the cosmic lotus is their generative organ. The cosmic lotus is called "The highest form or aspect of Earth," also "The Goddess Moisture," "The Goddess Earth." It is personified as the Mother Goddess through whom the Absolute moves into creation.

III.73. It isn't even a burning point

See perhaps Zimmer, p. 147: "The Absolute is to be visualized by the concentrating devotee as a vanishing point or dot, 'the drop' (*bindu*), amidst the interplay of all the triangles [of the Shrī Yantra]. This Bindu is the power-point, the invisible, elusive center from which the entire diagram expands."

III.73. a single arrow

See note above to "the three Towns."

III.73. the Flower / will grow down

The cosmic flower, the Lotus (Zimmer, p. 144), but also the Golden Flower (*Maximus* III, 18 and note).

III.74. gloire

French, 'glory.'

III.74. The Elephant / moves easily . . . He is Ganesh . . .

The elephant-headed god Ganesha. See Zimmer, *Myths and Symbols*, p. 70: "Ganesha forges ahead through obstacles as an elephant through the jungle . . . The elephant passes through the wilderness, treading shrubs, bending and up-rooting trees, fording rivers and lakes easily; the rat [traditionally pictured with him in Indian iconography] can gain access to the bolted granary. The two represent the power of this god to vanquish every obstacle of the Way." See plate 53 in Zimmer for a relief portrait of Ganesha "with big hands." See also the Elephant in the final portion of "West 4 and 5" from 1964.

III.74. the adamantine

See Zimmer, p. 145: "the term *tatha-tā*, 'such-ness,' represents the utterly positive aspect of Nirvana-enlightenment, the only really real state or essence, not to be undone or dissolved. All other states of consciousness are built up and dissolved again—the waking-state with its sense experiences, its thinking and its feeling, the dream-state with its subtle apparitions, and even the states of 'higher' experience. But the state *tatha-tā* is indestructible; for it is at once the experience and the reality of the Absolute. And it is termed 'adamantine' (*vajra*); for it is not to be split, disintegrated, dissolved, or even scratched, either by physical violence or the power of critical-analytic thought."

▶III.76. George Decker . . .

Written ca. 29 March 1965. The handwritten original is on the back of one page of a manuscript of the preceding poem, which is dated March 29th. A xeroxed copy, preserved among Olson's papers, was made of a typescript of the original, and the typescript itself, with two minor revisions, given Edward Budowski for publication in *Fubbalo* (now in Spencer Library, University of Kansas).

See Ingstad, "Vinland Ruins Prove Vikings Found the New World," esp. pp. 727ff. Ingstad's assumption "was that Vinland itself, the Viking's first land base, would logically be found in northern Newfoundland," and he had undertaken a search for the evidence of that earliest settlement:

> . . . One day, after many disappointments, I asked yet another fisherman my routine question. He scratched the back of his head and said, "Well, not so long ago George Decker over at L'Anse au Meadow [possibly L'Anse au Meduse, 'Jellyfish Bay'] was talking about some ruins there."
>
> We were off at once to L'Anse au Meadow, near the tip of Newfoundland Island. Here a few houses huddled at the sea edge.
>
> The village had only 11 families, all fishermen, people who speak English with a characteristic accent. No road reached the place.
>
> George Decker, a domineering man, but with warm, humorous eyes, was there to greet us. I asked about ruins, and Decker said: "Yes, there is something like that over at Black Duck Brook."
>
> "Has anybody been digging there?"
>
> "No stranger has seen them, and here at Lancey Meadow nobody tramps around without me knowing it," said Decker firmly.

> A few minutes' walk to the southwest brought us to Black Duck Brook, splashing through scrub willow and grass down to the shore. Cattle and sheep grazed on some of the most northerly good pastureland on Canada's Atlantic coast. An inviting place, peaceful and untouched.

In 1962—63 a smithy with a quantity of iron slag, small bits of iron, and some natural bog-iron, was uncovered at the site. Olson's date of 1006 A.D. for the settlement would seem to be a misprint (although in his "Vinland Map Review" he has an equally unconfirmed date of 1004), for Ingstad reports, p. 731: "Material in the blacksmith's fireplace gave two radiocarbon readings, one A.D. 860, plus or minus 90 years, and the other A.D. 1060, plus or minus 70 years."

Ingstad's find is also reported in Oxenstierna, *The Norsemen*, pp. 257—263. See, in addition, Olson's "Vinland Map Review" (*Additional Prose*, pp. 60—68).

III.76. Los Americans

As in "Los Americanos," Spanish for 'The Americans.'

III.76. Skraelings

The Norse name for the native Americans, as it appears in the sagas.

III.76. Norse are / Rus (Russia)

The Rus were the Swedish settlers in the ninth and tenth centuries A.D. of what in the nineteenth century became known as Russia, the name being derived from a Swedish word for seafarers (*Rods-men*, 'men of the oar-way'). See Oxenstierna, *The Norsemen*, pp. 99 and 104ff., also Brondsted, *The Vikings*, pp. 60—64.

III.77. Strzegowski only / removes the division / of Mesopotamia and / European.

Josef Strzygowski (1862—1941), an Austrian art historian whose *Origin of Christian Church Art* Olson valued highly. See e.g. p. 2 of that study: "Christianity in the first years of its growth embraced a vast territory inhabited by peoples widely differing in culture, among whom those of the Mediterranean coast-lands formed a minority, representing, intellectually, perhaps a third of the whole. The other two-thirds were Semites and Iranians, both Eastern peoples; and it will be one object of the present book to show how much these achieved for the growth of Christian art during the thousand years after Constantine. It must be remembered that at first there was neither East nor West in the modern sense. . . ."

▶ **III.78. ramp . . .**

Written in Gloucester; typescript dated 1 April 1965. A slightly longer earlier version bears the following note: "[*typed Sept 4 1964*) was written in fly of old Webster's used in kitchen—dates (spring 1963?)" The original poem referred to, written in pencil, can be read with difficulty on the back flyleaf of one of the poet's copies of *Webster's Collegiate Dictionary*, 5th edition.

See also *Maximus* II, 122 and note.

III.78. to eat God's food / raw

An allusion to the Aztec name for the sacred hallucinogenic mushroom, *teonanacatl*, meaning 'God's flesh' (the earlier version of the poem has "to eat God's food / to eat life's flesh . . ."). In "Under the Mushroom," the poet declares, "The Aztecs called the mushroom 'God's meat.' You *bit* God when you took the mushroom. This is literally *carne*, the earliest Spanish translation of the Nahuatl for the mushroom" (*Muthologos*, I, 50). It should also be noted that there is a buried etymological pun in the passage: both Latin *caro* 'flesh' (from whence *carne*) and English *raw* have same root, CRV- (Lewis, *Elementary Latin Dictionary*, p. 939, marked in Olson's copy, and see use of the root and cognates in "Experience and Measurement," *OLSON* 3, pp. 60–61).

▶III.79. Maximus, in Gloucester Sunday, LXV

Written in Gloucester upon the poet's return from teaching the previous spring at Buffalo and reading at the Festival of the Two Worlds in Spoleto, Italy, and at the Berkeley Poetry Conference that summer; dated 22 August 1965.

III.79. Osmund Dutch, and John Gallop, mariners . . .

See the letter written by John Winthrop *to* John White, 4 July 1632, in *Winthrop Papers*, III, 87 (marked in the poet's copy), in which is mentioned, "I wrote to you by the last returne, how I had vndertaken to paye them of Dorchester for Jo: Gallop and Dutche their wages, which Mr. Ludlowe did accompt to receive parte heere and parte in England, so as I mervayle you should have any further trouble about it." Also mentioned in Rose-Troup, *John White*, p. 300.

For Dutch, see also *Maximus* I, 158 and note, and II, 60 and 65; for Gallop, *Maximus* II, 65.

III.79. Abraham Robinson

See *Maximus* I, 160 and note, and II, 60 and 65.

III.79. Beverley . . . Bass River

See *Maximus* I, 45 and note.

III.79. John Tilley

See *Maximus* I, 99 and note; also *Winthrop Papers*, III, 256, 264, and 320.

III.79. Slews are named still / after them

See, e.g., *Maximus* II, 144 and note; also "John Gallop's Folly" below, III, 145–146 and note.

III.80. 28 / Stage Fort Avenue

A curious slip for 28 Fort Square (Stage Fort Avenue was where the poet spent his youthful summers in Gloucester).

▶**III.81. The Savages, or Voyages of / Samuel de Champlain of Brouage**

The original was probably written ca. 24 September 1965, after Olson had flown back to Gloucester from Buffalo, in the margins of his copy of Saville, *Champlain and his Landings at Cape Ann,* beginning on p. 6 and working backwards. It was copied and sent to Albert Glover ca. 7 October 1965.

The title is the first part of Champlain's account of his voyage to the North American coast in 1603. See Saville, pp. 8–9:

> [Champlain] was the son of a sea captain and must have received a very careful training in the principals [*sic*] of navigation and cartography, as well as in drawing, as his later career reveals. His maps and colored drawings of the fauna and flora of the New World, are evidences of a high degree of skill. That he was industrious and a quick worker is shown by the fact that on his first voyage to Canada, he left France on March 15, 1603, landed again in France six months later on September 20th, and the report on "The Savages, or Voyages of Samuel de Champlain of Brouage made to New France in 1603," was composed and ready for the press in five days less than two months after his return . . .

III.81. <u>1529</u> . . . <u>Ribiero</u> / (or 1537 anyway) . . .

Saville, pp. 5–6, quotes the historian J. G. Kohl: " 'From Cape Cod along the shores of our gulf to the north, we find no other more prominent point than Cape Ann, the extreme point of the rocky peninsula of Essex county. It is high and conspicuous, and was probably often seen by early navigators. I believe that I have found traces of it in the reports of the old Norsemen on our coast, and I suppose that it was the same cape, which, at a later date, the Spanish called 'Cabo de Sta. Maria (St. Mary's Cape).' " Saville points out that Kohl is "quoting from Oviedo (1537), who in describing the coast bases his description on the lost map of Chaves, 1536, and the map of Ribiero, 1529. . . ."

III.81. land discovered by the pilot Estevan / Gomez ...

From Saville, p. 6:

> The great map of the Spanish cartographer, Alonso de Santa Cruz, accompanying his Isolario General, quarta parte, composed as early as 1541, was published for the first time in 1908 ... On plate III is the map of the northeastern part of the United States, and the territory of New England is denominated "land discovered by the pilot Estevan Gomez." We find designated "cabo de Santa Maria" (Cape of Saint Mary, Cape Ann) ... From these credible sources it is clearly evident that Cape Ann was skirted and named Cape Saint Mary by the Spanish explorer, Gomez, in 1525, eighty years earlier than the visit of Champlain.

III.81. as early as 1506 / fishermen / of Portugal ...

From Saville, p. 7: "During the sixteenth century also, apart from the geographic voyages of exploration, it is well known that beginning a little after fifteen hundred, French, Spanish and Portuguese fishermen came regularly to fish off the banks of Newfoundland. Indeed, we know, that as early as 1506, the King of Portugal gave order, 'that the fishermen of Portugal at their return from Newfoundland should pay a tenth of their profits at his customhouse.'"

III.82. I fell down from the skies ...

I.e., conceivably his air flight from Buffalo to Logan Airport in Boston, 23rd September.

III.82. the scene of Cabot's landfall ... Land of the / Bacall / a o

From Saville, p. 4: "The great island of Newfoundland, the scene of Cabot's landfall, and the adjacent region appears on the earliest maps as the land of the Bacallao, the Spanish and Portuguese name for codfish." The phrase, "the scene of Cabot's landfall," in the original manuscript is not copied out but left as part of the source, with simply a line drawn to it so that it would be included when the poem was typed out.

The voyages of John Cabot and his sons are discussed in Saville, pp. 3–4. See also *Maximus* I, 79, and note above.

III.83. Gomez / pushing / his nose into everything westward . . .

Saville, p. 5:

> In 1525 the Spaniards sent out a Portuguese navigator and pilot, Juan Gomez [also known as Estevan Gomez— see above]. At this time the southern coast of the United States was comparatively well known and, as has been shown, the northern section had not been neglected. The official expedition sent out by the Spanish Government sought to find a passage through the continent between Florida and the land of the Codfish, which would lead to China and the Orient. What they really tried to do was what Verrazano had failed to accomplish the previous year. It is generally believed that Gomez sailed across to the shores of Labrador, which he explored, and then cruised slowly from Cape Race to Florida. He failed naturally to encounter the desired strait, and no detailed account of this voyage is known. In his minute examination of the coast Gomez entered many bays and ports of the coast of New England, and gave names to them, which names appeared for some time in new maps. New England is called The Land of Gomez on early Spanish maps of North America.

▶III.84. Physically, I am home. . . .

Written in Gloucester and dated 29 September 1965. Holograph manuscript only.

III.84. the Necco

Possibly the variously-colored candy wafers known as Necco Wafers, packaged as a roll, which are manufactured by the New England Confectionery Company of Cambridge, Mass.

III.84. necessary woman   not go away / renders service / of an essential / and intimate / kind . . .

See the definition of "necessary" in *Webster's Collegiate Dictionary*, 5th ed., p. 664: "[L. *necessarius*, fr. *necesse* necessary, fr. *ne-* not + *cedere* to go away.] 1. Essential to an end or condition; indispensable. . . . 4. Rendering service, esp. of an essential and intimate kind;—now only in phrase *necessary woman*."

III.84. hypsissimus

'The highest'—from Greek ὑψος. 'high,' and the Latin superlative suffix -*issimus*.

III.84. Tower / of Zyggurat Mount hypsistos / Purgatory "Heaven" / in that 7, or <u>Colored</u> / such

See Levy, *Gate of Horn*, p. 170n: "Classical authors describe the stages of the Ziggurat of Babylon as coloured to represent the various Worlds. The Ziggurat of Borsippa was called the seven rounds of Heaven and each reappears for instance in Mithraism and in Dante's *Divina Commedia*" (marked in Olson's copy).

"Hypsistos" is true Greek (unlike the earlier amalgam "hypsissimus") for 'highest.' It was also used earlier by Olson in "A Work" (*Additional Prose*, p. 33) as a name for the oldest father of all gods according to Sanchuniathon (q.v.) as discussed by Guterbock, "Hittite Version of the Hurrian Kumarbi Myths," p. 133, who also mentions (note on that page) that a "Hypsouranios," or the 'Highest Heaven,' occurs in the same source.

III.84. saecula / saeculorum

Latin, literally 'age of ages'; in Christian liturgy, 'time without end.'

III.84. 82,000,000,000 / years

A date far beyond current estimates of the age of the earth (at least 4,000,000,000 years old); more an epoch or aeon or *kalpa,* as Olson seems to suggest when he uses the same figure only a few weeks earlier at the Berkeley Conference: "at the end of eighty-two billion years, the earth starts again" ("Reading at Berkeley," in *Muthologos,* I, 115).

III.84. condition (conditio

Conditio is an alternate spelling of the Latin *condicio* meaning 'an agreement, stipulation, condition.' Olson writes in a letter to Mary Shore, ca 29 March 1966: "*condicio* con-dition [*not* condītīo, a *preserving*] actually—& condition as you might not have reason yet to know is as STA- [bene] in *my* book——" (see e.g. his "Statement for the CAMBRIDGE magazine," *Additional Prose,* p. 56). Lewis, *Elementary Latin Dictionary,* points out in his definition of *condiciō* (p. 158) that it is not the same word as *conditīo,* and it is there that *condiciō* is defined as 'a preserving' (p. 159).

III.84. saeculum . . .

Latin, 'a race, generation, age' (Lewis, *Elementary Latin Dictionary,* pp. 744–745).

III.84. Charles ◎

In the index to his copy of Levy, *Gate of Horn,* which the poet read in at this time, he makes similar spirals for the C and O of his name in the margin of p. 347, near "spiral, symbolic . . . 'spiral of entry.' "

III.84. Video

Latin, 'to see, perceive,' from the root VID-, knowledge through sight (see *Additional Prose,* p. 21 and note on p. 87).

III.84. View Point

See note to *Maximus* II, 100.

III.84. skope

From the Greek σκοπεω 'to look at,' as in "landscape" (*Additional Prose,* p. 21). See also *Maximus* II, 126 and note.

III.85. masts, of Winthrop fleet in Western / Harbor seen / from Salem . . .

See also *Maximus* III, 127: "Endicott / sighted the Winthrop fleet's / top-mast from Salem as / they sat here. . . ."

There is no clear historical evidence that Winthrop's fleet stopped over in Gloucester Harbor on its way down the coast toward what would become Boston, though there is a local tradition that the flagship of that fleet anchored briefly at Manchester, not far from Gloucester Harbor (see "Did Winthrop Land at Manchester?" in the *Essex Institute Historical Collections*). However, this was after the fleet had arrived in Salem, or at least anchored within "Baker's Isle and Little Isle" outside Salem Harbor. In his *Journal*, Winthrop only says that on the 12th of June, 1630, "most of our people went on shore vpon the lande of Cape Anne which laye verye neere vs, and gath[ered] store of fine strawberr[ies]," although as his editor points out, "The name of Cape Anne at that time was applied to the shore from the tip of the Cape to Beverly Harbor" (*Winthrop Papers*, II, 263 and n.). In the margin of his copy, next to Winthrop's entry, Olson writes: "probably Plum Cove on the Beverly shore?," seeming to accept the editor's identification of the anchorage.

Winthrop's fleet did pass along the coast of Cape Ann on its way to Salem where Endecott was waiting, and maybe even through Gloucester's Western Harbor, if the map of the coast (cover of *Maximus* III) said to have been drawn by John Winthrop himself from the deck of the *Arabella* on June 11th or 12th of 1630 is rightly attributed to him. The editor of the *Winthrop Papers* points out that this map or portulans "is the most accurate chart we have of the Cape Ann shore previous to the one in *The English Pilot, The Fourth Book*, edition of 1765"; however, he goes on to say that it is "much too accurate to have been made by any one merely sailing along the coast, as Winthrop did" and suggests it was a tracing of a larger chart made under Endecott's orders and sent back to England earlier to aid the *Arabella's* navigation.

That the masts of Winthrop's ships could have been seen

from Salem is apparently based on the poet's own calculations from the table, "Distance of Visibility of Objects at Sea," on the inside back cover of his *United States Coast Pilot,* which gives the approximate range of visibility for an observer whose eye is at sea level. Olson writes the following note there: "Pennants, of fleet of 1628(?) at Cape Ann (11 nautical miles [the distance from Salem]) were flying on masts 85 ft or better high?"

III.85. Wm Saville's / drawing, of Gloucester Harbor . . . better than / Champlain's

In the start of an essay from 25 October 1965, almost a month later, Olson would write: "my sense, of the Harbour and the River, and of such drawings as I am here examining—Saville's, and Champlain's—is that a lack of an ideal, a 'secular' condition arising sometime *after* Shakespeare's birth and *by* Descartes has transferred itself to this side of the Atlantic already in Champlain's drawing of Gloucester Harbor 1606 and is since, when one finds it in Saville, for one happy instance of drawing without necessarily any particular art—or such usefulness of history as John Smith's maps, or any of the great discoverers or pilots, La Cosa for example. . . ." For Saville's 1813 "Plan of the Harbour of Gloucester," see *Maximus* III, 100, and notes to *Maximus* II, 201; for Champlain's map, see also *Maximus* I, 151 and note.

III.85. Breughels / Didimus

Perhaps Pieter Brueghel the Elder, who painted such scenes as "Winter Landscape with Skaters and Birdtrap." His "Hunters in the Snow" and "Numbering of the People at Bethlehem" also portray persons skating or walking on ice, if that is what is being referred to. "Didimus" may be the Greek διδυμος 'testicle' (known to Olson, judging from a comment on the author's paper written for the Myth and Literature class at Buffalo, May 1965), though also 'twin, twofold, double'—and thus possibly either of Brueghel's sons, Pieter (1564—1637) or Jan (ca. 1569—1642), also painters. Olson did own a volume of Brueghel reproductions, Gluck's *Pieter Brueghel the Elder.*

III.85. Prometheus

The Greek culture-hero who stole fire for man.

III.85. Erectus

As in *homo erectus*, upright walking man.

III.85. Winthrop's / First Map here re-produced . . .

See the cover of *Maximus* III and note above to "masts, of Winthrop fleet . . ." There is a space in the original manuscript following this.

III.85. logo rhythm

I.e., *logos* (Greek 'word, thought, speech') rhythm, in a pun with "logarithm."

III.86. Face / of God

Cf. perhaps *Maximus* I, 88: "I have known the face / of God. / And turned away . . ."; also III, 106 and 126.

III.86. Night sky / is an air / of Heaven

Echo of "Imbued / with the light / the flower / grows down / the air / of heaven" (*Maximus* III, 18); also III, 178.

III.86. de bout

Apparently, French *debout* 'upright, standing up,' or *de* 'of, from' etc. and *bout* 'end, extremity, tip.'

III.86. stlocus

See *Maximus* II, 164 and note.

▶**III.87. North, / in the ice . . .**

Written in Gloucester, 29 September 1965 (note on original manuscript dated). Holograph manuscript only.

III.87. the Bulgar / and his 3 sons

See *Maximus* III, 35 and note above; also III, 44.

III.87. NNW, Novoye / Sibersky Slovo

See *Maximus* I, 151 and note; also III, 37.

▶**III.88. Lost from the loss of her dragger . . .**

Written in Gloucester around same time as previous two
poems (same paper and ink); "full fall tide" mentioned.
Holograph manuscript only.

III.88. Salt Island

Off the eastern coast of Cape Ann at Good Harbor Beach,
near Brier Neck.

▶**III.89. THE OCEAN**

Typed manuscript dated 30 September 1965; original
holograph manuscript in notepad.

III.89. Ganesha

See *Maximus* III, 74–75 and note.

III.89. St Sebastian

Christian martyr, ordered bound to a stake by the emperor Diocletian and shot with arrows. See esp. the portraits
by Andrea Mantegna and Tintoretto.

III.89. the God punished each year . . . the Solar King . . .

See Frazer's *Golden Bough* of course, but esp. Graves'
account in *Greek Myths* of ancient calendars and the solar

year, at the decline of which a king, identified with the sun, was sacrificed (I, 12–13 and 18–19).

III.90. the Real

Cf. Olson's essay, "Equal, That Is, to the Real Itself," where he writes of "Reality" as being "without interruption"; also that "the structures of the real are flexible, quanta do dissolve into vibrations, all does flow, and yet is there, to be made permanent, if the means are equal" (*Human Universe*, pp. 118–119, 122).

III.90. life is 13 months long each year. Minus / one day (the day the sun turns).

Cf. Graves, *Greek Myths*, I 16 (marked in both of Olson's copies):

> As a religious tradition, the thirteen-month years survived among European peasants for more than a millennium after the adoption of the Julian Calendar. . . . Thus the sun passed through thirteen monthly stages, beginning at the winter solstice when the days lengthen again after their long autumnal decline. The extra day of the terrestrial year, gained from the sidereal year by the earth's revolution around the sun's orbit, was intercalated between the thirteenth and the first month, and became the most important day of the 365, the occasion on which the tribal Nymph chose the sacred king, usually the winner of a race, a wrestling match, or an archery contest. . . .

▶ III.91. Dogtown—Ann / Robinson Davis . . .

Written ca. Sunday, October 3, 1965. Original in notepad with "The Ocean" (*Maximus* III, 89–90), which is dated September 30th, and following a dream dated "Fri-to Sat October 2nd"; typed version has a note to Robert Kelly (confirmed by phone conversation, 30 May 1974) dated "Sunday."

For Ann Robinson, sister of Captain Andrew Robinson (*Maximus* II, 25 and note) and wife of Samuel Davis, see II, 37 and note, also II, 53 and 152.

III.91. who is Goodwoman Josselyn? Margaret Cammock? . . . John / Josselyn's brother Henry's / wife. Margaret Josseline

See *Maximus* II, 25 and 37, and notes above; also III, 195—196. Olson's source for information concerning Margaret Josselyn is Babson's *History*, pp. 108–109, entry for Henry Joslyn, and Baxter's notes to *The Trelawny Papers*. E.g., Baxter, p. 2n, writes that Thomas Cammock, early settler at Black Point, Maine, under a patent from Sir Ferdinando Gorges, lived there "for several years with his good wife Margaret and faithful friend Henry Josselyn . . . So great was his friendship to Henry Josselyn, that previous to a voyage to the West Indies, from which he never returned, he bequeathed his property to him, reversing for his wife five hundred acres. After his death in 1643, in Barbadoes, Josselyn married Margaret Cammock, and so came into possession of his friend's entire estate" (marked in Olson's copy, with an exclamation point in the margin).

The attempt to establish the first of the Dogtown settlement had been a concern of Olson's since the early 1960's, when he writes in notes among his papers drawn from Babson and Baxter as well as the town records:

> Margaret Josline widdow 1707—is Margaret Cammock? If so c. 84 & *all* the coast history of the 17th century . . . The matter turns on Henry Josselyn original Maine settler's birth and death. Babson says he came originally 1634, and, guessing he was 20 then (impossible—his father Sir Thomas, of Kent, was 78 in 1638, suggesting his sons John & Henry would be at least 50 by that date (??). Henry Josselyn was Thomas Cammock's friend at Black Point fr 1638 to Cammock's death on voyage to West Indies 1643. Baxter says he was driven out by King Philips' War (1676) and ended his life at Pemaquid *1683* (his son shows in Gloucester on marriage to Bridget Day 1678)
>
> It is most unlikely, is it, that Margaret Cammock wld have survived to 1707? Is she therefore "Mother Joslin" of the "funeral" 1745? . . .

In *Maximus* III, 195–196 later, Olson will be convinced she is.

III.91. Black Point

Settlement at what is now Scarborough, south of Portland, Maine; attacked by Indians in October 1676 (Babson, *History*, p. 108).

III.91. Casco Bay

On coast of Maine north of Cape Elizabeth (see also *Maximus* II, 24 and note).

III.91. Baron Castine

Jean Vincent, Baron de Saint-Castin (1636—after 1701), gentleman adventurer, who came to the Penobscot Bay region about 1667 and built up a lucrative trading business. He led the Abnakis in raids against English settlements in Maine during the tumultuous 1690's (see e.g. Parkman, *Count Frontenac*, pp. 229, 342–345, 380–381; also Hull, *Seige of Fort Loyall*, pp. 27–28) before he returned to France in 1701.

III.92. Gorges

Sir Ferdinando Gorges, the founder of Maine (see *Maximus* II, 25 and note).

III.92. St Joe

St. Joseph, Missouri, outfitting center for Oregon and California bound immigrants, including the Mormons, in the 1840's and 1850's.

III.92. Essex

Town about ten miles west of Gloucester off Ipswich Bay. It was settled in 1634 and underwent a period of economic revival in the early nineteenth century when a canal built in 1820 from Essex Bay to the Ipswich River facilitated shipping of lumber from New Hampshire, which in turn led to the expansion of the town's shipbuilding industry.

III.92. How is it they speak of her . . .

See the close of Babson's entry for Henry Joslyn (*History,* p. 109): "One member of this family received at death a special mark of distinction from the town; which paid, February, 1745, eight shillings and tenpence for four pounds of sugar and two ounces of allspice, and twenty-six shillings for four pairs of gloves 'for Mother Josselyn's funnerall.' " Olson has the following note in the margin of his copy: "is she the Margaret, of Dogtown: 1687—? 1745. . . ."

III.93. the lower of the two Dogtown / roads

Cherry Street (see *Maximus* II, 46 and notes). Later poem has the site of her grant as "out either / upper Cherry or of Gee Avenue itself" (III, 195).

▶III.94. To make those silent vessels go . . .

Written late September or early October 1965. Undated holograph original only, found among Olson's papers in a pile from 1965; in pencil, on same pale yellow paper as earlier poem from 29 September 1965 (*Maximus* III, 87) and as "Cornély" which will follow. A note on the final page of the original manuscript deals with "Vinland Map Review" materials, viz. *The Vinland Map and The Tartar Relation* itself and Brooks Adams' *Law of Civilization and Decay,* both read by October 17th for Olson's review.

It is possible that the present poem, with its tribute to James Connolly's description of fishing voyages to Georges Bank, is an earlier attempt at *"3rd letter on Georges, unwritten"* (see *Maximus* II, 107 and note).

III.94. dinkies–Pinks

Perhaps "pinkies" and "pinks"; a "dink" is only "a small boat used in duck shooting" in local U.S. usage (*Webster's New International,* 2nd ed., p. 628). Chapelle writes in his *History of American Sailing Ships,* p. 15, that "Pinks were not anything like the later fishing 'pinkies' except in having a sharp stern and false overhang of a similar design. They were about the same size as the colonial ketch and, as a rule, were also off-shore fishermen. No particular rig distinguished the type, as in the later 'pinky,' and so pinks are noted as being rigged as ships, brigantines and ketches."

III.94. Joseph Collins

Capt. Joseph W. Collins (1839—1904), a former Glouces-ter fishing schooner master employed by the U.S. Fish Com-mission in numerous capacities and co-author of "The Sea Fishing Grounds of the Eastern Coast of North America" in Goode's *Fisheries* (used for *Maximus* II, 19). For a summary of his career, see Chapelle, *National Watercraft Collection*, pp. 3—6 and 169—170. See also " 'I know men for whom everything matters,' " *OLSON* 1, pp. 26—27 (for Connolly as well).

III.94. Joseph B. Connolly

James Connolly, as Olson well knew (indicating the haste of the poem's composition)—see *Maximus* II, 107 and note.

III.94. energy ergon the Mass . . .

Ergon is Greek 'work,' root of our "energy" (with "Mass" oc-curring as a pun—the term from physics as well as the ritual of the Mass). In a letter to his former student Albert Glover dated "Passover Eve [i.e. March 26th] MDCCCCLXVI," Olson writes: "One is then in a presence more interesting than simply at least what the *word* energy too immediately—unless as an Eastern Catholic you'd have the experience, say, of the *Mass* to qualify *Ergon* (!) [I tease my *Roman* Catholic 'family' or better my compadres! with *that* one . . ."

III.94. the / able handsome "ladies" Connolly says

Chapter X of Connolly's *Book of the Gloucester Fishermen* is entitled "The Able Handsome Ladies," referring to the schooners.

III.94. "Home" and "Mother" Melville taught the Typee / natives these two words in English

See Melville's *Typee: A Peep at Polynesian Life,* chapter XXXIV entitled "The Escape" (Constable ed., p. 333): "Before I had proceeded a hundred yards I was again surrounded by the savages, who were still in all the heat of argument, and appeared every moment as if they would come to blows. In the midst of this tumult old Marheyo came to my side, and I shall never forget the benevolent expression of his countenance. He placed his arm upon my shoulder, and emphatically pronounced the only two English words I had taught him—'Home' and 'Mother.' I at once understood what he meant, and eagerly expressed my thanks to him."

Olson had written years before in an unpublished essay from 1947 or even earlier, entitled "Herman Melville and the Civil War": "Pathetically Dionysian he [Melville] fought to get back to 'home' and 'mother' all his life, not just when he left Typee with these words, the only words he had taught the natives, on his lips." D. H. Lawrence makes a similar observation (*Studies in Classic American Literature,* pp. 147—148: "[Melville] even pined for Home and Mother, the two things he had run away from as far as ships would carry him. HOME and MOTHER. The two things that were his damnation."

III.94. he was, / like Whitman was . . .

Walt Whitman (1819—1892), the great American poet. In a letter to Donald Allen, 27 February 1958, concerning Melville's poem "After the Pleasure Party," Olson wrote: "I suddenly paid attention to the *MSS* of the poem—and wow the variants, in his own hand, trying to get the crucial lines *covered* (what he was hiding: it's the same dodge as Whitman by the way made in 'A Woman Waits for Me'—which I shld want to set beside the Melville to bring the full SEX story into the strongest straightest light . . ."

III.94. Michelangelo who thought his family / came from distinguished "blood," the Canossa's

(1475–1564), the most famous of the great Florentine artists of the Renaissance; son of Ludovico Buonarroti, a poor gentleman of Florence. "The Buonarroti Simoni were an old and pure Florentine stock of the Guelf faction: in the days of Michelangelo's fame a connexion of the family with the counts of Canossa was imagined and admitted on both sides, but has no foundation in fact" (*Encyclopaedia Britannica*, 11th ed., XVIII, 362). See also Michelangelo's *Letters*, II, 64n., 86 and n.

III.94. passages from Reykjavik or / from Georges to the Boston market . . .

See Connolly, *Port of Gloucester*, p. 186:

> For quite a while Gloucester halibut catchers fished off the coast of Iceland. On a passage to Iceland one time Captain Patsy Vail in the schooner *Pauline* made the coast of Ireland in one tack, and the harbor of Reykjavik, Iceland, on a second tack. She made that passage in thirteen days, great sailing, and Captain Vail put no soft pedal on his tongue when he went ashore in Reykjavik to acquaint the natives with the sailing qualities of his *Pauline*. When the Icelanders doubted the time, Captain Vail produced a copy of the Boston *Globe* that was only thirteen days old. "Maybe," said Patsy to the doubters, "I printed that newspaper aboard the *Pauline*."

See also *Maximus* II, 107 and note, with reference there to Connolly's chapter "Driving Home from Georges" from his *Book of the Gloucester Fishermen*.

▶III.95. Cornély. . . .

Written in 1965, around the same time as the previous poem (same ink and paper); also same paper and ink as the poem following, which is dated 12 October 1965.

The material for the poem is mostly drawn from a section in Levy, *Gate of Horn*, p. 146, concerning Megalithic monuments around Carnac in northwestern France:

> This locality is still a place of gathering for the annual *pardon* celebrated at the Church of S. Cornély. The legend of this saint's arrival in the vicinity, after his flight from the Roman soldiery on the backs of two oxen, and his transformation of the pursuing army, when the sea barred farther progress, into the ranked megaliths of the alignments, lights up the perpetual Neolithic association with the animals of the pastures. The horns of the two faithful beasts are set on either side of the West door of the church, a cross standing upon each pair . . . , exactly as the double axe stands in the Aegean Bronze Age. It is recorded that the pilgrims from all countries whose sick cattle came to be healed by the saint in memory of his rescue 'passed between the stone soldiers'; that is, they used the Pathway still.

Interestingly, this material had actually come to Olson's attention as early as February 1953, while preparing lectures for his Institute on the New Sciences of Man at Black Mountain College (notes from Levy among the poet's papers from that time).

III.95. Libya's feather / stuck out on the front of the Crown of Egypt . . .

See Levy, *Gate of Horn*, p. 114: ". . . the texts based on older legends reveal the early greatness of the Western Delta, where contact with the Libyans greatly influenced the future of Egypt. The Western group of nomes retained in historic times the hunting emblems derived from that common past, and the hieroglyphic sign of the West included the Libyan ostrich feather." Also Levy, pp. 176–177, a section called "The Crowns," with an illustration of the crown of Egypt with feather standing out from the front, which Levy refers to as "the spiral of entry, whether or not that descends from the Libyan head-feather" (underlined in Olson's copy).

Mentioned also in an essay beginning "I am not the first poet who happily finds material (subject-matter) in the past . . ." from 11 October 1965: "the Libyan feather curled out counter clockwise above the uraeus at the forehead . . ."

III.95. the Cape Ann Fisheries

Right on Fort Square, across the street from the poet's house (see *Maximus* I, 107 and note).

III.95. Isle Madame

Also, Madame Isle; in the Atlantic just south of Cape Breton Island.

III.95. F.H. Lane and I stand up / on this shore

See also *Maximus* II, 191: "I stand up on you, Fort Place." For the painter, Fitz Hugh Lane, see e.g. *Maximus* II, 100 and note.

III.96. I pass between / these stone soldiers, remembering / my dreams I continue to walk into the alley . . .

An alternate ending in the original manuscript—"I walk / the night of dreams, *se promènent* / dans ces allées"—makes the debt to Levy even more obvious. Cf. *Gate of Horn*, p. 164n. (a note to passage previously quoted on S. Cornély): "Z. Le Rouzic . . . mentions the local belief: 'souvent la nuit des revenants se promènent dans ces allées' [French 'often at night the ghosts go out for a walk in these avenues,' although Olson has mistaken *revenants* 'ghosts' for *rêves* 'dreams']."

III.96. the Church of Our Lady of Good Voyages

See "my lady of good voyage," *Maximus* I, 2 and note.

III.96. The alignments or avenues . . .

Cf. Levy, p. 145: "The alignments or avenues of frequently huge, undressed monoliths, composed of local granite broken by the primeval glaciers, stretch across the plains round Carnac sometimes for a mile . . ."

▶**III.97. "cromlech" of course it is (Settlement Cove . . .**

Holograph original only, dated 12 October 1965.

For the opening line, see *Maximus* II, 85: "the rocks in Settlement Cove / like dromlechs . . . ," and note. The repeated first phrase, with "cromlech" in quotation marks, may indicate the poet is here catching the earlier error.

III.97. where the Parsons / had their first wharf

Jeffrey Parsons and a number of his descendants settled in Fisherman's Field. His son Nathaniel "engaged in mercantile business; and, at the time of his death [1722], was the owner of several vessels and a shop and wharf" (Babson, *History*, p. 123). This may be the wharf the poem refers to, unless a smaller one the Parsons as fishermen had constructed near their land is known from the Town Records.

See also *"Of the Parsonses," Maximus* II, 63–64.

III.97. Champlain shows Stage Fort . . .

See *Maximus* I, 151 and note, and esp. II, 136.

III.97. Fred Parsons, the elder

Probably the Fred Parsons (d. 1934) who is listed in the Gloucester city directory for 1899–1900 as a fisherman with a house on Old Salem Road, in the direction of Stage Fort Park, where Olson grew up summers. Later, about the time Olson knew him, he was assistant drawtender of the Blynman Bridge with a house at 110 Western Avenue, in back of Stage Fort Park.

III.97. Curcuru's first wharf, / the Fort

Benney Curcuru, fish wholesaler on Fort Square, or the Curcuru Brothers on Commercial Street nearby.

III.97. Roland Strong

See *Maximus* II, 137, and note to "Cressy- / Strong," *Maximus* II, 63. His "City-robbery garage" was one that apparently figured in scandals involving Strong's friend Homer Barrett, when he was in charge of the Gloucester Highway Department (see *Maximus* I, 109 and note).

III.97. that "Cove" . . . a 2nd / half-moon

Like Half Moon Beach (*Maximus* I, 30 and note).

III.97. the "picture" / (painting) by Fitz Hugh Lane . . .

Possibly Lane's "View of Half Moon Beach in Stage Fort Park from Gloucester Harbor," oil on canvas, ca. 1848, owned by the Cape Ann Historical Society (Wilmerding, *Fitz Hugh Lane*, 1964, p. 55)—apparently, judging from size and subject, the same as "Stage Rocks and Western Shore of Gloucester Outer Harbor," assigned new date of 1857 and reproduced in Wilmerding's later *Fitz Hugh Lane* (fig. 73).

III.98. the Holy / Circle

Like Stonehenge or other Megalithic circular stone temples (see e.g. Levy, *Gate of Horn*, pp. 142 ff.).

III.98. a place of / Ridge

Cf. perhaps the poem "The Ridge," companion to "*Letter 27* [withheld]" (*Maximus* II, 14–15), although that concerns the Harbor area not Dogtown.

▶III.99. echidna is the bite / of the asp . . .

The original was written at the same time as the previous poem (begun on the final page of the manuscript of that). Holograph manuscript only.

Echidna is Latin 'viper, adder,' from the Greek ἔχιδνα; in Greek myth (Hesiod, *Theogony*, ll. 295ff.), the half-nymph with "glancing eyes," half-serpent mother of the Lernean Hydra after mating with Typhon. Thus see *Maximus* II, 84 and note, II, 81 and note, 94, 95, etc., and connections with Gloucester's own "Monster," the Gloucester Sea Serpent (*Maximus* II, 32, 121, and III, 59–60, 61).

III.99. the uraeus (ouraios) . . . the headdress / of rulers

Ancient Egyptian emblem of power. Cf. definition of "uraeus" in *Webster's Collegiate Dictionary*, 5th ed., p. 1100: "[NL., fr. Gr. *ouraios*] *Egypt. Relig.* The representation of the scared asp on the headdress of rulers."

III.99. the Horned Viper

The cerastes, or horned viper (*Cerastes cornutus*) of northern Africa and Arabia, is supposed to be the asp which Cleopatra used to end her life. Mentioned in the *Encyclopaedia Britannica*, 11th ed., article "Asp," to which one is directed if looking up "uraeus" in Index.

III.99. the special Hydra, / the particular worship of the City . . .

See *Maximus* II, 84 and note.

III.99. the Armed Virgin

The goddess Athena. A phrase actually from Melville's poem "After the Pleasure Party" (underlined in Olson's copy of the *Poems*, 1924 ed., p. 258, with the line continued to a note in the margin: "Athena?"). Mentioned also in an untitled poem by Olson on Melville from 22 January 1966, which begins:

> Melville's sense of blooming late.
> The "Century" Plant.
> From staying up all night as
> Urania, for example. And "warning" all Virgins
> "everywhere". "Armed", etc. As though he could hide his
>   own love affair
> or condition. . . .

(After this last, see also *Maximus* III, 94, where Melville is compared to Whitman and Michelangelo.)
Athena as "the Armed Virgin" also occurs in the poem called "The Horses of the Sea" from 12 March 1963.

III.99. The Monster shall rise / from the Deep . . .

Possibly the Gloucester Sea Serpent, but also the Midgard Serpent (see *Maximus* III, 61 and note), which arises at the end of the world, when Tyr loses his hand.

III.99. the Armed Man / shall have no Right Hand

Tyr, Norse god of battle (see *Maximus* II, 34, 38—where the "Armed Man" is Enyalion—47,177).

III.99. the War / of the World

See *Maximus* II, 198 and note.

▶III.100. "Cut Creek," the River is . . .

Holograph manuscript only; dated 25 October 1965. Saville's drawing is the one referred to earlier, along with Champlain's 1606 map of Gloucester Harbor, in *Maximus* III, 85; see also *Maximus* II, 201, and notes. On that 1813 "Plan of the Harbour of Gloucester" by Saville, the Annisquam River appears designated "Cut Creek."

III.100. Alfred Mansfield Brooks, / in his clever and sentimental-pictorial- / Portrait of Gloucester as of 1800 . . .

See Brooks, "A Picture of Gloucester About 1800," p. 335: "On the port side of a vessel coming through the 'Stream' rose the steep promontory where, 1743, 'the town naked to the enemy,' a breast work was thrown up and eight twelve-pounders set. Hence the name Watchhouse Neck. Here in 1794, covering both Outer and Inner Harbors and the 'Stream' the United States Government built a real fort which now long gone, survives in the name of this part of Gloucester."

▶III.101. MAXIMUS OF GLOUCESTER

The original, but for the final two lines, was written in pencil on a small "calling card" presenting a deaf-mute manual alphabet; a typed manuscript dated 5 November 1965 was sent to the *Literary Magazine of Tufts University* for publication, with xeroxed copy retained. The size of the card on which the poem was originally written accounts for such things as the division of the word "conventual."

III.101. The con- / ventual

The word appears underlined in the poet's copy of Brooks Adams' *Law of Civilization and Decay*, p. 133, which he had been reading in October 1965. Olson wrote to Edward Dorn around that same time: "I really do prefer the soul to society; and think that the conventual is now solely the imagination which applies . . ."

III.101. "robe and bread"

Cf. Adams, *Law of Civilization and Decay*, p. 347, a passage marked in Olson's copy and quoted by him in the "Vinland Map Review" 17 October 1965, three weeks earlier: "Before the opening of the economic age, when the imagination glowed with all the passion of religious enthusiasm, the monks who built the abbeys of Cluny and Saint Denis took no thought of money, for it regarded them not. Sheltered by their convents, their livelihood was assured; their bread and their robe were safe; they pandered to no market, for they cared for no patron."

III.101. Half Moon beach ("the arms of her")

See specifically *"The View," Maximus* II, 55.

III.101. the Padma

See *Maximus* II, 11 and note.

III.101. the arete

Greek *areté* (ἀρετή), 'goodness, manly excellence' (similar to "virtue").

III.101. myself (like my father, in the picture, a shadow) / on the rock

Rewritten on poet's xerox of typed version as follows:

Later: myself (like my father, in the snap-shot, taken by himself) a shadow, thrown, on the rock, taken

Original handwritten version has: "Yourself, nothing but a shadow on the rock."

Cf. perhaps *Maximus* I, 32: "the Whale's Jaw / my father stood inside of / I have a photograph, him / a smiling Jonah . . ."

▶III.102. Tall in the Fort . . . the fortune said. . . .

Typescript of original holograph manuscript is dated 18 November 1965. Apparently written in response to an "oracle" practiced by Joan Hart, then wife of poet Robert Kelly, named "Kenkyusha" (cf. the following from a poem written in Berkeley "Wednesday July 28th [1965]" to Suzanne Mowat, a friend at the time: "Charles Peter and I "Men" strong / in the Fort Kenkusha say . . ."). In response to the author's query, Mrs. Hart wrote 24 June 1974, confirming the lead provided by the other poem: "On April 12, 1964, soon after Betty's death, we'd been concerned about Charles Peter, as I asked Kenkyusha to 'tell me about Charles & Charles Peter' to wch the response was 'Tall in the Fort.' "

"The Fort" is again Fort Point or Fort Square, home of the poet.

III.102. Fixed Will, Foreknowledge Absolute

See *Maximus* II, 126—"the foreknowledge / is absolute"— and note.

▶**III.103. Here in the Fort . . .**

Written late November 1965 (original among pile from that period). Holograph manuscript only.

"The Fort" is Fort Point, Gloucester.

III.103. the Diagram

Possibly, but not at all necessarily, one of the eight fundamental Diagrams (later expanded to sixty-four) of the *I Ching* or *Book of Changes*, or even the "diagram" mentioned by Zimmer in note to "the burning point," *Maximus* III, 73.

▶**III.104. Migration in fact . . .**

Also referred to as "The Rose of the World" poem. Holograph original dated 20 November 1965. See also the later, "linear" version below, *Maximus* III, 176.

Edward Dorn inquired of Olson, 18 July 1966, following its reproduction in the *Wivenhoe Park Review*, "is that rose of the world thing of yours . . . after the manner of the Phaistos disc???? I mean outside to inside / right to left," while Olson wrote back July 24th: ". . . it was 'product' [result of *experience* or *practicing*] of a thing I have found out does happen after hours & getting hopelessly *tired*, one—or I—go widdershins, & write both outside in [as you say] & R to L."

III.104. the Aesir-Vanirs

Rival families or races of Norse gods. The Aesir, among whom were counted Odin and Thor, originally dwelt in Asia; their travels northwest from Troy are sketched in the prologue to Snorri's *Edda*. The Vanir, too, migrated from the south and included such deities of fruitfulness as Njord, Freyr, and Freyja.

III.104. Animus

Latin, 'reason, consciousness'; in Jungian terms, an archetypal projection, essentially masculine, of the feminine unconscious.

III.104. the rose is the rose is the rose of the World

Echo of Gertrude Stein's "a rose is a rose is a rose," also written as a circular device (e.g. as epigraph to her *The World is Round*), or perhaps most appropriately as it appears in her statement, "Civilization began with a rose. A rose is a rose is a rose is a rose" (quoted as epigraph to J.M. Brinnin's study, *The Third Rose*).

Jung identifies the Rose (of the World) with the Golden Flower (*Psychology and Alchemy*, p. 104), and interestingly William Butler Yeats has a poem entitled "The Rose of the World" concerning the movement of life (*Early Poems and Stories*, p. 109), which Olson read as a young man.

▶ **III.105. The winter the <u>Gen. Starks</u> was stuck**

Both original holograph manuscript and typescript dated 21 December 1965.

The story of the Gloucester privateer, *General Starks*, is told in Babson, *History of Gloucester*, pp. 417–423, Olson's source.

III.105. the land . . . going westward at a known / rate

Cf. *Maximus* III, 37: "the earth / rushing westward 2' / each 100 / years . . . ," and note.

III.105. the Great Circle

The navigational term also.

III.105. by this date December 1779 . . . solid frozen salt ice . . . from Black Bess Point across to Dolliver's Neck

Babson reports in his account of the *General Starks*, p. 422: "During the winter of 1779–80,—which was of excessive coldness,—she lay frozen up in the harbor from the middle of December to the 20th of March. Her provisions and wood were hauled alongside by teams. The harbor was frozen over from Black Bess to Dolliver's Neck,—a state in which it has not been seen for many years. It is said, that, at this time, a number of persons went on the ice to Ten-pound-Island Ledge, and took the marks and bearings." Marked in Olson's copy and with a marginal note indicating he read the section on "Dec. 12th," probably 1965.

Black Bess Point projects from the Harbor shore of Eastern Point, directly opposite Dolliver's Neck on the western shore of Gloucester Harbor below Freshwater Cove.

III.106. 207°

Bearing of Ten Pound Island Ledge from magnetic north (determined from Coast and Geodetic chart 233 of Gloucester Harbor).

III.106. Ten Pound Island Ledge

Rock in the middle of Gloucester Harbor southwest of Ten Pound Island. Mentioned in the Babson account.

III.106. the tightest Rose is the World

See previous poem, but with additional sense here possible of a compass rose.

III.106. the Vision / is the Face of God . . . its Perfection

See *Maximus* III, 86, 126, and especially I, 88.

▶III.107. December 22nd

Written that date in Gloucester, either 1965, 1967, or 1968 (during December 1963 and 1964 the poet was in Buffalo, 1966 in Berlin, and 1969 in New York Hospital). Holograph manuscript only, undated; found in a 1968–69 pile of papers, but the poem has the same image (of floating island) as others from early 1966.

III.107. Shag Rock . . . away from / the Island, the Island itself a floating / cruiser . . .

See also *Maximus* III, 113, 114−116, and 123. For Shag Rock, off Ten Pound Island, see *Maximus* II, 91 and note.

III.107. Monitor

Ironclad vessel of the Northern forces during the American Civil War, with single revolving turret; it defeated its Confederate counterpart, the *Merrimac*, in 1862.

III.107. Japanese / Buddhism and maybe, behind it . . . Chinese / Buddhism . . .

The distinction would not seem to be along doctrinal lines, but mainly historical: that the major forms of Japanese Buddhism are developments from Chinese Buddhism (although possibly, since geography is the issue, Chinese Buddhism is also "behind" Japanese Buddhism in the sense that China occupies the mainland, and Japan—like Shag Rock and Ten Pound Island—floats offshore).

III.107. pertinax

Latin, 'perservering, unyielding, obstinate,' root of "pertinacious."

▶**III.108. The whole thing has run so fast away . . .**

Typed manuscript only, dated 9 January 1966; part of an unsent letter by the poet to his daughter.

▶**III.109. like mountains   Stage Head & Tablet Rock floated up . . .**

Written around 1966. Holograph manuscript only, undated but in materials from early 1966 among the poet's papers.

For Stage Head, see *Maximus* I, 102 and note; for Tablet Rock, "the rock I know by my belly and torn nails," I, 48.

III.109. the Fabrick

See perhaps *Maximus* III, 53; also possibly III, 171 below, and notes.

III.109. Sonnetina

Apparently a coinage for 'little sonnet,' from a combination of sonnet and sonatina.

▶**III.110. My shore, my sounds, my earth, my place . . .**

Holograph manuscript only. Written ca. January 1965 on stationery from The Tavern, restaurant and inn in Gloucester, where Olson was staying on return to his city between semesters at the University in Buffalo. Dream notes on back of manuscript dated "Friday, Saturday January 15th / 16th," i.e. 1965. Date not determined at time of editing of volume; poem should be placed after III, 69–70.

▶**III.111. Sunday, January 16, 1966**

Original typed manuscript titled *"Sunday, January 15, 1966,"* with holograph note added: "date above shld be Jan. 16th."

III.111. the Playground

On Fort Point's western shore, near Pavilion Beach.

III.111. Mason A. Walton

(ca. 1838–1917), author of *A Hermit's Wild Friends, or Eighteen Years in the Woods.* His "Note" to this volume is actually dated April 5, 1903, and exhibits the same precision that Olson's observations in the poem do:

> During my eighteen years of hermit life, I claim to have discovered several new features in natural history, namely:
> That the cow-bunting watches over ⸱⸱ young, assists the foster parents in providing food, and gradually assumes full care of the young bird, and takes it to the pasture to

associate with its kind; that the white-footed mouse is dumb, and communicates with its species by drumming with its toes; that the wood-thrush conducts a singing-school for the purpose of teaching its young how to sing; that the chickadee can count; that the shad-bush on Cape Ann assumes a dwarf form, and grows in patches like the low-bush blueberry, fruiting when less than a foot in height . . .

Walton's choice of Bond's Hill in Gloucester for his hermitage is described on pp. 13–14 of his narrative. On pp. 15–16, he speaks of "a massive spur of bed rock" near his tent, which must be what Olson calls the "Poles" (see *Maximus* III, 35 and note).

A marginal note on p. 18 of Olson's copy reveals the poet had been reading Walton on January 15th, 1966, the day before the poem was written. On p. 21, Olson notes: "lovely / What a quiet & exact man this Mr. Walton is / Mason A. Walton."

▶III.112. IF THE DEATHS DO NOT STOP WE'LL HAVE NO EARTH OR YEARS LEFT

Original typescript only, dated 21 January 1966.

III.112. Has March now been added . . .

March formerly had been "the holy month" (*Maximus* II, 162). It was in March of 1964 that the poet's wife Betty had been killed in an automobile collision.

III.112. Odin or Christ stretched on that Living Tree

In the Old Norse Poem *Havamal* the god Odin sacrifices himself in order to win the runes of poetry, by hanging on the World Tree for nine days and nights, paralleling, as is commonly observed, Christ's crucifixion. See e.g. Turville-Petre, *Myth and Religion of the North*, pp. 42–43, although as Davidson points out: "despite certain resemblances, it would seem that here we have something whose roots go deep into heathen thought, and which is no late copy, conscious or unconscious, of the central mystery of the Christian faith. By hanging on a tree, Odin is not sharing in the suffering of the world or saving men from death, he is there to win the secret of the runs . . ." (*Gods and Myths of Northern Europe*, p. 220).

III.112. our Own Dog

Like Fenris the wolf who devours Odin at the End of the World (see *Maximus* III, 47 and note; also II, 36 and note).

III.112. Harry

Harry Martin (b. 1927), Gloucester artist, friend of the poet and his wife. Olson's notebook "MONDAY JANUARY 18 . . . [1966]" (in which the writing of this poem is mentioned) reflects an evening of intense talk between the two men. Martin's friend Jack Hammond (q.v.) died in February of the previous year.

III.112. Kenward

Kenward Elmslie (b. 1929), New York poet and friend of Harry Martin's, whom Olson had met at Hammond's Castle. See also *Maximus* III, 219 and note.

Olson had made the following note ca. late January 1966 in another notebook: "For Kenward Elmslie and Harry Martin—to these two friends of mine, in hope & in wish that I may in this way console them for the loss now of their friend Ruth Yorck: 2 lights on sea if there be distress." Ruth Landshoff Yorck, a novelist and poet living in New York, had died suddenly on 19 January 1966.

▶III.113. February 3rd 1966 High Tide 10.6 Feet / 8:43 AM

Written that date in Gloucester. The original was handwritten on an envelope, with a typescript made later. Notes on the original holograph indicate the *Gloucester Daily Times* was used for the time of high tide: "No no no: *today* is / oh— I was a day off yesterday! *That* was today's times I was using! . . . Tuesday's paper!!" In the *Gloucester Times* for February 2nd, the time for high tide for the next day is given as 8:43 a.m., as Olson has; however, its depth is listed as 10.3 feet, unless the poet had also consulted *The Old Farmer's Almanac*, as he did with the next poem, where high tide at Boston is given as 10.5 feet for the evening of February 4th.

III.113. Ten Pound Island

See *Maximus* I, 115 and note.

III.113. Shag Rock / is floating off by itself . . .

See also *Maximus* III, 107 and note, as well as the poem following this.

III.113. Eskimo Pie

Brand name for a chocolate-covered ice cream on a stick.

▶III.114. a 3rd morning it's beautiful . . .

Holograph manuscript only, dated 7 February 1966. Data in title is from *The Old Farmer's Almanac* for 1966, pp. 12–13, although Olson's copy has not survived (see also note to "JUST AS MORNING TWILIGHT," *Maximus* III, 137).

III.114. the Island floating

Ten Pound Island. See also *Maximus* III, 107, 113 and 123.

III.114. like a swordfish's tail stiff / in the Sun Blaze

Cf. perhaps earlier association, *Maximus* I, 26.

III.114. its 'sleek head' / the verse he sd in his work emerges

In an essay from 1948 based on his experience of visiting Ezra Pound, Olson had written: "Joyce, apparently, was not a man to give praise out easily, and Pound told me once, with what pleasure, the only thing he ever got out of Joyce, this comment one day when he had read something new, 'The

sleek head of verse, Mr Pound, emerges in your work'"
(*Charles Olson & Ezra Pound*, p. 104). See also Pound's poem,
"Medallion" (*Personae*, p. 204):

> The sleek head emerges
> From the gold-yellow frock
> An Anadyomene in the opening
> Pages of Reinach.

III.114. Shag Rock

See *Maximus* II, 91 and note; also *Maximus* III, 107.

III.114. the 'head' of the / Sea-Serpent (its 'first-fold' . . .

The Gloucester Sea-Serpent (see *Maximus* II, 32, 121; III,
59–60, etc., and notes). One observer reported "eight distinct portions, or bunches" to it, another that "the first part
of the curve it made resembled the link of a chain" (Babson,
History, p. 521).

III.114. the Queen Mary

The luxury liner, built in England in 1936 and retired in
1967; it was one of the world's largest ships in its time.

III.114. the 'Land' Below

Possible faint echo of title of a poem by Edward Dorn,
"The Land Below," in his *Hands Up!*.

III.114. aglaia

Greek, 'brilliance'; one of the three Graces, daughter of
Zeus and Eurynome, according to Hesiod, *Theogony*, l. 909
(quoted in Havelock, *Preface to Plato*, p. 102, and marked in
Olson's copy).

III.114. this Jewel / in her Eye

Cf. "Coiled, / throughout the system . . . ," *Maximus* III, 61
and note.

III.114. the Breakwater

See *Maximus* I, 22 and note (also for "Dog Bar").

III.114. Round Rock Shoal

See *Maximus* II, 70 and note.

III.114. the buildings on it like the old Light itself ...

A house and wharf of the U.S. Fish and Wildlife Service were on the north end of Ten Pound Island at the time, in addition to a conical lighthouse, a cottage for the lighthouse keeper with brick walls and a wooden roof, and a small utility shed which had housed an old fog signal. The lighthouse keeper's cottage was burned down in September 1968, to help clear the island, it was claimed, for the eventual construction of a park area. Olson protested the burning in a letter to the *Gloucester Times*, 28 October 1968.

III.115. Wide-Law, the 3rd Wife

Eurynome, daughter of Okeanos and Tethys, who becomes Zeus' third wife, after Metis and Themis, and mother of the Graces (Hesiod, *Theogony*, ll. 906ff.). Havelock, in quoting the passage in his *Preface to Plato*, pp. 101–102, translates her name as "Wide-Law" (marked in Olson's copy). Her name is akin to εὐρύνω 'to make wide or broad' and which in its passive form means 'to be spread abroad' (Liddell and Scott, *Greek-English Lexicon*, p. 615, consulted by the poet and marked in his copy).

III.115. John Temple

(b. 1943), an English poet, studying at the time in Buffalo.

III.115. a cormorant / on the Black Rocks / spindle

See *Maximus* III, 68 and note.

III.115. the entrance / to the Inner Harbor, to the Stream itself

See *Maximus* II, 144 and note, also II, 84.

III.115. my own / target-area

Cf. the occurrence of the phrase in "The Ocean," *Maximus* III, 89.

III.115. Euronyme

Eurynome (see note to "Wide-Law" above).

III.115. the property of / shag . . .

I.e., the shag or crested cormorant.

III.116. that in matter alone, the soul said, / you shall not walk about in the heaven of intelligence . . .

See Jung, *Psychology and Alchemy*, p. 254, quoting from the Harranite alchemical text known as "Liber Platonis quartorum" in a discussion of the spiritual transformation that might accompany the alchemical process, the results of the mind's working on matter: "The philosopher in the Book of Dialogues said: 'I walked round the three heavens, namely the heaven of composite natures, the heaven of discriminated natures and the heaven of the soul. But when I wished to walk round the heaven of intelligence, the soul said unto me: "That is no way for thee" '" (marked in the poet's copy). See also the quotation from Gerhard Dorn on the "truth" in "matter," note shortly below.

In his Beloit Lectures, Olson remarked: "If I understand this think that I'm seeking . . . to carry here, it is that efficaciousness is in matter. That when Kābir [i.e. Dorn] says natural things, he means matter" (*Muthologos*, II, 46).

III.116. I had successfully walked / round the Three Heavens

See quotation from the "Liber Platonis quartorum" in note above.

III.116. the Three Towns, the / trimurta

See *Maximus* III, 73–75 and note. "Trimurta" should then be "Tripura," which Olson had pronounced as "Triporta" in his Berkeley reading in 1965 (*Muthologos*, I, 102). It was transcribed by Zoe Brown as "Trimurta" (*Reading at Berkeley*, 1966, p. 5), and it may be this confused spelling, which Olson would have seen while assisting Brown with her transcription, that led to the error in this poem.

III.116. the 'prison' the soul says / you shall stay in

The "fetters" spoken of by the sixteenth-century alchemist Gerhard Dorn, as quoted in Jung, *Psychology and Alchemy*, p. 256 (marked in Olson's copy):

> In this [truth] lies the whole art of freeing the spirit [*spiritus*] from its fetters, in the same way that, as we have said, the mind [*mens*] can be freed [i.e., morally] from the body.
>
> As faith works miracles in man, so this power, the *veritas efficaciae*, brings them about in matter. . . .

See also "Poetry and Truth," using Dorn: ". . . as creatures of organism, the original difficulty is that of the soul having its chance to realize its separateness from the body; but that only the mind can free it from its fetters to the body" (*Muthologos*, II, 46).

▶III.117. I have been an ability—a machine . . .

Holograph manuscript only, dated 9 February 1966.

III.117. John

The poet John Wieners (b. 1934), who had been a student of Olson's at Black Mountain College and again at Buffalo in

1964–65. He would publish a book entitled, appropriately, *Nerves* in 1970.

III.117. Vincent Ferrini

See *Maximus* I, 20 and note.

III.117. Ben Kerr's house

House at 215 Western Avenue, opposite Stage Fort Park, owned by Benedict Kerr, who operated a furniture store in Gloucester.

III.117. Half Moon

Half Moon Beach (see *Maximus* I, 30 and note).

III.117. Tablet Rock

See *Maximus* I, 48, "the rock I know by my belly and torn nails," and note.

III.117. "washing rock," of the Parsonses

In the "Settlement of estate of Jeffrey Parsons late of Gloucester deceased. 1717 March 28," preserved at the Essex County Probate Court in Salem, there occurs the following reference: ". . . also to John hath another piece [parcel?] on the South Side of the Bass Rock point lying betwixt James's land and Ebenezers, with a sufficient way to carry fish to and from the washing Rock."

See also below, "Great Washing Rock . . . ," *Maximus* III, 185. For the Parsonses, see esp. *Maximus* II, 63–64.

III.117. the Great Auk

This bird, now extinct, was once plentiful on the Massachusetts coast. See, e.g., Allen, "The Fauna of Eastern Massachusetts," in Winsor, *Memorial History of Boston*, I, 12–13:

> The former presence of the great auk (*Alca impennis*) along the coast of Massachusetts is not only attested by

history but by the occurrence of its bones in the Indian shell-heaps at Ipswich and neighboring points. It seems to have existed in the vicinity of Boston till near the close of the seventeenth century, but probably did not survive to a much later date. . . . From Josselyn's account of the "Wobble," which is evidently the same bird, it may be inferred that it was not uncommon on the coast of Massachusetts Bay as late as 1672. He says: "The *Wobble*, an ill shaped Fowl, having no long Feathers in their Pinions, which is the reason they cannot fly, not much unlike a *Penguin*; they are in the Spring very fat, or rather oyly, but pull'd and garbidg'd, and laid to the Fire to roast, they yield not one drop."

III.118. Dollivers Neck

See *Maximus* III, 14 and note.

III.118. Hesperus Avenue

Along the shore, from Western Avenue near Dolliver's Neck in Gloucester, into Magnolia; named for the ship made famous by Longfellow's "Wreck of the Hesperus," said to have been wrecked on Norman's Woe (q.v.) nearby.

III.118. Rafe's Chasm

See Babson, *History*, pp. 4–5:

> . . . a remarkable fissure in a ledge on the seacoast between Norman's Woe and Kettle Cove. Its length forms a right angle with the shore, from which it extends more than two hundred feet. Its width is irregular; but the greatest is about ten feet. The depth from the highest part of the rock, forming one of its sides to low-water mark, is computed at sixty feet. The ledge is one of the most remarkable on the Cape; being compact, of great size, and presenting, ocean-ward, an aspect of singular boldness and grandeur. The view of the spot, and the hollow, thundering noise of the sea, as it is dashed back from the rocks at the upper end of the chasm, cause every visitor to feel the presence of a sublime and majestic influence.

III.118. this eye-view line Lane so also / used

See, e.g., Fitz Hugh Lane's "View of Half Moon Beach in Stage Fort Park from Gloucester Harbor" (ca. 1848) in the Cape Ann Historical Association museum. For more on Lane's "eye-view," see *Maximus* II, 100 and note.

III.118. he paid / with his life . . .

For this and other details of his father's post office career, including the fateful trip down the coast to Plymouth for the tercentenary celebration, see Olson's memoir, *The Post Office*. Also *Maximus* I, 33 and note; III, 30–34 and notes.

III.118. Doherty

William C. Doherty (b. 1902) had been president since 1941 of the National Association of Letter Carriers. Albert S. Burleson, Postmaster General at the time Olson's father's harassment began, is mentioned in *The Post Office* (pp. 44ff.).

III.119. Leroy

LeRoi Jones (b. 1934), poet and black nationalist leader (later Imamu Ameer Baraka), who had been a friend of Olson's in the late 1950's and early 1960's. His father, Coyette, was a postal supervisor.

III.119. Malcolm / X

(1925–1965), the black American leader, assassinated in February of the previous year.

III.119. Cagli

Corrado Cagli (b. 1910), Italian painter and friend of the poet. They first met in July 1940 while Cagli was visiting Gloucester and remained close for a number of years (see, e.g., the University of Connecticut Olson-Cagli exhibit folder). A photograph of the two men in Gloucester during

the summer of 1946 can be found in Crispolti and Marchiori's *Cagli*.

From the withheld "MAXIMUS TO GLOUCESTER,
LETTER #29" from 1953 (*OLSON* 6, p. 19):

> And sd (my cricket, of Ancona, painter, teller of tarots:
>
> > "I do not feel rest here. I cannot sit
> > on this grass as, anywhere else, I can
> > sit, as at home I can."

III.119. the Industrial League . . . Cut Eagles

During the summer of 1940 when Olson and Cagli met,
Gloucester had an amateur baseball Twilight League—which
included a team called the Eagles—playing its games at Stage
Fort Park in the evenings.

III.119. my Father / in a dream said / Ad Valorem / Cagli

The dream is recorded in Olson's notebook, "FAUST
BUCH #1 / Washington Spring '47," under the date 16
May 1947:

> A dream of my father asking me ad valorem Cagli! With
> the Latin phrase in the dream. His question pointed: what
> are you getting from Cagli in exchange for your friendship.
> And I pushed punched him on the shoulder, as much
> as to say, get away with you.
> But at the same time sore at this interference, thinking
> all the time, my mother put him up to this!
> He did not push the matter.

The Latin "Ad Valorem" ordinarily means 'according to
the value'; here it might be translated, 'to' or 'of what value.'

III.119. Seine's bank

The French river, flowing through Paris.

III.119. coming from Da Vinci Airport / into Rome

The poet had arrived there in June 1965 to read at the
Spoleto Festival. In a letter to Frances Boldereff from Rome,

ca. June 27, he writes of "Having Flown Through the Empyrean and Arriving here in the Host of Human beings.— Incredible [paper torn] of Ancient Human Life, the light [tear] close beautiful condition of every possible matter, trolley cars, old dirt walls, hay (made into perfect solid houses on edges of fields . . ."

III.119. Memphis-time

Related to the city of ancient Egypt where the "Memphite theology" flourished (see Frankfort, *Kingship and the Gods*; also note to *Maximus* II, 147, "to enter into their bodies . . . ," and to II, 160).

III.119. Acropolis

The citadel of Athens on which the Parthenon stands.

III.119. Mr Brown the Postmaster / of North Plymouth

Olson remembers this aspect of the trip to Plymouth in *The Post Office*, p. 35:

> For my father the irony of that week must have been that the family we stayed with was that of the Postmaster of North Plymouth! It was one of those gentle houses the New Englanders of the 17th century built and the pleasure of it, of the trees at Duxbury and the sea at Plymouth meant more to me (at least I am stained more with the traces) than the excitements we had come to Plymouth to enjoy. The Postmaster was a Mr. Brown. My father had met him at some convention and it is a measure of how much my father's heart was set on this trip that he had arranged our room with Mr. Brown ahead of time.

III.120. Obadiah Bruen

See *Maximus* I, 145 and note. Babson says nothing of him coming from Strawberry Bank (see next note), rather it would seem he came to Gloucester from Plymouth.

III.120. Strawberry Bank

Early name for Portsmouth, N.H., at the mouth of the Piscataqua River, named for the many wild strawberries growing there.

III.120. Ararat

Mountain in eastern Turkey where Noah's ark came to rest; the highest peak in Turkey. Curiously, and perhaps significantly, because of the references that follow, there was a hill called Mount Ararat in Worcester, Mass. (later Indian Hill, but Ararat Street survives), although it was farther north in the city than the section where Olson grew up (see e.g. Lincoln, *History of Worcester*, p. 293).

III.120. rats my father and I shot / off the back porch Worcester . . .

See also the poem "The Thing was Moving," written ca. May 1952:

. . . the meadow near the house
which was later covered by a dump to make an athletic field
and the brook was gone to which we tried to speed our sleds
from the hill the house stood on and which the dump
was meant to join, the loss punctuated by the shooting
my father taught me with the rifle he gave me from the back porch
of the three-decker, the rats living among the cans and peat
as the dump came closer, and I hated
all of it . . .
the smoke from the dump-fires all the time the thing was moving
toward us, covering the meadow . . .

III.120. Beaver Brook

Located in Worcester, Mass. It flows from Beaver Brook Park into Middle River in South Worcester, passing through the field in back of the poet's boyhood home on Norman Street. With a pun on William Maxwell Aitken, Lord Beaverbrook (1879–1964), British newspaper publishing magnate.

▶ III.122. Outer Darkness   Inner Schoodic . . .

Holograph manuscript only, written in blue ink in long yellow notepad; undated, but most probably written ca. 23 July 1968, the date of the following fragment among the poet's papers (discovered after the editing of the volume), which was written—as noted on the manuscript—following a conversation with Gerrit Lansing the previous evening:

> Time's
> unbearable complexity—as though our souls
> could never be the equal of our bodies, its
> devouring
> occurring at such a rate only knowing
> Ko Hung says
> white and preserving
> black (that the mystery-unity is seen only in the sun
> as against the truth-unity
> ["which is full of color & events" crossed out]) and will make us
> unsuccessful
> in the desire for death

The poem should thus be placed in the sequence immediately before the one beginning "above the head of John Day's pasture land . . ." (*Maximus* III, 195–196), written 24 July 1968.

Ko Hung (ca. A.D. 280–340), who is mentioned in the fragment though not in the poem, was a Taoist philosopher and alchemist of the Chin period. In the flyleaf of his copy of Needham, *Science and Civilisation in China*, Olson notes: "1st used with use July 22nd ('LXVIII) as of Ko Hung [learned of his existence from Gerrit Lansing this day—Monday July 22nd." Lansing recalled the occasion for the present author in a letter ca. 9 December 1975: "That evening, on the lawn behind the house in Riverdale where I was living at the time, I read aloud to Charles the whole first chapter (not very long) of Ko Hung as translated & edited by James Ware. The book is called *Alchemy, Medicine, Religion in the China of A.D. 320* (it is all Ko Hung, but is not listed as such in catalogs), edited by James Ware, published in 1963 by MIT Press. Charles was stunned . . ."

See then, Ko Hung's *Nei P'ien* as translated by Ware, pp. 305–306 (actually well into the volume): "Preserving Mystery-Unity is much easier than preserving Truth-Unity. The latter has names, size, uniforms, and color. Mystery-Unity is seen only in the sun . . . The search for It begins in the sun, and is described as 'knowing white and preserving black' or 'unsuccessful in the desire for death.' "

Inner Schoodic Ridge, like its counterpart Outer Schoodic Ridge nearby, is a coastal bank and fishing ground off the coast of Maine near Mount Desert Island. In another poem (not a *Maximus*) among his papers, probably written 9 February 1966, Olson again speaks of Inner Schoodic as his inner or spiritual "bank": ". . . to internalize my / Schoodic to make my rivers run / for me to make Inner / or Outer / Schoodic one piece from conception . . . all one"; while a fragment from ca. 1968, beginning "Inner & Outer, Schoodic . . . ," concludes: "no 'outside' except as as knowable as every inside."

"Schoodic" is an Indian word meaning 'a place where water rushes,' and may be related to "schooner" (see e.g. Thoreau, *The Maine Woods*, 1906 ed., p. 357—quoted in a letter to Olson from Peter Anastas, 8 February 1966).

III.122. the 'colours'

Cf. probably Snell, *Discovery of the Mind*, p. 13: "*Noos* is akin to *νοεῖν* which means 'to realize', 'to see in its true colours' . . ." Marked in Olson's copy and referred to in an essay among his papers entitled "The Great Origins of European Thought" (a variation on the subtitle of the Snell book), dated "Valentine's Day," probably 1966.

III.122. the 'unity' / seen only in the / sun

See passage from Ko Hung quoted in note above, and cf. perhaps Olson's own experience mentioned in "Poetry and Truth": "an experience of, say, twenty years ago, which was to me dogmatic, when I knew there was a sun . . . inside myself" (*Muthologos*, II, 35).

III.122. the pin / does penetrate / the crown

See *Richard II*, III.ii.160−170:

> . . . for within the hollow crown
> That rounds the mortal temples of a king
> Keeps Death his court . . . and . . .
> Comes at the last, and with a little pin
> Bores through his castle wall, and farewell king!

▶III.123. That island / floating in the sea . . .

Written ca. 1966 (holograph original found among Olson's papers with other material from 1966).

The "island" is presumably Ten Pound Island in Gloucester Harbor, elsewhere described as "floating" (*Maximus* III, 107, 113, 114−115, 123).

III.123. <u>Moeurs de Societé</u>

French, 'manners of society, social customs.'

▶III.124. the Mountain of no difference . . .

Written in a notebook and dated 11 February 1966.

III.124. that Angel . . .

See Corbin, *Avicenna and the Visionary Recital*, p. 148, quoting from the "Recital of Ḥayy ibn Yaqẓan":

> "He who succeeds in leaving this clime enters the climes of the Angels, among which the one that marches with the earth is a clime in which the terrestrial angels dwell. These angels form two groups. One occupies the right side: they are the angels who know and order. Opposite them, a group occupies the left side: they are the angels who obey and act. Sometimes these two groups of angels descend to the climes of men and genii, sometimes they mount to heaven. It is said that among their number are the two angels to whom the human being is entrusted those who are called 'Guardians and Noble Scribes'—one to the right, the other to the left. He who is to the right belongs to the

angels who order; to him it falls to dictate. He who is to the
left belongs to the angels who act; to him it falls to write."

The passage is repeated, with a commentary and Corbin's
notes, pp. 357–361.

III.124. the modus

Latin, 'measure.' The term "mode" occurs frequently in
Whitehead's *Process and Reality* (see e.g. the quotation from
p. 471 in note below).

III.124. visione

Latin (though ablative case), 'the act of seeing'; also
'vision,' 'apparition,' 'mental image,' 'idea,' 'notion.' Also
Italian, 'vision,' though just as likely the word has been made
"foreign" for stress or freshness.

III.124. modulus

Latin, 'a small measure.'

III.124. measurement / "throughout the system"

See Whitehead, *Process and Reality*, p. 471, at the close of
his chapter on "Measurement": "Measurement is now possible throughout the extensive continuum. This measurement
is a systematic procedure dependent on the dominant societies of the cosmic epoch. When one form of measurement
has been given, alternative forms with assigned mathematical relations to the initial form can be defined. One such
system is as good as any other, so far as the mathematical
procedure is concerned. The only point to be remembered is
that each system of 'coordinates' must have its definable relation to the analogy which constitutes congruence." (Olson
has this and an earlier passage dealing with congruence as
analogy marked.)

Note also the earlier appearance of the phrase in both
"entwined / throughout / the system" (*Maximus* II, 121) and
"Coiled, / throughout the system" (*Maximus* III, 61).

III.124. "There are no infinitesimals"

See Whitehead, *Process and Reality*, p. 465:

> Measurement depends upon counting and upon permanence. The question is, what is counted, and what is permanent? The things that are counted are the inches on a straight metal rod, a yard-measure. Also the thing that is permanent is this yard-measure in respect both to its internal relations and in respect to some of its extensive relations to the geometry of the world. In the first place, the rod is straight. Thus the measurement depends upon the straightness and not the straightness upon the measurement. The modern answer to this statement is that the measurement is a comparison of infinitesimals, or of an approximation to infinitesimals. The answer to this answer is that there are no infinitesimals, and that therefore there can be no approximation to them.

Also, p. 472: "The current physical theory presupposes a comparison of so-called lengths among segments without any theory as to the basis on which this comparison is to be made, and in ignorance of the fact that all exact observation belongs to the mode of presentational immediacy. Further, the fact is neglected that there are no infinitesimals, and that a comparison of finite segments [see "precise finite segments" in the poem] is thus required."

III.124. all does rhyme

Echo of Heraclitus' "All does flow," quoted in Whitehead, p. 437 (underlined by Olson), and used also in "Equal, That Is, to the Real Itself" (*Human Universe*, p. 122).

III.124. like is the measure of / producing like

The principle of analogy, that "things are perfected by their like," and its use in alchemy as discussed in Jung, *Psychology and Alchemy*, p. 255. As Jung observes, p. 315n., "The pairing of like with like is to be found as early as Heraclitus."

See also *Maximus* III, 128.

III.125. the Guardian / does <u>dictate</u>

See the section from the "Recital of Ḥayy ibn Yaqẓan" in Corbin quoted above.

III.125. the message / is a discrete & continuous conduction . . . a sequence of events measurable / in time

Cf. "The Kingfishers": "And what is the message? The message is / a discrete or continuous sequence of measurable events distributed in time." For which, then, see Wiener, *Cybernetics*, pp. 15–16: "On the communication engineering plane, it had already become clear to Mr. Bigelow and myself that the problems of control engineering and of communication engineering were inseparable, and that they centered not around the technique of electrical engineering but around the much more fundamental notion of the message, whether this should be transmitted by electrical, mechanical, or nervous means. The message is a discrete or continuous sequence of measurable events distributed in time—precisely what is called a time series by the statisticians."

III.125. Dixit

Latin, 'he said.'

▶III.126. Bottled up for days . . .

Written ca. February 1966. Holograph original (on back of which is opening line from a poem concerning the poet's deceased wife which is datable at 1966), revised and copied out again by hand. An earlier start was given the title "*Desire*" but abandoned after two lines.

III.126. <u>petere</u>

Latin, 'to strive for, seek,' 'to beg, desire.' Also used in essay "The Great Origins of European Thought," written Valentine's Day, i.e. February 14, [1966].

III.126. to construct knowing back to image

> See: an actual earth of value to
> construct one, from rhythm to
> image, and image is knowing, and
> knowing, Confucius says, brings one
> to the goal . . .
> —*Maximus* III, 190 and note.

III.126. God's face . . . turned as mine / now is to blackness . . .

See *Maximus* III, 86 and 106, and esp. *Maximus* I, 88 and note; also the "preserving blackness" of *Maximus* III, 122.

III.126. the rate / reason hath

Cf. *Maximus* III, 129 and 168, and notes.

▶ III.127. Got me home, the light / snow gives the air, falling

Typescript of the original holograph manuscript is dated 16 February 1966.

III.127. 127

The shore route from Salem through Magnolia to Gloucester.

III.127. Lookout / or what was Hammond's / Castle

Lookout Hill, overlooking the Atlantic, off Western Avenue on the approach to Gloucester; where John Hays Hammond, Sr. formerly lived, now site of the Cardinal Cushing Villa nursing home. See the third section of the original four-part sequence beginning "having descried the nation . . ." (see note to *Maximus* III, 1):

> Lookout
> Hill (J H H Senior's
> & before Charles

Hovey's and in Lane
always
a thin tower
(example Miss Proctor's
view of
Freshwater
Cove

  an aerial
tower long before
Mr John Hays Hammond Junior's
imitations
of Marconi's

Hammond's Castle itself (further down the road toward Magnolia than his father's residence), finished externally in 1928, is now operated as a museum by the Archdiocese of Boston, to which Hammond left the structure upon his death. See also *Maximus* II, 7 and note.

III.127. Endicott / sighted the Winthrop fleet's / top-mast from Salem . . .

See *Maximus* III, 85 and note.

III.127. Magnolia

See *Maximus* I, 11 and note.

III.127. The Binnacle . . .

A poem by Olson written ca. December 1958 and sent to Robert Creeley, then living in Albuquerque, for publication in a local weekly newspaper, *The Albuquerque Review*. Creeley wrote Olson to ask for it on 20 November 1961; he had heard it earlier on a taped reading Olson had made for him as a Christmas present in 1958, where the poem is termed "the latest *Maximus*" and titled, significantly enough for the present poem, "Maximus, Home Again, Crying Out to All." At Cortland, N.Y. in 1967, Olson remarked on the inscription to the poem before reading it: "Mr. Creeley, unfortunately, stood me up—unbelievable—one night, when I left my house to get the hell out of there . . . to meet him, and from then I was to go into the [world?]. . . ."

▶III.128. same thought—2

Begun as a quick note by the poet to himself, but then copied out again, with final lines added, and dated 16 February [1966].

III.128. to / make such shapes etc / in the universe . . .

Echoes a section of "Letter #41 [broken off]" from *Maximus* II, 1:

> Where it says excessively rough moraine,
> I count such shapes this evening in the universe
> I run back home out of the new moon . . .

III.128. likes to / likes / efficacy

See "like is the measure of / producing like" as a principle of alchemy, *Maximus* III, 124 and note. Jung quotes on p. 256 of *Psychology and Alchemy* the alchemist Gerhard Dorn on the "efficacy," or more precisely the *veritas efficaciae*, which is to be found in matter (and see Olson's use of this in "Poetry and Truth," *Muthologos*, II, 45).

▶III.129. valorem is / rate . . .

Original holograph manuscript dated "March 11th" and found among the poet's papers from 1966. A page of notes written at the same time and dated "Friday March 11th VILXVI," includes the following:

> ratio is
> rational is society "Nation" . . .
> reason *and* art
> ratio and rate
> society and *Dogtown*
> the Nation and *value*
> *ad valorem*
> Cagli . . .

For "*valorem*," then, see *Maximus* III, 119 and note. Olson also uses "rate" in the phrases "the rate reason hath" (*Maximus* III, 126), "rate of rate" (*Maximus* III, 168), and "rate of ratio" in his "Vinland Map Review" (*Additional Prose*, p. 68).

▶ **III.130. As of Parsonses or Fishermans Field or Cressys Beach or Washington, the Capital, of my Front-Yard?**

Dated 29 March 1966. Holograph manuscript only. For the Parsonses' field, with its well and spring, see *Maximus* II, 63–64; for Fishermans Field as the poet's "front yard," see *Maximus* I, 100; and for Cressys Beach described with this same feeling, see *Maximus* I, 9–10.

III.130. Otter

In Norse mythology, the son of Hreidmar, killed by Loki while eating a salmon by a waterfall. See the story of "The Ransom of Otter," from the *Reginsmol* or *Ballad of Regin*, in Davidson, *Gods and Myths of Northern Europe*, p. 43.

III.130. Gassire's / fate

Gassire is the hero of the African folktale, "Gassire's Lute," who because he cannot be king (his father although old refuses to die) becomes a bard with a lute to sing the *Dausi* or songs of heroes. The smith who makes the lute for Gassire explains to him: "This is a piece of wood. It cannot sing if it has no heart. You must give it a heart. Carry this piece of wood on your back when you go into battle. The wood must ring with the stroke of your sword. The wood must absorb down dripping blood, blood of your blood, breath of your breath. Your pain must be its pain, your fame its fame. The wood may no longer be like the wood of a tree, but must be penetrated by and be a part of your people. Therefore it must live not only with you but with your sons. Then will the tone that comes from your heart echo in the ear of your son and live on in the people, and your son's life's blood, oozing out of his heart, will run down your body and live on in this piece of wood. . . ." (Frobenius and Fox, *African Genesis*, p. 103).

III.130. 1 FA-

The root of *fātum*, Latin 'an utterance, prophetic declaration, fate,' in Lewis, *Elementary Latin Dictionary*, p. 940.

III.130. the Well

The well of Mimir, whose waters yield wisdom, located beneath the roots of Yggdrasill, the Norse World Tree. Odin gave one of his eyes for a single draught of the precious water in order to gain knowledge of his fate.

III.130. the / Liquid of the / Eagle's mouth

The magic mead which conferred the power of poetry. It was stolen from the giant Suttung by Odin, who had changed himself into an eagle to do so. As he was flying over the earth, hotly pursued by Suttung, some drops spilled out of his mouth, and in this way men received the gift of poetry.

III.130. teonanacatl

Nahuatl for 'God's flesh,' a name for the sacred mushroom (see *Maximus* III, 78 and note; also "Under the Mushroom," *Muthologos*, I, 50, and "Experience and Measurement," *OLSON* 3, pp. 60−61).

III.130. Ymir's trunk / the 'Tree' is

Ymir was the Norse primeval giant from whose body the world was formed.

III.130. the / 'Head' of Mimir's

Mimir was the guardian of the spring beneath the World Tree to whom Odin sacrificed his eye. His head had been cut off in a dispute but preserved by Odin and is consulted by him in times of difficulty.

III.130. the <u>son</u> of Poseidon's fate

Poseidon was the Greek god of the sea and of springs (which he produced by striking a rock with his trident).

III.131. Altgeld the Eagle

Both an American political figure and Olson's name for the eagle of Geoffrey Chaucer's *House of Fame*: a clever pun, bringing together (as the poem does) both poetry and politics in the English and American varieties. John Peter Altgeld (1847–1902), governor of Illinois from 1892 to 1896 and sympathetic to radical causes (he pardoned three anarchist leaders convicted of provoking the Haymarket Riot), occurs as an emblem or embodiment of democratic virtues, the American eagle. As such, he was already subject of a poem by Vachel Lindsay entitled, significantly, "The Eagle That Is Forgotten" (as well as a novel by Howard Fast, *The American*, published in 1946).

At the same time, "Altgeld" is German for 'old gold.' (The golden eagle, it is to be remembered, is the national bird of the United States.) The eagle in Chaucer's poem (see next note) is unnamed, but both golden and old: "Hyt was of gold, and shon so bryghte / That never sawe men such a syghte . . . ," and " 'For y am now too old.' / 'Elles I wolde the have told,' / Quod he 'the sterres names, lo . . .' " (11. 503–504, marked in Olson's copy with the note in the margin, "The Gold Eagle"; 11. 995–999).

III.131. as Chaucer in the eagle's feet, going up to see the / House of Fame is taught . . .

See the dream-vision in Book II of Chaucer's *House of Fame* (read by Olson at least as a graduate student), in which the poet is carried heavenwards in the "grymme pawes stronge" of a garrulous eagle. The direct address on the part of the eagle is present in the original (e.g. line 729, "Geffrey, thou wost ryght wel . . ."). See also *"Paris Review* Interview," *Muthologos*, II, 117.

III.131. the Partridge in the bushes

The partridge who sat under a bush and sang the *Dausi* to Gassire (Frobenius and Fox, *African Genesis*, pp. 101–102).

III.131. the street / I lived on in Washington

Randolph Place, N.E., during the 1940's and early 1950's.

III.131. Cressy's beach a nightingale

See the early version of *"Thurs Sept 14th 1961"* (*Maximus* II, 59–62) in which the poet speaks of a mockingbird:

> It flies slowly
> in full song
> from perch to perch
> why the scoundrel
> who gave me the hard
> time Cressys beach
> that May night
> 1959 seemed such
> a pistoleer!

Also the non-*Maximus* poem, "May 20, 1959," where a whip-poorwhill or other bird follows the poet home "pistoling me with his / message."

▶III.132. white ships all covered with ice . . .

Holograph manuscript only, written 29 March 1966. The original appears on the same sheet as the start of a letter to Robert Duncan; in the letter finally sent Duncan, dated March 29th, Olson adds as a postscript the following, which can be considered a first version of the present poem:

> To greet you with 17° degrees of *Spring*
> here —silly spring   And a ship just
> came in flying ICE like Theseus' wrong-flag (from
> St John's, Newfoundland.
> But the men *were* chopping
> ice off the capstan (on the foredeck) as she passed by, all
> white, out my bedroom window. So it was
> cold out there also

III.132. black as Theseus' wrongly-flown / sail . . .

Theseus, in the legend, had been given a white sail by his father Aegeus to hoist in place of the traditional black sail if he should return victorious from his mission to the Cretan labyrinth. However, Theseus forgot his promise on his return to Greece after slaying the minotaur, and his father watching from the Acropolis cast himself into the sea for grief, which was thenceforth named the Aegean.

III.132. Blue Peter

A dragger or a beam trawler, presumably.

▶III.133. light signals & mass points . . .

Dated 14 April 1966. Original holograph manuscript sent to George Bowering for publication in *Imago* and returned. The original of part II occurs in Olson's copy of Weyl, *Philosophy of Mathematics and Natural Science*, pp. 94–95.

See Weyl, p. 103 (marked in Olson's copy): "As a matter of fact it can be shown that the metrical structure of the world is already fully determined by its inertial and causal structure, that therefore mensuration need not depend on clocks and rigid bodies but that light signals and mass points moving under the influence of inertia alone will suffice." Also Weyl, p. 104: "It is impossible objectively, without resorting to individual exhibition, to make a narrower selection from among the 'normal mappings'. . . ." Again Weyl, p. 106: ". . . it is impossible, according to an earlier remark, to eliminate the field of inertia, or the 'ether,' as an independent power from the natural phenomena."

III.133. to perambulate the bounds   a cosmos / closed in both respects . . .

See perhaps Weyl, pp. 108–109: "It is possible, however, that space is finite and yet unbounded; indeed it may be a closed manifold, like the two-dimensional surface of a sphere. It is an appealing interpretation of A. Speiser's . . . that Dante, without denying the validity of Aristotle's conception of perceptive space, assumes the real space of creation (of which the former is but an image) to be closed rather than bounded."

▶ **III.134. having developed the differences . . .**

Written in a spiral-bound notebook identified by the poet on the cover as "Pocket book starting Wed March 16th [1966] . . . If lost, & found PLEASE RETURN TO Charles Olson . . . Award!" and dated 25 April 1966.

III.134. Abraham Robinson . . . and William Brown and, James Babson rent a shallop Lechford / is information of

See *Maximus* I, 160 and note; also II, 60–61. However, it is Thomas Ashley not James Babson (first son of the widow Babson) that rents the shallop along with Robinson and Brown for purposes of fishing. For Robinson, see also *Maximus* II, 65 and note.

III.134. James Babson's mother was born 1577

Babson reports that Isabel Babson died in 1661, aged about eighty-four (*History*, p. 59), so that her birth would be around 1577.

III.134. his wife Elinor Hill is born 1603

Babson states in his *History* that James Babson's wife, Elinor Hill, "died on March 14, 1714, aged eighty-three" (p. 59).

III.134. Robinson . . . who dies 1646 . . .

Babson, however, reports that Abraham Robinson died at home on February 23, 1645 (*History*, p. 135).

III.134. William Brown marries his widow, raises his son Abraham . . .

Babson, p. 135; also see *Maximus* III, 16 and note.

III.134. Wm Stevens himself first of all ship builder . . .

See earlier poems and notes, beginning with I, 30 ("my carpenter"); most notably, II, 48; and III, 28–29, 30–34.

III.134. John Coit who chose to leave when the New Londoners—or Pequots did in 1651 . . .

After residing in Gloucester a few years, thirteen of the early settlers, including John Coit, removed to New London, Connecticut (see Babson, p. 52, also his notice of Coit, p. 71), where the Pequot Indians had their home on the Mystic River, although their power had been broken by the colonists in 1637.

III.134. his son John Coit . . . had married Mary Stevens . . .

Babson, p. 71: "[Coit] had land granted to him in New London; but, not removing thither, the grant was forfeited. He married Mary, daughter of William Stevens, May 21, 1652."

III.134. Nathaniel Coit, raised with Robinson's & Brown's two . . .

See Babson, p. 72, also p. 175; for the children from previous marriages raised by Henry Walker, see *Maximus* III, 16 and note.

III.134. Henry Walker . . . left the largest accumulated sum at death 1692, / 287£

Walker died in 1693, and "his estate, the largest that had then been accumulated in town, was appraised £922.10s . . ." (Babson, p. 175—marked and noted in the margin of Olson's copy).

III.134. the Davises at Mill River

For John Davis and his descendants who held land along the Annisquam River, see Babson, pp. 75–79 (marked throughout in Olson's copy); also *Maximus* II, 42.

III.134. the Parsons at Fishermans Field

See especially *Maximus* II, 63–64 and 136–137, also III, 170—and respective notes.

III.134. by 1742 Thomas Sanders, / coming as a ship builder direct from England . . .

See Babson, *History*, p. 241; also *Maximus* II, 48 and 49 and notes. Babson, in his *Notes and Additions*, II, 74–75, says: "Tradition reports that the [Sanders] family came to Gloucester direct from England," and that Thomas Sanders "left a clear estate of £3160; one of the largest that had been accumulated in town to the date of his death, 1742."

III.134. in Boston say by 1676 already Edward Randolph reports . . . there are 30 millionaires

See Morison, *Maritime History of Massachusetts*, p. 17: "Edward Randolph, an unfriendly but accurate English observer, describes Massachusetts in 1676 as a thriving maritime colony. Thirty of her merchants have fortunes of ten to twenty thousand pounds." (This last sentence is underlined in Olson's copy with the following note in the margin: "NOT Gloucester! (cf. Stevens, 1667—not a cow!") Randolph had arrived in Boston in June of that year as an agent for the Committee of Trade and Plantation in London to report on conditions in the Massachusetts Colony.

III.134. Squam River

Name, more common in earlier times, for the Annisquam River.

III.134. Lobster Cove

See *Maximus* III, 43 and note.

III.134. Edward Harraden and Francis Norwood . . .

Among the earliest settlers on the east bank of the Annisquam and Mill River just below Dogtown, the region generally known as Squam or Annisquam. Harraden arrived
in 1657; Babson says he "appears to have been the first
permanent settler in that section of town. The place of his
residence and business was undoubtedly Squam Point"
(*History*, p. 98). While Francis Norwood, according to Babson, came to Gloucester about 1663, settling at nearby Goose
Cove (see *History*, p. 118).

III.134. Planters Neck . . .

The peninsular portion of Annisquam west of Lobster
Cove, with convenient access to Mill River, the Annisquam
itself, and Ipswich Bay. It was divided up into house-lots
by the early settlers, or planters, in 1642. Copeland and
Rogers write that "One of the generally accepted stories
about the early settlement of the Cape is that in 1631 a band
of Pilgrims came across Massachusetts Bay and settled at
Planters Neck, where they set up a fishing stage. . . . The
leader of that band is said to have been Abraham Robinson,
and it also has been generally accepted that he was the son
of Reverend John Robinson who had been pastor of the
Pilgrims in Holland before they migrated to Plymouth"
(*Saga of Cape Ann*, p. 11). However, they are quick to point
out that "That legend is subject to considerable revision."
Indeed, Babson writes: "Abraham Robinson and his companions may have set up their fishery there [Planter's Neck],
as early mention is made of a 'stage' at that place; but no evidence exists now to show that any of the earliest families
resided there" (*History*, p. 185 and again on p. 292, at which
point there are notes in Olson's copy made in 1966, probably
at the time this poem was written).

III.134. story / in the Robinson family has it . . .

See Copeland and Rogers quoted immediately above; also Babson's entry for Abraham Robinson, *History*, p. 134:

> A traditionary account of the most respectable character affirms that this individual was a son of Rev. John Robinson, whose name and praise are familiar to New-England ears as the faithful pastor of that band of Pilgrims, who, after bitter persecutions in their native land, and a sojourn of several years at Amsterdam and Leyden in Holland, found a final resting-place at Plymouth in New England . . . The tradition before alluded to asserts that Abraham, another son, settled at Cape Ann, and had several children born here; one of which (Abraham) was the first child born of English parents on this side of the Bay . . .

III.135. John White

See above, *Maximus* I, 45 and note, and especially, II, 65 and 187.

III.135. sd Rev. Eli Forbes in 17—, a church was here in 1633 . . .

See *Maximus* II, 65 and note.

III.135. Ferry / Street . . .

Ferry Street runs west from Washington Street (north of Route 128) to Wolf Hill and the site of Samuel Hodgkins' ferry across the Annisquam (*Maximus* I, 150).

III.135. each lot 2 mo 42 / were divided up among newcomers—Stevens Coit Elwell . . .

See *Maximus* I, 156 and note to "what Endecott / and Downing divided . . ." The Elwell mentioned is Robert, grandfather of Joshua Elwell of Dogtown (*Maximus* II, 38). The family gave its name to Elwell's Neck near Hodgkins Cove on the Annisquam.

III.135. Abraham Robinson left where he was, head of Harbor Cove . . .

Robinson's grant of land at the head of Harbor Cove is not specified in Babson (who in fact says, p. 185, the exact location of Robinson's house is not known), and the passage actually reflects Olson's ready familiarity with the town records as well as the actual mapping he had patiently done over and over for himself (and which is preserved among his papers).

III.135. Osmund Dutch alongside Thomson's fishery

See *Maximus* I, 156−160, and II, 60−61, and notes; also III, 53.

III.135. Edward Harraden in 1656 buys from Robert Dutch / his stage . . .

In writing about Planter's Neck, Babson reports: "It is known that Robert Dutch had 'a house upon the stage-neck with the stage and all belonging to it, and thirty acres of land, bounded with the river, and upon a line from Lobster Cove to the sea.' This property, in 1656, came into possession of Edward Haraden; who, from the best information now attainable, settled upon it, and became the first permanent settler in Annisquam" (*History*, p. 292). The information in the passage is written in the margin of Olson's copy, part of notes dated 1966.

III.135. Squaw Rock

The poet uses the original name for Squam Rock, quite appropriate in terms of what follows in the poem as well as the "17th Century" feelings mentioned earlier. Copeland and Rogers give the history of the rock's name (*Saga of Cape Ann*, p. 154):

> Squam Rock . . . which stands high in the old pasture above Lighthouse Beach, and has been the climbing delight of generations of Annisquam children, got its pres-

ent name by accident. It once was known as "Squaw Rock," since an Indian girl was said to have been fatally injured there by falling or by throwing herself despondently from its top. When the first picture postcards of this region were printed, one of them portrayed that famous landmark, but the printer assumed that an error had been made in the spelling so he changed "Squaw" to "Squam."

III.135. a woman cut into field stone . . .

The "great Algonquin sculpture" that Olson tells Herbert Kenny about (" 'I know men for whom everything matters,' " *Muthologos*, II, 159), found in 1922 under a sail and spar shed at the Madam Goss House, 47 Leonard Street in Annisquam, immediately north of the bridge across Lobster Cove (mentioned a few lines later in the poem). There is a drawing and description of the piece in Willoughby, *Antiquities of the New England Indians*, pp. 164–165 (see *OLSON* 1, pp. 38–39), which Olson had consulted around 20 November 1960, judging from notes among his papers, and in 1961 he had a plaster cast made for himself of the original which is in the Peabody Museum, Cambridge.

III.136. Madam Goss's lawn

In back of the house at 47 Leonard Street in Annisquam, built by Captain Thomas Goss in 1728. "A few years later Richard Goss became the proprietor and his wife, the former Elizabeth Harraden, was the 'Madam Goss' whose name became permanently attached to the house and to the hill where it stands" (Copeland and Rogers, *Saga of Cape Ann*, p. 171). (On the next page the authors write, "The site where the Madam Goss House was located previously had been a summer camping ground for Indians, as evidenced by relics uncovered during later excavations"—which is marked by Olson in his copy.)

III.136. the Panic of 1837

Financial panic and depression in the United States following, in part, Andrew Jackson's Specie Circular which required hard money (gold or silver) in payment for public land. For its particular effect on the residents of Annisquam, see Copeland and Rogers, *Saga*, pp. 161–162:

> At one time, during the height of the shipbuilding boom in the 1829–32 period, seventy-five vessels of various sizes made Annisquam their home port ... That was a prosperous period for Annisquam and in the ten years following 1828, the number of dwelling houses in the village doubled, from thirty to about sixty. The prosperity came to an end, however, with the Panic of 1837. Some of the local shipowners and traders had been borrowing heavily from the banks, and when they were unable to renew their loans, they suffered losses from which their businesses never recovered.
>
> After 1837 Annisquam declined as a commercial port, partly of course, because it could not accommodate the ships of larger size which by then were coming into general use.

III.136. Lanes & Yorks & Robinsons ... Goss' Gees Dennisons Harradens ...

Some of the seventeenth and eighteenth century families in the Lobster Cove area—descendants of original settlers John Lane, Samuel York, Abraham Robinson, Thomas Goss, William Gee (who gave his name to Gee Avenue, Dogtown), George Dennison, and Edward Harraden.

III.136. ships then carrying again to south'ard to Dutch Guiana / to Virginia ...

For trading voyages by Gloucester merchants to Virginia and the West Indies, see *Maximus* III, 16; Copeland and Rogers, p. 161; and Babson, pp. 384–385 (quoted in part in note to *Maximus* III, 16).

III.136. the bridge / rattles ...

Old planked bridge from Washington Street across Lobster Cove into Annisquam, since closed to traffic.

III.136. Champlain and Lescarbot show / map & story

For Champlain's portrayal of Gloucester Harbor, see *Maximus* I, 151 and note; also II, 136 and III, 85 and 100. Marc Lescarbot (ca. 1590–ca. 1630), a lawyer and poet, visited Port Royal, Acadia, and traveled down the coast from there with de Poutrincourt (q.v.) and Champlain. He recorded his experiences in his *History of New France* (1609), which includes a description of Gloucester Harbor and which Olson calls "one of the greatest books . . . more interesting than Champlain's report, because Lescarbot talks with some vivacity about Gloucester" (" 'I know men . . . ,' " *Muthologos*, II, 164).

▶ III.137. JUST AS MORNING TWILIGHT . . .

Holograph original only, dated 3 May 1966. The designation "Full Flower Moon" can be found, e.g., in the *Old Farmer's Almanac* for 1966 (p. 19). The poem was written very early that morning (the sun was scheduled to rise at 4:37 that day), apparently after the poet had returned home from a visit with his friends.

III.137. principle acausal

See Jung, "On Synchronicity," in *Man and Time*, p. 210 (notes in Olson's copy indicate he had been reading it the day before): "The Rhine experiments [in ESP] have demonstrated that space and time, and hence causality, are factors that can be eliminated, with the result that acausal phenomena, otherwise called miracles, appear possible." Jung had previously pointed out on p. 204 that in certain so-called coincidences, such as those that occur in ESP experiments, "the law of causality does not hold . . . For we cannot conceive how a future event could bring about an event in the present. Since for the time being there is no possibility whatever of a causal explanation, we must assume provisionally that improbable accidents of an acausal nature—that is, meaningful coincidences—have entered the picture." See also Jung's essay, "Synchronicity," subtitled "An Acausal Connecting Principle," in Jung and Pauli, *The Interpretation of Nature and the Psyche*.

III.137. solar piston ion force

See Jung, "On Synchronicity," in *Man and Time*, p. 207: "In the light of the most recent astrophysical research, astrological correspondence is probably not a matter of synchronicity but, very largely, of a causal relationship. As Professor Knoll has demonstrated at this meeting, the solar proton radiation is influenced to such a degree by planetary conjunctions, oppositions, and quartile aspects that the appearance of magnetic storms can be predicted with a fair amount of probability." Olson has underlined "the solar proton radiation" in his copy.

See also "ion-conditioning" of the human personality in Knoll's article in *Man and Time*, "Transformations of Science in Our Age," esp. pp. 296ff., which Olson had read at an earlier point (also for the passage, "effected [i.e., affected?] too in birth and or conception or / in both by either ions stored in earth . . .," and see *Maximus* III, 54 and note).

III.137. these two friends, a man & woman / I have had reason to say were my only brother-sister . . .

Vincent Ferrini and Mary Shore, his wife at the time— whose mother's maiden name was Hynes, similar to that of Olson's mother, so that Olson would often address her as his "sister" (Mary Shore in conversation, June 1972). See also "Olson in Gloucester," *Muthologos*, I, 182.

▶III.139. AN ESSAY ON QUEEN TIY

Written in Gloucester and dated May 1966. The holograph original appears in a notebook among the poet's papers and was written after May 18th, when a copy of *Oceanus* containing Mavor's "Mighty Bronze Age Volcanic Explosion" (a definite source for the poem) was sent him from the Woods Hole Oceanographic Institution. The poem was sent to Andrew Crozier for publication in his *Wivenhoe Park Review* apparently in an envelope postmarked 25 May 1966, on the verso of which is written: "You cld call it an Essay on Queen Tiy! if you wanted to or TIY—1, 2." A poem of migrations, continuing the earlier "Chronicles" and "Sanuncthion lived / before the Trojan War . . ." (*Maximus* II, 102—105).

See Stubbings, "The Aegean Bronze Age," in Hayes et al., *Chronology*, p. 75 (marked in Olson's copy):

> The latest datable Egyptian object in Crete in a context before the destruction [of the Minoan palaces at the end of Late Minoan II] is a seal of Queen Tiy (consort of Ameno-phis III, who reigned 1417—1379 B.C.) from a chamber tomb at Hagia Triada. The earliest Egyptian cross-link *after* the destruction is a scarab of the same queen found at Mycenae with Late Helladic III pottery. Our date can hardly, therefore, be more than a quarter century wrong, but until new and preciser evidence comes to light it seems idle to try to adject the '*c.* 1400' figure by the odd decade.

This information was apparently sent to Mavor (see below) by the poet, for there is a letter from him dated 8 June 1966 thanking Olson for his "letter on the dating of Queen Tiy's seal and scarab" and enclosing a reprint of his article which, however, had already been seen and used by Olson in the writing of this poem.

III.139. Phoenicians / before / —or by 1540 BC says . . . the / Parian Chronicle

See *Maximus* II, 102 and 104 and notes.

III.139. Zeus / rolled up / on the shore . . .

See *Maximus* II, 102 and note.

III.140. Gortyna

Ancient city on the southern side of the island of Crete.

III.140. Minos ... Rhadamanthys ∠ Semitic names ...

The identification of the names of Minos and his brothers as Semitic would not be derived from the source for the earlier migration poems, Graves, *Greek Myths*, as he mentions, I, 295–296, "whether inscriptions in Linear A are written in Greek or Cretan has not yet been established" at the time of his writing. Rather, Olson's suggestion that the names are Semitic in derivation follows from Cyrus Gordon's discoveries in 1962 that the Cretan Linear A is a Northwest Semitic language brought to Crete by migrating Semitic settlers some time before 2000 B.C.

See also *Maximus* II, 102 and 111.

III.140. the earth's crust once—& mantle or at / least the depth of the asthenosphere broke ... apart

See Wilson, "Continental Drift," p. 93:

> Most oceanographers now agree that the ridges [of the ocean floor] form where convection currents rise in the earth's mantle and that the trenches are pulled down by the descent of these currents into the mantle. The possibility of lateral movement of the currents in between is supported by evidence for a slightly plastic layer—called the asthenosphere—below the brittle shell of the earth. . . . It is easy to believe that where the convection currents rise and separate, the surface rocks are broken by tension and pulled apart . . .

III.140. 150,000,000 years ago to the t ...

Wilson (b.1908), a geophysicist at the University of Toronto, explains elsewhere in his article, "The ages of the islands [along the mid-ocean ridges] and of the coastal formations suggest that about 150 million years ago, in mid-Mesozoic time, all the continents were joined in one land mass and that there was only one great ocean" (p. 98). See then the cover of *Maximus* II and Olson's note on the copyright page of that volume.

III.141. runs right down the middle / such as when / India ground a path for herself ...

Wilson describes the ridges of the mid-ocean floor as "submarine trails" which are "records of the motion of the continents as they receded from one another," and points out that "three such ridges have already been well established by surveys of the Indian Ocean . . ." (p. 97). On p. 99 he speaks of India having moved northward, "away from the still intact Australian-Antarctic land mass."

III.141. Mozambique

Portuguese colony on the southeastern coast of Africa opposite the island of Madagascar (now Malagasy Republic); area of oceanic ridges (see map in Wilson, p. 96).

III.141. Tethys

Wife of Okeanos (*Maximus* II, 168), for whom the sea between Africa-Arabia and Europe-Asia on the map of the single supercontinent prepared by Wilson, p. 97 (cover of *Maximus* II), was named.

III.142. 10,000 people by or about 1637 plus say 2 / years ...

Olson's source for this figure is not known. The first official census of the United States was not taken until 1790, although figures for earlier years have been compiled in Greene and Harrington, *American Population Before the Federal Census*. Their section, "General Estimates of the Thirteen Colonies as a Whole," p. 3, lists 50,000 English inhabitants of America for 1641 (the closest date to 1637–39 available), according to a colonial New York source. At the same time, 21,200 men, women, and children are given for New England alone in 1637, according to Josselyn's "New England Rarities" (p. 9); while the compilers estimate a total of 7,912 inhabitants for Massachusetts in 1637, 8,592 in 1639 (p. 13). Olson's figure, therefore, is quite low.

III.142. the breaking out of Civil War / in England

I.e., 1640, when the Scottish army crossed the border into England (see also *Maximus* I, 157 and note).

III.142. 1623

The founding of the fishing plantation on Cape Ann by the Dorchester Company.

III.142. 1630 when / the Big Travel started . . .

The Puritan migration under John Winthrop which led to the founding of Boston.

III.142. 2100 from Maikop

Village in southern Russia near the Black Sea, site of a royal tomb from Early Kuban culture (see, e.g., Childe, *Dawn of European Civilization*, pp. 147−148; also Piggott, *Prehistoric India*, pp. 62−63). Also, "Advantages of Literacy": ". . . even the Amorites stir at the same date that the Indo-Europeans appear via or from Maikop at before or after 2100 BC . . ."

III.142. Aia the / Golden / original name for Colchis . . . cld be Kuban

Colchis was the location of the Golden Fleece sought by Jason and the Argonauts. See *Maximus* II, 164 and notes.

III.143. Bristol

Home of merchant adventurers such as John Jay (*Maximus* I, 80) who encouraged early exploration of North America. ("It was . . . the fisheaters of Bristol / who were the conquistadors of my country . . ."—*Maximus* I, 58). See also I, 77 and note.

III.143. Plymouth

Seaport of England which gave its name to the Plymouth Colony in America.

III.143. Weymouth

Port from which the Dorchester Company settlers sailed (see *Maximus* I, 99 and note).

III.143. Hercules born 1340

See *Maximus* II, 104 and note.

III.143. Santorin / practically like / Herculaneum / dropped / herself / ashes . . .

See Mavor, "A Mighty Bronze Age Volcanic Explosion," an account of the eruption of the island of Santorin (known in ancient times as Thera) which is linked directly to the decline of the Minoan civilization, esp. p. 20: "The Minoan eruption carried ash primarily toward the southeast under the influence of prevailing summer northerly winds. The extent of substantial ash fall included all of the Aegean islands south of Andros, west to Khania on Crete, east to Rodhos and south half way from Crete to the mouth of the Nile. The depth of ash fall on all land areas within this region was enough to cause desertion of the land by the people who survived."

Herculaneum was the Roman city, named for Hercules, destroyed along with Pompeii in 79 A.D. by an eruption of Mount Vesuvius.

III.143. exactly / 1400 BC

See Mavor, p. 18: "Since 1939 evidence has come to light establishing the date of the bronze age eruption of Santorin. Galanopoulos reported in 1960 that Carbon-14 dates have been obtained from a piece of wood found under the top

40-meter thick layer of pumice. The date is 1405 B.C. plus or minus one hundred years. The demise of the Minoan civilization has been dated at 1400 B.C. by examination of Egyptian artifacts found on both Santorin and Crete."

III.144. Tiryns or Thebes or My / cenae

Cities of mainland Greece, centers of the Mycenaean civilization which, as Mavor points out, arose after the volcanic destruction of the power of Minoan Crete. Tiryns and Mycenae are in Argolis on the Peloponnesus, Thebes in Boeotia.

III.144. Europe was beautiful / 800 AD to 1250 . . . Iceland was, Greenland, Vinlanda

Roughly, the Age of the Vikings. The first Norse settlement in Iceland was 870; in 982–986 Eric the Red explored the coast of Greenland and established a settlement there; and in 1003, Eric's son, Leif, explored "Vinland" on the North American coast.

III.144. Java

Large island of Indonesia. A huge tidal wave, or tsunami, nearly one hundred feet high drowned 86,000 inhabitants of low-lying settlements there and on neighboring Sumatra in 1883, following the eruption of the nearby volcanic island of Krakatau. Mentioned in Mavor's article, p. 17.

III.144. a tsunami

Mavor describes the destruction of Santorin, p. 17: "For the people of the Eastern Mediterranean this tremendous explosion must have produced thunderous noises and aerial vibration, followed by ash which on Santorin included boulders as large as a house, noxious fumes, darkness, lightning, earthquakes, and gigantic tsunamis, the first one of which reached Crete 30 minutes after the collapse and flooded the coastal areas. Probably there were no surviving eye witnesses to the eruption. A 30 to 40 meter thick layer of ash covered Santorin, and in 1939 it was reported that a five-meter thick layer of ash was found on neighboring Anaphi, 25 kilometers to the east at 250 meters above sea level."

▶ **III.145. The usefulness / of tramping out with great care . . .**

Written in 1966 (as mentioned in the poem), probably early June. A note in the poet's copy of Perry Miller's *Orthodoxy in Massachusetts*, one of the poem's sources, indicates Olson had been reading that volume May 29th to May 30th 1966, so the poem was probably written then or shortly thereafter. The opening portion, down through "Westcountry comment of these new shores / Little-Good . . . ," was written on an invitation to the poet Joel Oppenheimer's wedding to be held 5 June 1966. The poem was then continued (from "Gloucester Stark-Naught or Pure Zero . . ." through "the younger Hugh Peter pastor North Church Salem before . . .") in the same notebook where "[to get the rituals straight . . ." (*Maximus* III, 173–174), dated 19 June 1966, appeared. (Other dates from mid-June 1966 occur in the notebook, of which the earliest is June 13th.) Finally, the section beginning "going home to England . . ." was found only in typescript among the poet's papers, and since this was clearly not the beginning of the poem, the remaining, earlier portions had to be pieced together.

III.145. as Whitehead did then, 1927–28

The philosopher's great achievement, *Process and Reality*, was first delivered as a series of lectures at the University of Edinburgh during those years, as indicated on the title page of the published volume. See also *Maximus* II, 79.

III.145. 300 years from then . . . the true <u>style</u> of thought from Descartes

Cf. *Maximus* II, 129: "exactly / 300 / years / writing / at the stile . . ." (and reference to "stile" below in this poem). For Descartes, see *Maximus* I, 128, and II, 79, and respective notes.

III.145. the year by year Annals Winthrop thought to / make his History

See the editor's introduction to Winthrop's *Journal* in *Winthrop Papers*, II, 234: "Apparently Winthrop intended to edit his Journal at some future time, using it, perhaps, as the basis of 'The History of New England,' which it has often been inaccurately called—a title suggested by the words which Winthrop wrote on the cover of the third volume of the manuscript, at the top: '3: [Vol *cancelled*] Booke [*written in above*] of the Annalls of N: England.' " Olson has copied in the margin of his copy in the same red ink as on the Oppenheimer invitation and manuscript notebook: "3: Booke of the Annalls of N: England"; while a note on the flyleaf indicates he had been using the volume on May 23rd and May 25th 1966, shortly before the poem was written.

III.145. Thos. Dudley

(1576–1653), Winthrop's deputy-governor of the Massachusetts Bay Colony and later governor; he sailed with Winthrop on the *Arabella*. The quotation promised from him is never actually delivered in the poem.

III.145. that stile

See *Maximus* II, 129 and 130 and notes. With a pun on "style" (see note above).

III.145. <u>incita</u>

From Latin *incito*, 'to incite, encourage, hurry, hasten.'

III.145. <u>pratum</u>

Latin, 'a meadow.'

III.145. universum

Latin, 'universe'; also 'whole,' as in the phrase *in universum*, 'as a whole.'

III.145. 50 English fishing vessels on this side / in 1624

See *Maximus* I, 112 and note.

III.145. by 1637 was 15 reported

From Innis, *The Cod Fisheries*, p. 80 (marked in Olson's copy in red ink): "The 50 vessels which had sailed from the West Country to New England in 1624 had dwindled to 15 in 1637."

III.145. 1636 the / <u>Desire</u> built [Marblehead? & by Wm Stephens

See Winthrop, *History*, I, 230, entry for 26 September 1636: "A ship of one hundred and twenty tons was built at Marblehead, and called the Desire."

For William Stevens at Marblehead, see *Maximus* III, 28, 134 and note; also Philips, *Salem in the Seventeenth Century* (where the name is spelled "Stephens"), in the note following.

III.145. on Salem / Neck, & therefore Richard Hollingsworth's?

See Phillips, *Salem in the Seventeenth Century*, pp. 96–97 (marked in Olson's copy):

> . . . in 1637 a grant of land 'nere unto Richard Hollingsworth's works' is mentioned. Hollingsworth was a ship-

builder of note and had evidently got his yards well started by 1637, and the same year William Stephens was 'to have 18 poole of ground by ye waters side and 12 poole in bredth in ye narrow of ye neck for the building of Shipps, provided yt shalbe imployed for yt ende.' This Stephens had already built in England a vessel called the Royal Merchant of six hundred tons, so he was a real ship-builder. He may have moved to Gloucester and built ships there about 1661.

A ship or ketch called the Desire was built at Marble-head in 1636. She was one hundred and twenty tons, so must have been quite a vessel for those days. Her owner or master, Captain William Peirce, was furnished with armament and anchor from the bark Warwick for £24-19-0. She made various voyages, one to the West Indies in 1638, on the return from which she elicited from Winthrop the remark that 'dry fish and strong liquor are the only commodities for those parts,' but she brought back cotton, tobacco, salt, and Negroes! Whether the latter were slaves the record does not say, but, anyway, we do know that the Desire did take Pequot captives to the Bahamas to sell for slaves the year before.

For Salem Neck, see *Maximus* III, 28 and note.

III.145. Made / trip Feb 26 1638 . . .

See Winthrop, *History*, ed. Savage, I, 305, entry for that date: "Mr. Peirce, in the Salem ship, the Desire, returned from the West Indies after seven months. He had been at Providence, and brought some cotton, and tobacco, and negroes . . ." Savage notes at this point that "a few years later, we shall see a very honorable testimony of our fathers against the horrible practice of taking the negroes from their native land." He is referring to Richard Saltonstall's petition, quoted in a note below.

The voyage of the *Desire* to the West Indies is also noted by Innis, *Cod Fisheries*, p. 78 and n., where it is marked by Olson in his copy.

III.145. by 1638 how many of the 10,000 / people who came in the 1st decade . . .

See previous poem, "10,000 people by or about 1637 plus say 2 / years" (III, 143), and note.

III.145. Smith's deliberate / naming of the other landmark as bold on the ocean . . .

Probably Smith's Isles, earlier name for the Isles of Shoals (on *Maximus* I, 157–158, Olson refers to "Smith's Isles of Shoals"); see *Maximus* I, 109 and note. Of the list of place-names on his map of New England (*Travels and Works*, I, 232; II, 699-700), no other names as obviously fit this passage, unless it might be Cape Tragabigzanda (q.v.) or the Three Turks' Heads (q.v.).

III.145. the rock Upper Platte /. Sioux later

The North Platte river in Wyoming and Nebraska, so named—from the French 'flat,' a translation of the original Siouan designation transliterated as Nebraska, 'flat water'— because of its shallowness. See, e.g., DeVoto, *The Year of Decision*, 1960 ed., p. 165: "The gentle hills that bordered the valley of the Platte, known as the Coast of the Nebraska, suddenly became eroded monstrosities. Jail Rock, Court-house Rock, Chimney Rock, Scott's Bluff, were individual items in creation's slag heap that had got named, but the whole formation was fantastic." There was also the dis-tinctive Independence Rock, where travelers on the South Pass route across the Rockies traditionally painted their names.

III.145. Land's End

The westernmost point of England, a promontory of Cornwall. The southern tip of Emerson Point on Cape Ann, looking toward Milk Island, also bore that designation.

III.145. Haste and Little Haste Bay

Great Haste, a bare rock surrounded by ledges, and Little Haste close by, bare at low water, are in the main channel outside Salem Harbor.

III.145. Westcountry

See *Maximus* I, 99 and note.

III.145. Little-Good

See Copeland and Rogers, *Saga of Cape Ann*, pp. 74–75:

> One of the traditions of Cape Ann is that Little Good Harbor Beach was so named by an Indian whose English vocabulary was so limited that to him "little good" meant "not good." The Indian was referring, of course, to the harbor outside the beach, not the beach itself. That is an intriguing tradition, but there is evidence that it originated in the mind of one of the imaginative citizens of Gloucester rather than in the mouth of an Indian.
>
> At the southwestern end of the beach, a creek, after winding through the marsh behind the beach, flows into the cove. When the Cape was first settled, that creek apparently was considerably wider and deeper than it is today. And on an old map we have found a basin in the creek, near the mainland, designated as "Little Good Harbor." The boats of the early residents of the Cape were small craft, and that basin in the creek, though little, would have been large enough to accommodate them. Inasmuch as it was fairly well protected from the sea by the marsh, it was also "good"; hence "Little Good Harbor."

III.145. Stark-Naught

See Copeland and Rogers, *Saga of Cape Ann*, pp. 77–78:

> One other spot of minor historical significance in this general area should be mentioned for the record. We had run across several casual references to Starknaught Harbor, but it was not until we examined an old map of the shore that we found out where it was located. That map designated the shallow cove beyond the eastern end

of Brier Neck, where Long Beach begins, as Starknaught Harbor. It was not well protected from the sea, and apparently was used commercially for only a short time.

The site appears on Babson's map accompanying his *History of Gloucester*.

III.145. Matinicuns

Inhabitants of Matinicus Island in Penobscot Bay. A Tenpound Island is nearby, less than a half mile off its southeast side.

Shortly before this poem Olson had written his friend and former teacher Wilbert Snow, who was born on Penobscot Bay and had a summer home there, about the island, and Snow replied, 11 May 1966: "The library failed to help us any at all. So we telephoned to people who lived on Matinicus. They think it was called '10 Pound' because of its size—a little shrimp of an island, an attempt to emphasize its diminutive character."

III.145. Folly

Folly Cove (see next note).

III.146. John Gallop's Folly

The present Folly Cove on the north shore of Cape Ann west of Halibut Point. The history of its name is given in Babson, *History*, p. 247 (marked in Olson's copy), who writes that, according to tradition,

> a man named Gallop once carelessly ran a vessel into the cove there, and lost her, mistaking it for the entrance to another haven; and that, to perpetuate the memory of his fault, it received the name by which it has ever since been known. It might be supposed that the unfortunate man was Benjamin Gallop of Boston, whose sloop was cast away near Pigeon Cove in 1712; but the name was given many years before: and a last resort for conjecture as to its origin may be found in the possibility that it came from John Gallop of Boston, an early pilot, who may have had charge

of the "great shallop," which, in 1635, was cast upon the rocks, coming out of Annisquam Harbor.

Also, Copeland and Rogers, *Saga of Cape Ann*, p. 137. For Gallop, see *Maximus* II, 65 and note, and III, 79–80.

III.146. Winthrop says Gallop lost / a great shallop

This is the vessel referred to by Babson in the preceding note. See Winthrop, *History*, Savage ed., I, 208, entry for 28 November 1635: "A great shallop, coming from Pascataquack in a N.E. wind with snow, lost her way, and was forced into Anasquam; and going out with a N.W. wind, through the unskilfulness of the men, was cast upon the rocks, and lost £100 worth of goods."

III.146. August 27 1639 a vessel in from the West Indies ...

See entry for that date in Winthrop, *History*, Savage ed., I, 369–370: "Here came a small bark from the West Indies, one Capt. [*Jackson*] in her, with commission from the Westminister company to take prize, etc., from the Spaniard. He brought much wealth in money, plate, indico, and sugar. He sold his indico and sugar here for £1400, wherewith he furnished himself with commodities, and departed again for the West Indies."

III.146. the / General Court action_____1639 had finally decided that / John White Rector of St Peter's Dorchester ...

The rulings of the General Court of the Massachusetts Bay Colony, as preserved in *Records of the Governor and Company of the Massachusetts Bay*, ed. Shurtleff, I: 1628–1641, make no mention of John White for any part of the year 1639. Possibly the date should be 1629, the founding of the church at Salem.

Concerning the blank space, Pound's words in Canto XIII (quoting Confucius) might be recalled:

"And even I can remember

A day when the historians left blanks in their writings,
I mean for things they didn't know . . ."

III.146. the younger Hugh Peter pastor North Church Salem . . .

. Peter ("younger" because younger than John White) came to New England on the *Abigail* in 1635 and became the fourth minister of the church at Salem in December 1636. He returned to England in August 1641, was active on Cromwell's side during the Civil War, and was executed as a regicide at the return of Charles II.

III.146. had been chosen . . . by John White for the Salem post

See, e.g., Miller, *Orthodoxy in Massachusetts*, 123−124 (noted in Olson's copy): "Probably through the influence of John White, whom he called 'my dear firm Friend,' Peter became one of the patentees of the New England Company in May, 1628. . . . He finally went to Massachusetts, he says, because 'many of my Acquaintance going for *New-England*, had engaged me to come to them when they sent.' " Actually, however, John Endecott was more directly influential: "Endecott himself was a friend of Hugh Peter, whom he had asked the Company to secure as minister for the post [at Salem]" (Ibid., p. 129).

III.146. Hugh Peter's service in the Hague or Rotterdam

See Miller, *Orthodoxy*, pp. 106−108 and 112, for mention of Peter and other Puritans in Holland.

III.146. Perry Miller's sure / Peter was / one of the secret / non-separating / Congregationalists . . .

See Miller's discussion in *Orthodoxy*, pp. 123−124, which concludes: "Peter's devotion to the Congregational polity was well known at this time, and his affiliation with the [New England] Company may very possibly have been the entering wedge of the Congregationalists' control."

III.146. John White / was patsy . . .

As Miller points out, White was a Presbyterian "conspicuously" to the end of his life and "the last thing he would ever have desired to behold in New England, next to an episcopal hierarchy, was a Congregational state. Although he kept up his connection with the enterprise, it is evident that after the reins had been seized by the bumptious Easterners the Company's ecclesiastical complexion was radically transformed. Thereafter the ministers whom it attracted were, almost to a man, either confirmed Congregationalists or on the highroad to becoming so" (*Orthodoxy*, p. 105).

III.146. the Planters Plea

See Maximus I, 102 and note. Miller, *Orthodoxy*, pp. 140–141, suggests that the tract was written to suppress rumors that the Puritan migration to New England was inspired by Separatism.

III.146. Norfolk

County on the east coast of England.

III.146. York

The city and county (Yorkshire) in northeastern England, home of emigrants such as William Bradford and Richard Saltonstall.

III.147. Nowell

Increase Nowell (1590–1655), one of the original grantees named in the Massachusetts Bay Company patent. He arrived in the *Arabella* with Winthrop in 1630.

III.147. big Saltonstall

Sir Richard Saltonstall (see further below and note).

III.147. great Winthrop

John "Wanax" Winthrop (see *Maximus* II, 135 and III, 41).

III.147. this use of Craddock

For Matthew Craddock, see *Maximus* II, 65 and note. The "use" referred to was the transformation by a number of wealthy men from the Eastern counties of England, of the Dorchester Company's fishing and trading enterprise into the Massachusetts Bay Company's factional religious one. As Miller writes, "it was certainly by the timely support of the newcomers, Easterners like Winthrop, Dudley, Pynchon, Johnson, and one or two Londoners, Saltonstall and Increase Nowell, that Craddock's motion [to transport the charter of the Massachusetts Bay Company to New England] was carried and the great migration precipitated" (*Orthodoxy*, p. 104).

III.147. Charles I

(1600–1649), King of England from 1625 until his execution by Cromwell and the Puritans during the Civil War.

III.147. the Charter of / the Company was as slidded . . .

See note to "the docquet" below.

III.147. Richard / Saltonstall cried Havoc here / when Guinea ship / came to Boston . . .

See Winthrop, *History*, Savage ed., II, 298–300, and the "petition of Richard Saltonstall, Esq., for justice to be done on Captain Smith and Mr. Keyser for their injurious dealing with the negroes at Guinea," included as an appendix to Savage's edition of Winthrop, II, 462–463, in which Saltonstall writes: "The act of stealing Negers, or of taking them by force, (whether it be considered as theft, or robbery) is (as I conceive) expressly contrary both to the law of God, and the law of this country." The petition was granted by the General Court in its session of 7 October 1645, and Smith and Keyser were punished. Saltonstall (ca. 1610– 1694) was a magistrate and held the office of 'assistant' in the Massachusetts Colony. His father, Sir Richard Saltonstall (1586–1658), was an original patentee of the Massachusetts Bay Company, came to New England in 1630 but returned to England the next year, and was appointed ambassador to Holland in 1644, where his portrait was painted by Rembrandt (see below).

III.148. John Robinson

(ca. 1576–1625), pastor of the Pilgrim Fathers. He settled in Amsterdam in 1608, but removed the following year to Leiden where he ministered to the Nonconformist community, and died before he could accompany his people to Plymouth. His position is discussed in Miller's *Orthodoxy*.

III.148. Rembrandt painted Saltonstall

See *Winthrop Papers*, II, 241n. (marked by Olson): "Sir Richard Saltonstall remained in New England less than a year. In 1644, while he was ambassador to Holland, his portrait was painted by Rembrandt. In 1858, a copy of this portrait was presented to the Massachusetts Historical Society by Leverett Saltonstall, Esq., and reproduced in I, *Proceedings*, IV." Also reproduced in Morrison, *Builders of the Bay Colony*, opposite p. 68. Compare that to the frontispiece portraits of John Winthrop in *Winthrop Papers*, I and II.

III.148. he / found instead he / waked with Christ . . .

See John Winthrop's "Christian Experience," written in a notebook "the 12th of the 11th month, 1636. in the 49th year of my age just compleat," in which he tells, "I was now growne familiar with the Lord Jesus Christ, hee would oft tell mee he loved mee, I did not doubt to believe him; If I went abroad hee went with mee, when I returned hee came home with mee. I talked with him upon the way, hee lay down with mee and usually I did awake with him. Now I could goe into any company and not loose him: and so sweet was his love to mee as I desired nothing but him in heaven or earth" (*Winthrop Papers*, I, 159—pages uncut, however, in Olson's copy).

III.148. says in so many words / (1644) "we / with money & with power . . .

Not an exact quotation; see note to "the docquet" below.

III.149. John White's study / was raided . . .

See Rose-Troup, *John White*, ch. XXIII: "In the Toils: The Raided Study," describing the search of White's parsonage in Dorchester in 1635 for documents which might implicate him with some unauthorized non-conformist plot. During a siege of the city a few years later in 1643, his library was plundered by Royalist soldiers (ibid., pp. 312−313):

III.149. William Ames's library, / rather than himself, came over . . .

Ames (1576−1633) was a leading Puritan divine who had settled in Holland. He hoped to join the Massachusetts Bay Colony but died before the opportunity came to pass. As Miller points out, "his family ultimately crossed over in 1637, bringing his books with the intention of making them 'the first furniture' of the college library" (*Orthodoxy*, p. 126).

III.150. in England, sd the docquet . . .

See Miller, *Orthodoxy*, pp. 144−145:

> Contrary to the universal custom, this document [the charter of the Massachusetts Bay Company] entirely omitted to specify a particular residence for the corporation's headquarters. The evidence we possess seems to indicate that this hiatus was not accidental. Winthrop wrote in 1644 that heretofore it has been the manner for those who

procured patents to keep the chief government resident in England, and "so this was intended & with much difficulty we gott it abscinded." The docquet containing the application for a charter asked the privilege of "electing governors and officers here in England," and the strange failure of this restriction to be transcribed into the final draft appears, to say the least, providential.

III.150. Cape an

Cape Ann, a common enough older spelling (see, e.g., *Maximus* I, 109).

III.150. J. Prynne

Jeremy Prynne (b.1936), English poet and Director of Studies at Gonville and Caius College, Cambridge, at the time. A regular correspondent of Olson's since November 1961. See his address, "On Maximus IV, V, VI," as well as his review of that volume in Andrew Crozier's magazine *The Park* (and Olson's response to the review in his interview with Gerard Malanga, *Muthologos*, II, 105ff.). See also *Maximus* III, 157 and 184.

III.150. Edward Dorn

(b.1929), American poet, student of Olson's at Black Mountain College (see *A Bibliography on America for Ed Dorn*) and author of *What I see in the Maximus Poems* (1960). His *From Gloucester Out* (1964) directly portrays Olson and his *Geography* (1965) was dedicated to Olson. At the time, a Fulbright lecturer in American Literature at the University of Essex.

III.150. Andrew Crozier

(b.1943), English poet who had studied with Olson in 1964–65 at Buffalo, editor of *Wivenhoe Park Review* and publisher of Ferry Press in London.

III.150. Tom Pickard

(b.1946), English poet, editing at the time the magazine *King Ida's Watch Chain*.

III.150. "the light cloud / blowing in from the ice of Norfolk thrust"

From a poem by Jeremy Prynne entitled "The Glacial Question, Unsolved," a xeroxed copy of which was sent to Olson by its author; later collected in Prynne's *The White Stones*. On the bottom of his copy, Olson has noted: "date? pre-June 1st, 1966—by a few days?"

III.150. "the top and head", / he had it, / Men / of Power

John Keats, in his letter of 22 November 1817 to Benjamin Bailey (*Poems and Letters*, p. 274): "Men of Genius are great as certain ethereal Chemicals operating on the Mass of neutral intellect—but they have not any individuality, any determined Character—I would call the top and head of those who have a proper self Men of Power." See also *Special View of History*, pp. 32–33.

III.151. the moskitoes of Beverly Farms

A resort village outside Beverly, Massachusetts; home of such persons of political influence as Henry Cabot Lodge (b.1902), U.S. ambassador to South Vietnam, 1963–1964, 1965–1967.

Olson's "moskitoes" might be read as a diminutive of "WASPs."

III.151. streetcars, in Athens, made / Prime Minister's of England's money

Probably an allusion to political developments in Greece toward the close of World War II, specifically, British intervention against the Communist guerrillas in the Greek civil

war—the Prime Minister at the time being Winston Churchill, who visited Athens on Christmas Day, 1944. The British
program gave way to American involvement in the form of
the 1947 Truman Doctrine, a program of financial and
military assistance, the beginnings of a foreign policy which
would culminate in the Southeast Asian entanglement of the
1960's. The poet had a number of Greek friends in Washington during the 1940's (see "Name-Day Night," *Archaeologist of Morning*, p. 8) who were concerned with the turn of
events in their native land, most notably Constantine Poulos,
who reported on the strife in Greece for the Overseas News
Agency.

III.151. Nahant Head

High rocky peninsula on the Massachusetts coast near
Lynn, site of a resort town with an exclusive yacht club.

III.151. Manchester Port

Formerly, Manchester-by-the-sea. Manchester Harbor is
about five miles west of Gloucester Harbor and is the location of a fashionable yacht club.

III.151. Chatham

Resort town on the Atlantic shore of Cape Cod.

III.151. "like a heart", Edward Johnson said in / The
Wonder-Working Providence of . . .

See Johnson's *Wonder-Working Providence*, Jameson ed.,
pp. 70–71, concerning the fourth Church of Christ at
Boston:

> So that the fourth Church of Christ issued out of Charles
> Towne, and was seated at Boston, being the Center Towne
> and Metropolis of this Wildernesse worke (but you must
> not imagine it to be a Metropolitan Church). Invironed it
> is with the Brinish flouds, saving one small Istmos, which
> gives free access to the Neighbour Townes by Land on

the South side; on the North west, and North East, two
constant Faires [Ferries] are kept for daily traffique
thereunto. The forme of this Towne is like a heart,
naturally scituated for Fortifications, having two Hills on
the frontice part thereof next the Sea, the one well fortified on the superfices thereof, with store of great Artil-
lery well mounted, the other hath a very strong battery
built of whole Timber, and filled with Earth. At the
descent of the Hill in the extreme poynt thereof, betwixt
these two strong armes lies a large Cave [Cove] or Bay, on
which the chiefest part of this Town is built, over-topped
with a third Hill; all three like over-topping Towers keepe
a constant watch to fore-see the approach of forrein
dangers, being furnished with a Beacon and lowd babling
Guns, to give notice by their redoubled eccho to all their
Sister-townes.

Also in Shurtleff, *Topographical and Historical Description of
Boston*, pp. 43–44. The passage was used by Olson earlier
in "Letter # 29" omitted from the first *Maximus* volume.

III.152. a London, Company

Not the earlier London Company, which founded James-
town in 1607, but the New England Company which grew
out of the Dorchester Company (a "Westcountry" company)
and in turn became the Massachusetts Bay Company (see
Miller, *Orthodoxy*, pp. 103–105).

III.152. turned even Boston Neck / into / Fortress' "loud-babbling guns" . . .

From Johnson's *Wonder-Working Providence*, Jameson ed.,
p. 71 (see note above).

III.152. John Smith's Southern Palisadoes / blew his hand off . . .

See Smith, "A Map of Virginia, with a Description of its
Commodities, People, Government, and Religion" (1612):
"But this hapned him in that Iournie [*about the beginning
of September 1609*]. Sleeping in his boat, for the ship was

returned 2 daies before, accidentallie one fired his powder bag; which tore his flesh from his bodie and thighes 9. or 10. inches square, in a most pittifull manner: but to quench the tormenting fire, frying him in his cloath[e]s, he leaped over board into the deepe river, where ere they could recover him he was neere drown[e]d" (*Travels and Works*, I, 165).

III.153. Wm Blackstone's / home, and apples

See *Maximus* II, 57 and note.

III.153. "had one small isthmus" / to the neighbor towns . . .

From Johnson, *Wonder-Working Providence*, Jameson ed., p. 70, in passage quoted in note above.

III.153. Murmansk

Arctic seaport on the Kola Peninsula, Russia; on the fur trade route. According to Fisher, *The Russian Fur Trade*, p. 24, "during the last quarter of the sixteenth century and the first decade of the seventeenth a substantial trade in furs was carried on along the Murmansk coast of the Kola Peninsula. All foreign vessels had to pass along this coast, and undoubtedly a few of them made it, rather than Arkhangelsk, their destination, although no outstanding center of trade arose there, unless it was the Pechenga monastery. After 1613, however, the Murmansk coast seems to have lost whatever importance it had possessed in the trade with Europe."

III.153. White Sea

Inlet of Barents Sea in northern Russia. See note following; also, *Maximus* II, 92 and note.

III.153. Muscovy Company, headquarters York

Fisher, *The Russian Fur Trade*, p. 198, writes:

English trade with Russia began in 1553 when Chancellor discovered the White Sea route. His discovery led to the formation in 1555 of a joint-stock company, variously named but known usually as the Muscovy Company, which obtained from Queen Mary and from her successors a monopoly of the Russian trade. From the Russian tsars it acquired various privileges, the most important of which were a monopoly of the White Sea route—which it enjoyed until the Dutch appeared there—full exemption from customs tolls, and the right to trade and to maintain factories within Russia. The last three privileges it retained until 1649.

By virtue of the monopoly grant to the Muscovy Company from the English crown the company's activities constituted practically the whole of English-Russian commerce down to 1669, when the company's existence was terminated.

That the Company had its headquarters at York is not evident from any other source. On the contrary, although there were merchants from York who were members of the Company, the majority were from London and the headquarters was located there (see e.g. Willan, *Early History of the Russia Company*, p. 25).

III.153. Armenia

Area of southwestern Asia, between the Black and Caspian seas and south of the Caucasus Mountains.

III.153. the Caspian

Inland sea in Russia, east of Armenia and the Caucasus Mountains.

III.153. Karakoram

City of Mongolia, capital of Genghis Khan. It was visited by Carpini in 1246 and by Marco Polo in 1275, but destroyed by a seige toward the end of the thirteenth century. See Olson's review of *The Vinland Map and The Tartar Relation*.

III.153. Hugh Peter preached, / fish / as White by mail . . .

See *Maximus* II, 65 and note.

III.154. Endecott & Downing

See *Maximus* I, 156 and note.

III.154. see a fishing on this side as / more valuable than shop-keepers

See John White's letter to John Winthrop (referred to previously in *Maximus* II, 65) in which is written: "I heare shopkeeping begins to growe into request amongst you. In former age all kinde of retailing wares (which I confess is necessary for mens more convenient supply) was but an appendixe to some handicraft and to that I should reduce it if I were to advise in the government." White continues by saying he prefers employment for men "wherein their labours might produce something for the common good which is not furthered by such as drawe only one from another and consequently live by the sweat of other mens brows, producing nothing themselves by their owne endevours," and advises Winthrop to develop a fishing industry, "which is the first means that will bring any income into your lande" (*Winthrop Papers*, III, 322, marked in Olson's copy).

III.154. 2 years / or 7 . . .

See *Maximus* I, 135—"About seven years / and you can carry cinders / in your hand . . ."—and note; also III, 41.

III.154. the lice / of policy, on the body / Politick

Cf. Whitman's "lice of politics" in his 1855 Preface to *Leaves of Grass*.

III.154. "a / entire and Independent body- / politic . . .

See Miller, *Orthodoxy*, pp. 77 and 78, quoting the Puritan authors Henry Jacob and William Bradshaw:

> Jacob defined a church, in 1605, as "a particular Congregation being a spirituall perfect Corporation of Believers, & having power in it selfe immediately from Christ to administer all Religious meanes of faith to the members thereof." It was, he later put it more happily, "an entire and Independent body-politic." . . . Bradshaw declared, "We confine and bound all Ecclesiastical power within the limits onely of one particular Congregation, holding that the greatest Ecclesiastical power ought not to stretch beyond the same."

▶ III.155. OCEANIA

Originally written the night and early morning of 5–6 June 1966 in a pocket checkbook, over and on the backs of unused checks, and then copied by the poet, with an effort to regain the original order of writing, in a small notepad.

III.155. since 1650 this / infestation . . .

The figures are from an article in an unidentified journal, a torn page of which, bearing Olson's underlinings and calculations, was found among the poet's papers from 1965–66:

> According to Professor Edward S. Deevey Jr., writing in *Scientific American*, world population went up from five and one third million some 10,000 years ago to 86.5 million 4,000 years later, and then for centuries increased only slowly until some 300 years ago another revolution in man's control over his environment set in. This revolution is still under way, although it has entered a new stage in our own life time. With the coming of industrial methods of environmental exploitation and control, it became possible to change the ecological balance once again in a most drastic fashion and to support a vastly increased world population: 545 million in 1650, 906

million in 1800, and 2,400 million in 1950. For the year
2000, Deavey predicts 6,270 million.

Further calculations from the journal article were made on
an envelope from Jeremy Prynne postmarked Cambridge,
Eng., 9 May 1966.

III.156. as I had / 5 yrs ago called it   Oceania!

In "*The River Map* and we're done," written in 1963,
where Olson describes the Annisquam as "a salt Oceania or
lake / from Baker's field to Bonds Hill" (*Maximus* II, 202).

III.157. Robert Hogg

(b.1942), Canadian poet, former student of Olson's at
Buffalo.

III.157. Dan Rice

(b.1926), American painter. He studied at Black Mountain
College while Olson was there and received a degree in
painting and drawing under Franz Kline in 1953.

III.157. Jeremy Prynne

(b.1936), English poet and teacher at Cambridge University; a regular correspondent with Olson since 1961. See also
Maximus III, 150 and 184.

III.160. at / 16, 17 . . . the <u>Riggs</u> . . .

The gill-netter *Eliza Riggs*, owned by Captain William
Lafond (see *Maximus* I, 34 and note).

III.160. the Fisherman's / statue

See *Maximus* I, 152 and note.

▶ III.162. MAREOCEANUM

Possibly written ca. 1966–68, at time when preparing
cover for *Maximus* II. Updated holograph manuscript only.

Note on original manuscript is addressed to "Tom"—possibly Tom Maschler, editor at Jonathan Cape, or the English poet Tom Raworth, whom Olson had met in 1967.

The title is formed from Latin *mare* and *oceanus*, 'ocean sea.' According to *The Shorter Oxford English Dictionary* (3d ed., rev.), II, 1356, 'ocean' was, "down to *c* 1650, commonly *ocean sea*, representing L. *mare oceanum* . . ."

III.162. Forming a lake . . .

See the surface of the North Atlantic floor as portrayed on Heezen and Thorp's "Physiographic Diagram," a copy of which was mounted on Olson's kitchen wall.

III.162. Tethys

See *Maximus* III, 141 and note above.

III.162. Tripolitanic

I.e., North African (from the former Roman province Tripolitania, capital Tripolis—now part of Libya).

III.162. Biscay

See *Maximus* I, 77 and note, and especially III, 65 and 189.

III.162. Cape Race

Newfoundland (see note to Cap Raz, *Maximus* I, 77). Cape Raz is on Finisterre.

III.162. Finisterre

The most western portion of France, thrusting out into the Atlantic.

III.162. Gondwanaland

See *Maximus* II, 1 and note, and cover of that volume.

▶**III.163. To my Portuguese . . .**

Holograph manuscript only, dated 15 June 1966. Maximus refers to "my Portuguese" earlier, in *Maximus* I, 10 and 79.

III.163. the Guanches . . .

See Osborn, *Men of the Old Stone Age*, sections on "The Crô-Magnons of the Canary Islands" and "Guanche Characteristics Resembling Crô-Magnon," esp. p. 507 quoting the anthropologist Verneau:

> Without doubt the race that has played the most important rôle in the Canaries is the Guanche. They were settled in all the islands, and in Teneriffe they preserved their distinctive characteristics and customs until the conquest by Spain in the fifteenth century.
>
> The Guanches, who at that time were described as giants, were of great stature. The minimum measure of the men was 1.70 m. (5 ft. 7 in.). . . .
>
> Their skin was light colored—if we may believe the poet Viana—and sometimes even absolutely white. . . . The hair of the true Guanche should be blond or light chestnut, and the eyes blue.
>
> The most striking characteristic of the Guanche race was the shape of the head and the features of the face. The long skull gave shape to a beautiful forehead, well developed in every way. Behind, above the occipital, one notices a large plane contrasting strongly with the marked prominence of the occipital itself. In addition, the parietal eminences, placed very high and very distinct from each other, combined to give the head a *pentagonal form*.

Parts of the passage are marked in Olson's copy.

III.163. Gloucester itself comes from the / Canaries

Cf. also: "Portuguese / are part Phoenician (? / Canary Islanders / Cro-Magnon" (*Maximus* II, 81). Also in the sense that Gloucester, like the whole of North America, is a product of continental drift, and was once joined to the original single continent just at that point of the African coast where the Canaries lie offshore. See, too, *Maximus* III, 205.

III.163. the Muses / told Hesiod / there was / 4 things got / genet

See Hesiod's *Theogony*, 11. 116–122 (Evelyn-White trans., pp. 86–87): ". . . at the first Chaos came to be [χάος γένετ], but next wide-bosomed Earth, the ever-sure foundation of all the deathless ones who hold the peaks of snowy Olympus, and dim Tartarus in the depth of the wide-pathed Earth, and Eros (Love), fairest among the deathless gods, who unnerves the limbs and overcomes the mind and wise counsels of all gods and all men within them."

See also "[MAXIMUS, FROM DOGTOWN—IV]," *Maximus* II, 163–172.

III.163. muspilli it is called in Norse . . .

See Fowler's discussion of the root of Muspellsheim, the realm of fire in the Norse cosmogony, in "Old Norse Religion," p. 247: "*Muspell*—(the word occurs in ON, OS, OE, and OHG) may mean 'fire'; but it may also mean something like 'the end of the world'. For an excellent brief discussion and a useful bibliography see the notes to the Bavarian poem *Muspilli* (c. 830 A.D.) in W. Braune, *Althochdeutsches Lesebuch . . .*" Also Davidson, *Gods and Myths of Northern Europe*, pp. 206–207.

In his "Reading at Berkeley" (*Muthologos*, I, 115), the poet says: "I believe in the end of the world, in the sense that it's knowable. I also believe that the only thing that offends the end of the world—I mean, that's what war is: the way we offend the end of the world . . ." See also Olson's conversation with Ed Dorn the next day (*Muthologos*, I, 159), and "the War of the World," *Maximus* II, 198 and note.

III.163. wetness or moisture or like cloud nebel / in German

See Fowler, "Old Norse Religion," p. 247: "Niflheim (ON *nifl*; German *Nebel*, 'cloud') is known later as the home of the dead ..."

III.164. Niflesheim

The place of mist and cold and darkness in Norse cosmogony.

III.164. Red Cloud ... Man-Afraid-of-His-Horses High / Backbone Little Wolf / Red Dog American Horse

Names of chieftains and warriors of the Oglala Sioux during the later nineteenth century. All but Little Wolf occur, e.g., in Hyde, *Red Cloud's Folk*, which Olson read in the late 1940's; while a Little Wolf is mentioned as an Oglala scout in Sandoz, *Crazy Horse*, p. 397. See pp. 316–317 in Hyde for notes on Red Cloud's name. High Backbone, the teacher of Crazy Horse, was also known as "Hump" for short (Sandoz, p. 18), while Man Afraid's full name was Man Whose Enemies Are Afraid of His Horses (ibid., p. 13).

III.164. acyanas

Harrison, *Themis*, p. 457n., points out that Ocean is related to *acayanas*, 'surrounding.' Also, *Encyclopaedia Britannica*, 11th ed., XIX, 967: "The Greek word ὠκεανός is related to the Sanskrit *açāyanas*, 'the encompassing.' "

III.164. Hunger Himself ... χαω the Muses said ...

An onomatopoeic variation on Greek χάος, 'Chaos.' For Chaos as "hunger," see *Maximus* II, 164 and note.

III.164. Norse is / Ginunga Gap ...

See *Maxmius* II, 164, "appetite. Or / as it reads in Norse / hunger ...," and note. Olson writes to Joyce Benson, ca.

13 November 1967: "Ginnunga Gap—Norse for condition of [un-]Creation *before* even Earth—were genet: simply a organic condition G a gaping mouth standing for 'hunger.' "

III.164. when Earth Herself was One / Continent, Ocean-Tethys were the Single Ocean . . .

See the map on the cover of *Maximus* II, of "the Earth (and Ocean) before Earth started to come apart at the seams," with Oceanus and Tethys Sea and bodies of water surrounding the continents.

III.164. topos

Greek, 'a place.' As Olson says in "Poetry and Truth": ". . . that sense of place as in the same sense that I think names are almost always proper, of the earth, as sort of the place of our habitation, at least, But that that literal globe or orb is our lamp or clue to the whole of creation, and that only by obedience to it does one have a chance at heaven" (*Muthologos*, II, 34).

III.164–165. Tartarus . . . is outside Ocean

See *Maximus* II, 164–165, "Tartarós / is beyond / the gods beyond hunger outside / the ends and source of Earth / Heaven Ocean's / Stream . . .," and note.

III.165. mid-Mesozoic / time, 150,000,000 years ago

See *Maximus* III, 140 and note.

III.165. Terceira

An island of the central Azores.

III.165. Cape Jolly

Should be Cape Juby, headland on the coast of Morocco, some seventy-five miles from Fuerteventura in the Canaries (an error in decipherment). On the second holograph manuscript of *Maximus* III, 205, the poet has added more clearly: "at Cape Juby across from the Canary Islands."

III.165. Atlas Mountains

System of mountains across northwest Africa.

III.165. Fish or Aquarius Time

See *Maximus* II, 9 and note.

▶III.166. Same day, Later

Written 15 June 1966, following previous poem.

III.166. my Neolithic / neighbors

See previous poem, "the Guanches . . . Gloucester itself comes from the Canaries," and note.

III.166. family relations among contemporary Americans and . . . the baboons as a kin group in / Africa

Discussed in Sahlins, "The Origin of Society" (marked by Olson).

III.166. mid Mezozoic at / the place of the parting of the seams of <u>all</u> the Earth

See previous poem; also *Maximus* III, 140–141 and note, and map on the cover of *Maximus* II with the poet's note on copyright page there.

▶III.167. When do poppies bloom . . .

Dated 15 June 1966 on original holograph manuscript. A note in one of Olson's notebooks from the time (same one containing original of *Maximus* III, 173–174) indicates this was written after *Maximus* III, 163–165. See also the poet's letter to the editor of the *Gloucester Times*, written 7 February 1968 (published February 12th): "There was a kitchen garden by a house right next to Birdseyes just recently

removed where each early summer I cld be sure, one day, to
be bombed right out, walking up Commercial Street, by suddenly a poppy, or maybe one or two more, lying there up on
its stalk like crepe paper, and swinging, in the least of all possible air, in a mad dance of toss and tremor. And the woman
who had those seeds there as well as tomatoes, knew it. . . ."

III.167. Mrs. Frontiero's yard

At the side of a house at 47 Commercial Street where Mrs.
Catherine Frontiero lived at that time, since torn down to
make way for a parking area for O'Donnell-Usen trucks
(Olson's letter above reports it "recently removed").

III.167. Birdseyes (or what was once Cunningham / & Thompson's and is now O'Donnell-Usen's)

Building at 88 Commercial Street, site of the fish-processing plants mentioned. Owned by Sylvester Cunningham
and William Thompson at the turn of the century, and then
by Clarence Birdseye, where in the 1920's he developed his
process for preserving fish by deep freezing, it is presently
the site of a branch of O'Donnell-Usen's "Taste O'Sea"
Fisheries.

III.167. Dennison's Crepe

Crepe paper manufactured by the Dennison Maufactur-
ing Company of Framingham, Massachusetts.

III.167. the King of the Earth

Hades or Pluto.

III.167. Penelope

A curious slip or perhaps substitution. Penelope was the
wife of Odysseus, remembered for her patience and ingenu-
ity while awaiting his return from Troy; whereas it was
Persephone, daughter of Demeter, who was stolen by Hades
and had to return to the underworld every six months,

having eaten the pomegranate seeds. It might be noted that the flowers Persephone was picking at the time of her abduction are said to have been poppies.

▶III.168. <u>AN ART CALLED GOTHONIC</u>

Dated "Thursday June 16th [1966]" in both the typescript (of which a carbon also survives) and the original holograph version, which was written in a small spiral-bound notebook.

Gothonic is a term suggested by the ethnologist Gudmund Schütte as an alternative for "Germanic" and is mentioned in Jespersen, *Growth and Structure of the English Language*, p. 18n. In his copy of Jespersen, on top of p. 18, Olson has written:

> the
> Goths
> > *Gothonic*
> > 400 the lowlands
> > > occupied (as invasions discontinued . . .

Also, on top of p. 24 of his copy, the poet notes: "word formation is by *endings* in Gothonic," while marking the following statement by Jespersen there: "As it is characteristic of all Aryan languages that suffixes play a much greater role than prefixes, word formation being generally by endings, it follows that where the Germanic stress system has come into force, the syllable that is most important has also the strongest stress . . ." Also marked is this passage on p. 26: ". . . we have here a case of *value-stressing*; that part of the word which is of greatest value to the speaker and which therefore he especially wants the hearer to notice, is pronounced with the strongest stress." Which might be true for this poem and may account for its halting rhythm, esp. in sections like:

> We trace wood or
> > > > path
> > > will not
> > > > hasten
> > > > > our
> > > step-wise ad-
> > vance

So that the poem as written embodies certain linguistic patterns or characteristics, like "A FOOTNOTE TO THE ABOVE" (*Maximus* I, 144). Indeed, in notes from ca. 11 September 1969 in a pad among his papers, the poet does make the suggestion that the present poem is an "instance . . . in principle of ap-pli / cation? Leading to syllabary-poems [of which "From the Song of Ullikummi" is perhaps another example]."

III.168. ARMENIAN . . . MEASURE

An "Ideal Scale," synonymous with "Lake Van measure" below. "Armenian" in the general sense of "northern," or non-Greek, non-classical in Strzygowski's (q.v.) terms. In an interview with Swedish visitor Inga Loven in August 1968, Olson says that "for an American the Northern condition at this point is more interesting than any Mediterranean," and that "if I continue to write what I do, I get closer and closer to what I call the Armenian or the Gothonic than I do to anything else" (*Muthologos*, II, 87). And in his "Continuing Attempt to Pull the Taffy Off the Roof of the Mouth," Olson writes (*Additional Prose*, p. 70):

> It is a wholly otherwise than metal, and administrative,
> time. I hope I can be followed
> in registering it as *Armenian* or
> wooden-runic and Goth   −   landers'
> water-paths and wave-motion than
>   all this cruel and iron-mongers time between

"Armenian," because derived, according to the poet in conversation August 1969, from a consideration of Armenian church architecture as discussed by Strzygowski in his *Origin of Early Christian Church Art*. One of the churches under discussion there which apparently caught the poet's attention is a cruciform church of Achthaman, on Lake Van, built between 904 and 938 A.D., which would then summarize the achievement of non-Western art. Beneath plate 33 of the volume, showing the south side of the building, Olson noted to himself in his copy: "what abt Scale here."

Of equal and related significance is that Armenia, in western Asia just south of the Black Sea and west of the Caucasus, was on the path of the Indo-European migration, or might even be considered an Indo-European homeland, although as a language Armenian has not yet been clearly located in the Indo-European group. Albright and Lamdin report, "the Armenian language appears to be a late offshoot of Hittite" (*Evidence of Language*, p. 20; and see also pp. 23– 24 there). Olson has marked the following passage in Sanford, *The Mediterranean World*, p. 105: "the racial type that we know as Armenoid or Caucasian reasserted itself and persists in Armenia today."

III.168. George or Isaac   and James / Dennison s   building a house . . .

See note to "George Dennison's store," *Maximus* II, 38. R. Babson and Saville report (*Cape Ann Tourist's Guide*, p. 80) that the "Dennison House is on Revere Street, leading from 628 Washington Street, Bay View. It was built in 1727. 'In March, 1727, John Day obligated to George Dennison to build the cellar of this house 6½ feet deep with two stone stairways, one laid out and one laid in, for 51 pounds in payable money.' " See also Mann, quoted in note below.

III.168. the ways leading from / Town to Squam   and to / Sandy Bay

On John Mason's 1831 "Map of Gloucester, Cape Ann" there appears a "Road from Sandy Bay to Squam Meeting House through the Woods," which begins in the vicinity of Lobster Cove. Another road, to present-day Washington Street, is identified on that map as simply "to Town Parish," and extends from the Town Landing to "Squam River" at Wheeler's Point. Mann identifies the old Squam to Sandy Bay road as present Revere Street, and writes further (*In the Heart of Cape Ann*, p. 11): "Coming from 'Squam, one may leave the church, walk a mile through the same road, past the Cape

Ann Granite Co.'s quarries, the road passing through the upper end of one, to the house of David Dennison, an ancient gambrel-roofed lean-to, built by Mr. Dennison's first ancestor on Cape Ann, and a fine sample of the better class of the Dogtown homes." Mann earlier quotes (pp. 7–8) a passage by Thomas Wentworth Higginson, which is of some interest in terms of this poem:

> So much of the charm of American pedestrianism lies in the by-paths: For instance, the whole interior of Cape Ann, beyond Gloucester, is a continuous woodland, with granite ledges everywhere cropping out, around which the high-road winds, following the curving and indented line of the sea, and dotted here and there with fishing hamlets. This whole interior is traversed by a network of foot-paths, rarely passable for a wagon and not always for a horse, but enabling the pedestrian to go from any one of the villages to any other, in a line almost direct, and always under an agreeable shade. By the longest of these hidden ways, one may go from Pigeon Cove to Gloucester, ten miles, without seeing a public road. In the little inn at the former village there used to hang an old map of this whole forest region [Mann, in a note at this point, identifies this as Mason's map], giving a chart of some of these paths, which were said to date back to the first settlement of the country. One of them, for instance, was called on the map 'Old road from Sandy Bay to 'Squam Meeting-House through the woods'; but the road is now scarcely even a bridle-path, and the most faithful worshipper could not seek 'Squam meeting-house in the family chaise. These woods have been lately devastated; but when I first knew the region, it was as good as any German forest. . . .

III.168. Lake Van

In far-western Turkey, site of the Armenian cruciform church at Achthaman (see note to "*ARMENIAN . . . MEA—SURE*" above, also the occurrence of the phrase "Lake Van measure" in "The Vinland Map Review," *Additional Prose*, p. 63 and editor's note pp. 99–101 there). This church interested Olson as early as 1952, when he mentions it in a letter to Robert Creeley, January 31st of that year.

III.168. rate of rate

The phrase occurs in several ways throughout Olson's writings and notes. See, e.g., "*valorem is* / RATE: the Dogtown . . . ," *Maximus* III, 129 and note; also, "the rate of ratio 1:1200" in "The Vinland Map Review," where the phrase is linked to the "Ideal Scale" as determined from another John Mason map of Gloucester (*Additional Prose*, p. 68 and editor's note pp. 99–101 there), and where "ratio" carries the sense of 'reason,' of which the Latin *ratio* is the root. Again, in an unfinished essay from ca. 6 October 1965, Olson stated that "the rate of ratio" gives "the distance-speed of any (every) feeling," while across the tops of pp. 38–39 of his copy of Sawyer, *Age of the Vikings*, the poet has written: "the new science—*reason*: RATIO of man: rate of rate, 'true' "Numbers"—Measure of quantities as continuous not compositions / art as *real* not personsyncratic."

III.168. Harraden-Dennison store

See note to "George Dennison's store," *Maximus* II, 38. Notes among his papers indicate Olson examined the account books of the store preserved in the Cape Ann Historical Society; these include entries for provisioning of vessels owned by Harradens (in-laws of George Dennison, who married Abigail Haraden in 1725), from which Olson is able to conclude in those notes that the Dennison store may have been "a 'company' in the 19th century Gloucester sense," with the Harradens owning the vessels. Another Harraden store, operated by John and Martha Harraden, was said to be located in an inn built by Joseph Harraden at River Road and Leonard Street in Annisquam.

III.168. B. Ellery . . .

See *Maximus* II, 34 and note; also II, 200. For "the lower of two and Back / road," see *Maximus* II, 25 and note.

III.169. two further / movements into / the woods, the Germanic / (and Celtic?) "forests" . . .

This poem might be read in conjunction with other migration poems in the series (such as *Maximus* III, 104). In his essay "A comprehension . . ." two months later, Olson would write of an earlier such "movement"—"the greatest single movement yet, of man & language, the Indo-European dispersion . . ." (*Additional Prose*, p. 46). Thus—and in terms of what follows in this poem—the movement into the woodlands of Dogtown is paralleled to the Indo-European migration (Germanic and Celtic both being offshoots of the original Indo-European language), or at least the later Gothic or Germanic migrations (in which case, Gloucester itself might be considered the result of a *first* or Indo-European migration—as suggested previously in *Maximus* II, 81, 102ff., etc.). Earlier, in his "Vinland Map Review," the poet had called attention to the "Teutonic Migration" along with that prior Indo-European one which culminated in the Mycenaean Age, expressing his belief in the advantages to be gained from knowledge of these two "strikeouts," and how this knowledge "can be shown to have already effected language and poetic results" among "young English and somewhat older American poets."

III.169. silva / John Singer Sargent called a book . . .

The Silva of North America, subtitled "A description of the trees which grow naturally in North America exclusive of Mexico" and published in fourteen volumes from 1893 to 1902, is by Charles Sprague Sargent (1841–1927), not the American painter John Singer Sargent (1856–1925). Both are descendants of Epes Sargent of Gloucester, it might be added.

Silva is Latin for 'a wood, forest, woodlands.' In notes made in 1966 inside the back cover of his copy of Cook, *Classic Line*, Olson writes of *silva* in terms of 'primary woods, original growth unburned & uncut except for small pieces to plant maiz[e].''

III.169. James Audubon's / bird book

John James Audubon (1785–1851), artist and ornithologist. He is the author of *The Birds of America* (1827–38).

III.169. Henry Wallace

Henry A. Wallace (1888–1965), American agriculturist from Iowa, Secretary of Agriculture (1933–1940) and Vice-President of the United States (1941–1945) under Franklin D. Roosevelt, and the populist Progressive Party's candidate for the Presidency in 1948.

III.169. Ezra Pound

See *Maximus* I, 27 and note. He was born in Hailey, Idaho. In his poem, "A Lustrum for You, E.P.," Olson alludes to the older poet's mid-western or "frontier" origins (*Charles Olson & Ezra Pound*, p. 4 and editor's note p. 117).

III.169. Pliny

Pliny the Elder (ca. A.D. 23–79), Roman natural historian, author of *Naturalis historia*, which in its present form consists of thirty-seven books. See "Reading at Berkeley" (*Muthologos*, I, 127) where his name, curiously, occurs shortly after mention of Ezra Pound; also p. 145 there, where Olson calls his work, not a classic, but "a very interesting 'pre-scientific' book." As a cavalry commander Pliny saw service in Germany, Gaul and Spain, where he learned something of the Celtic language; he also wrote a *History of the German Wars*, since lost, which was probably a principal source for Tacitus' *Germania*.

III.169–170. one <u>does</u> quote Saxus / Germanicus to / locate early enough Tys . . .

I.e., Saxo Grammaticus (ca. 1150–ca. 1216), Danish historian, author of *Gesta Danorum*, a history of Denmark to

1186, which does include the Germanic forebears of the Danes, thus perhaps Olson's epithet "Germanicus." Writing in Latin, Saxo speaks of Mars (I. 28), but does not mention Tys (also Tyr), war god of the North, by name (although Tys of course is the Germanic equivalent of Mars).

III.170. the GOTHIC condition

See especially "The Vinland Map Review" (*Additional Prose*, pp. 60–68).

III.170. Italic

One of the European branches of the Indo-European language; the prototype of Latin. See Albright and Lamdin, *Evidence of Language*, p. 19.

III.170. Hittitic

The language of the Hittites. For the relationship between that and Indo-European, as well as Armenian, see Albright and Lamdin, pp. 21ff.

III.170. "Hattic"

Albright and Lamden mention the "so-called Proto-Hittites, called *Hatti* by the 'Hittites.'" Their language was ultimately displaced by cuneiform Hittite (*Evidence of Language*, p. 23).

III.170. HURRIAN

Another early Anatolian language, traceable back to 2400 B.C. (Albright and Lamden, pp. 33 and ff.). One of the principal Hurrian texts is the Kumarbi myth (see Guterbock's "Hittite Version of the Hurrian Kumarbi Myths"), which includes the "Song of Ullikummi," part of which Olson had translated. See also *Maximus* II, 98, 104, and notes.

III.170. KELTIC

One of the Indo-European family of languages, the language of Britain before the Roman conquest; discussed in Jespersen, *Growth and Structure*, pp. 19 and 36ff.

III.171. Sapphite

After Sappho (fl. 610–580 B.C.), the Greek lyric poet; probably in the sense of the self-centered or individualistic lyric (Olson had very likely looked through "The Rise of the Individual in the Early Greek Lyric," chapter 3 of Snell's *Discovery of the Mind*, at this time—see next note), or the Sapphic meter invented by her, which is quantitative in nature and different from the "value-stressing" of "Gothonic" (see earlier note).

III.171. Solonic

Characteristic of Solon (ca. 640–ca. 560 B.C.), the Athenian lawgiver and poet, or his age. See especially Havelock, *Preface to Plato*, p. 121: "Solon provides the surviving classic example of Hesiod's 'prince' on whom Calliope has breathed her inspiration and so given him effective functional control over the preserved word. He was not a politician by profession and a poet by accident. His superior command of metrical composition gave him his efficacy as a policy-maker. His policies became inscribed upon the memory of his audience so that they knew what they were and were able to carry them out." Also Havelock's note to that passage, on p. 131: "The relevant poems of Solon are, I assume, not retrospective justification for political acts (this tradition grew out of 'literary' conceptions of poetry) but contemporary directives, prescriptions and reports"—to which Olson has added in the margin of his copy: "! Join *this* to Else—& to letter to J[oyce] B[enson] [June 1966]."

See then also Else's *Origin and Early Form of Greek Tragedy*, chapter II entitled "Solon and Pisistratus," in which he writes, e.g., on p. 33:

> ... Aside from the shadowy Thespis and his equally
> shadowy successor Choerilus, Solon is the only Athenian
> poet or man of letters whom we can even name from the
> whole sixth century. It is not that the works of the others
> are lost; there were no others. Solon *is* Athenian literature,
> down to Aeschylus, except for the beginnings of tragedy
> itself.
>
> Solon was, of course, not primarily a literary person but
> a public man, a statesman. . . .

Or, on p. 35: "Solon stands forth as the first discoverer of
that inner balance which has remained the life principle of
free societies ever since, between freedom and responsibility,
consent and authority, the morally autonomous individual
and the demands of society." These passages, as well as much
else on Solon throughout the chapter are marked and annotated in Olson's copy.

In his letter to Joyce Benson, 2 July 1966, the poet refers
to Solon "in whom there was already total absence of mythology . . . *and* the righteousness hypocrisy of virtue that 'poetry tells lies,' " as well as the "switching on the iambic and
trochaic, in preference to the elegaic couplet, for exhorta-
tion." (Else, p. 38, writes: "A kindred feature of Solon's
poetry is the total absence of mythology. Partly this belongs
to the style of elegaic and iambic poetry; partly, no doubt, it
reflects the sober, present-oriented temper of Solon's own
mind.")

There is one other particular aspect of Solon that interested Olson. Havelock writes: "Herodotus uses the verb
'philosophies' in connection with Solon's travels and his
desire to see the world . . ." (*Preface to Plato*, p. 280), and
Snell, *Discovery of the Mind*, p. 144, says that Solon "is said to
have been the first to travel round the world for the sake of
theory (Herodotus I.29)." Both passages appear to have been
read by Olson at this time, judging from annotations in his
copies.

III.171. suits / they called sails

John Smith, e.g., refers to "a suit of sayles" in his *Accidence
for Young Sea-men* (*Travels and Works*, II, 795).

III.171. John Smith / in "Accidence   A / Sea-Grammar says / <u>fabrick</u> . . .

It is in his *Advertisements for the Unexperienced Planters* that Smith writes, "Of all fabricks a ship is the most excellent, requiring more art in building, rigging, sayling, trimming, defending, and moaring . . ." (*Travels and Works*, II, 950; quoted in Innis, *Cod Fisheries*, p. 60n., where it is marked in Olson's copy).

For the designation of Smith's *Accidence for Young Sea-men* as his "Sea-Grammar," see *Maximus* I, 50 and note.

III.171. Goose Cove

See *Maximus* III, 43 and note.

III.171. Lobster Cove

See *Maximus* III, 43 and note.

III.171. "corners"

Perhaps as in the translation of the Dutch *hoeck* (as in Wyngaerds hoeck) as a cove or 'corner.' See specifically "grapevine corner," *Maximus* II, 94 and note; also " 'I know men for whom everything matters,' " *Muthologos*, II, 162, and note to "Wyngaerds hoeck" there.

▶III.173. [to get the rituals straight . . .

Written 19 June 1966 (date given in text) in small spiral-bound notebook; typed manuscript sent Robin Blaser for publication in *Pacific Nation*.

III.173. Intichiuma

Sacred rituals of the Central Australian tribes. Described in Harrison, *Themis*, p. 124: "By *Intichiuma* are meant magical ceremonies performed by members of a totem-group to induce the multiplication of the totem." See also pp. 273–274 of that volume (marked in Olson's copy); also her *Prolegomena*, p. 83.

III.173. John & Panna

John Wieners (b. 1934), poet and student of Olson's at Black Mountain and again at Buffalo, living in Riverdale for the summer on Dennison Street at the edge of Dogtown; and Panna Grady, who would become for a while Olson's patroness.

III.173. Riverdale mills

At the southern end of Mill River, where now Washington Street crosses and divides Mill Pond from the river. For the saw- and grist-mills constructed in the area, see R. Babson, *Cape Ann Tourist's Guide*, pp. 89ff., and Copeland and Rogers, *Saga of Cape Ann*, pp. 21–22.

III.173. that / Indies captain had his Chinese boat / on Mill pond

Olson also mentions him in a letter to the *Gloucester Times*, 21 December 1965: "It is not one of the known and thank God therefore I hope not quaint facts, that a Gloucester captain of the China trade, who retired and lived on Washington there on the uplands going down to the marsh of Mill Pond so longed for the feeling of the view he knew he had a small junk made and floated her there in the Pond for himself and anyone else who therefore had occasion to see."

The captain was James A. Clarkson (ca. 1816–1849), who lived at 394 Washington Street, overlooking Mill Pond. His miniature junk, not mentioned by Babson or any of the historians of Cape Ann, is pictured in a lithograph competently drawn by his brother-in-law Lodowick Bradford entitled "Mills, Riverdale, 1849" (collection of Paul Harling of Riverdale).

III.173. comed

Like "combed out"? Spelled "comed" also in the original. Read as "cōmèd out" on tape of interview in Gloucester with Inga Loven, August 1968.

III.173. rituelle / Sabeen . . . ismaëllienne

From the title of Henry Corbin's study, "Rituel sabéen et exégèse smaélienne," as it appears in a footnote to his essay "Cyclical Time in Mazdaism and Ismailism," p. 139 (marked in Olson's copy). The Sabaeans were an Arabic people, Saba being an ancient name of the people of Yemen (Biblical Sheba); the Ismailians, an Islamic sect.

III.173. topi

Greek 'places' (from *topos*), although actually an improperly constructed plural, probably after Latin *loci* (also 'places'). See also "topos," *Maximus* III, 164 and note.

III.173. 3 year old Ella

Daughter of Panna Grady.

III.174. John Wieners

See note to "John & Panna" above.

III.174. Edward Dorn

See *Maximus* III, 150 and note.

III.174. Allen Ginsberg

(b. 1926), the American poet, whom Olson had known since the late 1950's. He and Olson were together at the Vancouver Conference in 1963 and more recently at Berkeley in July 1965.

III.174. a poem like The Telephone

Probably "I am a Victim of Telephone" (collected in Ginsberg's *Planet News*), written in 1964 and read at the Berkeley Poetry Conference, 21 July 1965, with Olson in the audience.

III.174. his unbelievable ability to make a picture / postcard alive . . .

On 10 June 1966, Olson sent Ginsberg a postcard of Italian fishing boats on the beach at Gloucester Harbor "in return for all your many from all over to myself . . ." (with letter that date, in Butler Library, Columbia University). Among the three or four picture postcards which Olson received from Ginsberg over the years, the one closest in time to this poem was from Moscow, 6 April 1965, showing Red Square. An earlier one from 6 October 1963 shows a Japanese garden and is signed by Ginsberg, "love—belly flowers," and another is from Athens from 1961.

III.174. Robert Creeley

See the dedication to *Maximus* I and note to that above, and esp. Creeley's collection *For Love: Poems 1950–1960*.

III.174. lusimeles

Greek λυσι-μελης, the result or power of love, translated as 'limb-relaxing' in Liddell and Scott, *Greek-English Lexicon*, p. 908, and as 'unnerves the limbs' in Evelyn-White's Hesiod (see *Maximus* II, 2 and note)—both marked in Olson's copies. Olson preferred 'loosens the limbs' ("Reading at Berkeley," *Muthologos*, I, 147), suggested by Ed Sanders, although in a letter to Joyce Benson ca. 14 June 1966 he translates the word as "Love which makes the limbs all-fire."

III.174. Joyce / Benson

(b. 1927). Teaching at the time in Oxford, Ohio, she had written Olson enclosing some poems containing references remarkably close to a few in his own work. See her "First Round of Letters," *Boundary 2* (1974), pp. 358–366.

Olson wrote as part of his letter of 16 June 1966 to her:

> I *can* in fact send you this. For I *just* found the added note—I mean, on the 'reed', so that I am playing to you, to *your* requirement: I can tell you it this way—:
>   "de reglement des senses" (?)
>   le abaissment, c'est necessaire [de niveau mental] pour participation mystique!
>   a very low threshold *to* disorder . . .

III.174. poets whose / mental level . . .

An allusion to the phrase, *l'abaissment de mental niveau* (French, 'the lowering of the mental level'), a term originated by Pierre Janet in his *Les Névroses* (1909) and used throughout Jung's writings, where it is defined variously as "depression" (*Two Essays on Analytical Psychology*, p. 227); "fatigue" (*Symbols of Transformation*, index); "a diminution or execution of consciousness" which "is equivalent to that 'peril of the soul' which is primitive man's greatest dread" (*Psychology and Alchemy*, p. 320); and a "reduced intensity of consciousness and absences of concentration and attention" which "correspond pretty exactly to the primitive state of consciousness in which, we must suppose, myths were originally formed" (*The Archetypes and the Collective Unconscious*, pp. 155–156).

III.174. participation mystique

A term originated by the French philosopher and anthropologist Lucien Lévy-Bruhl in his *Fonctions mentales dans les societes inferieures* (1912) and adopted by Carl Jung. See especially Jung's *Psychological Types*, pp. 572–573:

> It connotes a peculiar kind of psychological connection with the object wherein the subject is unable to differentiate himself clearly from the object to which he is bound by an immediate relation that can only be described as partial identity. . . . It is, of course, a phenomenon that is best observed among the primitives; but it occurs not at all infrequently among civilized men, although not with the

same range or intensity. Among civilized peoples it usually happens between persons—and only seldom between a person and thing. . . .

▶III.175. This town / works at / dawn . . .

Original written on an envelope postmarked 1966 and dated "Monday June 20th."

III.175. washed as gods in the Basin of Morning

Cf. Levy, *Gate of Horn*, p. 174, speaking of the sacred texts on the walls of ancient Egyptian tombs: "They describe the journey by water, in the barque which is itself a Goddess; the entry through the Gates of rebirth—'the two hills are divided; the God comes into being'—beyond which the newly dead is suckled by the Cow-Mother, and his soul, purified in the Basin of Morning receives its immortal body." In the margin of his copy, Olson copied the phrase: "purified in the Basin of Morning."

▶III.176. Migration in fact . . .

A version of the earlier "Rose of the World" poem (III, 104), arranged in couplets. Holograph manuscript bears date, 8 August [1966].

▶III.177. This living hand . . .

Original written in grey ballpoint ink on a plain, otherwise unused envelope; undated but possibly from ca. 1966, the period of variously colored inks for Olson. It was found among the poet's papers from 1966, and is actually almost exactly the opening lines of a poem by John Keats written ca. 1819–20 on a manuscript page of his unfinished poem, "The Cap and Bells," and believed to be the last lines of poetry that Keats wrote:

> This living hand, now warm and capable
> Of earnest grasping, would, if it were cold
> And in the icy silence of the tomb,
> So haunt thy days and chill thy dreaming nights

That thou wouldst wish thine own heart dry of blood
So in my veins red life might stream again,
And thou be conscience-calmed—see here it is—
I hold it towards you.

Olson had written about the lines in a letter to English writer Ronald Mason, 15 July 1953: "I am sure those lines which Forman [M. Buxton Forman, early Keats scholar] found written on the margin of the mss of Cap & Bells, and then called Lines Written to Fanny Brawne—the ones abt this hand, in the chill of the grave, etc.—ARE NOT KEATS'. In fact, are Jacobean, probably Massinger's (or Webster) . . ." See them in the present context, however, in terms of Tyr's hand lost to Fenris, which Maximus identifies as his own and progressively regains (*Maximus* III, 34; III, 47; and III, 63).

▶III.178. Out of the light of Heaven . . .

Written ca. 24 December 1966 in Berlin, where Olson had been invited to read at the Akademie der Kunstes. Original on Hotel Steinplatz stationery, notes on verso of which are dated December 24th. Also copied out in endpapers of Wolfskehl and von der Leyden, *Alteste deutsche Dichtungen* (see notes to the next poem). Another version was written in London, ca. 18–23 February 1967:

> Imbued
> with the light of heaven the flower
> grows down, the air
> of heaven

Both are variants of the earlier poem on *Maximus* III, 18.

▶III.179. HOTEL STEINPLATZ, BERLIN, DECEMBER 25 (1966)

Holograph original with later typescript, slightly revised. Written in Berlin, where the poet had been invited to read at the Akademie der Kunstes and where he was to suffer a mild heart attack. The poem draws upon Davidson, *Gods and Myths of Northern Europe*, and an anthology of Old German poetry presented to Olson by his German translator, Klaus Reichert.

III.179. rots at the side the Tree of the World

Yggdrasill, which forms the center of the Norse universe. Beneath its roots lie the regions of the gods, the giants, and the dead. Davidson writes, p. 194:

> ... we learn from the *Edda* that the tree constantly suffers attack, both from the serpent at the foot and from the hart that gnaws its branches ... :
> The Ash Yggdrasill endures anguish,
>   more than men know.
> A hart gnaws it on high, it rots at the side,
>   While *Niðhoggr* devours it below.

In the margin of his copy, after underlining "the tree constantly suffers attack," Olson adds exclamation marks and "the Crocodile"—for which see *Maximus* III, 48.

III.179. the lance by which watery fluid ...

Similar to the lance which pierced Christ's side (John, xix. 34).

III.179. the female animal in the boughs / of the Tree ...

The hart, which gnaws on its branches (note above), and whose milk becomes shining mead (note below).

III.179. the End / of the World Tree

At the coming of Ragnarok or the End of the World (see *Maximus* III, 163 and note to "muspilli" there, and esp. Davidson, pp. 202ff.) Yggdrasill was said to shake and tremble.

III.179. Serpent, of the Earth

Niðhoggr (see note to "rots at the side of the Tree" above).

III.179. I want need, hail and ice, need-nail   fingernail of Abwehr

From a ninth-century Norman runic poem published with German translations in Wolfskehl and von der Leyen, *Älteste deutsche Dichtungen*, a gift to Olson in Berlin, 14 December 1966, from Reichert, and which he read in with the assistance of his copy of *Langenscheidt's Pocket Dictionary of the English and German Languages*. Von der Leyen offers two translations of the poem, working in the second case from a revised text:

Viehstand vorne •	Viehstand (ist) das erste
Urochs andringt •	der Stier bedroht es
Thurs draut am	die drei Runenstabe
dritten Stabe •	des Riesen
As der ist ihm uber •	Der Ase (Donar) ist oben
Rad ritz am Ende •	(Sein) Eagen rennt
Knistern klebt daran •	Fackel (sein Blitz) spaltet
Hagel hegt die Not •	Hagel (ist) hart
Eis • Anfang und	Not-Nagel (schutzt)
Sonne •	Eis-Jahr
Tiu • Birke und	Sonne scheint
Mann inmitten •	TiuBirke bebt
Lache die Lichte:	Das leuchtende Wasser
Yr umhegt alles.	In der Mitte der Mann
	Eibe alles
(p. 31)	
	(pp. 128–129)

"Not" in the seventh line of both versions is translated as 'need, want' in Olson's German dictionary (p. 953—where he has underlined the word). "Hail" and "ice" are also to be found in the poem (*hagel* and *eis*). "Not-Nagel" in the eighth line of the second translation is the source of Olson's "need-nail." In his commentary to the text, p. 129, von der Leyen explains that the rune *Not* is drawn on the fingernail for purposes of defense (*Abwehr*), i.e. as a sign or charm to ward off need or misery.

III.180. the staves / the three staves of my giants

From the rune-poem cited above. The three staves, according to von der Leyen, symbolize hail, need or difficulty (*not*), and ice.

III.180. TiuBirka's bebt, Tiubirka / s shaking

In his commentary, von der Leyen explains that Tiubirke or TiuBirka is the sacred birch tree, dedicated to the god Tiu, pointing out that TiBirke is also the name of Tiu's sanctuary which has been discovered and excavated in Zeeland. *Bebt*, also in the rune-poem, is present tense of German *beben*, to 'shake, tremble.'

III.180. dew dew aurr sprinkling

From Davidson, p. 195: "It is said that the ash is sprinkled with *aurr* from the spring; the meaning of this word is uncertain, but De Vries takes it to mean clear, shining water. We are told that dew comes from the tree, and that when the hart feeds on its branches, her milk becomes shining mead which never gives out, and is used to provide drink for the warriors in Valhalla." Very likely, "Das leuchtende Wasser," 'the shining water,' in the second translation of the runic poem has called to mind the "clear, shining water" sprinkled on the World Tree (see also Olson's piece with that title in *Additional Prose*, pp. 71−73).

III.180. who is this man who drives me all the way . . .

Davidson, p. 146:

> Like the shamans also, Odin seeks knowledge by communication with the dead. In *Baldrs Draumar* [*Balder's Dream*] his approach to the dead is shown as it were in double symbolism: he rides down the road that leads to the underworld, and then he proceeds to call up a dead seeress from the grave until she replies to his questions.

She is shown in the poem as being forced to answer him
against her will:
> Who is this man, unknown to me,
> who drives me on down this weary path?
> Snowed on by snow, beaten by rain,
> drenched with the dew, long I lay dead.

Olson has copied the verse into his copy of Wolfskehl and
von der Leyen, p. 130.

▶III.181. 11 o'clock at night . . .

Written ca. 24 July 1967 (another version with that date
found among the poet's papers). Holograph manuscript
only.

▶III.182. Celestial evening, October 1967

Holograph manuscript only. A new moon occurred on 3
October 1967, so the poem was possibly written at that time.

III.182. the time I did actually lose space control . . .

In a note dated 19 July 1966 from a notebook among his
papers, Olson writes:

> In the early 60s—that would be sometime after the fall
> of 1959—I lost my space control, not my *sense* of it but
> literally lost succession of event in time, memory of when
> things happened—that is, were done. So that, in effect,
> the result was I 'lost' my space control—or *physical* act
> [art?] in sequence, as important to my confidence of my
> space majority as in fact my space-tone ['History] itself.
>   And it lasted—? Until at least spring, 1964(?

In conversation, June 1968, the poet spoke of a sudden
disorientation or vertigo, apparently localized in his ear, that
occurred when setting out for a walk one evening, so that he
had the utmost difficulty finding his way back home although not very far from his house.

III.182. my star-nosed mole batted / on the head

See *Maximus* III, 26−27.

III.182. one further / ring of the 9 bounding / Earth . . .

The ring of Ocean (see *Maximus* II, 70 and III, 19 and notes) or the "nine silver-swirling streams" by which he encircles the earth; a tenth flows into the abode of Styx, Ocean's eldest daughter (Hesiod, *Theogony*, Evelyn-White trans., pp. 135–137).

III.182. whose waters then / are test . . .

See Hesiod, *Theogony* (as above):

> . . . when strife and quarrel arise among the deathless gods, and when any one of them who live in the house of Olympus lies, then Zeus sends Iris to bring in a golden jug the great oath of the gods from far away, the famous cold water which trickles down from a high and beetling rock. . . . For whoever of the deathless gods that hold the peaks of snowy Olympus pours a libation of her water and is foresworn, lies breathless until a full year is completed, and never comes near to taste ambrosia and nectar, but lies spiritless and voiceless on a strewn bed: and a heavy trance overshadows him. But when he has spent a long year in his sickness, another penance and an harder follows after the first. For nine years he is cut off from the eternal gods and never joins their councils or their feasts, nine full years . . .

Also referred to by Olson in "The Animate Versus the Mechanical" (*Additional Prose*, p. 75): "the water or turgor 'test' of the Gods as whether they are or are not telling 'truth'—tested and failing. They are abandoned by 'God' from 'his House of Mountain' for precisely '9' *Years* . . ."

III.183. Amoghasiddi

Amoghasiddhi, one of the five Dhyani-Buddhas, or Buddhas of contemplation, of Tibetan Buddhism. His characteristic gesture, or *mudrā*, is either that of concentration (hands together in lap) or of granting tranquility (right hand raised)—see Saunders, *Mudrā*, p. 88.

▶III.184. (LITERARY RESULT)

The poem has survived in an original holograph version and a final typescript, both dated 18 October 1967.

III.184. Jeremy Prynne

See *Maximus* III, 137 and note; also III, 144. Prynne has suggested in a letter to the author, 9 September 1974, that there may be a "glancing reference" to his poem "FRI 13" (collected in his volume *The White Stones*, p. 23), which had apparently been written while he was staying at Olson's flat at Fort Square (Olson was on the West Coast at the time for his Berkeley reading). The poem had been sent as part of a letter to Olson from "Friday 13th August [1965]" and in it Prynne speaks of the presence of "gulls, squarking / in the knowledge / of time" and of a life-situation which is "to be gauged / by the most / specific & / hopeful / eye." He concludes his letter by referring to the view from Olson's window.

The more immediate occasion of the present poem, however, may have been Prynne's letter of 15 October 1967, in which he proposes a community of English and American poets despite the distance of the Atlantic—a new "home" or "land," even "if we have to build an ark to find it."

III.184. Larry Eigner

(b.1927), poet living in Swampscott, Mass. Shortly after the occasion in Gloucester referred to in the poem, Olson wrote to Robert Creeley, 30 September [1954]; "Maybe the most of the trip was coming on EIGNER in Ferrini's house! What a beautiful thing! . . . So direct and witty and delightful—and hammering hell out of me for leaving it, he says, each man must save his own soul! And, complaining, that a lack of subtlety! Christ, I was taken! He's beautiful."

Cid Corman provides the full context for Eigner's question in his introduction to *The Gist of Origin*, quoted in note to *Maximus* I, 41. See also Eigner's "Letter to George Butterick" in *Athanor* 2 (1971), esp. p. 61.

III.184. eye-view

Used several times previously, most often in relation to painter Fitz Hugh Lane (*Maximus* II, 100 and note; III, 118).

▶ III.185. Great Washing Rock . . .

Holograph manuscript only, dated 24 December 1967.

The view is from 28 Fort Square across the Harbor to Fisherman's Field (Stage Fort Park), where the Parsons family first settled. The Parsons' "Great Washing Rock," where a catch of fish brought to shore could be cleaned before salting and drying on the stage, is known to the poet from the probate records of the family. See *Maximus* III, 105 and note; for the Parsons family, see esp. *Maximus* II, 63–64 and notes. Notes on the bottom of the last page of the manuscript likewise attest to Olson's working with the probate records.

III.185. I was born . . . on the day of the year / when the sun returns . . .

The poet was born on December 27th, 1910.

III.185. their division of land, 1707 . . .

The poet is a digit off in his date; the land settlement in which "the washing Rock" appears is from 1717.

▶ III.186. The sea's / boiling . . .

Written in small pocket memo pad from 1968 and dated January 8th, a period of below zero cold on Cape Ann and throughout New England.

▶ III.187. the salmon of / wisdom . . .

Holograph original written in blue ink, with corrections made later (or at least with a different pen) and a note added at the bottom: "sent [Robert] Kelly, for new Matter / June 29 1968" (an uncompleted typescript among Olson's papers had been begun verso a page of notes dated 29 June 1968). The original has the following title crossed out: "Cuchulain, born of impregnation by / a may-fly"—a story told in Graves, *White Goddess*, pp. 342, 348–349, and esp. 408n., where it is marked in one of Olson's copies with a note added: "again!—my 'Soul' or psyche: Salmon of Wisdom."

For the figure of the Salmon, see *Maximus* III, 72 and note.

▶III.188. That's / the combination . . .

Holograph manuscript, dated 2 February 1968, sent Jack Collom for publication in *the*; no other manuscript among poet's papers.

III.188. automorphism

Cf. Weyl, *Philosophy of Mathematics and Natural Science*, p. 72: "We now consider the special case when our domain of objects is mapped not upon another domain but upon itself, and thus arrive at the notion of *automorphism*: an automorphism is a one-to-one mapping $p \rightarrow p'$ of the point-field into itself which leaves the basic relations undisturbed . . ."

▶III.189. That there was a woman in Gloucester, Massachusetts . . .

Original holograph manuscript dated 18 February 1968; typescript sent to G.F. Butterick for publication by the Institute of Further Studies.

Among Olson's papers is an article by Gardner entitled "New Theory Offered on Beothuk Canoe Origin" from the newspaper *National Fisherman / Maine Coast Fisherman* which had been given the poet by Brian Shore, son of his friend Mary Shore, ca. December 1967. Gardner's article mentions an earlier one by E.F. Greenman in *Current Anthropology* entitled "The Upper Palaeolithic and the New World," which argues that the sea-faring canoe of the Beothuk Indians of Newfoundland "may be of Upper Palaeolithic origin, and that its prototypes"—which could have easily made Atlantic crossings—"were quite possibly in use in the Bay of Biscay by Late Old Stone Age people as early as 15,000 B.C., or even earlier." Gardner also reports that Greenman had identified "an hitherto unexplained Upper Palaeolithic painting in the Cave of Castillo in northern Spain, not far from the Bay of Biscay, as a representation of a craft that could well be the direct prototype of the Beothuk canoe" (see Greenman, p. 46), while pointing out that the Beothuks, who became extinct in the early nineteenth century, "were much addicted to the use of red ochre, whence they got the name of Red Indians."

After reading Gardner's report, Olson wrote to the present author on 8 January 1968 for a xeroxed copy of the original Greenman article (which was sent but lost in the mails so that another request, dated 9 February 1968, was necessary). It is Greenman himself who reports that the noted authority on Maine Indian cultures, Frank G. Speck (1881–1950), had discovered a description of the use of the Beothuk canoe "that would have been admirably adapted to the ocean habitat in Pleistocene times among the ice floes. He found an elderly Indian woman in Gloucester, Massachusetts, who said her father was a Beothuk, of Red Pond, Newfoundland. Her mother was a Micmac. The woman was born in Newfoundland about 1837, and she described the boat in which she remembered traveling with her family during her childhood. This boat had a skin covering over its framework; its bottom was round and Speck emphasizes that it was a kayak type of boat. The most interesting feature was that its whole front half was covered with a skin 'forming an enclosure large enough to contain the whole family, including women, children, dogs, and property'. . . ."

There is a discrepancy between the date of 1828 which Olson gives and the date of 1837 in Greenman's account (as well as in Speck's original account). The date of 1828 is found in Greenman as that in which the last surviving Beothuk Indian, a woman named Shanawdithit, was taken to the Beothuk Institute in St. John's, Newfoundland, established for the welfare of the tribe (p. 48); however, she is not the same Indian woman interviewed by Speck in

Gloucester, whose name was Santu Toney (Speck, *Beothuk and Micmac*, pp. 55–61). When asked by the author in conversation shortly after the poem was published in 1968, why the confused date, Olson replied that the 1828 date was purposely wrong, purposely further back in the nineteenth century, to avoid "current history," which he said is "ours alone."

III.189. Biscay shallop . . . Biskie Island

See *Maximus* I, 160 and note.

▶III.190. * Added to / making a Republic / in gloom on Watchhouse / Point

Holograph original, begun on back of open envelope and continued on back of letter within from Joyce Benson; typescript dated 6 March 1968 sent to the present author for publication by the Institute of Further Studies.

See the initial poem of this volume and notes above for an understanding of the title.

III.190. to / construct one, from rhythm to / image, and image is knowing . . .

Cf. "ABCs (2)," from ca. 1950:

one sd:
                of rhythm is image
                of image is knowing
                of knowing there is
                a construct . . .

Also "Equal, That Is, to the Real Itself" from 1957 where the passage is prefaced, "As the Master said to me in the dream . . ." (*Human Universe*, p. 121). In lecture notes from 1956 appended to Charters' *Olson / Melville*, p. 87, it is called "the syllogism as passed to me by the fathers in said dream." See also "The Bezel" from 1962 in *Io* 8, p. 81.

III.190. knowing, Confucius says, brings one / to the goal

See *Secret of the Golden Flower*, p. 37 (marked in Olson's copy): "All holy men have bequeathed this to one another: nothing is possible without contemplation (*fan chao*, reflection). When Confucius says: Knowing brings one to the goal; or when Buddha calls it: The view of the Heart; or Lao Tzu says: Inward vision, it is all the same."

III.190. malgre

French *malgré*, 'in spite of, notwithstanding.'

▶III.191. Wholly absorbed / into my own conduits . . .

Holograph original, with typescript sent Institute of Further Studies for publication dated simply "March 1968."

▶III.192. Take the earth in under a single review . . .

Written in 1968, probably around June 17th judging from Olson's reading at that time of Cyrus Gordon's *Forgotten Scripts* (see note to "a peri-Mediterranean syllabary" below), although the poem was written in ink verso a letter from Vincent Ferrini dated much earlier, "Sat March 23–24." Holograph manuscript only, with revisions made at the time of writing. Another version written on the back cover of Barbara Guest's *The Blue Stairs*, published in 1968.

The opening line is a variation of the definition of "landscape" as given in *Webster's Collegiate Dictionary*, 5th ed., used by Olson previously in "Postscript to Proprioception & Logography" (*Additional Prose*, 21). See, then, other of the poems with "view" in them, such as *Maximus* II, 81, 100; III, 118, 184.

III.192. Eratosthenes

(ca. 276–ca. 194 BC), Greek geographer and chief librarian at Alexandria (see also note to "1183," *Maximus* II, 104).

He was the first to attempt to scientifically measure the earth's circumference.

III.192. Ptolemy

The great mathematician, astonomer, and geographer. He was the author of a *Geographikē syntaxis*, a survey of the known world, ca. 150 AD. Of possible interest to readers of this poem (and of all the *Maximus* poems, for that matter) is the following from a discussion of Ptolemy in the article "Maps," *Encyclopaedia Britannica*, 11th ed., where all the other geographers mentioned in the poem are also discussed: " 'Geography,' in the sense in which he [Ptolemy] uses the term, signifies the delineation of the known world, in the shape of a map, while chorography carries out the same objects in fuller detail, with regard to a particular country" (p. 636).

III.192. Ptolemy's Tyrian teacher who had the name <u>marine</u> ...

Marinus of Tyre (2nd century AD), the Greek geographer whose work Ptolemy made the basis of much of his own. Mentioned also by Olson briefly in "Tutorial: the Greeks" (*OLSON* 2, 1974, p. 44).

III.192. John Gallop   John Tilley   Osman Dutch Ralph Green ...

All early Gloucester settlers. See, e.g., *Maximus* II, 65 and III, 79 and notes, for Gallop, Tilley and Dutch. Ralph Green appears here for the first time in the poems; he does not occur in Babson and would have been known to Olson only through the town records.

III.192. a peri-Mediterranean syllabary ...

That is, Phoenician or what Cyrus Gordon, *Forgotten Scripts*, pp. 164–165, calls the Aegean syllabary, which includes Minoan and the inscription of the Phaistos Disk (*Maximus* III, 50, 51, and notes):

> The Aegean syllabary is of unique significance because it expresses the first important written languages of Europe and provides the cultural background of the Greeks on what became Greek soil. Although the syllabary (as well as the contents of the Minoan texts) reveals Egyptian influence, the basic character of the script is not Egyptian. The main thrust of the Minoans may have come from Egypt but not from Upper Egypt; they hailed from the coast of the Delta, which is Mediterranean in more ways than one. The Minoans were a sea people, and it is possible that there was a peri-Mediterranean script that the Phoenicians (and perhaps other sea people too) used and transmitted not only to the Aegean but wherever they sailed or settled.

The passage is marked in pencil in Olson's copy and the date "June 17, 1968" added at the top of p. 165.

III.192. Pytheas

The early Greek explorer (see *Maximus* I, 62 and note; II, 81, 92).

III.192. Meander

Winding river in Asia Minor (familiar as the source of our word meaning 'to wander') flowing into the Aegean below Priene in ancient Caria.

III.192. Piryne

In the version written on Barbara Guest's *Blue Stairs*, "the Pierian spring"—near the slopes of Mount Olympus, in the district where the Muses were born. There was also the spring called Pirene flowing from the Acrocorinth, the citadel of ancient Corinth. However, because of the connection made here with the river Meander, undoubtedly Priene, the city on the coast of Caria, is meant. A confusion of spelling.

III.192. Alpheus

River in Greece emptying into the Ionian Sea, flowing underground for part of its course. In legend (Pausanias, Ovid, and others) it is said to flow under the Mediterranean (not the Adriatic) and emerge in the fountain of Arethusa in Syracuse. Olson would have known this story from at least *Moby-Dick*, chapter 41 (Constable ed., I, 227, marked in the poet's copy)—where Melville, too, transfers the original locale, as does Shelley in his poem "Arethusa"!

III.192. Adriatic

The sea between Italy and the Balkan peninsula.

III.192. Latinum

Ancient Latium, the land of the Latini; that portion of central Italy including Rome which was conquered by Aeneas. It bordered on the Tyrrhenian Sea, however, not the Adriatic.

III.192. Phoenician

See also *Maximus* II, 100, 101, 104, 111, and notes; also perhaps III, 50 and 51.

▶III.193. That great descending light of day . . .

Holograph original, with note: "to Robt Kelly Sunday / July 21st [1968]." This is the Golden Flower, which "grows down / the air / of heaven" (see *Maximus* III, 18 and note).

III.193. the wild geranium not the fringed gentian . . .

Whether there is any symbolic value to the two flowers is uncertain; however, in a letter to Robert Creeley from 19 February 1951, Olson refers to the fringed gentian in relation to D. H. Lawrence (his "Bavarian Gentians," presumably), writing that the sight of the Yucatan sky is enough "to make me wild, wild (not like beautiful Lawrence, I don't mean, who, fr the full of the moon, is sd, to have got like the throat of his fringed gentians) . . ." (*Mayan Letters*, in *Selected Writings*, p. 75), while in an early poem from 1952, "The Thing Was Moving," Olson speaks of "the fringed gentians I used to so love / I'd lie amongst them in the meadow near the house / which was later covered by a dump to make an athletic field." Closer to the time of composition of this poem, in his copy of Weyl, *Philosophy of Mathematics and Natural Science*, p. 102, the poet writes of the "twy-fringed Gentian of Creation" ("fringe" is Weyl's term, p. 109, in speaking of the topological difference between closed and open space: "two fringes as opposed to one"—which is marked by Olson).

See also his brief poem or fragment written possibly as early as 1961–62: "I was stretched out on the earth so that a wild geranium / was looking down into my face / at a wild geranium." There is another version from the spring of 1963 (on start of a typescript of "*Civic Disaster*," *Maximus* II, 185): "the wild geranium / who looked at me / and my own face / was of the same size."

In any case, as with the "black cormorant" and the "gull" of *Maximus* III, 184, the poet chooses the less tame for his "eye-view" to "possess."

III.193. sawol

Old English 'soul.' Olson had read and marked a number of pages which Jeremy Prynne had xeroxed and sent him in 1966 from Swadesh, *Prehistoric Man in the New World*, in which the following occurs (p. 545): ". . . the modern English word *soul* corresponds to an older SAWOL. It is evidently cognate with the Greek HELIOS and Latin SOL *sun*."

III.193. Armenian

See *Maximus* III, 168 and note. In the manuscript, "Gothonic" has been crossed out, further strengthening the reading of "Armenian" in terms of its earlier appearance.

▶**III.194. flower of the underworld**

Undated holograph manuscript, probably written in 1968 (verso start of a letter to Loren Sears, a filmmaker Olson had met in San Francisco in April of that year); another version on the back of a letter from Joyce Benson dated Christmas Day, 1968. Another manuscript of the poem, apparently "scribbled on the back of an envelope," was, by his own admission, slipped "like a thief into the breast pocket of my Black Dyed Caracul coat" by Gerard Malanga (introduction to his interview with Olson, *Paris Review* 47, p. 179).

The "flower" of the title is also the Golden Flower of the earlier poems, *Maximus* III, 10 and 163.

III.194. to build out of sound the walls of the city

See the earlier occurrence of this allusion, *Maximus* III, 37 and note.

▶**III.195. above the head of John Day's pasture land . . .**

Both original holograph manuscript as well as typescript dated 24 July 1968. Sent Robert Kelly by Olson for publication in *Caterpillar*. The poem represents a final attempt to resolve the identity of Margaret Josselyn, thereby establishing the earliest settlement of Dogtown.

From an entry in the Gloucester town records for 16 June 1707 ("Transcript of Book Two, Town Records, in the Town of Gloucester, from 1694 to 1752," p. 160): "Margrett Josline widdow had granted to her a smale parcell of Land to sett a house upon dureing her naturall Liff above the head of John Days pasture Land and att her deceas the Land which she hath made use of to return to the towne again for the towns use." Olson had recorded this information in a notebook designated "D'Town Dec 8 1960 . . . *ENDED* abt Feb 21st? 1961" and in another begun "Wed January 25, 1961."

For Margaret Josselyn, earlier Margaret Cammock, see *Maximus* II, 25 and 37 and notes, and esp. *Maximus* III, 91–93, which this poem might be read as a successor to.

III.195. Black Point . . . just before the Indian attack, 1676

Information from Babson, *History*, p. 108. See also *Maximus* III, 91 and note. The date of 1671 would be when John Josselyn was still visiting at Black Point (see note below).

III.195. He died, Pemaquid, 1683.

Reported in Baxter, *Trelawny Papers*, p. 8n. For the location of Pemaquid, see *Maximus* I, 124 and note.

III.195. upper Cherry or of Gee Avenue

The "lower" road of Dogtown (see *Maximus* II, 3 and 46, and notes).

III.196. married after 1643 . . .

Her first husband, Thomas Cammock, early Maine settler, died that year (Baxter, *Trelawny Papers*, p. 2n—quoted in note to *Maximus* III, 91).

III.196. THE JOHN / "who was again with his brother in the eastern country", / July 1663 till / July 1671

The dates are of John Josselyn's second visit to New England, spent mainly with his brother Henry at Black Point, Maine—although in his *Account of Two Voyages to New-England* (1865 ed.), p. 162, Josselyn says he "took leave of my friends at *Black-point*" on 28 August 1671, not July of that year. For Josselyn, see also *Maximus* II, 37. The source of the quotation is not known.

III.196. Henry Josselyn, John's nephew born pre–1658 [here by reflux . . .

Possibly should be pre–1685 rather than 1658, since Henry Josselyn Jr. (the "Henry the 2nd" below) was driven from Falmouth with John Wallis in 1675—"probably the first reflux of the tide of emigration which, about twenty years before, began to set towards Maine from our town" (Babson, *History*, p. 108).

III.196. Margaret became Henry Josselyn's wife after Thomas Cammock's death . . .

See note above concerning her marriage after 1643.

III.196. Henry the 2nd   her son's child Margaret born / Gloucester <u>1687</u>

Reported in Babson, *History*, p. 109.

▶III.197. I'm going to hate to leave this Earthly Paradise . . .

What seems to be an original version of the poem survives as a typescript among the poet's papers, as does the thoroughly revised final version. The beginning portion of the latter (through "? Monday Aug 5th / —2 AM plus / [of the 6th]" was written in ink in a small yellow notepad; while the later section, from "burning gold water-strip setting" to "Beverly / Air Port possibly or Hanscom Air / Force Base," survives handwritten on two small pieces of white paper, laid by the poet into his copy of *Stony Brook* 1/2 with note on cover: "My own copy with correct original Ms." A typed manuscript was apparently sent George Quasha for publication in *Stony Brook* (four pages of a carbon of this— consisting only of the section of the poem written in the yellow notepad—are preserved among the poet's papers). Also among the papers are printer's proofs returned to Olson for correction, where the inconsistent accenting of Idrīs (see below) is insisted upon.

The poem actually draws upon the notion of alchemy as a spiritual process, as discussed by Nasr in *Science and Civilization in Islam*, which Olson had been reading at the time. In a letter to a geographer, Brian Goodey, 25 September 1968, Olson describes the poem as having been "written as though *below* low water!"

III.197. Mauch Chunk, P.A. is changed to Jim / Thorpe, P.A.

Town in the coal fields of the Lehigh Valley in eastern Pennsylvania; the original name, Indian for "Bear Mountain," was changed in 1954 to Jim Thorpe in honor of the American Indian Olympic and football star who got his start at the Carlisle Indian School in Carlisle, Pa.

III.197. Mollie McGuires are filmed . . .

Society of militant miners active in the coal fields of eastern Pennsylvania during the 1860's and 1870's; a number of them were tried and executed in Mauch Chunk. Filming of a motion picture entitled *The Molly Maguires* (released the next year) was reported in the press during the summer of 1968 (see e.g. New York *Times* for June 16th) and, according to Harvey Brown (see below), may have been a topic in his long telephone conversation with Olson.

III.197. Lane

Fitz Hugh Lane, the Gloucester painter (see *Maximus* II, 100 etc.), whose stone, seven-gabled house stands on a knoll on Duncan's Point overlooking the Harbor. Olson probably has in mind his view of Gloucester Harbor, "Moonlight on a Bay" (fig. 6 in Wilmerding, *Fitz Hugh Lane*, 1964—even though later identified by Wilmerding, *Fitz Hugh Lane*, 1971, as actually by Lane's student Mary B. Mellen).

III.197. boats hanging / over on their side . . .

See e.g. the foreground of the view "Moonlight on a Bay" mentioned above, or Lane's view of Duncan's Point from Rocky Neck entitled "Three Master on the Gloucester Railway" in the collection of the Cape Ann Historical Association, where Olson would have seen it (fig. 7 in Wilmerding, 1964; plate 7 in his 1971 book).

III.197. Dunkums Point & Rocks

Duncan's Point on Gloucester Harbor (see *Maximus* I, 156 and note), named for early settler Peter Duncan who owned the land. The rocks off the point are barely in evidence, probably those which are incorporated into a seawall built before the Coast Guard station now occupying the promontory; however, the name "dunkum point rocks" appears on a map by John Mason of the Gloucester waterfront, which Olson had a photocopy of (on another, faded copy, Olson had written in the name).

III.197. Moonlight on the / At Low Water Harbor / Scene

Lane's "Moonlight on a Bay" mentioned above.

III.197. my friend

Harvey Brown (see below).

III.198. the railway there

Either of two marine railways in operation on Duncan's Point at the time—Parkhurst's, in use in 1968 but since cleared away for the U.S. Coast Guard base, or Burnham Brothers Railway, subject of Lane's painting, "Three Master on the Gloucester Railway," mentioned above.

III.198. urban destruction . . .

Reference to Gloucester's Urban Renewal program begun in the 1960's, which altered the face of the waterfront.

III.198. the Atlantic Halibut wharf

The Atlantic Halibut Co. had its wharf on Duncan's Point west of the marine railways, a site now occupied by the Coast Guard station.

III.198. the Diner

Michel's Cape Ann Diner, on Main Street at the corner of Chestnut, a short walk through the A&P parking lot from Duncan's Point.

III.198. Ragged Arse Rock

An island off the coast of Maine, northwest of Matinicus Rock in Penobscot Bay. The full name is given in a footnote identifying points on John Winthrop's sketch of the coast of Maine in his *Journal* (*Winthrop Papers*, II, 261n—where it is underlined in Olson's copy). *The U.S. Coast Pilot* (Atlantic Coast section A, 1950, p. 214) gives simply a "Ragged Island" among a group which includes Tenpound and Matinicus (see *Maximus* III, 145 and notes)—at which point in the margin of his copy as well as in the index the poet adds the full explicit designation.

III.198. his weed-crippled legs

Lane had become paralyzed as an infant from an attack of what we would now know as polio and was obliged to walk with crutches the rest of his life, although in earlier times it was believed that the apple of Peru (our common tomato) was the source of his crippling: "At the age of eighteen months, while playing in the yard or garden of his father, he ate some of the seeds of the apple-peru; and was so unfortunate as to lose the use of his lower limbs in consequence, owing to late and unskillful treatment" (Babson, *History*, p. 258).

III.198. Hawthorne's / sweet contemporary

Nathaniel Hawthorne (1804–1864), the American writer, born in nearby Salem. Olson had noted the fact that Lane and he were born in the same year in his poetic tribute to Lane entitled "An 'Enthusiasm.' "

III.198. Noah Webster

The American lexicographer (1758—1843). His *American Dictionary of the English Language* first appeared in 1828. Olson cites him among other contemporaries of Lane's in a review (unpublished) of Wilmerding's 1964 book as follows: "Noah Webster, the creator of the only dictionary which has now permitted the English-American language to become the re-issue of the initial Indo-European experience. . . ."

III.199. Shiva . . . when war was nec- / essary even against the Goddess of the / Three Towns . . . draw his bow to kill Tripura

For Shiva as Tripurantaka, the god as "conqueror and liberator of the entire world" who puts an end to Tripura or the Three Towns (the earth, atmosphere and sky), see Zimmer, *Myths and Symbols in Indian Art and Civilization*, pp. 185—187 (quoted in notes to *Maximus* III, 61).

III.199. 4th condition God himself makes / necessary to a vision . . .

In notes from 14 December 1967 at the back of his copy of Zimmer's *Myths and Symbols*, Olson lists five "subjects of the Conversation" which may have some bearing (esp. with the previous mention of Shiva) on the "4th condition" referred to here. These subjects appear to be derived from a reading of pp. 137ff. in Zimmer on Shiva-Shakti (Olson writes nearly the same ones in the margin of his p. 143, calling them there the "5 subjects of Shiva-Shakti") and they are probably also patterned on the "five activities" of Shiva as Cosmic Dancer listed on p. 154 in Zimmer. In Olson's order, then:

> [1.] the Creation
> [2.] the War of the Worlds . . . [added to the side: "*the destruction of the world*"]
> 3. the worship of the Gods
> 4. the attainment of superhuman power
> 5. "*the four modes of union with the Supreme Spirit*"

They appear in earlier notes dated 5 September [1966] in a notebook, where Olson writes of "a dialogue between each [i.e. Shiva and Shakti] & ought in theory to treat of 5 subjects:

> the creation,
> the destruction of the world,
> the worship of the gods,
> the attainment of superhuman power &
> the 4 modes of union with the Supreme Power (Spirit) revealed by Shiva alone."

III.199. holy Idris

Prophet mentioned twice in the Koran and identified by commentators as Enoch of the Bible. See esp. Nasr, *Science and Civilization in Islam,* writing about the Islamic sect known as the Sabaeans, p. 31: "This religious community traced its origin to the Prophet Idrīs (the Enoch of the Old Testament), who is regarded in the Islamic world as the founder of the sciences of the heavens and of philosophy, and who is identified by some with Hermes Trismegistus." (The book was given to Olson on 28 July 1968 by Harvey Brown—see below—and a note by the poet on the flyleaf indicates he began reading it on July 31st. It would seem to be in part in response to the book that his phone call to Brown was made.) See also Nasr's *Introduction to Islamic Cosmological Doctrines* (which Brown had presented to Olson earlier, in February 1967), p. 13n: "By Hermeticists, or *haramisah,* the Muslim authors meant the followers of the ante-Diluvian prophet, Idrīs, or Ukhnukh (Quran, XIX, 57; XXI, 85), whom they regarded as the founder of the arts and sciences as well as of *hikmah* ['wisdom'] and philosophy" (marked by Olson). Also Corbin, *Avicenna and the Visionary Recital,* p. 14, a passage briefly mentioning Idrīs and marked by Olson 4 March 1966.

III.199. Trismegistus

Greek 'Thrice-Greatest'; title of Hermes of the Hermetic tradition, legendary author of alchemical and other sacred texts.

III.199. Enoch

A figure in the Hermetic tradition for whom the apocryphal *Book of Enoch* was named; Hebrew name of Arabic Ukhnukh or Idrīs.

III.199. the alemb the gold- / making juices lie in . . .

Nasr writes: "There are most likely elements of Chinese science in Islam, especially in alchemy, pointing to some early contact between the Muslims and Chinese science. Some have even gone so far as to claim—without much proof, to be sure—that the word *al-kimiya* from which 'alchemy' is derived, is itself an arabization of the classical Chinese word *Chin-I*, which in some dialects is *Kim-Ia* and means 'the gold-making juice' " (*Science and Civilization in Islam*, pp. 31–32).

III.200. the / Groaner and the Whistling Buoy . . .

The "Groaner" is undoubtedly the poet's name for a fog signal (an air-diaphone horn) on Thachers Island off Eastern Point, while about two and a half miles to the east is a lighted whistle buoy (definitely identified in the early unpublished "Maximus, West" as "the Whistling Buoy / off Eastern Point").

III.200. Bach

Johann Sebastian Bach (1685–1750), the composer. In commenting on a performance of Pierre Boulez's Second Sonata at Black Mountain College, Olson said: "I hadn't heard anything as interesting as that since I once heard Bach" (quoted in Clayre, "Rise and Fall of Black Mountain College," p. 412); while in his "Notes for a University at Venice, California" Olson proposed, for one of the courses in music, "if Boulez not available . . . solely *Bach* complete . . ." (*OLSON* 2, p. 66). Later, as part of his 1968 "Plan for a Curriculum of the Soul," he proposes the study, "Bach's belief."

III.200. God festen Berg

Echo of Martin Luther's hymn, "Ein' feste Burg ist unser Gott" ('A mighty fortress is our God'), set to music by J. S. Bach (his Cantata No. 80).

III.200. Robeson Channel

Separating northwestern Greenland from Ellesmere Island (see particularly the photograph in Wilson, "Continental Drift," p. 87).

III.200. Wegener Fault

Fault or rift in the earth's crust above Greenland, marked by Robeson Channel; named after Alfred Wegener, who proposed a theory of continental drift (again Wilson, "Continental Drift," p. 87).

III.200. the Chinese / word of Al 'chimiya . . . the / Gold-making machine

See note to "the gold- / making juices" above; also "I am the Gold Machine . . . ," *Maximus* II, 131 and note.

III.200. Harvey Brown

Friend and patron of the poet, as well as publisher of Frontier Press; living in West Newbury, Mass., about twenty miles away.

III.200. Natalie Hammond

(b. 1904), sister of John Hays Hammond, Jr. She had lived on her father's estate overlooking Dolliver's Neck, which included a series of cottages of Tudor design (now part of Cardinal Cushing Villa), before founding her own museum at North Salem, N.Y. in 1957.

III.200. Sausalito Over the Bay

City north of San Francisco on San Francisco Bay.

III.201. the school bell rings the hours ...

"The 1851 bell from the former Point Grammar School on Plum Street can be heard striking the clarion hour across the water from 'the copper paint'"—Garland, *Gloucester Guide,* p. 82, writing of the Wonson Paint Manufactory on Rocky Neck (next note).

III.201. Wonsons Paint Manufactory at / point above Black Rocks on Rocky Neck

Tarr and Wonson's on the tip of Rocky Neck, manufacturers of copper paint for boat bottoms since 1863. The red-painted wooden building with "Wonson's Paint" prominent on its side is easily visible in daylight at least from the Fort.

III.201. Beverly / Air Port

Small airport at Beverly, Mass., twelve miles down the coast.

III.201. Hanscom Air / Force Base

In Bedford, some fifteen miles west of Boston.

III.201. Frank Moore's birth face forceps / bent

Cf. "The Librarian," in which the following dream-figure appears: "He / (not my father, / by name himself / with his face / twisted / at birth)," and which ends: "Who is / Frank Moore?" Moore (b. 1923), a composer, was a friend of Olson's during the late 1940's and early 1950's in Washington. See also "Olson in Gloucester," *Muthologos,* I, 169–173.

▶ III.202. December 18th

Original holograph manuscript dated 18 December 1968, with a typescript also among the poet's papers.

See Olson's letter earlier that year to the editor of the *Gloucester Times,* dated 11 January 1968:

May I ask the attention of the City once more, despite all troubles and snow, to another threatened erosion of her handsomeness—and this one on a spot which is uniquely hers, and special in America: the corner on which Abraham Robinson sat down as early as 1638 and which, right now, holds buildings including still the beautiful old Town Hall which go back from whenever that was built to some certainly 1830. And at least a few which may date to the 18th century.

I mean of course what is too easily called the West End. If I read correctly further plans for the expansion of the Shell Station it sounds as though the house Alfred Mansfield Brooks was born in, the one which Tally's backs up to, is scheduled to go(?)

In any case what today's sun shows is that a composite of buildings which I don't believe are usually thought of as what is so easily called the West End are in danger: that is, given the old Mansfield house, built for Brooks' mother's marriage post-the 1830 fire, and going across the street, up Washington to the Middle Street corner, and including all of Angle Street and Lower Middle as well as the core house of the old Town Hall itself (now the Legion building), are a half a dozen of the rarest Federals or Colonials left anywhere—

And once a gap-tooth is blown in that complex, it is modern jungle immediately, and all the clash and error of like war wrong and ugly and depressing.

Is there no sense in the City that her beauty, by nature, and the support of man, is not to be slashed and gone forever simply to accommodate business men, who are no matter how progressive and that virtue, also profit-makers and so immediately or eventually greedy. And devouring. I BEG AGAIN for action.

Also, a photograph in that issue of the newspaper, 18 January 1966, of the "West End" of Gloucester showing the Mansfield house, under which is this caption: "Built on style of a Boston town house, the former Mansfield home at 15 Main St. in Gloucester is slated to be removed to make way for expansion of Tallys Mobil Service Station in the spring. Old Timers' Tavern occupies ground floor of the three-story brick structure built after great fire of 1830. . . ."

The Mansfield house is also referred to in Olson's "Rocking meter over desolation," dated 20 January 1968, while in a letter to the *Times,* 7 February 1968, the poet speaks of "looking out my door and seeing the early morning sun so differently striking . . . the ancient Gloucester House brick— how rosy red is that brick as against the Mansfield house's dark red's blood red's brick."

III.203. the Poles / of Bond's Hill

See *Maximus* III, 35 and note.

III.203. fake gasoline station / and A&P supermarket / construction . . .

In a postscript dated 1 April 1969 to still another letter to the *Gloucester Times* (published April 7th) denouncing the destruction of Gloucester, Olson protests: "Main Street was a snake in the sun until A&P plaza—and now even the spots are going to be rubbed out."

III.204. "We are not a narrow tribe of men . . .

See *Redburn, His First Voyage,* chapter XXXIII (Constable ed., p. 216):

> Settled by the people of all nations, all nations may claim her for their own. You cannot spill a drop of American blood without spilling the blood of the whole world. Be he Englishman, Frenchman, German, Dane, or Scot; the European who scoffs at an American calls his own brother *Raca,* and stands in danger of the judgment. We are not a narrow tribe of men with a bigoted Hebrew nationality— whose blood has been debased in the attempt to ennoble it, by maintaining an exclusive succession among ourselves. No: our blood is as the flood of the Amazon, made up of a thousand noble currents all pouring into one. We are not a nation, so much as a world . . .

▶III.205. Between Cruiser & Plato . . .

Holograph original, with another pencilled copy and a finally revised typescript (these last dated 1 January 1969). Written following a conversation with John R. Butterick the previous night on the subject of the lost Atlantis (note on second holograph manuscript apparently intended for present writer: "George—this is what at least your brother provoked! Charles").

Cruiser and Plato are both mountains on the floor of the North Atlantic and appear on Heezen and Tharp's "Physiographic Diagram" of the North Atlantic Ocean, which Olson had hanging on his kitchen wall. They are about 500 miles south of the Azores and some 750 miles west northwest of the Canary Islands.

III.205. Atlantis

A seamount, immediately northwest of Plato on Heezen and Tharp's map of the ocean floor. Named for the legendary island said by the philosopher Plato to have existed west of the Pillars of Hercules.

III.205. Gloucester / tore her way West North West ½ West . . .

See earlier, "Gloucester itself comes from the / Canaries" (*Maximus* III, 163), and note.

▶III.206. Full moon [staring out window . . . March 4th / 1969 . . .

Holograph manuscript only; blue ballpoint ink on yellow paper.

▶III.207. The first of morning was always over there . . .

Written in a small pocket notepad and dated 20 April 1969.

III.207. when I went to work . . . at the Post Office

The poet worked as a substitute carrier at the Gloucester Post Office during the summers of 1931 to 1936 (see *Maximus* I, 5; II, 96, 97; and especially *The Post Office*).

III.207. Geisha

A brand name of Japanese seafood products distributed in the United States.

III.207. Genji and/or Lady Murasaka

Lady Murasaki Shikibu (ca. 978–ca. 1030), author of *The Tale of Genji,* a prose narrative dealing with the loves and adventures of prince Genji and reflecting the declining splendor of Japanese court life of the eleventh century.

▶III.208. the left hand is the calyx of the Flower . . .

Written in pencil on the back cover of a copy of *Pleistocene Man* (1968) and dated 20 April 1969.

The "Flower" is both the "Golden Flower" (*Maximus* III, 18, 73–75, 178, 194, and notes) and the Lotus or *padma* of Buddhism (*Maximus* II, 11), formed here by a *mudrā* or symbolic gesture.

▶III.209. The Island, the River, the shore . . .

Holograph original only, dated 24 May 1969. The "Island" presumably refers to Ten Pound Island, prominent earlier in the poems (III, 113, 114–116)—unless it is Gloucester itself, separated from the mainland by the Annisquam ("water / on the 4th side"), which can be considered an island.

III.209. an arm / such as Enyalion's . . .

For Enyalion and his lost arm, see *Maximus* III, 29 and note.

III.209. Champlain's channel

See *Maximus* I, 151—the channel outlined by the numbers, the measurements of Champlain's soundings, in the text—and note.

III.209. Brace's Cove

See *Maximus* I, 6 and note.

III.209. strain locus

See Whitehead's chapter "Strains" in *Process and Reality*, pp. 439ff., which dated notes in his copy indicate Olson was reading the day this poem was written. On p. 439 he has underlined: "In a strain qualitative elements, other than the geometrical forms, express themselves as qualities implicated in those forms . . ."; also, "A strain is a complex integration of simpler feelings. . . ." On p. 453 he notes in the margin, "a strain-locus is . . . ," and draws a line to the following definition by Whitehead: "A strain-locus approximates to a three-dimensional flat locus; but in fact it is four-dimensional, with a time-thickness." And in undated notes among his papers from the 1960's, Olson has written (based on Whitehead, p. 439): "All night Sunday to Monday starting with Weyl on disorder, and from him to Whitehead, from '*rest*,' finding strain-locus a set of points the 'seat' of the strain & the set of lines—projectors—the 'future' in a sense which removes entirely Weyl's error of front & rear instead of end & back."

▶III.210. slownesses / which are an / amount . . .

Written "Monday June 23rd" on a letter from Albert Glover dated 20 June [1969], revised, and copied again on back of letter.

III.210. way into the woods . . . otter pond

See *Maximus* II, 33 and notes.

▶III.211. I was bold, I had courage . . .

Written in legal-sized yellow notepad, undated but between material dated 26 June 1969 and the following version of the poem dated the morning of June 27th:

> The tide so flat
> & the night so wet

I cld lie down
wrapped in it as Homer's rug
he went to sleep in,
the night in Smyrna
he fell out on the ruts
practically in the road-way
he was so tired, and had eaten
too little, spending too much time watching
those two boys fishing all afternoon into
evening time   it made so much
sense to him to see them it was
as it has been today for me such
a day & the wind is onshore
& southerly quite wet & moving
around 10 knots & the June tide
is very low like at 3.19
a.m. on the 27th

III.211. Piney's wharf

See *Maximus* I, 22 and note.

III.211. sleep / as Homer did that last night on Smyrna's / edge . . .

See also the following passage by the poet among notes from 1966–68:

> The loveliest story I know of the greatness of the Poet is the death (or at least I seem to have it) of Homer that, his last day on earth (unknown as such of course to himself) he spent the whole afternoon watching two boys fish (say in the neighborhood of Smyrna) & neglecting nightfall coming, had in fact to roll up in his own zarape or whatever heavier roll or blanket he did have wandering as it seems he was
>
>   And was found dead in the morning so sleeping by the roadside or the edge of some street in the city.

The story does not occur in any classical source, although Smyrna in Asia Minor was one of at least seven cities of antiquity that claimed the honor of Homer's death. On tapes made at station KQED in San Francisco on 2 April 1968 and particularly 4 April, Olson suggests the possibility he may have invented the story, saying: "It's a story I either know or made up . . . of how the poet [Homer] died." In other notes, difficult to read at times, in a notepad from ca. April 1969 (same one that "The first of morning . . . ," *Maximus* III, 207 occurs in), the poet repeats the story:

> . . . I'd like to live to die as Homer did—or at least as I have that story of how [he] did die at Smyrna, I mean the story of his last day, that he got so interested watching two boys fishing he was careless abt taking care of himself, & fell out after the chill of evening where he [found?] himself on the road and was found there dead in the morning wrapped out [inadequately?] in a rug for his sleeping [purposes?].

III.211. the Bosporus

The strait separating Europe from Asia and, with the Sea of Marmara, joining the Mediterranean with the Black Sea.

III.211. Samarkand

Oldest city of Central Asia; west of the Caspian Sea, it was on the trade route east to the silk of China.

▶III.212. Golden Venetian Light . . . June 28th 1969 . . .

Original written in ink on envelope torn open and flattened out; copied out later in notepad, with final lines added; final manuscript typed with slight changes to final lines.

III.212. Agamenticus Height

See *Maximus* I, 151 and note.

III.212. Zeus' dust

The shower of gold that Zeus became in order to possess Danae, who had been confined in a tower because her father had been warned by an oracle that she would bear a son who would cause his death.

III.212. what the Arabs by / muezzin . . .

In Islam, every believer is summoned to pray five times each day, including just after sunset and at the close of the day. The worshipper faces the direction of Mecca; from the east embankment of the Cut, where the poet is stationed as he writes the poem, the position for prayer would be towards the southeast, or away from the Annisquam.

III.212. to quote pater / Helios

Cf. perhaps Pound's use of Pater Helios (Greek 'Father Sun') in Canto CXIII (*Drafts & Fragments,* p. 16—which Olson had received and read in April 1969).

III.212. if I understand Mohammed's / reasons . . .

The Koran in fact forbids the worship of the sun: "Adore not the sun nor the moon; but adore Allah Who created them, if it is in truth Him whom ye worship" (XLI.37, from Pickthall, *Meaning of the Glorious Koran,* p. 342).

III.212. Ra & the Sun Boat

Ra, the Egyptian sun-god, sails across the sky each morning in his boat and back again at sunset.

III.212. the Aldermens polished granite statement . . .

A polished granite marker, roughly four feet by five feet, laid in the embankment along the canal about one hundred yards from the bridge, recording the date the embankment was built and crediting the city officials at the time. Noticeably larger than the other granite blocks which make up the embankment, it can be read only with one's fingertips. On it are the names of the mayor (Harry C. Foster, 1914) and the aldermen of the town, including Charles H[omer] Barrett.

III.212. the old Newell Stadium baseball diamond

In the Gloucester High School field, off Centennial Avenue and along the Cut.

III.212. Jack & Mary Clarke's wedding day

John Clarke (b. 1933), "who gave me Blake" ("Reading at Berkeley," *Muthologos*, I, 110), teacher and Blake scholar at the State University of New York at Buffalo; later director of the Institute of Further Studies. He and Mary Leary were married that day in Oxford, N.Y. (Olson had received an invitation to the wedding).

III.213. the "homes" of my 1st / poems

No "homes" or houses as such appear in Olson's first poems concerning the Annisquam (see note to *Maximus* I, 82), but the houses along Kent Circle in Gloucester are meant here. See certainly *Maximus* I, 84–85 and notes, and II, 133 and notes, relative to the period of those "1st poems."

III.213. the Frazier Federal

House at 3 Essex Avenue, along Kent Circle, home of the mother-in-law of "Schwartz, the bookie" (*Maximus* I, 84).

III.213. Brooksie

Olson's nickname for Alfred Mansfield Brooks, the former director of the Cape Ann Historical Society (see note to "the house the street cuts off . . . ," *Maximus* I, 5).

III.213. the Aunt Vandla gambrel

See *Maximus* II, 133 and note.

III.213. the Waiting Station

See *Maximus* I, 11 and note.

III.213. Chas Peter

The poet's son, born in 1955.

III.214. the 'Other River' / coming in from the Bay

The Annisquam is a tidal river, open to the sea at both ends, and an incoming tide from Gloucester Harbor would encounter at some point in its channel the incoming tide—the "Other River"—from Ipswich Bay.

III.214. where . . . do they actually in fact / slowly impede each other?

At Done Fudging, beyond the Boston and Maine railroad bridge (see Garland, *Gloucester Guide*, p. 45), some distance from where the poet was positioned. Babson, for example, writes: "The opposite currents meet at Done Fudging; and there the vessels were sometimes anchored to wait a change of tide. The attractions of a tavern added other inducements to stop. The singular name given to this place is said to have been derived from the fact, that persons, poling or 'fudging' a boat or raft on the river against the current, here took a fair tide, and were therefore 'done fudging' " (*History*, 150n).

III.214. my Aunt Vandla's / unoffensive / egg at the front / of her / neck

Again, see *Maximus* II, 133 and note.

III.214. the Gloucester / revelations

Probable echo of the *Meccan Revelations* of Al'Arabi ("Poetry and Truth," *Muthologos*, II, 47 and note), and the revelations to Mohammed which constitute the Koran.

III.215. Isis-boat

The papyrus boat which the goddess Isis used to search for the scattered remains of her lost brother Osiris, slain by Typhon.

► **III.217. Short Possible Poem to Follow / Long Excessive "Venetian Job"...**

Written 28–29 June 1969, apparently back home at 28 Fort Square, in the same notepad in which the previous poem had been copied out from its original writing.

III.217. Mr. Browne on duty East Pt Light station...

Coast Guard Captain Fletcher W. Brown, whose responsibilities included the operation of a diaphragm fog horn installed on Ten Pound Island the previous summer. For Olson's dispute with Brown earlier over the disturbing noise of the horn, see Harrigan, "Neighbors silence Ten Pound's wail," *Gloucester Daily Times,* 8 August 1968, pp. 1, 12, and "Ten Pound answer: 'Militancy,'" *Gloucester Times,* 8 October 1968, p. 1.

► **III.218. Enyalion of / brown earth...**

Written on the front cover of a spiral notebook "*Started Sunday June 22nd / to . . . July 10th* [1969]," where it has been distinguished by the poet from other notes by enclosing it in a box with the opening lines connected to the body of the poem by a drawn line.

See Enyalion and the "brown-red" earth of *Maximus* III, 40. The bird-like call attributed to him here is related to the Northwest Semitic *krk* 'town' from *Maximus* III, 51.

► **III.219. His health, his poetry, and his love all / in one...**

Written 16 July 1969 in small notepad identified as "*Started Wednesday July 16th for the kitchen table.*"

III.219. the green glow of Glaowceastre...

The discoloration due to mercury vapor lighting installed throughout the business district of Gloucester (once *Glaowceastre,* the 'glowing city'—see *Maximus* I, 44 and note), which

Olson made frequent complaint against: "the Electric Company's / lights are there, every night, to destroy the color of color / in human faces . . ." (in "A *Scream* to the Editor") and "the color of the lights on the Main / Street turn the lips of women blue" (*Maximus* II, 88).

III.219. Reich was / right, the / race does seek / to resemble its own / experiments

Wilhelm Reich (1897–1957), psychologist best known for his orgone research and theories concerning the sexual basis of politics; imprisoned by the United States government for violation of an injunction against the sale of "orgone boxes." See also Olson's letter to the *Gloucester Times,* 29 January 1969, in which he writes: "Wilhelm Reich arises, as Saint (from death, in Lewisburg, Penitentiary)."

III.219. St Francis

(1182–1226), the saint of Poverty, founder of the Franciscan order.

III.219. Clara whose body still lies . . .

Saint Clare (1194–1253), founder of the order of Franciscan nuns known as the Poor Clares. Her body lies preserved in a glass-enclosed case in the Church of Saint Clare in Assisi and can be visited by tourists. The hands only are exposed, which the devout may kiss. Charles Boer, who visited the shrine in 1967, suggested in conversation that the "dark nun" may have been the same veiled one he observed, assigned to keep a vigil over the corpse and to wipe the hands after each kiss. Olson would have made his visit two years earlier in the summer of 1965, when in Italy to read at the Spoleto Festival.

III.219. Kenward Elmslie

American poet (see *Maximus* III, 112 and note). He had attended the Festival of the Two Worlds at Spoleto with poets Bill Berkson and Barbara Guest during the time Olson was there in July 1965.

III.219. Father / Carpini listening / at the tents . . .

Fra Giovanni de Piano Carpini, associate of St. Francis of Assisi whose mission to Central Asia in 1245–47 is reported in full in Skelton et al., *The Vinland Map and The Tartar Relation*. Olson writes in his review of that volume (*Additional Prose*, p. 67): "the leader [of the mission to the Tartars] is one of St. Francis' earliest adherents, a brother so able he was the Franciscan's first 'ambassador' to the Germans, and was so useful there in Europe, and in Poland, that when the Mongols looked as though they were in all likelihood going to smash Europe by 1250 . . . , it was Carpini who was sent to Karakorum, by the Pope, to see if he could smoke out, ahead of time, or in any way forfend the dreaded Destruction."

See also Olson's summary of the Carpini mission in "Poetry and Truth," *Muthologos*, II, 47–48:

> Carpini is the contemporary of Saint Francis and became Saint Francis's first political . . . I don't want to say agent, but body. Suddenly Francis, who himself was a sick soldier and had a dream in Spoleto which so caused him—or was sick in Spoleto, like a shaman can be—and had this vision of being Christ, actually, if possible, again. Suddenly he's joined by this man who becomes Carpini, and is already by the date of 1245, so useful and has been so, has been the ambassador of the Franciscans to the Germans originally—missionary, I suppose, in the first sense—then to the rest of Europe, and then suddenly about that date to Poland—is sent by the Pope, with two brothers, to the East to discover the Mongols' intention—the expectation of the whole West being that in 1250 they will raid again and destroy to the Atlantic. And the Carpini Mission goes to Karakorum and sits, or tries to, for three years to hear whatever they can hear in the marketplace, and come home, and arrive back in Poland at around 1248 to report that apparently the Mongols are not going to strike. I'd like to call that the end of the advantages of the mind, that we can reach to.

III.220. the slumberous / animal forms . . . in / Settlement Cove

See also *Maximus* III, 223 below.

III.220. Jack Micheline

Proletarian poet, born Howard Silver in the Bronx in 1929 (the "Jack" of his adopted name taken from Jack London). His visit to Olson in the summer of 1960 is mentioned by Olson in a letter to Robert Creeley (Creeley to Edward Dorn, 3 August 1960; the letter itself does not seem to have survived), and in letters from both 1965 and 1966 Micheline reminds Olson of the "pleasant walk" they had taken together in Gloucester at that time.

III.220. I come from the last walking period of man

Repeated in the poem following.

III.220. Brythonic

In the same notepad the poem was written in, two pages later, appear the following definitions (taken from *Webster's Collegiate Dictionary*, 5th ed., p. 131):

> *Brython:* A *Briton*
> *Brythonic*
>   that division of the Celtic languages which includes *Welsh*, *Cornish*, and *Breton*

III.221. the Park

Stage Fort Park.

III.221. the Woman Who Is Loved poem

A poem apparently called *"For Woman, Who is Loved / —& Hated if she say so & She Be,"* written the evening of the previous day, first on envelopes and scraps, then copied in a notepad "Started Sunday July 13th / 1969." It is a long, confused, personal poem (involving the poet's mother and deceased wife), also called "She-Bear Re-Visited Or Re-taken 19 yrs Later," with such lines as,

> God save my soul because it
> needs it for the horror it's
>   done
> for almost 20
>   years by being
>   sightless when it had
>   its eyes & didn't have its
>   beautiful fish like
>   scales of sight itself to
>   lay upon a bed & be
>   as bound to her as man when
>   [he] is lying in the arms of
>   the Signet [Serpent?] Goddess Hell herself
>   when woman
>   is his
>   form . . .

It is not, in any case, a *Maximus* poem.

▶III.222. Thank God / I chose a Protestant / Federalist / town . . .

Among notes three pages later in the same notepad as previous poem occurs the following: "FUCKING *CATHO-LIC* / BOSTON," with a line drawn from that to: "Thank God / I chose a Protestant / Federalist / town," which has been circled on the page and copied out again on the next page of the notepad with date, 16 July 1969. A typescript was prepared, with line added (from previous poem).

▶III.223. Father / Sky   Mother Earth . . .

Originally written in pencil on two small sheets, then copied out in ink in large legal-sized notepad and dated 19 July 1969.

III.223. Chomplain

I.e., Champlain. See esp. *Maximus* I, 151 and note, also *Maximus* II, 136, and III, 73 and 88.

III.223. Freshwater Cove

See *Maximus* I, 10 and note; also *Maximus* III, 6.

III.223. il

French 'he'; i.e., Champlain.

III.223. galliots

Also galiot; a small light galley.

III.223. a stream fell down steeply . . .

Probably the one mentioned earlier, *Maximus* III, 6.

III.223. Ravenswood "park" . . .

See *Maximus* I, 10 and note. The "nameless road" is probably the one eventually called Old Salem Road, which ran through the northern portion of Ravenswood and through Manchester to Salem.

III.223. Manchester was Jeffries . . . s creek

Town south of Gloucester on the coast, below Magnolia. Originally a part of Beverly and Salem, it was known at first as Jeffrey's Creek, from William Jeffrey who had settled there for a brief while.

III.223. Magnolia

See note to *Maximus* I, 11. As Copeland and Rogers point out, until 1867 the area between Freshwater Cove and Magnolia (then Kettle Cove) was almost wholly forest. The forests were cleared by an early developer, however, and roads and summer cottages constructed, and the area was called "Magnolia" from the swamp magnolias nearby (*Saga of Cape Ann*, p. 211).

III.223. Magnolia glauca

The swamp magnolia, which grows as a shrub on Cape Ann. Common in the South and Southwest, its only native place in Massachusetts and the northernmost point at which the species is found in a natural habitat is in a swamp in Ravenswood (see Babson, *History,* pp. 6–7, and Copeland and Rogers, pp. 213 and 226).

III.223. Dollivers neck

See *Maximus* III, 6 and note.

III.223. Dogbar breakwater

See *Maximus* I, 22 and note.

III.223. Clarence / Birdseyes

Birdseye (see *Maximus* III, 167) had his home across the harbor on Eastern Point, at Eastern Point Road and St. Louis Avenue.

III.223. charmant

French 'charming, delightful.'

III.223. Niles

Niles Beach on the western shore of Eastern Point, directly across Gloucester Harbor from Freshwater Cove.

III.223. Ten Pound Island channel marker (Nun Buoy 10)

See *Maximus* II, 132 and note.

III.223. loco

Probably Latin 'place,' rather than Spanish 'madman, crazy.'

III.223. Oakes Cove

Small cove on the west shore of Rocky Neck. It is identified as such on John Mason's "Map of Gloucester, Cape Ann" (1831) and also in the legend to Champlain's map as printed in Pringle ed., *Book of the Three Hundredth Anniversary*, opposite p. 36.

III.223. Worcester paper company . . . owner's house

20 Wonson Street on Rocky Neck, overlooking Oakes Cove; home of former owner of Shepard Envelope Co., Worcester.

III.223. Ben / Widdershins

The name, apparently a confusion with Ben Shahn, actually came to the poet in a dream. In a notepad from around this same time in 1969 appears the following record of the dream: "wanted to do piece—speak on Ben [added by Olson: Shahn] Widdershins. Where?—Florida! & I say why not someone who is already Widdershins? like Pound [feeling is young(?) Zukovsky." In the original manuscript, "Shahn," in parentheses before "Widdershins," is crossed out. Shahn, the painter, was a friend and associate of Olson's during the 1940's and early 1950's at the O.W.I. and at Black Mountain.

III.223. now hidden Algonquin corn / houses . . .

Portrayed on Champlain's map of Gloucester Harbor, 1606 (see *Maximus* I, 151; II, 136; III, 97, and notes).

III.223. O donell-Usen freezer . . .

On the Fort, to the right (from across the Harbor) of the main O'Donnell-Usen plant, which was Clarence Birdseye's original (see *Maximus* III, 153 and notes).

III.223. City Hall

In town, on Dale Avenue, its tall tower with cupola (see *Maximus* II, 190) visible from the Freshwater Cove area.

III.223. Tavern

The Tavern, restaurant (see *Maximus* I, 142) at the beginning of Western Avenue overlooking the Harbor at Pavilion Beach.

III.223. Tablet Rocks

See note to "the rock I know by my belly and torn nails," *Maximus* I, 48.

III.223. what Lane has so well drawn

See Fitz Hugh Lane's various drawings and paintings of the Freshwater Cove vicinity, such as "Fresh Water Cove from Dolliver's Neck," an oil at the Museum of Fine Arts, Boston; the pencil drawing "Fresh Water Cove, Gloucester" from ca. 1864 (Wilmerding, *Fitz Hugh Lane,* 1971, plate 56); and especially Miss Proctor's "Fresh Water Cove," mentioned in " 'I know men for whom everything matters,' " *Muthologos,* II, 160. Also see *Maximus* III, 97.

III.224. Charley Olson from over the like / Cut

I.e. the poet himself, who as a boy grew up summers "over the Cut," in the local phrase, on the other side of the Cut from the town (see also *Maximus* III, 55). "Like" is used here as an expletive, to provide a pause.

III.224. topknot

The poet at the time wore his hair in a knot at the back of his head (see photos in Charters, *Olson/ Melville,* and her photograph on the cover of the paperback edition of *Poetry and Truth*).

▶III.225. Melkarth of Tyre . . .

Holograph manuscript only, written on verso of a manila envelope and dated 11 September 1969; photo-reproduced in *Paris Review* 49, 1970, p. 176. Original in possession of Gerard Malanga, who interviewed Olson for the *Paris Review*.

For Melkarth, the Phoenician Hercules, see note to Melkart-Hercules, *Maximus* II, 104; also note to "What he drew . . . ," *Maximus* I, 78.

III.225. Lebanese

The ancient Phoenicians (see also *Maximus* I, 147), rather than Gloucester's small but distinct Lebanese-American colony (see interview with Joe Kyrouz in Parsons and Anastas, *When Gloucester Was Gloucester*, pp. 35ff.).

III.225. Herodotean / report

See *Maximus* I, 100 and note; also II, 79.

III.225. Egyptians said . . . speaking to Solon . . . as of Greeks . . .

Part of the original story of the lost Atlantis as told by Plato in the *Timaeus*. See, e.g., the summarization in the *Encyclopaedia Britannica* (11th ed.) article "Atlantis": "Plato describes how certain Egyptian priests, in a conversation with Solon, represented the island as a country larger than Asia Minor and Libya united, and situated just beyond the Pillars of Hercules (Straits of Gibralter). Beyond it lay an archipelago of lesser islands. According to the priests, Atlantis had been a powerful kingdom nine thousand years before the birth of Solon, and its armies had overrun the lands which bordered the Mediterranean. Athens alone had withstood them with success." Also told in Spanuth, *Atlantis,* and Donnelly, *Atlantis* (of books Olson is known to have read).

III.225. a thing does flow

Cf.—especially in this context amidst other borrowings from Whitehead—"all does rhyme," *Maximus* III, 124 and note there to Whitehead's use of Heraclitus' "All does flow."

III.225. intensity / is characteristic throughout / the system

Cf. "measurement / *'throughout the system,'* " *Maximus* III, 124 and note, and again as "measurement possible through the system" in "The Secret of the Black Chrysanthemum," *OLSON* 3, 1975, p. 73. While "intensity," too, is a term used by Whitehead in *Process and Reality,* p. 137 (marked by Olson), following a discussion in which he says, " 'measurement' is not determinable in a systematic way throughout the society" (pp. 135–136).

III.225. I raise monuments / by the River

See, e.g., *Maximus* II, 84 and 174 and notes.

III.225. have sd it does take a mole to join Gloucester to / the Nation

See *Maximus* II, 80.

▶**III.226. the Blow is Creation . . .**

Written in University of Connecticut notepad, ca. 26 November 1969 (page following "Notes Wednesday Nov 26th 1969"). Occurs in notepad three pages *after* poem designated as final one by the poet.

The "Blow" referred to is *typos,* Greek for 'a blow, the mark of a blow,' one of the terms in Olson's "basic trio" of "topos / typos / tropos, 3 in 1" (first published in "Letter to Elaine Feinstein"—see *Human Universe,* p. 97). See esp. "Poetry and Truth," *Muthologos,* II, 34:

> . . . it's type, and is typology, and is typification . . . We get our word type . . . from it. If any of you have ever seen a piece of movable type, at the bottom is the letter and the block is above. So that in order, really, to imagine a printer doing it . . . he's under your words in order to make the letters of them. Which always delights me, literally, as a problem of creation. In fact, literally, I would go so far—if you will excuse my Americanism—to think that you write that way. That you write as though you

were *underneath* the letters. And I take that a hell of a lot larger. I would think that the hoof-print of the creator is on the bottom of creation, in exactly that same sense.

III.226. the Twist   the Nasturtium

See *Maximus* I, 36–37, where the nasturtium or "nose-twist" first occurs; also the poem "The Twist" (I, 82–86) and the one following here. At the same time, the "Twist" is the equivalent of *tropos*, Greek 'turning,' one of Olson's "basic trio"—just as "Place" in the fourth line is *topos*, Greek 'place,' the first of the three terms. In 1968, Olson had spoken of his sense of "place" in a way that is relevant here: "in the same sense that I think names are almost always proper, of the earth," and that "that literal globe or orb is our lamp or clue to the whole of creation, and that only by obedience to it does one have a chance at heaven" ("Poetry and Truth," *Muthologos*, II, 34).

▶III.227. Nasturtium / is still my flower . . .

Written in a University of Connecticut notepad six pages after notes dated November 23 [1969] and three pages before "I live underneath / the light of day . . ." which follows.

The nasturtium or "nose-twist" appeared sixteen years earlier in the poems, in "Tyrian Businesses" (*Maximus* I, 36–37), where the poet had called it "my flower." See also *Maximus* I, 93, where it is referred to as "my shield."

▶III.228. I live underneath / the light of day . . .

Written in the same University of Connecticut notepad as the previous two poems, on 23 November 1969 or shortly thereafter (the date appears a few pages earlier).

Among the poet's papers from this time are pages torn from a copy of Brøndsted's *The Vikings* supplied him by the poet Tom Raworth on which the following passage is marked and "Gaian" added in the margin (pp. 195–196): "Another runic inscription, cut on the underside of a slab covering a grave of about a century before the Viking Age at Eggjum in Sogn (Norway), declares that neither stone nor runes have ever been exposed to the sun's light and that the runes were not carved with an iron knife. In other words: both stone and runes are dedicated in secret to the dead man and to none other. This, the longest of all the early inscriptions, commands further that the stone must never be brought out into the light of day."

III.228. Tartarian-Erojan, Geaan-Ouranian

For Tartarus or Hell, see esp. *Maximus* II, 163ff.; "Erojan" is probably derived from Eros, Love; "Geaan" (or more usually "Gaian" or "Gaean," pertaining to the Earth) appears in this irregular spelling elsewhere among Olson's notes at the time; while "Ouranian" pertains to Ouranos or Heaven. Together, they are among the first elements or aspects of creation after Chaos in Hesiod (see *Maximus* II, 163–172; III, 163–164).

III.228. time & exact / analogy

Variation of the phrase "time and exact definition" from the alchemical treatise "Liber Platonis quartorum," quoted in Jung, *Psychology and Alchemy,* p. 255 (in its full context: "Through time and exact definition things are converted into intellect"), reflecting the process of analogy in alchemy.

▶III.229. my wife   my car   my color . . .

The original was written in the same University of Connecticut notepad as the previous poems, between the 23rd and 26th of November, 1969. It was identified as the last poem of the *Maximus* series in instructions to the poet's literary executor, Charles Boer, made in the margin of Olson's copy of John Philip Cohane, *The Key,* p. 258, shortly before his death. The poem would seem to be a catalogue of losses or at least of concerns occupying the poet as he approached his last days.

The poet had lost his wife Betty, who was killed in an automobile collision, in March 1964. His own car, the second of

two of the same model and color Pontiac beach wagons he
had owned during these last years, had recently been abandoned in Gloucester, and in Connecticut during his last
weeks he had been driving a rented car (Boer, *Charles Olson
in Connecticut,* pp. 80–81).

"Color" is the most difficult and curious choice in the
series. It might be kept in mind that Olson had written in
1964, as "William Dorn," that

> Color is not social, color is not recognition. Color
> is the evidence of truth
>
>   it is a very trustworthy thing,
>   color
>
>   Color is the Fruits
>   or the Four Rivers of Paradise

(See the rest of that series, in *Archaeologist of Morning,* pp.
[223]–[225].) It also should be noted that the "color" of
Enyalion, the god of war, is "beauty," that "the color" is
what the Bulgar carries (*Maximus* III, 38–39), and that
there is a "world / constituted of color" (III, 44). Also, that
it is one of the functions of the mind or *noos* to see something
in its "true colors" (Snell, *Discovery of the Mind,* p. 13—see
Maximus III, 122 and note). Charles Boer has reminded the
author that the poet's own complexion, or "color" in that
sense, would also have been of concern to him, as his health
continued to decline.

If, however, there are "racial" or cultural implications to
"my color," it would have to be in the sense in which Olson
referred to himself at Berkeley half-mockingly as "that
famous thing, the White Man, the ultimate paleface, the
noncorruptible, the Good, the thing that runs this country,
or that *is* this country" (*Muthologos,* I, 133); or, in notes from
ca. October 1967 among his papers, where he writes of himself as a "WHITE guerrilla—who hates violence & hates
hate . . ." In other words, his "color" would be that of the
white man as the "dominant" form of man in the twentieth

century—Western, civilized, industrialized. In later jottings, written 12 August 1968, he refers to the automobile as the "automobilical" or substitute for the "independence of the white man's individuality," adding: "au-tō-mō-bile / [Mō-town Dē-troit . . . down the drain goeth the White man and / all his Ford Plant . . ."

Eleves, I salute you! come forward!
Continue your annotations, continue your questionings.

—Walt Whitman in *Song of Myself,* section 38

Works Cited

The following will provide full bibliographical information for all published works cited in the annotations. Titles preceded by an asterisk (*) are ones positively known to have been used by Olson, whether through textual or other evidence. Most of these titles, in the editions given, were owned by the poet as part of his personal library and are now preserved in the Literary Archives at the University of Connecticut Library, where they are accessible to researchers. (A complete listing of works known to have been read or consulted by Olson, with evidence of their use, can be found in the author's checklist, "Olson's Reading: A Preliminary Report," published serially in *OLSON: The Journal of the Charles Olson Archives* from 1974 on.)

In a very few cases—specifically, Banks' *Topographical Dictionary*, *The Dictionary of National Biography*, the *Encyclopaedia of Religion and Ethics* where Paton's articles appear, and the volumes by DeVoto, Donnelly, Whorf, and Wiener—the precise edition used by Olson is uncertain, although the work itself is known to have been consulted. All other titles—i.e., those appearing without asterisks—are books and articles that the author has found useful in preparing these annotations, either to support conjectures or provide further illustration for a subject.

The list includes titles of collections of the poet's own writings that are referred to in the text, although it is expected the reader will also wish to consult *A Bibliography of Works by Charles Olson* by Butterick and Glover (New York, 1967), or the checklist of Olson's writings appended to the author's 1970 Ph.D. dissertation, until these are superseded by a fully revised, definitive bibliography.

*Adams, Brooks. *The Emancipation of Massachusetts*. Boston: Houghton, Mifflin, 1887.

*———. *The Law of Civilization and Decay: An Essay on History*. New York: Knopf, 1943.

*———. *The New Empire*. New York: Macmillan, 1902.

*Adams, Charles Francis. *Three Episodes of Massachusetts History*. 2 vols. Boston: Houghton, Mifflin, 1892.

*Adams, Herbert B. *Salem Commons and Commoners: or the Economic Beginnings of Massachusetts.* I, "The Fisher Plantation at Cape Anne"; II, "Origin of Salem Plantation"; III, "House Lots, Ten Acre Lots, Widows' Lots, Maids' Lots." Reprinted from *Historical Collections of the Essex Institute,* vol. XIX. Salem, Mass.: Essex Institute, 1882.

*Adams, James Truslow. *The Founding of New England.* Boston: Atlantic Monthly Press, 1921.

*Albright, William Foxwell, and T. O. Lambdin. *The Evidence of Language.* The Cambridge Ancient History, rev. ed., fascicle 54. Cambridge: Cambridge University Press, 1966.

*Altsheler, Joseph A. *The Eyes of the Woods.* The Young Trailers Series. New York and London: D. Appleton, 1917.

The American Heritage Dictionary of the English Language. Edited by William Morris. Boston: American Heritage Publishing Co. and Houghton Mifflin, 1969.

*Anderson, Edgar. *Plants, Man and Life.* Boston: Little, Brown, 1952.

Andrews, Charles M. *The Colonial Period of American History.* Vol. I: *The Settlements.* New Haven: Yale University Press; London: Oxford University Press, 1934.

Asser. *Asser's Life of King Alfred.* Edited by William Henry Stevenson. Oxford: Clarendon Press, 1904.

*Athenaeus. *The Diepnosophists, or Banquet of the Learned.* Translated by C. D. Yonge. 3 vols. Bohn's Classical Library. London: G. Bohn, 1854.

Atwood, Albert W. "Northeast of Boston," *National Geographic Magazine,* LXXXVIII (September 1945), 257–292.

*Auden, W. H., ed. *The Portable Greek Reader.* New York: Viking Press, 1948.

Babson, David L. "Maritime History of Gloucester, 1600–1807." Washburn prize essay, Harvard University, 1932.

*Babson, John J. *History of the Town of Gloucester, Cape Ann, Including the Town of Rockport.* Gloucester, Mass.: Proctor Brothers, 1860.

*———. *Notes and Additions to the History of Gloucester, Part First: Early Settlers.* Gloucester, Mass.: M. V. B. Perley, 1876.

*———. *Notes and Additions to the History of Gloucester: Second*

Series. Salem, Mass.: Salem Press Publishing and Printing Co., 1891.

*Babson, Roger W. *Actions and Reactions: An Autobiography.* Rev. ed. New York: Harper, 1950.

*———, and Foster H. Saville. *Cape Ann Tourist's Guide, with comments on Business Cycles.* 4th ed. Gloucester, Mass.: Cape Ann Community League, 1952–54.

*Babson, Thomas E. "Evolution of Cape Ann Roads and Transportation, 1623–1955," *Essex Institute Historical Collections,* XCI, 4 (October 1955), 302–328.

*Bailyn, Bernard, and Lotte Bailyn. *Massachusetts Shipping 1697–1714: A Statistical Study.* Cambridge, Mass.: Belknap Press of Harvard University Press, 1959.

*Baker, William A. *Colonial Vessels: Some Seventeenth-Century Sailing Craft.* Barre, Mass.: Barre Publishing Co., 1962.

*Banks, Charles Edward. *The Planters of the Commonwealth: A Study of the Emigrants and Emigration in Colonial Times . . . 1620–1640.* Boston: Riverside Press for Houghton Mifflin Co., 1930.

*———. *Topographical Dictionary of 2885 English Emigrants to New England 1620–1650.* Edited by Elijah Ellsworth Brownell. 2d ed. Baltimore: Southern Book Co., 1957. First published Philadelphia: Bertram Press, 1937.

Baxter, James Phinney. *Christopher Levett, of York, the Pioneer Colonist in Casco Bay.* Portland, Me.: Gorges Society, 1893.

*———, ed. *The Trelawny Papers.* Documentary History of the State of Maine, Vol. III. Collections of the Maine Historical Society, 2d series. Portland: Hoyt, Fogg, and Donham, 1884.

Benson, Joyce. "First Round of Letters," *Boundary 2,* II, 1 & 2 (Fall 1973/Winter 1974), 358–367.

*Bérard, Victor. *Did Homer Live?.* Translated by Brian Rhys. New York: Dutton, 1931.

Berry, Robert Elton. *Yankee Stargazer: The Life of Nathaniel Bowditch.* New York and London: Whittlesey House, McGraw-Hill, 1941.

*B[ethell], J[ohn] T. Review of *Four Winds 1,* *Cape Ann Summer Sun,* 18 July 1952, p. 4.

*"Big Wave Swept Men Overboard," *Boston Post,* 7 January 1905, p. 9.

Boer, Charles. *Charles Olson in Connecticut.* Chicago: Swallow Press, 1975.

Bolton, Charles Knowles. "John Adams of Pitcairn's Island," *American Neptune,* I, 3 (July 1941), 297–300.

*Bowditch, Harold. "Nathaniel Bowditch," *American Neptune,* V, 2 (April 1945), 99–110.

*Bowditch, Nathaniel. *American Practical Navigator: An Epitome of Navigation Originally by Nathaniel Bowditch, LL.D.* U.S. Navy Hydrographic Office Publication no. 9. Washington, D.C.: U.S. Government Printing Office, 1962.

Bowditch, Nathaniel Ingersoll. Memoir of Nathaniel Bowditch, Vol. IV of Marquis de la Place, *Mécanique Céleste.* Translated by Nathaniel Bowditch. Boston: Charles C. Little & James Brown, 1839.

*Boyd, William C. *Genetics and the Races of Man.* Boston: Little, Brown, 1950.

*Bradford, William. *Bradford's History "Of Plimoth Plantation."* Boston: Wright & Potter Printing Co., 1898.

*Braidwood, Robert J. *The Near East and the Foundations for Civilization.* Condon Lectures. Eugene: Oregon State System of Higher Education, 1952.

*Brakhage, Stan. *Metaphors on Vision.* Issued as *Film Culture,* 30 (Fall 1963).

*Brandeis, Louis D. *Other People's Money, and How the Bankers Use It.* Jacket Library. Washington, D.C.: National Home Library Foundation, 1933.

*Brebner, John Bartlet. *The Explorers of North America 1492–1806.* The Pioneer Histories. London: A. & C. Black, 1933.

Brinnin, John Malcolm. *The Third Rose: Gertrude Stein and Her World.* Boston: Little, Brown, 1959.

Brodeur, Arthur G. *The Meaning of Snorri's Categories.* University of California Publications in Modern Philology, XXXVI, 4. Berkeley and Los Angeles: University of California Press, 1952. Pp. 129–148.

*Brondsted, Johannes. *The Vikings.* Translated by Estrid Bannister-Good. A Pelican Book. Harmondsworth: Penguin Books, 1960.

*Brooks, Alfred Mansfield. "The Pearce-Parrot Garden in Gloucester," *Essex Institute Historical Collections,* LXXX, 3 (July 1944), 283–285.

*————. "A Picture of Gloucester About 1800," *Essex Institute Historical Collections,* LXXXVII, 4 (October 1951), 333–338.

*Brown, Alexander, ed. *The Genesis of the United States.* 2 vols. Boston: Houghton, Mifflin, 1890.

*Carpenter, Rhys. *Folk Tale, Fiction and Saga in the Homeric Epics.* Sather Classical Lectures, vol. 20. Berkeley and Los Angeles: University of California Press, 1946.

*"Carrier Force Adds College 'Giant' to Fernwood Route," *Gloucester Daily Times,* 11 June 1931, pp. 1, 6.

*Caulkins, Frances Manwaring. *History of New London, Connecticut, From the first survey of the coast in 1612, to 1852.* New London: Published by the author, 1852.

Cech, John O. "Edward Dahlberg and Charles Olson: A Biography of a Friendship." Ph.D. dissertation, University of Connecticut, 1974.

Chambers, E. K. *Arthur of Britain.* London: Sidgwick & Jackson, 1927.

*Chapelle, Howard I. *The History of American Sailing Ships.* New York: Bonanza Books, n.d.

*————. *The National Watercraft Collection.* United States National Museum Bulletin 219. Washington, D.C.: U.S. Government Printing Office, 1960.

*Charters, Ann. *Olson / Melville: A Study in Affinity.* [Berkeley]: Oyez, 1968.

*Chaucer, Geoffrey. *The Complete Works of Geoffrey Chaucer.* Edited by F. N. Robinson. Student's Cambridge Ed. Boston: Houghton Mifflin, 1933.

*Cheyne, T. K., and J. Sutherland Black, eds. *Encyclopaedia Biblica: A Critical Dictionary . . . of the Bible.* New ed. New York: Macmillan; London: Adam and Charles Black, 1914.

Childe, V. Gordon. *The Dawn of European Civilization.* 2d ed. The History of Civilization series. New York: Knopf, 1939.

*————. *What Happened in History.* A Pelican Book. Harmonds-worth: Penguin Books, 1950.

*Church, Albert Cook. *American Fishermen.* Text by James B. Connolly. New York: W. W. Norton, 1961.

Clayre, Alasdair. "The Rise and Fall of Black Mountain College," *The Listener,* LXXXI (27 March 1969), 411–414.

*Cohane, John Philip. *The Key.* Intro. by Cyrus Gordon. New York: Crown Publishers, 1969.

*Collingwood, W. G. *Scandinavian Britain.* Introductory chapters by F. York Powell. London: Society for Promoting Christian Knowledge; New York: E. S. Gorham, 1908.

*Colum, Padraic. *The Voyagers: Being Legends and Romances of Atlantic Discovery.* New York: Macmillan, 1925.

*Conant, Frederick Odell. *Life of Roger Conant.* Reprinted from F. O. Conant's "History and Genealogy of the Conant Family." N.p.: Roger Conant Family Association, 1926.

*Connolly, James B. *The Book of the Gloucester Fishermen.* New York: John Day, 1928.

*————. *Gloucestermen: Stories of the Fishing Fleet.* New York: C. Scribner's Sons, 1944.

*————. *The Port of Gloucester.* New York: Doubleday, Doran, 1940.

*————. "Pride of Vessel," *Collier's,* CII (15 October 1938), 48–52.

*Cook, Albert. *The Classic Line: A Study in Epic Poetry.* Bloomington and London: Indiana University Press, 1966.

*Coon, Carleton S. *The Story of Man: From the First Human to Primitive Culture and Beyond.* New York: Alfred A. Knopf, 1954.

*Copeland, Melvin T., and Elliott C. Rogers. *The Saga of Cape Ann.* Freeport, Me.: Bond Wheelwright Co., 1960.

*Corbin, Henry. *Avicenna and the Visionary Recital.* Translated by Willard R. Trask. Bollingen Series LXVI. New York: Pantheon Books, 1960.

*————. "Cyclical Time in Mazdaism and Ismailism," in *Man and Time: Papers from the Eranos Yearbooks.* Edited by Joseph Campbell. Bollingen Series XXX. 3. New York: Pantheon Books, 1957. Pp. 115–172.

Corman, Cid, ed. *The Gist of Origin 1951–1971*. New York: Grossman Publishers, A Division of Viking Press, 1975.

Cornell, Julien. *The Trial of Ezra Pound: A Documented Account of the Treason Case*. New York: John Day Co., 1966.

Creeley, Robert. *Contexts of Poetry: Interviews, 1961–1971*. Edited by Donald Allen. Bolinas, Calif.: Four Seasons Foundation, 1973.

*———. *For Love; Poems, 1950–1960*. New York: Scribner's, 1962.

Crispolti, Enrico, and Giuseppe Marchiori. *Corrado Cagli*. Torino: Edizioni d'arte Fratelli Pozzo, 1964.

Cross, Tom Peete, "The Celtic Elements in the Lays of *Lanval* and *Graelent*," *Modern Philology*, XII, 10 (April 1915), 1–60.

Dahlberg, Edward, *Because I Was Flesh: The Autobiography of Edward Dahlberg*. New York: New Directions, 1964.

———. *The Confessions of Edward Dahlberg*. New York: George Braziller, 1971.

*———. *Do These Bones Live*. New York: Harcourt, Brace, 1941.

*———. *The Flea of Sodom*. Direction 18. Norfolk, Conn.: New Directions, 1950.

*———. "Laurels for Borrowers," *The Freeman*, II (17 December 1951), 187–190.

Darrow, Clarence. "The Edwardses and the Jukes," *American Mercury*, VI (October 1925), 147–157.

*Davidson, H. R. Ellis. *Gods and Myths of Northern Europe*. A Pelican Original. Baltimore: Penguin Books, 1964.

Davis, Adelle. *Let's Eat Right to Keep Fit*. New York: Harcourt, Brace, 1954.

Dawson, Fielding. *The Black Mountain Book*. New York: Croton Press, 1970.

Dean, John Ward, ed. *Capt. John Mason, the Founder of New Hampshire*. With memoir by Charles Wesley Tuttle. Boston: The Prince Society, 1887.

*DeVoto, Bernard. *The Year of Decision, 1846*. Boston: Little, Brown, 1943.

Dictionary of American Biography. Edited by Allen Johnson and Dumas Malone. 20 vols. New York: Charles Scribner's Sons, 1928–37.

*The Dictionary of National Biography. Edited by Leslie Stephens and Sidney Lee. Vol. IX. London: Oxford University Press, 1921–22.

"Did Winthrop Land at Manchester?," Essex Institute Historical Collections, XXXIV (July 1898), 209–218.

Diodorus Siculus. Diodorus of Sicily. Translated by C. H. Oldfather. Loeb Classical Library. Cambridge, Mass.: Harvard University Press; London: William Heinemann, 1939.

*Donnelly, Ignatius. Atlantis: The Antediluvian World. Modern rev. ed. by Egerton Sykes. New York: Harper, 1949. First published in 1882.

*Driver, Godfrey Rolles. Canaanite Myths and Legends. Old Testament Studies, no. 3. Edinburgh: T. & T. Clark, 1956.

*Duncan, Robert. "Notes on Poetics Regarding Olson's 'Maximus,' " Black Mountain Review, 6 (Spring 1956), 201–211.

Eckstorm, Fannie Hardy. "The Attack on Norridgewock, 1724," New England Quarterly, VII, 3 (September 1934), 541–578.

*———. Old John Neptune and Other Maine Indian Shamans. Portland, Me.: Southworth-Anthoensen Press, 1945.

*Eddy, Richard. Universalism in Gloucester, Mass. Gloucester, Mass.; Proctor Brothers, 1892.

*Edmonds, J. M., ed. and trans. Lyra Graeca: Being the Remains of all the Greek Lyric Poets from Eumelus to Timotheus Excepting Pindar. Vol. 1 of 3 vols. Loeb Classical Library. London: W. Heinemann; New York: G. P. Putnam's Sons, 1922.

Eigner, Larry. "Letter to George Butterick," Athanor, 2 (Fall 1971), 60–63.

*Else, Gerald Frank. "Aristotle on the Beauty of Tragedy," reprinted from Harvard Studies in Classical Philology, XLIX (1938), 179–204.

*———. The Origin and Early Form of Greek Tragedy. Martin Classical Lectures, vol. 20. Cambridge, Mass.: Published for Oberlin College by Harvard University Press, 1965.

*The Encyclopaedia Britannica. 11th ed. 29 vols. New York: Encyclopaedia Britannica Co., 1910–11.

*Essex County, Mass. *The Probate Records of Essex County, Massachusetts.* 3 vols. Salem, Mass.: Essex Institute, 1916–20.

*———. *Records and Files of the Quarterly Courts of Essex County, Massachusetts.* 8 vols. Salem, Mass.: Essex Institute, 1911–21.

Ferrini, Vincent. "A Frame," *Maps,* 4 (1971), 47–60.

*———. *The Infinite People.* New York: Great Concord Publishers, 1950.

*———. *In the Arriving.* Liverpool: Heron Press, 1954.

*———. "Two poems from *The House of Time,*" *Imagi,* IV, 4 (Spring 1949), 4.

Fisher, Raymond H. *The Russian Fur Trade 1550–1700.* University of California Publications in History, vol. 31. Berkeley: University of California Press, 1943.

The Fishermen's Own Book. Gloucester, Mass.: Proctor Brothers, 1882.

*"Flames Scorch Field: 3 Acres Are Burned Here," *Gloucester Daily Times,* 24 February 1960, pp. 1, 12.

Ford, W. C. "Dorchester Company at Cape Ann, 1635," in *Proceedings of the Massachusetts Historical Society, October 1909–June 1910.* Vol. XLIII. Boston: Massachusetts Historical Society, 1910. Pp. 493–496.

*Forsdyke, John. *Greece Before Homer: Ancient Chronology and Mythology.* London: Max Parrish, 1956.

*"14-Year Hunt Yields 'Missing Link' Fish," *New York Times,* 30 December 1952, p. 21.

*Fowler, Murray, "Old Norse Religion," in *Ancient Religions.* Edited by Vergilius Ferm. New York: Philosophical Library, 1950. Pp. 237–250.

*Frankfort, Henri. *The Birth of Civilization in the Near East.* Bloomington: Indiana University Press, 1951.

*———. *Kingship and the Gods: A Study of Ancient Near Eastern Religion as the Integration of Society & Nature.* Chicago: University of Chicago Press, 1948.

*Franklin Institute of the State of Pennsylvania for the Promotion of the Mechanic Arts. *Report No. 3333 Investigating the Works of John Hays Hammond, Jr., in Remote and Automatic Controls.* Philadelphia: Hall of the Institute, 1959.

*Frazer, James George. *The Golden Bough: A Study in Magic and Religion*. Abridged ed. New York: Macmillan, 1947.

Friedman, Albert B., ed. *The Viking Book of Folk Ballads of the English-Speaking World*. New York: Viking Press, 1956.

*Frobenius, Leo, and Douglas C. Fox. *African Genesis*. New York: Stackpole Sons, 1937.

*Gardner, John. "New Theory Offered on Beothuk Canoe Origin," *National Fisherman combined with Main Coast Fisherman* (August 1966), 8A and 31A.

Garland, Joseph E. *The Gloucester Guide: A Retrospective Ramble*. Gloucester, Mass.: Gloucester 350th Anniversary Celebration, Inc., 1973.

*————. *Lone Voyager*. Boston, Toronto: Little, Brown, 1963.

*Gates, Reginald R. *Human Ancestry from a Genetic Point of View*. Cambridge, Mass.: Harvard University Press, 1948.

Ginsberg, Allen. *Planet News, 1961–1967*. The Pocket Poets, no. 23. San Francisco: City Lights, 1968.

Gloucester, Mass. *The Gloucester Fire Department: Its History and Work from 1793 to 1893*. Gloucester: Proctor Brothers, 1892.

*Gloucester, Mass. *Vital Records of Gloucester Massachusetts to the End of the Year 1849*. Vol. I: Births. Topsfield, Mass.: Topsfield Historical Society, 1917.

*————. *Vital Records of Gloucester Massachusetts to the End of the Year 1849*. Vol. II: Marriages. Salem: Essex Institute, 1923.

*————. *Vital Records of Gloucester Massachusetts to the End of the Year 1849*. Vol. III: Deaths. Salem: Essex Institute, 1924.

*Gluck, Gustav. *Pieter Brueghel the Elder*. Translated by Eveline Byam Shaw. London: Commodore Press, 1937.

*Goode, George Brown, ed. *The Fisheries and Fishery Industries of the United States*. Section III: *The Fishing Grounds of North America*, edited by Richard Rathbun; Section IV: *The Fishermen of the United States*, by George Brown Goode and Joseph W. Collins. U.S. Commission of Fish and Fisheries. Washington, D.C.: Government Printing Office, 1887.

*Gordon, Cyrus H. *Before the Bible: The Common Background of Greek and Hebrew Civilisations*. New York: Harper & Row, 1962.

*———. *Forgotten Scripts: How They Were Deciphered and Their Impact on Contemporary Culture.* New York: Basic Books, 1968.

*———. "The Phaistos Disk." Hectographed abstract prepared for a Mediterranean Studies Colloquium held at Brandeis University, 5 March 1964.

*Graves, Robert. *The Greek Myths.* 2 vols. Baltimore: Penguin Books, 1955.

*———. *The Greek Myths.* 2 vols. A Pelican Book. Baltimore: Penguin Books, 1961.

*———. *The White Goddess: A Historical Grammar of Poetic Myth.* Amended and enlarged ed. New York: Vintage Books, 1958.

Greene, Evarts B., and Virginia D. Harrington. *American Population Before the Federal Census of 1790.* New York: Columbia University Press, 1932.

*Greenman, E. F. "The Upper Palaeolithic and the New World," *Current Anthropology,* IV, 1 (February 1963), 41–66.

*Guterbock, Hans Gustav. "Hittite Religion," in *Ancient Religions.* Edited by Vergilius Ferm. New York: Philosophical Library, 1950. Pp. 81–109.

*———. "The Hittite Version of the Hurrian Kumarbi Myths: Oriental Forerunners of Hesiod," *American Journal of Archaeology,* LII, 1 (January-March 1948), 123–134.

*———. "The Song of Ullikummi: Revised Text of the Hittite Version of a Hurrian Myth." Reprint from *Journal of Cuneiform Studies,* V (1951), 135–161; VI (1952), 8–42. New Haven: American Schools of Oriental Research, 1952.

Harden, Donald. *The Phoenicians.* Ancient Peoples and Places series. New York: Frederick A. Praeger, 1962.

*Harrigan, Paul. "Neighbors silence Ten Pound's wail," *Gloucester Daily Times,* 8 August 1968, pp. 1, 12.

*Harris, Zellig S. "Ras Shamra: Canaanite Civilization and Language," in *Annual Report of the Board of Regents of the Smithsonian Institution . . . for the Year Ending June 30 1937.* Washington, D.C.: U.S. Government Printing Office, 1938. Pp. 479–502.

*Harrison, Jane Ellen. *Prolegomena to the Study of Greek Religion.* Cambridge: Cambridge University Press, 1903.

*————. *Themis: A Study of the Social Origins of Greek Religion.* 2d ed. Cambridge: Cambridge University Press, 1927.

*Harrisse, Henry. "The Outcome of the Cabot Quater-Centenary," *American Historical Review*, IV, 1 (October 1898), 38–61.

*Havelock, Eric A. *Preface to Plato.* Cambridge, Mass.: Belknap Press of Harvard University Press, 1963.

*Hawkes, C[hristopher] F. C. *The Prehistoric Foundations of Europe to the Mycenean Age.* London: Methuen, 1940.

*Hayes, William C., M. B. Rowton, and Frank H. Stubbings. *Chronology: Egypt—To End of Twentiety Dynasty* (by Hayes); *Ancient Western Asia* (by Rowton); *The Aegean Bronze Age* (by Stubbings). The Cambridge Ancient History, rev. ed., fascicle 4. Cambridge: Cambridge University Press, 1964.

"The Hazards of the Fisheries," in *Thirty-Seventh Annual Report of the Gloucester Fishermen's Institute* (Gloucester, Mass., 1928), pp. 9–11.

*Heezen, Bruce C., and Marie Tharp. *Physiographic Diagram: Atlantic Ocean (Sheet 1).* Geological Society of America, Special Paper 65. New York: Geographical Society of America, c. 1957.

*Herrigel, Eugen. *Zen in the Art of Archery.* Translated by R. F. C. Hull. New York: Panthon Books, 1953.

*Hesiod. *Hesiod, The Homeric Hymns and Homerica.* Translated by Hugh G. Evelyn-White. Loeb Classical Library. New York: G. P. Putnam's Sons, 1926.

*Higginson, Stephen. "Letters of Stephen Higginson, 1783–1804," in *Annual Report of the American Historical Association for the Year 1896.* Washington, D.C.: Government Printing Office, 1897. I, 704–841.

The Holy Bible containing the Old and New Testaments—King James Version. New York: Grosset & Dunlap, 1931.

*Homer. *The Complete Works of Homer . . . The Iliad Done Into English Prose by Andrew Lang, Walter Leaf, Ernest Myers; The Odyssey Done Into English Prose by S. H. Butcher and Andrew Lang.* New York: Modern Library, n.d.

*Hull, John T. *The Seige and Capture of Fort Loyall, Destruction* *of Falmouth, May 20, 1690 (O.S.).* City Document. Portland, Me.: Owen, Strout, 1885.

"Hull Afloat for Short Time Then Sank Again," in *Thirty-Seventh Annual Report of the Gloucester Fishermen's Institute* (Gloucester, Mass., 1928), pp. 12–13, photo on p. 14.

*Husaini, Moulavi S. A. Q. *Ibn al 'Arabi: The Great Muslim Mystic and Thinker.* Lahore: Muhammed Ashraf, n.d.

Hutchinson, Thomas. *The History of the Colony and Province of Massachusetts-Bay.* Edited by Lawrence Shaw Mayo. 3 vols. Cambridge, Mass.: Harvard University Press, 1936.

*Hyde, George E. *Red Cloud's Folk: A History of the Oglala Sioux Indians.* The Civilization of the American Indian series. Norman: University of Oklahoma Press, 1937.

The I Ching, or Book of Changes. The Richard Wilhelm translation rendered into English by Cary F. Baynes. Foreword by C. G. Jung. Bollingen Series XIX. New York: Pantheon Books, 1961.

*Ingstad, Helge. "Vinland Ruins Prove Vikings Found the New World," *National Geographic,* CXXVI, 5 (November 1964), 708–734.

*Innis, Harold A. *The Cod Fisheries: The History of An International Economy.* Rev. ed. Toronto: University of Toronto Press, 1954.

*"Insists Upon Right to Live in Hogshead," *Boston Post,* 18 January 1932, p. 7.

*Jameson, John Franklin, ed. "Letters of John Bridge, 1623, and Emmanuel Altham, 1624," in *Massachusetts Historical Society Proceedings, 1910–1911,* vol. XLIV. Boston: Massachusetts Historical Society, 1911. Pp. 178–189.

*Jespersen, Otto. *Growth and Structure of the English Language.* 9th ed. Doubleday Anchor Books. Garden City, N.Y.: Doubleday, 1956.

*Johnson, Edward. *Johnson's Wonder-Working Providence 1628—1651.* Edited by J. Franklin Jameson. Original Narratives of Early American History. New York: Charles Scribner's Sons, 1910.

*Jonas, Hans. *The Gnostic Religion.* Boston: Beacon Press, 1958.

*Josselyn, John. "An Account of Two Voyages to New-England," in *Collections of the Massachusetts Historical Society*, 3d series, III. Cambridge, Mass.: E. W. Metcalf and Co., 1833. Pp. 211–354.

*————. *An Account of Two Voyages to New-England, Made During the Years 1638, 1663*. Boston: William Veazie, 1865.

*Joyce, James. *Ulysses*. New York: Random House, 1934.

*Jung, Carl Gustav. *Aion: Researches Into the Phenomenology of the Self*. Translated by R. F. C. Hull. The Collected Works of C. G. Jung, vol. 9, part II. Bollingen Series XX. New York: Pantheon Books, 1959.

*————. *The Archetypes and the Collective Unconscious*. Translated by R. F. C. Hull. The Collected Works of C. G. Jung, vol. 9, part I. Bollingen Series XX. New York: Pantheon Books, 1959.

*————. *The Integration of the Personality*. Translated by Stanley Dell. New York and Toronto: Farrar & Rinehart, 1939.

*————. "On Synchronicity," in *Man and Time: Papers from the Eranos Yearbooks*. Edited by Joseph Campbell. Bollingen Series XXX.3. New York: Pantheon Books, 1957. Pp. 201–211.

*————. *Psychological Types or The Psychology of Individuation*. Translated by H. Godwin Baynes. New impression. International Library of Psychology, Philosophy and Scientific Method. London: Kegan Paul, Trench, Trubner; New York: Harcourt, Brace, 1946.

*————. *Psychology and Alchemy*. Translated by R. F. C. Hull. The Collected Works of C. G. Jung, vol. 12. Bollingen Series XX. New York: Pantheon Books, 1953.

*————. *Symbols of Transformation: An Analysis of the Prelude to a Case of Schizophrenia*. Translated by R. F. C. Hull. Collected Works of C. G. Jung, vol. 5. Bollingen Series XX. New York: Pantheon Books, 1956.

*————. *Two Essays on Analytical Psychology*. Translated by R. F. C. Hull. New York: Meridian Books, 1956.

*————, and C. Kerenyi. *Essays on a Science of Mythology: The Myth of the Divine Child and the Mysteries of Eleusis*. Translated by R. F. C. Hull. Bollingen Series XXII. New York: Pantheon Books, 1949.

*————, and W. Pauli. *The Interpretation of Nature and the Psyche: Synchronicity: An Acausal Connecting Principle*, by C. G. Jung; *The Influence of Archetypal Ideas on the Scientific Theories of Kepler*, by W. Pauli. Bollingen Series LI. New York: Pantheon Books, 1955.

*Keats, John. *Poems and Letters of John Keats*. Boston and New York: Houghton Mifflin, 1925.

*Kerenyi, C[arl]. "The Mysteries of the Kabeiroi," in *The Mysteries: Papers from the Eranos Yearbooks*. Edited by Joseph Campbell, Bollingen Series XXX.2. New York: Pantheon Books, 1955. Pp. 32–59.

*Kierman, Irma C. *The Sea Serpent of Cape Ann: An Exciting and Authentic Narrative of the Visits of the Sea Serpent to Cape Ann in the Years 1817 and 1886* ... New England Historic Series Vol. I, no. 1. Rockport, Mass.: Published by the author, c. 1950.

*Knoll, Max. "Transformations of Science in Our Age," in *Man and Time: Papers from the Eranos Yearbooks*. Edited by Joseph Campbell, Bollingen Series XXX.3. New York: Pantheon Books, 1957. Pp. 264–307.

*Ko Hung. *Alchemy, Medicine, Religion in the China of A.D. 320: The Nei P'ien of Ko Hung (Pao-p'u Tzu)*. Translated by James R. Ware. Cambridge, Mass.: M.I.T. Press, 1967.

*Kramer, S[amuel] N[oah]. *Sumerian Mythology: A Study of Spiritual and Literary Achievement in the Third Millennium B.C.* 2d printing. Memoirs of the American Philosophical Society, Vol. XXI, 1944. Philadelphia: American Philosophical Society, 1947.

*Kroeber, A. L. *Anthropology*. Rev. ed. New York: Harcourt, Brace, 1948.

*Lake, Stuart N. *Wyatt Earp, Frontier Marshal*. New York: Bantam Books, 1952.

Langenscheidt's Pocket-Dictionary of the English and German Languages. 5th ed. Berlin, Munich, Zurich: Langenscheidt, 1956.

*Lao-tse. *The Wisdom of Laotse*. Translated and edited by Lin Yutang. New York: Modern Library, 1948.

*Lapham, Alice Gertrude. *Old Planters of Beverly in Massachusetts and the Thousand Acre Grant of 1635*. Cambridge,

Mass.: Riverside Press for the Beverly Historical Society and the Conant Family Association, 1930.

*Lawrence, D. H. *Studies in Classic American Literature.* A Doubleday Anchor Book. Garden City, N.Y.: Doubleday, 1953.

*Leary, Timothy. *High Priest.* An NAL Book. New York, Cleveland: World, 1968.

*Lechford, Thomas. *Note-Book Kept by Thomas Lechford, Esq., Lawyer, In Boston, Massachusetts Bay, From June 27, 1638, to July 29, 1641.* Transactions and Collections of the American Antiquarian Society, Vol. VII. Cambridge, Mass.: John Wilson & Son, 1885.

————. *Plain Dealing; or, News from New England.* Library of New-England History, No. IV. Boston: J. K. Wiggin & W. P. Lunt, 1867.

*Leland, Charles G. *The Algonquin Legends of New England.* Boston and New York: Houghton Mifflin, 1884.

*"Letter-Book of Samuel Sewall," *Collections of the Massachusetts Historical Society,* 6th series, I (1886).

*Levermore, Charles Herbert. *Forerunners and Competitors of the Pilgrims and Puritans.* 2 vols. Brooklyn, N.Y.: The New England Society in the City of Brooklyn, 1912.

*Levy, Gertrude Rachel. *The Gate of Horn: A study of the religious conceptions of the stone age, and their influence upon European thought.* London: Faber and Faber, 1948.

*Lewis, Charlton T. *An Elementary Latin Dictionary.* New York, Cincinnati, Chicago: American Book Co., [1915?]

*Liddel, Henry George, and Robert Scott, comp. *A Greek-English Lexicon.* 8th ed., rev. New York, Chicago, Cincinnati: American Book Co., [1897].

Lincoln, William. *History of Worcester, Massachusetts, From Its Earliest Settlement to September, 1836 . . .* Worcester, Mass: Charles Hersey, 1862.

Love, Kennett. "Cheops Treasure, Ship of the Dead, Found at Pyramid," *New York Times,* 27 May 1954, pp. 1, 4.

*Luce, Stephen B., ed. "Archaeological News and Discussions: Notes on Recent Archaeological Excavations; Summaries of

Original Articles Chiefly in Current Publications," *American Journal of Archaeology*, XLVII, 1 (January-March 1943), 102–124.

*Mackenzie, George Norbury, ed. *Colonial Families of the United States of America*. 7 vols. Baltimore: Seaforth Press, 1915.

*Malinowski, Bronislaw. *Magic, Science and Religion, and Other Essays*. Edited by Robert Redfield. A Doubleday Anchor Book. Garden City, N.Y.: Doubleday, 1954.

Malthus, T. R. *An Essay on Population*. 2 vols. Everyman's Library. London: J. M. Dent; New York: E. P. Dutton, 1933.

*Mann, Charles Edward. *In the Heart of Cape Ann, or the Story of Dogtown* (with *Beginnings of Dogtown: Data from Days Before the Village was Deserted*). 2d ed. Gloucester, Mass.: Proctor Brothers, 1906.

Markham, Clements R., ed. *The Hawkins' Voyages During the Reigns of Henry VIII, Queen Elizabeth, and James I*. The Hakluyt Society, LVII (1st series). London: Printed for the Hakluyt Society, 1878.

*Marsden, R. G. "A Letter of William Bradford and Isaac Allerton, 1623," *American Historical Review*, VIII, 2 (January 1903), 294–301.

*Marshall, Nina L. *The Mushroom Book: A Popular Guide to the Identification and Study of Our Commoner Fungi* . . . New York: Doubleday, Page, 1901.

Mathews, Mitford M., ed. *A Dictionary of Americanisms on Historical Principles*. 2 vols. Chicago: University of Chicago Press, 1951.

Maud, Ralph. "Merk and Olson," *Athanor*, 2 (Fall 1971), 49–51.

*Mavor, James W., Jr. "A Mighty Bronze Age Volcanic Explosion," *Oceanus*, XII, 3 (April 1966), 14–23.

*Maximus Tyrius. *The Dissertations of Maximus Tyrius*. Translated by Thomas Taylor. 2 vols. London: C. Wittingham, 1804.

McCausland, Elizabeth. *Marsden Hartley*. Minneapolis: University of Minnesota Press, 1952.

*Meier, Fritz. "The Mystery of the Ka'ba: Symbol and Reality in Islamic Mysticism," in *The Mysteries: Papers from the Eranos Yearbooks*. Edited by Joseph Campbell, Bollingen Series XXX.2. New York: Pantheon Books, 1955. Pp. 149–168.

*Melville, Herman. *Billy Budd*. Edited by F. Barron Freeman. Cambridge, Mass.: Harvard University Press, 1948.

*———. *Moby-Dick, or, the Whale*. 2 vols. The Works of Herman Melville, Standard Ed. Vols. VII-VIII. London: Constable, 1922.

*———. *Moby-Dick; or, the Whale*. Edited by Luther S. Mansfield and Howard P. Vincent. New York: Hendricks House, 1952.

*———. *Poems: containing Battle-Pieces, John Marr and Other Sailors, Timoleon, and Miscellaneous Poems*. The Works of Herman Melville, Standard Ed. Vol. XVI. London: Constable, 1924.

*———. *Redburn, His First Voyage* . . . The Works of Herman Melville, Standard Ed. Vol. V. London: Constable, 1922.

*———. *Typee*. The Works of Herman Melville, Standard Ed. Vol. I. London: Constable, 1922.

Memorial of the Celebration of the Two Hundred and Fiftieth Anniversary of the Incorporation of the Town of Gloucester, Mass. August, 1892. Boston: Alfred Mudge & Son, 1901.

Mensendieck, Bess M. *It's Up to You*. Portland, Me.: Southworth-Anthoensen Press, 1931.

———. *Look Better, Feel Better*. New York: Harper, 1954.

*Merrill, William Stetson. "The Vinland Problem Through Four Centuries," *Catholic Historical Review*, XXI, 1 (April 1935), 21–48.

*Michelangelo. *The Letters of Michelangelo*. Translated and edited by E. H. Ramsden. 2 vols. Stanford, Calif.: Stanford University Press, 1963.

Millay, Edna St. Vincent. *Collected Sonnets*. New York and London: Harper, 1941.

*Miller, Perry. *Orthodoxy in Massachusetts, 1630–1650*. Boston: Beacon Press, 1959.

*Moloney, Francis X. *The Fur Trade in New England 1620–1676*. Cambridge, Mass.: Harvard University Press, 1931.

*Morgan, Edmund S. *The Birth of the Republic*. 10th impression. Chicago: University of Chicago Press, 1963.

*Morison, Samuel Eliot. *Builders of the Bay Colony*. Boston and New York: Houghton Mifflin, 1930.

*————. *The Maritime History of Massachusetts 1783–1860*. 7th impression. Boston and New York: Houghton Mifflin, 1930.

Morton, Thomas. *New English Canaan*, in *Tracts and Other Papers Relating Principally to the Origin, Settlement, and Progress of the Colonies in North America* . . . Compiled by Peter Force. Vol. II. New York: Peter Smith, 1947.

*Muirhead, L. Russell, ed. *Ireland*. The Blue Guides. London: Ernest Benn, 1962.

*Murasaki, Lady. *The Tale of Genji: A Novel in Four Parts*. Translated by Arthur Waley. New York: The Literary Guild, 1935.

*Museum of Modern Art. *Lyonel Feininger / Marsden Hartley*. New York: Museum of Modern Art, 1944.

Myott, E. B. "Babson Reservoir—Built in Six Months," *American City*, XLVII, 3 (September 1932), 49–53.

*Nasr, Seyyid Hossein. *An Introduction to Islamic Cosmological Doctrines*. Cambridge, Mass.: Belknap Press of Harvard University Press, 1964.

*————. *Science and Civilization in Islam*. Cambridge, Mass.: Harvard University Press, 1968.

*Needham, Joseph, with Wang Ling. *Science and Civilisation in China*, Vol. I: Introductory Orientations. Cambridge: Cambridge University Press, 1965.

*Neumann, Erich. *The Great Mother: An Analysis of the Archetype*. Translated by Ralph Manheim. Bollingen Series XLVII. New York: Pantheon Books, 1955.

————. *The Origins and History of Consciousness*. Translated by R. F. C. Hull. 2 vols. Bollingen Series XLII. Harper Torchbook. New York: Harper & Brothers, 1962.

*Obermann, Julian. *Ugaritic Mythology: A Study of Its Leading Motifs*. New Haven: Yale University Press; London: Geoffrey Cumberlege, Oxford University Press, 1948.

*O'Callaghan, E. B., ed. *Documents Relative to the Colonial History of the State of New York* . . . Compiled by John H. Brodhead. Vol. I. Albany, N.Y.: Weed, Parsons and Co., 1856.

The (Old) Farmer's Almanac . . . 1966 . . . No. CLXXIV. Dublin, N.H.: The Old Farmer's Almanac, c. 1965.

Olson, Charles. *Additional Prose: A Bibliography on America, Proprioception, & Other Notes & Essays.* Edited by George F. Butterick. Writing 31. Bolinas, Calif.: Four Seasons Foundation, 1974.

———. *Archaeologist of Morning.* London: Cape Goliard, 1970.

———. Autobiographical note, in *The New Writing in the U.S.A.* Edited by Donald Allen and Robert Creeley. Harmondsworth: Penguin Books, 1967. Pp. 326–327.

———. *Call Me Ishmael.* New York: Reynal & Hitchcock, 1947.

———. *Charles Olson & Ezra Pound: An Encounter at St. Elizabeths.* Edited by Catherine Seelye. New York: Grossman Publishers, 1975.

———. *Gedichte.* Translated by Klaus Reichert. Edition Suhrkamp 112. Frankfort am Main: Suhrkamp Verlag, 1965.

———. "The Growth of Herman Melville, Prose Writer and Poetic Thinker." Master's thesis, Wesleyan University, 1933.

———. *Human Universe and Other Essays.* Edited by Donald Allen. New York: Grove Press, 1967.

———. *In Adullam's Lair.* Archetype One. Provincetown, Mass.: To the Lighthouse Press, 1975.

———. *In Cold Hell, In Thicket.* Issued as *Origin* 8. Mallorca: Divers Press, 1953.

———. "Letters for Origin." Edited by Albert Gould Glover. Ph.D. dissertation, State University of New York at Buffalo, 1968.

———. *Letters for Origin, 1950–1956.* Edited by Albert Glover. New York: Cape Goliard Press in association with Grossman Publishers, 1970.

———. "Letters to Vincent Ferrini," *Origin* 1 (Spring 1951), 5–6, 42, 53–54, 61.

————. *Maximus, From Dogtown—I*. Foreword by Michael McClure. San Francisco: Auerhahn Press, 1961.

————. *The Maximus Poems / 1–10*. Jargon 7. Stuttgart: Jonathan Williams, 1953.

————. *Muthologos: Collected Interviews and Lectures*. Edited by George F. Butterick. 2 vols. Writing 35. Bolinas, Calif.: Four Seasons Foundation, 1978.

————. *Poetry and Truth: The Beloit Lectures and Poems*. Transcribed and edited by George F. Butterick. Writing 27. San Francisco: Four Seasons Foundation, 1971.

————. *The Post Office*. Intro. by George F. Butterick. Bolinas, Calif.: Grey Fox Press, 1975.

————. *Selected Writings*. Edited by Robert Creeley. New York: New Directions, 1966.

————. *The Special View of History*. Edited by Ann Charters. Berkeley: Oyez, 1970.

OLSON: The Journal of the Charles Olson Archives, 1–6 (Spring 1974–Fall 1976).

*Oppen, George. "The Mind's Own Place," *Kulchur*, III, 10 (Summer 1963), 2–8.

*————. "Three Poets," *Poetry*, C, 5 (August 1962), 329–333.

*Osborn, Henry Fairfield. *Men of the Old Stone Age: Their Environment, Life and Art*. 2d ed. New York: Charles Scribner's Sons, 1916.

*Oxenstierna, Eric. *The Norsemen*. Translated and edited by Catherine Hutter. Greenwich, Conn.: New York Graphic Society, 1965.

The Oxford English Dictionary. 13 vols. Oxford: Clarendon Press, 1933.

*Parkman, Francis. *Count Frontenac and New France Under Louis XIV*. France and England in North America, part 5. 16th ed. Boston: Little, Brown, 1886.

Parsons, Peter, and Peter Anastas. *When Gloucester Was Gloucester: Toward an Oral History of the City*. Gloucester, Mass.: Gloucester 350th Anniversary Celebration, Inc., 1973.

*Paton, Lewis Bayles. "Phoenicians," in *Encycopaedia of Religion and Ethics*. Edited by James Hastings. New York:

Charles Scribner's Sons; Edinburgh: T & T Clark, 1924. IX, 887–897.

*———. "Sanchuniathon," ibid. XI, 177–181.

*Paullin, Charles O. *Atlas of the Historical Geography of the United States*. Edited by John K. Wright. Carnegie Institution of Washington Publication no. 401. Washington and New York: Carnegie Institution of Washington and American Geographical Society, 1932.

*Pausanias. *Pausanias's Description of Greece*. Translated by J. G. Frazer. 2d ed. 6 vols. London: Macmillan, 1913.

Pepys, Samuel. *The Diary of Samuel Pepys* . . . Edited by Henry B. Wheatley. 10 vols. London: George Bell and Sons, 1893–1899.

*Phillips, James Duncan. *Salem in the Seventeenth Century*. Boston and New York: Houghton Mifflin, 1933.

*Phippen, George D. "The 'Old Planters' of Salem, Who Were Settled Here Before the Arrival of Governor Endicott, in 1628," *Historical Collections of the Essex Institute*, I, 3 (July 1859), 97–110; I, 5 (November 1859), 185–199.

Pickthall, Marmaduke, ed. and trans. *The Meaning of the Glorious Koran*. Mentor Books. New York: New American Library, 1953.

*Pierce, Wesley George. *Goin' Fishin': The Story of the Deep-Sea Fishermen of New England*. Marine Research Society Publication no. 26. Salem: Marine Research Society, 1934.

*Piggott, Stuart. *The Druids*. Ancient Peoples and Places, vol. 63. New York and Washington: Frederick A. Praeger, 1968.

*———. *Prehistoric India to 1000 B.C.* A Pelican Book. Harmondsworth: Penguin Books, 1950.

*———, ed. *The Dawn of Civilization: The First World Survey of Human Cultures in Early Times*. New York, Toronto, London: McGraw-Hill, 1962.

*Plutarch. *Plutarch's Morals: Theosophical Essays*. Translated by C. W. King. Bohn's Classical Library. London: George Bell and Sons, 1908.

*Pound, Ezra. *ABC of Reading*. London: G. Routledge; New Haven: Yale University Press, 1934.

*————. *A Draft of XXX Cantos*. London: Faber & Faber, 1943.

*————. *Drafts and Fragments of Cantos CX-CXVII*. New York: New Directions, [1968].

*————. *Guide to Kulchur*. London: Faber & Faber, 1938.

*————. *Jefferson and/or Mussolini: L'Idea Statale; Fascism as I Have Seen It*. New York: Liveright; London: Stanley Nott, 1936.

*————. *Literary Essays of Ezra Pound*. Edited by T. S. Eliot. Norfolk, Conn.: New Directions, 1954.

*————. *Make It New*. New Haven: Yale University Press, 1935.

*————. *Personae, the Collected Poems of Ezra Pound*. New York: New Directions, [1949].

*————. *The Pisan Cantos*. New York: New Directions, 1948.

————. *Polite Essays*. Norfolk, Conn.: New Directions, 1940.

*————. *Section: Rock-Drill 85–95 de los cantares*. New York: New Directions, 1956.

*Pratt, Fletcher. *A Short History of the Civil War (Ordeal by Fire)*. Cardinal Ed. New York: Pocket Books, 1956.

*Pringle, James R. *"Gloucester": a Pageant-Drama of New England's Oldest Fishing Town . . . Presented at Stage Fort Park, Gloucester, Mass. August 28th and 30th, 1923*. [Manchester, Mass.]: Published by the author (printed at North Shore Press), 1923.

*————. *History of the Town and City of Gloucester, Cape Ann, Massachusetts*. Gloucester: Published by the author, 1892.

*————, ed. *The Book of the Three Hundredth Anniversary Observance of the Foundation of the Massachusetts Bay Colony at Cape Ann in 1623 and the Fiftieth Year of the Incorporation of Gloucester as a City*. [Gloucester]: Publications Board of the Three Hundredth Anniversary Executive Committee, 1924.

*Pritchard, James B., ed. *Ancient Near Eastern Texts Relating to the Old Testament*. 2d ed. Princeton, N.J.: Princeton University Press, 1955.

*Proctor, George H. *The Fisherman's Memorial and Record Book*. Gloucester, Mass.: Proctor Brothers, 1873.

Prynne, Jeremy H. "On Maximus IV, V, & VI," *Serious Iron* [*Iron* 12] (ca. 1971), [14]–[23].

*————. Review of *The Maximus Poems IV, V, VI, The Park*, 4 & 5 (Summer 1969), 64–66.

————. *The White Stones*. Lincoln, England: Grosseteste Press, 1969.

Radin, Paul. *The Trickster: A Study in American Indian Mythology*. New York: Philosophical Library, 1956.

*Rank, Otto. *The Myth of the Birth of the Hero and Other Writings*. Edited by Philip Freund. New York: Vintage Books, 1959.

*"Retiring Councillors Complimented," *Gloucester Daily Times*, 3 January 1958, p. 1.

*Rich, Walter H. *Fishing Grounds of the Gulf of Maine*. Appendix III to the Report of the U.S. Commissioner of Fisheries for 1929. Bureau of Fisheries Document no. 1059. Washington, D.C.: U.S. Government Printing Office, 1929.

Ropes, J. H. "Agrapha," in *A Dictionary of the Bible*. Edited by James Hastings. New York: Charles Scribner's Sons; Edinburgh: T. & T. Clark, 1907. Extra Vol., pp. 343–352.

*Rose, H. J. *A Handbook of Greek Mythology*. 6th ed. A Dutton Paperback. New York: E. P. Dutton, 1959.

*Rose-Troup, Frances. *John White, the Patriarch of Dorchester [Dorset] and the Founder of Massachusetts, 1575–1648 . . .* New York and London: Putnam's, 1930.

*————. *Roger Conant and the Early Settlement on the North Shore of Massachusetts*. N.p.: Roger Conant Family Association, 1926.

*"Ruins of Old City Found in Bahrein: Danish Expedition Unearths Trace of a Persian Gulf Civilization of 3000 B.C.," *New York Times*, 17 May 1959, p. 124.

*Sahlins, Marshall D. "The Origin of Society," *Scientific American*, CCIII, 3 (September 1960), 76–87.

*Sandoz, Mari. *Crazy Horse: The Strange Man of the Oglalas*. A Bison Book. Lincoln: University of Nebraska Press, 1961.

*Sanford, Eva Matthews. *The Mediterranean World in Ancient Times*. New York: Ronald Press Co., 1938.

*Sapir, Edward. *Language, An Introduction to the Study of Speech*. A Harvest Book. New York: Harcourt, Brace, c. 1949.

Sargent, Charles Lenox. *The Life of Alexander Smith, Captain of the Island of Pitcairn . . .* Boston: Printed by S. T. Goss, 1819.

*Sauer, Carl Ortwin. *Land and Life: Selections from the Writings of*

Carl Ortwin Sauer. Edited by John Leighly. Berkeley and Los Angeles: University of California Press, 1963.

*Saunders, E. Dale. *Mudrā: A Study of Symbolic Gestures in Japanese Buddhist Sculpture.* Bollingen Series LVIII. New York: Pantheon Books, 1960.

*Savage, James. *A Genealogical Dictionary of the First Settlers of New England* . . . 4 vols. Boston: Little, Brown, 1860–62.

*Saville, Marshall H. *Champlain and his Landings at Cape Ann, 1605, 1606.* Reprinted from the *Proceedings of the American Antiquarian Society* for October 1933. Worcester, Mass: American Antiquarian Society, 1934.

*Sawyer, P. H. *The Age of the Vikings.* London: Edward Arnold, 1962.

*Scales, John, ed. *Piscataqua Pioneers, 1623–1775: Register of Members and Ancestors.* Dover, N.H.: Charles F. Whitehouse, 1919.

**The Secret of the Golden Flower: A Chinese Book of Life.* Translated by Richard Wilhelm. Commentary by C. G. Jung. 6th impression. London: Kegan Paul, Trench, Trubner, 1945.

*Shakespeare, William. *The Complete Works of Shakespeare.* Edited by George Lyman Kittredge. Boston: Ginn and Co., 1936.

*Shaler, N[athaniel] S[outhgate]. "The Geology of Cape Ann, Massachusetts," in *Ninth Annual Report of the United States Geological Survey, 1887–88.* Washington, D.C.: Government Printing Office, 1889. Pp. 529–611.

*Sherwin, Reider T. *The Viking and The Red Man: The Old Norse Origin of the Algonquin Language.* Vols. 1 and 2. New York and London: Funk & Wagnalls Co., 1940–42.

**The Shorter Oxford English Dictionary.* 3d ed., rev. 2 vols. Oxford: Clarendon Press, 1950.

*Shurtleff, Nathaniel B. *A Topographical and Historical Description of Boston.* Boston: A. Williams & Co., Old Corner Bookstore, 1871.

*————, ed. *Records of the Governor and Company of the Massachusetts Bay in New England.* 2 vols. Boston: William White, 1853.

*Simpson, William. *The Buddhist Praying-Wheel: A Collection of*

Material Bearing Upon the Symbolism of the Wheel and Circular Movements in Custom and Religious Ritual. London and New York: Macmillan, 1896.

*Sitter W[illem] de. *Kosmos: A Course of Six Lectures on the Development of Our Insight into the Structure of the Universe . . .* Cambridge, Mass.: Harvard University Press, 1932.

*Skelton, R. A., Thomas E. Marston, and George D. Painter. *The Vinland Map and the Tartar Relation.* New Haven and London: Yale University Press, 1965.

*Smith, Bradford. *Captain John Smith: His Life & Legend.* Philadelphia and New York: Lippincott, 1953.

*Smith, John. *Travels and Works of Captain John Smith.* Edited by Edward Arber. 2 vols. Edinburgh: John Grant, 1910.

*Smith, Sylvanus. *Fisheries of Cape Ann.* Gloucester, Mass.: Press of Gloucester Times Co., 1915.

*Smith, W. Stevenson. *The Old Kingdom in Egypt and the Beginning of the First Intermediate Period.* The Cambridge Ancient History, rev. ed., fascicle 5. Cambridge: Cambridge University Press, 1962.

*Snell, Bruno. *The Discovery of the Mind: The Greek Origins of European Thought.* Translated by T. G. Rosenmeyer. Harper Torchbooks: The Academy Library. New York: Harper & Brothers, 1960.

*Snow, Edward Rowe. "Bullfight on Cape Ann," in *Mysteries and Adventures Along the Atlantic Coast.* New York: Dodd, Mead, 1948. Pp. 146–156.

*Spanuth, Jurgen. *Atlantis—The Mystery Unravelled.* New York: Citadel Press, 1956.

Speck, Frank G. *Beothuk and Micmac.* Indian Notes and Monographs. Edited by F. W. Hodge. New York: Museum of the American Indian, Heye Foundation, 1922.

"Start Work on Alewife Brook Water Basin," *Gloucester Daily Times,* 8 July 1930, p. 1.

*Stefansson, Vilhjalmur. *The Northward Course of Empire.* New York: Harcourt, Brace, 1922.

*———, ed. *Great Adventures and Explorations From the Earliest Times to the Present, as Told by the Explorers Themselves.* New York: Dial Press, 1947.

*Stendhal (Marie Henri Beyle). *On Love*. Translated by H. B. V. New York: Boni and Liveright, 1927.

*Stewart, George R. *Ordeal by Hunger: The Story of the Donner Party*. New ed. Boston: Houghton Mifflin, 1960.

Stokes, Francis Griffin. *A Dictionary of the Characters & Proper Names in the Works of Shakespeare* . . . Boston and New York: Houghton Mifflin, 1924.

Stow, John. *A Survey of London; Reprinted from the Text of 1603* . . . 2 vols. Oxford: Clarendon Press, 1968.

Strabo. *The Geography of Strabo*. Translated by Horace Leonard Jones. Loeb Classical Library. Vol. I. London: William Heinemann; New York: G. P. Putnam's, 1923.

*Strzygowski, Josef. *Origin of Christian Church Art*. Translated by O. M. Dalton and H. J. Braunholtz. Oxford: Clarendon Press, 1923.

Suetonius. *The Lives of the Twelve Caesars*. Translated by Joseph Gavorse. New York: Modern Library, 1933.

*Swadesh, Morris. "Linguistic Overview," in *Prehistoric Man in the New World*. Edited by Jesse D. Jennings and Edward Norbeck. Chicago: University of Chicago Press for William Marsh Rice University, 1964. Pp. 527–556.

Taylor, D. Foster. "The Piscataqua River Gundalow," *American Neptune*, II, 2 (April 1942), 127–139.

"Ten Pound answer: 'Militancy,' " *Gloucester Daily Times*, 8 October 1968, p. 1.

*Thomas, Gordon W. *Fast and Able: Life Stories of Great Gloucester Fishing Vessels*. Edited by Paul B. Kenyon. Gloucester, Mass.: William G. Brown Co., 1952.

*Thomson, J. A. K. *The Art of the Logos*. London: Allen & Unwin, 1935.

Thoreau, Henry D. *The Maine Woods*. New York: Thomas Y. Crowell, 1906.

*Thornton, John Wingate. *The Landing at Cape Anne; or The Charter of the First Permanent Colony on the Territory of the Massachusetts Company*. Boston: Gould and Lincoln; New York: Sheldon, Lamport, and Blakeman, 1854.

*Tibbets, Frederick W. *The Story of Gloucester, Massachusetts, Permanently Settled 1623*. Gloucester: Clark the Printer, 1917.

*Townsend, Charles Wendell. *The Birds of Essex County, Massachusetts*. Memoirs of the Nuttall Ornithological Club, No. III. Cambridge, Mass.: Published by the Club, 1905.

*———. *Supplement to The Birds of Essex County, Massachusetts*. Memoirs of the Nuttall Ornithological Club, No. V. Cambridge, Mass: Published by the Club, 1920.

The Trot-Moc Book of Indian Fairy Tales. Hudson, Mass.: Ashby-Crawford Co., n.d.

*Turville-Petre, E. O. G. *Myth and Religion of the North: The Religion of Ancient Scandinavia*. London: Weidenfeld and Nicolson, 1964.

*U.S. Department of Commerce Coast and Geodetic Survey. *United States Coast Pilot: Atlantic Coast Section A, St. Croix River to Cape Cod*. 5th ed. Washington, D.C.: U.S. Government Printing Office, 1950.

*Velikovsky, Immanuel. *Earth in Upheaval*. Garden City, N.Y.: Doubleday, 1955.

Voltaire, Francois-Marie Arouet de. *Oeuvres Complètes*. Vol. I. Paris: Hachette, 1908.

*Waddell, L. A. *Egyptian Civilization: Its Sumerian Origin & Real Chronology and Sumerian Origin of Egyptian Hieroglyphs*. London: Luzac & Co., 1930.

*———. *The Makers of Civilization in Race & History*. London: Luzac & Co., 1929.

*Walton, Mason A. *A Hermit's Wild Friends: or, Eighteen Years in the Woods*. Boston: Dana Estes & Co., 1903.

*Wasson, Valentina Pavlovna, and R. Gordon Wasson. *Mushrooms, Russia, and History*. 2 vols. New York: Pantheon Books, 1957.

*Webb, Walter Prescott. *The Great Plains*. Boston: Ginn and Co., 1931.

*Webster, T. B. L. *From Mycenae to Homer*. New York: Barnes & Noble, 1960.

Webster's Collegiate Dictionary, 5th ed. Abridgement of *Webster's New International Dictionary*, 2d ed. Springfield, Mass.: G. & C. Merriam Co., 1945.

*Weill, Raymond. *Phoenicia and Western Asia to the Macedonian*

Conquest. Translated by Ernest F. Row. London: George G. Harrap & Co., 1940.

Wegener, Alfred. *The Origin of Continents and Oceans.* Translated from the 4th ed. by John Biram. New York: Dover Publications, 1966.

*Weston, Jessie L. *From Ritual to Romance.* A Doubleday Anchor Book. Garden City, N.Y.: Doubleday, 1957.

*Weyl, Hermann. *Philosophy of Mathematics and Natural Science.* Princeton, N.J.: Princeton University Press, 1949.

*White, John. *John White's Planters Plea.* Intro. by Marshall H. Saville. Rockport, Mass.: Sandy Bay Historical Society and Museum, 1930.

White, Newman I. *American Negro Folk-Songs.* Cambridge, Mass.: Harvard University Press, 1928.

*Whitehead, Alfred North. *Adventures of Ideas.* New York: Macmillan, 1933.

*————. *Process and Reality: An Essay in Cosmology.* Cambridge: Cambridge University Press, 1929

*Whitman, Walt. *Leaves of Grass.* Philadelphia: David McKay, 1900.

*Whorf, Benjamin Lee. *Language, Thought, and Reality.* Edited by John B. Carroll. Cambridge, Mass.: Technology Press of Massachusetts Institute of Technology, 1956.

*Wiener, Norbert. *Cybernetics; or Control and Communication in the Animal and the Machine.* New York: John Wiley & Sons, 1948.

Wigley, Roland L. "Bottom Sediments of Georges Bank," *Journal of Sedimentary Petrology,* XXXI, 2 (June 1961), 165–188.

Willan, T. S. *The Early History of the Russia Company 1553–1603.* Manchester: Manchester University Press, 1956.

*Williams, Kenneth P. *Lincoln Finds a General: A Military Study of the Civil War.* 5 vols. New York: Macmillan, 1949–59.

Williams, William Carlos. *The Great American Novel.* Paris: Three Mountains Press, 1923.

*————. *In the American Grain.* New York: Albert & Charles Boni, 1925.

*————. *Paterson*. The New Classics. New York: New Directions, 1948.

*Willis, William. *The History of Portland, from its First Settlement.* 2 parts. Portland, Me.: Day, Fraser & Co., 1831; Charles Day & Co., 1833.

*Willoughby, Charles C. *Antiquities of the New England Indians* ... Cambridge, Mass.: The Peabody Museum of American Archaeology and Ethnology, Harvard University, 1935.

*Wilmerding, John. *Fitz Hugh Lane, 1804–1865, American Marine Painter.* Salem, Mass.: Essex Institute, 1964.

————. *Fitz Hugh Lane.* New York: Frederick A. Praeger, 1971.

*Wilson, J. Tuzo. "Cabot Fault: An Appalachian Equivalent of the San Andreas and Great Glen Faults and Some Implications for Continental Displacement," *Nature*, CXCV (14 July 1962), 135–138.

*————. "Continental Drift," *Scientific American*, CCVIII (April 1963), 86–100.

Winship, A[lbert] E. *Jukes-Edwards: A Study in Education and Heredity.* Harrisburg, Pa.: R. L. Myers, 1900.

*Winsor, Justin, ed. *The Memorial History of Boston, Including Suffolk County, Massachusetts, 1630–1880.* Vol. I (of 4 vols.): The Early and Colonial Periods. Boston: Ticknor and Co., 1880.

*Winthrop, John. *The History of New England from 1630 to 1649.* Notes by James Savage. 2d ed. 2 vols. Boston: Little, Brown, 1853.

**Winthrop Papers.* 5 vols. Boston: Massachusetts Historical Society, 1929–47.

*Wolfskehl, Karl, and Friedrich von der Leyen, trans. and eds. *Älteste deutsche Dichtungen.* Frankfurt am Main: Insel-Verlag, 1964.

*Wonson, Carlton W. "History of a Hall: The Independent Story" (in 6 parts), *Gloucester Daily Times*, 26 September–1 October 1960.

Yeats, William Butler. *Autobiographies: Reveries Over Childhood and Youth and The Trembling of the Veil.* New ed. New York: Macmillan, 1927.

*————. *Early Poems and Stories*. New York: Macmillan, 1925.

York Deeds. Vol. I. Edited by H. W. Richardson. Portland, Me.: J. T. Hull, 1887.

Young, Alexander. *Chronicles of the Pilgrim Fathers of the Colony of Plymouth 1602–1625*. Boston: C. C. Little and J. Brown, 1841.

*Zimmer, Heinrich. *Myths and Symbols in Indian Art and Civilization*. Edited by Joseph Campbell. Bollingen Series VI. New York: Pantheon Books, 1953.

Index to the *Maximus Poems*

Volumes and page numbers are to *The Maximus Poems* (New York, 1960) - Vol. I; *Maximus Poems IV, V, VI* (London, 1968) - Vol. II; and *The Maximus Poems: Volume Three* (New York, 1975) - Vol. III.

2622

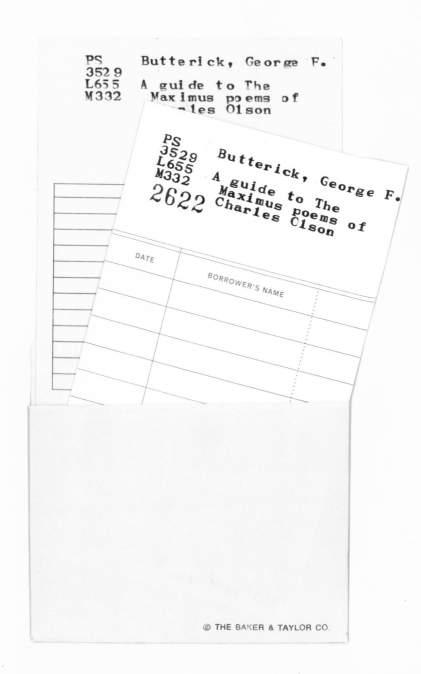